THE BOOKSHOP

Mrs. Neame occasionally passed a night
when she was not absolutely sure whether
had ~~been aslee~~ slept or not. This was bec
call it ~~that is to say~~ to invest
of her monies as to whether to buy the ~~uni~~
bookshop. The uncertainty probably kept her aw
or something must have made her ill as she
ever
She had once seen a cormorant ~~trying~~ over th
flying uncertain
as it were. The
estuary trying to swallow an eel, ~~which~~ was
twisting
to emerge from the ~~throat~~ of the cormoran wha
in a minute a half. occasionally astir quarter ma
sub. The indecision expressed by ~~of both~~ creatures was pitial
Mrs Neame felt that if she hadn't slept at all –
people often say that when they mean nothing
the kind – she must have been ~~being~~ kept awake by the
of the cormorant

~~In Anchestone~~ Mrs Neame ~~was known to be~~
~~tough as they were~~ her age was only guessed
The Like all human creatures, Mrs Neame was divi
a public & a secret personality
Mrs Neame's chief characteristic was self-p
in the sense of establishing her own sensa
of being alive & being known to be alive.
all the terms of 20th century ~~modern existence~~, even in ~~th~~ Happ
she was an exterminatee

.. good as adding area, of experience to
other

(Balzac) when people live v. close love or hate is
always growing; large things are simple to understand
small things are complicated, [but I want to show the
small evil aren't different from the great evil, but mirror it

Penelope Fitzgerald

PENELOPE FITZGERALD

A Life

❧

Hermione Lee

ALFRED A. KNOPF   NEW YORK   2014

THIS IS A BORZOI BOOK
PUBLISHED BY ALFRED A. KNOPF

Published in the United States by Alfred A. Knopf,
a division of Random House LLC, New York, a Penguin Random House company.
Originally published in Great Britain by Chatto & Windus,
an imprint of the Random House Group Ltd., London, in 2013.

www.aaknopf.com

Knopf, Borzoi Books and the colophon are registered
trademarks of Random House LLC.

Library of Congress Cataloging-in-Publication Data
Lee, Hermione.
Penelope Fitzgerald : a life / by Hermione Lee.
pages cm
"This is a Borzoi book."
Includes bibliographical references and index.
ISBN 978-0-385-35234-5 (hardcover)—ISBN 978-0-385-35235-2 (eBook)
1. Fitzgerald, Penelope.   2. Women novelists, English—
20th century—Biography.   I. Title.
PR6056.186Z74 2014
823'.914—dc23
[B]   2013047581

Front-of-jacket photograph by Tara Heinemann/Camera Press/Redux
Jacket design by Carol Devine Carson

Manufactured in the United States of America
First United States Edition

For John Barnard

If a story begins with finding, it must end with searching.

Contents

Illustrations

PLATE SECTION II

Every effort has been made by the publishers to trace the holders of copyright. Any inadvertent omissions of acknowledgement or permission can be rectified in future editions.

Preface

This is the biography of a great English writer who would never have described herself in such a commanding way. She wrote nine short novels, three biographies, some remarkable stories, many fine essays and reviews, and many letters. It is not a vast output. Her life is partly a story about lateness—patience and waiting, a late start and late style. In some ways she was like other women writers of her generation who began to publish in middle or old age. But she was not quite like anyone else.

She began as a brilliant young woman from an exceptional family, of whom much was expected. She spent many years as a housewife and mother, often in dramatically difficult circumstances, teaching, and, apparently, not writing. She started publishing books at sixty, and became famous at eighty. Her books were short, and hard to pin down. She wrote about her own life, but kept herself carefully concealed. She changed direction radically in her last four novels. They moved from using the material of her own life to creating astonishingly vivid and persuasive historical worlds, each one quite different, each one minutely researched, but with the research cunningly kept down. All are strange and original masterpieces.

Fitzgerald is elusive. She had a tragic view of life and a humourous style. Her art lay in reticence, quietness and self-obliteration, but her views on life, work, religion, politics and human behaviour were strong. Her deepest convictions were to be true "to the courage of those who are born to be defeated, the weaknesses of the strong, and the tragedy of misunderstandings and missed opportunities which I have done my best to treat as comedy, for otherwise how can we manage to bear it?" But she was cryptic as well as principled. Her writing is unsettling, and elusive; her style is plain, compact and subtle. She never shows off. She leaves much unsaid. There is often a sense of something withheld in her novels. She did not like to explain too much: she felt it insulted her readers. She likes to exercise her wit, and she likes her readers to have their wits about them.

She called herself an English liberal, which she said was an extinct species. She believed in the value of art as work, and in the usefulness of art to the community. Her heroes are Ruskin and William Morris. She is inspired by Morris's dedication to "the transformation of human existence throughout the whole social order." But she also sees the absurdity of utopias, and likes her idealists best at their most down-to-earth. She pays attention to craftsmanship, skills, well-made books. There is always a job to be done in her novels: running a bookshop or a school, keeping a barge afloat. She enjoyed painting or making things more than she enjoyed writing.

She is drawn to failures and lost causes, and her novels deal with people in a muddle, hopeless cases, outsiders; what she called "exterminatees." These include children, and women, whose lives she wrote about with deep sympathy, though you might not label her as a feminist. In telling any life story, whether in fiction, biography or in her essays, she is alert to cruelty, tyranny or unfairness. She does not think people get what they deserve in this world, but she thinks this is not the only world there is. Her novels argue, indirectly, over the relation between the soul and the body. Pity is one of the emotions—or qualities—she most values. But she is reticent about her beliefs. The people she admires are those who have a habit of "not making too much of things." She takes aesthetic pleasure in control and restraint, and felt drawn "to whatever is spare, subtle, and economical." She says of her father that "everything that was of real importance to him he said as an aside," and she inherited that sidelong manner. She kept her secrets, and she had a lot of time for silence.

She was not glamorous or self-advertising. On the contrary, she was evasive and reserved, and gave a misleading impression in public of a mild, absent-minded old lady. She wrote in a quiet voice, slipping unpredictably between comedy and darkness. For all these reasons, she did not become a popular writer. When she won the Booker Prize in 1979 for her third novel, *Offshore,* the decision was treated dismissively, as some kind of absurd mistake. Though *The Blue Flower* won a major award in America, and made her, for a time, into an international name, it was overlooked by literary judges in England. If you say her name, a few people will put their hand to their heart and tell you she is their greatest literary heroine; or they may just exclaim, with eyes shining, "The Blue Flower!" But more people, especially younger readers, will shake their heads politely and say "Who?"

This book, written out of love and admiration for her work, curiosity about her life and a belief in her genius, is meant to answer that question.

Family

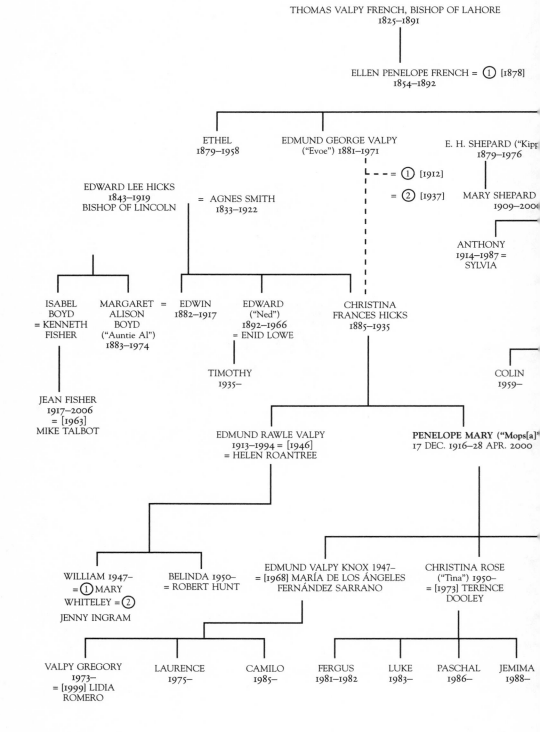

THOMAS VALPY FRENCH, BISHOP OF LAHORE
1825–1891

ELLEN PENELOPE FRENCH = ① [1878]
1854–1892

ETHEL
1879–1958

EDMUND GEORGE VALPY
("Evoe") 1881–1971

E. H. SHEPARD ("Kipp
1879–1976

= ① [1912]

= ② [1937]

MARY SHEPARD
1909–200(

EDWARD LEE HICKS
1843–1919
BISHOP OF LINCOLN

= AGNES SMITH
1833–1922

ANTHONY
1914–1987 =
SYLVIA

ISABEL
BOYD
= KENNETH
FISHER

MARGARET =
ALISON
BOYD
("Auntie Al")
1883–1974

EDWIN
1882–1917

EDWARD
("Ned")
1892–1966
= ENID LOWE

CHRISTINA
FRANCES HICKS
1885–1935

COLIN
1959–

JEAN FISHER
1917–2006
= [1963]
MIKE TALBOT

TIMOTHY
1935–

EDMUND RAWLE VALPY
1913–1994 = [1946]
= HELEN ROANTREE

PENELOPE MARY ("Mops[a])
17 DEC. 1916–28 APR. 2000

WILLIAM 1947–
= ① MARY
WHITELEY = ②
JENNY INGRAM

BELINDA 1950–
= ROBERT HUNT

EDMUND VALPY KNOX 1947–
= [1968] MARÍA DE LOS ÁNGELES
FERNÁNDEZ SARRANO

CHRISTINA ROSE
("Tina") 1950–
= [1973] TERENCE
DOOLEY

VALPY GREGORY
1973–
= [1999] LIDIA
ROMERO

LAURENCE
1975–

CAMILO
1985–

FERGUS
1981–1982

LUKE
1983–

PASCHAL
1986–

JEMIMA
1988–

Tree

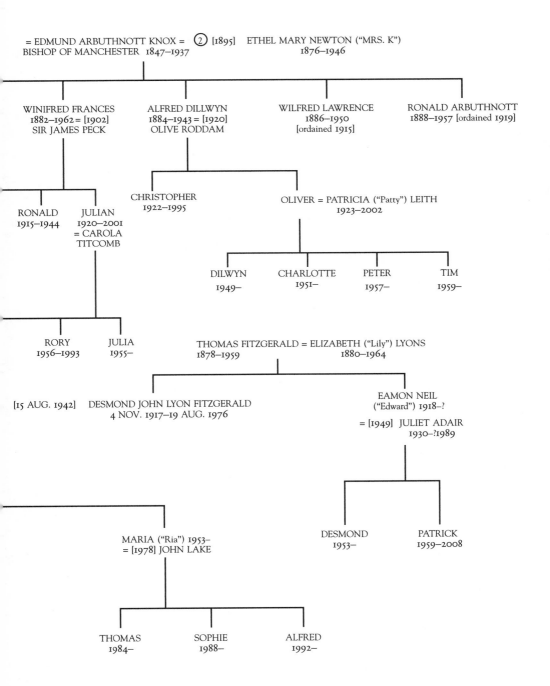

= EDMUND ARBUTHNOTT KNOX = ② [1895] ETHEL MARY NEWTON ("MRS. K")
BISHOP OF MANCHESTER 1847–1937   1876–1946

WINIFRED FRANCES
1882–1962 = [1902]
SIR JAMES PECK

ALFRED DILLWYN
1884–1943 = [1920]
OLIVE RODDAM

WILFRED LAWRENCE
1886–1950
[ordained 1915]

RONALD ARBUTHNOTT
1888–1957 [ordained 1919]

CHRISTOPHER
1922–1995

OLIVER = PATRICIA ("Patty") LEITH
1923–2002

RONALD
1915–1944

JULIAN
1920–2001
= CAROLA
TITCOMB

DILWYN
1949–

CHARLOTTE
1951–

PETER
1957–

TIM
1959–

RORY
1956–1993

JULIA
1955–

THOMAS FITZGERALD = ELIZABETH ("Lily") LYONS
1878–1959   1880–1964

[15 AUG. 1942] DESMOND JOHN LYON FITZGERALD
4 NOV. 1917–19 AUG. 1976

EAMON NEIL
("Edward") 1918–?

= [1949] JULIET ADAIR
1930–?1989

MARIA ("Ria") 1953–
= [1978] JOHN LAKE

DESMOND
1953–

PATRICK
1959–2008

THOMAS
1984–

SOPHIE
1988–

ALFRED
1992–

Penelope Fitzgerald

CHAPTER ONE

The Bishops' Granddaughter

"Must We Have Lives?"[1]

The Old Palace of the Bishop of Lincoln was freezing cold and full of hectic activity in the winter of 1916. The Bishop's younger daughter, Christina Frances, had said goodbye to her husband, Eddie Knox, in peacetime a journalist and poet, now second lieutenant in the Lincolns, a regiment he had joined because of its connection to her family home. He was waiting to embark for France. They had been married four years and had a three-year-old son, Rawle. Christina was thirty-one, and heavily pregnant. She and Eddie had set up home in rural Hampstead, but because of the war she had moved into the Palace with Rawle and a young nursemaid, to have their second child under her parents' care.

But the Bishop, Edward Lee Hicks, and his wife, Agnes, were under strain. They had thrown open the Palace at the start of the war to a group of pitiful Belgian refugees, some of whom were still living nearby and doing odd jobs for them. Lincoln, because it had munitions factories, was a target for Zeppelin raids. The town was full of war-wounded and displaced persons and housewives coping with bereavements, air raids and rationing. The Bishop was shocked to see police controlling huge queues for margarine at the shops. He was working so hard—visiting camps and hospitals, protesting against the ill-treatment of conscientious objectors, giving sermons all over the country—that he had come down with a dangerous attack of the flu. Agnes was doing everything.

He was too ill to see Christina when her baby, Penelope Mary Knox, was born, without much fuss, on the Sunday afternoon of 17 December 1916. The Bishop was still not well enough to officiate at the baptism on 18 January 1917. Penelope Mary was baptised by the Dean of Lincoln, with two aunts from either side of her family (Eddie Knox's sister Ethel and Christina's sister-in-law Margaret Alison Hicks) as her sponsors. Her given names, though, were never used by the family. She was always called Mops, or Mopsie, or Mopsa.

The great frost lasted into March. The Bishop had barely recovered from his illness, and his granddaughter was only a few months old, when the news came of his oldest son's death. Christina's brother Edwin Hicks caught trench fever at Amiens, then died of an attack of meningitis. The Bishop, a pacifist who opposed the war, asked that "nothing about 'victory' should be put on the grave of his dead son." The young widow, Margaret Alison, married for less than two years, bore up valiantly: this was a comfort to his parents. Weeks later, Bishop Hicks and his family turned the Old Palace over to the Red Cross for a hospital, and moved into a much smaller house, cramped quarters for Christina, her parents, her little boy and the new baby.

In September 1917, Eddie Knox, who had been shooting rats in the trenches, observing "ordinary behaviour under terrible conditions" and finding himself unable to write comic pieces from the front line for *Punch,* was reported missing. He had been shot in the back by a sniper at the Battle of Passchendaele, then found in a shell hole in a pool of blood. He was invalided out, operated on, and brought to a Lincoln hospital to convalesce. Christina, meanwhile, was playing her part on the home front, looking after the children, helping her father, and organising an exhibition of women's war work at the local branch of Boots.[2] In April 1919, when Eddie was finally demobbed, she was being visited by the Hickses in a Lincoln hospital for women and children, and was said to be only slowly improving; perhaps she had had a miscarriage. Just then, the Bishop, finally worn out, retired from his duties. He died in August 1919. Christina and her children were at his bedside, but Penelope, aged two, was too young to remember. Nevertheless, Bishop Hicks was a figure who mattered to her, among the bishops, missionaries, vicars and priests thickly scattered through her family tree. She liked the sound of him.

Edward Lee Hicks never refused to see anyone who came to his door for help. He was a great enemy of poverty and injustice, having come, while he was at Oxford, under the influence of John Ruskin. Ruskin he admired, not only for his teaching but also for his delight in even the smallest details of life. Ruskin, he said, would describe "with the keenest relish" the joy of shelling peas:

"The pop which assures one of a successful start, the fresh colour and scent of the juicy row within, and the pleasure of skilfully scooping the bouncing peas with one's thumb into the vessel by one's side." I can honestly say that I never shell peas in summer without thinking of Ruskin and of my grandfather.[3]

Shelling peas was the right association, since the Hickses were originally a farming family. So were the Pughs, the Bishop's maternal family. The Hickses farmed in Wolvercote, a village on the northern edge of Oxford that looks over Port Meadow and the River Thames. They were an old-fashioned Church of England family who didn't like Methodists coming into the village. But Edward Hicks, the future Bishop's father, married Catherine Pugh, a strong-minded person who lived to a great age, one of eleven poor children of a musical Welsh father and a devout Wesleyan mother. Because of his marriage, Edward Hicks became a Methodist. So his son Edward Lee Hicks grew up with a mixed religious background. Since the Hicks/Knox families contained Quakers, Ulster Protestants, Wesleyans, Evangelicals, Anglicans, Anglo-Catholics and Roman Catholics, some not on speaking terms with one another, Penelope Fitzgerald developed a belief that religious schisms are pointless, and that all different faiths are really one. She draws attention to this in *The Knox Brothers,* when calling the faiths that maintained the Knoxes in their dark hours, or "the Bishop of Lincoln's when his son died in the trenches, or Christina's when she got a telegram to say that Eddie was missing," not greater or lesser faiths, "but the same." Where she agreed with both her grandparents was that faith was necessary for life.

Both Edward Hicks and Catherine Pugh had fathers who died young (Edward's fell off a ladder pruning a Wolvercote fruit tree), and Edward Hicks, too, died early. An argumentative, musical, generous person, he was a hopeless businessman, who went into debt and died of consumption when his son Edward Lee was nine. Catherine ran the fatherless family, and got Edward Lee into Magdalen School as a chorister. He remembered the shame of being a poor boy at school among richer boys.[4] But he grew up into a scholar and an Oxford don, teaching at Corpus Christi College in the 1860s when Ruskin was there, and when Oxford was, in Fitzgerald's words, "spiritually in low water" after Newman's departure and the fiercely divisive Tractarian wars. One of Edward Lee Hicks's students at Corpus was Edmund Arbuthnott Knox. The Hickses and the Knoxes would keep on interconnecting.

Hicks was ordained in 1870; he was also by then an expert in Greek epigraphy, known at the British Museum for "a happy ability in restoring half-destroyed inscriptions."[5] So when he was offered the country living of Fenny Compton—a backwater between Banbury and Leamington Spa—for about £600 a year, in 1873, and married a vicar's daughter, Agnes Trevelyan Smith, he could have settled into a modestly comfortable combination of scholarship, rural ministry and domestic life, with six children (one of whom died in infancy) born between 1878 and 1892.

But Edward Lee Hicks was not an easy-living person. His years at Fenny Compton were a time of agricultural depression and farm workers' strikes. He sympathised with and worked on behalf of the "land-hungry" labourers. He was a Liberal who believed in grassroots social reform. In the 1880s he and the family moved to a huge, poor parish in Manchester, where he took his double life, as a social reformer and classical scholar, into a tough urban environment. But the move meant that scholarship, the quiet, happy deciphering of Greek inscriptions, had to give way entirely to public work. As Rector at Salford and Canon of Manchester Cathedral, he also wrote polemical pieces—for instance, against the Boer War—for his friend C. P. Scott at the *Manchester Guardian*. One of the clerics he disagreed with was his ex-pupil Edmund Knox, now his bishop at Manchester, who ran a loud national campaign for the retention of church schools, which were under threat—while Canon Hicks thought that parents should have the right to have their children taught according to their own beliefs.

Some people thought Hicks was too dangerously radical to be made a bishop, and the appointment came late in his life. He had nine years at Lincoln, but he made the most of them. His obituaries called him "a progressive prelate" and "a friend of the poor." It wasn't only for his pea shelling that Bishop Hicks admired Ruskin. Ruskin's dictum—*There is no wealth but life*—was his own, and he used Ruskin's attack on the immorality of capitalism, *Unto This Last,* as a text for his sermons. In "Christianity and Riches," given at Cambridge in 1913, he preached that the Church suffered from being associated with the comfortable, wealthy classes. But "all must refuse to value anyone the more because of his riches."[6] His granddaughter, who also admired Ruskin, agreed.

He understood poverty because he had experienced it. Fitzgerald wrote, with feeling, of Bishop Hicks's family: "Occasionally they would write down a list of all the things they wanted but couldn't afford, and then burn the piece of paper. This is a device which is always worth trying." All her life, Christina could never take a taxi without feeling guilty: "cabby" was her word for "expensive." There were other things, too, she got from her father. Hicks was a feminist, school of John Stuart Mill. He tried unsuccessfully to persuade his fellow bishops to take the clause about "obeying" out of the Marriage Service in the Prayer Book, and he supported women's suffrage. Christina Hicks inherited those beliefs. Her father gave her, and her brothers and sister, free choices. All the children, Christina wrote eloquently, were encouraged to talk to him as equals. They consulted him as though he were an encyclopaedia. "He never laughed at us, and always contrived to make us feel that we had asked something really interesting." They were taught that things should be "perfectly simple" but good of their kind—"a book well printed and bound, for instance, that didn't crack when it was opened." He liked games, music, walks, funny stories and beautiful objects; he hated tyranny and ugliness. He believed in equal opportunities for boys and girls. When he and Agnes moved to Lincoln in 1910—Christina was then twenty-five, with a university education—she was "offered the choice of going away to make a career for myself, or of being 'home-daughter,' whichever I pleased . . . I have never known a daughter so treated, and I have asked many."[7]

ॐ

We hardly hear that thoughtful, intelligent voice of Christina's in her daughter's family memories—either in *The Knox Brothers* or in other later pieces about her childhood—where the mother mainly exists as a silence or an absence, and appears first as "a gentle, spirited, scholarly, hazel-eyed girl, a lover of poetry and music . . . ready to laugh at herself " and later as "a quietly spoken woman whom nothing defeated."[8] In Granny Pugh's letters to her daughter-in-law Agnes about the children, Christina figures as an admirable granddaughter. In 1896, when she was eleven: "It is grateful to me to hear that Christina is fond of poetry. She always seemed to me a child of promise." In 1897: "I am so glad that Christina has distinguished herself."[9] At Withington Girls' School in Manchester, she took the lead in school plays. In 1904 she got a scholarship for £40 a year to Somerville, one of the first women's colleges in Oxford.

Her daughter would be amused by the letter which came with the scholarship, "reminding her that she must change her dress for dinner, but 'must bring no fal-lals, as they only collect dust.'" Her tutors thought her "decidedly promising" if a little immature, "animated and intelligent," with good skills in logic. Helen Darbishire, the Milton and Wordsworth scholar, then senior English Tutor, thought that she wrote with "taste and judgement," but needed "to cultivate more self-confidence." She was active on college committees, writing careful minutes as secretary ("Miss Hicks drew attention to complaints which she had received from members whose mackintoshes and umbrellas had been borrowed without permission") and allowing herself some light moments: "Miss Blake delivered a stirring exhortation on the subject of the Fiction Library" . . . "Rules about Sleeping Out: No one may consciously sleep out in the rain!"[10] She worked hard, went to dances, had a "beau" or two, won the College Coombs prize, made friends with the future novelist Rose Macaulay, and left in 1907 with a Second Class in English, though she could not take her degree until 1921, the year after Oxford at last started awarding degrees to women. Possibly Oxford's discriminatory attitudes, as well as her father's support, fuelled Christina's involvement, in 1908, in demonstrations and mass meetings in support of the Women's Suffrage Bill.[11]

Her father grieved over Edwin's death and over the defection of his youngest son, Ned, who, after being wounded on the Somme, converted to Roman Catholicism under the influence of Ronald Knox. But the Bishop was proud of "Tina" 's scholarly achievements. He was close to his younger daughter. When she went abroad after Oxford, he advised her: "Try to use all the chances that come to you of learning about the habits and conditions of the people." When she asked him about belief, he sent her a long letter, which concluded: "The sound Christian is largely an agnostic."[12] When he gave her the choice in 1910 of being a "home-daughter" or having a career, she went to teach at St. Felix School in Southwold. The Bishop approved of that as much as he did of her engagement to Eddie Knox, son of his old acquaintance the Bishop of Manchester, in 1912.

Christina and Eddie met in Oxford, probably introduced by her younger brother Ned, who, at Magdalen School, had already brought home an admirer for his sister, his fellow chorister Ivor Novello, who on family holidays followed her about devotedly. Nobody wanted the engagement to be long. One sensible bishop's wife, Mrs. Hicks, conferred with the other, Mrs. Knox: "Christina says . . . it *does* seem such a long time till May! She is anxious because he is lonely . . ."[13] They were married in St. Hugh's Chapel in Lincoln Cathedral on 17 September 1912. It was a family affair.

Her father-in-law-to-be, the Bishop of Manchester, officiated, assisted by the Reverend Ronald Knox, her new brother-in-law. The local papers made much of the event: "BISHOP'S SON WEDS BISHOP'S DAUGHTER." Christina was described as an active supporter of the women's suffrage movement, an amateur actress with a brilliant Oxford career. Joyful letters went back to Lincoln from the honeymoon in Porlock ("We are very happy"). After Rawle was born, in 1913, the Bishop enjoyed visiting the young

Knoxes in Hampstead. When war broke out, he wrote to his daughter: "Keep quite calm."[14] When Eddie went to war ("I knew, and he knew, that he would have to go," Christina wrote in her diary), it made perfect sense for her to return home.

Christina Hicks's marriage, at twenty-seven, to Edmund George Valpy Knox, aged thirty-one, was a love match between two exceptional people. Her reports on early married life in Hampstead, when she was pregnant with Rawle and Eddie was commuting into town in a heatwave ("Poor Teddy was nearly grilled alive down in Fleet Street . . . He is well though rather washed out"), and Eddie's longing notes from the front line ("Darlingest Christinissima, I do hope the babies will keep well, and your own darling squirrel self") set a lasting tone between them of deep affection and mutual concern.[15] Beyond that close personal relationship, in marrying a Knox, Christina became part of a remarkable tribe.

The Knoxes are the family that dominate Penelope Fitzgerald's life story. They set a tone and a standard. Her group biography of her father and her three uncles, *The Knox Brothers,* evocative, funny and deeply felt, makes it almost impossible to use any but her words, or to think in any but her terms, about her father's family. She was proud of belonging to that exceptional and eccentric clan, and they left a strong mark on her life and her writing. She describes them in *The Knox Brothers* as a brilliantly clever English family distinguished by alarming honesty, caustic wit, shyness, moral rigour, willpower, oddness and powerful banked-down feelings, erupting in moments of sentiment or in violent bursts of temper and gloom. Like them, she plays down her feelings, and describes these characters mainly in a spirit of comedy, but love and admiration keep breaking through, as when speaking of their truthfulness ("When you employed one of the four Knox brothers, you got absolute integrity"), or their reserve:

> It was not the habit of the four brothers to show enthusiasm about their own work. That would have gone contrary both to their real modesty and to the Edwardian habit of understatement, the habit which called the massacre of the Somme "a show," and an expensive lunch at Simpson's "something to eat."

Her index to the book sums up their "collective characteristics":

Bath, inspiration in; Bible, knowledge of; critical spirit; Edwardian; emotion at war with intellect; family feeling; fearlessness;
foreign travel, distrust of; games, love of inventing rules for; generosity; honesty; intellectual severity; love, need for; pipe-smoking;
poetry, love of; rhyming, skill at; speaking ability; temper, loss
of; tender-heartedness; transport, passion for forms of (railways,
trams, bicycles, motor-bikes); understatement, tendency to.

The key to them is the phrase "emotion at war with intellect." The
brothers had deep and largely inexpressible feelings for one another, which
came out in their "poetry, love of ": of Housman's *A Shropshire Lad,* or of
Cory's elegy for "Heraclitus" ("They told me, Heraclitus, they told me
you were dead . . ."), which she keeps returning to, like a sad tune. But
they also fought like devils in the schoolroom, went their different ways as
adults, and treated one another ironically and critically.

All the brothers were mad about systems. As children they insisted on
games "of which they invented or changed the rules, with the object of
making them as difficult, and therefore as worthwhile, as possible." She
sees this as symbolic. "A game is a classic method of bringing life to order
by giving it a fixed attainable objective, so that even if we lose, we are still
in control." But, "inconveniently enough, the emotions are exempt from
rules, and ignore their existence." This is the brothers' lifelong dilemma.
"If we are creatures of reason, what are we to do with our hearts?" It is a
particularly sharp question when it comes to matters of faith. *The Knox
Brothers* is as much about religious beliefs as it is about family life. Once an
Evangelical, she used to say, you never, ever get rid of it.[16] But what does it
mean for strong characters brought up in a strong faith when they lose it,
or leave it? This interests her very much, and she will often write about
it. As for all the Knoxes, "belief and unbelief " were vital concerns for her.

The sea of faith was at the full for the Knox brothers' parents and
grandparents. But the religious legacy from those generations could be
a harsh one. Fitzgerald cites Samuel Beckett (one of her favourite writers) and his character Watt, "who had never smiled, but thought that he
knew how it was done," when describing her eighteenth-century Knox
great-grandfather's gloomy Ulster Protestantism. George Knox, for a time
the East India Company's chaplain in Madras, brought his family up in
hard work and poverty, beating piety into them, a regime only slightly
softened by his sweet-tempered Quaker wife, Frances, who had eight chil-

dren and then took to her sofa. When Fitzgerald's nephew William Knox became a Quaker, she told him he was reverting to his roots.[17]

It was a rough childhood: "But hardship never destroys a family if the parents share it." Edmund Arbuthnott, the second son, robust, strong and determined, developed an unshakeable Evangelical faith, which means, as Fitzgerald explains it, a personal conviction of God's love, and "no real division between the seen and the unseen." Edmund went to St. Paul's School as a scholar (it only cost his father a shilling, for the porter's tip), and to Corpus Christi College at Oxford. He was taught by Edward Lee Hicks, lived on nothing, worked hard, was driven on by his father's grim ambitions for him, and became a curate and a Fellow of Merton, where he was known as "Hard Knocks."

In 1878, he married the daughter of a remarkable missionary, a delicate, selfless young woman called Ellen Penelope French, and in 1884, after nearly twenty years at Oxford, he moved his family (the six Knox children were born between 1879 and 1888) to Kibworth Rectory, in Leicestershire. This was the Knox family's paradise, a country childhood which Fitzgerald writes about with feeling, "where in memory it was always summer," in the big rambling house with its pastures and fruit trees and the Midland Railway line running past the bottom of the garden, turning the Knoxes into "passionate railway children." The children—Ethel, Edmund, Winifred, Dillwyn, Wilfred and Ronald—"were so happy there that in later years they could cure themselves of sleeplessness simply by imagining that they were back at Kibworth." She would say exactly the same thing about her own country childhood.[18] Elsewhere, though, she gives a harsher version of the "immensely hard-working Evangelical household where comfort and beauty counted for very little and money for almost nothing."[19]

The energetic, ambitious, broad-shouldered Rector of Kibworth decided in 1891 to accept a job in the big urban parish of Aston, in the "sulphur-laden air" of industrial Birmingham. It was an even more dramatic version of the Reverend Hicks's move from Fenny Compton to Manchester. The Knox children were plunged from country life into the dark, sooty slum streets of Aston. The only consolations were the trams, the good day schools and the Aston Villa football club. The parents worked all hours in the tough parish; but Ellen Penelope's health was frail. Soon after the move, at thirty-eight, she developed influenza, lingered for a few months (in an "atmosphere, so frightening to children, of things not being quite right, and of discussions behind closed doors"), and died.

The family's life changed utterly. The bereaved children, aged between four and thirteen, were sent away and moved around. The miserable rectory at Aston got more and more "seedy and neglected." The Knoxes were rescued by the shining, miraculous appearance of the immensely competent Ethel Newton, a wealthy vicar's daughter, who took on and humanised the "uncouth" Knox children and in 1895 became "Mrs. K." This was the support Edmund Knox required as his career marched on. He became Bishop Suffragan of Coventry and Rector of St. Philip's in Birmingham, where, among many other achievements, he supervised the installation of Burne-Jones's "Last Judgement" window in what would become the Cathedral of Birmingham. Fitzgerald writes with feeling about this window in *The Knox Brothers* and in her biography of Burne-Jones. But her grandfather hardly noticed it, since, she would say, "he had no aesthetic sense whatever."[20]

In 1903, Edmund Knox became Bishop of Manchester, where he stayed for nearly twenty years, and was renowned for "his energy and splendid powers of organisation." The see covered a huge swathe of Lancashire and three million parishioners, and involved him in "staunch battles" over religious education. There were battles, too, with his children, as their views left his behind, which painfully mixed deep, unexpressed affection with bewildered and angry conflicts over belief. In his retirement, in a large Victorian-style house in Kent, he continued to "peg away" against threats to the Evangelical Church and changes to the Prayer Book. His granddaughter remembered his "stout and wheezing" presence in old age as "perhaps more alarming than he knew." He was immortalised in what she calls a "delightful portrait, in which the Bishop is apparently about to rise from his seat and knock somebody down with a Bible."[21]

There was another model in the family, though, for spiritual dedication. Ellen Penelope Knox's father, the missionary-priest Thomas Valpy French, Bishop of Lahore, makes Christina's father, Bishop Hicks, look like a worldly hedonist. Innocent, learned and fanatical, French felt the call to be a missionary while he was at Oxford, went to Calcutta, learned so many Indian languages that he was known in the Punjab as "the seven-tongued Padri," lived in utmost simplicity, founded and taught in Christian schools in Agra and Lahore, married a Quaker, and travelled vast distances across the North-West Frontier on mule-back with his dictionaries and his teapot. As Fitzgerald observes, "Today he would certainly be asked: why not leave these people to their own beliefs?" Yet his Christianity increasingly took on the flavour of Hindu asceticism; he was "going native." In 1878 he became Bishop of Lahore and burnt himself out in his labours, but could never accept retirement. In his mid-sixties he set out again to preach Christianity to the Arabs. His solitary wanderings, which she recounts with entranced fascination, ended in the Bay of Muscat on the Red Sea coast, where he died alone in the blazing sun, book in hand, weighing next to nothing. Fitzgerald notes the profound effect of the news of her father's death on his daughter, Ellen Penelope Knox, who died a year later.

When Bishop French and his wife came home on leave, to Whitby or Lindisfarne or St. David's, there would be a big family reunion of Knoxes and Frenches. His granddaughter Winifred vividly remembered those holiday visits of the 1880s, when they would meet up with "a mighty army of sisters, cousins and aunts." The children would keep their heads down at teatime while "discussions raged above our heads" between their clerical relatives, all disagreeing about "doctrine and ritual." In between theological disputes, Bishop French would lead the family out on gigantic day-long walks in search of some religious ruin: "A runic Cross or a pre-Norman arch were to him what a pier or a promenade would be to an ordinary tourist." There would be no sandwiches, as the Bishop always relied on the kindness of strangers. His son-in-law, Bishop Knox, observed: "A wonderful man and a Saint was Bishop French, but I have known more sympathetic company for a family walk." Fitzgerald agreed. Thomas Valpy French "was a saint, holy in the noblest sense of the word, and as exasperating as all saints." For the Knox children, their authoritarian, conservative father and their wandering, ascetic grandfather provided contrasting versions of the religious life.[22]

Fitzgerald describes the Knox brothers, in youth, as a pack, often bossing around their sisters, Ethel and Winnie, but also chivalrously supporting them. They were quarrelsome, sarcastic, fearless, addicted to elaborate practical jokes and private languages, fanatical cyclists, ferociously competitive games-players bent on winning, and as one in their "inborn melancholy and natural relish for disaster." Like other big late-Victorian families (the Bensons, the Waughs, the Stephenses), they had a family magazine, *The Bolliday Bango,* which featured a long-running Latin play by Ronnie, a cypher by Dilly, sporting pages, family jokes and comic illustrations by Eddie. Fitzgerald would describe Evelyn Waugh's family, much as she described the Knoxes, forming "a conspiracy against the outside world, not feeling the necessity to explain itself." But she thought Evelyn Waugh did not understand "the deep, wordless affection between the brothers" when he came to write the life of Ronald Knox.

Pet names—such as Mops—are rife in this kind of English tribe. The family's names, inherited from different branches (Rawle from the Hicks family; Valpy, Penelope and Dillwyn—a Welsh trace—from the Frenches; Edmund from the Knoxes), got turned into nicknames. Dillwyn was Dilly, or "Erm," because he always hesitated in his speech. Edmund was Eddie, or Teddy, and later invented a *Punch* sobriquet for himself, "Evoe." This was meant to be pronounced "Ee Vee" but was sometimes read (and pronounced) as "Eave-oh," presumably with "Heave-ho" in mind. Ronald was Ronnie, inside and outside the family. Wilfred was Wilfie and Winifred was Winnie. Ethel used to call Ronnie and Wilfred "Iffie" and "Whooks."[23]

The tribe's sense of humour was relentless and surreal. For instance, when a journalist visited one of the rectories they used to stay in for their summer holidays, which had no servants, Mrs. K asked the Knox daughters, Winnie and Ethel, to act as cook and parlour maid. "Eddie told the reporter that both of them were deaf and dumb, and could be addressed only in sign language; this caused Winnie to drop the soup." They ganged up on the outside world, and also against one another. In Winifred Peck's words, which Fitzgerald quotes, they were "shy and sensitive and intensely critical, [imagining] that other people would think we were peculiar and yet . . . quite sure that our family stand-point on almost any question was absolutely and unquestionably right."[24]

Eccentric outsiders they may have been, but they also belonged to what was then, still, an influential and distinguished fellowship: "They were a vicarage family, and vicarages were the intellectual power-houses of nineteenth-century England."[25] Each of them broke away from the vicarage, but each of them retained a conviction of rightness and authority. One of these brothers became a sceptic, a comic journalist and poet, and a respected literary editor. One of them, a classicist with a mathematical bent, and an atheist, became a secret code-breaker whose brilliance was only fully appreciated posthumously. One became an ascetic, meditative, socialist Anglo-Catholic priest and teacher. One became a famous Roman Catholic priest, a dazzling preacher, a writer of detective stories, and author of an influential translation of the New Testament for Catholic readers. And one of the sisters (though her niece plays this down) became a writer of history books, memoirs and novels. Fitzgerald skilfully shows in her book how clannish they were, and how different they became.

Dillwyn, from the first, was the domineering imposer of rules, the one who could do maths in his head, and the genius of the family. He could be horribly "brusque and cutting," but "kind beyond belief " if a family member was in trouble. At Eton, a pipe-smoking sportsman and classicist, he became, with some private anguish, "an extreme agnostic." Later in life he would refer to Jesus Christ as "that deluded individual, J.C." But in Fitzgerald's view, "a violent reaction against an upbringing [is] a kind of faithfulness" to it.[26]

Dillwyn only studied and competed if he was interested: for his Cambridge exams he did two dazzling papers on maths and Greek verse, and ignored the rest. At King's College in the 1900s, where the term "noxian" ("noxious and anti-Christian") was coined for him, he had close friendships with some clever men: Lytton Strachey, the eccentric classical scholar Walter Headlam, his Eton school-friend Maynard Keynes, and later Geoffrey Keynes, who had connections to Bloomsbury. In his last two years at Eton, Dilly conducted some "intellectual and sexual" experiments with Keynes. At King's, for a short time, he was the object of Lytton Strachey's desire. Fitzgerald rather walks round this, making fun of Strachey's comical passions and implying that Dilly was "impervious" to the "golden glow of homosexuality" that suffused Cambridge in those days. She makes more of his passion for Greek poetry. He dedicated himself, under Headlam's influence, to editing the recently discovered papyrus of Herodas's "mimes," the bawdy satirical poetry of a "not very good" Greek poet. He became a Fellow of King's College when the ghost-story writer M. R. James was Provost, acted in comic plays produced by his theatrical friend Frank Birch, and spent his time deciphering Herodas and working on Greek metrical analysis. In *The Gate of Angels* Fitzgerald would evoke this Cambridge period.[27]

The war transferred his skills to Naval Intelligence. Dillwyn became a cryptographer in "Room 40," working with other Oxbridge dons who had been recruited to decipher German signals. It was secret, concentrated and difficult work, for which Dillwyn had a natural gift. "There was a certain art, a certain flair with which Dilly was born, for the shadow patterns of groups of letters, no matter in what language, revealing themselves, like a secret dance, only to the patient watcher." In 1917, he cracked the flag code used by the German commander-in-chief in directing submarine warfare, by recognising that one particular coded message must be in metre (it turned out to be a quotation from Schiller). Fitzgerald claims that this saved a great number of convoys from U-boat attacks.

Also, he fell in love, surprisingly, with his secretary, Olive Roddam. They got married after the war, and moved to a damp, draughty house in the Chiltern woods, near High Wycombe. Here, while Olive brought up their two sons, Dillwyn studied Greek poetry. In the 1920s he was hired by the Foreign Office, at the time of the General Strike, to monitor Russian activities in Britain and to try to break the codes of Soviet intelligence. His family knew nothing at all about his work—then, or in the next war—until much later. Olive was baffled by him: it was not an easy marriage. The neighbours thought him "an absent-minded dear," as he rode his motorbike dangerously from High Wycombe to London, played patience in his study, sawed down trees and expanded his woodland acres, a "gaunt and hesitant" figure, "amiable and abstracted." "Do what he could, he never looked, as he tramped up the overgrown paths, in the least like a landed proprietor."[28]

If Dillwyn was the genius of the family, Wilfred, like his grandfather Bishop French, was the saint. After his mother's death (he was only five) he and Ronnie were sent away to their Knox uncle in Lincolnshire, a mild, old-fashioned Evangelical household, where the little boys bonded together, for life as it seemed. Wilfred as a child had an astonishingly good memory, a sharp temper, a rich fantasy life and a passion for photography and for collecting "Bits of Old Churches." At Rugby, he struggled between "emotion and the obligation not to show it." He had a sensitive conscience and was more disturbed by the social conditions of Aston than any of his brothers. Under the influence of Ruskin, F. D. Maurice and an older boy at Rugby, Billy Temple (who became Archbishop of Canterbury), Wilfred came to feel that "a total change of heart in society" was needed. As a student at Trinity College, Oxford, when he went through a phase of "not particularly believing in anything," he was spending much of his time in the East End, in Stratford, at the college's Trinity Mission. Wilfred's support for the Labour movement and for the pacifist leader George Lansbury, his horror of materialism and of the effects of industrialisation, were moving him towards Anglo-Catholicism. The movement's "concern for the bottom of the heap" appealed to him as much as its commitment to tradition and authority. English Catholicism and social reform came together in his belief that society needed "to be unified before it could be healed."

In 1912 he went to study theology at St. Anselm's College in Cambridge, and took a vow of celibacy and poverty. He was not to keep more than £100 a year out of whatever he earned, and he was not to indulge in regrets for the things he had liked—good clothes, wine, tobacco. "Renunciation must never be seen in terms of loss." He became a priest when he was nearly thirty, in 1915. His convictions centred on the need for the purification of the Church. It should be freed from all "money and patronage derived from the State," and the clergy should give up all wealth and social status.[29] He found a home for these beliefs, from 1920 onwards, in the Oratory of the Good Shepherd, a celibate religious brotherhood, originating in Cambridge and partly inspired by the Anglican fellowship at Little Gidding, whose scattered communities were yoked under the rule of "unselfish action, loyalty and love." They set out to share what they had, not to judge others, and never to relax from mental labour. When he did take time off, he went fishing with Eddie in the Herefordshire/Welsh borders, on the River Arrow and the River Lug, a countryside they loved.[30]

Fitzgerald writes about the Oratory—one of those idiosyncratic communities which always fascinate her—with a mixture of wistfulness and humour, as though she would have liked to join it. She sees that its members are eccentrics. Wilfred by then was very odd. Extremely shy, with a peculiar nervous laugh, awkward and alarmingly honest, dressed in strange, messy old clothes, he spent his time in the Cambridge branch of the Oratory gardening and writing theological works on his "frightful typewriter." The best known of these, *Meditation and Mental Prayer,* was an important book for her. It recommends the self-discipline of silence, passive obedience to God, simplicity, poverty and "the mortification of our natural desires." The main object of religion is not "vague philanthropic enthusiasm" or "self-improvement," it is "to serve and glorify God."[31] When Fitzgerald left her copy behind on her travels while she was writing *The Knox Brothers,* she wrote asking for it to be returned, as "I value it highly."[32] And she valued the edicts of the Oratory, even if not judging other people, for example, is almost impossible, "because other people are not only infuriating, but boring." But impossible tasks had to be worked at. Stillness in prayer is hard, "because busy activity seems more rewarding. Stillness, however, does not mean inactivity, but peace." She thought of the Oratory as "one of the many unseen and unknown currents that quietly deepen the life surrounding it." Wilfred believed, and she believed, "that there will be a place for such small communities, still together, still understanding one another, in the life to come."

There was no possibility of Wilfred Knox's jumping from English Catholicism to Rome or of becoming a well-known public figure, like his beloved younger brother. Fitzgerald describes Ronnie Knox in childhood as sparkling and affectionate, "an exceedingly bright little boy," who learned Latin and Greek at four and soon afterwards embarked on Sanskrit and Welsh. He fell quickly in love with his stepmother, was petted by his sisters and bossed about by his older brothers. He wanted to be loved, and to please. At Eton, and later at Balliol, he was a star, a "brilliant, dutiful and rather delicate prize-winner," eager to conform to rules and traditions but also swayed (in the typical Knox struggle between reason and emotion) by romantic enthusiasms for the Pre-Raphaelites, or for seventeenth-century religious poetry. At school he "swam in a golden atmosphere of popularity and success," the cleverest boy in Eton's living memory. At Oxford he was famous for his "deceptively easy-looking brilliance" as a public speaker, his improvised limericks and his impromptu jokes. He was in demand among the Edwardian coterie of aristocratic young men—Grenfells, Balfours, Listers—children of that elite and powerful group "The Souls," who welcomed the brilliant, witty young intellectual to their house parties. Later, he would be a favoured guest in the Catholic households of the Lovats, the Actons, the Asquiths, and this raised eyebrows among the unworldly Knoxes. Fitzgerald disliked it when others wrote about Ronnie Knox as "a country-house priest with a keen enjoyment of upper-class society," and in *The Knox Brothers* she only hints that the family thought him too partial to his "carriage folk." Elsewhere, she is blunter: "Have nothing to do with these people, they'll destroy you sooner or later . . . but Ronnie was fatally attracted by them."[33]

Ronnie's intensest friendships were with two young men at Oxford before the war, when he was Chaplain of Trinity College: Harold Macmillan, future Prime Minister, and the classical scholar Guy Lawrence. Lawrence, clearly the love of Ronnie's life, converted to Catholicism, and was killed in the last weeks of the war. These events turned Ronnie, she thought, from a child into a priest. Beneath the witty amenable entertainer, a powerful mind was working its way towards Anglo-Catholicism, and from there, under the mentorship of the Jesuit priest Father Martindale, to Rome. This mental journey, though in parallel with Wilfred's, was different. Wilfred wanted a purification of the Church united with radical social reform; Ronnie was attracted to "the ideal of authority." Comfortable, tolerant Protestantism, or modernist religious leniency, dismayed him. Fitzgerald was fond of (and reapplied, in a lecture she gave on education) a phrase from his early book *Some Loose Stones:* "If you have a sloppy religion you get a sloppy atheism."[34] At Oxford he became "the irresistible apologist of the English Catholics." At home he was locked in painful battles with the Bishop, which his sister Winnie tried to mediate. Ronnie's conversion in 1912, and his ordination as a Catholic priest in 1919, was a great grief to his father, who cut him out of his will. "Well, they have got him now," he said. To his father, and to his brother Wilfred—though they did not quarrel about it—he was lost forever.

These public and private divisions over English religion seem remote now. But as Fitzgerald points out, "this was a time of furious interest in church affairs and in religious controversy." Ronald Knox's defection to Rome was not the mighty crisis that Newman's had been, nearly seventy years before, but it still caused a stir. In the 1920s, when he became a popular essayist, writing not just in the Catholic press, he was widely read. This populist touch helped with the task he had been given by his masters, to be an advocate for the Church of Rome in England—even if, as a new boy, he didn't always feel at home in it. ("Whoa! I'm only a convert!" he once said to an Irish priest who was pouring him out a triple measure of whisky.) He combined journalism, for a few years, with teaching Latin at a dull school in Hertfordshire. Then, though his media work made him suspect to some (too clever, too facile), he was appointed to the Catholic Chaplaincy of Oxford. At St. Aldate's, he settled, from 1926, into an unchanging routine. His niece noticed that one picture, "hung upside-down in the passage, stayed like that till 1938." He spent twelve years, not very successfully, trying to "encourage young men in their faith," and became "an Oxford institution," to be seen every day on the Thames in his canoe.

By his forties, Ronald Knox had turned himself into an anachronism, "a man who refused to fly or go to the cinema and whose idea of the last really good invention was the toast-rack." He supplemented his income by writing conventional detective stories (one of his early comic triumphs had been a spoof on Sherlock Holmes, much admired by Conan Doyle), padded with period details. Fitzgerald comments wryly: "Time has obscured these things, although time may well restore the wish to read about them." It is what she feels about the Knox brothers.

The oldest brother's attitude to the youngest never altered. Eddie always "marvelled at the prodigy," but thought that Ronnie needed protection and keeping in order. He treated his family, as he did most things in life, with sardonic detachment. Self-satire and understatement were his mode. When asked in old age if he might write his autobiography, he declined, but suggested the title "Must We Have Lives?" Eddie was especially attached to his brother Wilfred, and to his own small family, but did not speak of such things. In childhood an adventurous, short-tempered and darkly handsome boy, his mother's favourite, his emotions went underground when she died. His adoring sister Winnie described the painful change: "There was my eldest brother Eddie, my hero, driven into his own super-sensitive nature by the loss of my mother, by a miserable time alone at home afterwards and by an uncongenial school." Fitzgerald thought that he never quite recovered: "It gave him, at twelve years old, a spartan endurance and a determination not to risk himself too easily to life's blows, which might, at times, have been mistaken for coldness." It developed in him, too, "a certain dry response to life's unpleasant surprises," which he would put to good use.[35]

It took Eddie the longest to come round to Mrs. K, though from school he was writing letters to her as "mother." At Rugby, he put up, like Wilfred, with the roughhouse imperial training, but liked it best when people broke the rules. He liked truth-tellers and nonconformists and "the patient, self-contained, self-imposed pursuit of an entirely personal solution" within a rule-bound society. He completely bypassed the religious turmoil of his brothers. "Church did not seem to rub off properly," he would say. (Yet he would marry a deeply religious young woman.) Nor did scholarly competitiveness, another Knox tradition. At Corpus in the 1900s he played the Edwardian dandy, spending his allowance on fine clothes and cigars, making a reputation as a wit and a prankster, and doing very little work. He left without a degree and opted out of his destined path in the Indian Civil Service. What he did, single-mindedly, under cover of an air of dilettantism, was practise his craft. He was as determined to be a writer as Wilfred was to be a socialist priest or Dillwyn to crack his codes. His idols were Housman, Conan Doyle, Chesterton, Swinburne, Meredith, Yeats, Stevenson, Beerbohm and Twain, and he got into training, as many young writers do, through imitation.

Eddie did a year's teaching after Oxford, at the prep school for Manchester Grammar. Fitzgerald could easily imagine his state of mind: "He wanted to write, and suffered, as generations of authors have done, at the stuffy and inky boredom of the classroom." His ex-pupils would remember admiringly his "aura of good breeding, [with] a certain humorous movement of the lips," his well-built figure in light-brown tweeds, and his kind but firm discipline.[36] But in 1905 his comic verses and essays began to be printed, and the Bishop (who was willing to be convinced) gave him £150 a year to start off as a writer in London.

Fitzgerald writes with pleasure and interest, drawing on her father's reminiscences, about Edwardian Fleet Street, with its bohemian hard-drinking reporters and powerful idiosyncratic editors, who might lean down and give a young beginner a helping hand. Eddie's genius for pastiche, satire, ingenious punning and rhyming in comic verse, and his willingness to take on anything, from an epigram on "Women's Rational Dress" to an ode on a bus-horse, suited the market well, though at first, out of twenty contributions a week, he might get eighteen rejections. "Like every freelance, he could tell the sound of them as they fell through the letterbox onto the doormat." The editor of the *Observer,* J. L. Garvin, might write to him, regretfully turning him down: "We were so pressed last week that, much to my regret, I had to leave out the Ode to Tinned Beef, which I much loved." Or he might be lucky, telling his stepmother: "I wrote about a flea in this week's *Punch,* but with great delicacy suppressed my name."[37]

Eddie got his start at the *Pall Mall Magazine,* which made him subeditor on £200 a year, and as a contributor for the autocratic and conservative editor of *Punch,* Owen Seaman, in the days when the magazine was a British institution, read all over the colonies: "A joke was said either to be, or not to be, 'good enough for *Punch.'* " Alongside other juniors like E. V. Lucas and A. A. Milne, "Evoe" was a popular and satisfactory apprentice, though Seaman was a little wary of his occasional Knoxian bursts of "lunatic fantasy." Good-looking, funny and stylish, he was popular with women, too, and had a number of inconclusive girlfriends before he met and fell in love with Christina. By the time they were ready to marry, he had foreseen the coming war, with characteristic pessimism and clear-sightedness. His war experiences confirmed his darkly satirical view of the world.[38]

The women in *The Knox Brothers* are marginalised, apart from a strong sketch of the competent Mrs. K. The interesting sister, Winifred Peck, is pushed to the sidelines. When reproached about this, Fitzgerald would reply crossly that it was meant to be a book about the *brothers.* She is glimpsed as the emotional one in the nursery plays ("Enter Winnie, and kisses everybody"), as a romantic young reader with a passion for medieval history, as a family peacekeeper longing to get away from the religious rows, as Ronnie's particular friend, and as a young wife and mother in Edinburgh. But we hear little of her academic successes at school at High Wycombe and at Oxford, or her career as a historian and novelist, or of the memoirs which Fitzgerald makes much use of in her book.

Another woman who is kept almost concealed in the book is "the daughter," or "the niece," whose arrival is very quietly signalled as the birth of "Christina's second child" and who is the only member of the family to get no entry in the index. Only in the paperback reissue of the book, twenty-three years after its first appearance, is there a photograph of a young Penelope Knox, captioned "The niece." Blink, and you would miss her. Here she is, for instance, in relation to one of the book's most obscure and pathetic figures, the oldest Knox sister, Ethel, a "home-daughter" all her life, done here—like many of the characters in *The Knox Brothers*—in a novelistic miniature:

> Ethel was installed in her room with her typewriter and her work for the Christian Missionary Society, all the letters she had ever received, all the old toys, all the old books . . . It must not be thought, by the way, that Ethel, who had now become Aunt Ethel to three nephews and a niece, was at all discontented with her lot. Her Victorianism was not of the kind that appeared in twentieth-century novels. She did not like the outside world, and was proud to stay at home. Her bits of jewellery were put away for "the Miss Knox of the next generation." When her niece married, she put them away with a sigh, because now there would be no Miss Knox.

The niece, the one girl of her generation of Knoxes (since Dillwyn and Winifred had only boys), did want to be known as "a Knox," even though Ethel's kind of life would have been anathema to her. But she keeps her own story firmly back. That, for her, is not the point of this book, though it may be for us. Looking for Penelope Fitzgerald's autobiography inside *The Knox Brothers* is like bringing invisible ink to light. Every so often, a heartfelt comment—on the pain for children of leaving their country home or of their mother's death, on a remembered landscape, on the challenges for a writer's family or the frustrations of teaching when you want to write—reveal her presence. So she notes Dillwyn's preference, in painting, for "a certain kind of low-keyed, unassertive, but deeply felt English picture." This sidelong approach is part of her inheritance from the Knox brothers and their lifelong habit of understatement.

The tone also suggests that some things are not being said. The book was begun in 1971, after the death of the last surviving Knox brother, her father, and in consultation with his widow, Penelope's stepmother, Mary, to whom she was very close, and who also wanted to write something about Evoe.[39] It was published in 1977, dedicated to Evoe, and so it inevitably has an elegiac, loving and careful tone. And there were plenty of Knox relations alive when it came out. She admitted later to having had difficulty writing it "for fear of hurting people's feelings," and calls it "the opposite of the usual tell-all biography."[40] As she was reaching the end of the book, in 1976, she told her cousin Oliver, Dillwyn's son: "I haven't said what short tempers they all had, and what a gloom they could cast over the household, or anyhow my father did. No matter."[41] The terrible Knox

rages, the ambivalent sexuality of three of the brothers and Dillwyn's malfunctioning marriage, Ethel Knox being not "quite normal,"[42] any details
about her own mother and brother or her own life: there were personal
reasons for keeping such things back. But did she also romanticise the
Knoxes?

Being a Knox was not, in fact, an easy business. She said herself that
the truth was that "(like most children with conspicuous relations) I
tried to get away from them and do my own thing," and only much later
realised their importance to her.[43] Her nephew William Knox, Rawle's son,
remembers her saying: "The Knox men have a habit of flaunting their
superiority over others in a particularly nasty way."[44] Others speak of their
arrogance, their inhibitions, their clannishness, their neuroses and depres-
sions, and the pressure they created in their expectations of success. When
Oliver, Dillwyn's son, failed to gain the top scholarship to Eton, he was
told, to his chagrin, that his grandfather Bishop Knox was "appalled."[45]
Belinda Hunt, Rawle's daughter, thinks that "the Knoxes were just bad at
failure . . . If you didn't shine and were brilliant it was bad."[46]

But being expected to shine was also an inspiration. In the view of
Fitzgerald's close friend Jasmine Blakeway: "Being a Knox was so important. She knew in her heart that she was going to reach a high level."[47] The
Knoxes made her feel all her life that there was a standard to emulate. Writing in late life of all her ancestors, Hickses and Knoxes, she says: "I should
like to have lived up to them."[48] In her foreword to *The Knox Brothers,* she
wrote:

> In this book I have done my best to tell the story of my father and
> his three brothers. All four of them were characteristically reticent
> about themselves, but, at the same time, most unwilling to let any
> statement pass without question. I have tried to take into account
> both their modesty and their love of truth, and to arrive at the
> kind of biography of which they would have approved.
>
> When I was very young I took my uncles for granted, and it
> never occurred to me that everyone else in the world was not like
> them. Later on I found that this was not so, and eventually I began
> to want to make some kind of record of their distinctive attitude
> to life, which made it seem as though, in spite of their differences,
> they shared one sense of humour and one mind.

Returning to this foreword for a revised edition of the book, just before
her death, she added:

They gave their working lives to journalism, cryptography, classical scholarship, the Anglican Church, the Catholic Church. Since I wrote this book twenty-three years ago all these professions, all these worlds, have changed. If the four of them could be reborn into the twenty-first century, how would it treat them? I can only be certain that they would stand by the (sometimes unexpected) things they said. Evoe, my father, muttered to me, on the way to my wedding, "The only thing I want is for everyone, as far as possible, to be happy." Dillwyn: "Nothing is impossible." Wilfred: "Get on with it"—also "Why should we not go on, through all eternity, growing in love and in our power to love?" Ronnie: "Do the most difficult thing." I miss them all more than I can say.

CHAPTER TWO

Learning to Read

Twice in your life you know that you are approved of by everyone: when you learn to walk, and when you learn to read.[1]

Eddie and Christina Knox wanted to move back to Hampstead with the children after the war was over. Eddie was working, briefly, for the Civil Service, though, as "Evoe," he was also sending his contributions in to *Punch*. (One of the first things they asked for after he came out of the trenches was a "series of parodies on well-known poets of the day," including Charlotte Mew.)[2] He had rented a small house in East Heath Road in Hampstead, but there were tenants in place. These were John Middleton Murry and the very unwell Katherine Mansfield—the only recorded time her path crossed with Penelope Fitzgerald, then aged two. Christina, wanting a quiet, cheap place in which to bring up the children, and no doubt remembering Fenny Compton, suggested a move to the country, somewhere where they could "keep hens and grow vegetables and put up a swing for the children."[3] Evoe—no doubt remembering Kibworth—agreed, though they had to be near enough to London for him to commute to Fleet Street. He was hoping for an assistant editorship at *Punch*. They chose a small village in West Sussex, Balcombe, near Haywards Heath. Now it is close to the M23, and even then, as Evoe described it in *An Hour from Victoria* (his 1924 collection of *Punch* sketches about country life), it had motorcars humming through it all day long. All the same, "Bittleigh," as he called it, was "quite a little village," surrounded by oak and birch woods and within reach of the Downs. Evoe had fun with the Sussex "characters" speaking in dialect and wearing smocks who turn out to be "regional novelists," the non-stop activities of the village institute, golf and debating clubs. His "Bittleigh" is poised between age-old rural remoteness and commuting suburbia.[4]

For Penelope Fitzgerald, memories began at Balcombe, in a "homely mock-Tudor house with a lawn and a cherry-tree." Late in life, she remembered it as an idyll: the flowering cherry and the walnut tree outside her window, her secret hiding-place between the double rose hedge, the rabbit that was always getting lost, the low murmuring of the hens, the baker delivering bread in his pony-trap, the treat of riding home on the last cow going to the farm for afternoon milking, the feeling of utter security: "Balcombe was the place where for three years I had no real anxieties, and looked forward every night, as I fell asleep, to waking up the next day." There were some childhood horrors: the chained farm dog, the ganders, the "sudden smell of corruption in the lanes when you walked past a dead animal," moments of fear: "Sometimes I was overwhelmed, standing in a field under an open blue sky, by a kind of terror at the enormity of the turning earth."[5]

In retrospect she recognised how demanding post-war country life was for Christina, alone every day of the week with two small children while Evoe commuted to London on the train. There was no electricity, no telephone, no refrigerator, no washing machine, no nearby shop. A local lady came in once a week to help. Much of the day was spent on chores and on walking to and from the farms and the local tradespeople. Occasionally they would get a lift in the stuffy, evil-smelling Daimler of the village's Lady Bountiful, and eventually they had their own car, a new Citroën, parked in a "wild garage" which doubled as a hen roost. But everything was a long, slow process: picking over the raisins, pickling the walnuts, shelling the beans and peas, straining the redcurrant jelly, washing the brass rings of the curtains, drying the clothes on the kitchen airer.

Mops was "one of those children who don't at all mind being by themselves." Her childhood habits were ritualistic, secret ones: compulsively making, naming, and then burying, piles of rose petals in her hiding-place between the rose hedges, collecting feathers, shells, nuts and flowers on her walks to be "counted and recounted, one of the most reassuring activities of all for a small child." Her mother was at the centre of the memories: walking with her, reading to her. There is no sense of an intimate relationship with her older brother, but of a rather distant, even competitive, admiration. The three and a half years between them was "an unbridgeable gap." He was the one in command and the one in demand, the desirable one, she felt.

"Rawle" was the word she recognised in all the family prayers: "We thank thee, Lord, for Rawle thy mercies." She always describes him as doing something she couldn't—off playing cricket or at the village carpenter's, competing with his friends as to which of them could pee the furthest out of the upstairs window, absorbed in his war games, away at school.[6] Rawle—a pudgy, dark boy with a stammer—probably found his bright little sister a challenge. In later years he gave his family the impression that he felt outshone by her. They were never close, but they did feel loyalty and affection for each other, as children, and in later life.

Mops as a little girl was captured in her father's writings. When she was three, going on four, Evoe wrote an occasional column in *Punch* about the highly intelligent, strong-minded, articulate and imaginative "Priscilla," who would engage her father in Socratic dialogue and logical tests at which he always failed, because of her unbeatable combination of ruthless practicality and wild fantasy. Making allowances for the whimsical style of a *Punch* column of the time, the pieces create a vivid character. Here, Priscilla is painting a picture of some men in a boat:

Seven in all, they stood in their bright boat on a blue sea, beneath a round and burning sun. Their legs were long and thin, their bodies globular . . . and their faces large . . . Their countenances were all fixed in the same unmeaning stare. Take it all in all, it was an eerie and terrible scene. "I don't quite see how the boat moves along, Priscilla," I said; "it hasn't any oars or sail." It was a tactless remark and the artist made no reply. I did my best to cover my blunder. "I expect the wind blew very hard . . ." I said. "What colour is the wind?" inquired Priscilla. She had me there. I confessed that I did not know. "It was a brown wind," she decided, impatient at my lack of resource, and slapped a wet typhoon of madder on the page. There was no more doubt about the wind. "And is the picture finished now?" I asked her. "No, it isn't finished. I haven't drawn the pookin yet." The pookin is a confusion in the mind of Priscilla between a pelican and a toucan, because she saw them both for the first time on the same day . . . "Where were these men going to, Priscilla?" I asked. "They was going to Wurvin," she answered in the tone of a mother who instructs her child. "And what do you think they was going to do there?" "I don't know." "They was going to see Auntie Isabel." "And what did they do then?" "They had dinner," she cried enthusiastically. "And do you know what they did after dinner?" "I don't." "They went on the Front to see the fire-escape." It seemed to me now that the conception was mellow, rounded and complete . . . "And who is the picture for, Priscilla?" I asked . . . "It's for you," she said, presenting it with a motley-coloured hand, "it's for you to take to London town and not to drop it."

Here, Priscilla is showing her father how to dance. "'Dance!' she said to me one morning when I came down to breakfast. As a matter of fact I never dance my best before the first cup of coffee, and, after a few feeble steps had been taken, 'Very bad dancing indeed!' she cried; 'now I'll show you how to do it.'"

A year later, Priscilla is learning to read. "She grips the book furiously and her eyes blaze with excitement. I doubt if the author, in his most sanguine moments, dreamed how his story was destined to thrill. 'Pat is getting Dan hash from the pot. Crash! Pat has let the hash drop. Did it splash that pink sash? Yes, just a spot went on to it.' Just like that it sounds fairly simple, but to a beginner it is a much more breathless and dramatic affair. P—like blowing out a candle; A—as if you had scratched yourself on a pin; T—as if you were thoroughly shocked; and so on. When you come to DA-N it is really quite alarming."[7]

The real Penelope had her own vivid memory of the triumphant moment of suddenly learning to read, one of the two moments in your life when you know you are "approved of by everyone": "I began to read just after I was four. The letters on the page suddenly gave in and admitted what they stood for. They obliged me completely and all at once, in whole sentences, so that I opened a book in my lair under the dining-room table and read aloud, without hesitation: 'My hoop can only run by my side, and I often wish it was a dog and could bark.' I was praised, and since then have never been praised so much."[8]

So she was a "reading child" by the time she was five, in 1922, when the family left the country and went back to Hampstead.[9] Evoe was put on the staff of *Punch* in 1921; commuting to the country had become impossible. "The hens, the lawnmower and the rabbit hutches were sold; they would have to return to London." Rawle never forgot having to take the rabbit in the wheelbarrrow to its next owner. In the manuscript of "Thinking of Balcombe" she says that "she and her brother felt something like despair" at leaving the cherry tree, the rose hedges and the open fields. But "a child has no words to express" its feelings.[10] In her reminiscences, she cuts this sentence out: it is too raw.

Hampstead was where Penelope Knox grew up, where her father would live for the rest of his life, where she would come back, in her thirties, to live for almost ten years; and where she is buried. It was central to her life: that village was where she felt she belonged.[11] She does not use it as a setting in her fiction (though it comes into her biography of Charlotte Mew), but she wrote about it in *The Knox Brothers* and in scattered reminiscences. She re-created the vanished 1920s Hampstead of her childhood with pleasure and precision:

> The village—and Hampstead still felt itself very much a village—was a place of high thinking, plain living, and small economies. The steep, charming old streets were full of ham-and-beef shops, old bookstalls, and an amazing number of cleaners and repairers, all helpful to shabby refugees and literary men. There was even a jeweller's where one bead could be bought at a time, for all the Hampstead ladies wore long necklaces. The livery stables had only just turned into a garage . . . poets walked the streets, Stanley Spencer pushed his pramful of painting materials amiably across the Heath.[12]

This was a Georgian childhood. The streets, in her memory, were full not only of poets in their "wide-brimmed black hats," but also of lamplighters coming round to light the gas lamps, muffin men in winter and lavender-sellers in summer, knife grinders and chair menders, pony-carts bringing milk from the dairy farm at Highgate. Gazes the drapers had everything you needed in "the button, woollens, stocking, and knicker line"; Knowles Brown the clockmaker had a silver clock in the window in the shape of a spaniel "whose tongue moved up and down with every tick"; small shops sold "pennyworths of licorice." The Knox house was 34 Well Walk, a small house with a handsome green door, with two rooms on each floor, which Evoe rented for £40 a year—exactly the amount of a legacy he received at this time.[13] Well Walk is a pretty street of Queen Anne houses, dating from when Hampstead was still a spa. The ornate well sits across the road from Number 34. The street runs up to the Heath, where sheep grazed. Constable had lived there, and D. H. Lawrence, and Keats, from 1817 to 1818, with his dying brother Tom.

Hampstead was literary, poetic, artistic, rural, part bohemian, part genteel. It was not a bit like Bloomsbury, as Fitzgerald would often observe, with some edge to her voice. Bloomsbury was "brilliant" and "Cambridge-hardened"; Hampstead was "undemanding" and "homely." Hampstead had more poets, too. Some of them are buried near Fitzgerald in the Parish Church of St. John's, next to architects, sculptors, actors and editors. There lie the novelist George du Maurier, the actor-manager Herbert Beerbohm Tree, Thackeray's daughter (and Virginia Woolf's inspiration) Annie Ritchie, Arthur Waugh (father of Evelyn), the architect Basil Champneys, the novelist May Sinclair, the children's writer Eleanor Far-

jeon, Eva Gore-Booth the Irish poet, Cyril Joad of the Brains Trust and
the editor Alfred Orage, cheek by jowl with Hampstead tradesmen: the
owner of a popular 1920s fried-fish shop in Flask Walk, the livery-stables
man from Jack Straw's Castle, the chemist, the publican, the mason and
the coal merchant.[14]

The hill village, high to the north-west of the city—on a clear day you
could see the flag flying on the Houses of Parliament from the upstairs
bathroom window—felt a long way from foggy, polluted London. Evoe
went to the *Punch* office by Underground, but there were special trips
to go to a restaurant (there were none in Hampstead then) or to the theatre—*Peter Pan* for the children at Christmastime.[15] One frequent destination was the Poetry Bookshop in Bloomsbury, near the British Museum.
This remarkable small-scale literary concern was founded in 1913 by Harold Monro, who dedicated his life to poetry and was also a depressive, an
alcoholic and a repressed homosexual. He was one of Fitzgerald's lifelong
heroes. For her the Poetry Bookshop was the embodiment of Georgian literary London and a home for lost causes, dedicated craftsmen and undervalued geniuses. It was an important part of her childhood. She was taken
to poetry readings at its first shop in Devonshire Street (later bombed, and
renamed Boswell Street) and then, from 1926, at 38 Great Russell Street.
In her biography of Charlotte Mew, she gave a vivid picture of its first
home, in "a squalid bit of Bloomsbury, full of small workshops, dustbins
and cats."

> The shop itself was on the ground floor of a dilapidated eighteenth-
> century house, with only one cold-water tap for the whole building.
> However, as you came through the swing door you felt the warmth
> of a coal fire burning at the other end of the room. There was a
> dog stretched out there and a cat, which sometimes sprang about
> the shelves, apparently deliberately, knocking down piles of books.
> The furniture had been made by the Fabian master-carpenter
> Romney Green, and was exceptionally solid, the curtains were
> of sacking, and there were cushions in "jolly" colours. Across the
> walls rhyme sheets were displayed in rows, a penny plain, two-
> pence coloured, and bought mostly for children. A whole genera-
> tion learned to love poetry from these rhyme sheets.[16]

This place and its ideals had a profound influence on her. Here "all
the poetry in print by every living English poet" was for sale, anyone could

come in and sit down and read at the table by the fire, impoverished poets bunked down in the attics, and there were twice-weekly readings, hosted by Monro and his beautiful, intense Polish wife, Alida. Walter de la Mare, alternating with Eleanor Farjeon, would give afternoon readings for children upstairs in Devonshire Street. Though he did not look like a real poet ("I knew how poets ought to look, because at that time they walked about the streets of Hampstead"), "he was the man who had written *Peacock Pie.* That was enough."

Harold and Alida may have been "rather intimidating for a young child," but they were interested in publishing for children. Penelope Knox was one of many of her generation who went home from the Poetry Bookshop with their rhyme sheets, single poems with a woodcut illustration. Some, the "Nursery Sheets," were meant for children, like de la Mare's "The Huntsmen." Others were not, but became favourites all the same, like Charlotte Mew's "The Changeling," Frances Cornford's "To a Fat Lady Seen from a Train," or W. H. Davies's "Leisure." These went up on the nursery wall, next to her coloured print in a gold frame of the *Mona Lisa,* a picture whose "magic landscape" she always wanted to walk into: "There she sat, and beyond her in the distance heaven knows what mists and shining waters, a bridge that seemed to have very little support, and a road that led from the water margin, with extravagant bends and twists, apparently to nowhere." Like that inaccessible landscape, her childhood rhyme sheets vanished, over time, into the distance. Later, she would collect others, and put them up on her own children's walls, but all her life Fitzgerald regretted the loss of those first ones. In old age she wrote to a fellow enthusiast: "I'm perhaps the last person alive who used to go to sleep as a child with a coal fire and the PB rhyme sheets on the walls."[17]

The child who had poems pinned up all over her bedroom walls was the child of a writing household. Christina Knox wrote occasional pieces for the *Manchester Guardian* and contributed through the 1920s and early 1930s to the English Literature Series, editions of annotated, abridged classic texts, under the general editorship of J. H. Fowler. She did *Pilgrim's Progress, A Christmas Carol, Nicholas Nickleby, The Trumpet-Major, Pickwick Papers* and *Don Quixote*—abridgement, notes, "composition exercises," "helps to further study" ("The best further study of *Pickwick Papers* is to read more of Dickens himself"), and examination questions "intended to discourage cramming of unessential facts": "Was life in England happier in Mr. Pickwick's days or in our own?" In her commentary on *Don Quixote,* Christina's attitudes—passed on to her daughter—shine through. "To be 'quixotic' may be thought foolish and unnecessary by some people, but it can never be mean or cowardly or selfish." "Cervantes had the power of finding everything interesting and nearly everything amusing, and he never despised anyone . . . he makes jokes, and excellent ones, without a trace of bitterness or unkindness."[18]

The main writer in the family was Evoe, and, as Fitzgerald recalled with feeling, writers' families could "suffer greatly," especially if the bread-winner was a comic journalist with a relentless weekly deadline. You were not allowed to disturb him at work. "Lack of the right subject sometimes darkened Monday, difficulty in finishing it always haunted Thursday. Like Dilly, Eddie composed well in the bath, and could do nothing without tobacco. At three o'clock the printer's boy came up from the works for the copy." "Being funny is a hard way to earn a living, and as my brother and I listened to my father pacing to and fro in the study overhead, our hearts ached for him. Usually, the boy sat whistling cheerfully in the hall until past the last possible moment."[19]

The Knox children, "dipped in ink" from an early age, were supposed to be writers, since in their family "everyone was publishing, or about to publish, something." They were certainly supposed to be outstandingly intelligent, to join in the witty conversation at mealtimes, and to "perform" as clever Knoxes, which was often a strain.[20] They were given the back of their father's old galley proofs to write on, and like the previous genera-tion of Knoxes, they had their family magazine, produced on a "John Bull toy printing set," though why it was called *IF, or Howl Ye Bloodhounds,* Penelope could never remember. Back numbers of *Punch* were part of the furniture. She loved the illustrations as much as the writing: "As a small girl I used to sit on rainy afternoons in the corner of the dining room, where the old bound volumes of *Punch* were kept, turning the pages and enter-ing, without needing to understand, the quite different worlds of Keene and Du Maurier." Charles Keene did umbrellas, bony cab-horses, railway porters, drunks and stout wives; George Du Maurier did duchesses, draw-ing rooms, concert halls and drooping aristocrats.

Mops's own story-telling developed rapidly from the seven men in a boat going to Wurvin. From the age of six or seven both Knox children "expected to become rich by writing novels" or short stories. The maga-zines of the time were full of "yarns" and "tales," and at the back there were advertisements for "Plotfinders." These were cardboard circles with con-centric slots which you moved around until you had the perfect plot combi-nation: "seaside landlady, landlady's daughter . . . hero . . . jealous rival . . .

vicar . . . practical joker . . . comedy foreigner . . . mysterious lodger." Plots hinged on "the turn," signalled by phrases like *"after all, suddenly, to the general astonishment/consternation . . . through an absurd misunderstanding."* The juvenile short stories she wrote along these lines, none of which survive, did not bring her "the success I hoped for." Later she would realise, with some regret, that she was not the kind of writer who could be described as a "yarn-spinner."[21] But the "Plotfinders," like the Keene and Du Maurier *Punch* illustrations, were as much part of her education as the Poetry Bookshop rhyme sheets and *Peacock Pie*.[22]

She went to school, first, at Miss Lucas's nearby kindergarten. A retired infant-school teacher with a ferocious ginger tomcat, Miss Lucas believed in practical learning. When she found out that none of the six-year-olds could draw a cow, she marched them over the Heath to the farm at Highgate, to see for themselves. The school spelt safety and habit. Everything was in its place.

> I walked to school up flights of steps with my sandals in my shoe bag and my exercise books, which had on the back of them calculations in gallons, pecks, troy weight, furlongs, and farthings . . . I had a red tam o'shanter and a Liberty smock. The smock was embroidered in chain stitch, as was my shoe bag, which bore the words SHOE BAG. At home, at teatime, the hot-water jug was under a flannel cover marked HOT WATER. My mother seemed always to be at home, and by six o'clock my father was back from his work . . . I felt secure.[23]

Fitzgerald went back to 34 Well Walk about seventy years after she had lived there as child. By an odd coincidence, a neighbour from her later Hampstead years, Deborah Chorlton, had moved into the house, and, on leaving, she invited her to take a last look. Deborah observed her, reticent and self-contained, as she walked round the emptied house, remembering. A few years later Fitzgerald recorded the visit.

> Everything was packed up, they were going that very afternoon, would I like to see the house once again before she locked up? She meant, would I like to see my childhood once again? Yes, all things considered, I would.
>
> Because so much had been crated up, I could easily imagine our furniture back in the empty spaces. The little boiler . . . was

in the same place in the dark basement kitchen. The built-in solid shelves were still there, and with no effort at all I could conjure up the old stand-bys—arrowroot, suet, sago, blacklead, starch, Reckitt's Blue, Monkey Brand soap, Borwick's Baking Powder . . . A passage led from the kitchen . . . and out into the garden. In my time, the back of the house had been covered with a vine. The sooty grapes had ripened, I think, only in one year—the heat wave of 1926. The vines were gone, but the indestructible fig tree, usually figless, still offered its shade.[24]

There was no comforting shade or sense of "indestructible" security at the place she was sent away to in 1925, at the age of eight. Rawle was away too, at Oundle, not as eminent a public boarding school as Harrow or Eton, where previous Knoxes had gone, but with a good academic reputation and in a beautiful setting on the River Nene in Northamptonshire. The Knoxes chose it because the stalwart "Auntie Al," the widow of Christina's brother Edwin, who died in the war, had a sister married to Kenneth Fisher, headmaster at Oundle since 1922. The Fishers and their school would be very important to Penelope. But now, while Rawle was at Oundle excelling at cricket, she was sent off to a "young ladies" preparatory school in Eastbourne.

Deerhaddnn School was run, with great efficiency, by a Miss Godfrey. A pompous 1890s brick building with faux-Tudor gables and a glass-covered entrance stairway going up from the front porch, it sat on Bolsover Street, near but not on the seafront, next to four other very similar "ladies' schools." Eastbourne, with its healthy atmosphere and its genteel educational establishments, was the proper place to send a middle-class girl to prep school. But Fitzgerald's tone at this banishment, half a century later, is still baffled and indignant: "At eight years old I was sent . . . into exile and imprisonment." She remembered strictly regulated walks in straight lines in the bracing sea air, and miserable little girls (many of them with parents far away in the Colonial Service) crying themselves to sleep. A pall of anxiety, wretchedness and failure hung over these "horrible" Eastbourne years, which went on forever, it must have seemed, until she was thirteen. She would make comedy out of it: her uselessness at ballroom dancing, gym or geometry; her failure to move up from Brownies to Girl Guides because she couldn't cook a rice pudding and was told that she was "a disgrace to the ideals of Baden-Powell." "I still think that was putting things too strongly." It was a relief once to break her arm and not have to "join in" with anything, "particularly the dreaded Chocolate Box Dance." But the wretchedness was real, summed up by a horrifying memory of a little boy on the Eastbourne ice-skating rink whose finger had been sliced off by a skate. Her consolations were the poetry she knew by heart, and the sound of the sea.

Why did Christina and Evoe send their daughter away to school? It was a Knox tradition—Penelope followed her aunt Winifred to her second school, Wycombe Abbey—and, ambitious for their very intelligent daughter, they presumably felt it was her best route to an Oxford education. It may, as early as 1925, have had to do with Christina's health. Whatever their reasons, she noted grimly, "no one doubted that it would be best for me." But her unhappiness at Eastbourne, and her knowledge that "homesickness is a real illness and that reason has no power against it," profoundly affected her.[25]

Children are everywhere in Penelope Fitzgerald's writing: their feelings, their way of understanding life, their imagination, their rules and systems, their happiness and unhappiness. They come into her books as vivid characters, sometimes noticed in passing, but always entirely present and believable. The drawings she made all her life for friends were mainly of small children in domestic situations, and drawn on a child-friendly scale. She is always making observations about children. Here, a manuscript page for *At Freddie's* (working title, "What, Are They Children?") on how child actors think and feel: "They always want the game to be real . . . [They are] going through something they don't understand or only half-understand." Here, a remark in a 1992 interview: "I'm very interested in children and I try to put some in the novel because their battle to survive is totally different and so are their moral judgments." Here, a line from one of the BBC talks on "Books I've Been Reading Recently" she gave in the early 1950s: "My first book is about unhappy children, a subject which I find almost unbearably painful."[26]

The poignancy of unhappy childhoods is one of her best biographical subjects—as when she imagines the miserable neglected Knox brothers after their mother's death. Writing about "the pale, delicate, unassertive" little Edward Burne-Jones, living unhappily with his widowed father in Birmingham, she understands "the child's horrors, which are not less real when they are overheard and half-understood." Knowing that "the life of children is conducted on a totally different system from that of adults," she can capture Charlotte Mew as the "curly, brilliant, irresistible and defiant" little Lotti, who would "only learn what interested her." Fitzgerald is attracted to Mew's complete sympathy with children: "Charlotte used to read [her verses for children] to children of her acquaintance, giving no explanation, because she believed (quite rightly) that none would be needed. They understood her at once." Of Walter de la Mare, Fitzgerald says (and it applies to her, too): "He seems never to have lost the child's special faculties—daydreaming, make-believe, questioning." "To him, as to Blake, the child was an exile who must make the best of his way home."[27]

In her fiction, children are making their way home as best they can. She knows that they make up their own rules and live by them. We glimpse this in Vi's family home in wartime Hammersmith, in *Human Voices*. Vi goes into the house with the air of "the eldest child who expects to restore order," and finds one of the nine children at his serious games: " 'You can't come across the hall, it's the English Channel,' said a small boy who was sitting on the stairs." We glimpse it again with the small children of an Italian cook in *Innocence*, seen only once, solemn and reserved, "circulating slowly on their miniature tricycles, counting the red and black squares of the tiles." An adult asks them condescendingly, "How many are there?" "The little girl looked at him patiently. 'There are always the same number.' " The boy in the late story "Desideratus," who has lost the thing he most values and has to try and find it, thinks to himself, on his dark quest, "I am very far from home." Fitzgerald remembers and knows what it is like to be them.[28]

Wycombe Abbey School, to which the very bright Penelope Knox won a scholarship in 1930, at thirteen, was, for her, as bad as Deerhaddnn. She always said she hated it, though she knew it was a good school. It was founded in 1896 by a redoubtable High Anglican feminist, Dame Frances Dove, to prove that a girls' boarding school could be as good as Eton or Winchester, and to train middle-class girls for university and the professions, at a time when it was still unusual for girls to train for anything except marriage, or for parents to spend as much on their daughters' education as their sons'. The school buildings were clustered round the old country seat of the Carrington family, a Romantic eighteenth-century Gothic "Abbey," in a beautiful setting near High Wycombe. The school song, which Penelope sang every term-time morning of her life for five years, began: "Stands there a school in the midst of the Chilterns / Beech-covered hills encircle it round, / Ivy and creepers entwine the old Abbey, / Health and contentment within it are found."

Winifred Peck, Penelope's aunt, one of the first intake, gave a vivid picture of the school in its first ten years. Girls were required to be athletic and public-spirited. The regime was "daily cold baths, fresh air and games." Spartan simplicity was the rule; macaroni cheese and cocoa was the standard supper. Winifred noted that "the artistic, the gentle and the nervous" did not get on well. By her niece's time, the rules and regulations had eased up slightly, but the girls still wore "pig-tails, long skirts and black stockings." Central heating, hot baths and short hair came in a bit later. Penelope told her aunt that although "cosmetics were still forbidden, they would all put make-up on at night and wash it off in the morning." The point was to inculcate a no-nonsense ethic of public service. The headmistress in Penelope's time, Miss Crosthwaite, a "chilly authoritarian" figure known, perhaps ironically, as "Auntie," would write to the girls' parents: "Are your girls useful at home, are they learning to be unselfish?"[29] The facts of life, however, were not on the educational agenda. When Mops started her period, she thought she was bleeding to death, and no one explained to her what was happening.[30]

At the school the girls were cut off from their home life and bound by the school rules. Retrospectively, she exaggerated its muscular Christianity, here in a piece on her inability to swear for the *Cherwell Magazine* in 1939, writing in the witty mode that came to be expected of her at Oxford:

> When I was in the lower forms of my public school I was forced to play cricket, beaten with a skipping rope and thrown down two flights of stairs; I was made to do other people's essays for them and, justly enough, called Ratface. I only said "Dash." Later, when I grew strong and popular, I threw other little girls downstairs, and being of a later generation, they piped "Drat." If I heard them say this I had the power, which I exercised to the full, of making them write out three hundred lines. School developed our characters, but it did not teach us to swear.[31]

She may not have wanted, or needed, to have her character developed; she was a Knox, and she knew how clever she was. She read hugely, worked hard (mainly at Art, English, German, French, Latin, History) and excelled; and she had good friends. She was one of a trio, all in the same school "house," all contemporaries. The register which lists her as arriving on 25 September 1930 (and leaving in March 1935) also lists, arriving on the same day, Jean Whitworth Fisher, six months her junior, and Maryllis Dora

Tull, nine months her senior. This was her little gang. Jeanie and Mops had known each other since they were very small. They shared a godmother, "Auntie Al," sister-in-law both to Christina and to Jean's father, Kenneth Fisher. Confident, darkly handsome, determined, bright but not intellectual, humorous and practical, Jean Fisher was head-girl material, and would grow up to become a successful woman barrister. She was Penelope's equal. "Willie" Tull was a quieter, less confident girl, as homesick as Mops, missing her family in south Devon, miserable at school, keen on literature, and full of admiration for her more forceful friends. They were not always kind to her. One of the school's more brutal customs was the public notification, on the school noticeboard, of the termination of friendships. Girls who were friends were said to be "going about together"; if you wanted to stop going about together, you put up a notice to announce that you had "chucked somebody." At one stage, Jeanie and Mops "chucked" Willie; she never quite got over it, even though the trio made it up, went on to Oxford together and remained lifelong friends.

It was clear to Willie and to Jean that Mops was exceptional. She was the only girl who kept a commonplace book; they used to talk about "Mops and her Book of Quotes." Willie admired the illustrated news-sheet which Mops wrote and sent home every week. It was called the "Wuffine News" and—like *Punch*—was full of funny stories and pictures of dogs. In English lessons, very well taught by a Miss Day, known as "Daisy," Willie and Mops sat next to each other. In a class on Wordsworth's "Intimations of Immortality," at the lines "The moon doth with delight / Look round her when the heavens are bare," Mops wrote "RUDE" under the word "bare," much to the delight of these well-brought-up teenage girls. Mops wrote copiously for the school magazine, the *Wycombe Abbey Gazette,* in a mildly satirical tone: "The vast majority who knew nothing [about Modern Art], and were afraid the lecture would be unintelligible, were surprised to find that they could understand it." "Mr. Mackaness's lecture on Modern Poetry was unfortunately very much interrupted by the Monday night bell practice, though the School have heard so much classical music and so many lectures through this sound that they have become almost deaf to it." (In a franker account, written to her mother, she described the poetry man being "most frightfully riled" by the bells, "particularly as he read everything in a very small, reedy voice." "It's simply ruining the programme!" he kept complaining.) Occasionally her serious—and lasting—interests come through in these jovial school pieces: "Mr. Bertram explained that art was not merely applied beauty, but must have a close connection with ordinary life."[32]

. . .

The Fishers at Oundle provided an extra family for her. Kenneth and Isabel, Jean and her three brothers (one of whom, Jimmy, a brilliant ornithologist, went to Oxford at the same time as Jean and Mops and was part of their group) thought of her as one of them. She stayed there often in the holidays. "Auntie Al" was a regular visitor, too, taking a break from her active duties on the Reigate Borough Council. She and her equally domineering sister Isabel had a vigorous relationship, and as old ladies, in years to come, would sit on either side of the fireplace at Oundle, arguing. The school was two in one, a boarding school for well-to-do boys, and a day grammar school for locals. It had a strong practical bent, with science labs and workshops in design and technology. Kenneth ("Bud") Fisher, who had been head since 1922, lived in the large, comfortable School House, with seventy boys (including Rawle, until he went to Oxford in 1932, and the future ornithologist Peter Scott) living at the other end. The family and the boys ate together every day in the long dining hall. Isabel was a considerable presence in the school and the pretty market town; the family's life was completely involved with the school. For Penelope, it was a place where she overlapped with her brother, felt part of a community which she much preferred to her own school and spent a great deal of time with her closest friend, the next-best thing to a sister.[33]

Jean was one childhood friend who lasted for life; another, who went back even further, was Rachel Ollivant, Mops's exact contemporary. Rachel was the daughter of one of Evoe's colleagues, the remarkable Alfred Ollivant. A Fabian and ex-military man, he had broken his back in a riding accident at twenty-two and then taken up contributing to *Punch* and writing children's books and historical epics. Alfred and Hilda Ollivant lived near the Knoxes in Hampstead, and the girls had known each other from the age of about six, though Rachel did not go to school or university with Penelope. After her father's early death, when she was eleven, her schooling was erratic, partly in Germany, partly at Benenden, later at the Slade. Always travelling, reading, painting, a sympathetic fellow spirit, Rachel thought of Mops as "her longest friend."

At home, the safe steady life of Mops's Hampstead childhood was changing. Evoe celebrated his fiftieth birthday in 1931 with "an elegant family lunch at the Café Royal." The next year, he was appointed editor of *Punch*. "He had reversed his father's bitter disappointment when he failed to take his degree, and he had justified the confidence of Christina." But if he was moving more into the establishment—becoming a member of the

Athenaeum, getting a salary of £3,000 a year with a pension—he was as independent and inventive as ever. He brought *Punch,* Seaman's unchanging monument of Empire, into the twentieth century, hiring some fresh contributors, including the illustrator Ernest Shepard and the short-story writer A. E. Coppard, and trying out new kinds of surreal jokes. J. M. Barrie wrote to congratulate him on a cartoon of 1933, in which G. K. Chesterton had oysters for hair, eggs for eyes and a sausage for a moustache. Penelope remembered with delight the rumpus over "the Hippo joke" of 1937. "A drawing by Paul Crum . . . showed, in a few lines, two hippos almost submerged in an open swamp, miles away from anywhere; one is saying to the other: 'I keep thinking it's Tuesday.' This joke proved a breaking point for many subscribers." But the circulation continued to rise, as did admiration for Evoe's editorship.[34]

The brothers were always aware of one another's lives. Ronnie had taken the Catholic chaplaincy at Oxford a few years before Evoe became editor of *Punch,* Wilfred was still at the Oratory of the Good Shepherd in Cambridge, and Dilly was buried in the dank landscape of Courn's Wood, recovering from a much-predicted motorbike accident, inventing a new five-line verse form and emerging from his woods mainly to go to the Test match. More withdrawn than ever, he was beginning his highly secret work on the government's attempt to "break" Germany's brand-new encoding machine, the "Enigma." But no one knew anything about this.

The brothers' worlds in the 1930s were utterly different, but they took pains to keep in touch. Rawle and Mops were taken for memorable teas at Gunter's by Wilfred and Ronnie, at which the brothers might argue passionately over the rhymes in Vaughan's religious poetry, leaping up from their chairs to the amazement of the other customers. Wilfred came to Well Walk for Christmas every year, once with a mongrel dog he had just picked up, which wreaked havoc all over the house, and once eating his way without noticing through the "practical joke" chocolates bought from Hamley's, filled with soap and sawdust. Dillwyn had *his* fiftieth birthday party at the Spread Eagle Inn at Thame, a chaotic event at which the notoriously grandiose and eccentric landlord locked up all the lavatories, so that the guests had to pee in the gardens, pursued by ferocious bees, and the only food provided was a dish of boiled potatoes. (This story may have grown in Penelope's telling of it over the years.) But Dillwyn was a welcome sight to her at Wycombe Abbey; it was near enough to Courn's Wood for him to rescue his niece now and then from the endless games of cricket and the school routine. Once, driving as erratically as ever, he brought her back late to the school gates, and was confronted by "the outraged housemistress, who said 'Rules are made to be kept.' Dilly replied, in a phrase his niece never forgot, 'But they are defined only by being broken.' "[35]

Because of his new position, which involved giving dinner parties, Evoe and Christina moved in 1933 to a smarter house in Clarence Terrace, with tall windows overlooking Regent's Park. (The novelist Elizabeth Bowen moved to the same terrace two years later, and evoked it brilliantly in *The Death of the Heart*.) Well Walk, "where they had had so much happiness, where the floors were uneven and the children had grown up and there was not quite enough room for anything," was left behind. No one liked the house at Clarence Terrace, elegant though it was. To Jean Fisher it was never a very friendly house; Penelope remembered it as large, dank and "charmless."[36] But her memories were shadowed by the fact that this was the house where Christina fell ill.

She had been ill before, but from 1933 onwards began to suffer from the onset of a slow and dreadful bowel cancer. In the summer of 1934 she was unsuccessfully operated on. The doctors ordered her to a succession of nursing homes, the last one at Eastbourne. (The combination of associations meant that in adult life Penelope would never set foot there.) Christina's stoicism can be glimpsed in two brief fragments left over from a silenced life. One is a letter to a friend addressed from Reigate on 21 November 1934, and tucked by Fitzgerald into her first copy of *The Knox Brothers*. Christina apologises for having taken two months to reply to the friend's condolences.

> Truth to tell, I am only just coping with letters, and even now I find them an absurd effort. I suppose I had been ill for too long before they finally operated, and then the whole thing was not so straightforward as they hoped, so it seems to be taking me a long time to crawl up the hill again, though everyone is making encouraging noises and saying that I am doing wonderfully. An angelic sister-in-law [Auntie Al] has cossetted me for nearly 5 weeks, since I left the Home, and now I have persuaded the doctors to let me go home tomorrow so that will be a real step forward, even if I have to lie about most of the time. Really I should be quite pleased with myself if I had not such a perpetual back ache but I am promised that this will not be permanent. Evoe is fairly well, but has suffered horribly from loneliness and desertion.[37]

The other is her formal message to the Somerville Association of Senior Members, dated October 1934, thanking them for electing her Chairman of the Association, and apologising for having failed in her duties, a failure which she felt "keenly." "Had I a notion of what was going to happen to me I would, naturally, not have allowed my nomination to stand." But in early September she had been "ordered by a surgeon into a nursing-home at a week's notice." She hoped to resume her active participation in the winter.[38]

A few months after those letters, in March 1935, Penelope, now in her last year at the Abbey, was taking her entrance exams for Somerville, acutely conscious of following in her mother's footsteps. The school had very high expectations of her—when she was sixteen, the headmistress apparently told Evoe and Christina to take her away, as "she already knew more than any of the staff could teach her."[39] Penelope's letters to Christina at this time (the only correspondence between them that survives) are a touching mixture, full of excitement about her Oxford entrance, and of concern for—and a desire to amuse—her "dearest Ma." They are written in her impeccably neat, clear hand, almost like printing, interspersed with funny illustrations and signed off as Mops or Mopsa in big capitals, with a careful row of kisses. She gives her a blow-by-blow account of how the exams went, bubbling with youthful humour, self-consciousness, confidence and literariness:

> Now I will tell you all about the papers. I can scarcely write naturally for I am reading *Pamela* & queer expressions keep coming; I nearly wrote scarce instead of scarcely just then. Well, I started with Period, & this annoyed me very much, for would you believe it there was no question on Browne, Donne, Lamb or Hazlitt, & these are my specialties with the C[ompleat] Angler, which wasnt mentioned either. So I had to do Christabel & the Ode to a Nightingale for the 100th odd time, I also did a question on George Herbert about whom I know 0. But I usually write better about people I know nothing about. The next was the General Essay. We had for subjects either Propaganda, The scientific spirit, Or, Poetry is made of words, not of ideas.
>
> So yours truly did Poetry knowing Daisy wd. skin me if I didnt, though I think it's a difficult subject. Next I got criticism, which was a surprise to me, for instead of getting queer bits & spotting the author we had v. well-known ones. I didnt know what to do. I've been taught to look for internal evidence of authorship etc. but whats the use of doing that to "when I consider how

my light?" etc. I also did a v. weak essay on allegory. The French Unseens were awful. The Grammar was undoubtedly foul, but I expected it, as I never have known any grammar.

Three days later her spirits are lower. "Perhaps you will be able to get up soon, & crawl down to the 'front,' or over the Greens . . . I hope you arent lonely at Eastbourne, its full of terrible people. Oh Mother Im sure everyone else will get an interview and not me, and I did work hard, really. I knew tons, but they didnt give me anything to show it on. Never mind, all love, Mops."

She did get an interview, of course, and then came the triumphant news that Somerville had offered her a "Senior Scholarship," that is, for the best candidate in her year. She sent a telegram and a long letter to Eastbourne. "The old coll has turned up trumps . . . I cant help feeling that it is chiefly by indiscriminate use of your name that I have got through."

An excited account follows of her trip to Somerville with Jean (who was offered an Exhibition to read Classics). She described her first meeting with the English Tutor Mary Lascelles, the Jane Austen scholar, who "rather foxed" her by referring to all the characters by their first names, the interview at which she had to talk about Sir Thomas Browne and Gerard Manley Hopkins ("though completely out of my depth I did my best to keep talking") and all the meals she had had with Jean and Jimmy Fisher, who looked after them—"slightly soiled mutton pickles cheese & ginger beer" in a "low pub full of rustics," "welsh rarebit eggs & crumpets" for tea at Lyons. "Well this letter is all about me . . . I am so sorry you cant come home for I'm afraid it means you are not picking up as fast as you might . . . Dear Mother you must get better even if youre too unselfish to want to yourself then for Daddy & Rawle & me."⁴⁰

She left Wycombe Abbey School a few days later, and would always remember how wonderful it was to hear "Auntie" praying for the girls who were leaving: "I couldn't believe I wouldn't ever have to go back to it again."⁴¹ Like many girls of her time, she was sent off to France in the few months' gap between school and university. She was a paying guest in a house near Paris, in Le Perreux-sur-Marne. English girls went there to polish up their culture, with courses on fencing, dress-making, art and architecture, and French conversation. (But spare her the French conversation, Penelope said, she had had years of it at school.) The house was run by a fussy, eager lady, Madame Risler. Penelope called the family the Rissoles;

POST OFFICE TELEGRAPHS

TELEGRAM

86

Knox
Blackwater Hotel

INLAND telegrams may be handed to the Messenger for despatch.

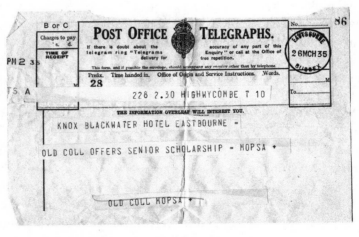

B or C	POST OFFICE ☤ TELEGRAPHS.	No.......	86

Charges to pay
's. d.

TIME OF RECEIPT

PM 2 35

If there is doubt about the telegram ring "Telegrams" delivery for

accuracy of any part of this Enquiry" or call at the Office of free repetition.

EASTBOURNE
2 6 MCH 35
SUSSEX

This form, and if possible the envelope, should accompany any enquiry other than by telephone

Prefix. Time handed in. Office of Origin and Service Instructions. Words.

28

TS A   M   228 2.30 HIGHWYCOMBE T 10   To....... M

THE INFORMATION OVERLEAF WILL INTEREST YOU.

KNOX BLACKWATER HOTEL EASTBOURNE =

OLD COLL OFFERS SENIOR SCHOLARSHIP = MOPSA +

OLD COLL MOPSA +

the whole family was "pocket-sized," and, according to her, rather odd. From mid-April she sent home a stream of comically illustrated, despairing letters. Rawle took her out there, but once he had left she felt lonely. Everyone else in the house had been a boarder longer than she had, she was nervous of the maids, she didn't like the radishes which came with every meal, the dog with an unpronounceable name ignored her and she spent a lot of time sitting in her cold room wishing she was better at Ping-Pong. Though they were taken to the theatre, to the Louvre and to ride in the Bois de Boulogne, the "jeunes filles anglaises" weren't allowed to go to Paris on their own as "all the workmen etc are v tiresome, not ½ so nice as English workmen." She was upset about missing George V's Silver Jubilee on 6 May. She wished Jean was with her. But "honestly," she reassured them, she was all right: "Ça va, as I say at least 1,0000 times a day on all occasions." And she watched everyone and everything:

> Heated discussions take place at dinner during which everyone waves their forks & knives, upsets glasses, & shouts at the top of their voices. One of the chief points of debate is as to whether England is the same as Gt. Britain . . . other great points are the pronunciation of "thistle" & "extraordinaire," whether English people talk too fast, what is intelligence, and the number of Italians in France. It is my ambition to join in one of these discussions. It is necessary to have rather a loud voice, also . . . some bits of bread for demonstration purposes, also some paper & a pencil which you produce at odd moments to draw diagrams on. To attract attention to yourself you shout "Tiens, tiens, tiens" at the top of your voice till you get an audience and then you start shouting and waving the fork & the bread.

In her last letter home, written on 8 May, she is upset to hear that Christina's jewel-box has gone missing from her wardrobe in the nursing home. She tries to cheer her up by promising that "one day when you are better you and I'll go & get something that really suits you & looks nice, you wait." She disagrees with her mother about possessions. "I don't think I like you saying one mustn't care for possessions & they don't matter— I think they do, unless you are very exceptional. Something to take a pride in, you know."[42] At this point, the intimate mother-and-daughter conversation came to an abrupt end. Christina was dying, and Rawle was sent to fetch Penelope home from France. According to Willie, she got home too late to see her mother. According to Jean Fisher, she did see her, and told Jean that Christina "was laughing before she died."[43]

On 30 May 1935, Christina died in Eastbourne of peritonitis and perforation of the intestine due to carcinoma of the colon. She was fifty; her daughter was eighteen. The obituaries idealised her as a perfect wife, a model of piety, refinement and sweetness. At the funeral on 4 June, at Golders Green Crematorium, all the family were there—Knoxes, Pecks, Hickses—with many of the *Punch* staff, alongside the Principal of Somerville, Helen Darbishire, and the novelist Rose Macaulay, who had been at Oxford with Christina. "Even on such a wretched occasion," Penelope wrote years later, "it was a memorable thing to see all the four brothers together. Wilfred took the service, Dilly, who rarely entered a church, stood in silent misery at the back, Ronnie, who had not been to an Anglican service for nearly twenty years, knelt in the aisle. Those who saw him, not cut off from the human grief around him, but totally absorbed in communion with God, felt that they had seen prayer manifest."[44]

Rawle went straight back to Oxford, in a state of shock, to take his Finals; he did badly, and got a Third. Penelope went to stay with her schoolfriend Willie's family in Devon, a difficult visit for them: "She was like a frozen person."[45] She no longer wanted to go to Somerville; everything was spoilt, wretched and dark. Evoe barely spoke about Christina, or let anyone talk about her, then or ever. In October, Mops left home; childhood was over.

CHAPTER THREE

The "Blonde Bombshell"

There is no need to introduce Penelope Knox; intellectually and socially she is well known in Oxford. Her name is famous at the Union and in the English School, and she has already appeared in these pages as the "blonde bombshell" who astonished the world by her spelling prowess.[1]

The Knoxes were famous in Oxford. Generations of them had been there. Ronnie Knox, in his time a bright Oxford star, was the Catholic Chaplain. All the Fellows of Somerville had been touched by Christina's death and had high expectations of her daughter. The College Record for autumn 1935 noted that Miss Dorothy Sayers had succeeded Mrs. E. V. Knox as Chairman of the Association of Senior Members, and that Mrs. Knox's daughter was "carrying on the tradition of scholarship and of close association with Somerville."[2] Penelope was extremely unhappy when she arrived. "I felt so proud to be going to the same college, then it all seemed so pointless when she was dead." But she also felt a sense of continuity.[3] She brought with her some of the books Christina had taken with her as a student in 1904; in her copy of Spenser's *Poetical Works,* Christina's notes were overlaid with her own.[4]

Rawle had just left Balliol, but she had ready-made friends in Oxford. Jean Fisher was going up with her to Somerville to read Classics, and Jean's brother Jimmy was already there. Willie Conder was going to read English at St. Hugh's. Her cousin Tony Peck, Winifred's son, was reading Philosophy at Trinity. She was sheltered by these associations, but she was also exposed. It was not an easy start, to have everyone point her out as the brilliant daughter of Christina Knox, who had just died. She protected herself with the Knoxian manner—brusque and indirect with those she didn't know, endearingly funny with those she did—which was as much a defence as a family inheritance. She was pretty, a slim short sturdy eighteen-year-old girl with her mop of tawny, reddish-blonde curly hair, a round rosy face and hazel eyes. She made her mark quickly.

·   ·   ·

The generation of students who went to Oxford in October 1935 coincided with Mussolini's invasion of Abyssinia, George Lansbury's defeat as leader of the Labour Party over the issue of rearmament, a general election fought over foreign policy and unemployment, and, soon after (in March 1936), Hitler's invasion of the Rhineland. They were too late for the famous Union debate of February 1933, which resulted in a vote not to fight for King and Country, or for the presence of the left-wing poets, Auden, Spender, Day Lewis and MacNeice. But they were starting their university life at a time of urgent political divisions. Some of the students who had voted against fighting for King and Country would do battle against Oswald Mosley's Fascist Blackshirts and join up to fight (and sometimes be killed) in the Spanish Civil War against Franco—including one Somerville student, dressed as a man.

The 1935 generation of students grew up at Oxford through the abdication crisis and the upsurge of Fascism and Nazism in Europe. Left-wing politics dominated the university, and a great many of them took up communism or the Labour Party. The debating clubs and political societies argued over pacifism, collective security, rearmament, the League of Nations, the political responsibilities of writers, unemployment, the fate of Europe. A short-lived Somerville magazine, *Lysistrata,* edited by Robert Graves's daughter Sally in 1934, passionately debated the causes of the day. "Politics mattered to us enormously in Oxford at that time," Fitzgerald would say in old age.[5] *Guernica* was the key painting of 1937. George Orwell was the writer she most admired, and everyone read *Homage to Catalonia.* As she said in *The Knox Brothers:* "Students of the Thirties were preoccupied with three subjects: sex, travel and European politics."[6]

There was still plenty of leftover 1920s-style frivolity. Iris Murdoch, who went to Somerville in 1938, just after Penelope left, noted the contrast: "There was a great deal of . . . idealism in Oxford at that time, which led people into left-wing politics . . . meetings, gatherings, demonstrations . . . peace groups and so on. And then just a lot of fun and dancing. There was plenty of perfectly ordinary frivolity. Many undergraduates weren't thinking about politics at all, they were just happy creatures enjoying the *dolce vita* and the Commem. Balls and so forth."[7]

There were many sets and cliques in Oxford, then as now, often exclusively male: upper-class communists and radicals like Jasper Ridley, Esmond Romilly and Philip Toynbee in Beaumont Street; Isaiah Berlin and John Sparrow at All Souls; Maurice Bowra at Wadham; admirers of Tolkien and C. S. Lewis and the "Inklings"; Wykehamists at New College, Etonians at Christ Church. At Magdalen, there was a rather wild and lawless little group of young men given to climbing on the roofs and heavy drinking, who included the future historian Robert Conquest and two handsome Irish brothers, Eamon and Desmond Fitzgerald. Women could get a foothold as speakers at the Union, or with the theatre people in OUDS, or as journalists writing for the *Isis* and the *Cherwell,* or as one of the swots to be seen only in the Bodleian Library. But men outnumbered women by six to one. This meant, on the one hand, that battles for equality were still being fought—women had only been allowed to take degrees since 1920, and in 1927 a vote had been taken to freeze their numbers in case the university was overrun—and on the other hand that girls with an appetite for adventure and society could have a great deal of fun.

Like all notable Oxford undergraduates, Penelope Knox had her own set. They were known as "Les Girls," and they were admired and envied. Barbara Chapman (later Craig), a classicist who became Principal of Somerville in the late 1960s, remembered "Les Girls" as a striking bunch. Barbara herself was slightly older, and not part of the set; nor was the clever, sensible Mary Fisher, the daughter of the Warden of New College, and a Knox family friend. (Mary, no relation to Jean Fisher, would be a lifelong friend of Penelope's, and become Principal of St. Hilda's.) Jean, and Willie Tull at St. Hugh's, whom Penelope helped all through her English degree, were still (with Rachel Ollivant) her closest friends. There was also Judith Hidelman, who became a lawyer, and Margaret Palmer, who was, notoriously, sent down for a term for spending the night with her boyfriend. But most importantly there was Janet Russell, bursting on the scene at Somerville at exactly the same time as Penelope. Janet was a forceful, stylish, strong-minded girl. Her mother was the Australian heiress to a big banking fortune; her father, son of an old English family, had been killed in the war, in Palestine, in 1917, when she was a baby. Janet's mother, who later worked in the UN, never remarried. She brought up Janet and her sister on her own, and educated them at home with governesses; Janet was deemed "too excitable" to be sent to school. Her mother wanted the girls to grow up practical, and useful to society. (The sister became a vet.) Janet got a scholarship to read History; but she had many other interests, including radical politics, French poetry, textile design, travel—and social life.

   She and Penelope became intimate friends, though they were never quite as close as Penelope and Jean Fisher (whom Janet could see were "like sisters"), and they would lose touch later on. But, like most of her friends,

Janet was influenced by her. "There was something in Mops which made her so lovable, beyond the wit and intelligence . . . a very private person, and extremely modest about her talent." It was because of Penelope that she too started to keep a commonplace book. She learned how miserable Penelope had been at school, and about her mother's death. Janet came to feel that "though she started life so brilliantly and was so well connected, she was not as fortunate as those of us with a more ordinary and supportive background . . . Having a much loved father, himself so damaged by his upbringing that he couldn't speak to her after her mother died," left its mark. She thought of Penelope, for all her sharp intelligence and comic irony, as a "romantic." Penelope once told Janet that she thought it would be wonderful to "hear the bells ringing for Christmas at Oundle and to be married."[8] Yet, on the whole, these intimate friends did not confide in each other. "At Somerville as a set," Janet recalled, "we certainly never discussed anything of real importance." The letters she had from Penelope at the time were "almost relentlessly frivolous and making fun of everything."[9] Janet noted "her inability or reluctance to discuss anything close to the heart, or anything important like religious feelings or politics, except in a witty comment."[10]

"Les Girls" had fun. They went to dances and balls and parties, travelled to Europe with their families, hired horses from the Longwall stables to go riding on Port Meadow or Headington Hill or to point-to-points, took trips to the theatre in London, went punting and canoeing and picnicking. Janet, looking back, felt as if "I didn't do anything except have a good time—my impression is that latterday students are in general much more serious-minded, and rarely as frivolous as we were."[11] Not everyone liked "Les Girls." A fellow student, Hope Rossitter, who was running neck and neck with Penelope to get that cohort's best English degree, resented her close friendship with Jean Fisher and her social life outside Somerville, and found her condescending, unfriendly and very conscious of being "a Knox." At their first encounter, Hope asked her: "Are you Penelope Knox?" "I—*am*," she replied, and turned away.[12]

"Les Girls" all had boyfriends; yet they were sexually very innocent. Lesbianism was not something they discussed, even though they might have "ploughed through *The Well of Loneliness*." "I reckon out of our group of six," Janet Russell reminisced, "4 went down [left Oxford] virgins, which is perhaps higher than the usual average for our year. Left-wing girls like me were subjected to a barrage of propaganda from their male friends in the Labour Club on the lines of Lenin's statement that having sex was no more important than having a drink of water! People like Philip Toynbee must have cut quite a swathe . . ."

Penelope too had her admirers. Even if she was, perhaps, one of the "4 who went down virgins," the few traces of her emotional life at Oxford suggest that she was having an interesting time. There was a lot of falling in and out of love, even if that only involved hand-holding and intense conversations. One of her Oxford "dates" was Max Beloff, then an up-and-coming—and anti-establishment—history student, who was, according to Jean Fisher, a "great admirer," and who proposed to her at a Christ Church ball. "Dear old Max," Penelope wrote next to his name in her address book, many years later. Also in the frame was a rich Etonian called Edward. They had their favourite jazz tune, and he gave her expensive presents, one of which showed that he knew how mischievous she could be. According to Janet, he sent Penelope a gigantic box of Charbonnel & Walker, with alphabet chocolates round the edge spelling out "Don't Gossip!" Later, he took up with a "suitable deb." After his engagement, and before he was posted abroad in the war, Penelope asked Janet to go with her to visit him, an awkward occasion, which he tried to make easier by putting on a record. On the way back, she told Janet it had been "their tune" he had played.[13]

She had a fondness for her cousin Tony Peck. One branch of the Knoxes (Dillwyn's son Oliver and his children) were strongly under the impression that Tony and Penelope had been attached to each other and may have been engaged. Oliver Knox, Penelope's cousin, used to say that Tony Peck was "the love of her life": but Oliver was given to exaggeration. The story went that they had consulted Ronnie Knox about their engagement, and that he had advised against it because they were cousins. But this is unverified family legend. Tony Peck's wife, Sylvia, long after his death, said that they were always "very dear friends." Although her husband (who went from Oxford into the Intelligence Corps and then into the Civil Service) had never mentioned an engagement, he did once tell Sylvia that he had "had a fling" with Penelope, "but that it had been a failure sexually, presumably on his part." Her husband was "somewhat reserved"—he was, after all, half a Knox—and they never discussed it again. All she knew was that Tony Peck, all his life, was extremely fond of his cousin Penelope.[14]

In the pages of the Oxford undergraduate magazines between 1935 and 1938, where Penelope Knox featured largely, she was known as "Our Penny from Heaven," "the Blonde Bombshell," and "Penelope (Belle-Lettre) Knox." She was one of the *Isis* magazine's "Women of the Year" in May

1937, with a fetching image of her sitting in profile, upright and jaunty in a tweed suit, and again a year later, with a romantic full-face photograph. In the *Cherwell* for May 1938 a paragraph headlined "Our Penny from Heaven" noted that "Miss Knox is taking schools this term, so you had better make the most of your opportunities."[15] That year, a story circulated around Oxford that she had gone to a party with one breast bared, and had stayed that way, nonchalantly, throughout the evening. One young man, Sinclair Hood (Harrow and Magdalen), thought that "Penelope Knox and Janet Russell were the two most attractive girls at Oxford" of his time.[16] He had friends who felt the same.

Two of them, Oliver Breakwell and Hugh Lee, became closely entangled for a time with "Les Girls." They were public-school boys from Harrow, talented, bright and gregarious. The fair-haired and dapper Hugh Lee, always known as "Ham," was reading Modern Languages at Oriel, and would have a career in the Ministry of Defence and the Treasury. His deep love was art, and he later became a good, modernist-influenced painter. His great friend from Harrow was Oliver Breakwell, a gifted linguist, mathematician and violinist, who read Politics, Philosophy and Economics at Magdalen, a degree he didn't finish because of the war. Oliver was bespectacled, unconfident and far from suave, but, according to another of this group, Douglas Stuart (Harrow and New College, and the future presenter of BBC's *The World Tonight*), "his charm was all-embracing." Oliver had a difficult family life. He was one of three brothers—the oldest, Raven, was a darkly handsome cad. His English father and American mother, Ellen Breakwell, had had a messy divorce while he was at school. Oliver sided with the mother, his brothers with the father, and he lived with her in her flat in Cornwall Gardens, where Penelope became a regular visitor. "Mrs. B," or "Mamma," as the group called her, was "quite a character," quarrelsome, "terrifying and unshockable."[17] (Later, she was sectioned with bipolar disorder.) Penelope left a few glimpses of her holding court during the war: "Mrs. B gave an amazing party . . . there was a strange babel of languages, Mrs. B pre-eminent in a torrent of mixed French and English, easily drowning the harassed player at the party." "Mamma is lying back on the sofa which is draped with an Indian carpet and telling Oliver he is repressed."[18] The powerful, eccentric older women in her novels (Freddie in *At Freddie's*, Aunt Maddalena in *Innocence*) perhaps carried a little trace of crazy, demanding Ellen Breakwell.

Oliver knew he had "an almost morbid need of affection."[19] He was always in love with someone—his mother, his friend Fred Warner (who became ambassador in Tokyo), "Les Girls." First Oliver was in love with Penelope, then with Janet; first Hugh was in love with Janet, then with Penelope. It sounds like an Iris Murdoch novel. Douglas Stuart remembered a picnic on the banks of the Cherwell in 1938 with himself, Oliver, Penelope and two other girls, at which his friend Oliver, who was "head over heels in love with Penelope," was completely ignored by her, and "became very glum." Douglas tried to attract their interest, but "Penelope was very sharp and crushing," and he told Oliver that he thought "his was a losing cause with an unpleasant female." After the war, though, when they met again, he was "charmed with her wit and good humour."[20]

Intense letters went between Oliver and Hugh about the two girls. Oliver would tell Ham what a "high intensity" relationship he had with Mops, then, a few months later, how he had had "feelings" for Mops but they were really more about Janet, and that now what he felt for Mops was a "kind of complete sympathy about everything outside oneself and no desire for sympathy *in* the relationship." Affectionately, he noted Mops's characteristics—what "sharpness of vision" she had, how she represented for him "gaiety and lightheartedness." He enjoyed her bursts of awkwardness. Both Oliver and Penelope reported to Ham on one unfortunate evening at Sinclair Hood's family home. In Oliver's version, Mops "opened on arrival by telling Mrs. Hood how antipathetical to her bulldogs were . . . [then] she produced deadly silences by 'I think this whole conversation is quite tasteless' . . . She passed her ice-cream on to me, and crossed the room unexpectedly to take a book by her uncle off the sideboard and read it. I felt strong in my knowledge of her, faced with the obvious bewilderment of everyone else. She is an angel!" Penelope called the dinner party "alarming": "For want of other conversation I told Mrs. H (quite accurately) that I couldn't abide bulldogs, and insulted the horrid but apparently precious specimen which she keeps . . . Oliver was kind and covered up my social errors as well as he could." In spite of these moments of Knoxian obstructiveness, both Hugh and Oliver evidently adored her, and were also rather in awe of her. As Hugh Lee said, "We in the Breakwell group of friends would never have dreamed of challenging any statement of fact by Mops. She was too clever, and infallibly accurate (though often herself professing utter ignorance, with a helpless giggle)."[21]

They were all very young—eighteen, nineteen, twenty, twenty-one. In old age, Penelope began to sketch out notes for a novel called "Why (or 'How') We Were Very Young." The setting is Oxford in the 1930s, and the main characters are to be J. R. R. Tolkien and C. S. Lewis. Tolkien lectured to her on Anglo-Saxon and "Middle English," with occasional readings from *The Hobbit* (published in 1937). She disliked him for his misogyny and used to refer to the "odious Tolkien." C. S. Lewis was "darkly red-faced and black-gowned," talking from the minute he entered the room, "the indispensable teacher, about whom all we personally knew was that he was pipe- and beer-loving, lived outside Oxford, and made a 'thing' of disliking the twentieth century. When T. S. Eliot came to read 'The Waste Land' to the Poetry Society, Lewis was not there."[22] Yet her notes sympathetically and comically reconstruct what their lives must have been like.

> Tolkien sleeps in dressing-room with bath in corner, not to disturb Edith with late work & snoring. Flannel trousers, tweed jacket . . . has to light stove in his study a.m. for tutorials . . . Lectures in East School . . . bell of Merton quarter a mile away strikes the hour, gathers up notes, clears out for next lecturer . . . shops at the Covered Market in High St. for sausages . . . Big typewriter with interchangeable type, Anglo-Saxon letters . . . Talked fast & not clearly, moved from idea to idea v fast . . . tended to talk in monologues . . . would dress up in Icelandic bearskin rug as a polar bear, or as A/Saxon warrior . . . Friendship with C.S. Lewis . . . companionship between men . . . C.S. Lewis drawn to Xtianity by T's explanation of it as a "myth that is true."

Mixed in with this draft of what might have been a characteristic Fitzgerald novel, vividly evoking a particular past, there are notes for the adventures of a first-person protagonist, a young girl at Oxford from a rectory family. She is given "worldly advice" by a character called Tony, who "meets me at the station and obviously doesn't want to be seen with me as I look terrible. No, not terrible. You're not either plain or pretty exactly the sort that gets picked up." Further down the page: "I'm staying with the Toynbees. To Bristol? I come down, I'm obsessed with P.T, confide in D . . . Meanwhile P off with someone else." So, did Penelope Knox have a crush while she was at Oxford on Philip Toynbee, her exact contemporary, who "cut such a swathe" with the girls, was head of the Labour Club, fanatical about the Spanish Civil War and like her a prolific student journalist? The facts are lost in time. What she remembered—as people do, looking back—was how very young and silly they all were: "At 18 although we thought highly of ourselves we were ignorant & hateful."[23]

Fitzgerald never did write her Oxford novel (instead she wrote a Cambridge one, set in Dillwyn's time). But Oxford's history made a strong impression on her. She liked to imagine "mid-Victorian Oxford" in the time of Bishop Knox and of Lewis Carroll, alias Charles Dodgson, with its eccentric dons and "nervous, stammering, opinionated, riddling and joking guests." Her grandfather at Corpus enjoyed hearing the jokes made by the author of *Alice in Wonderland:* "He knows a man whose feet are so large that he has to put his trousers on over his head." That Victorian Oxford surrealism appealed to her. Mavis Batey, who worked at Bletchley with Dillwyn Knox and whose husband was a Christ Church don, said that Penelope liked being taken round the college, talking about Lewis Carroll and Tenniel.[24] Most of all, Ruskin and Newman's Oxford deeply allured and fascinated her. In her biography of Edward Burne-Jones, she vividly evoked the intense friendships, the heartaches and passions between the young Pre-Raphaelites at Oxford in the mid-nineteenth century.

Somerville College's place in that Oxford history was a well-defined one. Christina Hicks was a typically Somervillian suffragist; her daughter had a typical Somervillian work ethic—and haughtiness about her own intellectual powers. The college was proudly nonsectarian (even though a new chapel was being built in Penelope's time), egalitarian and independent. It had a reputation for exclusiveness and "cussedness," and for producing formidable women. Winifred Holtby, one of the most famous of Somerville novelists (alongside Rose Macaulay, Dorothy Sayers, Iris Murdoch, Nina Bawden and Penelope herself), died and left the college some of her royalties in 1935, the year Penelope went to Oxford. Indira Gandhi was there for a year in Penelope's time. The tutors included Dorothy Crowfoot (later Hodgkin, and a future Nobel Prize winner for chemistry) and the difficult French scholar Enid Starkie. According to Janet, they all thought they were at the "top college . . . We mocked Lady Margaret Hall as the college for ladies," and used to say, "St. Hilda's, where's that?" The older generation of Somerville dons, a redoubtable bunch, complained in the 1930s that the students did not have the commitment to the college they used to have—a point of view noted by Dorothy Sayers. Penelope remembered her dining regularly in the college, "in black crepe de Chine, austere, remote, almost cubical." The students objected to her telling the dean that they were all badly dressed, since "we felt that, although most of us had not much money, we had done the best we could." *Gaudy Night,* based on Somerville life, came out in 1935:

"Responsibility bores 'em. Before the War they passionately had College Meetings about everything. Now, they won't be bothered . . . They don't want responsibility."

"They're all taken up with their young men," said Miss Burrows.

"Drat their young men," said the Dean.[25]

But some Somervillians wanted to shine academically as well as enjoy themselves, and Penelope Knox was one of these. English was taught then by Helen Darbishire, "the Darb," who had become Principal of the College, by the young Kathleen Constable (later Tillotson, an admired Dickensian) and by Mary Lascelles, a devoted Jane Austenite but—according to some of the girls—a hopeless tutor. She and Penelope did not get on. "They tell me Penelope Fitzgerald is very clever," she said to Barbara Craig, sniffily and donnishly, in old age. "I never noticed it."[26] Penelope requested to be "farmed out" for tutorials to Edmund Blunden and Lascelles Abercrombie. "Since it turned out that Lascelles didn't believe in education, and was dying anyway, poor soul, he spent all the time talking about his golden days before 1914 with Frost and E[dward]. Thomas in Gloucestershire." He often helped himself to a decanter on the sideboard, with the words "It's a sad thing that the best things in life are its poisons." Penelope asked him whether he considered poetry a poison, and he said that he did.[27]

Her tutorial partner, Jane Aiken Hodge, remembered vividly what it was like to be taught with Penelope Knox. "She was already very much of a character, and she may well have been as formidable to her tutors as she was to fellow students . . . We were 'doing' the romantic poets with Edmund Blunden, and I would sit in awe-struck silence as the two of them carried on their civilised, literary conversation. She used to spend the first ten minutes or so of the first lecture of the day in doing the Times crossword puzzle in her elegant small print." "Everyone else wrote [essays] at length," Hope Rossitter remembered, more grudgingly, "but Penelope Knox wrote one paragraph, and that was enough."[28] It always would be enough.

Penelope valued her Oxford education. They read no modern authors, but "we didn't feel the need to study modern literature, we imagined we were going to write it."[29] She always said that she "benefited from Oxford's wonderful libraries and the tutorial system—every student had individual teaching."[30] But even if she had had no teaching at all, she would still have excelled. There are traces of her undergraduate work in her old, battered edition of Milton (published in 1935 by OUP, so one of her first purchases), in which her pencilled student notes are overlaid with the much later notes she wrote when she was teaching. The student notes are detailed and investigative. Taught by "the Darb," who had just published an edition of the manuscripts of *Paradise Lost,* she notes Milton's spellings, his archaisms and dialect words, his "distrust of neologisms and the colloquial." "Milton obviously took great care in preparing his mss for the printer." "Milton had a sensitive ear." She ruminated on his choice of words. Next to the line in *Paradise Lost* about Eve waking at dawn "with Charm of earliest birds," she noted: "'Charm,' from *Cerm,* Anglian chirping, made a crowing noise. Cry of birds dialectically twittering. Goldfinches. Spenser: Tears of the Muses compare themselves to birds with 'free liberty to chaunt our charms at will.'" At times the voice of the future novelist speaks through the notes of the student. "Devil with Devil damn'd / Firm concord holds, men onely disagree," says Milton. "Even evil spirits keep in touch with themselves," says Penelope.[31]

No one was surprised when she got a First after a "congratulatory viva," at which the candidate is praised rather than quizzed. Legend had it that her papers were so outstandingly good they were kept and bound in vellum by her examiner, Roy Ridley. (This Oxford don gets a mention in Fitzgerald's review of a life of Dorothy Sayers: he wore spats and a monocle and was supposed to have been the original of Peter Wimsey.) Years later, her old tutor Kathleen Tillotson wrote to her, saying that Professor Ridley had given the scripts to her when he retired and that she still had them: Would Penelope like them returned? The answer, and the scripts, do not survive.[32] Nor does the prize-winning essay on "The Poetry of Matthew Arnold," which she entered for the Matthew Arnold Memorial Prize in 1939 (candidates for the prize could enter up to seven years after graduating, and the winner got £30). But one suggestive detail remains. Essays had to be sent in anonymously, with a motto attached to identify the candidate. Penelope's motto was *"Et praeterea nihil."* The phrase was Plutarch's: "A voice, and nothing more." It could refer to smoke without thunder, nonsense without meaning. Or it could mean that, after a writer is gone, only a voice remains.

Penelope's student voice lives on vividly in the journalism she wrote for the *Isis* and the *Cherwell,* practice grounds and playgrounds for plenty of future writers.[33] At school, for all her misery, she had been a chief contributor to and co-editor of the school magazine. By the end of her first year at Oxford, she was writing the first of many light, satirical pieces, which became her stock-in-trade. The tone is sophisticated and slightly world-weary, the observation ironical and acute, and the model is, clearly, *Punch.* In her first piece, she gives a guide to the real meaning of what people say to "freshers" at Oxford, with advice on how to respond:

> "I feel an irresistible urge to express myself in Art." Means: "I'm probably pretty stupid, and certainly no good at my subject." What to do: Smile mysteriously.

> ". . . as Voltaire remarks, "C'est que j'ai vécu'." Means: "I'm determined to get this quotation off at one point." What to do: Start talking in German.

> "My dear child . . ." Means: "You're beneath my contempt." What to do: Stay beneath it.

In her next, she satirises the tiresomeness of the traveller who insists on telling you his stories and showing you his photographs:

> Recital deferred makes him heavy at heart, and eventually embittered; the Ancient Mariner is an example readily consulted. The Mariner shows three prevailing characteristics; a periodical fit, or exaltation, during which he is spiritually forced to tell a travel story; a tendency to insist on the uniqueness of his experiences; a habit of always telling the same story.

A year later, she was co-editing the *Cherwell,* judging competitions, reviewing books and theatre, and—especially between February and October 1937—writing lots of pieces. Some of these were farcical fantasies, turning the *Cherwell* into a ship with a near-mutinous crew carrying potatoes to Spain, or sending a milkman's horse to compete in the Epsom Derby. Some were spoofs or critiques of popular genres, like romantic novels set in India, or detective stories—with a bold dig at her uncle Ronnie for letting in too much discussion, even "dullness." As in *Punch,* farce, which she defines as "horseplay and wisecracks," is presented in a dry, laconic tone. The art was to tell an absurd, even surreal story with the utmost formality or pomposity.

One or two pieces were fictional. "A Desirable Resident" told the story of a forty-year-old bookseller, a dealer in banned editions, who went bankrupt. He defaulted on £2,000 worth of payment to clients, abandoned his wife (who threw herself in the Thames) and ran away to the country, because he was a believer in Rousseau and the joys of nature. (Fitzgerald's juvenilia is like Jane Austen's in its distrust of Rousseau-inspired sentiment.) The local bore, Junior Treasurer of the Chelmsford Wordsworth Circle, takes the bookseller's confessions as an uproarious joke, until he says he doesn't play bridge: that makes him really undesirable.

In "A Curious Incident," a wealthy businessman, Sam Wetherby, has lent his large house for a meeting of the Meadington Higher Thought Society on a hot summer day, and keeps encountering their austere guest speaker, Professor Mortice, who is secretly as much in need of a quick whisky as his host. The title of "Beefsteak Damned Good" is the catch-phrase of an Italian waiter who belongs to a secret revolutionary group and is told to assassinate one of his best clients—a story told by a narrator who describes herself as having once been "a young and struggling journalist." These dark, surreal comedies, poised somewhere between Grossmith and Dostoevsky, point ahead to the inept male characters of her novels. The juvenile writer's boisterous, bouncy tone will be greatly toned down, but the oddity will last.

The most interesting of these Oxford pieces are some jokily contem-plative essays (a bit like Hazlitt, or Lamb), dressed up in the voice of an extreme personality. Though these are masked comic performances, they suggest some of her own feelings. They are bristling with up-to-the-minute literary allusions, as to Eliot, Joyce and Auden. "I Was Afraid" is told by a narrator so timorous that all the possible clichés about fear apply to her (or him): "Confront me with the slightest hazard, the most soluble crux, a dilemma whose horns are yet in embryo, and I shall be found unequal to the task of meeting it." The narrator is particularly terrified when travel-ling, and has to plan for every eventuality. "I have a padded deerstalker and boots to deaden the impact when the train is derailed (as I am always sure it will be) whichever way I am precipitated . . . I have a copy of *Ulysses* to drive clergymen out of the compartment, and I have given orders for a lunch hamper to be delivered at every stopping place."

In "The Curse of a Literary Education," a lover of literature has her visits to the countryside ruined because of all the quotations going round in her head, which she has to apply to everything she sees. "Look, Stranger" is a parody on a sensitive, alienated soul who has quarrelled with Nature, the Brotherhood of Man, and finally with herself: "I cut myself dead. I was surrounded by strangers." The last of these *Cherwell* pieces, "Wicked

Words," published after she left Oxford, tells her history of being unable to swear, with a caricatured version of her school life, and one or two autobiographical clues: "When I fall in love, which happens twice a year, and wish to end a tempestuous quarrel, I usually say 'Drat you.' When my heart is broken I say 'Cripes.'" At Somerville, they all knew how to cry, but not how to swear. "We should all have liked to do so, because we were young, and wanted to be thought vicious."[34]

She couldn't swear, but she could spell. In January 1938 she was selected as one of two women on the eight-strong Oxford team for the first "Spelling Bee" to be "conducted by wireless across the Atlantic" (as *The Times* reported it under the title "Hard Spells on the Air"). The opponents were from Radcliffe and Harvard, and the spelling had to follow the rules of the *Oxford Dictionary* (for the Oxford team) and *Webster's* (for the American team). They went to the BBC on a freezing cold Sunday train, hung about for ages while the engineers dealt with faulty headphones and microphones, were sent down to the cafeteria ("Cup of tea and Virginia cigarette, 2d, Cup of tea and Turkish cigarette, 2½d") and then did the forty-five-minute quiz, with thirty seconds allowed for each word, after which the other side had a go. The booby traps were "haemorrhage," "pettifoggery," "anonymity," "truncheon," "labyrinthine," "trachea" and "corollary." The Oxford team lost by four points, but "Miss Knox, like her listeners, found her early temerity an attractive pose and retained it throughout the contest with great effect." Her spelling of "daguerreotype" was "loudly applauded

---

10   THE ISIS   May 19th, 1938

PLACE AUX DAMES
Edited by ANNE WYNTER

IN THE NEWS.

Miss Penelope Knox (Somerville).

There is no need to introduce Penelope Knox; intellectually and socially she is well known in Oxford. Her name is famous at the Union and in the English School, and she has already appeared in these pages as the 'blonde bombshell' who astonished the world by her spelling prowess. She is now in her last term, and it seems likely that her undergraduate career will end with a flourish and a First. We could not improve on her own account of her experiences here:—

'I came up in 1935 as Senior Scholar from Wycombe Abbey. I was given to understand that Oxford was full of poets and unspeakable orgies, but that I would be all right if I kept my eyes open and my mouth shut. I followed this advice, but having seen very few poets and no orgies, I suppose I have wasted my time here to a great extent.

'Last term I went to the B.B.C. to take part in the first Spelling Bee against America. I was told there I was supposed to be a typical undergraduette. I spoke in the Union last term with the result that there were only two votes for my side of the motion.

'Since I came to Oxford I have had concussion twice and edited the *Cherwell* for two terms. I have been reading steadily for seventeen years; when I go down I want to start writing.'

MISS KNOX.

barges in our best bibs and tuckers, and watch them with adoring eyes. ('So clean, keen and upright, my dear.') We wonder why this is; rowing men may look ravishing sitting down, but they should never be allowed to stand up,

members of the 1936-37 teams will be playing again: M. S. C. Peters (Clifton High School and St. Hugh's) and B. J. K. Gracey (Royal School, Beith, and L.M.H.). Blues have been awarded to D. Keeton (Queen Anne's, Caversham, and L.M.H.), D. Berry (Malvern Girls' College and Somerville), and E. M. Ness (St. Dominics, Stoke-on-Trent, and O.H.S.).

The University played Birmingham University on Saturday, and the match resulted in a fairly easy win for Oxford by 5 matches to 1. The match with Norham Gardens L.T.C. on Thursday had to be adandoned owing to rain, when Norham Gardens were leading by 3 matches to 2.

The team is promising, but the pairs are at the moment suffering from lack of practice in playing together. If this difficulty can be overcome, they should be able to face Cambridge on Thursday with confidence.

Cricket.

We began the season well on Wednesday by winning our first match against Reading University by 111 for six against 53. Our high score was chiefly due to the good batting of Pike, who made 64 not out, and we might have made more runs but for the brilliant fielding of our opponents. Reading never settled down to Tunbridge's fast bowling, which was consistently good.

The first-year cricketers show great

by both teams." It was her first experience of the BBC, and she enjoyed herself. The Spelling Bee sealed her reputation, in her final year, as an Oxford star. "BLONDE BOMBSHELL BEATS THE LOT," ran the *Isis* headline, and its annual Valentine competition ("First Prize, One Hundred Oxford Memory Cigarettes and Two Seats at the Scala Cinema") listed for its recipients "Greta Garbo, Miss Penelope Knox, A Female History Don, or Mistinguett." The results of the competition largely consisted of verses written to the "evidently well-appreciated Penelope Knox": "O Bombshell with the golden thatch"; "Penelope, my Busy Bee, I love your voice, you must love me"; "Venus, Minerva, Spelling Queen, / All three in thy small Frame are seen; / Fair Goddess, thou hast caught me well, / Wrapped in the magic of thy 'Spell.' "[35]

Appearing again, in her final term, as an *Isis* "Woman of the Year," she gave this account of her Oxford experiences. It was the first of what would be, in years to come, many quizzical, self-concealing interviews. All the same it gives a sense of someone who knew exactly what she was going to do with her life. In retrospect she would sometimes say that she thought about staying on at Oxford to do graduate work, and did not, because "it hardly seemed to be the right thing to do at the time."[36] But there is no hint of this here.

> I came up in 1935 . . . I was given to understand that Oxford was full of poets and unspeakable orgies, but that I would be all right if I kept my eyes open and my mouth shut. I followed this advice, but having seen very few poets and no orgies, I suppose I have wasted my time here to a great extent. Last term I went to the BBC to take part in the first Spelling Bee against America. I was told there I was supposed to be a typical undergraduette. I spoke in the Union last term [no record of this speech survives] with the result that there were only two votes for my side of the motion. Since I came to Oxford I have had concussion twice and edited the *Cherwell* for two terms. I have been reading steadily for seventeen years; when I go down I want to start writing.[37]

She was going to be a writer, and she was not going to live at home—unlike Jean Fisher, who finished her Classics degree a year later and then went back to Oundle to teach Greek and Latin for a while, before reading for the Bar. Oundle had become more of a home than ever for Penelope while she was at Oxford. For two years after Christina's death, the Regent's Park House was a gloomy place. Every night, Evoe and Rawle ate dinner alone in their evening clothes. Rawle was trying, not very successfully, to find work as a journalist, at one point even writing copy for a ladies' underwear magazine. He knew he was a disappointment to his father; he missed his mother deeply; his stammer and his reticence had settled in.[38] Then, in 1937, Evoe fell in love again, with a much younger woman. She was Mary Shepard, the daughter of the brilliant *Punch* artist Ernest Shepard, the illustrator of Winnie-the-Pooh (always known as "Kipper"), who was not best pleased that his widowed boss, in his mid-fifties, was going to marry his twenty-eight-year-old daughter. Evoe and Mary moved away from the sad Regent's Park house to a house in St. John's Wood, and then back to Hampstead, near the Heath. But this, though close to her childhood scene in Well Walk, was not exactly "home" for Penelope.

All the evidence suggests that Penelope, eventually, got on extremely well with her stepmother. In later life they were very good friends, and helped each other out. Mary, like her father, was a gifted illustrator, and would be best known for the appealing pictures she did for *Mary Poppins*. She had spirit and adventurousness in her, but she was also domestically inclined, and eager to make Evoe happy. Jean, who found Evoe attractive and amusing, if a little daunting, thought that Mary was sweet and delightful. Just like "Mrs. K," and at exactly the same age, she took on a sad Knox widower and devoted the rest of her life to him. Like Mrs. K, she befriended the widower's children tactfully and affectionately. One friend of Penelope's observed that Mary was more like a sister than a stepmother to her. Between the 1950s and the 1990s Mops and Mary wrote hundreds of letters to each other, hardly any of which have survived.[39]

But to begin with she found it very difficult. Her father, who would never talk to her about Christina, only two years dead, had been swept away by a grand sexual passion for a young woman just seven years older than Penelope. Mary in herself was evidently not a threat. Her family were good friends of Rachel Ollivant's family; she was talented, friendly and benign, the opposite of a wicked stepmother. Nevertheless, she had taken Christina's place and Evoe's love.

Mops went home as little as possible, spending most of her vacations at Oundle. When she left Oxford, she and Rawle set up house at 130 Clarence Gate Gardens, in one of the heavy, purpose-built blocks of flats off Baker

Street. She had an allowance from Evoe, and a first job from him too, writing reviews for *Punch*. Her circle of friends came and went—Rachel Ollivant, who was at the Slade, Janet, Ham, the Breakwell boys, Jean's brother Jimmy Fisher, Willie Conder, who had a publishing job at Amalgamated Press and used to meet Penelope regularly for lunch in a Lyons Corner House near Sloane Square. London was their playground—cafés, restaurants, films, theatre, friendships.

She and Ham and Oliver and Janet continued their complicated four-way relationship. Mops to Ham: "I am very nervous of saying anything where people's feelings and sensitivities are concerned, which often makes me appear even stupider than I am." Oliver to Ham: "Forgive my regrettable series of half-utterances and petulances about Mops . . . Our relations had a high intensity of their own, due both to the soil on which they grew up, & to the exaltation of all conversation with her, & to the frequency of our meetings."[40] And there were other entanglements, now lost in time. Some were upsetting. She wrote to Ham: "I don't know whether Oliver ever told you that ever since I broke my engagement I have been mixed up in a rather stupid and unsatisfactory way, I suppose, but it is the only thing I can do, it goes on and on and it makes me appreciate my friends all the more." And some were absurd, like one unfortunate suitor who "proposed to her in a park in London—a pigeon messed on his head and she burst out laughing."[41]

But personal relations were all at risk; the air was darkening around them. Between 1935 and 1938, the atmosphere for undergraduates at Oxford had become more serious and intense. Now, in 1938, as they were launching on the world, "there was constant talk of Nazism, the Moscow treason trials, marching and raising money for arms for Spain, the bestial pogrom against German Jews in November 1938, Hitler's annexation of the Sudetenland."[42] Even *Punch* became sombre, Fitzgerald remembered. "After the Munich Conference and the abandonment of Czechoslovakia, Evoe wrote, for the Christmas of 1938, with a sense of bitter humiliation, a 'Hymn to the Dictators':

> O well beloved leaders
> And potentates sublime,
> We come to you as pleaders
> Because it's Christmas time.
> Illustrious banditti,
> Contemptuous of our codes,

Look down to-day in pity
On democratic toads."

His daughter looked back on that moment of history, as if writing an elegy for her youth, and said: "All the systems evolved by human beings for living on this earth were now shown to be either delusory, destructive, sadly outdated, or at risk."[43]

CHAPTER FOUR

Love and War

"Their lives were shaking into pieces."[1]

Mops, aged twenty-two, to Ham, 5 October 1939: "I am waiting in agonies for the reports of Hitler's speech, as any reference to unknown weapons will hypnotize me with fear . . . In spite of the somewhat ominous news I am in one of my optimistic moods, in which I feel that it will be a short war. Please concentrate on agreeing with this." 18 October 1939: "I am melancholy and terrified of the celebrated Blitzkrieg. I start at noises in the street, sleep with my head under the bedclothes, and listen to the owls hooting . . . with gloomy relish. When I get as depressed as this though, I must get better soon, it's a law of nature—but the really annoying thing is my fondness for doughnuts." 30 October 1939: "Everybody seems to be so mobile nowadays, and to flash to and fro past or through the metropolis leaving me glued to my desk. There is something to be said for remaining static, however, for it gives one an illusion of being nailed to the mast, or steadfast at the post."[2] Fear, hope, humour, stoicism, resilience: it is the Londoner's response to 1939 in miniature, a "People's War" of one. That autumn of the "phoney war," there were no bombs yet, but blackouts, rationing, gas masks, petrol shortages, enlistings, internments, evacuations and, over it all, the terrifying news from Europe, pouring through the wireless, on the cinema news bulletins, in the papers.

Everyone's lives were changed: almost at once the group of student friends began to be "broken up by war service overseas and war deaths."[3] Ham and Rawle were in training in the Officer Corps Training Units, as were many of their friends, at Catterick or Aldershot. Rawle was then posted to Scotland. Oliver joined the Coldstream Guards, his brother Raven was in Field Security. Some were gunners, some went into the Navy, some applied for exemption as pacifists. One of the group, Bill Cobb, was taken early as a POW. Penelope's own war work was, to start with, more escapist. Through 1939 and into early 1940 she sat at a desk in the *Punch* office in Bouverie Street, opposite the pipe-smoking subeditor from Lowestoft, Richard Mallet, whose habits she gleefully satirised, writing film reviews.

This niche suited her well. Like thousands of others in wartime, she had a passionate appetite for the cinema. The movies provided consolation and light relief, like doughnuts. She was equally keen on a rip-roaring Western, a Marx Brothers comedy, a new Hitchcock, or the "alarming and impressive" Ministry of Information short, *London Can Take It.* She often took Janet with her. They once excitedly spotted Clark Gable at Oundle, out at a dance from the nearby air force base, with a British nurse on his knee. And she had a tremendous crush on Rex Harrison.

Penelope Knox's 1940 film reviews, like her student journalism, were funny, knowing and evocative. They embraced the popular medium wholeheartedly, with no highbrow reservations. A spirited account of her hero Rex Harrison in Carol Reed's *Night Train to Munich* (much influenced, as she pointed out, by Hitchcock's *The Lady Vanishes*) describes him rescuing Margaret Lockwood "resplendent in the disguise of a Nazi officer . . . He penetrates through department after department of the Berlin Admiralty, orders champagne with attractive insolence, meets his enemy's eye with an unwavering glance, and fires not fewer than twelve rounds out of an automatic (without reloading) to cover the heroine's escape." In *The Westerner,* which she admired for its sepia tones, Gary Cooper is "the ideal cowboy, with very small boots and very large fancy spurs, and a Roman-nosed horse called Chickweed which starts cantering as soon as he gets on it and not a moment before." The showing of *The Doctor Takes a Wife,* with Ray Milland and Loretta Young, was interrupted before the end by the sirens, but not before a splendidly clichéd "accouchement" in a lonely farmhouse, "with the familiar accompaniment of a stricken gnarled old farmer, wide-eyed children, and continual demands for hot water."

She liked to use her reviews to talk about what the art form could do. Hitchcock is praised for his brilliant use of cinematic realism in *Foreign Correspondent.* He understands that "nothing is more sinister in a scene of violence than a quite familiar, or even an exceedingly ordinary object . . . That is why you get buses, railway refreshment-rooms, theatres, pierrots at the seaside, Sunday dinner, church services, lunch at Simpsons', music-halls and third-class carriages, instead of luxurious apartments, gambling-dens, dungeons, bearskins, jewellery and cloaked Master Minds." A review of *Pride and Prejudice,* with Greer Garson and Laurence Olivier, turns into an essay on comedy. Comedy is not, as Hollywood would have it, "uproariously good-natured." "It is nothing of the sort." It is about social distinctions and restrictions, and a film version of Austen which, "in an unlucky mood of universal benevolence," allows no one to be boring, sarcastic, unpleasant or snobbish, completely misses the point.[4] This analysis of comedy, one of her lifelong interests, dovetailed with a short anonymous piece she wrote in 1939 for the *Times Literary Supplement*. Goebbels, astonishingly, had issued an edict against "intellectual wit" in Germany, thereby, she said, "dealing another blow to those minor arts already on their deathbed—epigram and repartee." A brief history of the art of "badminton with words and meanings" in Wilde, Samuel Butler and Restoration Comedy follows. "One cannot help pitying the Germans, and if Dr. Goebbels is successful, pity will become despair."[5]

Evoe set up the job for her at *Punch,* and she in turn set up one or two *Punch* opportunities for Oliver Breakwell. But Rawle was left out of this cosy arrangement. He did once have a piece in *Punch,* but he sent it in under a pseudonym, because if Evoe had known it was his, Rawle thought that he would not have published it. While they were travelling on the tube together, Evoe remarked on this article admiringly, without knowing who the author was. Rawle said not a word.[6]

By June 1940, Penelope had joined the war effort: "I haven't been to any films at all lately as I have a vague feeling that it is wicked."[7] Instead, she was writing letters and copy for the Ministry of Food in Horseferry Road, under the fierce eye of a Mr. McAllister, whom she referred to as "my small short Scotch problem boss."[8] The Ministry was formed a week after the war broke out, as part of the Board of Trade, and it was needed because only 40 per cent of the country's food was produced at home. Its task was to co-ordinate all aspects of food imports, distribution and production, to regulate prices, and to propagandise for economies on the home front. The setting up of the Women's Land Army, the Dig for Victory campaign and the introduction of rationing all emanated from the Ministry, under Lord Woolton, Minister of Food from April 1940 to the end of 1943, after whom the famous meatless Woolton Pie was named. Rationing began in January 1940; by the end of that year the weekly ration was four ounces bacon, six ounces marge, two ounces tea, eight ounces sugar and two ounces of cooking fats and meat. The Ministry exhorted the nation to dig, save, and be inventive and thrifty in the kitchen. It issued posters ("Think of the potato as a weapon of war!"), "Food Flash Films" in all cinemas ("Waist not Waste: Food doesn't grow in the shops, you know!") and "Food Facts": "Those who have the will to win / Eat potatoes in their skin / Knowing that the sight of peelings / Deeply hurts Lord Woolton's feelings."[9]

Penelope spent her time sending messages to the British Beekeepers

Association, answering abusive letters about tea shortages and writing articles on "communal feeding." One older colleague remembered her as "an attractive young miss with bright eyes and a crisp wit, coping with the ceaseless output of [the Civil Servants] at the Ministry."[10] But this did not last long. She told her friends she had been sacked, but perhaps she just decided to move on. In any case, she left the Ministry in November 1940, after a "terrible leaving party" at which the messenger boy cried and they had Dundee cake.[11]

By December she was working for the BBC, where News, Talks, Music, Entertainment, Features, Variety, Schools, Drama, Foreign Language Channels, Forces and Overseas Services were all geared to "inspire determination to see the war through," yet the policy was "to tell the truth, and nothing but the truth, even if the truth is horrible."[12] She described herself, retrospectively, as a "Recorded Programmes Assistant—almost, I think, the lowest of the low," and that was the job description she gave to her alter ego in her BBC novel, *Human Voices*. But her BBC staff card suggests that she was slightly higher up the ranks than she made out: she was employed as a producer in the Features Department from 2 December 1940 and would keep that job description until 22 September 1945. In 1942 and 1944 she was also listed as a scriptwriter in the Transcription Production Unit (Programme Division), working under the actor, thriller-writer and radio producer Victor (V.C.) Clinton-Baddeley, a larger-than-life character, seventeen years her senior, about whom Ham and her other friends would hear many funny stories.[13]

She was living mainly at Clarence Gate Gardens, the nearby Baker Street flat, where Rawle, now in uniform, was an occasional visitor on leave from his battery in Scotland, or taking his troops from Aberdeen to Portsmouth. But like most wartime Londoners she moved about, depending on where the bombs fell, between Clarence Gate Gardens, a flat in NW8 (63 Eyre Court, Finchley Road), and, very near to that, 16 Avenue Close, Avenue Road, Evoe and Mary's house in St. John's Wood. The "alarming noises of the London night" followed her from place to place. One night a large oil-canister bomb came through her bedroom window, luckily while she was away, and all the windows of the flat collapsed; one day a land mine was safely removed from Avenue Close, "parachute, tassels, and all"; another night two bombs fell on one of the Baker Street "Show Flats," "which now has a sign Luxurious Flats to Let swinging over a crater."[14]

Her time at the Ministry, from May to November 1940, had kept pace with the retreat from Dunkirk and Churchill's coming to power, offering nothing but "blood, toil, tears and sweat." Hitler took over Northern Europe, the Germans entered Paris, the Battle of Britain was fought. "Never in the field of human conflict was so much owed by so many to so few," Churchill intoned on the BBC. From late August 1940, London was bombed. *Human Voices,* her novel about the BBC in wartime, published forty years later, is set precisely in that period, March to September 1940, though she did not start work at the BBC until December of that year. But from the start of the war, the BBC's "human voices" dominated the country's perception of what was happening. Everyone tuned in to Churchill's growling, nation-rousing rhetoric, Lord Haw-Haw's grotesque propaganda, J. B. Priestley's encouraging appeals to the man in the street and King George's speeches. (Fitzgerald has her BBC Recorded Programmes Director mention his "standby recordings for [the King's] speeches to the nation—His Majesty without stammer, in case of emergency.") Everyone listened to the nine o'clock news. "For those at home the sound of the war was the sound of the radio."[15] Accompanied by the reassuring stroke of Big Ben, the BBC poured out rhetoric, entertainment, bulletins and patriotic exhortations.

⚘

Fitzgerald's wartime novel was saved up in her mind for many years. *Human Voices* (1980), her fourth novel, published when she was sixty-three, looks like a light, funny, brilliantly accurate re-creation of the BBC in wartime. But inseparable from the comedy, there is danger and anguish, a strong idea about truth and a sad affectionate remembering of her younger self.

London in the Blitz is done as a series of quick vivid drawings. The silver-fleeced barrage balloons above Green Park go up like a flock of sheep in the evening light, seeming to "be fixed and grazing in the upper air." After the September air raids, "the buses, diverted into streets for which they were not intended, seemed to take the licence of a dream, drawing up on the pavements and nosing against front windows to look in at the startled inhabitants." The air was full of "fine, whitish dust." At night you counted your steps in the darkness, passing "doors with tiny slits of light, just enough to catch the eye, the rendezvous for Europe's Free Forces, soldiers who were sad and poor." In the Underground, during the raids, people settled down for the night,

> taking possession of their marked areas, bringing with them fold-
> ing chairs and tables, and in some cases cooking-stoves. Others

were waiting until the live rail was switched off at midnight to spread out their mattresses on the line itself. Meanwhile, the trains were still running, and those waiting to travel in them were confined to the extreme edge of the platform, nervously clinging to their bags and newspapers, aliens, where they had once been the most important people there. The shelterers, though friendly, crowded up to them, nudging them with kettles, and apologizing with the air of those in the right as they set up the evening's games of cards and chess.

The great ocean liner of the BBC in Portland Place, lapped round with sandbags, was once described by George Orwell, who worked there in wartime, as "half-way between a girls' school and a lunatic asylum."[16] Fitzgerald loves re-creating institutions or communities which have their own peculiar, fanatical systems and routines: the British Museum in her first novel, *The Golden Child,* the stage school in *At Freddie's,* the river community in *Offshore,* the Cambridge college and the hospital in *The Gate of Angels,* the printing works in *The Beginning of Spring.* In every case, the beauty of it comes from her complete mastery of detail, and the sharpness and inwardness with which she turns these self-absorbed environments inside out. And very bizarre they look, when the light of historical imagination shines in on them.

The BBC was perfect material for her because she observed it so closely at the time, and because it hovers between the absurd and the heroic. In her manuscript notes for the novel, the original title was one of the BBC's famous wartime catchphrases, "10 Seconds from Now," or "I Return You to My Colleagues at Broadcasting House." Her notes for the novel include a carefully drawn plan of the layout of the newsroom, technical terms (howl back, echo room), and a brisk account of what the novel is about: "BH is improbably in wartime dedicated to putting out the truth. It also keeps its old character—patriarchal & in that sense democratic: the lowest of the tribe may speak to the king. BBC people are affected by the character of BH and still more so as the vast building, sandbagged & darkened, becomes a kind of fortress."[17]

She understands the psychology of routines. Civilians in the war—women, especially—survive through concentrating on everyday details, in order to hold at bay what must be kept out of their thoughts, "helpless waves of flesh against metal and salt . . . the soundless fall of a telegram through the letter-box." "If you can't face living your life day by day, you must live it minute by minute." The British war effort, she notes, drawing on her experience at the Ministry of Food, consists to a large extent of "counting large numbers of small things into separate containers." The systems-ridden BBC provides an extreme version of that self-preserving effort to categorise and tidy everything, and to maintain "continuity." But of course there is chaos and anxiety swirling around inside the fussily patrolled bureaucracy.

Everyone is referred to by their acronym: RPD (Recorded Programmes Director), DPP (Director of Programme Planning), AD(E) (Secretary of Assistant Director [Establishment]), RPAs (Recorded Programme Assistants), IEP (Indispensable Emergency Personnel list). Long-term staff are known as the "Old Servants." In the canteen, there is one communal spoon "tied to the cash register with a piece of string." There you could eat "National Cheese"—"the manufacturers have agreed to amalgamate their brand names for the duration in the interest of the Allied War effort"—or herrings in mustard sauce, "the week's Patriotic Fish Dish." (Ros Goulder, a contemporary of Penelope's at the BBC, remembered whale meat and venison.) In case of siege, those on the right list can "draw a standard issue of towel, soap and bedding for the duration." Recordings, aluminium 78s smelling pungently of acetate (which Fitzgerald remembered as "the true smell of the BBC's war"), were always being misplaced. When "Atmosphere" recordings are needed, you could choose from "Air-Raid Siren, False Alarm" or "Cheerful Voices with Chink of Tea-Cups." The staff are in perpetual motion: "Men in brown overalls went round BH, fixing the framed blackouts in every window, circulating in the opposite direction to the Permanents coming downstairs, while the news readers moved laterally to check with Pronunciation, pursued by editors bringing later messages on pink cards." There are always shortages: "If you can tell me where to get any more steel filing cabinets measuring up to our specifications," says the exhausted supplies manager, "I'm prepared to go to bed with Hitler's grandmother." Up and down the seven floors of the building, "the air seemed alive with urgency and worry."

As the bombs start to fall and BH comes under siege, the absurd and the heroic increasingly converge. The young men manning the guns on the roof spend their nights "playing poker for margarine coupons, while the Regent's Park guns rocked them like ship's boys aloft." The unused concert hall is turned, first into a comical Red Cross classroom, then into a giant dormitory, with metal bunks and cubicles allocated on a ticket basis, the sexes divided by grey hospital blankets, the nights accompanied by a "great ground swell of snoring," amplified by walls "designed to give the best possible acoustics for classical music." All night long, people with deadlines strike matches to check their watches, muffled alarm clocks go off, announcers and continuity men speak their lines in their sleep, people burst out weeping. This strange and haunting scene is one of the novel's triumphs—and extremely close to the historical reality. "Twice in the concert hall I had to help out when someone had an epileptic fit," Fitzgerald recalled. "In my novel I changed this to the birth of a baby, but that wouldn't have surprised me either."[18]

All the BH types are caught. Among the RPAs, there are the serious boys—a utopian socialist, a Polish exile—and the very young women: sensible Vi, with her big family and her boyfriend away fighting, or the weepy half-French girl, Lise, whose fiancé has disappeared. There is Eddie Waterlow, the gay drama producer with a passion for music and for France. There are the refugees, like old Dr. Vogel, Europe's "greatest expert on recorded atmosphere," "disguising their losses, transcribing page after page of Nazi broadcasts in scholar's shorthand," and listening to late Beethoven quartets in their coffee breaks. (The BBC was often described, as it is in the novel, as another League of Nations.) Exploding onto the premises with sacks of oranges, gas mask, cameras and pistol is the American journalist "Mac," for whom "everything is possible, except to leave things as they were." And there is the famous newsreader, John Halliburton, known as "the Halibut," with a voice of such "hoarse distinction" that no German impersonator could ever be mistaken for him, and who is therefore "assigned to read in case of enemy landing."

Most of these are recognisable figures. "Mac" has more than a touch of Ed Murrow or John McBain, undaunted American reporters bringing home the European war to the States. Eddie could be Eddie Sackville-West. The Halibut closely resembles Alvar Liddell. Dr. Vogel is very like Ludwig Koch, the exiled German sound recordist and expert on birdsong and animal noises. A letter to Ham of March 1941 shows how close *Human Voices* would be to Fitzgerald's own experience of the time:

> The BBC . . . is rent with scandals and there are dreadful quarrels in the canteen about liberty, the peoples' convention, &c, and the air is dark with flying spoons and dishes. Miss Stevens poured some tea down Mr. Fletcher's neck the other day. He knew Freud who told him the term inferiority complex was a mistranslation and there was really no such thing . . . We are doing a programme

called "These Things are English," with the funeral of George V, beer, cricket, people singing in the underground &c. [In the novel, this becomes *"Lest we forget our Englishry."*] I think the people singing only express their own fierce triumph in getting the better of the London Passenger Transport Board . . . We had a mock invasion the other day. We were overpowered in 5 minutes as the officers in charge of the defence forgot their passes and couldn't get into BH.[19]

Fitzgerald used to say that she tried her best to disguise everyone in the novel, but that people were always contacting her after it was published, complaining that she had given them the wrong-coloured pencil.[20] This was the sort of joke the novel's laconic hero would have enjoyed. The DPP, Jeff Haggard, "a man with a pale ruined-looking face," "with dark eyebrows, like a comedian's, but one who had to be taken seriously," is a cross between Humphrey Bogart's Rick in *Casablanca* and Evoe Knox. A person of formidable integrity, his private life is a wreck, and his calmness is "really recklessness," as of "a gambler who no longer felt anything was valuable enough to stake." For all his apparent detachment, he is in touch with everything that's going on, and feels responsible to everyone. Mac tells him, and he tells himself, to be colder, to break free. But his Achilles heel is his protective friendship for the RPD, Sam Brooks. Sam is an irresistible force, an *idiot savant* or Holy Fool, unfit for ordinary human life. Childish, wildly enthusiastic, manipulative, self-pitying and charming, he is entirely obsessed with his craft as a recording engineer, at which he is a kind of genius. He also can't stop himself trying to seduce all the young women RPAs in his "Seraglio." Fitzgerald plays this as comedy, with a kind of innocence about it. But she also makes clear the damage it does, and, without labouring the point, the sexist assumptions and male hierarchy that made his behaviour possible.

Into the BBC, that "cross between a civil service, a powerful moral force, and an amateur theatrical company," comes Annie Asra, seventeen years old, an orphan from Birmingham. (Fitzgerald's notes for the novel include lists of Brummy diction and turns of speech.) She was "a little square curly-headed creature, not a complainer": just as Penelope Knox might have been described at her age. The chapter which introduces her—her school, her Saturday job at "Anstruthers" ("I was in the loose count sweets to start with, then they moved me to hosiery"), her life with her piano-tuner widowed father and her departure alone to London after his death—is a

poignant story in itself. Annie is a typical Fitzgerald heroine, sturdy, observant, honest, self-reliant and quietly passionate. She gets a job as a Junior
Temporary Assistant in the Department of Recorded Programmes, and she
falls in love, inevitably, with Sam Brooks. He magnetises her "like a ring of
magic fire," though she also knows he is a middle-aged man who "said the
same thing to all the girls" and who cares about nothing but his work. She
knows it is absurd and hopeless: "He existed, and so did she, and she had
perhaps sixty years left to put up with it."

There is a clue in her name. Placidly shelling peas (Fitzgerald's favourite
consolatory, Ruskinian activity), Annie tells Vi's mother that her teacher
once said that Asra was "the name of a tribe." The allusion, not recognised
by Annie, is to a famous poem by Heine, "The Asra." It tells of the slave
who grows pale for love of the Sultan's daughter; when she asks his name,
he replies: "My tribe it is the Asra / Who die, when they love." (Fitzgerald would be annoyed when A. S. Byatt failed to notice this allusion
when reviewing the novel.)[21] The novel puts this romantic extreme into a
historical context: "Hers must have been the last generation to fall in love
without hope in such an unproductive way. After the war the species no
longer found it biologically useful."

This is exactly what Fitzgerald says about herself, looking back on her
time at the BBC a few years after writing the novel. Whatever happened to
her now, this kind of silent, hopeless, perpetual love would become one of
the persistent themes of her fiction. But who she is talking about remains
one of her closely guarded secrets:

> I fell in love, with someone very much older and more important,
> without the least glimmer of a hope of any return. This was quite
> common in those days, but I suggested in *Human Voices* that we
> were the last generation to behave like this . . . Certainly, towards
> the end of the war or just after it we all of us married, had chil-
> dren, and forgot why and even how we'd managed to love without
> return.[22]

There may be a clue in that letter to Ham about the Mr. Fletcher who
had tea poured down his neck and had met Freud. Ros Goulder, who met
Penelope a few times at the BBC and saw her as a "jolly hockey-sticks"
type with a famous father, was quite sure who her love-object was. She
used to commute from the BBC on the train home from Victoria to Red-
hill with Mr. Fletcher, who often had one of the young women from his

department with him. "Everyone fancied him." H. Lynton Fletcher, a dark good-looking man then in his forties, was Head of Recorded Programmes, and a big name in the BBC. Penelope's relationship to him in the office would have been just like Annie's to Sam Brooks.

Over and over again Fitzgerald put into her fiction a version of a futile, unshakeable, lifelong love for the wrong person. Sometimes she lets it end happily. In *Human Voices,* there may possibly be a life after the war for Annie and Sam. But this is only in the context of the novel's other tragedies and drastic changes. The French girl, Lise, gives birth dramatically in the middle of the concert-hall dormitory. Vi's lovable family is bombed and scattered. The Polish boy goes off to fight for his country. Dr. Vogel is killed; Jeff Haggard is doomed because he goes to the help of his friend. But the most painful story in *Human Voices* is the story of France—compared with which, as Bogart says in *Casablanca,* personal tragedies don't amount to "a hill of beans."

Fitzgerald would write novels set in Italy, Russia and Germany, but not in the other two countries that fascinated her, Spain and France. *Human Voices* is the nearest she comes to a French novel, set at the time of de Gaulle's becoming leader of the Free French in London in opposition to the Vichy government. Occupied France overshadows the whole novel. Lise's absentee French boyfriend is found with a gang of French soldiers in Kensington Gardens who get into a sudden, distressing fight with the Free French boys. (Penelope took photographs of French soldiers in Hyde Park in September 1940.)[23] Annie's musical education is all in French music: Satie's *"Socrate"* is the novel's theme tune. "Less is more," Eddie says of it, as his author might have said of her own work. Eddie is trying to make a feature called "France Fights On," "a tribute to the country without which Europe could hardly be called civilised." Annie falls in love with Sam at an outing to Prunier's, a grand French restaurant which feels just as it might have done before the war, giving off "a whiff of the lost smell of Paris."

France walks into the novel in the person of the dignified and tragic General Pinard, just escaped from occupied France, who comes to the BBC on 14 June to give an unscripted broadcast to the nation. "Behind him lay France's broken armies." Jeff Haggard had encountered him in the trenches in the First World War (which haunts the novel all through). He alone has an inkling of what the General's message might be. He remembers him, in a dugout in France twenty-three years before, saying "Soyons réalistes." So when the General starts to tell the British nation, in "a quiet, moving, old man's voice," to give in to the Germans—"Don't think of resistance . . . Think of your selves . . . Give in when the Boche comes in. Give in"—the

DPP has already "pulled the plugs" on him, and the BBC is inundated with complaints about the ten minutes of silence on the Home network.

It is a beautiful example of how Fitzgerald plays with history. General Pinard is an utterly plausible character. Every "in-house" detail—the "switch censor" that could cut off a presenter at once, the fear of silence on the airwaves, the anxiety about unscripted programmes—is exact. So is the intimate relationship which the BBC created between France and Britain. "They were scattering human voices into the darkness of Europe." There were close BBC contacts with France from the moment of the invasion— regular programmes called *Vive la France* and *Ici La France,* well-known French presenters and producers like Jean Masson and Michel Saint-Denis. "If there is resistance in France," it was said by one of de Gaulle's men, "it is due to the BBC."[24]

In reality, Marshal Pétain broadcast on French radio in June saying he was going to sue for the end of hostilities. Then, on 18 June, the BBC was told "that a French general—unnamed—would be arriving at the studio." This was de Gaulle, who went on air at 10 p.m. to speak rousingly of the need for continuing resistance. (The broadcast is mentioned later in the novel.)[25] So Fitzgerald, true to her interest in failure and disappointment, imagines what might have happened if the famous French broadcast from London had been defeatist and appeasing, like Pétain's, rather than heroic, like de Gaulle's.

Instead, what the listeners get is silence: a silence which is a kind of lie. The truth would have been unendurable, and counterproductive. But the BBC's self-appointed task was to tell the truth, and an argument about truth goes all through the novel. "Without prompting, the BBC had decided that truth was more important than consolation, and, in the long run, would be more effective." In this the BBC was at odds with the various ministries who wanted it to be a propaganda machine, and this is a battle the DPP fights throughout the novel. There are heated arguments—in the novel, as there were in reality—about the use of pre-recordings, or any material that could be falsified or misleading. But, as fiction writers know, there is no such thing as absolute truth. Annie asks: "How can they find anything to broadcast that's got to be true, and couldn't be anything else?"

As Jeff Haggard goes out of Broadcasting House for the last time, he pauses to look up at the statue (which he remembers seeing Eric Gill carving in 1932, tunic billowing shockingly in the breeze) of Prospero and Ariel:

> Prospero was shown preparing to launch his messenger onto the sound waves of the universe. But who, after all, was Ariel? All

he ever asked was to be released from his duties. And when this favoured spirit had flown off, to suck where the bee sucks, and Prospero had returned with all his followers to Italy, the island must have reverted to Caliban. It had been his, after all, in the first place. When all was said and done, oughtn't he to preside over the BBC? Ariel, it was true, had produced music, but it was Caliban who listened to it, even in his dreams. And Caliban, who wished Prospero might be stricken with the red plague for teaching him to speak correct English, never told anything but the truth, presumably not knowing how to. Ariel, on the other hand, was a liar, pretending that someone's father was drowned full fathom five, when in point of fact he was safe and well. All this was so that virtue should prevail. The old excuse.

≈

The authorial voice, dry, disabused, concerned with truth and morality, is on the side of the Calibans of this world—and whatever other worlds there might be. But there is strong feeling, too, for Haggard, the Prospero of the novel, who looks and behaves so much like Evoe Knox. Fitzgerald's father had died a few years before she began the novel; part of its sadness is that it is an elegy for him, as well as a vivid recalling of her youthful time of love and trauma.

Evoe, wandering about London in the thick of the bombs with a bottle of whisky in his pocket, for whoever might need it, was editing a magazine that was as much a part of the British war effort as the BBC. "In the irrecoverably strange atmosphere of June 1940 countless letters of the simplest kind of appreciation came in response to *Punch'*s picture of a single aircraft, flying out to the attack into a darkened sky. Even at this point of danger, it mattered very much that *Punch* should appear every week."[26] There were plans to evacuate the *Punch* office to Manchester—or to America—if necessary, but in fact the Bouverie Street office kept going all through the war, though hit by fires and burst gas mains and with a much-depleted staff. At home in suburban St. John's Wood, Mary kept hens in the wasteland behind the air raid wardens' post, foxes ran wild and weeds took hold in the bomb craters.

The Knox brothers were having very different wars. Wilfred, more shabby and eccentric than ever, was standing in for the Chaplain of Pembroke College, Cambridge, for the duration. Privately, he was undergoing a "black night of the soul"; but he came through. Ronnie was thriving under the patronage of Lady Acton, at Aldenham in Shropshire, working on his version of the New Testament for English Catholics and looking after a convent school for Catholic girls evacuated from Kensington: "They were an easier generation than his own highly-strung nephews and nieces," wrote the niece.[27]

Dillwyn, preoccupied as always, was, by the start of the war, fully involved in trying to crack the German Enigma enciphering machine. He had begun work on it in the late 1930s. In 1938, though very ill, he had flown to Warsaw to meet the French and Polish cryptographers who were also working on Enigma. The leading Polish cryptographer described him as "grasping everything very quickly, as quick as lightning." (Fitzgerald's strong feeling for the Poles comes through, as it does in *Human Voices,* when she speaks in *The Knox Brothers* of the wartime connection to "these brilliant, suffering and heroic people.")[28] In 1939 the Department of Communications moved to Bletchley Park—"Station X." Learned cryptographers were billeted on the small Buckinghamshire railway town. Dillwyn slept in the office, a former coachman's cottage in the old stable-yard of the big Victorian Tudor-Gothic mansion, surviving on black coffee, chocolate, his pipes and his hot baths. He drove back to Courn's Wood at weekends, with his hands mostly off the wheel, reciting *Lycidas* as he went.[29]

Bletchley was growing all round him, while Dillwyn worked with Peter Twinn, Frank Birch, Alan Turing (Dilly was very fond of "the young genius") and a fleet of cyphering clerks, known as "Dilly's girls." Here he wrestled against time with the "Spy Enigma Variation," the code used by German embassies in neutral countries and in the occupied zones. The work was like a combination of solving crossword puzzles, playing chess, doing mathematics and deciphering Greek papyri. His methods seemed impenetrable and erratic, not helped by flare-ups of the "terrible Knox temper," his short-sightedness, his ignoring his colleagues, who were all devoted to him, for days on end, and his increasing ill health: he had stomach cancer. But in 1941 he had a breakthrough which speeded up the solving of the Enigma Variation by about six months, and led to some crucial gains for the Allies. One of the team, Mavis Lever (later Batey, and a friend of Penelope's), vividly remembered his working methods. She thought he was exactly like Lewis Carroll's White Knight, "the queerest bird" that Alice has ever seen. But perhaps, Mavis thought later, "the absent-mindedness was a smoke screen after all."[30]

Dilly's secret work was hidden from his family; but the Knox way, in general, was to react to the war with more than their usual reticence and ironic reserve. When a bomb in St. John's Wood made the cork pop out of a bottle of claret just as Evoe was opening it, no one got under the table: Evoe just said, "If one could rely on its happening regularly . . ."[31] One was not supposed to make a fuss. But, as the young men went to war, Penelope could tell Ham (even if she couldn't tell Evoe) how much she minded about her brother at this time. In October 1940 Rawle was back in their flat: "I do love having him on leave but a week is no good at all, a brother should be there all the time like the church and the post-office."[32]

In December, Rawle embarked from Portsmouth as a gunner, on a troopship to Bombay. In India he was seconded to the Indian Mountain Regiment, and then in 1942 he was sent to Malaya and Singapore, where he was captured by the Japanese. He spent three and a half appalling years as a prisoner of war, listening to the BBC while sweeping the floors, on a secret radio the prisoners had built inside a broom. His job in the camp was to get the news out to the other prisoners and to grow bean sprouts to make hooch. No one in the family knew if he was alive or dead.[33]

Hugh Lee was posted to Bucharest. Oliver Breakwell was sent to Egypt—Penelope told Ham she was extremely unhappy that he was going—where, well away from Janet and Mops, he rapidly fell in love with, and married, Hersey Williamson, a formidable ATS in Cairo.[34] Penelope's friends were scattered, her brother disappeared, her father was taken up with his second wife. Whoever she had fallen for at the BBC was a hopeless case; any involvements she had had before then had come to nothing. If she was feeling lonely and unhappy, she would have kept this to herself. But now, at the opportune moment, a new person turned up.

In July 1940, Oliver reported to Ham on a party at the Knoxes'. Rose Macaulay was there ("too awful: white ringlets, sack-shaped Chelsea long dress, and firm to embarrassment"); Oliver's batty mother; his current interest, a girl called Kate; Rawle and some American friends; Sir Frederick Leighton-Ross ("Economic Warfare"). And there were "the Fitzgeralds, whom Mops admires."[35] In October, Mops told Ham that she had visited Oliver at the Duke of York's Barracks (before he went off to Egypt): "Mrs. FitzG also came and delighted the sergeant with her fur, pearls, and smart black hat."[36]

We don't know how Penelope Knox first met Desmond Fitzgerald—"at a party," she used to say, vaguely. But their paths could quite easily have crossed. They overlapped at Oxford, and three of her group, Oliver Breakwell, Jean's brother James Fisher, and Sinclair Hood, had been under-graduates at Magdalen College at the same time as the Fitzgerald boys, Desmond and his younger brother Eamon.

They were the children of an Irish Catholic family with one foot in the Civil Service, one in the Church. The smart "Mrs. FitzG" had been Elizabeth Ellen Lyons (the family name came down to Desmond without the "s"), an Irishwoman from a family with its roots in Collon, County Louth. She had grown up in poverty—several siblings died of TB—but had made her way in the world, and she had some extremely effective relations. Her sister, Juliana, became a nun, "Mother Reginald," Mother Superior of the Dominican Order in Ireland. She was a major figure in Irish-Catholic education, President of the Conference of Convent Secondary Schools, in charge of the Dominican Convent for deaf children at Cabra, on the edge of Dublin, and of the Dominican Convent in Eccles Street. Mrs. Fitzgerald often sent her boys to visit their aunt the Mother Superior in their school holidays. Her brother Patrick, a handsome and imposing character, and "an unsurpassed story-teller," was made Bishop of Kilmore in County Cavan in 1937, when he was in his sixties. During his tenure, he had the old Roman Catholic Cathedral in Cavan rebuilt. Elizabeth—known as "Lily"—went out to Malaya in about 1916.[37]

In the social gatherings of the British Residency in Perak, she met a civil servant called Thomas Fitzgerald, who had also come up from a poor Irish family—his father was an Irish-speaking farmer in Tralee, County Kerry—to be Postmaster-General in Perak. Tom Fitzgerald and Lily Lyons were married in Malaya in wartime and had two sons, Desmond John Lyon (born on 4 November 1917), and Eamon Neil, born a year later.[38] After the war, Tom Fitzgerald's postings took him to East Africa, where he oversaw the Post Office and telegraph services of Kenya, Uganda and Tanganyika, while Desmond and his brother were put as boarders into Worth school, the Catholic prep school in Sussex linked to Downside School. So, like Penelope, and like very many middle-class children of the time, Desmond was separated early—aged six—from his parents. At ten, in 1927, he went as a boarder, with Eamon, to Downside, near Bath. It was a high-achieving, competitive, rigorous environment. The parents had no inherited money, so the fees were paid by the Colonial Service. In the holidays, Desmond and Eamon went to Ireland to stay with their aunt or their uncle.[39]

The colonial officer ("Thomas Fitzgerald, CMG, MBE") and his wife retired first to Sloane Street, and then to a solidly furnished, well-upholstered flat in Burton Court, next to Chelsea Barracks, stuffed full of imperial relics and heirlooms—an elephant's foot, embossed silver cutlery, bear and tiger rugs, assegais, treasures from Malaya and Africa. "Mrs. Fitzgerald" (as Penelope would always call her) became very active working with the East End poor for Catholic charitable foundations such as the Deptford Borough Youth Committee, and setting up an "Old Folks' Home" for Catholic ladies, Stella House in Ealing, where she herself spent her last years. She was also, according to Willie Conder, "clearly a serious toper." Teas with Grannie, in the memory of her grandchildren, involved fox furs, Harrods and huge amounts of gin. Old Mr. Fitzgerald developed a passion for the Law Courts, and would go every day (perhaps to get out of the flat) to listen to cases.[40]

At Downside, Desmond Fitzgerald was a star. The headmaster remembered him as a boy of "outstanding ability" who passed his School and Higher Certificate with Distinction, was a top-class rugby and hockey player, and a good boxer. He was "conspicuous" in the Officer Training Corps, and rose to the rank of Sergeant.[41] He was growing up to be a darkly handsome, attractive boy, athletic, bright, charming and a little bit wild. Eamon, the younger brother, was less good-looking and less of a charmer, but the two boys were close.[42] By odd coincidence, a well-brought-up Irish girl called Helen Roantree, whose family lived in Dun Laoghaire, a genteel little town by the sea near Dublin, where her father and brother were doctors, encountered the Fitzgerald boys there in the 1930s. Their parents took a holiday flat in the town, and the boys would come there from Downside. Helen Roantree would see them on the pier, reading. She thought they were "wonderful-looking fellows." Years later, she married Rawle Knox, and became the sister-in-law of one of those boys.[43]

Desmond went up to Oxford in 1936, to read History. He went on boxing and playing rugby, and he cut a swathe, with his clever, daring friends Bob Conquest and John Blakeway (a future diplomat). Robert Conquest remembered the group as anti-establishment, reckless, bawdy and rowdy. Eamon, he thought, was the more political of the two brothers, more of an Irish nationalist than Desmond. Their outrageousness was laddish and innocent—painting "VOTE FOR APES" on a conspicuous pediment during the Coronation celebrations, drinking a lot of beer. Desmond also had a serious and thoughtful side to him. He read a great deal, and was an admirer of the classical scholar Maurice Bowra and the philosopher A. J. Ayer. He was taught history at Magdalen by the formidable Bruce MacFarlane and by the influential social theorist G. D. H. Cole, and went travelling with John Blakeway, in the vacations, to Poland and Czechoslovakia.[44] Jasmine Blakeway, John's wife, who met Desmond after the war, remembered him as "one of the great charmers of all time," a mixture of "high seriousness" and "marvellous humour," "Irish to the core."[45]

He got a Second Class degree in the summer of 1939, and started to read for the Bar at the Middle Temple. Jean Fisher, who was doing the same, working with characteristic determination to become one of the very few women barristers in the country at the time, said that only about a year's training was required then. According to her, Desmond would have been cramming for the Bar, eating his requisite number of legal dinners and "soldiering" at the same time. In July 1940, he enlisted with the Officer Training Unit of the Irish Guards, stationed at Croydon. His military examiners thought him clever but slow: "Tries his utmost in everything . . . with a little more confidence he will not fail to make a very good officer."[46] The trainee officers were assigned to guard duty at sites like the Tower of London and Buckingham Palace. In his time off, he and Bob Conquest would go to London pubs and nightclubs together. They would buy a bottle of whisky between them and leave it at the club for the next time. At the end of the night, they would get a taxi and tell it to stop when their money ran out.

This was the summer when Penelope met Desmond. The word most often used about him then, in his early twenties, was "dashing": a young Guards officer, tall, dark and handsome, clean-cut and elegantly dressed, amusing, bold and energetic, fond of a drink and a good time, but also well travelled and well read. Presumably he was about to have a heroic war, and then to become a distinguished lawyer. He sounds like the next-best thing to her idols Cary Grant and Rex Harrison. And he seems to have fallen in love with her, then and forever. Some time between 1940 and 1942, they started going about together. She took him to Oundle to meet the Fishers, and to St. John's Wood to see Evoe and Mary; she introduced him to all her friends. He was her "Irish soldier," as she would often refer to him later: you can almost hear the word "gallant" before "Irish."

Under "Forthcoming Marriages" in *The Times* for 27 May 1942, it was announced that "the marriage will shortly take place between Lieutenant Desmond Fitzgerald, Irish Guards, eldest son of Mr. and Mrs. Thomas Fitzgerald, and Miss Penelope Mary Knox, daughter of Mr. E.V. Knox and the late Mrs. Knox."[47] There are no clues to Penelope's feelings or motives—no love letters, no diaries, no reminiscences. Friends, looking back, made their guesses. Hugh Lee said that during the war, the men all wanted to get married, and none of the women did. Jasmine Blakeway said that Penelope always knew Desmond was not going to be easy.[48] Everyone, repeatedly, said how charming and nice he was. Whenever she was asked about it, Penelope said: "I married an Irish soldier." Elizabeth Bowen's lovers, in her wartime novel *The Heat of the Day*, come to mind: "They were the creatures of history, whose coming together was of a nature possible in no other day."[49]

From 9 to 18 July, Desmond was ill, confined to the military hospital in Savernake in Wiltshire. A few weeks later, on 15 August 1942, they were married, at St. Thomas More Church on Frognal, in Hampstead, "according to Catholic rites." (In one of her autobiographical retrospects, she misremembered the date as 1943.)[50] Evoe and Mary—whose brother was killed in action that year on convoy duty—were the witnesses, Ronnie Knox officiated, Eamon was best man, Jean Fisher was the bridesmaid. (Her own fiancé, an American pilot, was shot down and killed during the war.) Willie Conder was present, and a few other friends. The absence of her mother, her brother and her uncle Dillwyn must have been felt. Penelope was registered as "Spinster, 25, Script Writer (BBC), 63 Eyre Court, Finchley Road NW8," Desmond as "Bachelor, 24, Lieutenant, Irish Guards, Student-of-Law, 50 Sloane Street. Father, Civil Servant." They moved into the Baker Street flat she had shared with Rawle.

There is no mention of a honeymoon; presumably they both went straight back to work. Penelope was keeping up reviews for *Punch* at the same time as her BBC work. At the end of July she had reviewed Gielgud's *Macbeth* ("no rough edges"); three days before the wedding she criticised a silly revue by Herbert Farjeon, in a piece beginning, perhaps tellingly, "Intimacy, however delightful, means friction." Through 1942 and until the end of the war, she would write over fifty pieces for her father's magazine.[51] Her uncle Dillwyn, now terminally ill, wanted her to drop the BBC and the journalism and go to work at Bletchley. Her friend Rachel Ollivant was working there, and Dilly had already asked Mavis Lever to persuade Penelope to join. He summoned her to Courn's Wood to talk it through. " 'You don't share the family pretence of not understanding mathematics?' he asked anxiously." It was their last conversation. And she did not go to Bletchley—which might have been a perfect setting for a Fitzgerald novel.

Dillwyn knew he was dying, but "all expressions of sympathy were brushed away." Evoe went to see him, and found him "smiling sardonically over a book called *The Art of Dying*," an anthology by Francis Birrell of "famous last words." He was awarded the CMG (the Order of St. Michael and St. George) for his work at Bletchley, by an emissary sent specially from the Palace, and just managed to get out of bed to receive it. He died on 27 February 1943, going, "unwavering in his disbelief, into what he believed was endless darkness," the first of the Knox brothers to die. The next day, 28 February, Lieutenant Desmond Fitzgerald, Intelligence Officer with the Irish Guards, embarked in Glasgow on the *Strathmore* with 926 other men, and sailed for North Africa. Penelope would not see him again for a year and a half.[52] Two weeks later, on 16 March, also just after his marriage, Oliver Breakwell was killed in the North Africa campaign, at Mareth, shortly before his twenty-fourth birthday.

As the *Strathmore* sailed past the coast of Northern Ireland, glimpsed through low cloud and mist, "for even the most unimaginative Irishman—and there are many such," Desmond wrote a few years later, "this was the real moment of parting." His job on board, as Intelligence Officer, was to "lecture all companies on the situation in Tunisia." Landing at Algiers, the Guards made their way east to Libya under General Alexander. In April, Desmond, now Captain Fitzgerald, led his battalion in the capture and defence of the Bou Massif in the mountains above Tripoli. For this he was awarded the Military Cross (on 6 July 1943), in recognition of "the highest degree of personal courage," "gallantry," "doggedness and tenacity." When Bob Conquest bumped into Desmond in London, back from the war, wearing his Irish Guards uniform and the Military Cross, Desmond said simply: "All the chaps who deserved it had been killed."[53]

After the Libyan campaign, the Irish Guards led the landings at Anzio and fought their way up to the siege of Monte Cassino. Jasmine Blakeway would say that Desmond "had a horrible war, and didn't talk about it." But he wrote about it, in a *History of the Irish Guards in the Second World War,* which he published in 1949. It was his only book, and he collaborated on some of it with his brother, who was with him in the Guards and whose trenchant views on "Awful Krauts" are occasionally mentioned in the *History.*[54] Though the tone is meant to be neutral, and Desmond mentions himself (like Penelope in *The Knox Brothers*) only in the third person, the narrative is remarkably vivid, personal and dramatic for a regimental history, as in these two detailed accounts of the fighting in Italy:

> The ambulance was running a non-stop shuttle service up and down the road direct to the Casualty Clearing Station just outside Anzio; but it could not cope with the pressure. The casual-

ties poured in and overflowed out of the culvert into an "annexe" in the drainage ditch at the foot of the embankment. Between bandaging wounds, the medical orderlies worked to deepen the ditch and roof it with old iron fencing and earth. The patience and gratitude shown by wounded men is one of the few things which it is worth being in battle to see. Not only on this occasion, but at all times, the silent courage of maimed, battered, bleeding Irish Guardsmen lying in the open or, if they were lucky, in some muddy ditch, was a living monument to the strength of the human will in the depths of human misery. A man drained of blood gets very cold; there is not much a man with a shattered thigh can do for himself; a man whose chest has been torn to ribbons by shell-splinters would like to be moved out of the barrage. But they did not say anything, they didn't ask for anything; they smiled painfully when the orderlies put a blanket over them or gave them a drink of water and a cigarette, and just shut their eyes for a moment when a shell exploded particularly close. The very men who complained most loudly about the few potatoes in the stew were the ones who assured the doctor most firmly that they had "no complaints."

For the past hour Colonel Andrew Scott, Captain Desmond Fitzgerald and their signallers . . . had been kneeling in two trenches at the side of a barn in "Dung Farm" . . . The Scots Guards were fighting beside, in front, behind and, it seemed, on top of them. The Germans pumped shells into the farm buildings, reducing the neat cow-byres, barns and houses into a blazing shambles. With painful monotony the high-velocity shells skimmed the ground and crashed into the farm-yard. Four lorries, towing the Scots Guards' anti-tank guns and carrying their ammunition, exploded one after the other in a sheet of purple flame. A charred mummy in each seat was all that was left of the drivers . . . There is something peculiarly fascinating about the flight of tracer bullets. They curve in a slow, graceful arc, glowing with a soft, almost friendly light. The eye is irresistibly drawn to them and then down the line of flight to the muzzle. There is a strong pull of attraction, something like vertigo, for it is hard to realize that anything so decorative can be so deadly. For the Commanding Officer and the Adjutant, the dark world was hung with a web of tracer. They could see the faint streaks down by the railway. Bright streams poured over them and over their heads to clatter into the walls and trees. The left-hand company of the Scots Guards went forward to attack the machine guns . . . the company commander decided to withdraw [them] round behind the barn . . . To withdraw troops from close contact with the enemy is always a difficult and dangerous operation. To do it in the dark invariably leads to chaos and often to rout. The men do not know what is happening; all they see is that their comrades are withdrawing, and they do not know why or whither.

The Scots Guards tramped back over the Irish Guards command post. Colonel Wedderburn stormed out of the dark and met the company half-way down the barn. His language was remarkable. Colonel Andrew and Captain D. Fitzgerald listened with amazement and admiration. The gist of his remarks were: "What were they doing? Why were they coming back? Where was the Company Commander? About turn; this is the way, follow me." That was all the Scots Guards needed. They had got confused in the dark, but now they recognized their Commanding Officer's voice and it was quite clear what he wanted. They were only too glad to do it and, headed by Colonel Wedderburn, they lumbered forward again into the woods and machine guns. Colonel Wedderburn came back panting. "That was a close thing," he said.[55]

The Libyan campaign, "Operation Shingle" at Anzio and the battle for Monte Cassino, some of the worst fighting the British saw in the Second World War, wiped out two-thirds of the First Battalion of the Irish Guards. "Of the 926 men who left Ayr in February 1943, 326 landed in Liverpool on the 22nd April 1944."[56] By 1944, Desmond had been promoted to Major. He stayed with the regiment till July, but that was the end of his fighting. Back in London with Penelope from the summer of 1944, he finished his legal training. He was apprenticed to the brilliant right-wing, Catholic criminal advocate Frederick Lawton (later famous for presiding over the second Kray brothers trial), who thought he would do well. He passed the Bar exams and was called to the Bar as a criminal barrister at the Chambers at 5 King's Bench Walk, in the Middle Temple. As for all young barristers, it was up to the Clerk of the Chambers which cases were sent his way. Desmond was doing only minor, jobbing criminal cases.[57]

In January 1945, he was mentioned for "gallantry" in the Italian action, and awarded the Defence Medal for his service in North Africa and Italy.

He was a hero: but he had been profoundly changed by the war, and, though not physically wounded, came back a different person from the dashing young officer Penelope had married in 1942. He had seen appalling things and lost many men; he had killed a large number of people. He would wake up in the night, screaming.[58] He could never bear fireworks.

Rawle, too, came back from the dead, and came back changed. In the Japanese POW camp, he heard the news of the bombing of Hiroshima from the broom-handle radio. It was 6 August, his thirty-second birthday. The first time that the family knew he had survived was when, after the prisoners had been liberated, the Red Cross arranged for them to send out postcards. Rawle mailed the Knoxes a crossword clue on his postcard, but no one could work out the answer. Just before his return, he sent a letter to Evoe, saying that if ever he wanted to ask him about what had happened in the camp, Rawle would tell him. He came back, and no one in the family ever asked him anything. He could hardly speak of it; though many years later, in a depressed state, he told Penelope that "the hopelessness of it reminded him of being a POW."[59]

The war ended. Penelope sent a satirical account of Americans celebrating in the Café Royal on VE Day, 8 May 1945, to Janet, now married and away from London. (The two friends went shopping together for her wedding clothes that year, but after the marriage they saw less of each other; her husband, Bill Probert, was jealous of her old Oxford friends.)[60] Desmond's war was not quite over: he attended the start of the Nuremberg trials. Penelope wrote to a friend at the BBC at the end of October 1945 that he had come home with yellow jaundice. "Not a *bit* the homecoming I expected, but it's a mistake to look forward too much to anything in this world."[61]

Like many other couples who had got married quickly in the middle of the war, they now had to construct a settled life for themselves in peacetime. Penelope stopped working as a producer for the BBC in 1945. She went on reviewing for *Punch* all through the 1940s, making her views clear on a wide range of post-war books. In poetry, she covered Edith Sitwell, MacNeice, Spender, Sydney Keyes, Lorca (showing signs of her passion for Spain), her old tutor Blunden ("a reticent mind, shy, guarding itself, intensely jealous of intrusion in the citadel where its treasures are hidden"), and Walter de la Mare, "one of the great poets of the century." Eliot's "Little Gidding" produced a mixture of awe at its lyric beauty and restiveness at the literary allusions: "It is for you to decide whether these really enrich the poetry or whether they are more like a nightmare parlour game, with the other side making up all the rules." She was as happy to review Trilling on Forster, Una Pope-Hennessy on Dickens and Wilson Knight on Shakespeare as she was to cover the latest Vicki Baum, Simenon or Angela Thirkell, or a new selection of Russian short stories, in which the "keynote to the volume," she said, was a sentence from Tolstoy's Ivan Illyich: "His life had been most simple and most ordinary and therefore most terrible."

Ordinariness interested her as always: A. E. Coppard, whom she likes, writes about "troubling behaviour on the part of ordinary people." She shows a constant interest in children, whether reviewing a batch of horsy books (*My Friend Flicka*), or the popular Christmas play *Where the Rainbow Ends,* acted by children from the Italia Conti school, her future haunt: "If you do not feel like reverting to childhood you will just have to lump it." Personal feelings occasionally shine through. A review of a novel by Elizabeth Taylor begins, forcefully: "Women, if they possibly can, *must* write novels."[62]

From 1944, she also wrote scripts for the BBC, mainly for the Schools Service. For a time the BBC went on addressing their letters to Miss Knox, so her correspondence ended up in the "Dead Letter Office": Miss Knox no longer existed. Though she sometimes used "PMK" when signing articles in the *World Review,* and though for a time the BBC continued to refer to her as "Miss Knox," she opted, then and later, for "Fitzgerald" as her writing name.

"Miss Knox," read an internal memo of 23 October 1945, "demands £300 a year for up to seven scripts a term" (i.e., twenty-one scripts a year) for the Schools History Programmes. These were a mixture of dramatised histories and abridgements of novels—the sort of work her mother had been doing in the 1920s—for instance, of Scott's *Ivanhoe* or Robert Louis Stevenson's *The Black Arrow.* "Stevenson is such a leisurely writer," she complained. Like her university essays and her reviewing, doing these scripts was a training in simplification and economy. Some of them fired her imagination, like the feature she called "The Friendly Arctic," on the explorer Stefansson's expeditions in Alaska. She loved putting in "the terrible noise of the grinding icepacks," and "how to cook and hunt seals." "We might have time for the bit where Stefansson is attacked by the polar bear," she wrote hopefully to her producer. The story gripped her because when Stefansson met disaster and discouragement "his determination hardens."[63]

The scriptwriting work started well, and she needed the money, though she went on getting a small annual allowance from Evoe well after her marriage. But in 1946 and '47 there were repeated apologies for lateness and missed deadlines and for letting people down because of hay fever, or travelling, or distractions. A disappointing first draft is noted as "not up to Penelope Knox's usual standard."[64] These were signs of strain.

Desmond was hoping to do some writing, too, and perhaps she encouraged him in this. He had promising connections with *Picture Post* and the Catholic-owned *Hulton Press,* and he started to write his book on the Irish Guards. Jean Fisher, called to the Bar in 1945, thought it was a pity that he was not concentrating more on his career as a lawyer. At the Baker Street flat, there were some awkward evenings. Willie Conder remembered going to supper and Desmond not turning up until very late: "When he came, you could see what the trouble was; he didn't speak much, afraid it wouldn't come out right, just smiled at us vaguely and walked off and didn't join us." Other friends remembered similar episodes, like an evening when Penelope was cooking and Desmond was "flapping around and picking up spoons and everything fell on the floor."[65] He was drinking, more than he had before the war. The same was true of Eamon, and Rawle Knox, and of a great many other young men who had survived fighting or imprisonment.

They wanted to have a baby. But between 1944 and 1946 Penelope had at least one miscarriage, and a "blue" baby (a baby with a congenital heart defect, or decreased oxygen-carrying capacity of the blood), which died soon after birth. She did not often speak of these tragedies, though she would tell her younger daughter that she had had one miscarriage while she was at the theatre. She must have thought, in these years, that she might never be able to have a family. Janet wrote to her, ten years later, with retrospective remorse: "I do hope I was sympathetic about yr depressing miscarriages."[66] But sympathy came from surprising directions. After one miscarriage, the notoriously silent "Kipper," Mary Knox's father, Ernest Shepard, "called on me [and] . . . handed me a bunch of flowers without a word."[67]

The anguish of these events, though rarely spoken of, was saved up and went sidelong into her novels, many years later. In *Innocence,* the newly, and stressfully, married Chiara becomes pregnant: "The child made its presence felt . . . only by an uneasy prickling, as though it was a faint-hearted pioneer awash in strange seas . . . But something must have been not quite right, Chiara miscarried and the baby's doubtful experiment came to nothing." In *The Beginning of Spring,* the young couple Nellie and Frank lose their first baby in a hot summer in Germany in 1905, with a barrel organ playing outside. "Nellie lay flat on her back, losing blood, hoping to save the baby. She told Frank to throw some money out of the window to the organ-man to bring them luck. But they had no luck that day."[68]

In April 1946 the Fitzgeralds went to Paris for ten days. She told her BBC contact that they were going to stay at the Bedford, rue de l'Arcade, a luxurious Right Bank hotel near the place de la Concorde. It was the time when British Europhiles could start to go to France and Spain and Italy again, and the Fitzgeralds would from now on be great travellers. This, Paris in post-war springtime, was their real honeymoon. She became pregnant again, and this time the baby hung on.

Her brother's life changed too that year. After he came home, he got a job in Dublin with the *Dublin Review,* and there he met Helen Roantree, daughter of a Northern Irish doctor and a "Dublin society" lady. He married her very soon after getting to know her. With some amazement, she realised that the clever, dark, stammering, vulnerable journalist she had rapidly fallen in love with was the brother-in-law of one of those Dun Laoghaire Fitzgerald boys. Helen was a lively, humorous, observant and immensely capable Irishwoman, and, like her Dublin mother, able for any social occasion. She was also completely unintellectual ("I couldn't spell!") and found the Knox clan—including Penelope, at first—rather alarming, especially at mealtimes, "a nightmare," when everyone was expected to be bright and amusing and play intellectual word games. But, like "Mrs. K," Christina Hicks and Mary Shepard before her, Helen was one of those sensible, affectionate women who found ways of dealing with the Knoxian cleverness, reserve and neurosis. She found Rawle kind, modest, a wonderful listener, unsure of his own worth, deeply affected by his POW experience and extremely shy. And she was immediately aware of the problems in the Knox family: that they all had to compete and perform brilliantly, and that they would never talk about the many things that went wrong.

She seems at once to have brought some lightness and fun into this clan. Tim Hicks, Penelope's young cousin, son of Christina's brother Ned, who was about fifteen when Rawle and Helen got married in 1946, fell madly in love with her. Evoe let his hair down at the wedding (as he sometimes could, to wild effect, especially when children were around or when he had had a few drinks) and crawled across the room to kiss the foot of Helen's elegant mother. And Penelope welcomed Helen into her life with great affection, even neediness. Helen and Rawle went all over Europe for their honeymoon; Desmond and Penelope, very pregnant by then, followed them to Paris. Helen felt this as an invasion. But, very soon, they got away from the family. Rawle, amazingly, wanted to return to the Far East. He wrote to the *Observer* asking if there was a job as a foreign correspondent, and the editor, David Astor, sent him as a freelance for a trial six months to India. Helen was pregnant with William, Penelope's nephew, who was born in 1947. In 1948 Rawle was appointed permanent foreign correspondent in Asia, and he would stay with the *Observer* for thirteen years.[69]

The three surviving Knox brothers had mainly good fortune after the war. Ronnie found a new, even grander haven, as chaplain and paying guest with his old friends the Asquiths at Mells in Somerset, and continued to be mildly ridiculed by the younger generation of Knoxes for his love of toffs. Wilfred carried on as the much-loved, saintly and very peculiar chaplain at Pembroke College. "Mrs. K," the Knox brothers' stepmother, died in grand old age, leaving a small legacy to all the brothers. Evoe and Mary moved to a beautiful old house, Grove Cottage, near Hampstead Heath, not far from Well Walk. His salary at *Punch* had reached £400 a year, and—to the great satisfaction of a man who had not taken a degree—he was awarded an Hon. D.Litt. from Oxford. But in 1949 he decided to retire from the editorship of *Punch,* though he carried on with some freelance reviewing and would regularly go down to see his Bouverie Street friends:

> On one occasion, when a few of the *Punch* staff were having a late drink together, the barmaid looked with curiosity at Eddie's neat dark overcoat, dark hat and impeccably rolled umbrella. "What do you do for a living?" Eddie folded his hands on his umbrella and looked down at the ground. "I live by my wits," he said. And that was true enough.[70]

Punch, like Evoe, would carry on for a few more decades. For many people, there were no sudden changes in peacetime. The war still affected everyone's lives; rationing continued; flowers and weeds were growing high in the rubble of London bomb sites. Penelope explored them with Rose Macaulay, whose haunting evocation of those "catacombs" in *The World My Wilderness* she admired.[71] But there was a new government, and post-war London was full of new music, art, writing. In June 1945, for instance, Penelope went to the second night of Benjamin Britten's *Peter Grimes* at Sadler's Wells, wearing a new black chiffon blouse, and was excited enough by it to write a long account to Janet and to keep her programme all her life.[72]

On 17 December 1946 she had her thirtieth birthday. On 30 January 1947, she gave birth to a boy, Edmund Valpy Knox Fitzgerald, in the Cromwell Road Nursing Home. (Desmond's appointment diaries would often put the birthday on 31 January, and it was sometimes celebrated on that day.) It was a terribly cold winter, and "all the patients crowded into her room because she had a new-born baby and so was allowed a coal fire."[73] The baby, who would always be known by the old family name Valpy, was to be brought up a Catholic, but Jean Fisher was allowed to be an "illegal" godmother, even though she was Church of England. Penelope told a BBC friend, Ursula Keeble, that February was a good month for a baby to be born into, as "after all it has to be wrapped in a shawl for the first 6 weeks or so, & then by the time it wants to kick and stuff its feet in its mouth the spring has got warm & you can leave the blankets off." The attention with which she watched her newcomer, and would watch all newborn babies, is glimpsed in a baby who makes a brief appearance in *Human Voices,* "wrapped in a silky white shawl" and breathing gently, "as though simmering, in a wicker basket." On waking, "he was quietened with some boiled water from a teaspoon, which he sucked, like an old man with a sweet, contemplatively, and then returned in the form of a fine spray." By summertime, Valpy had become "a very expert *roller,* and is difficult to keep in one place."[74] She was taking him off for a holiday in Southwold.

In 1948, Desmond, Penelope and Valpy Fitzgerald moved to a small house in Hampstead, very near to where her father and her stepmother were living, and a few streets away from her childhood home. It was ten years since she had left Oxford, with a brilliant independent future confidently ahead of her. Now she was going back, as a wife and mother, to the place of her childhood, without the books to her name or the life as a

successful writer she had confidently anticipated in 1938. It was not what she had planned, but life was not what anyone had planned. "Their lives were shaking into pieces . . . Goodbye, Asra, she thought," says the heroine of *Human Voices,* bidding farewell to her young self, as she puts her arms around her incompetent, bewildered lover. "God knows what's going to become of you now."

CHAPTER FIVE

The World

The electric touch of strong emotion. Don't let us be afraid of it . . .[1]

The little row of workers' cottages called Squires Mount ran up to East Heath Road, just off Cannon Place. Hampstead Heath was nearby, Well Walk a few streets away, and the Knoxes at Grove Cottage were within walking distance, in their old house with its walled garden and its cherry tree. Number 5 Squires Mount, which the Fitzgeralds rented in 1948, was the cottage furthest from East Heath Road, on the south side, a tiny house with the door opening straight onto the living room, and a small garden, where Desmond grew tobacco plants, his solution to rationing. Hampstead in the 1940s was not unrecognisable from Hampstead in the 1920s, though the muffin men, the lavender sellers and the lamplighters were disappearing. As ever it was a village for writers, musicians, artists, psychoanalysts and cultured refugees. Freud, in exile from Vienna, died there in 1939; the art historian Ernst Gombrich lived at the other end of Squires Mount. It was a shabby-smart bohemian environment which suited them—or suited Penelope—very well. Her friends noted her liking for the artistic Hampstead milieu and her desire to belong to it, partly because of Evoe, partly for her own sense of herself.

Some of their close friends had been killed in the war, some got married and moved out of London when the war ended, some started careers which scattered them across the world. Ham was working in Bucharest for the Allied Control Commission, where he got married in 1947. Janet's husband, Bill Probert, was distancing her from her friends. Desmond's friend John Blakeway was on his first diplomatic posting in Bulgaria. Rawle and Helen were leaving for India. Jean Fisher was starting work as a barrister in Birmingham, though she would go back to Oundle and would join her family for summer holidays in Harlech. Willie Tull, who had faithfully had lunch with Penelope once a week all through the war, got married in 1945 to Mike Conder, a forester and a plantsman (of whom Penelope became very fond), and moved first to High Dalby, on the North Yorkshire moors, and later to the Lake District. Rachel Ollivant married a vicar, Thomas Hichens, also in 1945, and went to live in Suffolk and then in Cornwall.

But the Fitzgeralds had plenty of acquaintances in London. They were an appealing couple in their early thirties: the handsome, charming lawyer–war hero and his brilliant literary wife, with their little boy and their stories of the BBC, Ireland, the Bar, *Punch* and the Knoxes. Penelope was taking pottery lessons at the Old Hampstead Pottery in Perrins Lane. She had a gift for ceramics, drawing and painting, and was enormously knowledgeable about books and bookmaking, plays and films, arts and crafts, English and European painters and writers. To Hampstead neighbours, to friends and colleagues, they seemed an enviable, talented couple with the world at their feet.

Her letters to her BBC producers give glimpses of what was happening in the Squires Mount years. She took the infant Valpy off regularly to the seaside, without Desmond: in the summers of 1948 and 1949 she went to the Swan Hotel in Southwold, and there were other trips to Gorham-by-the-Sea, near Worthing, and to Whitstable. But she and Desmond also went to Rome together for two weeks in the spring of 1949. As after their Paris trip in 1946, Penelope was pregnant again by May. A daughter, named Christina after her mother, but always known as Tina, was born in Queen Mary's House, a nursing home in north London, on 26 January 1950. Rawle and Helen's family kept pace: Belinda, their daughter, was born in the same year as Tina, as William Knox had been born in the same year as Valpy.

The new baby slept in a Moses basket and, like all the Fitzgerald children, would be "house-trained" by eighteen months.[2] With a boisterous little boy and a new baby to look after, Penelope was also doing a good deal of writing from home, and some studio recording. The BBC commissions were wide-ranging. Most of the work was still for Schools Programmes, but she also did film reviews, and a pre-recorded book review programme called *Bookshelf,* with the critic Walter Allen, and with Ernest Dudley, known as "The Armchair Detective," for a twenty-minute Sunday afternoon slot. She wrote occasional book reviews for the Overseas Service. The film reviews ("Coming Shortly"), also pre-recorded, were dropped into the Wednesday afternoon *Woman's Hour* on the Light Programme, in between items such as "Garden Soil," Carleton Hobbs reading *Middlemarch,* a "Household Forum" on "Wash Days," and a cookery item called "The Case of the Ominous Dumplings."[3]

Her letters show how seriously she took the work. She has been "lying awake" at night trying to remember whether she had left a sentence out of the feature she had just sent off. "Though I did write something about the Sikhs this weekend it was *no good* and I had to tear it up." "I enclose draft for the script on a medieval baker—was it a *day* in his life? I hope not."[4]

Her Schools adaptations are aimed at what children will enjoy and understand. For a dramatisation of Raleigh's discovery of Virginia, she noted: "I put in rather a lot about Red Indians, as children usually like them." Whether she is treating the revolt of a loyal band of Japanese samurai, "the 47 Ronin," or William Wilberforce's campaign against slavery, or an account of Jerusalem at the time of Jesus from the point of view of a small boy, she is at pains to make the historical language vivid and convincing, to bring the characters to life, and to see events, where possible, from the point of view of a child or an ordinary, unglamorous minor character.[5]

Occasionally, and surprisingly, she wrote for "General Science" programmes, where she always explains the facts by bringing them humanly to life. An item on "Heat: Keeping Things Warm" explains "the different ways in which heat travels" entirely through domestic examples: a rather disagreeable and bad-tempered family trying to keep warm in a badly insulated house, a mother telling her child to see if the potatoes have boiled yet. A feature on Edison's invention of the "electric lamp" makes him into a larger-than-life, unstoppable force of energy:

EDISON: Do you know what I'm thinking?
OTHER CHARACTER: No—what?
EDISON: I'm thinking that life's very short, and I've rather a lot to
    do . . . When do I think we start? We start right away![6]

With literary adaptations she was on secure ground. Asked by one producer (probably Robert Gittings, who worked on several of her programmes before his later career as a dramatist and a Keats and Hardy scholar) for her list of favourite literary characters, she offers him "Captain Cuttle in Dombey & Son, The Marchioness & Dick Swiveller in The Old Curiosity Shop, Colonel Newcome from The Newcomes, Dr. & Mrs. Lydgate from Middlemarch, Bruce Ottley from Ada Leverson's Love at Second Sight, Aunt Chloe from Uncle Tom's Cabin, Jeannie Deans from Heart of Midlothian, and the stranger with the *folie de toucher* from Lavengro." This fascinating collection of victims, self-deceivers, comic chancers, devoted women, mystery men and unworldly failures links to her Schools dramatisation of Dickens's *Dombey and Son* through the characters of Captain Cuttle and Susan Nipper. What she particularly likes in the novel is "the impression of how grown-ups don't understand you when you are a child . . . wonderfully real, I think."[7]

A 1948 feature for *Woman's Hour,* called "What It's Like to Be a Librarian," directed at younger listeners, describes a day in the life of an ordinary public library, largely from the point of view of a teenage girl just out of school. Mavis helps all the people who use this democratic space: the tramp who sleeps in the newspapers section, the German refugee who wants the scores of Mozart operas, the children thundering in after school, the man who is going to start making a garden outside his prefab house ("Well, gardening comes under Useful Arts") and a "sinister man" wanting "a book on poisons." It is a precursor of *The Bookshop,* and of her lifelong, passionate support of the public library system.[8]

One programme proposal, drafted in a letter in May 1950, suggests a treatment of the Red Cross through "four short stories." This is her idea for the first one:

> *Lost children*—a boy & his little sister in Vienna—they wander across from the Russian zone having been living from hand to mouth, their parents have been killed, or died, & all they know is that their grandparents are living somewhere in England. They are picked up by an Austrian policeman (unhelpful) who hands them over to a British military policeman & his Headquarters send them to the Red Cross. They stay in a hostel for the time being while the Red Cross gets in touch with British HQ & find that the grandparents are living in London & willing to pay the fare. Then they arrange for the little boy & girl to be escorted to England. [Cast]: 2 children—2 policemen (one with German accent)—Red Cross official (man)—& another assorted official.[9]

It is easy to imagine this as a Fitzgerald short story, but it remained one of the "lost children" of her pre-fiction years.

In her BBC reviews, she presents herself as an ordinary, domestic woman reader and viewer, looking for common ground with her listeners. She gives bits away about her own life in her film reviews: "If, like me, you have to do a considerable amount of manoeuvring to go to the pictures, if you have to get someone to mind the children and then have everything spoilt for you because you remember you've forgotten to turn the oven off when you're half way there . . ." After taking three small boys to *Robin Hood* (in 1952, when Valpy was five), she says it was "such a relief, after I got back home, to be held up with a bow and arrow instead of a machine gun." Watching the sufferings of the young girl in *Rawhide* made her feel "like going straight home to make sure my own little daughter was all right." Her review of *The Glass Menagerie* contains a sad premonition. The film, which she praises as subtle and delicate, is "about a mother who loves her children very much, but is doomed always to embarrass them and do the wrong thing for them." It gives "all mothers something to think about. You'll agree with me that letting your family alone is so much more difficult than simply loving them." She reveals more than she may have intended in her review of *Harvey,* a vehicle for James Stewart as "an amiable drunk" ("we all want to mother him"). "It's based on an idea that I personally don't agree with . . . that if you're amiable and good-natured it doesn't matter if you're drunken and lazy, you are the salt of the earth and more fitted for salvation than the busybodies of organised religion. I don't know what you think about this, but since it's an idea that seems to be gaining ground it's worth making up your mind about."[10]

There are some telling disclosures, too, in her book reviews. A biography of Arnold Bennett by her colleague on the *Bookshelf* programme, Walter Allen, makes her think that "perhaps there's always something rather satisfactory about hearing that fame doesn't bring happiness. It consoles the rest of us who have to rub along without being very famous." And a painful autobiography, *My Father's Son,* by Richard Lumford, seems to her to echo "the pattern you find in your own tired mind when it comes back time and again to the same worry."[11]

At the cinema, as when she was reviewing for *Punch* in 1939, she likes epics, musicals, film noir, comedies, Westerns. She embraces the great new American films of the early 1950s like *All About Eve* or *A Streetcar Named Desire* (and she adores Brando). She enjoys lavish spectacle, as in *Samson and Delilah* and a film called *The Wild North:* "It's the *first* time I've ever seen *wolves' eyes* shining through the dark in the firelight, and the avalanche (and I'm quite a connoisseur of avalanches in the films) is magnificent." But in her book reviews she likes exactness and realism, for instance, in a historical novel about twelfth-century French barons: "Not only did I get to know the least details of what they ate and what they wore and so on, but I began to understand how they thought." She never imposes her view. One film review ends: "But perhaps you won't like it, you must see what you think."[12]

Squires Mount was too small for a four-year-old and a baby, and the Fitzgeralds—particularly Penelope—had ambitions. Between the summer of 1950 and early 1951, there were two dramatic changes in their lives. They moved to a much larger house, and they took on a literary magazine.

All they did was to move next door, but it was an enormous step up, and seemed to mark a new sense of themselves as a couple with prospects. Chestnut Lodge, where the Fitzgeralds would live for six years, and bring up three children—Maria was born in 1953—was an imposing family home, quite unlike the London flats and the little cottage they had been living in so far. They took it on a seven-year lease. It was a five-storey redbrick Queen Anne house at the top end of Cannon Place, right next to Squires Mount. Originally it had been part of a huge mansion which had been divided into three houses, the main one owned by the Law Lord, Viscount Radcliffe (who at the time was busy organising the partitioning of Cyprus). It had a courtyard area in front, with a tree in the middle, where the children from all three houses could cycle round, and a long narrow garden at the back, contiguous with the neighbours' gardens, with trees at the end. An imposing front door opened into a red-tiled hall with stairs at the far end. You turned right into the drawing room, light and spacious, with a high ceiling and French windows, and left into the dining room. They did it up in 1950s style, very "à la mode," as their friends noted. The dining room was painted black, and there were black-and-white chequerboard tiles on the ceiling. There was a big Spanish wicker birdcage and wicker balls hanging down. There was no study or library, but books were everywhere, and magazines—including a whole run of the *Strand,* which Valpy devoured. There was pottery and ceramics, some of it her own.

Downstairs, a long basement-kitchen ran the length of the house, with ivy at the windows, and a separate side entrance with steps up to the street. There was a scullery, a coal cellar, a gas stove and a lift with a rope for food to go up to the dining room, where there was a dumbwaiter. Above the living rooms, there was the main bedroom on the right, and on the left another bedroom, which Desmond used as his dressing room. On the next floor up were the children's rooms, with stars painted on the wallpaper, and a spare room for a live-in help. In the attic, which had dormer windows in the roof, there was the nursery-playroom, with plenty of toys, notably a large rocking horse, the envy of the visiting Knox cousins.

For all the modern furnishings, Penelope wanted to create an old-fashioned nursery atmosphere for the children. Willie Conder thought she had a Victorian idea of family life and would have liked to have a big family. She dressed the children in Victorian-style clothes, Valpy in long breeches. There were children's parties with proper party dresses and sashes, and a wonderful tree at Christmas, with gingerbread men and homemade decorations. Helen Knox remembered, with amusement, one Christmas visit when they acted out a Nativity scene in the drawing room with Helen as the Virgin Mary and Desmond as a slightly plastered Joseph.

There were drinks and dinner parties, there was a charlady and an au pair, at one point an Italian girl. The children retained memories of coming down from the nursery to see their parents before they went out in the evening. Valpy was sent to a smart Hampstead prep school, the Hall. There was, even, a family memory of a limousine and a chauffeur with a peaked cap. The Fitzgeralds themselves bought a sizeable car, a Ford Consul. Penelope dressed up beautifully for outings: Helen remembered her on Easter day at Grove Cottage in a lovely black taffeta dress, wearing a yellow turban as her Easter bonnet. There were regular family holidays, at home and abroad: to Greece with Evoe, to Spain, to Ibiza, and to Harlech for beach holidays with the Fishers, the kind of 1950s family holiday where the adults all sat about on rugs with picnic baskets, sand got in the food and the children went shrimping with nets in rock pools. Penelope used to sit on a rock, wearing a cotton sun hat with flaps, and paint the scene with a little box of watercolours on her knee.

They were living a comfortable middle-class life: in fact, they were living beyond their means. But they were not smart, grand or tidy. Because the three houses shared the central courtyard, and the fence between the parallel back gardens was always down, the neighbours saw quite a lot of the Fitzgeralds. One of the three adjacent big houses, South Lodge, was lived in by Ursula and Arthur Thompson and their family. To Tina, as a little girl, South Lodge was something of a refuge. "They had biscuits," she remembered, with feeling: the implication being that the Fitzgeralds, in spite of their big kitchen, didn't. Certainly Helen Knox, visiting with Rawle from India, remembered there never being much food, or the food not being very good. "It was always spaghetti or things like that. Once, lunch was left in the oven. There were three plates, with the food on each plate. Once there was a fried egg cooked about two hours earlier, left in the oven." The Italian au pair made pasta and hung it to dry over the backs of the kitchen chairs.[13] She taught Penelope to make authentic spaghetti sauce: according to her daughters, this was her only good dish. Deborah, the Thompson daughter, at South Lodge next door, a bit older than the Fitzgerald children, thought of life at Chestnut Lodge as eccentric. She could tell that her parents viewed Desmond and Penelope as special, but also slightly disapproved of them. They seemed to the Thompsons to be living in "Hampstead artistic disorder." The house was a mess, with things lying around everywhere, prams parked haphazardly outside. There was not much evidence of house cleaning.

Nearby, in Hampstead Square, lived Harvey Frost's family. Harvey was about Valpy's age, and the two boys spent a lot of time thundering about together, raiding the Thompsons' garden across the fence and playing guerrilla wars. Deborah Thompson knocked Harvey down once, and Valpy jeered: "Floored by a woman!" When Harvey was baptised, Penelope gave him a prayer book and an African bongo drum, and he and Valpy raced around beating the drum and whooping like banshees.[14] There was quite a bit of wildness and chaos in the grand Hampstead house.

The guests at the house were often writers and journalists—friends remembered meeting Maurice Richardson (ex-boxer and literary journalist), or Malcolm Muggeridge, or Rose Macaulay, at dinner there. People who did not especially like Penelope Fitzgerald would refer snidely to her "Hampstead intellectual friends." The politics of the household were liberal, although the newspaper they took (which she would take all her life) was the *Daily Express*. One letter of hers to the BBC is headed "St. Marylebone Liberal Association," and Valpy had a vague memory of his mother standing—without success, presumably—as a Liberal local councillor. In later years she would often say that she no longer had a party to support: "My party was abolished, once and for all, while I went out into the kitchen to make a cup of tea."[15]

The older generation of the Knoxes were as much part as ever of the fabric of her life. Her aunt Winifred Peck was writing novels and memoirs all through the 1950s. Ronald Knox, staying on in comfort with the Asquiths at Mells, was trying to write his spiritual autobiography. When Penelope had to leave his sixtieth birthday party early to go and look after the one-year-old Valpy, one of the other guests, Evelyn Waugh (a friend of Ronnie Knox's and soon to become his biographer), was extremely scornful: "Children!" he snapped. "Nonsense! Nothing so easily replaceable!"[16] Evoe kept up his friendships and connections at the *Punch* table after his retirement. Malcolm Muggeridge, who took over at *Punch* in 1953, did not warm to him. He thought that "people like Evoe, who seem to be so shy and sensitive that they can scarcely endure human intercourse, are capable of being, when it's unavoidable, cold and calculating." He thought him a "great oddity," who "gives an impression of being unhappy, but defiantly so; complicated as to religion with background (and fears) of oppressive Evangelicism."[17] Family members, too, could still find him daunting. Helen Knox, newly introduced to the family, and sent upstairs to call him to lunch at Grove Cottage, where he had his papers spread all over the floor of his room, was made to feel she had come in at the wrong time. But with his small grandchildren he was funny and entertaining. He took time to teach Valpy chess. He would suddenly appear from the kitchen with a saucepan on his head, to amuse William and Belinda. Mary looked after him with devoted housewifely attentiveness—Helen Knox remembered her always rushing out to buy cake for tea.

Wilfred, the Knox brother whom Penelope most revered, was the guest of honour at family Christmases at Grove Cottage, where on one occasion he witnessed with serenity the table decorations going up in flames.[18] But, two weeks after the birth of Tina, on 9 February 1950, aged sixty-four, he died of cancer, leaving behind very few possessions (most of which were bequeathed to the Franciscans), the draft of a book on the sources of the Synoptic Gospels, and a belief dearly held by his niece that his life had a lasting spiritual effect on those who knew him.

Penelope would always think and talk of the Knoxes as her intellectual breeding ground, the background likely to produce a writer. But Desmond had his own network of journalistic and literary contacts, too. His Oxford friend Bob Conquest, who had been working for the Foreign Office in Bulgaria during the war and since 1948 with the Foreign Office, as Information Research Officer, where his job was to cultivate connections with journalists, became a freelance writer in 1956 and an expert on Russia. Desmond was also friendly with Tom Burns, a vigorous, unorthodox and determined Catholic publisher, who had backed the publication of Graham Greene's *The Power and the Glory* when he was at Longman. He had been director of the Catholic Tablet Publishing Company and became the editor of its magazine, the *Tablet*. (Penelope would later write for it.) Tom Burns and his Spanish wife and four children lived for much of the time in Spain, where they invited the Fitzgeralds in 1955 on a family holiday. He had a great deal of influence in the world of Catholic journalism and publishing. Desmond had a long-lasting friendship, too, with the journalist Clifford Makins, a big character with a passion for theatre, music, literature, drink and good talk. In the 1950s, Clifford was working for

Edward Hulton's publishing empire. It was this enterprise which drew in the Fitzgeralds.

Edward Hulton, illegitimate son of a newspaper proprietor and race-horse owner, was a wealthy right-wing Catholic with cultural interests, who inherited £6 million from his father in 1936. He used it to establish the Hulton Press, which from 1937 published an impressive range of popular, and specialist, journals including *Lilliput, Farmer's Weekly, Nursing Times,* and, most notably, *Picture Post. Picture Post* started in 1938 under the editorship of a young Hungarian, Stefan Lorant. His number two was Tom Hopkinson, an editorial genius, who soon took it over. Hulton also had an interest in comics for children, and in 1950 started publishing *Eagle* (with its hugely popular pilot hero, Dan Dare) and then *Swift* (which ran from 1954 to 1961), and the equivalent for girl readers, called, naturally, *Girl.*

Hulton was an interventionist proprietor. He came to grief in his relations with Tom Hopkinson, whose outspoken left-wing views clashed with Hulton's politics. In 1950, Hopkinson was sacked from *Picture Post,* after Hulton censored a story of his about South Korea which Hulton thought might arouse communist sympathies. In later years, the Hulton Press publications lost their way, or were sold on, first to the *Daily Mirror,* and eventually to Robert Maxwell. But, in spite of the row with Hopkinson, there was a sense of opportunity and success to the Hulton stable in the 1950s.[19]

Desmond and Penelope had interlinked connections here. Clifford Makins worked on *Eagle* magazine in the 1950s as deputy to its founder, Marcus Morris, an Anglican vicar with a passionate commitment to children's education. He had been at Oxford at the same time as Penelope, and he and his rather chaotic family lived near the Fitzgeralds in Hampstead, and became good friends. It was Morris's idea to start a morally sound, entertaining comic-strip magazine for children, and he sold the idea of *Eagle* to Hulton. Morris edited it through the 1950s, before quarrelling with Hulton, like Hopkinson, and leaving in 1959 (when Makins became the editor for a short time). There were other Hulton links. Rawle had contributed briefly before the war to *Lilliput,* the Hulton monthly magazine of short stories and photography, founded in 1937, and he had just been hired by the *Observer* editor, David Astor. Astor's inspired hirings at the *Observer* included Clifford Makins, who became, in the 1960s, after his stint with *Eagle,* the *Observer's* anarchic sports editor. He was known as "a legend in his lunch-time," who would arrive in the office at 11:00 and leave for lunch at 11:20 ("sometimes, he would not return"). Quite a few of those lunches were with Desmond.[20]

So the lively, literary young Fitzgeralds seemed a plausible choice of editors—probably brought to Hulton's attention through Makins and Marcus Morris—when Hulton came to revamp one of his periodicals, *World Review,* in 1950. This was a monthly cultural magazine which had begun life in the early 1940s as *The Review of Reviews,* and then became *World Review: Incorporating The Review of Reviews.* By 1950 it was being edited by Stefan Schimanski, a Hungarian photo-journalist and anthologist who was also the founder of *Lilliput,* and who often worked in collaboration with the poet and children's writer Henry Treece on anthologies of wartime poems and diaries. Schimanski's June 1950 "special issue" of *World Review* on George Orwell—who had died in January 1950—gives a good sense of the kind of magazine it was.

On the first page, under its title, its price (1s. 6d) and its provenance—produced from the Hulton Office at 43 Shoe Lane, EC4, printed at the Curwen Press in Plaistow—it gives a list of tributes recently paid to this "monthly devoted to Literature and the Arts and all other aspects of our cultural interests." Julian Huxley calls it "a much-needed forum for the discussion and presentation of serious themes." Bertrand Russell says that "*World Review* is always interesting, much more so, to me, than most other reviews." A list of the notable contributions of the year included T. S. Eliot reflecting on *The Cocktail Party,* Arnold Toynbee on the lessons of history, André Malraux on T. E. Lawrence, Rebecca West on Germany's refugees, Stephen Spender on Auden at Oxford, Eudora Welty on "The Art of the Short Story," stories by William Sansom and Henry Miller, and pieces by Shaw, Bertrand Russell, Schweitzer, Herbert Read, Ignazio Silone, Heidegger, Camus, John Rothenstein, Karl Barth and Orwell himself. The Orwell issue had extracts from his unpublished wartime diaries, and essays on him by Russell, Muggeridge, Spender and Tom Hopkinson. It also had "Art Notes" by Robert Melville, and new books reviewed by Max Beloff, Geoffrey Grigson, Michael Hamburger and Lettice Cooper. The issue concluded with an announcement from Schimanski that "the next issue will be the last under the present editorship." The new editorial regime, then, began in August 1950.

Helen Knox remembered a scene in the drawing room at Chestnut Lodge of "Mops telling Desmond to change his tie, to go for a job at the Hulton Press. She was trying to groom Desmond and make him look smart. Mops was telling him, 'Oh, Desmond, don't wear that yellow tie.' She was always telling him what to do."[21] Whatever the colour of the tie—and whoever was really in charge—the Fitzgerald charm prevailed, and

World Review

Desmond became the editor of the new-look *World Review*. An advertisement in *The Times* for 4 August 1950 read: "*World Review* has again changed its character and under a new editor (Mr. Desmond Fitzgerald) describes itself as 'a magazine of the Arts, Politics and Law.' It deserves a welcome under each of these heads."[22] The editor, writing in the first person in the first and second issues, described himself as an Irishman and a lawyer. Penelope, in a note to a BBC producer in January 1951, apologising again for the late delivery of a script, said: "I enclose the Christmas number of a magazine I am helping my husband to edit, there is no ulterior motive in this except to show I am not sitting about doing nothing when I should be finishing scripts."[23] Officially, Desmond was in charge. But many of their editorials were signed "D.F. and P.M.F." She contributed signed pieces to almost every edition; and some of the writing signed by him sounds like her. It is clear that *World Review* was as much her work as his.

The literary editor John Lehmann, lamenting the dearth of purely literary magazines in the new decade, and the demise of his own *New Writing* and *Penguin New Writing,* asked in 1950: "What will take the place of *New Writing*? Already the creeping frosts have claimed *Horizon* and *Life & Letters* as their victims. *World Review* has deserted the strait path of literature; soon there will be hardly any address at all to which a young poet or writer of short stories can send his MS."[24] Lehmann's fears, in this case, were not really justified. The Fitzgeralds' idea for *World Review* was that it should be a mix of politics, art, architecture, stories, poems, serialisations and reviews. It looked like a cross between *Encounter* (which began in 1953) and *Punch,* with an attractive colour illustration on the cover and plenty of artwork inside, including cartoons. There was political, economic or legal commentary at the front, meaty pieces on cultural subjects in the middle and reviews (of music as well as books) at the back. Real-world concerns were addressed, and the editorial tone was brisk, unpretentious and often humorous. The political and social pieces were conspicuously international, covering land reform in Italy, political divisions in France, the North Atlantic Treaty, the Persian oil dispute, refugees in Germany, British relations with China, the atom bomb and the Cold War. *World Review* was modern and anti-insular, Europhile, liberal, sceptical and cultured without being snooty. It valued bold new art of all kinds, and the crossing of borders. Jean Fisher thought it "progressive." It was part of a post-war British cultural resurgence, as celebrated in 1951 by the Festival of Britain, which *World Review* treated, however, with marked disrespect.

Some of the contributors—Henry Treece, Bertrand Russell, Michael

Hamburger, Henry Cecil, André Malraux—were already part of the Schimanski stable. Some were writers with whom the Fitzgeralds already had contacts or friendships: Bob Conquest, Max Beloff, Walter de la Mare, Neville Braybrooke. There was even one review by "E.N. Fitzgerald," Desmond's brother. Some contributions would have come in because the word went round—quite quickly, since writers were always looking for likely venues for their work—that *World Review* was a good place to be published. Raleigh Trevelyan, a writer who would become a publisher, and who, just over twenty years later, would publish Penelope's first book, sent a story to *World Review* in 1953 because he had heard it was *the* place to go to. It had gained an immediate reputation, he said, as "the magazine of the moment." He got to know the editors and visited them in Hampstead. "Desmond seemed to be full of go, a handsome Guard-ee type. Penelope would be bustling away in the background, running the whole show. They seemed very different types—Desmond Etonian, she more housewifey. He did most of the talking, but she was the brains."[25]

The list of contributors in the three years between August 1950 and May 1953 was extraordinary. They were the first publishers of two of Louis MacNeice's poems, "Suite for Recorders" in October 1950 and "Didymus" in April 1951. They published stories by Muriel Spark, Joyce Cary and L. P. Hartley, who would become Penelope's friend. So would the young novelist Francis King, and Stevie Smith, who did idiosyncratic book reviews for them and published some poems from *Harold's Leap,* with their illustrations, in March 1951. (Reviewing *Harold's Leap,* Fitzgerald comments: "Noble human beings at the height of their tragedy are usually grotesque.") They published Patrick Leigh-Fermor, Geoffrey Grigson, Roy Harrod, William Sansom, Cyril Connolly, Francis Huxley, Stuart Hampshire, James Kirkup, Alan Brownjohn and Anthony Thwaite. They had some adventurously modern music reviews—on Schoenberg, on *Wozzeck,* on Menotti, on Britten. In January 1952, the editors single out Britten's *Billy Budd* (they were at the first night) as a powerful expression, in the conflict between Claggart and Billy, of "the instinct that says 'the best must go.'" This would be one of Fitzgerald's subjects.

The most impressive thing about their *World Review* was its internationalism. Perhaps their most remarkable scoop was publishing J. D. Salinger the year before *The Catcher in the Rye* came out. They began with his story "For Esmé with Love and Squalor" in their first issue of August 1950, and published him again in 1952 ("De Daumier-Smith's Blue Period"), when they described him, with justifiable pride, as a brilliant "young

American writer, who has already appeared in *World Review*." They also captured Camus, Henry Miller, Bernard Malamud (a story called "The Death of Me," in April 1951), Norman Mailer, Allen Tate, Alberto Moravia (in whom Penelope was intensely interested) and the French novelist Julien Gracq, whose gesture in turning down the Goncourt Prize they wrote about admiringly.

They used the magazine as a forum for their own international interests. In all Fitzgerald's work so far—student journalism, reviewing, scriptwriting—European literature, art and culture had been important to her. Now she had the chance to explore and write about it in much more depth. Some of the most interesting pieces in *World Review*, which have her mark on them, are about Italian sculpture, art nouveau, French and Italian novels or Spanish painting. In these pieces there is a fascination with extremes and with ruthlessness, as when writing about the characteristics of farce: "characters in the grip of their fate," "complete absence of pity." Jarry's *Ubu Roi*, which she treats with confidence and mastery, embodies "the incarnation of the shapeless power" whose "prayer is to be spared from thinking," and which can "turn government into a nightmare." A life of Edvard Munch reveals "a northern genius, in his moral earnestness [and] the joylessness of his conception of love (a kind of bitter contest between the sexes)." An extract from a 1950 Italian novel, *The House Moves,* by the anti-Fascist writer Guglielmo Petroni, which she calls "a tragic masterpiece," has in it an almost entirely silent character, Ugo Gattagni, slowly dying in a wartime big house, attended by his faithful housekeeper: "To know how to wait is the most difficult task," it is said of him. She will bear him in mind for the stoical, silent Cesare in *Innocence*.

Alberto Moravia profoundly attracts and repels her. *The Conformist* is praised for the "abnormal hero who tries in vain to make a perfectly dull middle-class marriage." She admires his cold correctness and "the disconcerting and yet familiar way in which his people, even while we look at them, change and reveal different selves." "For all its realistic approach, and deliberate understatement, the *effect* is not realistic, but strange beyond all conception." His astonishing control is, she says, "a school for novelists." Fitzgerald's interest in this chilling genius is a vital stage in the long journey she was making towards writing fiction. The obliqueness and strangeness of her work, its surprising un-Englishness, its mastery of deep emotion, link back to these years of thinking about modern European art and writing.[26]

There is a powerful example of this in June 1951, in a long piece on the late-nineteenth-century Italian sculptor Medardo Rosso, titled "We Are All of Us Lighting Effects." She had seen his work when she and Desmond were in Rome in the spring of 1949. Her piece tells the story of "a boy of terrifyingly strong will," who felt that the art of the 1880s had nothing to do with reality as he saw it. Depressive and obsessional, he went into "open warfare" against the conventions of his time. He was an Impressionist in stone, who became very famous, and then very obscure. She particularly admires his "child portraits," like one where "the squat face looks out from under the enveloping shawl with a matchless expression of timidity and greed." Her thoughts on his work end with a passage which points ahead to her own future work, in which "strong emotion" is kept under formal control:

> The first effect of an exhibition of Rosso's work is the electric touch of strong emotion. Don't let us be afraid of it—don't let us be persuaded that it is "literary," for puritanism, never to be killed, has reappeared among critics today in this deadliest of all forms. Don't let us hold our noses if Rosso shows "a woman of the people" snatching a kiss before the last spadeful of earth covers her husband's corpse, or a sick child in hospital whose pathos we may like to think is easy. Pathos, indeed, is the keynote of the Impressionist Movement, as morbidity is of the Pre-Raphaelites. It is implicit in the very idea of the moment that will not return . . .
>
> It is not by coincidence that both Rosso and Renoir both set themselves to render, with miraculous success, the rubbery, puppy-like, irresistible faces of childhood. Both of them perceived the stubborn determination to get its own way that lay under the peach-bloom contours; both of them were masculine and were drawn to the tender, but, above all, both of them understood that in women and children they could study not only the appearances but also the tragedy of light which will betray minute by minute the terrible altering, foreshadowing and falling away of flesh.[27]

There is a similar intensity in her writing about Spain and Spanish art. She and Desmond travelled at least three times to Spain during the 1950s. A funny letter to Evoe and Mary from Barcelona, where she sprained her ankle at a bullfight and had mixed feelings about Gaudi, shows how the literary editors fared abroad—and, also, how freely and warmly she wrote to her father and her young stepmother:

Dearest Daddy and Mary . . . Our chief trouble here has been the literati to whom we had introductions as they are all "advanced" Catalans and speak Catalan to each other which means they write notes . . . to us beginning "Estimat amic." Well, these amics, who all keep rich-looking galleries (full of pictures we can't think of anything to say about) and book-shops and seem to have plenty of time and money, keep calling at the hotel and leaving cards (it's very awkward that we haven't any cards as they didn't get printed in time) and then we have to go and see still more frightful pictures which are brought down from attics by Spanish workmen who <u>always</u> display them upside down (angry gestures from the owner) and we've insulted one amic terribly by not meeting him where we said, though this may make us popular with the others, as I believe they really all hate each other like poison. (Incidentally when they want to go out of their flats they ring and <u>two</u> maids come and open the door for them.) Well, we conduct our conversations in terrible French . . . They all talk very fast.[28]

In *World Review,* she wrote about Spain and its arts with passion, knowledge and inwardness. A co-authored piece on "The Arts in Modern Spain" (December 1950) describes the "difficult genius" Solana, "eccentric, single-minded, and dearly loved by his friends." An essay on "Spanish Painted Sculpture" (July–August 1952) takes pains to connect the artists with their society. The ceremonies of Holy Week in towns in southern Spain like Seville, where these artists' painted religious sculptures are carried in procession, are "moving and austere": "The crowds wait motionless in the streets often in the rain, or with the cold night wind guttering the candles, for the hooded ranks of the Nazarenes to pass, with their long shadows going before them, and behind them the slowly moving *pasos.* There is nothing theatrical here, but an intensity and concentration." Singling out Montañés, the "astonishing" artist of Seville, she praises his "amazingly controlled energy," and the "very simple forms" in which he expressed himself.[29]

"The manual arts give the deepest satisfaction of all," she says of the wooden painted images of Seville. The same principle applies when she is writing—as she also often does in *World Review*—about English art and Englishness. In a review of a book called *The Unsophisticated Arts,* by Barbara Jones, she takes pleasure in learning about "the things that people make for themselves or that are manufactured in their taste": "which includes not only tattooing, shop-signs, wax-works, rustication, comic postcards, but 'early industrial' designs for crackers, fireworks and toys and half-deliberate arts such as the arrangement of food."[30] A people's art is "a most important field," she maintains, and she is ahead of her time in thinking so. Her passion for the useful arts, derived from Ruskin and Morris, points towards her book on Edward Burne-Jones. Writing about him in a co-authored piece on "Art Nouveau," she refers to Morris's insistence on morality in the arts (he contends that "handicrafts [are] *morally better* than easel-painting") and to Burne-Jones's "sympathy and honesty." "In spite of the intense morbidity of many of his designs," he was regarded by his contemporaries as "a healthy antidote to the sickliness of the Yellow Book."[31] She will return to these moral and aesthetic concerns.

Integrity in the arts was a concern to the editors of *World Review*. Fitzgerald's June 1952 review of *High Victorian Design* by Pevsner draws a "depressing comparison" between the Great Exhibition of 1851 and the Festival of Britain of 1951, "palely dictated by a cultural committee to a docile public anxious only 'not to miss anything.'" The post-war national cheer and optimism of the Festival was not to their taste. They associate it with an outbreak of "Festival English," by which they mean sentimental euphemisms ("Heritage bred in the blood and bone = Hazy memories of history learnt in school"), rusty patriotic flourishes ("It is a small island, this England of ours") and faux pastoral: "Over all the London street markets is the gay mantle of good nature." They like satirising sloppy ideas and the misuse of language. By contrast, they call William Empson's 1950 *The Structure of Complex Words* the "most valuable book of the year."

The issue of October 1950 has an illustrated ABC, scathing about the culture and politics of the time (next to a poem by "PMF" to mark George Bernard Shaw's death at ninety-four, calling him a "childless old fellow" and a "bitter success" who "still will not give in"). In January 1952 the editor's New Year resolutions take on current fashions in literature. He (or she) proposes "to set my face against decent ordinary everyday folk as heroes, and worse still, the presentation of heroes as ordinary everyday folk . . . To oppose all forms of You-Can't-Take-It-With-You-ism in literature"—like the good alcoholic in *Brideshead Revisited* or the good adulterers in Graham Greene—and to continue to look for writers who "are interested in human behaviour and its results rather than in motives and 'states of mind.'" (This is like her BBC review of the James Stewart film *Harvey,* suggesting she is the main author here.) The next issue has a "chart of Half-Baked Ideas" in current literature "particularly disliked by the editor." These include plays in which a mysterious stranger is "really" Death or Christ (like Eliot's *The Cocktail Party*); mishmashes of mysticism (Rosicrucianism, Swedenborgianism), as in Aldous Huxley; utopias and model communities; pastoral fallacies; and versions of H. G. Wells's "Little Man."[32] This cultural satire feels dated now. But it does express an independence from literary fashions.

Penelope Fitzgerald published no fiction in *World Review*, but a curious pair of editorials in March and July 1951 arouse suspicions. Slipped in among the essays on Korea, the U.S. budget and local government, "A Letter from Tisshara" invites the editor, Mr. Fitzgerald, to be the tutor to Tisshara's heir apparent, a solitary, sickly, nervous eight-year-old boy who has never met his mother, has bad dreams and thinks he is "growing smaller and smaller as the days go by." The anxious Chamberlain of Tisshara describes a country of self-deceiving political illusions, divided between left and right, with a folkoric puppet theatre for light relief, possibly "of interest to your British Council." His second letter tells of the little prince's increasingly pathetic condition, and of a festival of Tisshara's literary critics and biographers, observed by visitors from PEN, who come together every year to dig up the bones of dead writers in a strange desolate, windy landscape of wailing grasses. This peculiar exercise in satirical fantasy was perhaps intended as a regular column. After two episodes it peters out—but its vulnerable innocent child in a compromised adult world leaves its trace in Fitzgerald's later fiction.[33]

In spite of its adventurousness, *World Review* was not doing well. Later, Penelope would say to Maria: "I don't know why we thought it would make any money." In 1952 there began to be signs of turmoil and anxiety at Chestnut Lodge. In January 1952, Penelope wrote an urgent note to one of her BBC producers about a promised script: "I want to tell you that I have just been asked to write 4 other scripts in a great hurry & as I am very short of money, could I leave Queen Anne half way through till the end of February? This means everything to me."[34] In October 1952, leaving Desmond to manage the house and the magazine, and parking Tina with the Fitzgerald grandparents at Burton Court, she went away, taking the six-year-old Valpy with her, on one of the most improbable trips of her life. It was all the more startling because she was three months pregnant.

She and Valpy travelled to Liverpool, and boarded the *Queen Mary* to New York. What Valpy remembered of this journey was that Bing Crosby was on board, and at one point Penelope managed to infiltrate first class so that Valpy could get his autograph. And he remembered an indoor saltwater swimming-pool, with real waves. Arriving in the autumn, they went to 36 Amherst Road, Port Washington, in New York State, to stay with friends. Valpy recalled a family with children. The address is that of a splendid old grey-stone house, which at one point was lived in by the NBC reporter John McBain. He had worked with the BBC during the war, and was one of the models for the American reporter in *Human Voices*. He may have been their host. They stayed there for a few weeks, while the weather got colder—Valpy remembered being bought a weatherproof jacket with a polar bear fur collar. In November, they took a Greyhound bus down the length of the country, via San Antonio, Texas, to Saltillo, a small town in northern Mexico, near Monterrey. Valpy remembered the segregated lavatories for whites, blacks and Mexicans at the bus stops in Texas, and arriving at a grand house in the colonial style, lived in by old ladies, with (this especially impressed him) a gardener called Jesus. They stayed there for about two months, during which time they did some travelling in Mexico. On one trip, they climbed the Teotihuacan pyramid, leaving their picnic lunch at the bottom. From the top of the pyramid, they watched a small boy running off with their picnic basket. In January they made the bus journey back to New York and then Halifax, to board the *Franconia*. They landed in Liverpool on 26 January, Tina's third birthday. Just over ten weeks later, Maria was born.

What was she doing in Mexico, and why did she take Valpy? Why did she go when she was pregnant, leaving Desmond and Tina behind, and why did she stay so long? Friends and family, looking back, made up their reasons. Jean Fisher said, admiring and baffled, it was just the sort of outlandish thing she *would* do. She was restless, she was escaping, she was trying to raise some money, her children supposed, looking back.

Fitzgerald never answered any of these questions, but she told a version of the story, nearly thirty years on, as part of a 1980 essay on plots in fiction. She says that she went to try and persuade the old ladies, in the town she calls "Fonseca"—but where is Fonseca on any map of northern Mexico?—to leave Valpy "all their money" (in which case, taking him with her made sense). She says they had invited her, and that they were distant Irish connections of the family. The money came from the family silver mine; the two old ladies were called Delaney. This is how she tells the story:

The old ladies lived in a shuttered mansion in the French style, surrounded with pecan trees; the house was always cool because of the double height of the rooms. In the half-darkness of those rooms, as I discovered the very first evening I arrived, they were drinking themselves steadily to death. For two hours or so every morning there was a lucid period, and that was the time for callers. The manager of the mine came then, and so did everyone in Fonseca who was interested in the Delaneys' wealth and therefore wanted to get rid of me and my son as soon as possible . . .

. . . As time went on, more pretenders . . . arrived, even one who claimed to be a Delaney, and moved into the house. On the other hand, the manager was eliminated. Seeking to extend his sphere of influence, he began to drink level with the old ladies, slipped on the polished French Provincial staircase, and cracked his skull. My son and I were blamed for these and other disasters, and we left on the long distance bus without a legacy, but knowing what it was to be hated.[35]

It sounds, as she says herself, like "a yarn," a play by Tennessee Williams or a story by Conrad: the moribund old Irish ladies drinking themselves to death in their grand French-Mexican villa, the divisive legacy of the silver mine, the hostile intruders crowding into the house, the unwanted, anxious, pregnant English visitor and her little boy. But the journey itself was not a fiction. The Fitzgeralds' names are on the passenger lists. In 1987, she wrote a pleading letter to Tina and her husband about the brightly coloured "serape" she had brought back to use as a bedspread and which they were using as a living-room carpet. She asked them not to: "It is the only thing I have left from Chestnut Lodge . . . [and] I carried the serape all the way from Mexico City, through N. York, then Halifax and back to Liverpool on the old Franconia . . . it is 35 years old—I could never buy one like it now."[36] In 1997 she mentioned to an American friend that she had "been to San Antonio on the way to Mexico." The details of the story match the facts about the Saltillo area: that is where serapes are made, where there were silver mines, and where many Irish and English émigrés settled in the early twentieth century.

When she came back, by now five months pregnant, she wrote up the journey to Mexico for the magazine, in two impressive pieces that confirmed her interest in a people's art. In an essay on "El Muralismo," she puts the art of the Mexican revolution into its historical context, and connects the Mexican artists' manifesto for "an art for the people" to the "principles of William Morris." Their "muralismo" was "the kind of painting [that] would teach the people, express the revolution, transform the buildings of the past and remain in tune with both the Indian 'arte popular' and the art of ancient Mexico." She follows this "idea in action" with fascination through the work of individual artists like Siqueiros, Orozco and Rivera.

She describes her own visit to the site of the New University, to the south of Mexico City, to see the gigantic—and to her eye often confusing and unsatisfactory—murals being painted there. What she likes even more than the murals, though, are the popular, native homemade arts done by the women and children in Mexican villages, what she calls "expendable art," which she writes about in an another essay on "Mexican Art and History." Here, she makes much of her own experiences travelling around the country, referring to a city "which can be reached nowadays by a bus from Merida," or having "been out to see the Temple of Quetzcoatl," or her visit to the village of Melepec, where "almost every other household is full of children making clay toys." Historically, in Mexico, "manual crafts and fine arts were not distinguished from each other," and she approves of this. Her precious serape was a memento of these useful arts.[37]

At some point during, or after, her Mexican adventure, she wrote a story called "Our Lives Are Only Lent to Us." (It is not dated, but it overlaps in several details with the 1953 essays on Mexico.) Very compressed, it reads as if a whole novel about cultural and racial interrelations in northern Mexico—a novel by Conrad, or Graham Greene—has been concentrated into a brightly coloured fragment. The story is set in San Tomás de las Ollas, an old silver-mining town now dominated by incomers from across the border, where Americans, Europeans, Indians and Mexicans exist alongside, but without understanding, one another. Engineers, businessmen, well-meaning educationalists, experts on Mexican arts and crafts, tourists—all pass through. A shrewd Mexican observes that "the two cultures"—the incoming colonialists and the indigenous—"are complementary, but in the way that death is to life. The two cannot exist together, but just as surely they cannot exist without each other." Mrs. Sheridan, the benevolent widow of the mine owner, living in a stately old house (like the house Penelope stayed in with Valpy), is concerned for the family of her Indian chauffeur Pantaléon, who is slyly taking advantage of her to support his network of dependants. A heart-stoppingly beautiful little girl in his household, Esperanza, clearly the result of a mixed-race alliance, looks after the new baby, and sells fish in the decrepit, rotting old market, where the peasants "scrabble through on the right side of starvation," right next to the brand-new "supermercado." It is Esperanza who, asked by Mrs. Sheridan about the health of the baby, replies: "*Venimos prestados.* Our lives are only lent to us." In a house up in the hills, an American colonel with throat cancer, whose young wife has left him, listens to his talking starling repeat, all day long: "My God I can't bear it. My God I must get out . . . Get out you bitch." The old market goes up in flames, Esperanza is killed in the fire and all trace of her "perishes completely from the earth." The colonialists fork out large sums of guilt money to build a new market, and the Indians resignedly endure the catastrophe. This dark early story shows her turning her own experience, as she would do again, into a minutely observed fragment of historical fiction.

Her essays on Mexico were her final contribution to *World Review.* In the summer of 1953, the editors announced: "This is the last issue of *World Review* in its present form. For a number of reasons, already familiar to most of us, we have had to suspend publication. We hope after an interval *World Review* will appear again in a new form and devoted entirely to literature."[38]

Hardly a trace of *World Review* remains in the scattered and incomplete papers of Penelope Fitzgerald. Somewhere—perhaps at the bottom of the Thames, or in the long-lost archive of the Hulton Press at Shoe Lane—there would have been boxes full of correspondence between authors and editors, marked-up proofs, account sheets, galleys, letters to the editor. Nothing remains, except for one or two of her markings in the run of the magazine kept by Evoe and Mary Knox. There is a page of her notes slipped into an essay of December 1950 on the *Punch* illustrator Richard Doyle, who sounds like a character for a Fitzgerald novel, with his darkening thoughts, his strange imagination, a face that always "looked rather tired," and personal wounds concealed with humorous shyness. And there is one note pencilled next to a reference to a "young English poet, I.R. Orton": "Never heard of since."[39] It seems apt.

But she kept one tribute to the magazine in her archive, a fan letter which clearly meant a great deal to her. In 1990, Dr. David Painting, of Swansea, wrote to tell her that he had a complete run of *World Review* in his library: "I would like you to know that after forty years those old copies are still cherished reminders of the exceptional quality of *World Review.* To a provincial undergraduate they opened up new worlds of interest and provide the kind of intellectual stimulus which lasts a lifetime . . . When you ended *World Review* with the Mexican special number of April–May 1953 I wrote to the Hulton Press pleading for its return—but in vain!" She told him how much his letter meant to her: "I only wish my husband was alive to read it with me . . . I'm afraid we hadn't much idea how to edit a paper, but we did care, as I still do, about writers & artists & their ideas & what can be brought about by ideas."[40]

Her work for the Hulton Press was not quite ended, though, and took a surprising direction after *World Review* folded. Their friends Marcus Morris and Clifford Makins were involved in the setting up of a companion comic-strip magazine to *Eagle*, for younger children, *Swift*, which ran from 1954 to 1961, when it was merged with its older brother. For about two years, 1956 to 1958, Fitzgerald wrote a serial for *Swift* called "Jassy of Juniper Farm." It was illustrated by Bill White, a freelance graphic artist whose daughter, Francesca Zawadzki, coincidentally became a close friend of Tina's at university. Bill White liked working for the Hulton Press because they were reliable about paying on time. They paid Fitzgerald £7 an issue. Bill and his daughter noted that she was not snobbish or embarrassed about writing the strip. She needed the money.[41]

"Jassy of Juniper Farm" was a 1950s pastoral idyll—perhaps drawing on memories of Balcombe—with some useful information slipped in about country life. Jassy Thompson lives with her younger brother Jack and baby Jenny, with a loving housewifely mother and a practical, sensible farming father—all straight out of "Happy Families"—on a farm near the picture-postcard village of Great Puddingthorpe. The nearest town is Oxminster, the local hostelry is called The Mumpton Arms, there is a church, an old mill, a friendly blacksmith, a teashop and an eccentric but benign local aristocrat, Lord Crumley, who wears the skin of a dead pet hedgehog for a winter hat. The episodes are emphatically seasonal: skating and sledging and gathering holly for the church; harvest festival, ploughing, lambing, threshing. Mr. Thompson is always busy "lifting the mangolds" or checking the clover for mowing. Dramas are the elm tree falling on the pigsty in a storm, the tea lady objecting to the school holiday camp (bathing and rounders for the girls) outside her garden, a solitary wild man discovered in the woods who turns out to have a heart of gold. In moments of fear, Jack says to himself: "Courage, Thompson! Dan Dare would think nothing of this!" Opportunities are taken to show that you shouldn't cheat, even if you mean well, that you shouldn't show off, that you should be adventurous and observant. Jassy, who is drawn with blonde hair and a rather fetching black beret, is always content. "I wouldn't live anywhere else in the whole world."[42]

In the real world, on 10 April 1953, Maria was born. Three days after the birth, Penelope wrote to Evoe and Mary from Queen Mary's House,

Jassy
of Juniper Farm

Jassy and Jack Thompson live on Juniper Farm. They wouldn't live anywhere else in the whole world. Now it is nearly spring, a very important time when you live on a busy farm.

Jassy finds that she always has a large family to look after. It is difficult to name them all.

And every day there are newly hatched chicks to care for.

One day, Mr Crawley calls for Jassy and Jack.

He has decided to take them round the old Catchpole Mill for a treat.

t is very dark inside the mill nd full of old flour dust.

Sharp-eyed Jack finds a bit of the old cogwheel.

Mr Crawley explains how the mill used to work in the old days.

ut he tells them it would be angerous if it worked now.

They enjoy their visit, but as they cycle home from school next day . . .

. . . they see the sails of the mill turning! *More next week.*

the nursing home in Hampstead, thanking them for their letters and flowers. The nursing home was "difficult about visitors," even though it was meant to be just like home and not like a hospital, "so we have dainty traycloths and screens that fall down on top of us." The staff were kind, but she would be "glad to be home again."

> Maria is a dear little baby and so far has dark blue eyes, but I don't know whether they will last. She is on the greedy side, rather like Tina. It was such a relief when she was born and they held her up and I was able to count her toes and see they were all correct. I was getting quite worried with all the messing about. The surgeon who gave me the induction is a frightful old show-off and stopped at the last minute to say "Where are my students? Why are no students watching me?" He sounded like Beerbohm Tree.
>
> I do hope the children will approve of Maria, Valpy wanted a brother, of course, but I think she will be convenient for dollies' tea-parties and fit in quite well.[43]

The light, comical, self-deprecating Knoxian tone covers, and reveals, pride, anxiety and strong emotion. These three post-war babies had been struggled for; they would be at the heart of her life forever. And she had wanted a bigger family. Maria remembered being told by her mother that there had been more miscarriages after her birth; she thought that Penelope might have been rhesus negative and Desmond rhesus positive, which could lead to lost pregnancies, before the condition became treatable in the 1950s.

Maria (pronounced "Mar-eye-ah" and shortened to Ria) spent the first four years of her life at Chestnut Lodge, while Tina was going, unhappily, to St. Mary's, the convent school halfway down Fitzjohn Avenue. Valpy was still at school at the Hall. Family life muddled along, accumulating much-repeated, unverifiable anecdotes. One of Penelope's favourite stories of that time was that she was driven round London with Jean's brother James Fisher, now working at the Regent's Park zoo, with the first panda from China in the back of his car, "together with a supply of bamboo shoots."[44] More plausible reminiscences of the 1950s came from friends and family. Helen, visiting from India, remembered fetching the children from school with Penelope, and, if they were early, sitting on the benches outside the Hampstead pub and having a glass of cider. Jasmine Blakeway, back in London by 1955, remembered driving Penelope to take Valpy to the dentist. "Mops said to him: 'Now, darling, the dentist is going to ask whether you've worn your plate all along. Don't answer, because you've just been to confession, and I don't want you to tell a lie. I will say, yes.' "[45]

Her own scruples involved sticking consistently to the bargain she had struck in marrying a Catholic: she sent the children off to Mass every Sunday, while she went to her own Anglican service. On trips abroad with Valpy, though, she would happily go to Catholic Mass with him.

The only Catholic convert of the Knox family made one final public appearance. Ronnie Knox, very ill with liver cancer at sixty-nine, gave the prestigious Romanes Lecture at Oxford, on English translation. The example he gave of a perfect translation was the poem which had been the signature tune of the Knox brothers, Cory's "They told me, Heraclitus, they told me you were dead." He died a few weeks later, and there were extensive obituaries. Less remarked on was the fading away, at eighty-one, of "not quite normal" Aunt Ethel, who had stayed on in her unchanging Victorian room even after the death of Mrs. K. Now there were only two Knoxes left from that generation, Evoe and Winifred, both in their late seventies. Penelope had half expected to inherit some of "Uncle Ronnie's Money," but all she got was "a small plaster bust of Shakespeare."[46]

There was not much income coming in. Desmond went back to "lawyering"; he had kept his name up in the Middle Temple chambers and may also have been doing some work for a circuit court in Norfolk.[47] But the time spent on *World Review* cannot have done his legal career any good. To Jean Fisher, by now a successful barrister, that seemed a great pity. And Chestnut Lodge could not have been easily kept up by an allowance from Evoe, small sums from journalism and patchy lawyer's fees.

No sense of direction or ambition comes through from this disappointing time after the closure of the magazine. But there are two intriguing signs that there was some writing going on. In 1958 Fitzgerald wrote an experimental story, left unpublished in her papers, called "The Mooi." It was a surreal, experimental narrative written in a third-person, present-tense monologue, in a strange dialect veering between a kind of patois ("How know anyone the Mooi tell true when he say what he say?") and literary formality ("inevitable questions ensue"). The narrator observes but does not understand the Mooi. But we also get inside the Mooi's head, and the closer we get to him, the more challenging he is: "Strange to have a march stolen on one by one such as the Mooi." It is rather like Melville's Bartleby and his narrator, and very like Beckett's novels (*Watt, Molloy, Malone Dies*), which came out in the 1950s, and which Fitzgerald read and annotated with fascinated admiration. Like Beckett's tramps and unname-ables, the Mooi has his own kind of eloquence. He is a "margin man," bedraggled, homeless, "despised by the civilised such as we." He has lost his bicycle (Fitzgerald loves the bicycles in Beckett), drinks heavily, wears filthy clothes and talks to himself. But he is also a philosopher, a stoic, a kind of Wilfred Knox–like hermit-prophet. Plato and Ecclesiastes are invoked. He sits in the sun, hums like a bee and does not fear death. Like many of Fitzgerald's later characters, he embodies the power and value of failure in the world. As she would say of *Offshore:* "It seems to me that not to be wanted is a positive condition."[48]

Desmond, too, wrote a story in the late 1950s, though it may have been partly her work. His was a farcical comedy called "The Soldier in My Throat," which was published in *Lilliput* in November 1957, and was based on a real incident. A father swallows his small boy's plastic soldier by accident. He rushes himself off to hospital, unable to speak, but they can't find anything on the X-ray, and send him home looking foolish. The tone is straight out of the Grossmiths' *Diary of a Nobody,* one of Penelope's favourite books (and first published in *Punch*). It is the first outing for the Pooterish persona which Desmond and Penelope—and later the children—were inventing for him, and which her letters, and his, would play up: the comical, incompetent and accident-prone husband and father. The dashing soldier who fought so gallantly in the war has become the absurd plastic toy soldier, stuck in his own throat.[49]

They were beginning to struggle; they had overstretched themselves. Penelope was trying to make ends meet, cutting down her clothes, for instance, to make Valpy's dungarees.[50] The Thompson neighbours had the sense that all was not well at Chestnut Lodge. Deborah remembered worried discussions between her parents about the family next door, some anxious tut-tuttings ("that child hasn't got shoes on"), and feeling irritated with her mother because she was always busy "looking after the Fitzger-alds." She remembered her mother, Ursula Thompson, going to check on Maria, who had been left in her pram for ages in the back garden. The little girl looked up "in defiance," as if to say she did not need help. Tina and Maria, in particular, struck them as loyal and courageous small children. Certainly all three children would have to become stoical and independent very quickly.

In 1957, quite suddenly, the life the Fitzgeralds had made at Chestnut Lodge fell apart. They left Hampstead, and went to live in Southwold on the Suffolk coast. The Thompsons took the opportunity to move from

South Lodge to Chestnut Lodge. When they moved in, they could see it had been an emergency departure. The empty house was left in a chaotic state. They assumed that the Fitzgeralds had not been able to pay the rent, and had had to leave in a hurry.

Much of this part of her life Penelope Fitzgerald consigned to silence. The editing of the magazine, her life with Desmond and three young children in the 1950s, the adventure in Mexico, the flight from Chestnut Lodge: she hardly ever referred to these things, when, years later, she became well known and people asked her questions about her life. Of her attempt to use her trip to Mexico as material, she said: "My story . . . gives me the impression of turning fiction into fiction . . . Reality has proved treacherous. 'Unfortunate are the adventures which are never narrated.' "[51]

CHAPTER SIX

The Bookshop

Her courage, after all, was only a determination to survive.[1]

In the catastrophic floods all along the east coast of England in January 1953, which drowned 378 people and destroyed huge swathes of homes, livestock and farmlands, the small east Suffolk town of Southwold was badly hit. Five people died, the sea wall collapsed, great damage was done and for a time the town became an island, cut off on all sides. Traces of the havoc remained for years. The heroine of Fitzgerald's novel *The Bookshop*, set in a fictional Southwold in 1959, has lived in the town since 1951 and often thinks back to the great flood, as when she notes sadly that there are no herons nesting anymore in the pinewoods; not since "the sea had drowned the woodlands in salt."

Even in better times, Southwold was hard to get to, isolated and open to all weathers. Out on the edge of the flat marshes, facing the sea, with the River Blyth to the south and Buss Creek to the north, it can feel more like a promontory than a securely anchored part of the mainland. For centuries, boats and horses, cart and foot, were the only ways to get around. A railway, connecting Southwold to inland Halesworth, came and went: it lasted from 1879 to 1929. The defunct railway bridge over the River Blyth was replaced by a Bailey bridge for pedestrians and cyclists. A chain-ferry river crossing for cars was discontinued in 1941; a rowing-boat ferry continues to operate. Tidal flooding can still cut the town off and residents still have cause to fear a big storm, as in 2007. From the sea, Southwold is exposed to attack. In the famous 1672 Battle of Sole Bay, many bodies were washed ashore. In the First World War, the German fleet battered the coast; in the Second World War they bombed the town, narrowly missing the church.

St. Edmund's, the fine Suffolk flint church with its magnificent porch, "whose tower protected the marshes," is one of Southwold's landmarks, standing out starkly in "the cold and clear East Anglian air." In the flinty churchyard are "the Suffolk sea-dead, midshipmen drowned at eleven years old, fishermen lost with all hands." There is also the lighthouse, unmanned since 1938, the pier (broken down in the mid-1950s from war and storm damage, and only restored in 2001) and the water tower. These days, Southwold boasts colourful beach huts, museums, elegant hotels and boutiques, a literary festival and a flourishing middle-class tourist industry—though, at the time of writing, its bookshops have all closed. But in the 1950s, the main occupations were fishing, farming, reed-cutting, manning the lifeboat, shop-keeping, teaching and working in the pubs. For light relief, you could walk over the marshes, bird-watch, take a dip in the chilly North Sea with the holidaymakers, sail, ride and drink. Adnams, the brewers, founded in 1872, owned almost all of Southwold's many pubs. In *The Bookshop,* the opening of the town's first fish-and-chip shop is a major event; there was "no launderette, no cinema except on alternate Saturday nights." The bookshop which gives the novel its name was based on the Sole Bay Bookshop, run by Mrs. Phyllis Neame, and it was indeed the only one. Walberswick, across the river, was more of an artists' colony: there were little galleries set up in old fishing warehouses, actors and painters, a bohemian atmosphere. Down the coast, the Aldeburgh Music Festival had been started by Benjamin Britten and Peter Pears in 1948; but that was miles away. Orwell had lived in Southwold as a teenager (and turned it into "Knype Hill" in *A Clergyman's Daughter*), but there were no other notable literary associations.

The beauty of its setting was—and is—incomparable. "I still miss, and shall always miss," Fitzgerald wrote in 1989, "the wide shining horizons of East Suffolk, and the sight of the rooks and the seabirds balancing themselves on boundless currents of air."[2] On a bright summer day Southwold could be enchanting. Guidebooks of the time delighted in it. Pevsner called it "one of the happiest and most picturesque seaside towns in England; happy, but not cheerful in the cheerio-sense, and picturesque, but not in the quaint sense . . . It is a live little town, and it has . . . hardly a building that is a visual nuisance." In the 1960 *Shell Guide to Suffolk,* it appears as "a most distinguished little old borough . . . a residential resort for discriminating persons." But to live in it, in foul as well as fair weather, was another matter. Huddled against its exposed sea- and marsh-scape, the town in the 1950s was inward-looking, parochial and set in its ways. In mist and darkness, wind and cold rain, it could be a strange and gloomy place. Local stories of hauntings and spooky phenomena abounded. A poltergeist plays a dramatic part in *The Bookshop,* and Fitzgerald always maintained that it was an absolutely real manifestation. She was just as matter-of-fact about other Southwold legends mentioned in the novel: "The ghost at the

Southwold–Walberswick crossing is said to be a mother waiting for her child who was supposed to be coming back on the last ferry. The white dog, which I have actually seen, was something to do with Dunwich, I think, and the poltergeist was horrid."[3]

Fitzgerald exaggerates the solitariness of the place, and deviates from historical fact only slightly, at the start of *The Bookshop*—in which Hardborough is Southwold, the Laze is the Blyth, and Saxford is Blythburgh. (In the matter of "calling names," she commented on her choice of the name "Hardborough" for Southwold, "writers have an advantage.")[4]

> The town itself was an island between sea and river, muttering and drawing into itself as soon as it felt the cold. Every fifty years or so it had lost, as though careless or indifferent to such things, another means of communication. By 1850 the Laze had ceased to be navigable and the wharfs and ferries rotted away. In 1910 the swing bridge fell in, and since then all traffic had to go ten miles round by Saxford in order to cross the river. In 1920 the old railway was closed. The children of Hardborough, waders and divers all, had most of them never been in a train. They looked at the deserted LNER station with superstitious reverence. Rusty tin strips, advertising Fry's Cocoa and Iron Jelloids, hung there in the wind.
>
> The great flood of 1953 caught the sea wall and caved it in, so that the harbour mouth was dangerous to cross, except at very low tide. A rowing-boat was now the only way to get across the Laze. The ferryman chalked up his times for the day on the door of his shed, but this was on the far shore, so that no one in Hardborough could ever be quite certain when they were.

Why did the Fitzgeralds choose Southwold? Their reasoning is never explained. They seem to have been offered a house there, presumably to rent, via their Hampstead friends the Frosts.[5] There might have been health reasons. Asthma ran in the family: Evoe, Penelope and Valpy all suffered from it, and the brisk sea air could have been an incentive. And Southwold had associations. Christina had taught at St. Felix School in Southwold before she married Evoe. Penelope had been there more than once with Valpy when he was very small, staying at the Swan Hotel. It was not an unknown destination. For the children it felt, at first, like a splendid adventure.

Their house was on the River Blyth, at the end of a long road. It was next to the Anchor Inn, near the ferry, in the part of Southwold called Blackshore. That was the name of the house, too, though it was also known as the Old Oyster Warehouse, since it had been built for that use. "It had been plastered with sea salt, which meant that it was never quite dry."[6] The tidal river came lapping into the flood-cellar (just as in the Old House in *The Bookshop*), so they lived on the first floor. Like Chestnut Lodge, Blackshore was a spacious house, and Penelope made it look stylish. There were big framed mirrors, wickerwork basket-chairs, sisal matting on the floors. As in Hampstead, her Christmas decorations, like her homemade, beautifully lit ceramic crib, were a feature.

The children went to local schools. Maria, aged five in 1958, went to Miss Bonzie's Nursery School—a room in a nice lady's house where the children painted and ate biscuits. Tina, aged eight, went to Southwold Primary. Then both girls went on the bus to the Wangford PNEU school (Parents' National Educational Union schools, known for their liberal approach to schooling and wide curriculum). Valpy went by bus to the Sir John Leman High School in Beccles for a few months. The Fitzgeralds were paying for him to have private Maths and Latin tuition, clearly with a view to a public school and university education. In July 1958, Penelope took another trip with him, away from the rest of the family. They went on a canal boat to Holland with John Shaw, Valpy's Latin tutor, his wife, and fourteen Southwold schoolboys, sailing from Harwich. It was all very outward-bound and progressive. The boys were lined up naked in the mornings and soaped, and then they dived into the canal to wash. Penelope's job, as they went around Holland, was to find somewhere for the boys to sleep "*free* every night on land, as there wasn't enough room on the boat."[7] Perhaps the escapade gave her a taste for river life.

Early in 1960, Valpy went as a boarder to Westminster School. But he came home for the holidays with the girls, and they became full-time country children, in love with boats and horses. The girls rode ponies over the marshes all day, went to gymkhanas and were out from dawn to dusk. They got chased by bullocks, fell off the front steps of the house and played by the river on their own. "The children lived like acquatic animals," Penelope remembered, "taking no harm." Valpy boated up and down the River Blyth—sometimes rowing at night with a storm lantern—and went hunting. Penelope took to country habits, making cowslip wine and pickling apples. Still, for all their free outdoor lives, she could be a strict mother. If they broke something, or were rude, or told lies, she would be angry with them. As she had been with Evoe, they were often nervous of her. Valpy came home from school once and said the shocking word "fuck," and she made him wash his mouth out with soap.[8]

As in Hampstead, she made friends locally. Phyllis Neame at the bookshop became a stalwart friend.[9] At Walberswick, there were the Fienneses and the Freuds, Clement and his family, and a striking local character called Iris Birtwistle. Iris was a bohemian grande dame, a Catholic, literature- and music-loving painter with three adopted sons, who had run away from her upper-class family and opened a gallery in Walberswick in 1950. In 1955, she acquired a seventeen-year-old au pair called Jennifer Lash, a strikingly beautiful and emotional girl whom Iris took under her wing, renamed Jini, sent to an analyst and encouraged to paint and write. Jini fell in love with an older man, a farmer and photographer, Mark Fiennes, and married him in 1962. They had six children, including the future actors Ralph and Joseph Fiennes. Jini Fiennes published novels as "Jennifer Lash." Tina, in particular, later got to know the Fienneses well, though Penelope was wary of Jini.

Iris became very fond of Penelope. Herself an expansive and dramatic person, who would suffer increasingly from blindness, she described Penelope as being like a little robin, with her ruddy complexion and unbrushed mop of reddish-blonde hair. She always looked as if she had been out all day sailing with no hat on; she was bright, alert and cheerful. Iris thought her honest, generous, extremely artistic, self-deprecating, "loyal to the bone" and heroic. She never complained, and, though she was friendly, "you never knew what she was thinking." Iris never had the slightest idea that there were any problems, and Desmond, who was very quiet when he did appear, was not mentioned in his absence. Iris also found Penelope "quite terse." Iris's gallery was an old battery-hen-house next door to her house, where she would offer all her visitors mugs of coffee at her big scrubbed pine table (those were early days for scrubbed pine). She remembered Penelope, mug of coffee in hand, being "stringent" about some of the painters. Of one deep-sea fisherman who painted in his spare time, she said: "H'm! Very *people-friendly.*" She remembered arguing with her about music. Penelope accused Iris of having "written off Mozart." "You never quite knew what she really meant."

There were also the local gentry, who at first were tremendously gracious: a Major Brookes, with a niece called Gloria, lived in Sibton Park, a grand old house in Yoxford, shabby but full of exquisite things, like hand-painted Chinese wallpaper. She invited Penelope to visit, and the girls spent a great deal of time there. Iris Birtwistle summed up the class structure of Southwold in the 1950s pithily as "meat pies and grand pianos."[10]

In 1959 Tina wrote a children's story called *Mrs. Killick's Luck* and sent it off to a *Daily Express* children's story competition, which it won. The prize was a pony, and the adjudicators and reporters came to the house to present the four-footed award to ten-year-old Christina Fitzgerald. The story was picked up by Methuen's children's series and published as a short novel in 1960, complete with misspellings, charming illustrations by Mary Knox and an introduction by Penelope's friend from *World Review* Stevie Smith, who admired its child's "sense of character . . . with such sharp eyes at work and sharp wits like little white teeth." The little book was a spirited mix of Daisy Ashford, juvenile Jane Austen, the Grossmith brothers—and Penelope Fitzgerald. It was closely based on Tina's experiences and extremely revealing about her anxieties at the time: the whole thing was about money, and what it could do for, and to, people.

It is set in a small village called Blacklebury, which is like a dysfunctional version of the idealised village in "Jassy of Juniper Farm." One particularly awful couple, Mr. and Mrs. Raton, spend the whole time quarrelling. On the first page, we hear that Mrs. Killick's husband is dead and she is very poor, and two children come to stay in her shabby rented room, without their parents.

> "Shsh Tom," said Penelope Jane, "I think I hear somebody crying." "It must be Mrs. Killick."
> "What is the matter Mrs. Killick" asked Penelope Jane.
> "Its allright" said Mrs. Killick "Ecxept that we are terribly short of money."

Luckily, the elderly Lord Eric Poshenuff (whose mansion closely resembled Sibton Park) offers her his hand in marriage, as he has a "very poty" housekeeper: "I hope you will accept. You will be dressed in splenduor with a silken apron and a feather mattress." The poty housekeeper, Mrs. Algrumbel, who lies on a sofa ignoring the sampler on the wall which reads "I am, I can, I ought, I will," leaves in a huff and goes to live with her sister-in-law in Hampstead, who does good works. "She was very religious and went to a lot of committees and it got worse as she grew older." Mrs. Killick, now Lady Poshenuff, gets above herself, "would not daign to speak to the cook," eats huge meals and insists on refurnishing the Hall: "What are we going to sit on," asks poor Lord P, "getting more and more dipressed." Tom and Penelope Jane move to stay at the pub, the Golden Horse, where Penelope Jane helps the nice publican's wife make the "sandwidges." "Don't put the fish paste on two thick, one jar has to go round

fifteen people." There is an old pony and trap. They try to visit Lady P,
but she sends them away angrily, and Penelope Jane writes a poem about it
called "Dissapointment, dissapointment." All the money Lord P keeps in
a big chest is stolen by Mrs. Algrumbel in disguise, who knows when she
can get into the Hall because the servants are always "sliping and sloping
out to the pub," where they often have "a drop too much." The children
unmask Mrs. Algrumbel and are rewarded by Lord P with ponies, "a box
of toffees and a pound note each." All ends happily: "Mrs. Raton died and
Mr. Raton had some peace at last." Mrs. Algrumbel goes to live in a bus in
a field and "earnt a living by helping in a book shop." Mary Knox's illustration has her terrifying the customers, with books flying everywhere.[11]

But at the time Tina's little book was published, everything had changed
for the worse for the Fitzgerald family. Their luck was out.

Desmond stayed in London with his mother, at Burton Court, during the week, for work, and came down to Southwold at weekends. The
children would wave him sadly goodbye at Halesworth station. Penelope
kept the Ford Consul, which she drove around Suffolk without a licence,
on one occasion into a lamp-post. Presumably Desmond was not much
in demand in Chambers after his long deviation from the law with *World
Review,* and she had no work, apart from "Jassy." The BBC commissions
had dried up. Desmond was drinking, alone in London. On their visits
home, Rawle and Helen (who had their own problems) had the impression
at this time that Desmond felt "Mops had abandoned him." They began to
have rows, every weekend, terrible rows in the kitchen about money, with
the children listening. They ran up huge bills in the Southwold grocers,
and had to avoid the shops which would no longer give them credit. They
would buy things for the house on approval, like a refrigerator, and then
send it back and get another one. The children overheard their mother,
more than once, on the phone to the bank, asking how much money there
was in the account. They spent quite a bit of their time, at weekends, sitting outside various pubs waiting for Desmond to come out.

Phyllis Neame offered Penelope some part-time work in the Sole Bay
Bookshop. This was a godsend, but it was not a financial solution. Selling
books in 1950s rural Suffolk was not easy—even more so if your shop was
haunted by a poltergeist. In interviews, she would look back on it with
feeling:

[I worked] in a bookshop in a very lonely town we were living in
on the east coast in Suffolk, sort of watery and marshy, with Con-

stable skies. A very definite place. The shop was haunted as well, which I didn't realise when I went there. I wrote about the shop and about the poltergeist, which was only part of the struggle the bookshop had against the opposition in the town to it being there at all. Not on any rational grounds, but the feeling that reading the kind of book that we sold was sort of putting on airs . . . We didn't sell *How to Improve your Sex Life Through Vegetable Cookery* because the shop was frightfully respectable, and when *Lolita* came along there was a row about whether to carry it. But we did.[12]

She would remember "the poor old Sole Bay bookshop" fondly, as more of a community refuge than a thriving commercial concern. Forty years on, it seemed to her part of a lost history of England, rather like the public libraries:

It seems like another world . . . Mrs. Neame . . . would have been horrified at the idea of on-line bookselling, and so would the customers, who thought of the shop as the one place to go on a wet day (and the weather can be very bad in Southwold). They would hang about for *hours* and go away without buying anything—except perhaps one greeting card—but we never complained, that would have been against the tradition of book-shop keeping.[13]

There were no secrets in a town like Southwold, a community "divided into friends and enemies." As she says in the novel, "Everyone could be seen coming over the wide distances and everything seen was discussed." "Everybody in the town knew . . . who was in financial straits."[14] The crash, when it came, was a public event. Early in 1959, Adnams the auctioneers (no connection to the brewers) were called in, and all the contents of Blackshore were put out on the pavement outside the house. Everything had to go. Like the flight from Hampstead, it was all done in a great hurry, and, as she remembered, painfully, "I wasn't allowed the opportunity to say what I wanted to keep from the sell-up at Blackshore, and all the things I cared about most were sold."[15] She managed, at least, to salvage the Mexican serape. With the girls, she moved into a hotel on the seafront for a few weeks, and then into a very small terraced house, nothing more than a worker's cottage, at 8 High Street, inland from the sea. They were very crowded there, and the bitter, reproachful scenes went on for months, all through 1959 and 1960. To his lasting mortification, Valpy was taken out of Westminster School after two terms, because the fees could not be paid. (Penelope's friend Stevie Smith's acid lines of 1957 come to mind: "Parents who barely can afford it / Should not send their children to public schools / ill will reward it.")[16] An arrangement was made with Desmond's old school, Downside, which had a long tradition of taking care of the Catholic sons of former Catholic pupils. Later, there was a society of Old Boys called "The Bruised Reed," who looked after "Old Gregorians" who had fallen on hard times. Valpy was accepted without fees having to be paid.[17] The smart Suffolk acquaintances fell away. There were no more visits to Sibton Park. Iris Birtwistle was staunch, and let them use her land to graze Tina's pony. Outside the little house, Penelope kept up a brave front. It was obvious to everyone who knew them that Desmond was drinking heavily. Iris said he was not the kind of drinker who got rowdy and difficult, he was the kind who got "quiet and useless." But Penelope uttered not a word about this, or their troubles. As for Desmond, whatever was going on at work, he was not saying.

She did not want to ask her family for help. Evoe was honoured in 1959 by Cambridge University, who asked him, at seventy-eight, to give the Leslie Stephen Lecture. His subject was satire, and he argued that the right spirit for the century was "self-satire, the ability to see humour in the constant small defeats of life."[18] Whether this observation was useful to his daughter is not known. But she did not want to go to him with her own "small defeats." Desmond did ask Evoe and Mary for money, without telling her, and she was appalled when she discovered this. She felt it was her job to sort out the mess they were in. She was a forty-three-year-old wife and mother with an ineffective husband, and next to no income. They had taken on too much, like many other people brought up between the wars at a certain level of comfort and gentility, who had lost direction in the war years and had to make shift for themselves afterwards, without inherited wealth and at a time of social change, yet who still kept some of the old assumptions about how they ought to live. Now it was up to her to sort things out and to make sure they all survived. Early in 1961, Tina remembered, "Mother said: we're going to move to London." It was entirely her decision.

৯০

But *The Bookshop* (her second novel, started in 1977 and published in 1978) begins with an object lesson in indecision:

In 1959 Florence Green occasionally passed a night when she was not absolutely sure whether she had slept or not. This was because of her worries as to whether to purchase a small property, the Old House, with its own warehouse on the foreshore, and to open the only bookshop in Hardborough. The uncertainty probably kept her awake. She had once seen a heron flying across the estuary and trying, while it was on the wing, to swallow an eel which it had caught. The eel, in turn, was struggling to escape from the gullet of the heron and appeared a quarter, a half, or occasionally three-quarters of the way out. The indecision expressed by both creatures was pitiable. They had taken on too much.

The opening perfectly sets up the novel's story of struggle, worry and failure, and its watery, fluid, borderland setting. The light, the air, the sky, the sea, fill the margins of the book. "The sky brightened from one horizon to the other, and the high white cloud was reflected in mile after mile of shining dyke water, so that the marshes seemed to stand between cloud and cloud." The watercolourists who come there entirely fail to capture it. "All their pictures looked much the same. Framed, they hung in sitting-rooms, while outside the windows the empty, washed-out, unarranged landscape stretched away to the transparent sky." The North Sea is destructive to humans, eroding the coast, destroying the houses built too close to the edge, a brutal indifferent force: "The tide was running out fast, pausing at the submerged rocks and spreading into yellowish foam, as though deliberating what to throw up next or leave behind, how many wrecks of ships and men, how many plastic bottles." Conditions aren't really suitable for human beings; the natural creatures (treated with great beauty and care in the novel) need all their instincts for survival, like the aged Suffolk Punch marsh-horse, "the intensely watching old beast," or the broody hen "sunk into a soft tawny heap, scarcely opening her slit-like eyes, her whole energy . . . absorbed in producing warmth."

The human plot is simple, and, except for one sentence on the last page, is set entirely in one bit of England between early 1959 and late 1960. Fitzgerald makes her fictional self, Florence Green, one of the many lonely figures to be seen in the clear cold light of Hardborough, "the observed of all observers." She has no husband anymore, no family and no children. "Life passed you by in that respect, then," says the implacable ten-year-old Christine Gipping, who comes to help in the shop, and is allowed briefly to be a surrogate daughter for Florence. It is revealing that, in 1977, when

Fitzgerald reinvented her time in Southwold, she made her heroine a solitary, childless widow, whose husband died at the beginning of the war: "I loved him, and I tried to understand his work. It sometimes strikes me that men and women aren't quite the right people for each other." Florence is "small, wispy and wiry," insignificant-looking, but not to be cowed. Like Annie Asra in *Human Voices* (or Daisy in *The Gate of Angels*), she has been self-supporting from a very young age. She feels she has a duty "to make clear to herself, and possibly to others, that she existed in her own right." Walking along Southwold's wet sand and shingle, and watching her footsteps fill up with water, she thinks, as her author thinks: "To leave a mark of any kind was exhilarating."

Florence resolves to turn the ancient, long-empty, waterlogged Old House on the foreshore into her shop. Her supporters are the marshman, Mr. Raven, one of the solitaries of the countryside, "who never asked for anything unless it was absolutely necessary"; Christine Gipping and her stoical mother; the Sea Scout boys, in particular helpful young Wally, "square and reliable as a straw-bale"; and the obscure Mr. Brundish. He is one of the last of Suffolk's old families (she took the name from a nearby village), closeted away in Holt House like a badger in his lair, but still an authority in the town. He turns out to be a kind of hermit-philosopher, not unlike Wilfred Knox, a respecter of truth and courage, asking difficult and important questions: "whether there is such a thing as an action which harms no one but oneself." His archaic family china bears a motto which contains a warning for her: *"Not to succeed in one thing is to fail in all."*

Her chief opponent, by contrast, is the queen of the local gentry, the appalling Violet Gamart. The surname echoes Balzac's wicked Mademoiselle Gamard in *Le Curé de Tours,* a novella of petty provincial conflicts which lay behind *The Bookshop.* Violet is the "natural patroness of all public activities in Hardborough," who bullies the town as she bullies her poor old husband, the General, still stuck, in his mind, in the trenches of the First World War. Mrs. Gamart's determination to run Southwold's "culture" (a hateful word to Florence) in competition with Aldeburgh and Glyndebourne, and her Machiavellian deployment of her contacts in Parliament, the law and the local authorities, is done with relish, in Fitzgerald's caustic Jane Austen vein: "From long habit, Mrs. Gamart rejected the idea that her husband might be necessary for anything." In her wake lounges the feline, charming, treacherous Milo North, a glamorous figure in Hardborough because he commutes to the BBC and has a live-in girlfriend who wears tights and drinks Nescafé. Milo is insidious and utterly unprincipled. "His fluid personality tested and stole into the weak places of others until it found it could settle down to its own advantage." Fitzgerald likes "doing" this sort of young, often gay, man: there are variants in *Human Voices, The Golden Child* and *Offshore*. Milo, in this severely ethical novel, is a particularly harshly judged version of the type.

As a funny novel about selling books in 1950s Suffolk, *The Bookshop* is a joyous exercise in precise, eloquent detail. Here, Florence is setting out her stock in an order that reflects the class structure of the country. It was from Phyllis Neame that Fitzgerald learned all this. In her notes for the novel, Florence is called Mrs. Neame and the working title is "Mrs. Neame's Dream."[19]

> As she sorted them out, they fell into their own social hierarchy. The heavy luxurious country-house books, the books about Suffolk churches, the memoirs of statesmen in several volumes, took the place that was theirs by right of birth in the front window. Others, indispensable, but not aristocratic, would occupy the middle shelves. That was the place for the Books of the Car—from Austin to Wolseley—technical works on pebble-polishing, sailing, pony clubs, wild flowers and birds, local maps and guide books. Among these the popular war reminiscences, in jackets of khaki and blood-red, faced each other as rivals with bristling hostility. Back in the shadows went the Stickers, largely philosophy and poetry, which she had little hope of ever seeing the last of. The Stayers—dictionaries, reference books and so forth—would go straight to the back . . . She opened one or two . . . old Everyman editions in faded olive boards stamped with gold. There was the elaborate endpaper which she had puzzled over when she was a little girl. *A good book is the precious lifeblood of a master spirit, embalmed and treasured up on purpose to a life beyond life.* After some hesitation, she put it between Religion and Home Medicine.

Fitzgerald enjoys herself with the comedy of the bookshop's customers, competing ferociously for their favourite title, like the fishmonger demanding his vocal score of the *Messiah* ("I'd have thought you would have a thing like that in stock. Handel's *Messiah* is sung every Christmas, you know"), or the Sea Scout "who came in every day after school to read another chapter of *I Flew with the Führer*. He marked the place with a piece of string weighted down with a boiled sweet." Like Balzac, she is specific about all the sums of money involved: £3,500 for the freehold of the Old House, 12s. 6d the average price of a book (and Christine's weekly wage), 1s. 6d for a paperback, a turnover of £70 to £80 on her first week, £2,500 worth of stock-in-hand and a capital of £3,000, after nine months.

In this context of scrupulous book-keeping, minute comic detail and intense evocation of place and time, the irruption of Florence's most alarming opponent, the "rapper," is entirely convincing. The matter-of-fact way that all the locals accept the reality of the poltergeist which inhabits the Old House ("Your rapper's been at my adjustable spanners," said the plumber), and the malign physical presence it emanates, make it as plausible a force as the sea or the wind. It comes at the house at night, when she is sitting inside with Christine, both trying not to show fear, in one of the strangest and most violent scenes in Fitzgerald's work. The woman and the girl make common cause against it.

> The noise upstairs stopped for a moment and then broke out again, this time downstairs and apparently just outside the window, which shook violently. It seemed to be on the point of bursting inwards . . . There was a wild rattling as though handful after handful of gravel or shingle was being thrown by an idiot against the glass.
>
> "That's the rapper. My mam knows there's a rapper in this old place. She reckoned that wouldn't start with me, because mine haven't come on yet."
>
> The battering at the window died to a hiss; then gathered itself together and rose to a long animal scream, again and again.
>
> "Don't mind it, Christine," Florence called out with sudden energy.
>
> "We know what it can't do."
>
> "That doesn't want us to go," Christine muttered. "That wants us to stay and be tormented."
>
> They were besieged.

Sometimes in Fitzgerald's work there is a haunting, or the suggestion of a miracle, or an inexplicable event, insinuated into the carefully woven realistic world of the novel. This is the nearest she gets in her fiction to making clear her belief that there are things beyond our control or which we might have to accept without understanding. The poltergeist is the most dramatic and hostile of these irruptions into everyday life. Florence would have liked to ask the Vicar whether it is an example of what William Blake means when he says that "everything possible to be believed in was an image of Truth"—that even the most malignant phenomena might be a way of testing faith. But between running the flower-arranging rota and the fund-raising, she doesn't think the Vicar will be much use.

The crisis for Florence Green comes out of her decision (as Mrs. Neame decided) to sell large numbers of copies of the latest literary sensation, *Lolita,* in the bookshop. This bold modern gesture proves to be the comical turning-point in her fortunes, and—in spite of some surprising support from old Mr. Brundish—she is driven out by a combination of legal pressure, a compulsory-purchase order and the setting up of a rival bookshop in the next town, all the ruthless work of Violet Gamart, abetted by Milo's treachery. Fitzgerald doesn't choose to say anything about the sexual content of *Lolita* and whether it shocked the Hardborough readers—and, in general, sexuality is played down in *The Bookshop,* though not ignored. Christine knows that it's adolescent, menstruating girls who are usually vulnerable to poltergeists; Wally the Scout thinks that Hansel and Gretel are an incestuous brother and sister, like a lot of the families he knows. But the saucy title of the French translation of *The Bookshop, L'Affaire Lolita,* was misleading. The point about Florence's stocking *Lolita* is not so much that it is scandalous but that it pinpoints the exact point in time when the 1950s turn into the 1960s. Fitzgerald likes to set her books on the cusp of change. Christine uses a jacket of *Lolita* for her fancy-dress costume: she calls her costume "Goodbye, 1959."

The Bookshop uses its small-scale comic plot for a serious moral argument. Florence, even in middle age, is naive. She believes that success must reward effort, and that if you tell the truth and try hard you will prevail. She is sensitive to beauty, and allows herself to be weakened by this—as when buying two hundred unsellable hand-painted silk Chinese bookmarks, just because she likes looking at them. She values kindness above everything. But most of these principles are proved to be ineffectual or self-deceiving. A more ruthless survival of the fittest is really what prevails. Machiavelli, Hobbes or Nietzsche should have been Florence's mentors, not Ruskin or William Blake: "She blinded herself . . . by pretending for a while that human beings are not divided into exterminators and exterminatees, with the former, at any given moment, predominating." This message, given more forcefully and directly in *The Bookshop* than anywhere else in Fitzgerald's work, is something she repeated, all her life, in her own voice.

The moral questions raised by *The Bookshop* are not abstract, but carefully tied to the political and social world which the novel describes. Florence tries to take on "the establishment," and suffers the consequences. The place she is trying to operate in, like most places in England after the war, is based on a long-maintained class structure. The ruling classes will always stick together: "They were all of the same kind, facing one way, grazing together. Between themselves they could arrange many matters." If you are not part of them, you can be a parasite, or fight them, or go under, or accept your status as an outsider.

These class divisions start at the beginning of life—what family you are born into, how much money you have, where you live, how you are educated. The one chance for many 1950s children to move up or out from where they were fixed was the eleven-plus exam. The most poignant episode in the book is Christine's failure to pass it, and the effect that has on her. Everyone in Hardborough knows that there is an utter, life-long division between those who pass and those who fail. On this subject, Christine's mother is given the most eloquent speech in the book. It speaks for the 1950s class structure of post-war rural England, and the average working woman's life: "She's the first of ours not to get to the Grammar. It's what we call a death sentence. I've nothing against the Technical, but it just means this: what chance will she ever have of meeting and marrying a white-collar chap? She won't ever be able to look above a labouring chap or even an unemployed chap and believe me, Mrs. Green, she'll be pegging out her own washing until the day she dies." "What is natural justice?" is Florence's last question to her solicitors.

Fitzgerald said of this novel that she wanted its small story to have a larger political resonance. In her notebooks to *The Bookshop* she wrote down:

Out of the ability to govern and the desire not to be governed . . . comes whole achievement of English nation.

And, from *Le Curé de Tours:*

Cette tempête dans un verre d'eau . . . développait néanmoins dans les âmes autant de passions qu'il en aurait fallu pour digner les plus grands intérêts sociaux." (This storm in a teacup developed, nevertheless, in the souls [of those involved], as violent passions as those excited by the greatest concerns.)[20]

At the sad end of the novel, Florence leaves Hardborough, with dark feelings of shame and failure, and nothing to show for her efforts. At least she has validated one of her beliefs—that "courage and endurance are useless if they are never tested"; though "her courage, after all, was only a determination to survive." And we are allowed, on the last page, one glimpse of a world elsewhere. The two books Florence takes with her, both Everymans (*A good book is the precious lifeblood of a master spirit, embalmed and treasured up on purpose to a life beyond life*), are Ruskin's *Unto This Last,* his powerful mid-nineteenth-century polemic on the true value of human labour and the dignity of the ordinary working man, and Bunyan's *Grace Abounding.* "The Ruskin had a pressed gentian, quite colourless. The book must have gone, perhaps fifty years before, to Switzerland in springtime." When it was picked, the gentian would have been a blue flower.

CHAPTER SEVEN

Clinging On for Dear Life

*"It's his own fault if he's kind. It's not the kind who inherit the earth,
it's the poor, the humble, and the meek."*
 "What do you think happens to the kind, then?"
 "They get kicked in the teeth."[1]

In 1960, Penelope Fitzgerald, aged forty-three, took her family back to
London and set up house offshore. This is how she describes the move,
nearly thirty years later:

> At the beginning of the Sixties we had to go back to London, and
> not being able to find a house that we could afford, we settled for
> a boat; it was moored on Chelsea Reach, between Battersea Bridge
> and Albert Bridge, so that we were in one of the very grandest
> parts of London. On the other hand, we were living on an old
> wooden barge which for many years had carried cargoes [of coal]
> up and down the east coast under sail, but was now a battered,
> patched, caulked, tar-blackened hulk, heaving up with difficulty
> on every rising tide. Her name was *Grace,* and she had never been
> fitted with an engine, so that there was plenty of room for us in
> the huge belly of the hold. There was a very old stove, in which we
> burned driftwood. Driftwood will only light when it has paint or
> tar on it, and we knew its bitter fragrance well from the foreshore
> at Southwold, just as we were used to a more or less permanent
> state of damp and to the voices, at first light, of the seagulls. Now
> we had to get used to the movement of *Grace,* rocking on the high
> tide, and the echoing wail of the hooters from the passing colliers
> on their way to the Port of London.
> *Grace* was anchored next to the wharf, so that she was the
> first of a long line of lived-in craft—barges, landing craft, and
> one minesweeper. They were connected by a series of gangplanks
> which were anything but safe, so that the postman and the milk-

man had, very sensibly, refused to go on delivering. There were other drawbacks, too—the boat owners were only allowed to let out wastewater, and to use the lavatories, on a falling tide. Our great consolation was that a Thames barge, because of the camber of the deck, never sinks completely.[2]

She would always be irritated when people referred to or represented *Grace* as "a trim houseboat in a backwater," "whereas she had served an honourable career at sea and still had part of her mast—the only trouble was that she was beyond repair."[3]

Fitzgerald made very good use, eventually, of this experience. Her third novel, *Offshore,* published in 1979, a fictional version of life on board the barge, dedicated "To Grace, and all who sailed in her," won the Booker Prize and made her name. When, in later life, she reminisced about her two years on the boat, she would make a dramatic, fascinating story out of it. But in reality this was a bleak, difficult and dangerous time for the Fitzgeralds. The untranslated epigraph for *Offshore*—"*che mena il vento, e che batte la pioggia / e che s'incontran con sì aspre lingue*"—referring to the souls in Book XI of Dante's *Inferno* "whom the wind drives, or whom the rain beats, or who clash with such bitter tongues," invokes all the desperation of their life on board.

For a few weeks, when they left Suffolk, they stayed at Burton Court while she looked for an affordable place to live. (Tom Fitzgerald, Desmond's father, died in 1959. Tina retained a faint memory of walking down the King's Road with her grandfather to buy some lamb cutlets, and of him sitting, unwell, in a huge armchair listening to his ancient wireless, built like a piece of furniture.) Penelope sometimes said that they bought the barge, but her children insist that this was not the case. She never bought a piece of property in her life, she never had a mortgage: according to her daughters, she hardly knew what a mortgage was. Sometimes she would say that they rented *Grace* for £1 a week. Whatever the exact rent, it was the cheapest way of moving back to central London in the early 1960s. And the bohemian in her liked the romantic idea of life on a boat.

But living on the boat was no gypsy-like idyll—in fact, as Willie Conder observed, the barge was much more uncomfortable than a caravan. It was exceptionally cold in the winter of 1962–63, their second winter on board *Grace,* a terrible white-out with freezing blizzards. The boat was always chilly and damp: "rough, cold, grim, wet," as Tina remembered it. *Grace* was insanitary, bleak and unsafe. "A total disaster area," in Valpy's view.[4]

The big black tarred hulk with its stump of a mast, "fifteen foot of blackened pine," sat on its flat bottom on the stinking mudflats of the Thames at low tide, and started to leak as the tide rose. It was always on a slope. Every time the tide went out, the boat sank slightly to one side, and all the cupboards jammed—the girls had to remember to get out everything they needed, like their school uniforms, while the tide was up. They got onto the barge by going through the iron gate on the Embankment just west of Battersea Bridge, down the ladder to the wobbly gangplanks that connected one boat to the other and in through the door at the bow end, nearest the wharf. Or they could jump across from the side of the next-door boat and walk round the edge of the barge, with a low rail only on one side, to the narrow door at the wide stern of the boat, the end furthest from the shore. This rocking, slippery walk was an acquired skill.

At the bow end was the bedroom shared by the girls, who were often woken up at night by Desmond, making his way late and drunk through their room to his bedroom next door. There was a high-sided bath. They had to pump water in from the river to make the lavatories work. In the middle of the boat there was a living room on one side, with a Belling electric fire (a backup for the wood-burning stove), a few chairs and a wireless, where the girls remembered sitting down to *Children's Hour* and *Listen with Mother*. Jean Fisher, on one of her visits, found, to her horror, the girls toasting bread on an electric fire turned upside down on the damp floor. ("We had much anxiety over what went on," she said.) There were frequent electricity failures. Penelope slept in the living room on a single day-bed. From this time onwards, she and Desmond never slept together. What grew out of conflict and disappointment turned into habit. For the rest of her life she would not have a bedroom of her own, but would sleep in a bed that turned into a sofa in a sitting room. She would be up before anyone else and fastidiously tidied her bed away, so that the room did not look like a bedroom, and she would go to bed after everyone else.

Across from the living room there was a dining room with a built-in, tip-up red Formica-topped table with benches around it, but they only used it when there were visitors. Mostly they ate on chairs in the living room, and the tip-up table made space for a bed when Valpy came home from school. At the end further from the shore was a galley kitchen with Calor gas rings. There was never very much to eat, and the girls were not allowed to help themselves to food. They didn't have any lunch money.

They lived off fried potatoes, fried eggs, toast. The potatoes had to be carefully divided up at dinner. There was fruit. There was a stew that came out of a tin, called "Morning Song Stew," and they often had that. They had no oven and no clothes washer. In between the kitchen and the living room there was a dip in the floor where a pool of water collected at every high tide and had to be bailed out. The wooden bung that let the water out then had to be hammered back in. When the tide went down, a permanent muddy swamp was left on the floor. Desmond went down into the river mud up to his waist most days, to patch up the boat to stop it sinking. They had a scrawny ship's cat, which lived in perpetual terror of the huge Thames water rats.

They often used the public baths in the King's Road, where they would be issued with rough towels and a bar of soap; the bath was in a cubicle, and the water supply was limited. *Grace*'s address was 106 Cheyne Walk, now a luxurious and expensive neighbourhood, but in the early 1960s the beautiful Chelsea Embankment houses rubbed shoulders with a shabby, deprived area of London. The barge sat at Chelsea Wharf just at the point where Cheyne Walk turned into Lots Road. Lots Road Power Station loomed over it; across on the south side of the river you could glimpse the spire of St. Mary's Church, Battersea. The office for the boats, Dakins Yard, where they picked up the post, was a small shabby enclosure with a few sheds and a wooden fence. Rent was paid to the Chelsea Boat Company at the other end of the moorings, and Tina would be sent to run up with the payments. *Grace* was moored opposite Dartrey Walk, a row of old slum tenement buildings, now long demolished. At the other end of Dartrey Walk (Partisan Street in the novel) was the King's Road, five minutes from the boat and a world away, where the "swinging Sixties" were just getting going. The big tower blocks of World's End had not yet been built. Hidden away through a side entrance between Chelsea Wharf and the King's Road was—and is—the "peaceful garden where the faithful of the Moravian sect lie buried," tenderly mentioned in the novel.

When they first moved to London, Penelope sent Tina and Maria, now aged eleven and eight, to the French Lycée in South Kensington, which Maria hated, but this only lasted a few terms—presumably they couldn't pay the fees—and for a while, between 1961 and 1962, they had no schooling. In the summer of 1962 they went to Our Lady of Sion school and then to the Catholic London Oratory in Kensington—Maria to the primary school, Tina to the main school. But they spent much of their time left alone on the boat or running wild. Like the girls in *Offshore,* Mar-

tha and Tilda, they would scavenge and mudlark, finding De Morgan tiles
and other treasures on the shore, running and climbing between the boats,
making up games and adventures, reading in the Chelsea Public Library
and roaming round their favourite places in this part of London—the
Embankment, Albert Bridge, the leftover amusements from the Festival
of Britain in Battersea Park. They would sell sweets, go carol-singing,
beg for a penny for the Guy. For days on end they went unwatched and
unsupervised, often cold and on the edge of hungry, but taking this raga-
muffin life for granted.

Valpy, meanwhile, aged fourteen, was at his well-appointed, respectable boarding school, Downside. On his holidays, he sometimes brought
his school-friends home to the boat. (One visitor, a smart Austrian boy,
was used for a character in *Offshore*.) But he found the whole set-up morti-
fying and chaotic; and he was a teenage boy, inevitably growing away from
the family. When he came to read *Offshore,* he found it interesting that he
did not feature in the novel.[5]

All this while, family outings and holidays did continue. Tina's and
Maria's ponies were still in Southwold, and Desmond took the girls back
there to stay in a caravan or a B&B for weekends and short holidays. After
a time, Jini and Mark Fiennes took over the care of the ponies, and Tina
grew very close to Jini, whose family provided a comforting and welcoming
bolt-hole for her. Penelope went to Germany with Valpy to visit Rawle, and
took a couple of trips to Spain, also with Valpy. The second of these trips
was to Córdoba, at Easter 1962, where she enrolled on a Spanish-language-
for-foreigners course. This would, later, have unexpected consequences.

Worried friends—Jean Fisher, Willie Conder, Helen Knox, Iris
Birtwistle—visited occasionally, though on the whole Penelope kept them
at bay. They brought helpful gifts, like woolly hats and scarves, but didn't
like, or weren't allowed, to ask how and why the family had come to this.
To a degree they thought living on a barge a characteristically adventurous
and original thing for the Fitzgeralds to have done. But they could also see
that things were very difficult. Janet Probert remembered going to lunch
there, not having seen Penelope for a while. They ate hard-baked biscuits
with watercress and cream cheese. As she was leaving, Desmond turned up
on the quay, on his way to collect the girls from the Lycée. There was an
unease between them; it seemed clear to Janet that they were not getting
on well. How could things have gone so wrong for her friend? she asked
herself.[6] Looking back, the children were equally amazed. Why did she put
the family there, in these conditions? Why didn't she ask for help? How
could they have become so poor?

Evidently Penelope was determined to keep the ship afloat herself. She was a Knox, she was a Hicks. Knoxes and Hickses, on the whole (Ronnie had been an exception), did not believe in luxury or comfort; they prided themselves on their independence, on their stoicism, on living on their wits. (The last generation was dwindling: Winifred Peck, still writing books in her nursing home, died in 1962; now only Evoe was left.) She refused to complain to her friends. She would not go for help to her father or her stepmother; she could not depend on Desmond. She knew—had known since they left Chestnut Lodge and the *World Review* folded—that Desmond was a failure. He was kind and devoted to her and the children. But he was not earning enough for the housekeeping; his professional life was going nowhere; he was spending money on drink. Her son was away at school; inevitably, his close childhood intimacy with his mother was shifting, and she found his absence painful. Her job was to keep things going for the girls. So, from 1960, when they moved onto the boat, she started teaching: first at the Italia Conti stage school in Clapham and, from 1962, at Queen's Gate School in Kensington and at Westminster Tutors. For very many years, teaching was her day job and her main source of income. She was always tired.

To Tina and Maria she seemed fraught and bad-tempered; they realised later she was under great stress. They squabbled and fought a lot, as sisters do, in their shared room, and Penelope would be irritable with them. She would fly off the handle easily, and they would try to avoid bothering her. Sometimes they would find her eating blackboard chalk from a packet— "I feel I need it," she said. Perhaps she was worried by the calcium deficiency in their diet. But, looking back, the girls felt that there was something odd in her behaviour then. She was "at her wits' end." So was Desmond. The children remembered going to the courts with him, and his meeting them from school, but for long periods of time he was away—perhaps working in circuit courts, perhaps staying at Burton Court, they didn't know. When they did see him, he was unhappy, adrift, often drunk. He was never violent or aggressive, but he was spending money foolishly. He would come home loaded with presents, guilt-offerings, toys from Hamleys which they did not want. One night he came back drunk, started to walk round the edge of the barge, lost his footing and fell. The tide was low and rising, he struck his head and gashed it open, and landed in the mud and the garbage. It was amazing that he was not killed. Penelope heard the thud, and called an ambulance. Desmond was taken to St. George's Hospital at Hyde Park Corner. In the morning she told the children he was in hospital, but they weren't allowed into the ward to see him. He had cracked his skull, wore a huge bandage for weeks, and thereafter had a scar and a dent in his head.

A disconcerting piece from 1989 looks back with unusual candour on this phase in her life, and on how she used it in *Offshore:*

> A few years ago we were living on a Thames barge, and on the boat next door lived an elegant young male model. He saw that I was rather down in the dumps, a middle-aged woman shabbily dressed and tired, and he took me on a day out to the sea, to Brighton. We went on all the rides and played all the slot machines. We walked for a while on the beach, then caught an open-top bus along the front. What happiness!
>
> A few days later he went back to Brighton, by himself, and walked into the sea until it had closed over his head and he drowned. But when I made him a character in one of my books, I couldn't bear to let him kill himself. That would have meant that he had failed in life, whereas, really, his kindness made him the very symbol of success in my eyes.
>
> I am drawn [she goes on immediately] to people who seem to have been born defeated or, even, profoundly lost.[7]

The word "failure" is placed at the start of *Offshore,* when the boat-dwellers are being described: "A certain failure, distressing to themselves, to be like other people, caused them to sink back, with so much else that drifted or was washed up, into the mud moorings of the great tideway." Looking back on the novel, she regretted that "the title was translated into various European languages with words meaning 'far away' or 'far from the shore,' which meant the exact opposite of what I intended. By 'offshore' I meant to suggest the boats at anchor, still in touch with the land, and also the emotional restlessness of my characters, halfway between the need for security and the doubtful attraction of danger. Their indecision is a kind of reflection of the rising and falling tide, which the craft at anchor must, of course, follow."[8]

That liminal uncertainty seeps through the whole book. It performs a balancing act between being enclosed and being at risk, between comic lightness and tragic depth, between the short term and the long haul. The specialised rules and habits of the riverboat community are seen as fragile defences against chaos and danger. They provide what most attracts her imagination, "closed situations that created their own story out of the twofold need to take refuge and to escape, and which provided their own limitations."[9]

Almost everything in *Offshore* is ambivalent. The world it describes is temporary and makeshift. The heroine Nenna James's first words are "I wish I knew the exact time." She answers most questions with yes and with no, or with "I don't know." She is partly married, partly not; half respectable, half bohemian; half Canadian, half English; part Catholic, part sceptical. She accuses herself of deliberate unkindness, and also tells herself: "I don't do anything deliberately." She would like to "ebb and flow without volition." She puts off the single obvious course of action open to her, to seek out her estranged husband, because to act decisively would be to close down her last chance: "While I've still got it I can take it out and look at it and know I still have it." Her two girls, Martha (aged twelve) and Tilda, or Mattie (aged six), are partly childish and innocent, partly grown-up beyond their years. At the turning-point of the story for Nenna, "reality seemed to have lost its accustomed hold, just as the day wavered uncertainly between night and morning."

Everything is betwixt and between. Even the date of the book's setting wobbles, perhaps intentionally, between 1961, 1962 and 1963.[10] Though the boat-people live on Battersea Reach, within a few minutes' walk of the King's Road and its hippy boutiques, trendy fashion and new music, reached via the slums of Partisan Street, they are "creatures neither of firm land nor water," and all have mixed motives for being offshore.

She sets them all up with deftness and speed in the first pages. Richard Blake is the "skipper," the natural commander, the kind of man who wears a smart blazer at all times and "who has two clean handkerchiefs on him at half past three in the morning." Unlike all the other boat-people, he is gainfully employed in an office on shore. His temperament and his war service in the Navy make duty his watchword: "Duty is what no one else will do at the moment." Yet Richard's reasons for living on the river are obscure. His resentful, "shires-bred" wife, Laura, is longing to live in a nice country house in somewhere like Norfolk. The river speaks "to his dreaming rather than his daytime self." Evidently living there has to do with his experiences in the war—which shadows the whole book—but this is not discussed. He cannot explain his own motives. His romanticism is invoked in the name of his houseboat, *Lord Jim*.

Beside him, the rest of the river-people are a "ramshackle assembly," particularly Maurice, clearly based on the "elegant young male model" who lived next door to *Grace*. He is a homosexual prostitute with some shady friends. He picks up his clients in the local pub and his boat is used to store their stolen goods. He is drawn to excess and excitement, so as to drown out loneliness. But he has a gift for intimacy, and stays up half the night with Nenna, talking about "sex, jealousy, friendship and music." This seedy, unmoored urban character is imagined with affection and tolerance. He often speaks for the novelist.

> There isn't one kind of happiness, there's all kinds. Decision is torment for anyone with imagination. When you decide, you multiply the things you might have done and now never can. If there's even one person who might be hurt by a decision, you should never make it. They tell you, make up your mind or it will be too late, but if it's really too late, we should be grateful. You know very well that we're two of the same kind, Nenna. It's right for us to live where we do, between land and water.

Nenna's failed marriage to Edward James is hovering between land and water, rescue and disaster. Edward is sulking in a remote flat in Stoke Newington, which she refuses to visit. But "all distances are the same to those who don't meet." Their stupid quarrel plays out in her head, in the form of "a kind of perpetual magistrate's hearing," in which she is the accused, Edward is the plaintiff and her conscience "holds a watching brief." "Mrs. James. Do you like your husband?" . . . "Have you made any effort to go and see the plaintiff, Mrs. James?" . . . "You are very dependent on praise, Mrs. James." . . . "You could be described as an obstinate bitch?"

Nenna is angry with Edward because he won't "give." She wants to be looked after and made much of, as she was as a little girl, boating on Bras d'Or Lake in Nova Scotia with her father. She does not like living alone, as she explains to Richard and Laura in a comically heartfelt speech. "I can't do the things that women can't do . . . I can't turn over *The Times* so that the pages lie flat, I can't fold up a map in the right creases, I can't draw corks, I can't drive in nails straight, I can't go into a bar and order a drink without wondering what everyone's thinking about it, and I can't strike matches towards myself . . . There's a number of much more essential things that I know how to do, but I can't do those ones, and when they come up I feel like weeping myself sick."

When Nenna finally goes in search of Edward, the meeting is as painfully disappointing as the novel leads us to expect. Setting out on the long journey to Stoke Newington with her cheap one-day ticket, changing from bus to bus, she gets at last to 32B Milvain Street, where she encounters, not Edward, but the gloomy, "heavy-treading" Gordon, son of Edward's nosy, hostile landlady, whose mother's house Edward is living in. These two are wonderfully dismal apparitions. Nenna tries to persuade Edward to come home with her, but the old quarrels flare up, about money, about *Grace,* about his work ("I'm not going to pretend anything about my job. It's clerical"). There is a love scene of sorts, down on the floor, Nenna clinging onto Edward for dear life, scorched by "Gordon's mother's horrible gasfire," to the accompaniment downstairs of Gordon playing along to a record of Chopin, "always two or three notes behind." Then Edward turns on her "and once again a trial seemed to be in progress, with both of them as accusers, but both featuring also as investigators of the lowest description . . . And the marriage that was being described was different from the one they had known, indeed bore almost no resemblance to it, and there was no-one to tell them this." "You're not a woman!" he shouts at her. Nenna rushes out weeping, leaving her purse and her ticket behind, and becomes a fugitive in a nightmare, who can only pray: "Prayer should be beyond self, and so Nenna repeated a Hail Mary for everyone in the world who was lost in Kingsland Road without their bus fares." She asks herself, what would Tilda do?

Nenna is extremely dependent on her daughters, who often seem more competent and independent than she is. The two girls, like all Fitzgerald's children, are entirely convincing. Martha is the worrier, efficient and anxious, "armed at all points against the possible disappointments of her life." She is long past the moment "when children realise that their parents are younger than they are." A convent-educated child, like her mother, she has an exaggerated sense of sin and an expectation that life brings unhappiness. She has one moment of ordinary teenage pleasure towards the end of the book (with a charming visiting boy from Vienna, who briefly brings into this very English novel a little glimpse of Europe). And the two girls are, in a way, normal sixties children, clutching their records and photos of Cliff and Elvis, devoted to *Dr. Kildare* on the TV. Tilda, though, is odder than most six-year-olds. "Waterproof," mud-caked, wellington-booted, she is a child of the river, a water sprite or "daemon from the depths." Stripey, their dreadful river-cat, is her familiar. In her fantasies she is an adventuring boy setting out alone for the high seas. She is also unbiddable, opportunist, interfering and a ruthless mimic. She knows how to get out of danger—and there are real dangers out there, like an encounter with a violent, sexually threatening criminal. This is not a gentle book. Tilda knows that it's "the kind who get kicked in the teeth."

The girls' solidarity, true of most children of separated parents, is touchingly done: "Between the sisters there was love of a singularly pure kind, proof against many trials." The scene where they go scavenging on the mudflats on the Surrey side from the wreck *Small Gains* (the best anyone can hope for in this book), find two beautiful De Morgan tiles, take them to a disreputable antique shop on the King's Road and get £3 for them, a fortune to spend in Woolworth's, is one of the novel's most entrancing set-pieces.

Tilda has a comprehensive knowledge of all river-craft, tide times, flag markings and boat signals. Martha worries that "with so much special-ised knowledge" she would be qualified for "nothing much except a pilot's licence." But Martha also believes that "everything you learn is useful." And Tilda's knowledge is useful to the reader, as well as funny, as it pro-vides one kind of language, a detailed, technical one, for the boats and the river, the novel's dominant characters. The language of painting is used, too. Tilda and the marine artist Willis visit the Tate (a disreputable pair, closely watched by the gallery attendant) to look at the Thames paintings by Whistler and Turner. Tilda criticises them for inaccuracies, but Willis puts her right: "Whistler was a very good painter . . . There's Old Battersea Bridge. That was the old wooden bridge. Painted on a grey ground, you see, to save himself trouble. Tide on the turn, lighter taking advantage of the ebb."

Fitzgerald daringly infiltrates a whole paragraph of Whistler's famous 1885 lecture "Ten O'Clock" into Nenna's mind. The prosecutor in her head asks her if she knows Whistler's description of the time "when evening mist clothes the riverside with poetry, as with a veil, and the poor buildings lose themselves in the dim sky, and the tall chimneys become campanili, and the warehouses are palaces in the night, and the whole city hangs in the heavens, and fairyland is before us." There are other kinds of grand lan-guage sounding through this plain-spoken, low-key novel. A curate visits the barge to complain about the girls' irregular attendance at their convent school. ("Ma, it's the kindly old priest," bellows Tilda.) This allows in a solemn biblical note: "You've decided to make your dwelling place upon the face of the waters," he says. All through, the sound of the water, the changing tides, the light, the smell, the air, the wind, the feel of living on the Thames, is invoked with a mysterious, melancholy eloquence. One of her notes to herself in the manuscript of *Offshore* sums up the mood she wanted to invoke: "Slack tide, calm, knocking sound on boatside, peace, it doesn't matter when & how sordidly you live, happiness."

The magical moment of the changing tide is conjured up, when "the Thames had turned towards the sea," and the moment as night falls when "the darkness seems to rise from the river to make it one with the sky." We hear the groaning of the old boats as they stir and long "to put out once again into mid-stream." Maurice and Nenna think of the Thames, in a faint echo of Eliot's *Four Quartets* ("I think that the river / Is a strong brown god—sullen, untamed and intractable") as "a powerful god, bearded with the white foam of detergents, calling home the twenty-seven lost rivers of London, sighing as the night declined." This is a pagan god. The river's edge is where Virgil's ghosts "held out their arms in longing for the further shore."

Conventional religion does play a part in this book, but it is not of much help. Tilda and Martha, innately musical children, can sound like angels singing the night-time prayer of the two lost children in *Hansel and Gretel,* taught them by the nuns (*"Abends wenn wir schlafen geh'n"* . . . "When I lay me down to sleep, fourteen angels watch do keep . . .") But a Catholic education, here, mainly leads to a burdensome sense of guilt and sin. It is the natural power of the river which prevails, or the kindness of ordinary human beings, like the taxi driver who rescues Nenna from the Kingsland Road in the middle of the night, and takes her safely home. Perhaps he did come in answer to her prayer.

In the anxious lives of these characters, everyone is vaguely hoping for better things, "small gains," what Nenna thinks of longingly as "melting ice-floes." After her terrible scene with Edward, she spends one night on the river with Richard, very touchingly and quietly done. There is no future in this, though. Everything we are reading about is going to be swept away. A sense of transience gathers towards the end. We see the colourful "riot of misrule" in the King's Road, "a paradise for children," "fated to last only a few years, before the spell was broken." A note of regretful nostalgia creeps in: the decrepit, Dickensian brick houses of Partisan Street, "the refuge of crippled and deformed humanity," are going to be "swept away and replaced by council flats with rents much higher than they could afford." The characters and boats we have become fond of are all under threat. *Dreadnought* sinks, and is filled with the "unmistakable dead man's stench of river water." It is one of many violent moments in the novel: a horrifying drowning, a sexual assault, a homicidal attack. Several times we think that a character has been killed. For all her gentle manner, Fitzgerald does violence, fear and cruelty unblinkingly.

By the end we know they are all going to leave. The wounded Richard will be taken away by Laura from the river to their country home. Nenna and the girls will go to live with her bossy older sister and her rich husband in Nova Scotia. The book breaks up and dissolves—rather than concluding—in a catastrophic, exhilarating storm, in which the two truly hopeless and incompetent characters, Maurice and Edward, are swept away, very drunk, into the darkness, "clinging on for dear life."

Her original plans for the ending were more explicitly tragic. One note reads: "Last chapter. Maurice has already drowned himself. His boat goes down in the storm." Another: "End. Husband to fall into the mud & cries not heard, boats sail away."[11] It is what could easily have happened to Desmond. There is a thick layer of autobiography in *Offshore*. As with the other novels which draw on her own experiences, she uses her memories at once very closely, and very loosely. But of all of them, *Offshore* has the most painful look of writing salvaged from personal anguish, translated into fiction long after the event. Edward looks at Nenna with eyes that are "without much expectation from life." When he tells her that he can't get a job, she "realized in terror that he was right and that he would never get anywhere." Contemplating life without him, she tells Richard that she "feels unemployed . . . I don't know what I'm going to think about if I'm not going to worry about him all the time." The mixture of pity, shame, exasperation, hopelessness and anxiety seems to re-enact Penelope's feelings about Desmond from that time. She would often apply to herself Nenna's litany of complaints about living alone without a man. Asked once whether Nenna's bringing up the children alone on the barge was autobiographical, she said yes. Her children, as adults, would note the fictional accuracy of the absent husband, and of there being two daughters and no son in the novel. In the manuscript, the girls are called Tina and Maria; she had to keep reminding herself to change their names.[12]

But in life, Penelope's silence on the subject of Desmond's failure was almost impenetrable. She buried the catastrophe, she refused to complain to her friends, and she barely spoke of it, even—or least of all—to her children.

They all knew that there was hardly any money coming in and that Desmond was drinking (and smoking) heavily. Valpy remembered him at that time as "alcoholic and rambling." Tony Babington, a criminal lawyer in the Middle Temple (a remarkable man who had been shot and paralysed in the war and went on to have a distinguished career as a judge), remembered him being drunk in court, and thought him "terribly feckless."[13] But the family did not realise quite how desperate he was. He was trying to get hold of money however he could. He was going to old friends for loans. Bob Conquest, then living in a basement flat in south London where Desmond used occasionally to visit, could see that he was "under the weather," but couldn't afford to lend him anything.[14]

Early in 1962, the second year on the barge, Desmond began to steal from his Chambers. Solicitors' cheques came to the barristers in the Chambers as payment for work done. Desmond intercepted the cheques made out to his colleagues, took them to the nearest pub, countersigned them with the colleague's forged signature and pocketed the cash, either for drink, or for the housekeeping, or for paying off debts. This went on for months, until he was found out. His case went to trial on 3 June. On 4 July *The Times* reported, under the heading "Barrister Placed on Probation for Forged Cheques," that Mr. Desmond Fitzgerald had been placed on probation for obtaining money by means of forged cheques and for "obtaining solicitors' cheques for fees paid to barristers in his Chambers and cashing them in a public house." Nine offences were listed, and it was asked that seventeen others be taken into consideration.

These were three of the charges, in their banal and shaming detail:

On or about 29th January, at 1, Red Lion Court, with intent to defraud, did obtain from Walter Frank Douglas Herman the sum of £19–13–0 by virtue of a certain forged instrument purporting to be an endorsed cheque on Barclays Bank Ltd. knowing the same to be forged. Plea—EST. G. Probation Order 2 years West London.

On or about 22nd March, at 1, Red Lion Court, with intent to defraud did obtain from Walter Frank Douglas Herman the sum of £9–14–0 by virtue of a certain forged instrument purporting to be an endorsed cheque on the Co-operative Wholesale Society Ltd Bank knowing the same to be forged. Plea—EST. G. Probation Order 2 years West London. Similar offence—£29–7–0, on or about 12th April. Plea—Est. G. Probation Order 2 years West London.

Six similar offences were listed in detail, for sums ranging from £27 7s. to £5 10s., on all of which his plea was established as "guilty." He would have been charged with "obtaining money by false pretences" under the Larceny Act of 1916. The offence was being tried summarily in a magistrates' court, where the maximum prison sentence that could be handed down was a year. Possibly he had agreed to plead guilty and the prosecution therefore did not object to trial before a magistrates' court—as opposed to a trial under the Forgery Act of 1913, which would have been heard in an assizes court under a judge and jury, and where the offence could be punishable by up to fourteen years' penal servitude.

So Desmond was, in a way, fortunate. By pleading guilty to all charges and asking for the other offences to be taken into consideration, he wiped the slate clean. And he may have been treated leniently because of his war record. He was put on probation for two years, which meant he had to check in with his probation officer every few weeks. This was not a grave or arduous punishment, though a humiliating one. But the Bar took a very serious view of his offences, and decided to disbar him and to eject him from the Chambers. On 12 December 1962, *The Times* announced that Mr. Desmond Fitzgerald had been disbarred and expelled from the Inn of the Middle Temple at a meeting held on 4 December. The joint disciplinary procedure committee had referred him to the Masters of the Bench, and they had found him "guilty of conduct unbecoming a barrister in that on his own confession he had been guilty of 26 offences of obtaining sums of money totalling £373 by virtue of forged instruments." His membership of the Honourable Society of the Middle Temple, to which he had been admitted in November 1939, and his career at the Bar, to which he had been called in July 1946, had ended, in public ignominy, at the age of forty-five. At Downside, one of the boys, reading *The Times* in the common room of the school, said to Valpy, "Isn't that your father in the paper?" Valpy at once knew that it was him, and at once denied it. He was a Catholic boy at a Catholic school. Peter's denial of Christ would come readily to mind, and in his adult life Valpy often remembered and regretted the moment when he betrayed his father.[15]

There were other family consequences. Desmond had to pay back the money he had stolen and to clear his debts. He wrote to his old friend John Blakeway, now First Secretary at the Embassy in Athens, and told him he was in trouble and had been disbarred. John sent him £600, a great deal of money in 1962. Years later, in a rare breach of her silence on the matter, Penelope told John's wife, Jasmine, that it would have been better if John had sent the money to her. Desmond also went to his brother, Eamon, to whom he had been so close all through childhood, Oxford and the war. Eamon, now working for Lloyd's, had married into money. His wife, Juliet Adair, whom he married in 1949 when she was nineteen and he was in his early thirties, was the daughter of a Major General Adair, one of the inheritors of the Tate & Lyle sugar fortune. Eamon changed his name to Edward, and he and Juliet had two sons, Desmond (born in 1953) and Patrick (born in 1959). Now Desmond asked Eamon to pay off his debts. Eamon did so, but said that he would never speak to his brother again. (After their mother's death, it was Eamon who took possession of Burton Court.) This rift was not explained to Penelope and Desmond's children, who knew that the brothers had become estranged but did not know why. The story was told to me, nearly fifty years on, by Antonia Southern, a colleague of Penelope's at Westminster Tutors, whose husband, Hugo Southern, a solicitor, had been a close friend of Eamon's.[16]

In spite of Penelope's loyal silence, exaggerated and unprovable rumours flew around in Desmond's legal circles. Tony Babington thought that Desmond must have gone to prison. In a series of Chinese whispers, this story filtered through to later friends of Penelope's, Babington's partner Josephine Pullein-Thompson, who knew Penelope through PEN, and the novelist Francis King, a friend of both women, and a great gossip. Francis thought Desmond an awful rogue with whom Penelope was "besotted." Both Josephine and Francis maintained that Desmond went to prison and that he and Penelope were estranged for a time. It was said by some that he had "disappeared from the scene for two years or so."[17]

In the family, the court case was never discussed. Valpy wrote home to "Dear Mum" from Downside (in neat italic writing very like hers), saying that the headmaster was worried about him "after Daddy was dis-barred." "He told me there was nothing to worry about as far as I am concerned, and if I am ever short of pocket-money or anything, he does not want me to be embarrassed and I can come and ask him for some any time." But the headmaster is "rather worried" that he has not "heard a word from you or Daddy."[18] Tina and Maria knew only that their father had left the Bar and that it was something to do with money. But what they saw was a father adrift and at a loss. He had no work, and signed on for the dole. He would turn up at the playing fields of the London Oratory School and wander about aimlessly. He was still drinking with cronies like Clifford Makins, and a few months after his disbarment he got a job selling encyclopaedias door to door, for a basic monthly pay of £10.

No record exists—other than her fictional version of painful marital estrangement in *Offshore*—of Penelope's reaction when she found out what was happening. One glimpse of her response survives, at the end of a letter to her old friend Rachel Hichens, written from *Grace* on 18 December 1962, a week after the announcement of Desmond's being disbarred: "I have had a hard year but everything is straightened out now thank heavens." It suggests that she had accepted what had happened, was relieved that the outcome was no worse and was determined to get on with life. "There is a point with living conditions when things *have* to get better," she wrote years later to her friend and publisher Richard Ollard, "I felt this when we were awash in the Thames."[19] In fact, things would now get worse.

For some relief, Penelope took Valpy to Bonn in April 1963 to see Rawle and Helen. (Rawle, too, was falling on hard times, hating his life in Bonn, struggling to keep his work going for the *Observer* and heading for a breakdown, the long-term aftermath of his time as a POW.) There would be other getaways that year, to Rachel and Thomas Hichens, then living in Zennor in Cornwall, to an oast house in Sussex belonging to Diana Ladas, a generous colleague at Queen's Gate School,[20] and to a farm in Wangford, in Suffolk, to stay with Jini Fiennes. But these were brief escapes from their difficulties.

On the morning of 24 June 1963, the girls woke up to find that there was water in their bedroom. "That was not a good sign," Maria thought. They went off to school, and Penelope went to her teaching. During the day, *Grace* began to sink, and that evening she was towed away from the other boats, still afloat but sinking. Two days later, *Grace* sank—not "completely," but enough for most of their possessions to be lost and for the barge to be fit for nothing except, eventually, to be "towed away to the Essex marshes to be broken up."

The sinking of the most decrepit boat in *Offshore*, the *Dreadnought*, drew closely on Fitzgerald's memory of the sinking of *Grace*: the old boat "struggling to rise against the increasing load of water . . . like one of those terrible sights of the racecourse or the battle field where wallowing living beings persevere dumbly in their duty although mutilated beyond repair"; the half-sunk wreck having to be towed away by the salvage craft, "still under water, but surfacing from time to time, as though she had still not quite admitted defeat"; the salvage men returning what they could to the family. Fitzgerald humorously dramatised the scene when she described it in 1989:

We went down twice, and on both occasions the deck stayed just above water. We were taken off the first time by a kindly Swede in a dinghy, and the second time by the river police in their patrol launch. Among our drenched and floating possessions I saw a bottle of champagne that had been intended for a party. I was glad to be able to retrieve the champagne so as to have something to give, in gratitude, to the police, who reminded me that they were not allowed to drink on duty but agreed to put it aside for later.[21]

This does not quite correspond with the versions given by her daughters, who only recall the shock of coming home to find their home gone. Maria remembered her dolls' tea set floating out of the hold. The cat was found clinging to the mast, and had to be rescued. Most of Penelope's family documents, photographs, letters from her mother and childhood mementoes were lost, to her great distress. Some books were salvaged, and remained in her possession, their pages forever crinkled and stained. She went back to her teaching the next day, looking more than usually dishevelled, and said to her class: "I'm sorry I'm late, but my house sank." Desmond was no help: "God knows where Daddy was." On 1 July an official letter from the boatyard office noted that "Mr. Fitzgerald appeared to be on board at the moment," presumably trying to rescue some family possessions before the twice-sunk wreck was finally towed away. The sinking became legendary on Chelsea Reach. The Blakeways, who lived on a houseboat there a few years later, in the late 1960s, when they came back from Greece, would often hear the story of the end of *Grace*. It was evident to Jasmine Blakeway that Desmond had been useless when the boat went down. Friends were shocked, but it also seemed the kind of thing that *would* happen to them. Iris Birtwistle said: "I can't think of anything more like the Fitzgerald family than that boat sinking."[22]

For the first two nights, Penelope and the girls were taken into a shelter on the King's Road. On 27 June they were rehoused by the Council Welfare Department. Homelessness was a major post-war concern, and the 1948 National Assistance Act had given local authority welfare departments a duty to provide temporary accommodation for those in urgent need "whose homelessness could not have been foreseen." Most local authorities offered accommodation to mothers and dependent children, but not to homeless fathers.[23] So Penelope, Tina and Maria were sent to the London County Council Reception Centre for the Homeless at 205 Morning Lane, Hackney Wick, E9, along with large numbers of other homeless mothers and children. This large, 1930s, black-and-white modernist building had been the Berger Paint Factory until 1957, when it was turned into a reception centre. (In 1964 it became a centre for adults with learning disabilities; it was later demolished.) Families lived in one room with bunk beds, and ate in a communal canteen in the basement. There was a permanent smell of carbolic and stewed cabbage. They stayed there for four months (with a long summer break for the girls, who went to stay with the Fienneses), until 21 October, when they were moved to another temporary reception centre in Bromley, south-east London, for a few weeks. Desmond was not with them. Possibly he was with his widowed mother, who was herself drinking heavily as always and was now in the early stages of dementia, soon to be moved from Burton Court to Stella House in Ealing. Possibly he was living in a room in north London, like Edward in *Offshore,* since Penelope sometimes said that Nenna's night flight down the Kingsland Road was something that had happened to her.

For the children, this was a traumatic time. The homeless centres were the worst thing that had ever happened to them; they were at the very bottom of their fortunes. Maria remembered Hackney as "a ghastly place." She and Tina had to make a long bus journey from Hackney to the London Oratory School in Kensington, and were often late. Valpy, who took a temporary job working in the Hackney Metal Box Factory, was aghast at how "down and out" the family had become. They were even applying to the Lord Mayor's Fund for money to buy clothes. To him, none of this seemed necessary. He could not understand why they did not go for help to Evoe and Mary, or to Jean Fisher and her family. Looking back, it seemed to him a drastic act of defiance on his mother's part, entirely her own decision. The girls were more stoical; Jean Fisher remembered Maria saying grimly, "Well, we've got to stick to it."

On 13 November, they moved, now with Desmond, to temporary housing at Flat 5, 144 Earls Court Road, where they would stay for just over a year, until the end of 1964. They lived in a corridor of four adjacent rooms in a Victorian house (since demolished), which Penelope made as comfortable and homely as she could. Maria remembered her mother making her a doll's house there, with furniture built by Valpy. There were baths in the basement (a penny in the slot for hot water) and a "terrible smell of cooking" from the other flats. The other tenants were homeless families with their own problems; many of them, however, were kind and neighbourly to the girls.[24] The welfare officer called regularly.

While they were living in Earls Court, Penelope carried on with her teaching. In June 1964, she wrote to one of her old producers at the BBC, Ivan Gilman, giving Queen's Gate School as her address. She had heard one of her Schools programmes rebroadcast, and "this gave me courage to write & ask whether there is any chance of my writing for the schools department again." She added that she knew more about "conveying information" than she used to, as she was now teaching "English up to Oxford & Cambridge Entrance, & English, History & Religious Knowledge from 9 year olds up to GCE level." Gilman replied that he was very pleased to get a letter from "a friendly voice from my past," and circulated her details to the history producers, noting that ten or twelve years before "she was very tied up with family matters and unreliable regarding delivery dates," but that she had written many history scripts in the past and "may well have something to offer." A note scribbled on the memo said "Will bear her in mind." But nothing came of it.[25]

Desmond began to put his life back together. He spent many days doggedly looking for work, and after a time found a low-level but secure job as a travel agent's clerk. Sir Henry Lunn, Methodist philanthropist and founder of Alpine travellers' clubs, formed a travel company in the 1890s. In 1965 it was merged with the Polytechnic Touring Association, or Poly Tours, and became "Lunn Poly" travel (later taken over by Thomson Holidays). Henry Lunn's son Arnold, who inherited an interest in the business, was a skiing pioneer, a Catholic convert and a religious controversialist. Coincidentally, his conversion had been helped along, in the 1930s, by a correspondence with Ronald Knox.

Early in 1964 Desmond started work at Lunn Poly in their office at Marble Arch House in the Edgware Road. He worked in the back office, issuing train tickets. ("I'm not going to pretend anything about my job," says Edward in *Offshore*. "It's clerical.") To Valpy, his father seemed "a broken man." It was obvious to all his family that he was ludicrously overqualified for this job, which he kept for the rest of his life. But at least he had an income, of about £700 a year. His job also entitled them to cut-price or free travel with Lunn Poly tours, so they were able to resume family holidays and trips abroad together. But they were done on a shoestring. The girls well remembered going into a succession of restaurants with their mother, eating the bread and olive oil while looking at the menu, throwing down the menu as if in disgust and going on to the next place for more free bread.

Tina took a school trip away to Barcelona at Easter. The first of many longing letters from her mother followed her there. ("Of course you are very much missed especially by Maria who finds me boring in the extreme . . . Do remember to wash your stockings or socks every night.") The girls were moved from the London Oratory to Godolphin & Latymer school in Hammersmith. Maria passed her eleven-plus exam. After his A levels, Valpy stayed on for a last autumn term at Downside to take his Oxford entrance exams, and got into Trinity College. Desmond's mother, whom he and the girls would dutifully visit in the convent home (to be met with cries of "Who are you? Go away!"), died in September. Tina and Desmond went to the funeral, a Catholic Requiem Mass. Tina's veil smelt of turpentine, she had holes in her shoes, her stockings were laddered and she spent the whole service praying that Daddy would remember how to serve Mass, which he hadn't done for thirty years. She saw her uncle Eamon, grown very fat, and his wife, Juliet, who whispered to him all through the service. Desmond must have had dealings with his brother over Burton Court, which Eamon and Juliet had moved into, and over the funeral, but there was no rapprochement.[26]

On 17 December 1964, the family went to see *Mary Poppins*, as a forty-eighth birthday treat for Penelope. Mary Knox had been invited specially, as the illustrator of the original books. It was a celebration, too, of leaving Earls Court—though there was some delay with the move, as the letter which told them they had been found a permanent council flat

was sent to Desmond, and he put it in his pocket and forgot to give it to Penelope. She found it six weeks after he received it. ("That's how hopeless he was," Maria recalled, bitterly and fondly.) On 30 December 1964 they moved into council housing in south London. The address was 185 Poynders Gardens, SW4. It was a flat in a large, redbrick, 1930s estate on one of the wide trafficky roads that ran south from Clapham Common towards Streatham, quite a long haul from the Clapham South Underground station. The rent was £7 a week. Each block had a gateway entrance to its main door, a stone stairway up to the flats, and a shared balcony running along outside the upstairs flats. There was no garden, but Penelope could put pots on the balcony, and next door was a forlorn little municipal park with a few scrubby trees, Agnes Riley Gardens. She would sneak out at night and get earth from the beds there for her plants, and on fine days would often sit on a bench there and read, so as to get out of the flat. She furnished and decorated it as best she could, painting the kitchen and the bathroom in the same bright strong colours she had used in Hampstead and Suffolk, constantly inventing improvements, putting lino remnants down for the kitchen and the lavatory floors, stripping pine furniture, hanging the Mexican serape. Jean Fisher thought it "not at all a bad council flat." Lis Hichens, Rachel's daughter, found it bohemian and welcoming.

There were three bedrooms, one for Desmond and one each for the girls. When Valpy came to stay, he shared a room with Maria. As on the boat, Penelope slept on a bed in the dining/living room. She used the Clapham Branch Library for books and shopped in the market in Balham High Road, slogging up and down the long south London streets with her heavy shopping bags, cooking on the gas stove, knitting and mending and making clothes from material bought in the sales. One of Desmond's jobs was to get the clothes washed in the nearby launderette and do the ironing. At the time, Valpy considered this humiliating for him. Maria, by contrast, thought of it as Desmond making his best efforts to lighten Penelope's load. Every weekday she went doggedly off to work, typically wearing her father's tweed jacket over smocks and full skirts and sensible flat shoes, her hair bushy and unkempt (no hairdressers' bills were possible), with no make-up. But also, all the time, she wanted beauty and art and fine language and ideas, listened to the Third Programme on the radio constantly (they had no gramophone), watched television avidly from 1965 onwards, went to art galleries and cinemas and the Old Vic and to pottery classes, made ceramics, drew Christmas cards, studied Spanish and Russian, read incessantly and widely, and travelled as much as she could inside and outside England. Her spirit, her will, her appetite for life, her interests, her energy, were vital and powerful.

Poynders Gardens was her home for eleven years, until December 1975, all through her fifties. A profile of Penelope Fitzgerald in these years might describe her as a middle-aged teacher, recovering from a traumatic period of homelessness and deprivation, living in a dreary council estate in south London with a disgraced alcoholic husband in a dismal low-paid job, her children coming and going from school and university, her early ambitions to be a writer catastrophically thwarted, her life obscure. This was not, in fact, the whole story—or at least was only the bleakest version of the story. Something else was bubbling under the surface, all this time. But she was certainly a very long distance away from the "blonde bombshell" of Oxford, or the wartime BBC employee, or the literary editor in Hampstead, and she felt that distance acutely. She headed a letter to Tina in April 1965, "Squalid Council Estate." It was barely a joke.

CHAPTER EIGHT

Family Matters

*So much pain is caused by the illusions and dreams you can't
help making for yourself—no-one can—when your children are
tiny and just sit on your lap and can't speak and tell you that
they'll soon be individuals with quite other ideas.*[1]

Valpy was seventeen when his family moved to Poynders Gardens. He
was finishing school that year, and had a place to read Chemistry (though
he soon switched to Philosophy, Politics and Economics) at Trinity College, Oxford, where Wilfred Knox had been an undergraduate and Ronnie
Knox had been chaplain. No written evidence of Penelope's pride in her
son's success has survived; on the contrary, he remembered that, critical
as always, she thought he should have got into Balliol instead. She did
not praise her children to their faces; Valpy felt that nothing he did was
ever quite good enough for her. But she was proud of him; other people
told him so, even if she did not. He had always been the apple of her
eye. Everyone in the family knew it was a special relationship. Helen, her
sister-in-law, noting how Mops always took Valpy with her on her travels,
felt she was training him up to be a Knox.[2]

In some unpublished notes (probably from the 1980s or early '90s), she
exposed some of her feelings about her son.

> I wanted him (& I also wanted this for his 2 younger sisters) to
> like all the things I liked & to do the things that I did, & at the
> same time to be able to do all the things I couldn't, & to be sure to
> be able to earn a living . . . Mothers fall in love with their sons of
> course, & remember everything they do or say [*deleted:* I suppose
> Nature provides for this.] Sons also fall [*deleted:* deeply] in love
> with their mothers, but only to the age of five, or eight, or perhaps
> occasionally thirteen . . . After that they love them still/there is a
> special feeling but which has become less intense & . . . has turned
> into a mixture of embarrassment and tolerance . . . I do not know

the name of this emotion. Does "tolerance" suggest patronising of the most affectionate sort?[3]

The tangle of the manuscript suggests the knottiness of this relationship. All three children describe her as a devoted mother, but also often awkward and severe. All through the difficult years she slogged away, teaching and shopping, sewing and cooking and cleaning, to keep them going, determined that all of them should be educated, independent and professionally qualified. She did everything she could to fill their lives with culture and beauty, queuing for tickets for the ballet, taking them to exhibitions, sharing her passions for Morris and Burne-Jones, Velázquez and Patrick Caulfield, Arts and Crafts and Victorian stained glass, telling them the story of Shakespeare plays before they went to the theatre. But she was not effusive with them, except in her letters when they were away. She did not hug or kiss. She was not the kind of mother who let her children win when they were playing games: she was ferociously competitive and a notorious cheat at Ludo. "She couldn't not win," Valpy recalled. There were things she drew the line at or disapproved of. Maria remembered, aged six or seven, asking her mother in a public lavatory what sanitary towels were for; she was embarrassed and wouldn't reply. As teenagers, the girls would never ask her for practical advice, or tell her about their boyfriends. She would often avoid answering their questions. And she had fastidious, even snobbish standards, those of her class and generation. Some things were "common." They were to speak well, not eat in the street, not use certain "non-U" words like "serviette, toilet, lounge, settee." They were poor—all three children felt this acutely at school and university—and they were brought up to despise opulence and extravagance, for which "£££" was her shorthand.

Maria was a much naughtier, wilder teenager than the responsible Tina, messing about at school and staying out late. Her mother found this hard to deal with. When Ria went through a phase of writing daringly "dirty" notes about sex to impress her school-friends, her mother found one of these and said to her: "Sex is like eating a piece of cake." Maria cheekily responded: "But you wouldn't be cross if I wrote a note about a piece of cake," and Penelope was furious with her.

There were plenty of squabbles and mishaps at Poynders Gardens. Tina was fourteen, Maria was eleven, when they moved in. In their teenage diaries—emotional, banal and self-absorbed as all such diaries are—the daily life of the Fitzgeralds is displayed in sometimes bruising detail. The family shorthand for feeling off-colour, or for being drunk, was "bonking" or "bonky." Desmond is often reported on as coming home late, drunk, and with no money: "Daddy bonking again, had to put him to bed." "Daddy late and bonking." "Daddy came back penniless." "Daddy borrowed 2/– in morning." The girls pick up on their mother's moods, and her responses: "Mother quarrelled with Daddy at supper." "Daddy's new name is Sordissimus." "Mother in awful mood." "Daddy <u>very</u> sulky and cross." "Daddy was very self-righteous." There was a particularly bad phase, not long after the move and after Desmond's mother's death. Tina noted: "Mother upset as found out Daddy had gone on drawing Granny's pension after she died." "Mother cross with Daddy as she found out he'd been charging up a bill at newspaper shop for 16/–." Sometimes she was just as cross with the girls, and they (especially Tina) with her: "Mother said I read nothing but trashy historical novels." "Mum did Beckett essay. I know I'm lucky to have a clever mother ready to help me but oh she does annoy me." "Mother is childish and some of the things she says are fantastic."

There are the usual daily anxieties about homework and being late to school and staying up too late. Food is a major item; clearly Penelope was doing standard 1950s low-budget cooking: macaroni cheese, Welsh rarebit, baked beans, eggs, bacon, fried bread and fruitcake feature largely. But mixed in with the daily grind a sense comes through in these diaries of endless activities—walks, outings, films, expeditions—and of parents who wanted the best for them: "Daddy tested me on my Latin until late." "Mother told me plot of Hamlet and heard my Spanish."[4]

Her driving ambition for them was that they should all be able to earn their living, should be as well educated as possible, and should be bilingual. That was why she sent the girls to the Lycée, even though she couldn't afford it. "Then they need never starve because they could be teachers of languages." This was a practical, but also a cultural, aspiration. She wanted her children to understand, and if possible emulate, her passionate interest in European art and literature. Her own French, German and Italian were good, and she was trying to learn Russian and Chinese in the 1960s.

She was immensely attracted to Spain, and went there often in the 1950s and '60s. In 1961, just after they moved onto the barge, she took Valpy to Peñiscola for a school holiday, on one of their many journeys together. In 1962 they went together to Córdoba, the Andalusian city on the River Guadalquivir, with its rich Roman, Jewish and Moorish history, and its traditions of flamenco and bullfighting and good cooking. She wanted to go there, she used to say, because she had read a piece by Salvador Dalí in *Vogue* describing Córdoba as a city of "magic and moonlight."[5]

She had also read a recent book about a language school in Córdoba, by John Haycraft, a pioneer of English-language teaching to foreign students, and brother of her future publisher Colin Haycraft.

She and Valpy enrolled together on a Spanish language course at the "Casa Internacional," Academia Británica, on San Fernando Street. Valpy also began to read Spanish, to her delight, from the "funnies," the comics that were lying around in the dressmaker's house where they were lodging. One day, they went on an expedition high up into the Sierra Morena above the city, with a picnic of cold tortilla and cold veal steak. Valpy accidentally broke his bottle of Coca-Cola and cut his hand, very deeply. Two boys on a scooter offered them a lift, and so they "sailed" down through the particoloured landscape of olive trees to the Red Cross centre. The only person to hand was the local vet, who treated Valpy as he would his cows, giving him "three tremendous smacks on the haunches by way of an anaesthetic followed by a tetanus injection, then the needle & thread." "I thought that perhaps Valpy might take against Spain, but that wasn't at all the case." The story, told many years later, is loving, vivid and wistful.

In the break between finishing at Downside and going to Oxford, Valpy went back to Córdoba, in the spring of 1965, and took a job teaching English at the same language school where he and his mother had studied together in 1962. He also gave private classes in various "palatial mansions." He was proud of his independence, and wrote letters home describing the friendliness and hospitality of the Spaniards. He told Tina that he was her Walter Mitty brother, pretending to be twenty-one rather than eighteen.[6]

In the files of the school office, he found an application from his mother—sent at some point between 1962 and 1965—for a job at the school. It was a startling moment for him: he realised that during the crises at home, she had had an idea of another life. She was still thinking of it while he was away in Spain. In April, she signed on for evening classes at John Haycraft's International Teacher Training Institute in Shaftesbury Avenue. She started a new notebook, headed "Fitzgerald, Teacher Training; English as a Foreign Language."[7] The first page has a list of instructions for teachers, taken down from a lecture: "Beware of teachers temperament; show that you care about their progress; don't show favour; teach through encouragement . . . Remember to let class speak more than you do . . . ask questions as much as possible . . . don't concentrate on one person . . . don't rely on text book . . . Try to get students who do understand to explain to those who don't." But the notes run out after a few pages.

Within weeks of arriving in Córdoba, the eighteen-year-old Valpy fell in love. María de los Angeles Fernández Serrano, known as Angelines, was a dark, attractive young tourist guide and translator, two years older than Valpy. She was the daughter of a Córdoban civil servant, called "the Don," a domineering, womanising, heavy drinker, who had fought on Franco's side in the Civil War and acted, as his daughter put it, "as God's representative in the family." He would not allow his daughter (unlike her brothers) to go to university—instead she studied French in Switzerland—and she had to give him half her earnings. Her mother was bullied and submissive. The Don expected his daughter to take her place, in due course, as his household slave. Angelines was as keen to free herself from this family situation as Valpy was to get away from home, and she liked the clever, stick-thin, long-haired English boy, who (unlike the Spanish boys) treated her as a person and not as a sex object. Though they were both very young, they were, as time would show, a good fit. A few months after they met, Valpy went to the courtyard of Córdoba's Great Mosque, with a bunch of flowers, and proposed. Angelines, though terrified of her father's reaction, agreed to a trial engagement. Valpy told her that his parents were very poor, had lost everything and lived in a council flat. "If we get married," he said, "we'll have to look after my two sisters." He presented the Don with a CV, his photograph, a description of his family and an account of his prospects. The Don was not pleased. But dealing with his future father-in-law was not as delicate a challenge as telling his mother. He broke the news in a letter written on 30 March 1965. "Dear Mum," she read, in Poynders Gardens:

I suppose, in a way, this is the letter that arrives from every son to every mother, the one every mother expects but doesn't believe will ever come, but it must arrive sooner or later.

I have met the girl I am going to marry, that's all there is to it really, ten words which mean so much that spell my future, from now, in the spring of 1965, until the day I leave this world. You realize, of course, that here in Spain, an engagement is for keeps, and so I haven't rushed into this without a lot of thought . . . You are thinking, perhaps, one of two things, firstly that this is just a romantic illusion of mine which I will soon grow out of, or secondly that I have foolishly flung myself into something that I will regret afterwards. Let me assure you that this is nothing of the sort, and that I am quite sure in what I am going to do. You have always trusted me, and I try and return this trust by telling you everything and although [*in Spanish:* I am only 18] I think I am old enough in spirit to make up my mind on this.

I know that you will never actually forbid me to get engaged but I could not do it feeling that you did not approve.

Another thing is that I am not going to get married at once only after I finish at Oxford, that will be in the spring of '69 at the very earliest.

. . . One more thing, it is that, of course, I need a ring, I was wondering if there was one in the family, or that you knew of one I could have as it would mean so much more than one bought in a Spanish jewellers. If you can find one, can you send it out as soon as humanly possible, meanwhile I hope you will pray for me and Angelines, Your loving son Valpy.[8]

Maria was with her mother when this bombshell arrived. Penelope was distraught, wringing her hands. "It was heartbreaking." The letter from Valpy is blurred in patches where the ink has run, as though she had been weeping over it. Every detail—not least the request for a family ring—was hurtful to her. Tina wrote in her diary: "Mother very upset as letter from Valpy saying he's going to get MARRIED!! to a Spanish girl . . . I'm sure it'll all pass over but it's a worry."[9] Penelope immediately wrote a letter which Valpy showed to Angelines. It has not survived. (Valpy did not keep his mother's letters, and replied to them only intermittently. Hundreds of these missives, in her blue italic hand, beginning "Dearest Valps" and signed "xxx Love Ma," full of anecdotes about her daily life, are gone.) This letter said, in essence: it's impossible, you are too young. More anguished letters must have followed, and Valpy kept replying: "I don't think you realise that I am formally engaged" . . . "I wanted to cool down a bit before replying to your last letter . . . I do wish . . . that you would stop thinking it is a wild idea of mine that I will get over as soon as I return to England. As soon as you realize this I think you will understand me better."[10]

Valpy came back from Spain and went up to Oxford. For the next three years, his mother must have hoped that he would change his mind; and he had to keep telling her that he meant it. Tina, whose Spanish was excellent and who visited Valpy in Córdoba on her own, was something of a go-between. Valpy wrote to her from Oxford in October 1965, when Tina was still at school and living at home: "If you do write to Angelines, don't forget to reassure her about Mother. I'm sure we all need it . . . Thanks too for all your moral support." He tried to encourage her, in a big-brotherish way, as from one who has his own course mapped out: "I know that life seems pretty black and hopeless, but perhaps its because you're not looking at anything more than your immediate surroundings." But however difficult family life was, Valpy recognised that they owed everything to their mother: "I think you (and I) must realise that Mama has been through absolute Hell to keep us together and finish our education. You know perfectly well where we'd have ended up if we'd been left with Daddy! So I think we should permit her any point of view she may have, and thank her for all she has done and is doing."[11]

For all that, relations were strained. There are glimpses of this in Desmond's appointments diary, which he kept, patchily, between 1963 and 1976. On one occasion in January 1966, during his first Christmas vacation from Oxford, Valpy brought an old school-friend home to dinner at Poynders Gardens. "Mops very agitated," Desmond recorded, "and I had instructions not to talk." After dinner Desmond drove the school-friend home and was invited in by his father, who gave him a whisky and soda. "Called me Major and assumed I was at the Bar—awkward." So Desmond's everyday humiliations continued. At the end of that vacation, Valpy's parents drove him back to Trinity. "Mops had bad flu, but nothing could have stopped her going."[12]

Penelope, too, made some entries in a little appointment diary for 1966, covering April and May. They are a mixture of comments on her reading (on Nietzsche, for instance) and laconic, fragmentary notes to herself, some in Beckettian style, suggesting deep depression. "Constructive total loss in maritime terms costs more to salvage than it will be worth to sell." "That's where Christianity helps. It helps!" "I shall leave university and get married, because people do that . . . because people do that . . . Nietzsche complained of the 'smell of failed souls' in modern civilization." "And yet it is all the same—so terribly the same, every morning one must get one's body up, consult it, wash it—somehow . . . To live in the country with dog cat an apple tree books a listener—not only good but the only good." "After all, yes, & one is only middle aged once. The feeling of autumn before it is quite there, the leaf, not about to fall, but about to be tinged with yellow . . . which gives me the confidence to ask you to clear out of my room." "We aren't really constituted to bear our memory, it's so painful . . . fantasies produced by a glass of sherry: is it a good thing?" "If you find a person who is really alone in the world, they would be a test-case for an action (eg suicide) which hurt no-one but themselves." "Glass of wine makes you absolutely happy for about 5 seconds then deterioration." "When Mrs. Thing was 47 years old a fairy appeared & said, 'You need never do anything you hate doing again: you need never find on catching sight of yourself that your face is red & foolish, you need never not quite catch what is said, never try to keep up with things, never feel cold water coming in through your "ordinary" shoes which admit water at ever step.' Mrs. Thing replied, such offers are not made except as a bargain . . ." "Going to work neat & clean—coming back a total wreck." "Making a list of things you've done for the last time." "Idiot evening." "Idiot afternoon." "The tragic figure knows when to abandon hope." After that there are mostly empty pages, a few appointments, class times, staff meetings, the start of Russian evening classes and one entry in red letters for 3 October: "Valpy comes back."[13]

But Valpy never did come back. "By 1965 I had left home," he recalled.[14] His mother had to accept his decision, and she also had to get to know Angelines. This did not go well. Tina had paved the way on a visit to Córdoba in the spring of 1966. "I felt tremendous relief," Penelope wrote to her, "when you told me that Angelines was very sweet and that you feel sure they'll be happy . . . I trust your judgement absolutely . . . and after all she'll be your sister-in-law long after I'm dead and buried."[15] But she was not looking forward to the meeting with Angelines, when she, Desmond and Maria set out for Andalusia that summer. As usual she confided in Tina (who was away on her own holiday): "I got very upset before we went away and said I wouldn't go at all, I felt I was really going to have a nervous breakdown, like other people's friends do, and Daddy and Maria were very fed up naturally." Once they were settled in their "Residential Club," courtesy of Lunn Poly, in the seaside town of El Puerto de Santa Maria, it was really quite a nice holiday. Maria was being very patient with her "fusty old parents," there were trips to Cádiz, Seville and Sanlúcar, and bullfights, which Penelope unreservedly relished.

On the morning of 3 September, Valpy and Angelines were due to arrive at Puerto station at 11 a.m.; the family were waiting there for them by 9 a.m. They went for the day to Sanlúcar, further up the coast. Penelope left no record of the meeting, but Angelines would always remember it vividly. In her version, after an initial brusque hello, Penelope and Valpy talked to each other the whole day—"probably about me"—and Penelope ignored Angelines completely. The young couple stayed with the Fitzgeralds overnight, and then took the train back to Córdoba the next morning. While they were waiting for the train, Penelope took Valpy aside, talking to him "like a confessional," and leaving Angelines standing by herself. Hurt and insulted, she cried all the way back to Córdoba.[16] Hers were probably not the only tears shed over this first encounter.

Things did not go much better when Angelines visited Poynders Gardens for the first time in December 1967.[17] There were many features of her future parents-in-law's lives which Angelines found peculiar. It didn't help that Penelope decided to paint the bath white on the day she arrived—and surely, Angelines thought, you can't paint an enamel bath with oil paint? On offering to help in the kitchen, she was appalled to find that no one rinsed the plates at Poynders Gardens. She thought the house was messy, and that Desmond was put-upon and neglected. He clearly idolised the girls, whom Angelines thought spoilt.[18]

This memory is coloured by years of pent-up feeling, and perhaps runs more than one visit together. Tina noted in her diary for January 1968, on the next visit, that Angelines was "cross" and "sulky," and that the mood was fractious: "Bit of a 'to do' with Angie. All lost tempers."[19] Valpy confirmed that his mother would always "blank out" Angelines. He did not attribute this to jealousy, but to her disappointment that he was not marrying the right sort of girl: a clever Somerville graduate, a well-educated English rose.

Valpy graduated from Trinity College in June 1968 with a 2.1. No doubt he felt that his mother would have been expecting him to get a First. He went straight off to Spain for the wedding preparations. Penelope went shopping for "wedding garments." She wrote to Tina, who was away doing a summer au pair job in Frinton before going up to Oxford:

> I should so much have liked someone with me to try on wedding hats—many other middle aged ladies were doing the same . . . Finally got cheap (10 shilling) hat hideously made of plastic netting, the sort of material sink cleaners are made of, and an American silk dress at Peter Robinson top shop, much too short but I think I can let it down . . . Dreading going to Córdoba, although I'd always expected to enjoy my children's weddings, and wish them well amid a mist of tears.[20]

On Wednesday, 31 July, at 9:30 a.m., in the Cathedral in Córdoba, Edmund Valpy Knox Fitzgerald and María de los Angeles were married, followed by a wedding lunch at "La Torrecilla." An elegant joint invitation had gone out to "Desmond Fitzgerald and Penelope Mary Knox," but only she and Maria went: Desmond and Tina were both working. Her description to Tina of the wedding is a Fitzgerald tour de force, in which her desolation is turned into broad comedy, with herself at the chaotic centre.

They arrived in a terrific heatwave. The bullying Don Rafael ("who *is* as bad as ever") was showing off his wealth and his English and his relations, and had ordered "a complete morning-suit" (with velvet edges) "and winkle-pickers" for the wedding. "But I feel I don't care about him any more and answer back recklessly." Angie seemed much better on her home ground: "I am now experiencing the familiar 'Córdoba feeling.'—Angie is being very charming and helpful and I feel a swine for having been so bitter and criticising last Christmas . . . In Córdoba she just seems a completely different person from in London, I can't understand it . . ." Valpy, who was suffering from food poisoning, was looking "rather pale" and "very smart in his C&A tropical outfit, ironed every day by his landlady, but has bought a queer wideawake panama, rather like Mr. Pooter's, but it's a matter of dignity and we try not to complain about it." They are taken to a prolonged family al fresco evening picnic with nothing to eat until 1:00 a.m. "and then too much," to a country bullfight and on moonlit rides.

On the day of the wedding her dress felt all wrong ("bunchy and very broad"), and "of course no one else had a hat." Valpy was late arriving, and amid scenes of family chaos she rushed round to his flat with one of Angie's brothers, to find him ill, "pale as death, quite green" in his "lovely new 4 gns frilled shirt and absurd Cordobés suit," looking like "a sick little boy." At the boiling hot church, while Valpy was "crumpling," Angelines arrived looking "v.nice, with the sweet rather pathetic smile that very short sighted people give." A stout, perspiring, cross-looking priest began the Mass, during which Valpy fainted and had to be fanned in a side seat, surrounded by Don Rafael's "coarse and horrible" sisters. He recovered during the long sermon, in which the Virgin was described as a young woman "perfectly content with her house [who] never wanted any modern furniture or 'cosas automáticas,'" and the papal encyclical about the pill was summarised. Valpy fainted again, but got through the responses. Penelope found she suddenly had to kiss "a filthy, silver relic." Then it was over and a crush of relatives pushed down the aisle while she tried to stop the Don "from treading on Angie's train with his winkle-pickers." Interminable photographs were taken in the blazing heat of the Alcázar, the Don insisted on showing off various aspects of Córdoba, and eventually they got to an air-conditioned restaurant where "the guests had obviously been waiting impatiently." After "further endless confusion" the young couple were seen off "in a nice refrigerated train for Madrid."[21]

Once they were back, they settled into a little flat on the north side of Clapham Common, within walking distance of Poynders Gardens. Penelope's efforts to like Angelines often relapsed. Angelines continued to feel humiliated by Valpy's family, the more so because she was in exile: "In Cór-doba, I was someone."[22] She thought that Penelope encouraged the girls to be nasty to her. Valpy's first job was at the Economist Intelligence Unit, an organisation which carried out economic research for international governments. Angelines took a job at Peter Jones, the department store in Sloane Square. Desmond and Penelope would go to lunch with them on Sundays at their little flat on Clapham Common, and Penelope would report to Tina on the conversation: "Angie now tired of Peter Jones and says they are all jealous of her because she is a foreigner and can manage all the department[s] better than they can, as they are common and haven't the power to command: so I think it's a good thing she's leaving there soon." And, with an almost audible sigh, of Valpy: "He's a good boy and I'm sure he's happy, what else matters?"[23] The same tone gets into Desmond's letters to Tina: "Angelines gave us a blow by blow, or munch by munch, account of Valpys eating habits . . . which Mother may have found interesting but which was a bit yawny for Maria & me."[24] Their meetings were always a strain. "Valpy and Angie are coming to lunch tomorrow, I must keep off controversial subjects and be sensible."[25]

In 1970, Valpy went to Churchill College, Cambridge, to do a doc-torate; he was later made Assistant Director of Development Studies. In 1975 he got a job in The Hague as Professor of Economics, from where he travelled widely; he would get a Readership at Oxford in 1992. Their son, Valpy Gregory Fernández, was born in April 1973. Penelope and Desmond and Tina attended the baby's naming—a "trendy mass" in Cambridge, where Penelope presented Valpy with a drawing: "Valpy says my drawing of him and baby was not like him, but like Solzhenitsyn, but I still think it wasn't a bad likeness. They seem very happy and baby is a dear."[26] But she was not allowed to do as much as she would have liked for this first grandchild ("grannie's ideas are always hopeless"),[27] and felt Valpy's career taking him further and further away. "Feeling rather low," she told Maria in August 1972, "as I've just rung Valpy and he was rather grand and said I'm afraid I can't talk to you now as we have dinner guests . . . They're so rich and grand now, to think I used to cut down my things to make his dungarees!"[28]

After one of their regular trips to Cambridge, Desmond reported to Maria that on the way back in the car, "Mother started to cry saying 'Why should they treat us like that.' I really felt sorry for Valpy, & even sorrier for myself, as Angelines had refused to prepare any lunch & Valpy produced bread & cheese."[29]

It was always small things which rankled, on both sides. Penelope, for instance, would never ring them up herself, but would get Desmond to ring, so that she wouldn't have to speak to Angelines. Such tiny slights would rankle for years. Relations would ease, and Angelines would even develop some admiration for her mother-in-law, and a recognition of how remarkable she was. But they were never friends, in the way that Mary and Penelope, or Penelope and her sons-in-law, became friends. Even much later, the sharp tone recurs, as to Tina in 1993, when Valpy and Angelines were moving to Oxford: "He's worked so hard and so long to get back to Oxford, it just has to work. If only A likes it! There are lots of extramural courses and consciousness-raising events there, after all."[30] Valpy never quite forgave his mother for her treatment of his wife.

Penelope's unpublished notes about her son tenderly recall scenes from their early life together: the accident in Córdoba; a time in Suffolk when "the mechanics of daily living" had got too much for her and he took her out, silently, for a day's boating on the river and she felt "more at peace than I had ever done before"; the funny things he said as a child which made her think he might be literary (going under the water in the bath was "too hippo" for him); her looking after him when he had asthma: "I sat up with him at night as I remember my mother used to sit up with my father." Mixed with these anecdotes are melancholy self-reproaches. "I don't get letters from my son because he doesn't write them . . . The truth is & was that I am an ineffective person, not the sort who is ever noticed when they come into a room, & although this is difficult to swallow, your children see you much as the rest of the world does. I don't know how early Valpy saw through me . . . It wasn't difficult for him to see that I was quite incompetent . . . It sometimes seems to me that Valpy might like to take my advice on the very few things I know a little about . . . . But if I'm not of much use to him, and perhaps don't understand him as I should like to do, he certainly understands me."[31]

The girls, her dear companions and her friends, were also on their way. Tina left home in 1968, Maria in 1972. But both girls went away from home on summer jobs or holidays while they were still at school. In the summer of 1967, all three children were away from home at the same time. She wrote them affectionate, wistful letters: "Dear Tina, rather miserable that you have gone away, but trying to be sensible about this—I can't always expect you to be here to manage things for me." "Dearest Tina, I wasn't able to say the many things I intended . . . but I must say now that I miss you very much—as we all do—and what to do without you I cannot think." "Dearest Ria, The place certainly seems empty without you, but I should be grateful I know, because if you have 3 children and they leave home gradually you at least have a chance to get used to it . . . So much pain is caused by the illusions and dreams you can't help making for yourself—no-one can—when your children are tiny and just sit on your lap and can't speak and tell you that they'll soon be individuals with quite other ideas."[32]

She dramatised and fixed their characters in her letters, as she would in *Offshore*. Quite often she mildly satirised one to the other. Tina was the dependable, bossy rock of strength, frequently described to Maria as working too hard and "staggering on gallantly." Maria was the stroppy, independent adventurous one. After a "spin" with a boyfriend on a motorbike: "She loves going fast—she always enjoys things so much." One evening at home: "Maria has much depressed me by 1. Looking at Daddy and me and saying: 'What a funny old couple you are!' and 2. Telling me that studying art and literature is only a personal indulgence and doesn't really help humanity or lead to anything, and, I suppose, really, that is quite true: she said it very kindly. My life seems to be crumbling into dust."[33]

Tina got into Somerville in 1967, to read Spanish, and went up in 1968. Maria stayed on at school for another year to do her Oxford entrance, after her science A levels, and then went to Lady Margaret Hall in Oxford to read Physiological Sciences, in 1972, the year Tina graduated. It would not have occurred to any of Penelope's children not to go to Oxford.

Both the daughters met, and settled for, their partners very early in life. But Penelope seems to have been less upset by her daughters' youthful marriages than by Valpy's. Perhaps she liked their choice of partners better; perhaps she was not as possessive of the girls as she was of her son. This was not the sort of thing they would have discussed. It does appear that all three children wanted to get away from home as soon as possible. But it is also the case that the daughters, and their partners, stayed closely involved with Penelope for all of her life.

Maria met her future husband, John Lake, when she was sixteen, at a party in London. By 1970, when she was seventeen, they were going out together, and they were married in 1978. John Lake was practical, steady, clever, a mathematician who moved out of academic life and became an investment banker. He thought Penelope bohemian and eccentric. He had never met anyone like her before or seen anything like Poynders Gardens, with its darkly coloured painted walls. She also struck him as extremely hard-working, always reading, marking homework, shopping, cooking, doing the housework. "He never saw her doing nothing." He found her, at first, difficult to talk to.

Tina, in her first year at Oxford, met her future partner, Terence Dooley, at a poetry group. Terence, a long-haired poetry-lover, was a passionate reader and a compulsive book-buyer, imaginative, unworldly, serious, creative, with two literary siblings (his brother and his younger sister are both poets). Terence Dooley and John Lake could not have been less like each other. But both were conscious that Penelope was not, at first, friendly or welcoming to them. They both came from "ordinary" families—Terence's parents lived in a suburban semi in Bristol, John's in a bungalow in Isleworth—and there was some snobbery towards them. Terence's parents, on the other hand, especially his mother, who had left school at fifteen and not been to university, uncritically admired Penelope. It took a while for Penelope to warm to John, but she got used to him because he was always doing useful chores for the often helpless Fitzgeralds: "John came round this morning and kindly helped with collapsed tyre and total non starting of car."[34] Gradually, she became very fond of him. And she slowly grew close to Terence, too—who realised very quickly what an extraordinary person she was—though she disapproved of the fact that he and Tina were living together, after Oxford, before they got married in 1973. At first, Terence thought, she regarded her daughters' partners as "obstacles to work round." But over the years, this changed. Tina and Maria worked hard to draw their husbands into the family. They knew that they were at the centre of their mother's life and she found it hard to let them go. But Terence and John were both tolerant of Penelope's capacity for brusqueness. They became good friends whose lives were intimately involved with hers.[35] She asked Terence, quite soon, to call her Mops. Whenever she thought ahead to her old age, she hoped it would be with the daughters and their families close by: "My long-term serious plan," she wrote to Maria in 1974, "is that somehow or other I must be near either you or Tina, when either of you 'settle down'—not to call in every moment and brood, but just so as to have a human link—I know it would be asking too much to hope to be near both of you."[36]

Terence would vividly remember the moment when their lives became fused together. It was in the early 1970s and he was walking with her in the rain across the open space of Parker's Piece, in Cambridge. He was holding his umbrella over her. Suddenly, "lightning struck us both glancing off a tree to the point of our shared brolly, an electric frisson went through both of us, our hands shook, I dropped the umbrella, then picked it up again, neither was hurt, no damage done; we walked on together."[37]

It was important to her to keep in touch, too, with the rest of her family and her old friends. She was known for travelling long distances to family weddings and christenings, baptisms and funerals. She wrote regular letters and sent her hand-drawn Christmas cards and careful presents to long lists of relations and friends. Jean Fisher got married late in her life, in the 1960s, to a circuit judge who became a High Court judge, Mike Talbot. An impressive professional couple, they lived in Hampshire, then in Bath; Penelope often visited. Willie Conder and her husband, Mike, and their children moved to a beautiful Jacobean house, Terry Bank, in Kirkby Lonsdale, where Mike the forester made a wonderful garden, and they had a summer home by the sea in Alderney. These two places were important to her: there are many affectionate letters thanking the Conders for walks in the Lakes or days on the sand. Willie's daughter Anne, born in 1958, had strong childhood memories of Penelope's visits. She described her mother's oldest friend as eccentric, precise, very upright, wearing bohemian pinafores, with a childlike look of innocence in her eyes, dreamy and gentle but also strict. She would say things edge-on, and would draw out the person she was talking to. She was truthful, selfless and down-to-earth.

Rachel Hichens's daughter Lis, Penelope's god-daughter, who got to know her when she visited the Hichens family in Zennor, was fascinated by her. She was much her most interesting godmother: no one else she knew lived in a council flat, or sent hand-drawn cards, or gave presents like unusual-coloured scarves or a little handmade mug with cream handle, engraved with a Christmas holly wreath and "Elisabeth Hichens: 1956." Lis, an energetic and charitably minded person, became a missionary in a leper colony (Penelope had her down as a missionary from the age of about eleven) and spent much of her adult life in remote parts of the world. Sometimes her undaunted do-gooding made the Fitzgeralds feel rather faint. Penelope wrote to Maria in 1972: "Lis has taken on Guide Camp as well as the lunatics' outings, crippled classes &c. She really deserves some reward because she's a good girl. I always feel an absolute swine when I hear what she's been doing."[38] But she admired and respected her, and these emotions were returned.

All the children who knew Penelope felt she was extremely interested in them. She paid great attention to her nephews and nieces, and wanted to know about their lives in detail. Tim Hicks, her first cousin, the son of Christina's brother Ned and his garrulous Yorkshire wife, Enid, remembered her being sharp with his mother ("she could nip") but always kind with him. She made the same strong impression on Dillwyn's branch of the family, who called her Mopsa rather than Mops. Her cousin Oliver

Knox, son of Dillwyn and Olive, had had a miserable childhood, with his ill-matched parents; his eccentric father was always buried in mysterious work. In marked contrast, Oliver grew up to be a gregarious, widely travelled, bucolic character, full of expansive bonhomie and very good with young people. He had started life as a brilliant classicist, like his father, but he turned his back on family tradition, went into advertising, and made enough money to retire at fifty and to buy a house in Italy, in Pesaro, near Urbino. He wrote a number of not very good novels, published by an old Etonian friend working at Collins, the charming and clever Richard Ollard, who, through Oliver, became Penelope's publisher.

The household of Oliver Knox, his Irish wife, Patty, and their four children, whether in Italy or in Notting Hill Gate, was always full of people and conversation and jollity and fast-flowing wine, the very opposite of Courn's Wood. Mopsa, as they called her, would go regularly to Sunday lunch (sometimes with the girls, never with Valpy, rarely with Desmond) wearing one of her Liberty pinafore dresses. She would sit at the end of the table next to Oliver, joking clannishly, rather to the exclusion of Patty, who was not always happy. Oliver's daughter Charlotte and his sons Tim and Dilwyn (an accidental alternative spelling of the family name) remembered her speaking to them as children exactly as she did to the adults. Tim Knox recognised a razor sharpness under the apparent gentleness. She would talk to you "with an apologetic, stammering approach, and an air of gentle puzzlement"—and "half an hour later you realized you'd been a complete idiot." Both Tim and Dilwyn identified in their father and in Mopsa the Knox characteristics which they thought the next generation also inherited. Dilwyn listed these as pig-headedness, commitment to a work ethic, refusal to take no for an answer, a ferocious temper, distrust of wealth, inability to share or express emotions, liberalism and belief in independence for children. Tim defined them as "a great distrust of pomposity and an ability to laugh at life's ridiculousness. Taking silly things seriously and serious things in a light way. Rationality. Thinking you can find by logic your way from A to B. Great distrust of showiness."[39]

That Knoxian solidarity kept her feelings for her brother strong and affectionate. She visited Rawle abroad whenever she could. "She'd go anywhere," Helen Knox commented, not entirely admiringly. Her niece and nephew, William and Belinda Knox, became very attached to her. They were vaguely aware of the Fitzgeralds' problems, though these were not discussed. They felt, as adults, that Rawle had always been rather jealous of Mops. William trained as a lawyer and went into charity work, lived in

Kenya and Sri Lanka for years, and had a troubled first marriage. When he became a Quaker in his thirties, his aunt told him—referring to her great-grandmother Frances Knox—that he was reverting to his roots, and gave him a book by William Penn to take on his travels. He was keenly aware of her paying intense attention to him and later to his three children. She would ask "inquisitive," "pertinent" questions, and tell funny little stories that showed her power of observation. Belinda, who became an artist, was similarly alert to her wryness and love of narrative. "Never tell Mops anything," was the family mantra, "she always turns it into a story and elaborates it."[40]

In the years after Rawle came back to England it was more difficult than ever for Penelope to have a close relationship with him. After twenty years or so abroad—Hong Kong, Cairo, Singapore, Delhi, Bonn—he gave up his job with the *Observer* and came back from Germany in 1967 in a bad state. He and Helen had very little money, and no permanent home. They were given some support—as the Fitzgeralds were, occasionally—by Mary and Evoe. Evoe, in his late eighties, was going blind, and Mary's life's work was to look after him. But a note of February 1972 from Mary to Penelope suggests some regular gestures of support for Evoe's grown-up, struggling children: "I can let you and Rawle have £500 each this year."[41]

Helen, who taught herself to cook, took jobs catering for wealthy families in a series of stately homes. In a situation curiously similar to Penelope's, she kept the family going and looked after a broken husband. In 1968 they moved to Ireland, and lived for a year with Winifred Peck's son Julian at Prehen. Helen cooked and worked as a caretaker. Later—because, as Penelope put it, "they can't stand it at Prehen"[42]—they moved back to England, to Marlborough, where Helen did the same kind of work. They lived in a council house.

Prehen was a vast, ramshackle Georgian country house, complete with romantic window-seats, holes in the ceiling, creaking floorboards and vaulted cellars. Julian Peck had married a rich American from New Orleans, Carola, who, according to Helen Knox, became Russian Orthodox and constructed her own chapel in the cellar, next to Julian's wine collection and their son Colin's disco. She was interested in cultivating the Knox family, and repeatedly issued invitations to Penelope, to Dillwyn's son Oliver, and to Julian's brother Tony—Penelope's dear friend—and his wife, Sylvia. Penelope would arrive bearing her usual gift for Rawle, a bottle of vodka. According to Helen, she was satirical about the impractical grandeur of life at Prehen, and deliberately put Carola's back up by quizzing her about her religion. They took an instant dislike to each other, and she always resented Carola's influence over Rawle.[43]

Rawle was unhappy at Prehen, but would have been unhappy anywhere. He was drinking heavily. In old age he would develop Parkinson's. Mixed with the after-effects of his POW experience was a lasting sense of guilt. He had fallen in love with someone else while he and Helen were in India; he felt he had betrayed his family. In 1968, while his son William was at Balliol and his daughter Belinda was eighteen and at boarding school, Rawle had a serious breakdown. He disappeared from home, checked himself into a hotel in Dublin, got very drunk, wrote to Belinda telling her that she would "have to pretend that he had *never been*" and cut his wrists. He was found in time, rescued and taken to hospital. But, as Helen put it, stoically and matter-of-factly, in very old age: "He wasn't well—everything caught up with him . . . so that was that, really." The Knox family believes that Penelope must have known about this suicide attempt.[44]

For Penelope, in her early fifties, domestic life improved. There is no trace of any recurrence of those bleak, even suicidal diary entries of 1966, though there were regular lamentations about missing the girls and feeling tired, sad or worried. But, after their crises, she and Desmond settled into, or settled for, an affectionate, forbearing companionship.

To the girls, Penelope caricatured Desmond—as he caricatured himself—as comically inept: "Alas, poor Daddy couldn't manage the paint-spray and didn't dare scrape off what he'd done, so the bath is not a great success." "Daddy's dirtied up his new room <u>already</u>."[45] This was a comedy played out for the girls, a running family joke, affectionate but also revealing. But she did the same to herself. She was the accident-prone, muddle-headed Mrs. Thing, always embarrassing herself or coming a cropper:

On the way back [from Oxford] one of my shoes fell off just as I was getting into the train—it fell right under the train—but just before we started a kindly man managed to hook it up with his umbrella—I was so grateful—but his wife, in a white plastic hat, seemed rather annoyed. How could I have arrived in London with only one shoe?[46]

I've just been dragging the furniture about [while painting Maria's room olive green] and I <u>think</u> I have broken my leg, but I'll tell you whether I have or not in my next letter: in any case I am stained indelibly olive green. It won't come off my legs at all, and makes me look like something from a horror movie.[47]

Desmond's own brief diary entries from the mid-1960s suggest slightly more competence than his comic persona, but have a rueful tone: "Cleaned stairs." "All to Panto, except me. Sad." "Get sewing-machine needles." "Meet Tina at Victoria from France." "Spring cleaning." One typical slice of family life in January 1966, when the girls were at school and Valpy was briefly home from Oxford, went like this: "Drove girls to school, first day. Knocked off early [from work] with alleged cold. Drove Mops, V and T to Aldwych to see Hamlet. Return to disconsolate Maria. There was no film worth seeing. Drove in at 11 to fetch theatre party. M[ops] much distressed as lost one glove—also she has flu."[48]

When the girls were away, he wrote them tender, self-caricaturing letters. One, to Tina in November 1968, gives the tone. There has been a tiresome visit from Valpy and Angie, but luckily everyone then went out, "so I had a bit of peace, to get on with my ironing." One of the neighbours—there was always neighbour noise and trouble next door at Poynders Gardens—had knocked violently on the ceiling while he was quietly sitting by himself. "I didn't say anything about it to Mother." Maria had got home late with her new boyfriend, John, "and kindly made me a cup of coffee." He has decided to write his letters with an ink pen, rather than a biro, "as writing in biro is bad for my noble Celtic script," so "has requisitioned a whole bottle of ink for myself" from the Lunn Poly stationery store. "I expect the auditors will query the extravagance." They are planning an outing: "I've got Thursday off which is nice . . . so I'm meeting Mother at lunch time & we're going to the V&A for the [Charles Rennie] Macintosh exhibition—the old folks treat; so think of us kindly as we hobble round . . . afterwards we shall have a feast in the canteen on our luncheon vouchers." He signs off wistfully: "I wish I had seen more of you over your visit, aber so ist das Leben, mein Herz."[49]

Desmond was often alone, with the girls away, and Penelope off visiting Evoe and Mary in Hampstead, or the Conders in Kirkby Lonsdale, or Rachel down at Zennor, or Jean Fisher. On the rare occasions when he was travelling without her, he left her loving notes. One scribble on the back of an envelope read: "Even though I am always late—I do hate going away as I miss you so much. All my love, Your unsatisfactory Tour Operator." In a card sent in May 1972, he wrote: "Every day & every year I love you more, if that were possible, but it is." One long letter to "My dearest Mops" survives from July 1973. It gives a good idea of their shared interests and ways of amusing each other.[50] Rain has started, and this has him "all confused because I had planned to wash and wax the car this morning . . . but instead, I've had to do my ironing, which I had planned to do this evening,

& this has thrown me all in a tizzy." He has been on one of the "Antiquarian Walks" they sometimes did together, with a large turnout "including the sandyhaired nice woman whose name we can never remember & who calls you Penny." Disappointingly, they had seen no Victorian houses, but they looked at a Georgian house which had once been lived in by the architect of Westminster Cathedral "& now occupied by a sinister German doctor Herxheimer (sexual aberration specialist judging by his books at which I peered)." Tea was at "the Hostel of God, which is actually called a Hospice for the Dying, and is run by an Anglican Order of Nuns, of St. Margaret of East Grinstead (who was she? Martyred by Danes? Jutes? Saxons? Normans? Parliamentarians?). Anyway it was very familiar to me . . . long habits & large white head-dresses, ancient potty maids, plaster statues of the Sacred Heart, texts in Latin, and a special invocation to St. Thomas of Canterbury (I see from the Times Lit Supp we must not call him à Becket) 'defender of the liberties of the church, killed by wicked men.' No news from the laundrette—the price of school uniforms is considered outrageous, but surely it is the wrong time of year to be discussing this subject? . . . I miss you very much, but you really do need a break, & I hope a rest, after the past weeks of so much work. All my love dearest, Desmond."

They went on many Lunn Poly trips together in the school holidays. Their first one, with Maria, in 1965, was a coach tour ending with a week in the Alps. Desmond bought a book of alpine flowers, with a blue gentian on the cover, and wrote a dedication:

To dearest Mops, August 15 1965 (when we were in the bus).
Whenever I'm in trouble you're there to help me out,
You are my better half of that there is no doubt
If I had never had you, dear, to be my loving guide
Beneath the roaring waves of life my heart it would have died.[51]

In August 1967 they went with Maria to Elba and Florence (Penelope's first sight of the city); in the summer of 1969 to Turkey; in 1971 to Madrid, Greece and Palma; in 1972 to Austria, Crete and Paris. In May 1973, Desmond was made redundant from Lunn Poly (his final weekly pay packet was for £36.96), but he got another travel agent's job at Cook's in June, and they went to Sicily that summer. In April 1974 they went with Maria for a short trip to Venice. As quite often on these holidays, Penelope made a great fuss about their room, because it was not facing the canal, and sent Desmond to argue with the manager. As they usually did in these circumstances, Desmond and Maria went downstairs, had a walk and a drink in the nearest bar, and then went back to explain to "Ma" that they would have to stay in the same room, by which time she had calmed down.[52] Apart from these stroppy moments, she was an adventurous travel-ler, always rousing Desmond up—as she used to rouse up Valpy—to look at one more museum, one more church or bazaar. Turkey, in particular, made a powerful—and lasting—impression, which she transmitted to the girls with the warning note "Travel description!"

> You get into Istanbul on the public minibuses and taxis and more and more helpful and unintelligible people squeeze in as you get nearer to the city . . . Old Istanbul is very dirty and seedy but tipico beyond words . . . You have to look out as the porters carry vast loads of mattresses, chests of drawers &c through streets and there are horses and donkeys wearing blue beads against the evil eye, and everything including hair-cutting, bread-baking and furniture-making going on in the street . . . I think it's lovely in the mosques, the big ones are so empty and quiet and when you've taken your shoes off you shuffle over very soft lovely Turkish rugs with a green one here and there, grass green really, then there are very wide alcoves near the windows where people sit for hours mumbling over a Koran looking completely peaceful and it's so noisy outside.[53]

In England, whenever work allowed, there were weekend outings to the countryside—to Penshurst, or to Dorset via Stonehenge in the rain when the car broke down, or to Rodmell to see Monk's House and the walk Virginia Woolf took to the river "(morbid)." They often went to the cinema (Desmond, with Maria, preferred Westerns; Penelope would have shed tears at *Dr. Zhivago* if she'd "been able to bear Julie Christie seen through a blue filter").[54] They saw all the good things: the film of the Russian *Hamlet* in 1965, a big Van Gogh show in 1968, *Boris Gudunov* at Covent Garden in 1971, John Arden picketing the production of his *King Arthur* at the Aldwych in 1972 ("I wonder if we'll be the only people in the theatre?"), a show of her "favourite artist" Patrick Caulfield in 1973, and a production of *The Misanthrope* for which they sat in the slips and took a "pie and a half bottle of wine." They saw Nureyev in *The Sleeping Beauty* in 1975, and even Desmond was converted, though really he preferred Fred Astaire. "Nureyev had a spotlight on him the whole time . . . but why not,

I expect he *has* to be vain."[55] There was always a birthday outing for her on 17 December, *Hair: The Musical* in 1968, a visit to Leighton House in 1970, *The Beggar's Opera* in 1972.

Hair, like the hippies she saw sitting in the road in Istanbul, or Maria's unsuitably thin "flower-power" dress worn on the boat to Elba, was part of the tone of the times; she would slip such details sideways into her novels of the 1960s and 1970s. She and Desmond spent a lot of time in front of their black-and-white TV. By 1975 this had begun to seem "rather dowdy." They watched the Eurovision Song Contest with a passion. (In 1968: "We felt sure Cliff should have won, though doubtful about his dress of nylon ruffles and dandy's velvet-effect suit.") They watched cricket and the Olympics and the Commonwealth Games. They were in agreement about some of the high art on the BBC: "We are watching some dreary music by Michael Tippett and Daddy keeps saying 'When does the shooting start?'" World events were closely followed. She took the blackouts and candles of the winter of 1972 in her stride, hardened by the Blitz and life on the boat.[56] She was in tears watching the funeral of Martin Luther King. Another funeral, in 1967, was more ironically noted:

Murdered Joe Orton was cremated in a maroon coffin at Golder's Green and Harold Pinter read a poem, part of which ran

If you're sad that he's dead
you'd make him sad
that you'd missed the point
of his best bad joke

When the wretched man was hit on the head with a hammer![57]

In the summers of 1970 and 1972, Penelope set off alone on a journey to the island of Iona (train from Clapham to Edinburgh, bus across Scotland to Oban, ferry through the Inner Hebrides to Mull, fishing boat to Iona), where she joined a retreat for meditation, prayer and pilgrimage. Of course she sent back comical accounts of her fellow pilgrims at the Iona Community, where rooms were shared and everyone mucked in with lunch duty and washing-up: "One American pastor in jungle survival kit and a tartan bonnet marked Commonwealth Games 1970." But most of the days were spent getting fat on "porridge, bacon and eggs, scones, Scotch pancakes and gingerbread," going for long walks, "pebbling" on the beach and sitting in silence looking at the sea, "which is a kind of silvery colour, locked in by islands, with 2 white doves and a sheep staring at me from about a yard away." In gratitude, she sent the Community a book about wildflowers, one of her passions, and was politely thanked by the priest in charge: "I am so glad that you felt the benefit of your stay in Iona." Many years later, the scene would reappear in a story called "Beehernz," about a reclusive composer living alone on an imaginary island off Iona. "Time passes more slowly in small places."[58] Only with difficulty is he persuaded to return from his retreat to the mainland.

CHAPTER NINE

The Teacher

Why don't you teach? people used to ask me,
for women are supposed to be able to do this.[1]

From the moment the Fitzgeralds moved back to London in 1960 to live on the barge, Penelope Fitzgerald started teaching, and she went on doing so for twenty-six years, from her mid-forties until she was seventy. She taught, to start with, because she had no other means of support—and because, as she would wryly say, that's what women do when they have no choice. No teacher training was required of her. She had her brilliant First in English from Oxford, her wartime work experience, her scriptwriting for the BBC Schools programmes, her magazine editing, and her remarkable literary knowledge and high intelligence. Any shrewd head of school—at a time when employment requirements were not so regulated as they are now—would have snapped her up.

Teaching was not her preferred profession. It confirmed her, for many years, in her sense that much of her life was obscure drudgery, and not what she had intended. Her passport for 1973 reads: "Teacher. No distinguishing marks." A poignant sentence of resignation is written inside the back cover of a teaching notebook for 1969: "I've come to see art as the most important thing but not to regret I haven't spent my life on it."[2] But in the memories of her ex-pupils, in her teaching books and her essay markings, there is evidence of passionate interest, vigilance and dedication—and of a writer practising in secret. What began as a makeshift necessity became a useful vocation.

Her first job was at the Italia Conti stage school, where she taught general subjects to aspiring child actors. This peculiar posting did not last long, but was saved up in every detail for *At Freddie's,* twenty years on. In 1962 she took two part-time posts teaching older students. One was at Queen's Gate School in South Kensington, where she taught A level—at first Religious Knowledge, then English—on Mondays, Wednesdays and Fridays. The other was at Westminster Tutors, then known as "Miss Freeston's," after its remarkable founder. Here, on Tuesdays and Thursdays, she taught A-level students and trained students for their (now defunct) Oxbridge entrance exams. The teachers at Westminster Tutors in the 1960s were paid about 10 shillings an hour; the hours were 10:00 till 1:00 and 2:00 till 4:00. (In 1976, the hourly rate went up dramatically, to between £7.50 and £10 an hour, under a new head.) She also marked A-level English scripts, in vast numbers, over many years. Whenever she felt tired out and wanted to give it all up, it would always seem impossible. She wrote to Maria in 1974: "I can see poor Daddy is appalled at the idea of my giving up work—he says he would have to earn double the salary." (His pay was £750 a year.) "But I'm getting so old I feel I must give up Queen's Gate some time. I have tried dyeing my hair with a tea-bag, but it did not make much difference."[3] She worked at Queen's Gate until 1977, and at Westminster Tutors until 1987, long after she had begun to publish. So teaching was in great part her life's work, though it is not what she is remembered for, except by the students whose lives she changed.

The Italia Conti stage school was founded in 1911 by the woman who gave it her name. She had been training child actors for a long-running family show for children, *Where the Rainbow Ends,* and then set up the school in central London. It attracted stage-struck parents who wanted to get their children into the theatre. (The school's most famous graduate, Noël Coward, would satirise such parents in "Don't Put Your Daughter on the Stage, Mrs. Worthington.") It catered to ten- to sixteen-year-olds, and provided training in music, dance, Shakespeare and modern drama, elocution, dialects, movement, impersonation, audition technique and so on. It also guaranteed to give a good all-round education. Italia Conti died in 1946, and her niece, a singer, Ruth Conti, took the school over and moved it in 1960 to a large shabby Edwardian house, Avondale Hall, in Clapham. This is where Penelope went to teach, making the journey from Battersea Reach to Clapham North tube station, or taking her schoolbooks backstage for the children who were "in work." The "academic department" was squashed into four tiny little offices on the top floor of Avondale, where the nontheatre staff tried to drill these self-conscious children in the subjects they might have to fall back on. The successful graduates of the school, from Noël Coward, Freddie Bartholomew and Charles Hawtrey to Nanette Newman, Googie Withers and Lena Zavaroni, were always held up as shining models, but many of the children would not succeed.

Fitzgerald described the house and its inhabitants in "Curriculum Vitae" (1989), a few years after she published *At Freddie's.* The stage-school children are recognisably the same in the novel and in her reminiscences.

I had to help give the pupils what was called their "education," and they did not disguise their lack of interest in it. I don't mean that they were bored—it was much more positive than that, a fierce electric thrill of rejection that ran from one end of the class to the other. They wanted not education but "work." Work was largely in TV commercials and small movie roles, but there were those, especially around Christmastime, who actually got a stage part, and this gave them a certain dignity, the almost vanished magic of belonging to a venerable profession. The authorities allowed them to stay in one show for six months at a time, and to make up for their lost schooling I had to go round backstage and attempt, as they came back to their dressing-rooms in a state of pitiable excitement, to calm them down and give them their lessons. A little arithmetic (we still taught arithmetic then), a little spelling. They were brilliant with confidence. "How was I, Miss? Why don't you go and see it from the front?" But after a certain age—say ten or eleven—these children, particularly the dancers, were never likely to get another part. That was why I was being paid to teach them to spell. They might, in the future, need a tedious everyday job, such as I had. And under their bravado, they knew this, and even knew that I knew it.[4]

Queen's Gate, by contrast, was an upmarket institution, in a grand row of Kensington houses. Classes were taught in a large first-floor room, with French windows looking out over the plane trees. It had been founded as an independent girls' school in 1891 by a progressive educationalist called Miss Wyatt. By the 1960s, Diana Ladas was the headmistress. Queen's Gate was an expensive school for posh girls, described by one ex-student as a "deb factory." Camilla Shand, much later the Duchess of Cornwall, was a not untypical Old Girl. In between their lessons and their cultural add-ons—cookery, dress-making, theatre outings, dress shows, voluntary work, talks on "careers and the art of make-up"—they were delighted to be let loose on sixties London, and sneaked out to the local clubs in the Cromwell Road in their "mini-skirts, fish-net stockings and Mary Quant smudgy eyes and white lipstick." It could be as hard work getting some of these girls to concentrate on Jane Austen or Gerard Manley Hopkins as to get the child actors to do their sums. And there were tedious hours having to take tea with the students (Hovis toast, butter and strawberry jam or Marmite) and supervise their homework in the ice-cold library.[5] Still, some impressive young women went through the school (including Nigella Lawson, Eliza Manningham-Buller, Vanessa and Lynn Redgrave, and Harriet Cass), and it attracted some fine women teachers. The cultured French teacher Marielle de Baissac, Margaret Macintyre, who taught Greek and Latin, and the tiny, ebullient Berliner Susie Swoboda, the art historian and German teacher, became Penelope's friends.[6]

Others did not. There was all too much staffroom life and the teachers frequently got on her nerves. She sank her teeth into them in her letters:

> I can't get on with Mrs. Smith the new English teacher. She is Warm and Generous and Splendid and has blonde hair, sometimes in a pigtail though she isn't much younger than I am, and calls Kuala Lumpur "old K.L." and says she misses the cocktail parties. I wonder why she left?[7]

> I'm very anxious to go in on Monday as I'm fighting a battle with Mrs. Odescalchi, who says she has too much correcting to do and wants to reorganise things in such a way that she does even less.[8]

Westminster Tutors, in Artillery Row, off Victoria Street, was a more raffish outfit. It had been started in the mid-1930s and catered to sixteen- to eighteen-year-olds (a few boys, as well as girls) who needed intense schooling for their A levels and their seventh-term Oxbridge entrance. Some had not been doing well at previous schools, or had come back into education after a break. The tutors did their teaching in small-group classes, or one to one, and spent much less time with one another than the staff at Queen's Gate. There was a bohemian, shabby air to the place. Miss Freeston's aura hung over the premises; literally so, since she was inseparable from her very old dog, Topsy, "dirty, blind and smelly beyond words."[9] It sat in a sagging basket in the hall, and was given to chewing up the new timetables. A. S. Byatt, who was a colleague of Penelope's there in the 1960s, remembered a terrific smell of "rich upholstery and decaying dogs"; Fitzgerald lent this aura to Freddie's office in *At Freddie's:* "Everyone who knew the Temple School will remember the distinctive smell of Freddie's office. Not precisely disagreeable, it suggested a church vestry where old clothes hang and flowers moulder in the sink."[10] Miss Freeston, like Freddie, was a cunning, cajoling, bullying character who ran the school on a haphazard system. She often did not pay the staff their wages, but she had a sharp eye for a promising teacher. She retired, and developed Alzheimer's, but was still to be seen stomping around the backstreets of Victoria, draped in many shawls and wielding her stick, long after Topsy was no more.

Things became more orderly when the history teacher, Antonia Southern, took over as Head in 1976. Antonia Southern was devoted to Penelope, and they became good friends. By coincidence, she and her husband, Hugo, a solicitor, knew Eamon Fitzgerald well, and knew that there had been an irrevocable breach between the brothers over Desmond's professional disgrace. She and Hugo watched Eamon's own tragic decline with regret. Both he and his much younger wife, Juliet, were addicted to drink; Juliet, not well treated by her husband, died in her mid-fifties, and Eamon, once so charming and handsome, became seriously overweight and diabetic, and was eventually confined to a wheelchair, having had a leg amputated.

Antonia Southern and Penelope did not discuss Eamon or Desmond. She admired Penelope enormously. She loved her cleverness and her wit, and, unlike some of her colleagues, found her practical and not at all vague. Antonia noted that she gave the same attention to the bright students as to "the terribly thick ones." Her reports on individual students were always acute: "She's got a certain obstinacy which I've observed before in people who think for themselves."[11]

Other colleagues were not quite so at ease with her. Antonia Byatt found her contradictory. She could be sharp; she could appear vague and self-effacing; she was also knowledgeable, perceptive and generous. "She was interesting to know, but not easy to get to know well." When Penelope was teaching Antonia Byatt's daughter at Westminster Tutors in the late 1970s, she took it upon herself to rebuke Byatt for not realising how clever her daughter was. Byatt knew it perfectly well, took offence and did not forget. Nor did Penelope forget criticism. She would tell other friends that she had disliked Antonia for correcting her use of the word "protagonist" when she was teaching. As her ex-colleague began to publish, Byatt watched her career with fascination and close attention. She hugely admired her work, and gradually came to think of her as "one of the major writers of my time." But, remembering their period together as colleagues, she thought that Fitzgerald was "not a nice person. Geniuses are not nice people."[12]

A less-well-known ex-colleague, Jane Darwin, could not get on with her at all. Like some of the students at Somerville in the 1930s, she felt put down by her and wary of her brilliance. Jane Darwin thought her a bit of a "poseuse," putting on an act as a charming absent-minded middle-aged lady. Since there was no staffroom at Westminster Tutors, colleagues would wait outside the rooms they were teaching in until the class before had finished. But Penelope used to come in while Jane Darwin was still teaching and "rummage around" at the back of the room. Jane found this particularly off-putting when, for instance, she was trying to explain the sex in *Sons and Lovers,* and was getting slowed down by this difficult task; it was a terribly long book to teach, and she had only got to Chapter 31 when she should be at Chapter 35. Every time she looked at Penelope's back view she felt it was suggesting: "I don't have to prepare, I can do it off the cuff." Jane found *The Waste Land* "awfully difficult" and had to prepare it with student guides, the Bible and dictionaries. "Oh," said Penelope dismissively, "but do the students really need all this apparatus? It just makes them feel safe."[13]

She did not want to make her students feel safe; she wanted to make them think and concentrate. But she never felt like a natural teacher. "Right to the end at Queen's Gate," she told Tina in the early 1990s, "I had classes I just dreaded, and even at Westminster Tutors there were often classes I didn't look forward to because I knew some of them wouldn't have done their essays—I just hadn't the courage—call it the temperament—for teaching, or indeed, I'm afraid, for <u>any</u> job—and then I'd get tired of pretending to mind whether they'd done their essays or not."[14] There are many, many complaints, in her letters of the time to Maria. "Monday tomorrow, my worst day, really hard." "Faced by piles and piles of foul A level scripts I have a sensation of wasting my life, but it's too late to worry about this anyway." "Very hard work at Queen's Gate as many staff absent and I feel I'm getting very nasty to the girls, I said something nasty yesterday. I must check this."[15] Year by year, she had to get them through a certain number of set texts and practice essays in a certain number of weeks. Her notebooks are full of deadlines and assignments ticked off: "Next term do 'Vision of Judgment' . . . Give back essay on *Passage to India* . . . Anna Wintour read essay on Capital Punishment and how authors do not live up to their books . . . Sarah Bellord, do importance of Marabar Caves."[16] She did not always enjoy the extracurricular activities, either:

On Tuesday I went to the Old Vic with some of the girls to see Olivier in Long Day's Journey into Night and we went in a coach and had a chicken dinner first, but even so I could hardly keep awake! It was wonderfully acted, but Olivier got <u>very</u> red and I was afraid he would collapse.[17]

The students at Westminster Tutors were mostly brighter and keener than those at Queen's Gate. Many of them became writers, journalists, arts administrators, fashion editors or actors, among them Byatt's daughter Antonia, Marina Warner, Anna Wintour (who would remember nothing of Penelope Fitzgerald), Patrick Marber, William Sieghart, Edward St. Aubyn, Helena Bonham Carter and Tilda Swinton. A few girls went from one school to the other, and were taught by "Mrs. Fitzgerald" at both: they could see she was much more at ease with the smaller classes and the more interesting students at Westminster Tutors. But ex-pupils from both schools agreed on the impression she gave: short, dishevelled, softly spoken, harassed-looking, dressed oddly in homemade smocks and pinafores, with unkempt hair, watery blue eyes, ruddy cheeks, "John Lennon specs," her mild high voice often straying off into silence, and with a surprisingly sweet, warm smile. To the less perceptive, she seemed like "a caricature of a schoolmarm": "Odd socks wouldn't surprise you." At Westminster Tutors, she would heat up her lunch on the school radiator between twelve and one, so that teaching was done to the smell of warming sausage rolls.

She was not an imposing presence, and had trouble keeping order with the large classes of spoilt girls at Queen's Gate. A cruelly observant schoolgirl diary of the time records her almost pleading with the class for their interest:

> January 22 1965. Morning, treble English To the lighthouse. Suzanne Judy & me drawing talking. Please I mean I am so sorry but honestly if you don't like it please try to understand you see. Write about something like making the tea no please I mean I expect you don't do such low things as that . . . Mrs. Fitzgerald double First Oxon.

> May 4 1965. Morning went to a vague Mrs. Fitzgerald lesson. Onerstly [*sic*] she's wasted here, should be doing something better than teaching.[18]

But she had ways of taming or shaming these unruly girls. When two of them, sitting in the back row, started writing a book about school life, she made them stand up and read it aloud, and offered constructive criticism.[19] She sometimes handed back essays in front of the whole class, giving one very glamorous girl who had written four elaborate pages and was expecting a good mark a C−, and an A to an insecure but clever student:

"You haven't written very much," she said, turning it over for effect, "but you seem to have said everything that needs to be said." The nervous student thought "she enjoyed knocking the beautiful girl off her perch."[20]

She was not a motherly or affectionate teacher. She did not invite confidences and she hardly ever talked about herself. She could get very emotional when teaching, for instance, *The Mill on the Floss*—"poor, poor Maggie!," with tears in her eyes—but the students felt she was much more bound up with George Eliot than she was with any of them. She did not suffer fools; she was droll and laconic. One ex-student described her as "a little beady-eyed hedgehog. She seemed so sweet; but her spikes were sharp." She could use silence for effect: "If one offered something, she'd think about it, or think about how bloody silly it was, or maybe what she'd be having for lunch, or doing next Tuesday. One never knew. The response when it came would be a question ('Do you?' 'Is it?') but never a satisfying rumbustious response." But with the unconfident students she was consistently encouraging and stimulating. "She tolerated all opinions and made us want to impress her." With some of the bright boys at Westminster Tutors, she could be twinkly and flirtatious—"brilliantly disarming," said one. They fell a little in love with her and tried to catch her attention. Edward St. Aubyn, whose life was in disarray when he went to do his Oxford entrance exam in the autumn of 1979, was struck by the mixture of the soft and the steely in her, the air of tolerance and patience underpinned by a strong sense that she shouldn't be there at all. She taught him Joyce, fielded all the usual clichés about the stream of consciousness, and saw that he was passionate and serious about *Ulysses*. "She raised our game."[21]

St. Aubyn was one of the exceptional students who was profoundly influenced by her teaching. She made them read differently and "reach into the work." She liked to speak conversationally, biographically, about writers' lives. The young Antonia Byatt remembered her, speaking of Yeats's view of the artist, telling the story of Yeats in his tower coming downstairs and finding two children (his) and saying, "Who are they?" She remembered how clear and wise Fitzgerald was. She had not been well taught before, but Fitzgerald "gave her intellectual rigour." "I trusted her—she showed me and told me things and pushed me into places . . . you had a real conversation with her . . . She was never intolerant or sarcastic . . . She put stuff in my bones." The museum curator and art editor Jane Martineau remembered her classes well. "She was attempting to get us 16-year-olds to empathise, if not sympathise with Manley Hopkins, wretched, lonely and homosexual in a benighted parish in Wales. I was trenchantly anti-religious, but she made me think about Hopkins's Catholicism and respect his belief . . . We got deeply involved with the writers, their fictional characters and their style. She was always prompting me: 'Have you read Elizabeth Bowen? James Joyce? Beckett? Any Henry James short stories?' "

When Jane Martineau read *The Blue Flower* in 1998, she wrote Fitzgerald a fan letter, reminding her that she had been her pupil over thirty years before. "You gave me a passion for reading and involved us in the process of writing—I remember encouragement in red biro written in your clean italic hand over blundering attempts to write in the style of Virginia Woolf." Fitzgerald thanked her for her praise. "What makes me happiest of all is the thought that I really was of some use to you as a teacher."[22] Another ex-student from the 1970s, Lucy Wadham, who got back in touch with her years later when she published her own first novel, and received an encouraging letter in return, remembered that "she had that gift for making you feel as though your ideas were infinitely interesting . . . which at that age was not only new but immensely empowering. Though I wasn't aware of it at the time, she taught literature like a novelist, always bringing the text back to the stuff of experience and getting us to look at *how it was being done*."[23]

Evidence remains which confirms these reminiscences: a scatter of thank-you letters from students at the time ("I would like to thank you very much for helping me in the past two years, in spite of the fact that Wordsworth remains a complete mystery to me!"),[24] and a few of those red-biro-marked essays, though not, sadly, the ones where, as one student remembered, if you used the word "overall" she marked it with a picture of an overall in the margin. She enjoyed teasing them, as with one girl's essay on *The Winter's Tale*. "Perdita is found, yet sixteen years later she is lost again to her rightful position, and lost to her shepherds' home." "I can't say that she seems to regret this," Fitzgerald wrote in the margin.[25] Her own views come through. Jane Martineau's essay on Mr. Ramsay in *To the Lighthouse* ended: "It is only after his wife dies that he can make this journey to the lighthouse and completes the pattern of the book—it ends with his triumph—he has faced up to reality." Fitzgerald crossed out "has faced up to reality" and wrote "has overcome the need for sympathy." On Jane Martineau's "Appreciation" of Thomas Hardy's great poem of leave-taking, "Afterwards," next to "The poet is wondering what people will remember him by . . . wondering whether to come or go [through] . . . the postern-gate," Fitzgerald writes musingly in the margin: "You enter life I suppose at the front and leave slipping quietly out of the back gate . . . will any one remember you were ever here?"[26]

The "General Paper" entrance exam for Oxford had questions designed to test the candidates' capacity to think. Westminster Tutors prepared the students for this paper by using past examples; Lucy Wadham was impressed by what a range of subjects Fitzgerald took in her stride. A paper from November 1974 survives with her annotations. "How would future generations suffer if we falsified the evidence about ourselves on the basis of which they write their history?" Fitzgerald: "Historians would show we were falsifiers & assume we attributed great value to history, and historians." "Should there be limits to curiosity?" Fitzgerald: "Scarcely an adult quality in itself—what is it an element of? Ambitious search for truth etc in biography."[27]

Fitzgerald's teaching notebooks, shabby green exercise books with lists of their contents on the cover, are full of clear, painstaking notes on books she was consulting (*A Reader's Guide to the Contemporary English Novel, The Moral and the Story* by E. J. Spottiswoode, *Character and the Novel* by W. J. Harvey, George Steiner's *Language and Silence*), and her own summaries of the authors she had to teach. Some of these notebooks cover twentieth-century writers. One of them has notes on the English Stage Company, on 1950s and '60s English drama, including Osborne, on Wittgenstein and Borges ("Borges likes to keep complications but reduce them to their most economical form"), and page after page on Beckett.[28]

Everywhere in her schoolwork, her own feelings emerge. Her notes on Crabbe, for instance, say nothing about her own experience of the Suffolk landscape, or of poverty, but those things inform what she tells her students:

First thing strikes us is his quiet sincerity. He writes because he really does want to "form the real picture of the poor." He knows them through & through (son of a poor collector of salt tax who got extra money by getting election votes). He doesn't hide that village girls get pregnant, that children are cruelly treated, poor people steal. At the same time Crabbe, in this way more like 18th c, does not "see through" their eyes . . . Heroic couplet gives dignity to simple stories but doesn't make them ridiculous, because Crabbe understands the dignity of the poor . . . Genuine poetry comes from sober picture. Crabbe was well aware that your own emotions make landscape change but aimed himself at scrupulous accuracy (nothing vague). His Suffolk picture is true poetry because born into him is the feeling that land sea & people share one mysterious life.[29]

Many of the books Fitzgerald used for teaching have survived, some crinkled and with pages stuck together from having been in the Thames. This is the battered, much-used library of a working woman, mostly dog-eared paperbacks stuffed full of notes, marks, clippings and reviews, their margins annotated all through in Fitzgerald's clear, italic handwriting. They are the teaching texts of an enormously conscientious person, with (as she said of herself) an unshakeable Evangelical work ethic. There are plot summaries, chapter résumés, careful tracing of themes (as in her much-marked copy of *Ulysses,* keeping pace with what she calls Joyce's "terrifyingly exhaustive mind") and specimen exam questions with her stamp on them: "Robert Browning is always unwilling to speak the whole." "In what respect is Leo's story [in Hartley's *The Go-Between*] an illustration of English social history during the first fifty years of the 20th century?" "A short enough book to contain 2 suicides, 2 ruined lives, a death, a girl driven insane: it may seem odd to find that the keynote of the book [*The Good Soldier*] is restraint." In her copy of Graham Greene's *The Power and the Glory* she has drawn an elaborate map of the whisky priest's journeyings, complete with little towns and mountains. There are attentive marginal notes, made in 1968, to Barthes's *Elements of Semiology,* or to the first volume of the *Pelican Guide to Modern Theology* (the second volume seems to have got lost), where she shows, in 1969, particular interest in the relation between religion and unbelief: "How are we to be Christians when God is dead?" she marks, in the chapter on Bonhoeffer. Her comments on 1960s thinkers were sometimes sardonic. Susan Sontag's *Styles of Radical Will* is marked: "She thinks . . . we must advance from rhetoric and ritual to shared experience of revolutionary feeling, which she apparently did on a trip to Hanoi."[30]

Her copies of Joyce and Beckett are full of little jokes to herself, as when the citizen in the "Cyclops" episode of *Ulysses* goes out "to the back of the yard to pumpship," and she notes: "Has to pee just like Bloom. We're all human." In *Molloy,* in the early passage about "Ma," the line "I got into communication with her by knocking on her skull" has the marginal note: "How to communicate with your parents." T. S. Eliot's *Murder in the Cathedral* is given the subtitle: "The Archbishop Murder Case." On the title page of Frank Kermode's *Romantic Image,* for the benefit of whichever student she had lent it to, she writes: "My only copy of this work of culture—please return."

Often, the teacher's notes take fire, and you see the future novelist having a conversation with her books. When she is reading Jane Austen, her notes are all about education, morality and self-deception. Of Emma on Box Hill: "Emma has failed in her great virtue—generosity. We love her spirit and hate to see her humbled." Of Lady Russell in *Persuasion:* "A right-feeling but wrong-judging parent, who does as much harm as an unfeeling one." On the last page of that novel: "Autumnal shadow even at the end of the book." Of Elizabeth in *Pride and Prejudice:* "She punishes herself too much." Of the characters in *Mansfield Park:* "We like Tom, though not Julia or Maria—how does JA do this?" "Mrs. Norris is terrible, but there *is* a great fund of misdirected energy here." Of Fanny's mother: "We see relentlessly what a difference some money makes."

She often waxes eloquent in her margins, as on Virginia Woolf's *The Waves* ("The virtues of courage, sympathy and intelligence cry aloud from her books"), or Browning ("My opinion: B's problem is, why so much, and why so odd?"). Ted Hughes strikes her as "a mime, [who] can take on the voices and thoughts of creatures . . . And these birds, animals and situations give him a sense of certain possibilities of instinctual life or simple moral life, while the failure, cruelty and inefficiency of human life fills him with contempt." She gets irritated by E. M. Forster, noting his "unsuccessful poetic passages," places where "he is lecturing us," and his "childish religious beliefs: God must be like Forster."

Beckett always involves her. In her teaching notebooks she copied out passages that particularly strike her:

"To be literally incapable of motion at last, that must be something!" says [the nameless speaker] in *Comment C'est* "and mute into the bargain! and perhaps deaf as a post! And who knows blind as a bat! And as likely as not your memory a blank! And just enough brain left to allow you to exult! And to dread death like a regeneration."

When Ada speaks [in *Embers*] she's only in Henry's mind. Tells himself stories of past. Trying to recall his father "in his old red dressing gown might go on fire any minute like when he was a child, no that was his pyjamas, standing there waiting in the dark, no light, only the sound of the fire, and no sound of any kind, only the fire, an old man in great trouble."[31]

She is particularly interested in his dialogues between mind and body, as in her copy of *Waiting for Godot:* "Are they [Vladimir and Estragon] mind and body? . . . Beckett is drawn to this dualism. He represents it as a man riding a bike and reading a newspaper, ringing a bell from time to time—mind and body going about their own business." It is an early warning of one of her deepest fictional themes, especially in *The Gate of Angels,* which begins with a man riding a bike in a high wind and calling out his views on thought and blood.

Beckett's stoicism attracts her. *Waiting for Godot* is "an attempt to show how man bears his own company . . . The play is about the way we endure daily life." Of *Molloy,* she notes: "The Beckett plot is the attempt to escape from loneliness." She likes his formal choices, too. Of *Happy Days:* "The form is to remain strictly formal, yet the subject is to be chaos." That relationship fascinates her, as in an annotation of Thom Gunn's poetry: "The poems seem lucid and orderly, but what they are describing is irrational."

What interests her most is the way novelists deal with technical challenges: how to move large numbers of people around in a room, as at the ball in *Mansfield Park* ("JA's confident management of a large scene"), how to drop in clues to be picked up later (like Ford's use of "know" and "heart" on the first page of *The Good Soldier*), how to use colloquial speech, as in the funeral scene in *Ulysses* ("Joyce's Irish dialogue at its absolute best").

Her own future fictional interests are often glimpsed. She particularly likes to see emotions kept down, as in the section about Dorothea in Rome in *Middlemarch,* "a delicate chapter—low-keyed emotions but minutely traced." Her concluding note on *Middlemarch* is: "The characters' prospects narrow as the novel closes." (She will return to that idea in old age.) Above all she notices minor characters, obscure onlookers to the main action whom other readers might not have spotted. So she takes note of someone called Christopher Jackson, the carpenter, mentioned once, hired to build the stage for the family theatricals in *Mansfield Park:* "JA's art, this character never appears." In Bunyan's *Pilgrim's Progress,* it is not the glorious and triumphant utterances of Honest and Valiant-for-Truth crossing the river ("Death, where is thy sting?") which she marks, but the presence of the unnamed "many" who accompanied them to the riverside. Her note reads: "Real people in background." It is those people she notices; the poor, the ordinary, as represented by the chorus in *Murder in the Cathedral:* "Who will intercede for them?"

As her students noticed, she is a sympathetic reader, unembarrassed about feeling sorry for fictional characters. Pages are often marked "poor

Fanny," or "poor Fred" (*Middlemarch*) or "poor Elizabeth-Jane" (*The Mayor of Casterbridge*). Her sympathies are often for women's lives, as in her heart-felt notes about the cruelty done to Catherine Sloper in *Washington Square* ("No-one sees her as she really is"), or her underlining, in her collected Shakespeare, of these lines in *Two Gentlemen of Verona:* "Of many good I think him best . . . I have no other but a woman's reason; / I think him so because I think him so." Many of her notes on writers are biographical, as in her absorbed annotations of Dorothy Wordsworth's journals: "What was the affecting conversation with William? . . . Coleridge comes, tension rises . . ." You can see her wanting to write a life story—or a novel—about her. The conversations she was having with writers in her teaching books show her thinking intently and deeply about art and writing. They show how the deep river was running on powerfully, preparing itself to burst out.

Hannah, the young teacher in *At Freddie's,* likes to get to her classroom the night before, so she can put the day's work up on the blackboard. "This would mean that she needn't turn her back on the class first thing, which is as unwise in junior teaching as in lion-taming." Fitzgerald put her hard years in the classroom to good use. *At Freddie's,* her fifth novel, published in 1982, while she was still teaching, was the last of her novels to draw closely on her personal experience. It takes off from her own life more loosely and freely than *Human Voices, The Bookshop* or *Offshore,* and so it stands at the turning-point between the "autobiographical" novels of the 1970s and the "historical" novels (though neither term quite fits) of the 1980s and 1990s. But it drew recognisably on her early 1960s teaching experience at Italia Conti, and on Miss Freeston, who is used for one of her grandest comic inventions. The novel is dedicated to "Freddie."

The fictional Freddie's origins are cloaked in mystery. Traces of her past emerge unexpectedly, when she needs them to. She began life as Frieda Wentworth, a vicar's daughter, and has had phases in the East End, with the Manchester suffrage movement, and with the Land Army in the Great War. But her claim to fame is the time she spent at the Old Vic working with its legendary founder, Lilian Baylis, from 1917 to 1924, after which she started the Temple School, with the help of a mysterious legacy. Many of these details are unverifiable, though Freddie does have a brother, a harassed solicitor who despairs of her managerial methods but who, like every other man in the book, is no match for her. Nobody is.

Freddie's peculiar power—over the school, the children, her employees, her family, other members of the theatrical profession and people she has never met but can still bend to her will—is comically and compellingly done. She is partly just a huge joke, a female Falstaff, a vast, shambolic, sedentary creature frowsting in her smelly, shabby, crimson lair, where "the margin between alarm and fascination was soon crossed." With her pale blue eyes glinting behind round spectacles, her heaving layers of shawls and crumpled skirts, her outsize costume jewellery hanging off her at random, her croaking voice and lopsided smile, she is a figure of fun who is also a monument of magnificence. When she ritually kisses her child actors as they go off to a first performance, they yield at the same time as recoiling: "The Temple children all dreaded this embrace, the odour of Mothaks, unmade beds, sandalwood and old woman that issued cloudily from blouse and cardigan, and with it often the painful scrape of the great brooches—and Freddie knew very well what they felt—but not one of them would have wanted to open in a new show without it." In one creakily farcical scene, she tumbles out of her great chair and has to be levered up, like the White Whale, but "without loss of dignity."

There is no one she cannot charm or browbeat. Such as it is, the plot of *At Freddie's* centres on her control of her school, which, in spite of sagging floorboards, torn-up bills and unpaid debts, she manages by making all events work to her advantage. Being "Freddied" is a well-known state for those who try to challenge or outmanoeuvre her, clinched with the phrase "Shakespeare would have been pleased, dear." A house manager ringing to complain that one of her boys has played a dangerous practical joke at his theatre ends up promising to send his discarded chair and carpet covers to the school; an employee bullied into doing twice as much work for next to nothing ends up feeling "slightly in the wrong" for having complained; a plan for a rival stage school at the, as yet unbuilt, National Theatre on the South Bank is quashed by her appeal to sentiment and tradition. Anyone who tries to reorganise her finds themselves outwitted. All suggestions for improvement "met with frustration, like efforts in a dream, where the way to escape is clear enough, but one can't remember how to walk." Infuriatingly, she resorts to mystic inspiration for her decisions: "I'm in need of a bit of guidance. A Word may come to me." Her closest assistant, the long-suffering Miss Blewett, known as the Bluebell, is sceptical about these messages from a higher plane, as about many of her employer's tactics, but even she can't free herself from Freddie's thrall: "She was, perhaps, under some form of mild hypnosis."

Fitzgerald is extremely interested in power and weakness. In many of her novels one preys on the other, true to her belief in the struggle of the human race between exterminators and exterminees. In her working notes for the novel, she remembers, "A class at Conti's already divided into choosers and chosen."[32] Freddie's power edges over the borders of comedy into something dark and sinister, a kind of "cheery malignity," a cold "tactician's joy." Those who turn against her come to think that she "cared neither for art nor tradition nor for the theatre nor even for her children. She loved only power, indeed she loved Freddie's." But she is also passionately committed to a school which will train up Shakespearean actors for the English theatre. Her office is decorated with a vast piece of gilt-edged canvas which quotes, in gigantic capital letters, the last line of *King John:* "NAUGHT SHALL MAKE US RUE IF ENGLAND TO ITSELF DO REST BUT TRUE." Freddie has inherited this from the proscenium of the Old Vic; it was her leaving present from Lilian Baylis.

In her working notes for *At Freddie's,* Fitzgerald quotes a description of Miss Baylis as "ruthless, dedicated and sentimental," but adds a warning to herself: "Not too many refs to Lilian B."[33] But Baylis is certainly used. She was notoriously penny-pinching. She used to depend on prayer for practical decision-making (one apocryphal story, of which a version gets into *At Freddie's,* had her telling the young Olivier that she couldn't pay him any more because God had advised her against it).[34] She was dedicated to working for the underprivileged: the origin of the Old Vic was her philanthropic aunt Emma Cons's Royal Victoria Temperance Hall for the poor of the Waterloo Road. She was the great enabler of Shakespeare productions in England between the wars, and she was, like Freddie, a patriotic defender of national culture. But Fitzgerald was upset when a harsh review of *At Freddie's* by Paul Bailey accused her of having lifted the character of Freddie from a biography of Baylis which, in fact, she hadn't read.[35] She wanted to create the opposite effect, to have Baylis both there and not there in the book. In her later novels, set back in their remoter historical moments, real characters would boldly enter her fictional worlds.

Here, real figures hover at the margins. When Freddie, like the Kraken rising from the vasty deeps, makes a spectacular appearance in public at the end of the book, the Bluebell dresses her in an ancient, glimmering dress "entirely crocheted from black silk with a deep border of . . . real beetles' wings. The great Maria Casarès, it appeared, had worn it as Lady Macbeth." The beetle-wing dress, over which Freddie drapes a moth-eaten

fur-trimmed university gown (from a long-ago honorary degree), gives her the appearance of "a hugely moulting royal raven sprinkled with gems," or something from an early horror film in which "mummy cases opened wide to show their inmates." In fact, the dress is a replica of the famous green gown "shimmering with the iridescent wings of 1,000 beetles," worn by Ellen Terry as Lady Macbeth in 1888, as painted by Sargent.[36] This is one of several allusions to the grand old world of English theatre. The fussy, difficult actor who plays King John, forever complaining about having his lines cut and giving irritating little notes to the other actors, has a slight air of Gielgud about him. Noël Coward, "the Master," makes a funny appearance, out of sight but in earshot, singing a pastiche Coward song in his "unmistakable toneless half-voice, a kind of satire on itself, blandly enticing."

> Even in the
> Mediterranean sun . . .
> When day is done
> And shadows fall
> We can recall . . .
> All those long Shakespearean speeches
> Once more unto the breaches
> Those All the worlds a stage, dear, every one . . .
> Because . . . Freddie, you made it fun . . .

In her notes she warns herself not to overdo the pastiche: "No, wait, no funny accent producers."[37] But she does enjoy inventing a now dated caricature of a ridiculous 1960s production of *King John,* set in the Edwardian period, in which King John's mother, Eleanor, is Queen Victoria, and the lighting has to be exactly as in Sickert's drawings of the Old Bedford Music Hall, but in which, as in the *Marat / Sade* (Peter Brook's 1964 production of Peter Weiss's play), large numbers of lunatics have to come onstage to act out Constance's madness, to show that "politically speaking she's the only sane person on stage." (Some knowledge of *King John* is assumed.) The theatre-land of 1960s London is invoked with brio. Every small character part—the stage doorman buried in his *Racing Standard,* the old actor who used to understudy the part of the dog in *Peter Pan*—evoke a time poised between post-war and modern London. She does her homework: in her notes there is an elaborate drawing of the Old Vic stage, a list of theatrical turns of phrase, notes about great actors (Gielgud on technique, Tynan on Olivier, Scofield as Lear, who "never appears to be working hard"), and details of the time: "1963 snowbound winter and spring. Beatles 'Please Please Me' No.1. in March 1963. Papers took up Beatlemania as Profumo scandal had come to an end."[38]

But she would not have needed to research the atmosphere of 1960s Covent Garden. She puts the Temple School, with a nod to a famous comic actress, in "Baddeley" Street, and has the stage children run wild "through the alleys of the great market" "like little half-tame animals on the scavenge." She does the all-night queuers for opera tickets (of whom she had sometimes been one) asleep on piles of netted carrots or in empty barrows, the evangelists distributing tracts to them, the early morning starlings, the debris of straw and crushed baskets, or "frails," the theatre programmes blown round the gutters.

The stage-school children live in this setting as in their "village lane." They wheedle for leftover vegetables, hang around the coffee stall at the actors' church, St. Paul's, buy cheap make-up from the little local shops, run in and out of the "character-shoe store, which also did duty as a sex shop." She laconically underplays the sexuality buzzing around them: the "local flasher," the men on the Underground who follow the boy actor, still in make-up, the girl who tries to get off with everyone and whose future profession is clear to see, the possibility that one of the boys is gay, Freddie's queer appearance. She presents these things by inference but does not make a fuss about them. There is no sense of the children being looked after or policed; as in *Offshore,* they fend for themselves. Her books, she says to the publisher of *At Freddie's* in 1981 (meaning, by then, *The Golden Child, The Bookshop, Offshore* and *Human Voices*), are all set "before the 1960s as this was the last period when anyone was stopped from doing anything for moral considerations."[39]

At Freddie's is on the cusp of that period. She chooses historical moments when the tide is on the turn. The old London theatre world is changing. Traditional character actors and long-running shows are on their way out; the stage school is being pressurised to give up training Shakespearean actors and concentrate on TV commercials and film roles. Plans for the new National Theatre "threatened the existence of the shabby tiny hopelessly outdated Old Vic." Fitzgerald's heart is with the shabby and hopelessly outdated. But she also has a nostalgia for that sense of infinite possibilities. She calls the plans for the National Theatre one of the "strange symptoms of hopefulness in the early nineteen-sixties." If the novel had a title like *Innocence,* it might have been *Hopefulness.*

Her working titles for the novel were "Born Survivors," and Hamlet's exclamation about boys in the theatre, "What, Are They Children?"[40] Like the bruised, thrown-away fruit or the crushed "frails" of the market, she thinks of the stage children as "expendable products."[41] Hannah sees them "as taking their place in the whole world's history of squandered childhood." But this Dickensian view of them is also sentimental, since they partly aim to produce this effect on soft-hearted adults.

Freddie's child actors, known by old hands as terrible little shits, but also as dependable professionals, are regularly employed as the fairies in *A Midsummer Night's Dream,* and as the tragic little Prince Arthur in *King John,* who avoids having his eyes put out with a red-hot poker, but then jumps to his death trying to escape from prison. At Christmastime they get work in pantomimes and in *Peter Pan.* Currently she has them in an imaginary musical of *Dombey and Son* (her fictional improvement on *Oliver!,* which was running at the time). Drawing on the Italia Conti children, she brilliantly catches their mimicry, their cunning and competitiveness, their overexcited exhibitionism. She inhabits their lives completely. Her blurb for the novel says: "This story is not only for theatre-lovers, but for people who care about children, or hate them, or were children once themselves."[42]

The child actors are different from ordinary children because of their consuming dedication to one pursuit. "Happy are those who can be sure that what they are doing at the moment is the most important thing on earth. That, surely, is a child's privilege. Reality is his game." This comes quite early in the novel, but in her manuscript notes it was to have been at the very end. She tells herself: "THE POINT: the intense concentration of those whose lives have genius for one thing." She is fascinated, too, by the difference between genius and talent, and acts this out in her two main child characters, Mattie Stewart and Jonathan Kemp.

Mattie is an addicted impersonator, "as hard as iron" under his charm, who will become a film star: Fitzgerald sees this as the reward of the superficially talented character who really has no deep gift for acting. Mattie is obsessed with the school's real genius, Jonathan, first seen as a "very small preoccupied boy who did not speak." He is like a hibernating animal. His intense imagining of himself into his future roles make him, we can see, a potential Olivier or Scofield. In his imagination, he practises and practises. Watching Mattie playing Prince Arthur, not very well, "he sat in passive detachment," imagining precisely how he could do it. Backstage, he is "a creature in his natural habitat." The school is the only home he knows; he is in effect Freddie's child.

The boy actors are regularly cast as the Lost Boys. In a 1987 essay about Alain-Fournier's *Le Grand Meaulnes,* a novel she loves, and in which children seem at one point to have taken over the adult world, Fitzgerald compares it to *Peter Pan:* "James Barrie noted in 1922 that 'long after writing P.Pan its true meaning came back to me—desperate attempt to grow up but can't.' *Le Grand Meaulnes* is about adolescents who want to want not to grow up, but fail."[43]

The child actors in *At Freddie's* would prefer not to grow up. But they are fanatically attentive to the adult world. They are ventriloquists and chameleons. They use whatever is to hand, particularly their teachers. Mattie does an outrageous imitation of Freddie, and in one of their double acts, Mattie and Jonathan gang up on Hannah and do a rapid, cruel mimicry of her Belfast accent.

The two underpaid, temporary teachers at Freddie's, Hannah Graves and Pierce Carroll, are both from Northern Ireland. Hannah is from a repressive, parochial Catholic Belfast home. Her messy bedsitter above an Italian grocer's is where "for the first and last time in her life, she knew what it was to be free." She is one of Fitzgerald's sturdy, optimistic, romantic girls. "She had the kind of temperament which always goes forward rather than back." She is also stage-struck, as perhaps Fitzgerald was when she was teaching at Italia Conti. Like her narrator, she responds to the "noble" illusion created every night by "a handful of human beings about to risk their professional future." She falls in love with a middle-aged character actor, Boney Lewis, a "charming drunk" who is well aware of "the waste of his talent." It is another unequal pairing, like Annie and Sam in *Human Voices*.

Pierce Carroll is a "black Protestant" from rural Northern Ireland whose family always thought the theatre "a place of sin." He has no charm or humour, is implacably truthful and believes that "we should never give up . . . It's a great mistake to live with the past victories." He is driven by a "terrible quiet decisiveness which should have been able to move mountains." Pierce has taught in a "deaf and dumb school" in Ireland (a detail borrowed from Desmond's Mother Superior aunt, Juliana Lyons). In her notes for the novel, Fitzgerald wonders whether one of the child actors' parents might run a deaf-and-dumb school, to explain why his gestures are so expressive.[44] But it is Pierce who is unable to communicate normally. When she wrote about her grim eighteenth-century Knox ancestor, she compared him to Beckett's Watt, "who had never smiled, but thought that he knew how it was done." Pierce, from the same background, is her most Beckettian character, silent except for alarming bursts of terrifyingly loquacious utterances, like Lucky in *Waiting for Godot*. His love for Hannah is absolute and obsessive; there is something sinister about it. She admires his "stubborn incorruptible intensity," goes to bed with him out of embarrassment and pity, and then has to resist his assumption that they are bound to marry. All this is terrible to him; he is a Beckettian "inconsolable."

What will happen to these people? We suppose Freddie will die of a heart attack, the school will go under or be rebranded, the expendable children will float adrift like flotsam, Boney Lewis will carry on drinking and acting and forget Hannah, Hannah will go on to other jobs (we hope she doesn't marry Pierce) and Pierce will remain in love with her for the rest of his life. None of this is told; we only know that Mattie becomes a film star. All are suspended in the pocket of time and place that is Freddie's. All must "melt into air, into thin air."

Nor do we know what happens to Jonathan, the future great actor of his generation. The novel ends with his practising his jump to freedom, for his imminent appearance as Prince Arthur. He has an exact vision of how he wants it to look. In the dark, snowy yard at the back of Freddie's, alone and unseen, he jumps and jumps off the high wall, his object "to get so used to the jump that he could do it without thinking, and exactly the same way every time." In interviews, Fitzgerald said that she had meant him to die, or for us to think that he would die. But she does not tell us. Comedy hovers on the edge of tragedy; the balance is kept perfectly unresolved. "He went on climbing and jumping, again and again and again into the darkness."[45]

٭

For Fitzgerald to move from being the person who was teaching those stage children to the person who, twenty years later, was impersonating them in fiction required the determination, the patience and the single-mindedness she gives to her own characters. She said that she began—at last—to write books "during my free periods as a teacher in a small, noisy staff room, full of undercurrents of exhaustion, worry and reproach."[46] Much of her writing would jostle for space and time with her teaching work. Drafts of *Innocence* would be filed away next to Oxford entrance exams for 1974; notes for the biography of Charlotte Mew would be written on the back of A-level papers for June 1978.[47] But she was trying, already, to clear a space for her own work in the 1960s.

In 1965, she sent off her 1950s Mexican story, "Our Lives Are Only Lent to Us" to a *Blackwood's Magazine* short-story competition. It did not win, and remained hidden away until it was published, after her death, in the 2001 paperback edition of her collected stories, *The Means of Escape*.

Another vivid, personal, unpublished fragment survives from 1969. This was a typed sheet of paper dated 30 January, tucked into the copy which Stevie Smith had given her, in 1966, of *The Frog Prince and Other Poems*. Her friendship with Stevie Smith—as with Leslie Hartley—dated back to the *World Review*. Here, she describes a visit she and Tina made to Stevie Smith's house in Palmers Green. Smith would die two years later, in March 1971:

> Stevie opened the door [of Adelaide Road] after a long wait. She was, as always, very small, grey hair cut very short like a ragged boy or an inmate of an asylum, very bright dark eyes, huge nose, birdlike. Combination of shrewd business woman, genuine artist, lonely middle aged woman anxious to please, and mad-woman. House where she had lived for sixty-one years with her aunt after her father had run away to sea when quite old, abandoning her mother. House not changed in all that time. Hall with dark oil-cloth and peg hatstand; Stevie said she was fond of hats, but when she went to try them on the assistant asked her to stop as it might discourage other customers . . . Upstairs, aunt's bedroom just as

she left it when she died, freezing cold, white painted cupboard, hair-tidies, dressing table with muslin cover . . . Downstairs in the basement, stone sink, ancient stove with stovepipe, might have come out of La Boheme, faint mould . . . a cupboard with bits of tarnished silver . . . fluted gilt teacups, Japanese teapots, no lids, nutcrackers, dim cruets; Stevie struggling mysteriously with the lunch, a large tough chicken—was not allowed to do anything in the house by her aunt for sixty years, then her aunt became bedridden and she had to do everything and struggle upstairs with trays. There were squares of carpet on the floor—we thought they were samples and she was choosing a new one—they <u>were</u> samples, but she had got them free and was sticking them together to make a carpet. Evidently it was too late for her now to learn to cook; she looked dwarfed by the huge thick plates and forks; she had bought some large white tombstone-like meringues from the local shop; felt distressed by her going to this trouble.

Afterwards, walk through Palmer's Green; said she couldn't decide to make the break and leave the house where she'd lived for so long; Palmer's Green had been country when they arrived and she still loved it. Pointed to dismal, pollarded trees in dreary road: how beautiful they look against the sunset! Stopped on the banks of a dirty lake in the park surrounded by depressed-looking bushes; said this was "all the lakes in the world, and all the water in my poems." . . . She seemed half aware and half not aware of how very odd the house was; she seemed to stand half inside and half outside herself. Shrewd about money and people. The decision to leave seemed to be the great one in her life. She said she must stay unhappy to write poetry . . . We had a bright pink and yellow Battenburg cake for tea. Stevie put on a strange hat to see us down to the bus. She kissed me good-bye.[48]

A third group of writings from the late 1960s are a few laconic, Stevie-ish poems. She carefully typed these out, with illustrations on the facing page, and bound them into a handmade book with laminated pink covers, for family circulation.[49] One of these reached the finals of the 1969 Poetry Festival held in St. John's, Smith Square. Fitzgerald described to Tina the excitement of reading "The Kitchen Drawer Poem," sandwiched between Roger McGough and "a compassionate coloured poet," with Desmond sitting encouragingly in the audience. "Many contestants," she noted, "read very long poems about priests and sex and oppressions and snow-queens." The next day she took her students to hear Ted Hughes read, who, "strangely mumbling with his eyes close to the paper read . . . lengthy extracts from this 'autobiography of the crow' he's doing, of himself really I suppose."[50] Her poem was also "of herself really":

> The nutcracker, the skewer, the knife,
> Are doomed to share this drawer for life.
>
> You cannot pierce, the skewer says,
> or cause the pain of in one place.
>
> You cannot grind, you do not know,
> says nutcracker, the pain of slow.
>
> You don't know what it is to slice,
> To both of them the knife replies,
>
> with pain so fine it is not pain
> to part what cannot join again.
>
> The skewer, nutcracker, and knife
> are well adapted to their life.
>
> They calculate efficiency
> by what the others cannot be
> and power by the pain they cause
> and that is life in kitchen drawers.[51]

The other poems are equally dry, quirky and bleak.

The Later Middle Ages

> Look at me, I am a sign
> of the Middle Ages in decline.
> You evolve legs like mine
> by natural processes
> through entering fortresses
> up spiral staircases.

Late Autumn; The Prophet at the Bus Stop

The lighted bus towards him rolls
But 'twill not stop, 'tis full of souls,
And through the streaming glass they cry
"We in you out you wet we dry"
And therefore through the streaming glass
He wet he cold he looked and said
And instantly it came to pass
That all the passengers fell dead
And there were 56 free seats, and 5 standing
Inside, for it was the rush hour.

Feeling and Reason

Feelings are treacherous
Reason speaks truly.
Good-morning, Reason,
Good-morning, bully.

These small-scale, private writings, and all her reading and teaching notes, show her limbering up, as if she was waiting for a signal to start. In 1969 and '70, she began to do some research on Edward Burne-Jones. In January 1971, Evoe Knox died. It was expected. He was ninety, and had been frail and almost blind for some years, tenderly looked after at Grove Cottage by Mary, who was in deep distress: "She felt that her life had lost its point." Penelope was with them, and described it to Tina: "There's something majestic about seeing a natural death, not from an illness, but when nature just decides a life is at an end & he gradually ceased to breathe, fainter & fainter." (Next to this she noted: "The district Nurse biked up next day & said 'He's passed away? What a shame dear, can I have my case notes?' Bless her.") Retrospectively, she gave more details: "He complained gently as people do when they're dying that the room was getting dark. We said that the lights were on. My father said 'of course they are. How absurd one is. [Very Edwardian. We've lost the secret.] But there's an awkward thing about dying—one gets so little practice.' I treasure that 'how absurd one is' & hope I won't forget it when the time comes."[52] The cremation was at "grim depressing Golders Green," and the memorial service was at Hampstead Parish Church, where his ashes were interred. Valpy noted that his mother did not weep.

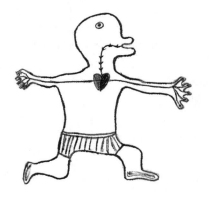

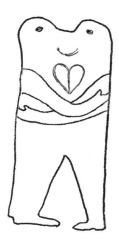

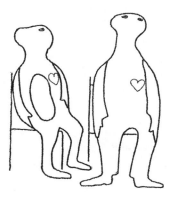

She was fifty-four. Valpy was married, gainfully employed and soon to start his own family. Tina was at Oxford, Maria was about to leave school. Desmond, though not very energetic or effective, was again her good friend and companion: their life together was steady. The last of the older generation of Knoxes had gone. Had she disappointed Evoe, not achieved what he had expected of her, what her mother would have wanted for her? She never spoke of such feelings. But there was space in her life now for her to make her own mark, and for her half century of reading, thinking and learning to be shaped into the books she had always known she would write.

In 2000, at the end of her life, Fitzgerald published an essay about her friend J. L. Carr. Of one of his novels, *The Harpole Report,* she noted: "The death of the spirit is to lose confidence in one's own independence and to do only what we are expected to do. At the same time, it is a mistake to expect anything specific from life. Life will not conform."[53]

CHAPTER TEN

The Useful Arts

If I had left these images hidden in my emotions,
they might have torn me in pieces.[1]

Penelope Fitzgerald wrote her first book, the biography of the Victorian painter and designer Edward Burne-Jones, between 1971 and the start of 1975. It was published in September 1975, when she was nearly sixty. Looking back, she gave several reasons for her choice of subject. The first was that Burne-Jones designed the stained-glass window of the Last Judgement for Birmingham Cathedral, "through whose ruby red glass the light streamed through at evensong," when her Knox grandfather was bishop there. "I was taken to see it when I was very little and, I suppose, held up to it. It was the first time that I'd seen something that I realised was stunningly beautiful."[2] In *The Knox Brothers,* she gives her own childhood emotions to Ronnie Knox, at age thirteen, with his intense feelings "for the poetry of the Rossettis and for the splendour of the west window at St. Philip's."[3] The window becomes the symbol of her passion for Burne-Jones. It links her work on him to her family history and her family feeling: and her research for *The Knox Brothers* overlapped with her writing of his biography.

Burne-Jones was a deeply religious child who lost his faith as a young man and translated it into his dedication to art. But the idea of being called to account on the last day stayed with him: "There were only two questions asked in Judgement—why did you, and why didn't you? The artist has the opportunity to supply the beauty which most lives noticeably lack and for which they cry out, even if they scarcely know it. In so far as he fails to show beauty to other people the artist will be asked, 'Why didn't you?'" His deep sense of the artist's responsibility is one of the things that attracted Fitzgerald to him.

She would give other, more prosaic, motives for writing this book, such as: "I found I hadn't enough money." Also, she said, a biography of Burne-Jones was needed. She described him "making all safe behind" when he left his home or his studio: that, she said, was also what he did about future biographies. They were kept in the family. He made sure that his son-in-law, J. W. MacKail, wrote the biography of his lifelong friend William Morris. His widow, Georgiana Burne-Jones, wrote his memoir, "one of the most firmly door-closing of Victorian biographies." There was room for more work on him. Why? "The reasons for looking further into Burne-Jones's life . . . is to understand his pictures better."[4]

These hints do not quite add up to a full explanation (she did not like full explanations) of why she dedicated five of her middle years to Burne-Jones. But the clues are everywhere. Beginning with her childhood pleasure in the rhyme sheets of the Poetry Bookshop, she loved the concept of the "useful arts," artwork drawn from nature, made for everyday use to improve the lives of ordinary people, but also full of romantic and spiritual feeling. This was the gospel of Ruskin and Morris, her intellectual heroes. Many of Fitzgerald's pieces for the *World Review* were concerned with the values of a "people's art," and bore in mind Morris's view, in *News from Nowhere,* that "there is such a vast number of things which can be treated as works of art."[5]

She loved Victorian novelists and poets, particularly Christina Rossetti, Tennyson and Browning. She had a passion for the meaning and symbolism of flowers, especially in nineteenth-century literature. Maria remembered her thinking about a book on this subject before she began work on Burne-Jones. The theme runs through the biography and would continue to haunt her. She took pleasure, in every detail of her life, in arts and crafts. She made pots and ceramics, she drew and painted expressive cards on domestic subjects, she painted her rooms in strong dark colours, she dressed her children in Victorian-style clothes when they were little, she wore Liberty prints, she carried her things in a capacious William Morris bag. She went to every exhibition and every gallery she could reach where there was Pre-Raphaelite or nineteenth-century art, and her pursuit of Burne-Jones's stained glass in churches and cathedrals all over the country was pleasure, as much as research. Mavis Batey remembered a funny search with her for Burne-Jones's trademark wombats in the Christ Church cathedral windows; Jasmine Blakeway remembered looking for Burne-Jones in Salisbury Cathedral, and Penelope's saying: "You'd think I could find a Burne-Jones window with my eyes shut."[6] *Edward Burne-Jones* was the beginning of her public, recognised literary career. But it also came out of a lifetime's interest. In her will, she would leave her friend and publisher Stuart Proffitt her copy of Ruskin's *The Seven Lamps of Architecture:* he took it as an emblem of her life's values.[7]

Burne-Jones attracted her, too, because she felt a strong imaginative pull towards characters at odds with their world: the depressives, the shy, the unworldly, the emotionally inarticulate. Wilfred and Dillwyn Knox, Charlotte Mew, many of her fictional characters, Burne-Jones and Fitzgerald herself fall into this category.

For all her books—novels as well as biographies—Fitzgerald amassed huge amounts of information (not always in a very orderly-looking fashion, though she knew her own systems), much of which she then buried, or rendered obliquely. This process is less assured in *Edward Burne-Jones* than it would become later. It was her first biography, and there was a vast scatter of materials. She knew her subject well, but she still did a prodigious amount of research. She worked hard, and she reproached herself for not working hard enough. At the end of a long week's teaching, in bed with the flu in February 1973, she wrote to Maria: "I'm very annoyed with myself that I can't manage to do more in the evening. All this dropping off must cease. After all I hardly ever go out so I should be able to get more done. One must justify one's existence."[8]

The quest for Burne-Jones began at St. Deiniol's Library, in Gladstone's Victorian Gothic house, Hawarden, near Chester, where she went first in July 1969 and then in the summers of 1971, 1973 and 1974. Burne-Jones was a friend of Gladstone's, devoted to his daughter Mary, and often went to Hawarden, for which he designed, at the end of his life, a Nativity window in St. Deiniol's church. When Fitzgerald visited St. Deiniol's, it was a combination of a research centre for Gladstone scholars and an Anglican theological college. She, too, used it partly for research and partly as a place to get away to, like the Iona retreat. She developed an affection for it, but felt ill at ease when she first arrived there on a very hot July day, wearing what she felt sure must be a too-short dress, the only woman surrounded by eccentric elderly clerics, "amiable lunatics" who were not spared in letters home:

The dinner bell has just interrupted me—I went down five minutes late, which I thought was about right, but they were half way through dinner already, the sub-warden absurdly presiding in a gown—a new, ancient deaf cleric has arrived from the Canary islands—he says that in 3 weeks he is going back to the Canary Islands—q. Why did he come at all?—another cleric said to me—I saw you soaking up the sun on the back lawn—I shall sit on the front lawn tomorrow—another cleric who seems to be wearing a

wig (they've all *got* wives but haven't brought them) has asked me
if I'd like to come to the Castle tomorrow to see the interesting
chapel, but I shan't go, as he gives me hysterics . . . There are some
little figures in a glass case which I at first thought might be pin-
football, but turns out to be <u>a model of St. Deiniol's in the 13th
century made entirely of edible materials</u> (ie marzipan). I asked the
sub-warden when he meant to eat it and he replied <u>oh, not yet,
we've only had it for three years.</u> Everyone nodded, and an ancient
vicar who comes here every year said <u>we hope to keep it indefinitely.</u>[9]

But the Gothic Gladstone library was wonderfully quiet, the grounds
were lovely, and she was "in and out" of the church all day long to see
the Burne-Jones windows "both morning and evening, to get the different
lights through them." In the biography she describes "the concentration of
all the lines on the Mother and Child, the last thing visible in Hawarden
Church today as the evening light falls."[10]

Hawarden was the first of many "B-J" destinations. There are frequent
reports in her letters or in Desmond's diaries of their setting off in Bes-
sie, their old 1950s car (Mary Knox's gift to them), in pursuit "all over
the country" of B-J's "many hundreds of letters," or to Kelmscott or the
William Morris galleries in Walthamstow, or to visit Brompton Cemetery
to find the grave of B-J's Aunt Catherwood ("Childless, but beloved," the
tombstone reads). She got squashed by the football crowds on the Underground on the way to Stanmore Hall near Harrow, where B-J designed tap-
estries for a rich patron. She went to Christ Church in Oxford to consult
a "trendy" B-J expert. Valpy paved her way to do some research in Fitzwilliam College Library in Cambridge. She went with friends to a terribly bad
lecture by David Cecil on Rossetti.[11] One of her companions on that outing was Mary Chamot, a White Russian émigré in her seventies, a distinguished art historian and curator who had been the Assistant Keeper at the
Tate Gallery, wrote books on British and Russian art, led cultural tours to
Russia and gave tea parties, with her companion Lulette Gerebzov, in their
house in Kensington full of "samovars, ikon-lamps and silver candlesticks."
Chamot knew all about Burne-Jones and lent Fitzgerald one of her treasures, the Italian notebook he kept in 1871, "and so began my researches."
This impressive woman was the link, in the 1970s, between Fitzgerald's
interest in Burne-Jones and her fascination with Russia.[12]

Her archive is bursting with inventories of letters, lists of contacts, descriptions of artworks and places, reprimands to herself about

disorganisation ("This bit shouldn't be here . . ."), moments of despair ("There is a terrible lot of glass"), annotated reproductions of B-J's paintings, pencil notes taken in museum archives, book slips from the British Library, summaries of many books (on the Pre-Raphaelites and Arthurian myth, on Giorgione and George MacDonald), chronologies, trial contents pages, lists on the language of flowers, little drawings to remind her of what she's seen, unanswered questions ("What is the High History of the Holy Grail by Perceval le Gallois 1898?") and vivid accounts of interviews, for instance, with Lance Thirkell, Burne-Jones's great-grandson. Her Morris and Burne-Jones books are bulging with clippings, cards and bits of Morris fabric.

In her notes, the story she wants to tell keeps breaking through the research. Of Burne-Jones's early days with Rossetti: "B-J had like the rest of us an instinct for which was the happiest time in his life, the best time we can all look back [on] and identify it with absolute security—for B-J it was the time in London with DGR." In the book this becomes one sentence: "So sure an instinct has the human heart for its happiest time."[13]

All this work began without a contract. But she must have started in the reasonable hope that a biography of a much-loved, major Victorian artist would be a viable proposition for a publisher, and might sell. She used the connections she had, which pointed her towards the firm of Michael Joseph. The managing director was a distant relation, Edmund Fisher, the grandson of the Kenneth Fisher who had been headmaster at Oundle, brother-in-law to "Auntie Al" (Christina's sister-in-law) and father of Penelope's dear friend Jean. The editorial director at Michael Joseph was Raleigh Trevelyan, who had published stories in the *World Review* in the 1950s and met the Fitzgeralds then, and who had written about the Pre-Raphaelites. He was a learned gentleman-publisher-writer of the old school, the first of a series of male editors in whom she would put her trust. Raleigh "pushed" her book through, though the firm preferred more popular titles, and negotiated her a contract in April 1972. She was to deliver at the end of 1973 (she would be about a year late), and they paid her an advance of £500, half on signature and half on delivery. They would cover £50 of picture costs. Royalties started at 10 per cent on the first 3,000 copies and would go up to 15 per cent after 7,500. There were, immediately, problems about how many illustrations she could have and whether they could afford colour. Trevelyan gave her some help: she was particularly interested in the painting *Green Summer,* which she wanted on the cover, and he helped her to track it down. But he left Michael Joseph (for Hamish

Hamilton, who would do the first paperback of *Burne-Jones* in 1989) before the book was published.

The story Fitzgerald tells of Burne-Jones is partly, like her own, the story of a dedicated worker. She shows him as heroically determined, prolifically inventive, always with multiple projects in hand, but also as disorganised, slow, easily exhausted and discouraged, surrounded by unfinished work. "Often the canvases were put aside and he allowed the subject to grow in his mind, perhaps for years, consulting no-one." But hard work, always, was his need and his solace. In his dark times, "work continued to be what Morris called it, 'the faithful daily companion.'"

She takes it as a given that his art is beautiful and that it matters. She assumes that her readers are fans of the Pre-Raphaelites and that they will agree with the message of Ruskin and Morris about the need for "honest" art and for "scorning" worldly materialism, a message which, she tells us severely, "it is to the credit of humanity that whenever it has been clearly put, there have always been people to attend to it." She assumes that her readers will be cultured and educated and will know about things like *Unto This Last* or Gladstone's pamphlet on the Eastern Question. She establishes a tone of sympathy with her subject from the first page: "He never knew his sister, who died in infancy, nor his mother, who died a few days after his birth, but he felt all through his life that he had lost them and sorely missed them." The virtue of this biography, we see at once, will be its inwardness. But it also opens windows, bright and minutely detailed like the background of a Pre-Raphaelite painting, on the world surrounding its subject. In her plans for the book, there is a notebook headed "main lines to follow," with an entry reading: "Raptus: Beethoven's word for slow succession of musical statements: you meditate over each."[14] This was her instruction to herself about how the book might be shaped.

The "disconsolate" little family of the bereaved, unsuccessful artisan father, the philistine housekeeper and the delicate small boy, prone to nightmares and fantasies, are set touchingly in the grim context of 1830s industrial Birmingham. "Ruskin warns us"—in *Praeterita,* one of her key books—"that those who are starved of beauty in childhood will find the love of it in later life 'rampant and unmanageable.'" She quickly tracks the young man's escape towards art, through love of nature, religious faith, the influence of Newman and the instant Oxford friendship with the pugnacious, fist-clenching William Morris. In the formation of their artistic creed, their reading is all important: "Without the concept of the book as hero, Victorian idealism can hardly be understood." She plunges happily into their books: Charlotte Yonge's *The Heir of Redclyffe,* Malory's *Morte D'Arthur,* Kenelm Digby's *The Broadstone of Honour* (Catholic revivalist legends of wandering medieval knights), De La Motte Fouqué's *Sintram* (more knights, inspired by Dürer woodcuts) and Friar Colonna's *Hypnerotomachia,* a fifteenth-century "maze-like" quest for a lost love.

The people and places who changed his life are strongly drawn. We see the "careless and lordly" chaos of Rossetti's studio and private life, Ruskin's shrinking, fussy, neurotic disposition, the enchanting "perpetual summer" of Little Holland House (benign shelter for Watts and Tennyson and Holman Hunt), and the noisy, truthful household of the "great unorthodox preacher and writer" George MacDonald, whose many children "never began a sentence without knowing how it would end." His daughter Georgie MacDonald, ten years old when she met the young painter Ned Jones and fifteen when they got engaged, is Fitzgerald's pet. In everything Georgie has to put up with in her long marriage to Burne-Jones—the death of her second baby, her husband's roving heart, financial struggles, Morris's infatuation, problems with her son Phil and the pressures of her husband's fame—she is described as behaving "with the dignity of a true daughter of the manse." Fitzgerald plays down Burne-Jones's gloom about his marriage in late years, and Georgie's relentless involvement with local politics. For Fitzgerald, there is only one view to take: "Not many painters, and not many men, deserve such a wife."

Before their problems arise, she gives a spirited account of the early days of discovery and adventure: the idyll of Burne-Jones's friendship with Morris and Janey at the Red House in Kent, the life-changing trips to Italy, the optimistic Ruskinian ambitions of the Morris "shop" at Red Lion Square "to bring into the Victorian revival of the useful arts the spirit of the medieval workshop," and the outpouring of Burne-Jones's incredibly varied talents, for watercolour painting, stained glass, tapestry, wood engraving, furniture decoration, jewellery and illustration. The crash came in the 1860s with his disastrous passion for the wild redheaded Greek beauty Mary (or Maria) Zambaco. Everything went awry. Morris fell in love with Georgie, Rossetti fell in love with Janey Morris, Mary Zambaco attempted suicide. Burne-Jones's startling and recognisable nude portrayal of her in *Phyllis and Demophöon* shocked the conservative Water-Colour Society, and his work, after a promising start, went back into obscurity. Fitzgerald comments, with feeling: "The fact that Morris, Burne-Jones and Rossetti could live through these days and months and maintain such a convincing everyday life will only seem strange to those whose marriage has experienced no crisis."

She is guarded about the sex, and puts the emphasis on Burne-Jones's hopeless romanticism and on Georgie's endurance. The same is true of her treatment of his series of intense, but probably platonic, feelings for much younger women, and of his possessive relationship with his daughter Margaret, whose marriage made him wretched. She does not remotely mention the possibilities of paedophilia or incest, though in her notes she reports Lance Thirkell's saying, in interview, that "Ruskin wrote hundreds of obscene letters" to the young Margaret Burne-Jones—a story she chooses not to use in the book.[15] She takes a sympathetic attitude to the sentimental Victorian idealising of young girls, and sees it as a vital, not a perverse, preoccupation in Burne-Jones's work. Innocence points to "the terrible falling short between expectation and reality." In *The Golden Stairs,* with its procession of palely beautiful virginal maidens going down to a mysterious doorway with expressions of "increasing tension," or in his *Briar Rose* paintings of the Sleeping Beauty before any intrusive prince arrives ("the princess must not wake up"), he keeps returning to the theme. "Only if we are afraid to lose a daughter shall we understand Briar Rose."

Mary Zambaco was painfully shed, more comforting young admirers took her place, hard work substituted for happy love, fame and popularity arrived in the 1870s, and Ned Jones became the influential Sir Edward Burne-Jones, reluctant member of the establishment. Fitzgerald shares his approval for the Arts and Crafts movement, noting that Morris and Burne-Jones, for all their love of "decorative richness," cared also for "simplicity, whitewash and fine line." But she comes down hard on the fin de siècle Aesthetes. "The Aesthetic Movement, like all movements led not by artists but by their followers, would first dilute, then copy, then exaggerate, then become ridiculous, then grow out of date. It was, after all, a consumer movement, with time and money to spare." She reports with tender sorrow on the phase of estrangement between Morris and Burne-Jones, as Morris's socialist activism filled him "with a deep sense of waste." Morris's death is seen as the greatest loss of Burne-Jones's life. "But the loss of a friend is not, of course, a recognised clinical condition."

The picture she paints throughout is of a "tensely-charged nature" prone to "fainting, weakness and nightmares," shrinking from attention, a lovable and faithful friend. He is earnest "about things that really mattered," but he is funny, too, though his humour surfaces only occasionally in her version. (Asked to paint a picture of "Faith, Hope and Temperance," he suggests that Drink and Polygamy might do instead.) She sees him as elusive and self-concealing. "Burne-Jones was to find increasingly over the years that there was a solace in manoeuvring the different aspects of his own personality, sometimes to disconcert people, often to keep them at a distance." It is one of many moments in this subjective and emotionally charged book where she appears to be talking partly about herself.

Fitzgerald is interested in technique and methods, commissions and patterns of work, studio life, income, sales, exhibitions, deadlines and reputation. She sketches the minor characters as if writing a novel: "Wherever [Charles Eliot] Norton enters the course of events, there is a breath of Bostonian high-mindedness, goodness and tedium." William Allingham "became finical and difficult, was obsessed with germs, refused to touch door-handles, and had to be forcibly got up and dressed, though his Anglo-Irish charm never faded." She can be dry about the collision between dreamy romanticism and the real world: while Burne-Jones is reading *Morte D'Arthur* in Birmingham, steel screws are being manufactured in their thousands just up the road. She has a theory that Kipling (Burne-Jones's nephew by marriage) based the spiritual, unworldly Lama in *Kim* on Burne-Jones: "But if he thought that his uncle's art had little connection with his real life, then he did not altogether understand Burne-Jones."

At the heart of her book is the secret interior life of the artist accessed through his paintings. She believes that, for some obsessive, unconfident artists, their images will destroy them if they remain unexpressed. Burne-Jones might have said, "with Jung": "If I had left these images hidden in my emotions, they might have torn me in pieces." Art for such people is a form of exorcism. It is the job of the biographer to enter the inner life, understand the obsessive images and see how they become the "burden" of the works. The "burden," she says, is "the totality of the given thing which is not complete until it has been understood by a sympathetic attention." And the obsessive images which correspond to the inner life are, for Burne-Jones, "the enchantment of the willing victim, sleep, waiting, imprisonment, loneliness, guiding, rescue, the quest, losing and finding, tending the helpless, flying, sea-crossing, clinging together, the ritual procession and dance, love dominant and without pity, the haunting angel, the entry into life."

She tracks these images through his work. The "burden" of *Green Summer* is "beauty guilty of its own mortality." *Chant d'Amour* gives off "the

sensation of music that has just been played and of listening to silences."
King Cophetua and the Beggar Maid tells the story of his marriage, "the
painter's consciousness that for thirty years he had been subjected to the
test of the highest purity and truth he knew and . . . could not feel that
he had met the test." Above all, the inner life is felt through the language
of flowers. This language, she says, is "a means of communicating, and
yet concealing, the secrets of the heart." Burne-Jones copied some of the
illustrations in Gerard's *Herbal,* which Morris also used for his wallpapers,
and which Fitzgerald would often say was her favourite book. Influenced
by Ruskin's *Proserpina,* he made a book, *The Language of Flowers,* out of
his interpretations of the mythical meaning of the names of flowers. "If the
name was right, it opened a direct access, like an intensified view through
a small round window, into the world where his own limited range of private images joins the world's store of archetypes." In his portrait of Georgie, she is holding her copy of Gerard's *Herbal* and a flower, heartsease,
which Ruskin called "the flower of those who love simply, to the death."
The biography ends with Georgie laying a small wreath of heartsease on
Burne-Jones's grave.

Burne-Jones connected to her later work in many ways. Four years
after it was published, Fitzgerald's publisher—by then Richard Ollard, at
Collins—presented his firm with the possibilities he had been discussing
with her for future nonfiction books. One of these was "a book on the use
of flowers in early Renaissance paintings." Her argument, he said, "and I
bet she is right because she is both scholarly and exceedingly acute, [is]
that flowers in early Renaissance paintings are entirely symbolic and not
merely decorative. Why, she enquires, is there a spurge, the dullest and
ugliest of flowers, in the middle of Botticelli's 'Primavera'?"[16] Her interest in the *Primavera* returns in her notes for *Innocence* (1986), where a
blue gentian is remarked on.[17] The blue flower is not the only legacy of
Edward Burne-Jones. The values of the Morris/Burne-Jones "firm" are often
invoked, in the William de Morgan tiles washed up in *Offshore,* in the
Swiss gentian pressed into the pages of Ruskin's *Unto This Last* at the end
of *The Bookshop,* in the Nottingham printing press of the Reid family and
Nellie's admiration for uncorseted Arts and Crafts women in *The Beginning of Spring.* George MacDonald, whom she so much admired, led her to
Novalis: she told Frank Kermode in 1995 that she thought MacDonald was

the only person who had really understood him. William Morris stays in her mind for Len Coker, the Marxist draughtsman at the museum in *The Golden Child,* dedicated to his craft, "politically exceedingly fierce" yet in his personal life "gentle and frequently embarrassed,"[18] and for Selwyn the Tolstoyan printer in *The Beginning of Spring.* The optimism and curiosity of the young artists at the Red House provides one model for the Cambridge students in *The Gate of Angels* and for Fritz and Jacob's student friendship in *The Blue Flower.* Fritz's love for the very young Sophie has a distant echo of Ned Jones's youthful love for the fifteen-year-old Georgie. The Greek community in London inspired an unfinished novel set in Istanbul, which was eventually turned into a story, "The Likeness." The oddest leftover from Burne-Jones comes in *The Gate of Angels.* Burne-Jones, Fitzgerald tells us, always regretted not learning to bicycle, but relished the anecdote he had heard of "two young bicyclists, a man and a woman, perfect strangers, who crashed at Ripley, were picked out of a hedge and woke up to find themselves in the same bed."[19] She saved up that story for many years.

During and after the work on *Edward Burne-Jones,* Fitzgerald became a dedicated member of the William Morris Society, going on trips, organising poetry readings, giving talks and sitting, not always happily, on committees. The talks she gave for the Society grew out of her book. One

was on Morris's attitude to women, praising him for "his condemnation of marriage and property laws, which made women the slaves of slaves" and for his treatment of Janey Morris as "a free agent." A later talk on the Burne-Jones house, The Grange—a demolished house, "a house of air"— conjured up the life of the house with undiminished inwardness and affection.[20] She treated the William Morris Society, as she did all the small-scale British cultural institutions in which she had a part, with a mixture of indulgence and satire. This characteristic tone is heard in her descriptions of meetings of the Clapham Antiquarian Society, here celebrating its fiftieth anniversary:

> [There was] a large cake, bearing the arms of Clapham and the Atkins family in blue and yellow icing, and (as it turned out) heavy as lead. The lady in charge of cutting it was very inefficient, particularly as before starting she felt it necessary to demonstrate how she had made a cake the year before exactly like the Tower of London, with a bridge that went down and up. Then came a lecture on "Clapham as I know it" and we crept quietly away and had dinner and watched the horse show.[21]

But members of the William Morris Society, Alyson Barr and Dorothy Coles, remembered her commitment, and her archive is full of these sorts of postcards: "Thankyou for your scintillating talk at the AGM, we were all enthralled."[22] A warm friendship also grew out of her work on Burne-Jones with the American academic Mary Lago, whom Penelope met through her old college friend Mary Bennett (née Fisher). Some thought Mary Lago a bore, heavy-going and relentlessly garrulous. But Penelope had a way of finding what was interesting and valuable in the most unprepossessing individuals. In 1982, Mary Lago edited Burne-Jones's studio conversations, collected by his assistant T. E. Rooke. She was at the University of Missouri, but came to England regularly, when she, Mary Bennett and Penelope would meet at the University Women's Club, a formidably intelligent trio. A long correspondence developed, mainly about their mutual interest in Morris and Burne-Jones and about Mary Lago's other subjects, Forster and Tagore.[23]

In 1980 Fitzgerald was asked by a small radical imprint, the Journeyman Press, to edit, with an introduction, the manuscript of an unfinished novel by William Morris. It came out in 1982 under her title for it, *The Novel on Blue Paper*, "because it was written on blue lined foolscap and Morris preferred to call things what they were." (The title was a nod, also, to Stevie Smith's *Novel on Yellow Paper*.) In Morris's fragment, two sons of a cruel, tyrannical country parson fall in love with the same grey-eyed, honest girl, clearly based on Georgie Burne-Jones. One son is sickly and imaginative, the other is sturdy and inarticulate. The setting is very like Kelmscott. Fitzgerald thinks the two young men are "two opposing sides of his own character." In a coda to her edition, imagining how the book might have ended, she says, with something like satisfaction, that "the book's repeated forebodings of unhappy old age will come true for all three of them."[24]

That edition, and her biography (twice reissued in paperback) were treated by future scholars with respect. Mary Lago inscribed the copy she sent her of *Burne-Jones Talking:* "Many thanks for showing the way to Burne-Jones!" The curators of the big 1998 New York Metropolitan Burne-Jones exhibition cited her approvingly. Fiona MacCarthy, her friend in her late years, spoke affectionately, in her 2011 biography of Burne-Jones, the first since Fitzgerald's, of her debt to her "still lamented friend": "Penelope had a phrase 'the squeeze of the hand' by which she meant an almost physical passing on of knowledge and enthusiasm from one generation to another. I like to think of this book being the squeeze of her hand onwards to me."[25]

Such tributes, however, came only gradually. The initial reception of the biography was muted and in some cases baffled. Russell Davies, in the *Times Literary Supplement,* described it as "a very odd book . . . very full of fact, but forever ducking back into a fog of exaggerated sympathy and discretion . . . Mrs. Fitzgerald either chooses, or has been forced, by lack of source material, to perpetuate Victorian reticence."[26] But the reception of her first book was not her main concern towards the end of 1975.

In her "B-J" archive, Desmond's handwriting often appears, mixed up with her own notes. He was helping her, they were working together. She gave him a copy of the book when it came out on 15 September 1975. It was dedicated, not to him, but "to Valpy, Tina and Maria." Nevertheless, she inscribed his copy: "To dearest Desmond—who understood what it meant to me, helped me with all my difficulties, and made it possible for me to write it at all. Mops." When that dedication was written and the book was given to him, Desmond was in hospital.

❧

All the time Fitzgerald was writing *Edward Burne-Jones*, she referred to it as "My Little Bit of Writing." To Valpy, it looked like therapy, something to "stop her going mad" amid the pressures of teaching and keeping house. She presented it to her family as a hobby and an enthusiasm, rather than the start, at long last, of her professional career.[27]

But family needs and activities were still paramount. The main anxiety after Evoe's death was making sure that Mary was all right. Having been the minder for so many years, she now needed looking after. Mops helped her move out of their beloved Grove Cottage in June 1971, into a nearby flat (paid for with money inherited from her father) in Frognal. The loss of the old house where Evoe and Mary had lived since 1948 was a wrench to Mops, too: she kept, in a small packet titled "Just a Few Memories," a brown envelope containing the "Last Rose from Grove Cottage." Mary at once wanted to write about Evoe and to edit his writings. Going through his papers and helping Mary to produce a book of his *Punch* poems, *In My Old Days,* which came out in 1972, took up a good deal of time. Mops thought Mary was "mad" to sell £1,000 of her stocks in order to finance the printing of 1,000 copies in hardback, and it seemed absurd to her that both she and Rawle had to write introductions.[28] But writing this piece confirmed her feeling that she herself wanted to do a book about Evoe, and his brothers. Her introduction to *In My Own Days* set the tone for her book:

> Light verse is a product of civilization, for it is a sign of being civilized to be able to treat serious things gracefully. The concern can be felt, however, beneath the surface . . . Just as light verse is based on strong-mindedness, so his kindness was based on courage, and what always goes with true courage, reticence. To be thanked was for Evoe a dreadful experience.

That year, 1972, which was filled with the work on Burne-Jones, Lunn Poly trips to Austria, Paris and Greece, and a return visit to Iona, in between school terms, was the year of their thirtieth wedding anniversary, which Desmond, unusually, noted in his diary; they left for their Greek holiday two days later. Tina graduated and set up house in Muswell Hill with Terence Dooley. Penelope disapproved: she would not visit them there because they were not married. Maria went up to Oxford to read Physiological Sciences, and Valpy was lecturing in Cambridge. It was the time of Heath and the miners' strike and then, in 1974, of the three-day week, sardonically noted: "Electrical blackouts are now in full swing and very boring, as I can't sew, and everybody talks about them the whole time. I'm hardened to them because of the not-to-be-mentioned Blitz and the frequent crises of the houseboat." In the 1974 election, they would both vote Liberal, as usual.[29] 1972 was also the year of the Tutankhamun exhibition at the British Museum. Penelope went more than once, observed the enormous queues and their carnival atmosphere, the suspiciously dim lighting of the exhibition and the fact that "you weren't allowed to pause anywhere for very long," and asked herself: what if the whole thing were a gigantic fraud? She made mental notes, and stored them away.[30]

In April 1973, she became a grandmother for the first time, though she did not see as much of Valpy Gregory Fernández Fitzgerald as she would have liked. "Am a grandpa," Desmond noted on 12 April. A few weeks later the new grandfather swapped one travel-agent's desk for another: "final weekly pay at Lunn Poly, £36.96."[31] That summer, on Saturday, 28 July, at 11 a.m., Tina married Terence at St. Mary's Church in Hampstead. Desmond gave his daughter away, and they all went for the wedding party to Mary Knox's flat. Desmond helped them move out of Muswell Hill—they were going to live in Leyton. Then the Fitzgeralds went on holiday to Sicily. In the autumn, Penelope and Desmond went to see Valpy get his doctorate at Cambridge. She held her grandson on her lap while he chewed her umbrella, and watched her son, "a solid impressive figure in hired crimson-lapel gown." She felt "very proud."[32] At home, she and Desmond were talking about moving out of Poynders Gardens, but they couldn't afford it: the GLC told them they could only borrow £7,000 "on our present so-called incomes." She longed for "somewhere quiet with a bit of garden." But "whatever happens I mustn't land us in real financial straits again," she told Maria, away at Oxford.[33] Throughout 1973 and 1974, she went restlessly on visits to friends all over the country.

She finished most of the writing of *Burne-Jones* in 1974, and started doing the index and the corrections, at the same time as beginning work immediately on her next biography. Tina recorded in her diary for Sunday, 12 May 1974, on a family visit to poor Auntie Mary in Frognal, "Ma told me of new plan to write biography of Grandpa & 3 brothers."[34] That spring and summer she set about writing letters, visiting libraries and making contacts with friends, colleagues and relations of the brothers. From 27 July to 11 August 1974 Tina and Terence rented a house in Cambridge and Penelope stayed with them (Desmond went down for two weekends), to research *The Knox Brothers*. Tina noted her visits to "various elderly clerics who knew Uncle W" and to sundry "ancients & dons." By the autumn of 1974 her Knox Brothers notebooks were bulging with information, plans and drafts, and her correspondence from clergymen, classicists and code-breakers was mounting up. Peculiar, intriguing letters came in about Evoe's brilliant after-dinner speeches, Wilfred having his socks darned by devoted parishioners, or making up a whole detective story on a walk, or his unconquerable fear of young women. The formidable David Kahn, Enigma expert, gave advice, and ex-colleagues of Dillwyn at Bletchley sent their reminiscences ("he had a curious way of not knowing quite what to do with his arms when he was talking to one"). Mavis Batey helped with code-breaking, Valpy with maths and computing. A huge box of materials arrived from Dilly's son Christopher. Oliver wrote his reminiscences of his father. Many of Evoe's letters were lent by Mary. Malcolm Muggeridge was encouragingly enthusiastic, though he told her that she shouldn't call it *The Knox Brothers,* as it would make them sound like a circus.[35] She wrote back carefully to all, for instance, to her cousin Oliver:

> I do like what you wrote so much, indeed it brought all of them back to me, particularly what Muggeridge (who has been co-operative) described to me as "the long Knox silences, during which one strained to hear what conceivably might be another remark." He [Dillwyn] was exceedingly proud of you really.[36]

Some of her interviewees were almost too eager to help, like the eighty-five-year-old Greek scholar Professor Lobel and his wife, in Oxford. She instantaneously turned them into characters for a novel (stored up for *The Gate of Angels*):

> Presently the Professor's wavering step was heard on the uncarpeted stairs (the whole beautiful little house was freezing except for a small coal fire in the drawing-room, but I'm used to this) and Mrs. Lobel said: "I hope Edgar will talk to you as he is very eccentric and sometimes takes dislikes," however, I got on rather too well with the Prof as he spent nearly all the time telling me about his emendations to Aeschylus ("You will of course be familiar with the first two lines") but he was very nice. There were some of those frightful cakes made of chocolate and cornflakes, in fluted paper cups, Mrs. Lobel had bought them specially, and the Prof had never seen them before and examined his critically, but neither of them could eat them, so I had to have one.[37]

Unlike *Burne-Jones,* which had been a slow, arduous process, *The Knox Brothers* raced along. She researched and wrote at speed through 1975 and

1976, in the middle of much other work and other pressing concerns. The book was powered by strong emotion as well as inward knowledge. Though she barely allowed herself in, it was a kind of elegy for her childhood and her remarkable family, and most of all for her father. And it was written at a time of great stress, anxiety and grief. This intense emotion, banked down and often translated into comedy, gave the book its particular, expressive, unaccountable atmosphere.

She had no publisher for it until the autumn of 1975. Raleigh Trevelyan had left Michael Joseph, and the firm was not interested in a book "on all four brothers together, but only one at a time—this is quite useless and I shall have to find a new publisher. I think I'd better get an agent?"[38] She never did. But she knew that her professional writing life was under way. In September she signed a contract with Macmillan's, with an advance of £1,000. Harold Macmillan had been one of Ronnie Knox's dearest friends at Eton and Oxford, and wrote appreciatively to her when it came out. Her editor there was Richard Garnett, and, like all the men who published her, he became an admiring friend, though she only did one book with Macmillan. She wanted to call it "Must We Have Lives?" The publisher had "considerable doubts."[39]

In the middle of working on *The Knox Brothers* and finishing off *Burne-Jones,* she produced a startling piece of short fiction. In 1974, she entered a story called "The Axe" for a *Times* ghost-story competition. It is told by a bureaucratic narrator, like the storyteller of Melville's "Bartleby the Scrivener," or one of M. R. James's rational characters to whom something indescribably horrible is about to happen. The narrator has made his ageing clerical assistant redundant. W. S. Singlebury, who has only two sets of clothes and "a defensive expression," lives alone, and has worked for years in his immaculately arranged cubbyhole. The office smells damp; Singlebury says it is "the smell of disappointment," because in 1942 the building was used by the Admiralty to give information to relatives about those missing at sea. Like Pierce in *At Freddie's,* he is a Beckettian figure. He takes the news of his dismissal very quietly, but invites his embarrassed employer home for an awkward supper. They discuss reading, which Singlebury says is his hobby. The narrator thinks that a hobby is something you do for relief. Oh no, Singlebury says, "the mind and the body are the same." Going back late to the office, the narrator feels a "creeping tension" as of danger behind him: "One might say the body was thinking for itself on these occasions." There in the corridor is Singlebury, advancing with his "unmistakable shuffling step," but with his head wobbling about, nearly severed above his cut throat; Singlebury is holding it on, trying to steady it, as he goes into his cubbyhole. The narrator locks himself into his office and sits with his back to the door, unable to bring himself to look behind him to see if blood is seeping in, writing his report.

"The Axe" was short-listed for the competition and was published in *The Times Anthology of Ghost Stories,* edited by Tom Maschler.[40] It was her first fictional publication since her student pieces of the 1930s and her experiments in the *World Review* twenty years before. She was paid £50. But the publications of 1975, *Edward Burne-Jones* in September and "The Axe" in November, were overshadowed by Desmond's illness. The warning signs appeared in 1974. They had taken their usual short holidays—to a wet, cold Paris in March, where they "trailed round" rather miserably, and to Venice in April. There are reports of "Daddy bearing up very well really." They went together to St. Deiniol's in the summer, after the family's stay in Cambridge; there are photographs of Desmond looking ashen and terrible. He spent most of the visit sitting about reading detective stories (his favourite kind of fiction) and drinking tea, though they did play some games of croquet. Penelope cheated to make sure of winning. In October 1974, she wrote to Maria: "Daddy going to the doc again on Wednesday to know result of test: I can't help feeling there must be some kind of microbe."[41] This test would be inconclusive.

In January 1975, Penelope went to Russia with Maria, on a two-week package tour with other tourists, whom she mostly ignored. She had been learning Russian now for several years, and going to events—lectures, films, theatre, exhibitions—organised by the Great Britain–USSR Association in Grosvenor Place. Mary Chamot, too, with her stories of old Russia, had fuelled her interest. An excited postcard went back to Desmond saying how interesting it all was and how well Maria was looking after her. They went to Moscow and Leningrad, to Tolstoy's house, untouched from the time he lived there, to the Bolshoi Ballet (*Don Quixote*), and to the Kremlin. Access to sights was then strictly regulated by Intourist. It was her only visit to Russia. Every detail stayed in her mind.

After her return, Desmond took a short trip to Nice, to interview, on her behalf, a French expert on Enigma. She and Desmond did some more research together at Bletchley Park. They were pleased to hear that Angelines was expecting her second child. In March, they went to Vienna; it would be their last trip abroad together. In May, while she was proofreading and indexing *Burne-Jones*, she was increasingly worried about Desmond's health. They had a GP whom they disliked, and Desmond decided to leave him. Penelope described to Maria what happened when Desmond went to get his cards: "Dr. M. was very angry, and shouted at him that he didn't want him as a patient anyway as he was always complaining, though Daddy has only seen him 3 times in 10 years. But Daddy told him he was unfit for general practice, and I'm glad someone has told him so at last." Clearly the GP had been fatally incompetent—"he said there was nothing wrong"—since the instant Desmond went to his new doctor, in late May, he was sent to St. George's Hospital in Tooting for an X-ray. Penelope told Maria, not wanting to worry her too much, that he was going to have an operation for "a nasty ulcer in the back passage." In fact, he had bowel cancer. "If they have to cut through his sphincter muscle poor old Da will have to manage with a plastic bottle for the rest of his days, but this <u>may</u> be avoidable. Pray it won't happen, won't you darling, and if it does, well this is just one more difficulty to face and we have already faced many."[42]

He was hospitalised on 6 June. On the ninth, Penelope went to Oliver Knox's launch party for his new book. Two days later, Desmond wrote a valiant letter to Tina, joking about the latest news (*Private Eye's* loathing of Tony Benn, for instance) and making light of what was to come: "I have just signed a document consenting to everything & absolving everybody from liability; it . . . bears a strong resemblance to a booking form prepared by a Tour Operator, except that there is no 60% cancellation charge."[43] On the twelfth, he had the operation: "abdomino-perineal resection," he noted in his diary. This, the removal of part of the rectum, left him with a colostomy and what medical textbooks call a "poor quality of life." During this month, while Desmond was in hospital, and Penelope was at home or visiting him, she started to write a story, which filled four red notebooks. It was to be a light comic thriller, inspired by the Tutankhamun exhibition and her trip to Russia. On the front of the first notebook she drew a scary, funny picture of a swaddled child-mummy. This would be her first novel, *The Golden Child*. When asked, later, why she had started to write fiction alongside biography in the 1970s, she would always say that she wrote it "to amuse my husband when he was ill."[44] She gave a slightly different version of her motives to Richard Garnett: "I did write this mystery story, largely to get rid of my annoyance 1. about the Tutankhamen [*sic*] Exhib: as I'm certain everything in it was a forgery, and 2. about someone who struck me as particularly unpleasant when I was obliged to go a lot to museums &c to find out about Burne-Jones."[45] But certainly the story was intended as a distraction: for herself, surely, as much as for Desmond.

She was told, after his operation, that "Desmond couldn't live." The children knew this, but Desmond, it seems, was not told: there was a "conspiracy of silence."[46] He recorded his condition in his diary in the summer. "June 25: Relapse. Food poisoning. July 4: Left Hospital 4 pm, lovely to be home. July 5: Great luxury—life of Pasha—but very tired. July 8: Went to library supported by Mops & Tina—big achievement."[47] The family were planning an emergency move. Tina and Terence were buying a house in Battersea, in Almeric Road, a side street of terrace houses near Clapham Common. The plan was for Desmond and Penelope to make the long-desired departure from Poynders Gardens and move in with them, so that they could share the burden of care. Terence, Tina and Desmond were eager to do this; Penelope was anxious and uncertain, and even though she longed to leave Poynders Gardens, she made difficulties for several months.[48]

Maria graduated from Oxford that summer with a Second Class degree ("the important thing is," Desmond wrote fondly, "it's a good second") and got a postgraduate place at University College London. In July and August, they went to Brighton for short seaside stays, but in between Desmond kept relapsing and going back into hospital. Penelope found his illness difficult to deal with; it made her angry and resentful as well as sad, and she would often sit glum and silent in the hospital.[49] On 17 August, Valpy's second son, Laurence, was born. On 3 September, Penelope signed her contract for *The Knox Brothers*. In September, Desmond tried to start work again, but he was soon back in hospital. The family—Penelope, Tina, Maria and John, and Desmond's old friend Peter Norton—were sitting round his bed on 15 September. It was the day *Edward Burne-Jones* came out. She said: "It's my publication day, and nobody cares."[50]

Desmond was not well enough to go to Laurence Fitzgerald's christening in Cambridge on 20 September. In December they moved from Poynders Gardens to Almeric Road. There is no record of Penelope's feelings on closing the door behind her on the council flat where she had put their lives back together and where they had lived for eleven years. In the winter of 1975–76, Desmond was continually in and out of the Royal Marsden, and was on doses of a "nauseating" drug.[51] In March, "Kipper," Ernest Shepard, died. It was sad for Mary Knox to lose her father a few years after her husband. And because Kipper had never quite forgiven Mary for marrying Evoe, only a small proportion of the fortune that was amassing from the *Winnie-the-Pooh* illustrations was left to her.[52] Rawle embarked on a book on *The Work of E. H. Shepard*, published in 1979, which Penelope would help him write. In April, she went away, alone, to Florence. She looked at churches and galleries and intensely took in the atmosphere of the city. It would stay in her mind: Florence, charged with strong emotion.

In May, Desmond told himself that "the cancer is under control. Things look better." But he had to go back into the Royal Marsden on 17 June, and was "rather grouchy" and disappointed that Mops could not take him: "I'm really a bit frightened." On the eighteenth he was told that all was well: "thanked every doctor in sight." Probably they knew now that nothing could be done, but chose not to distress him. If he knew he was dying, he did not utter it. Thirty years before, he had witnessed the "silent courage" of the wounded Irish soldiers at Anzio, "a living monument to the strength of the human will in the depths of human misery."[53]

It was a very hot June. He was worried about Mops, who was working hard. She was in the last stages of *The Knox Brothers,* and had finished *The Golden Child.* She had not "placed it yet, but that is no cause of despondency," Desmond noted on 24 June, in his only reference to the book in his diary.[54] On the twenty-ninth he wrote: "Mops overwhelmed with work. I can't do anything to help." Tina and Terence went for a holiday to Broadstairs and "Mops was quite envious, but I can't join in because I don't envy anybody, I am so lucky & happy myself just to be here." By mid-July he was feeling, in his word, "awful." "Pain-killers essential." Valpy, in Córdoba with his family, wrote on 9 July: "I am glad to hear that Daddy is bearing up, but as you know, all you have to do is send a cable and I can be in London by the next day more or less." At the end of July, she took Desmond for another weekend to Brighton. The sea air made Mops feel energetic and him feel very tired. At some point in these summer months, she rang Eamon Fitzgerald's number to tell him that his brother was dying. He refused to come to the phone. On 8 August, Desmond's diary entries ended. A week later she wrote to Oliver: "I'm staggering along to the end of the family biography after endless difficulties . . . Desmond alas, after hanging on for a year after the op, very much worse now, so much occupied with nursing. They gave me very good pain-killers though, much better than in the old days."[55] They got him home to Almeric Road. He died on 19 August, of carcinoma of the rectum and pneumonia, at the age of fifty-nine. His death certificate described him as "travel agent." He was buried in Putney Vale Cemetery. That autumn, she wrote to her old friend Willie Conder from Almeric Road:

> I was told a year ago after his op. that Desmond couldn't live, but didn't really prepare myself as I should have done, and I do feel it as a dreadful blow, only I really oughtn't to complain as I'm so lucky being here, with Tina and Terry upstairs, and their bicycles in the hall, and someone to talk to whenever I need to; the truth

is I was spoilt, as with all our ups and downs Desmond always thought everything I did was right . . . I'm so glad we were able to get the move over so that Desmond died at home, and not in hospital; the district nurse was there that morning, such a kindly person, not much of a nurse but a very good woman, and she helped me to see him out of this world and read a Bible chapter, absolutely naturally, as only a West Indian could do, and I have to be glad the suffering is over, but I do miss him.[56]

To her daughters, when he died, she said: Don't leave me to live on my own.

(*Above*) 1. The Knox family: an exceptional and eccentric clan
(*Left*) 2. The formidable Bishop Knox
(*Below*) 3. Bishop Hicks, enemy of poverty and injustice
(*Below left*) 4. Winnie Knox, the future writer Winifred Peck

(*Above*) 5. Eddie ("Evoe") Knox going to war, 19
(*Left*) 6. Christina Hicks, the Bishop's
daughter as debutante, 1903

(*Above*) 7. Bishop's son weds Bishop's daughter,
September 1912

(*Right*) 8. Christina Knox and baby Rawle, 1914

(*Above left*) 9. Mops on the beach, circa 1920

(*Above*) 10. Brother and sister, 1924

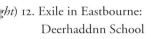

(*Left*) 11. The village of
Hampstead in the 1920s

ht) 12. Exile in Eastbourne:
Deerhaddnn School

(*Above left*) 13. Penelope Knox, 1930, the brightest girl in school

(*Above*) 14. Evoe Knox: the editor of *Punch* at his desk, 1930s

(*Left*) 15. A young stepmother: Evoe, Mary Shepard and Mops, late 1930s

(*Below*) 16. Penelope Knox, the "blonde bombshell"

ove) 17–19. "Les Girls": Willie Conder, Janet Russell, Penelope and Jean Fisher

(*Above*) 20. Penelope and Oliver Breakwell with Free French soldiers, Hyde Park, September 1940

(*Left*)
21. Oliver Breakwell

(*Right*)
22. Hugh Lee

(*Above*) 23. Lieutenant Desmond Fitzgerald, the "Irish soldier," 1940

(*Right*) 24. The wedding of Desmond Fitzgerald and Penelope Knox, 15 August 1942

(*Above left*) 25. The bridesmaid, Jean Fisher

(*Above*) 26. At the wedding: Evoe and Mary Knox, flanked by Mr. and Mrs. Fitzgerald

(*Left*) 27. Mary Knox and Penelope Fitzgerald, 1945

(*Above*) 28. Squires Mount, Hampstead, today

(*Right*) 29. Chestnut Lodge, next door to Squires Mount, today

(*Above left*) 30. Desmond and his daughters, Tina and Maria, 1954

(*Above*) 31. Penelope painting, on holiday with the Fishers, 1950s

(*Left*) 32. Penelope at Blackshore House, Southwold, 1957

(*Left*) 33. Tina and Valpy on holiday in Europe, 1955

(*Below*) 34. At home on *Grace:* Maria, early 1960s

(*Below*) 35. Temporary housing: Desmond in Earls Court Road, 1964

(*Right*) 36. "Squalid Council Estate": Penelope in Agnes Riley Gardens, next to Poynders Gardens, 1974

(*Above*) 37. The wedding of Valpy and Angelines, Córdoba, 31 July 1967

(*Right*) 38. Mother and son at his wedding

(*Left*) 39. Desmond and Penelope, early 1970s

(*Below*) 40. Penelope in 1975

(*Above left*) 41. In Russia, 1975

(*Above*) 42. In China, 1977

(*Above*) 43. Maria's wedding, 1978.
Left to right: Penelope, Terence and Tina, Mar~
and John Lake, Joan Lake, Angelines and
Valpy with Laurence and Valpy Gregory

(*Left*) 44. The writer at her desk,
Almeric Road, 1980

(*Above*) 45. Publisher Richard Ollard (left) and cousin Oliver Knox

(*Above right*) 46. Rawle Knox, *Observer* journalist, New Delhi, 1950

(*Right*) 47. With her dear cousin Tony Peck

(*Below left*) 48. Rachel Hichens, née Ollivant: one of the oldest friends

(*Below right*) 49. Colin Haycraft and Beryl Bainbridge at Gloucester Crescent

(*Above*) 50. Winning the Booker Pri[ze]
for *Offshore*, 23 October 1979, with,
left to right, Chair of Judges Asa Brigg[s]
Chair of Booker McConnell Michael
Caine, and runners-up Fay Weldon a[nd]
Julian Rathbone

(*Above*) 51. Winner of the Booker Prize

(*Right*) 52. Being congratulated,
with Maria

(*Left*) 53. Edward Burne-Jones with his granddaughter, Angela MacKail

(*Above*) 54. Penelope's hero, William Morris

(*Left*) 55. Charlotte Mew, 1923

(*Top*) 56. Living alone in St. John's Wood and writing *Charlotte Mew*, 1982–83

(*Above*) 57. Granny with Maria, Sophie and Tom Lake, 1990

(*Right*) 58. Granny with Alfie Lake, Highgate Woods, 1990s

(*right*) 59. At
Penelope Lively's
house, with Jack
Lively, 1981

(*right*) 60. Winning the Golden Pen
Award, with Maria, 1999

(*below*) 61. The eightieth-birthday party
at Bishops Road, 7 September 1996

(*below right*) 62. The eightieth-birthday
party at Café Rouge, Highgate,
December 1996, with Valpy
and sister-in-law Helen

63. Outside 27A Bishops Road, July 1999

CHAPTER ELEVEN

Enigmas

"The ideographs are absolutely clear; yet I confess myself baffled."[1]

Fitzgerald was in the middle of researching and writing *The Knox Brothers* in the summer of 1975 when she deviated into *The Golden Child*. Her head was full of the characters of the four brothers, now all dead, whom she had known as odd, unworldly, formidably clever older men, with the enigmas of their lives cocooned in layers inside them. Unravelling their secrets was like following a thread from the present back into the underworld. In the novel, her invention of an ancient mummified child, with its golden ball of twine, a code that has to be broken to crack open the mystery, all connect to her work on the Knoxes. (There is even a learned code-breaker in the novel who, like Dillwyn, has been studying the Mimes of Herodas.) The story of *The Golden Child* is closely intertwined with her thoughts about her family biography. For all its Knoxian tomfoolery, it has a serious question to ask: What is false, and what is true, and how are people deceived? That was the kind of question the Knoxes were interested in. The ominous plot also links to her family book. Any anxieties she may have had about pursuing the life stories of her father and uncles, none of whom had relished the idea of a biography ("Must We Have Lives?"), are indirectly voiced in the idea of a curse which hangs darkly over her light comic thriller. "Everything that is long hidden in the earth and is dragged by human beings into the light of day, brings with it its own danger."

She used the Knoxes in her first novel, and other pieces of her own experience: the trip to Russia in January 1975, her visits to the Tutankhamun exhibition in 1972, her Burne-Jones forays into the world of museum curators and art historians. The legend of the Golden Child echoes her fictional experiment of 1951, in the *World Review*, "A Letter from Tisshara," the story of the ailing young prince of a lost civilisation. And, hidden inside the manuscript notebooks for the novel, whose working title was "The Golden Opinion," was a painful subplot which, in the end, was written out of the book.

The "Museum" of *The Golden Child* is not, by name, the British Museum, and the new exhibition for which thousands of people from all over the country are patiently queuing in the bitterly cold January of 1973 is not the Tutankhamun exhibition. All the same, she took pleasure in exaggeratedly re-creating the stoic, carnival atmosphere of the vast crowds of tourists and schoolchildren queuing day and night to have a few minutes in front of the exhibit. The queuing itself, in her version, becomes an epic, legendary experience, recalling the endurance of the Blitz. "The length of time waited was . . . an important part of the experience of seeing the Treasure," badges are issued to those who had been among "the First Ten Thousand" and the scene in the courtyard becomes like "a great fair painted by Breughel." But she did try to distinguish her exhibition from its inspiration. She had been at pains, she said crossly in 1997, when the Flamingo paperback came with Egyptian artefacts on the cover, to "make it *not* Egyptian."[2] Her mummified golden child, with his toys and his ball of golden twine, has arrived, via Russia, from a remote and ancient African country called Garamantia.

The Garamantians, whose civilisation dates from the fifth century B.C., are found in Herodotus; they are one of the tribes he mentions when he is listing what he knows about the far-flung peoples of the world. In one of the "Golden Opinion" notebooks, Fitzgerald translates from Herodotus (Book IV): "The Garamantes, who avoid all communication with men, are ignorant of the use of any military weapons, and totally unable to defend themselves. Their language bears no resemblance to that of other nations, for it is like the screeching of bats." In the finished novel this is reduced to an enigma, a single untranslated line in Greek from Herodotus in a secret memo from the British Embassy in Garamantia, annotated by its recipient in the Foreign Office: "What the hell does the sod think he's talking about?" But the culture of the ancient Garamantians comes to be seen as a lost Utopia. The novel's William Morris lookalike, Len Coker, a draughtsman and restorer, a passionate Marxist, as clumsy in his personal life as he is meticulous in his professional skills, imagines ancient Garamantia as an ideal society, like Morris's in *News from Nowhere*. All men are regarded as alike, all is shared in common, the word for "buy" and "sell" is the same, and they have no present tense: "The Garamantians had no conception of the present. They thought only of the past and the future; hence, they were happy." Needless to say, they became extinct. The Garamantia of the present is a malfunctioning, underdeveloped African country, its young ruler, "Prince Rasselas," a weak figure under a military dictatorship. It is sending its ancient treasure to Western museums, with Russian help and with financial backing from a tobacco company, in the hopes of attracting aid and political clout. The contrast between the ancient Garamantians and contemporary Western civilisation is clear.

The comic energy of *The Golden Child* comes from Fitzgerald's satire on the hierarchical museum culture and its internal power-plays, which are of Darwinian ruthlessness, "a free-for-all struggle of the crudest kind. Even in total silence one could sense the ferocious efforts of the highly cultured staff trying to ascend the narrow ladder of promotion." It anticipates her comic treatment of the BBC in *Human Voices,* a few years later, but that institution is fundamentally benign, while the great museum is sinister and corrupt. Within it, though, there are forces working for good. There is the aged Sir William Simpkin, a working-class boy who became a great archaeologist, was trained by the pioneering Egyptologist Flinders Petrie before the Great War, and is world famous as the original discoverer of the Garamantian treasure. Sir William, whom the polished museum curators think of as an "old ruffian," looks like Elgar (she wants him to represent the Edwardian era) and is curmudgeonly, incorruptible, brilliant, intrepid, kind to unimportant juniors, given to practical jokes, fond of "poetry, games, puzzles—all arrangements of words," and hostile to showiness and worldly success. He is, in short, a Knox.

This legendary figure has "come to roost" in his den high up in the museum, with an endearing, useless Eastern European secretary, Dousha, and an ancient troll-like retainer, old Jones, who roams the corridors like a ghost, muttering about the curse of the treasure. And there is a kind of curse on the museum. Sir William knows all about its malignity. "The object of the museum is to acquire power, not only at the expense of other

museums, but absolutely," he says. Up against him are two perfect opera-
tors of this system. One is the Museum Director, Sir John Allison ("Coldbreath" in the manuscript), the "awe-inspiring, gently smiling, wondrous
blend of civil servant and scholar," based on Kenneth Clark (he has his own
long-running TV series, *What Is Culture?*), secretly filled with "the pride
and bitter jealousy which is the poetry of museum-keeping." The other
is the "effete" Hawthorne-Mannering, specialist in Funerary Monuments,
ex-Courtauld, "not quite as young as he looks," and known throughout the
museum as the Queen of the May. Hawthorne-Mannering shrinks away
"with a snail's-horn delicacy from complete commitment," takes frequent
sick leave, and dreams, ineffectually, of "revitalising" the museum. His
kind of treacherous, cultured young man is a favourite "type" for her: this
is the most outrageously homophobic version of it. (But she will make up
for it with the lovable and admirable gay prostitute in *Offshore*.)

Labouring away in another subdivision of the museum is Len Coker's
friend, the junior exhibitions officer, Waring Smith, in whom Sir William
takes a kindly interest because he is "young, normal, unimpressed, sincere
and worried." Waring is the first of her muddled, broke, well-meaning
male characters: his wife, Haggie, has left him because he is so hopeless,
and he spends the novel trying, not very effectively, to get her back and to
deal honestly with circumstances beyond his control. He sees that Sir William is his good angel, that Len Coker, for all his belligerence, is a friend
till death, and that Sir John and Hawthorne-Mannering are wicked. This
novel is implacably evangelical about who is a decent human being and
who is beyond the pale. But Waring Smith has to put up with unpleasant
people in order to earn his living. At the heart of the novel is his journey
towards independence, the point at which he can say: "Such as I am, I
want to be Waring Smith, true to the spirit that walks inside me." What
becomes of Waring? He grows up.

Brought in to inspect the treasure are two foreigners, one good and
one bad. The baddie is a ludicrous French cultural anthropologist and
mythologist, a spoof amalgam of Barthes, Derrida and Lévi-Strauss. Tite-
Live Rochegrosse-Bergson (who is gay, and lives in the rue Baron de Char-
lus in Paris) gives a fluent discourse on how the Ball of Golden Twine
is like "the cat's cradle . . . which, unlike string itself, has no end." "All
our thoughts are, to use my own word, my own chosen signifier, *la
pensée-stop*—the irresistible impulse to *stop thinking at all*." This "arrant
nonsense," eagerly mopped up by journalists, is as fraudulent as all the
other artefacts. Rochegrosse-Bergson, it will transpire, was once a crooked
provincial curator called Schwarz who used the Occupation to sell off

his museum's treasures for personal gain. The shadow of the war hangs over *The Golden Child,* as it will Fitzgerald's other novels of the 1950s. Its history is embodied in the other visiting expert, shabby Professor Untermensch, a learned European Garamantologist, and a highly cultured refugee, obsessed by the Golden Child. He lost his wife in 1935 and is well used to violence and dictatorship: "The Nazis used to make him do the street-sweeping in Vienna in 1937 . . . Madness, death, and destruction were not a new story to him." Untermensch, Coker and Waring are the novel's three musketeers—using courage, skill and determination to discover the truth about the exhibition and the terrible things that are happening in the museum.

Untermensch immediately realises that the Golden Child is a fake, and, laughing grimly, tells Sir John as much. There is a series of sinister events, including an attempt to strangle Waring with the golden twine. The Director, horrified at the prospect of being exposed, orders the lights to be lowered in the exhibition room, and sends Waring to Russia, with the Golden Child's toy in his suitcase, to consult with the world's only other Garamantian expert in the hope that he will authenticate the treasure. This unlikely plot twist (all the plotting in the novel is, in a phrase from her notebooks, "a bit steep") allows her to use her experience of Russia.

At the back of one of the "Golden Opinion" notebooks there is a hand-drawn map of Moscow, and details about routes to the House of Freedom, directions to Tolstoy's house, taxi fares ("10 kopeks whatever the distance") and entry times to the Lenin Mausoleum. Waring undergoes a surreal version of Fitzgerald's own visit. The long, frozen, patient queues to see "the mummy of Lenin" remind him of the queues for the Golden Child: "The true international solidarity was not between workers, but between queuers." The visit to Tolstoy's house ("wooden balconies and birch trees") transports him into "Moscow's past," which she will re-enter in *The Beginning of Spring*. Waring's quest for the elusive Garamantian expert takes him on a nightmarish adventure, like one of those dark thriller films she loved, *The Third Man* or *The Thirty-Nine Steps*. His visits to a violent circus performance, where the clowns are all really spies, to the frozen wastes of the Park of Economic Achievements and to the "gaunt" bazaars of Red Square, lead him, with Untermensch as his unlikely guide, to the revelation of the real Golden Treasure of Garamantia. The great Western museum has been conned by the great communist power, which has taken the real treasure into safekeeping in surety for a loan to the struggling African country, and sent a replica abroad to avoid "an international incident."

When Waring gets back, he finds that Sir William has been murdered.

The police and the Secret Service get to work, all with names like Rivett, Gunn and Mace, all completely incapable of solving anything. ("Police to find out *nothing*," she wrote in her notebook.) The increasingly wild plot culminates in Untermensch, Waring and Coker trying to decode a tablet of Garamantian hieroglyphics. As they get to work, "a strong current of excitement, generated from the love of knowledge simply for the sake of knowing, made itself felt in the darkening room." We are in Bletchley. The code, once cracked, reveals the murderer. For good measure, there is also a frenzied chase through the night-time museum, another attempted murder, a suicide, and the destruction and rapid reconstruction of the sham treasure. "It looks almost new," says the first person in the queue to be let in after the debacle. So the story ends, with the fake exhibit continuing to pull in the crowds, and Waring still waiting for Haggie to come back, but with "a physical sensation like the thawing of ice, or the melting down of gold," telling him "that the worst of his troubles were over."

This was not how she meant the book to conclude. Whenever she was asked about her first novel, she would always say that it was written to amuse Desmond when he was ill, that it was inspired by a fancy that the Tutankhamun exhibition might have been a fraud, and that it was meant to have several more chapters and characters, which she had been made to cut out by her publisher, who wanted her to write a series of subsequent thrillers with Untermensch as her detective. Looking back in 1994, she commented:

> I was brought up to believe that mystery stories should have clues, false clues, suspects and a complete explanation in the last chapter. With all these, when I started to write my novel, I did my best, although when I cut down the text some of the clues, and I think some of the suspects, disappeared . . . The Russians in it are villains of the simplest and most inscrutable kind, French Academicians are still structuralists . . . and a junior exhibition officer is bowed down by mortgage repayments of £118 a month. But I think of *The Golden Child* as a historical novel. All novels, in fact, are historical.[3]

One of the cuts she made was to a series of high-level Cabinet meetings, recounted in the bureaucratic diary of a Cabinet Secretary, discussing the possibilities of public disorder raised by the fake exhibition. These scenes involved homework on museum governance, the Foreign Office, diplomatic language ("'With great respect' indicates anger") and funding for the arts. The anti-establishment politics of the novel would have been even more explicit with these scenes kept in.

Then there was the subplot. In the manuscript, Sir John Coldbreath has a rich, idiotic daughter, Lush Coldbreath (the sort of girl who might have gone to Queen's Gate), who is keen on Dolly Spiller, the son of Waring's immediate superior at the museum, Franny Spiller. It's a pity that the needy and histrionic Mrs. Spiller was edited out. She has a "brightened eye and reddened mouth, with much metal about her, clashing ear-rings, small silver bottles containing both stimulating and tranquillising pills, bracelets and large bags which shut with a definitive snap." But her "impression of self-sufficiency" is an illusion. "In the most important relationship of her life Mrs. Spiller was at a loss. She dearly loved her only son, and he did not love her. She had called him Adolphus because 19 years ago it had seemed amusing to give your child a Victorian name; he was now lanky, languid Dolly Spiller, not interested in anything very much." Dolly despises her: "He says our life at Yeomans Row is poverty-stricken & he needs <u>money</u> to find out who & what he is." The pain this causes her, and her desperate need to get money for him in order to keep him, are sharply sketched. In a harsh scene in her dismal terraced house at the wrong end of Chelsea, Dolly walks out on her party, leaving his mother wailing: "I made gnocchi because he said he liked it so much in the Abruzzi . . . I made it myself and dried it over the back of the kitchen chairs." Waring tells Lush Coldbreath that she should ask Dolly to be kinder to his mother, but the awful girl replies: "He <u>is</u> good to her. She's intolerable. He gives her things and she just loses them." Perhaps these characters disappeared, not just because cuts were required, but because they were too close to Fitzgerald's feelings about her son.

The cancelled last chapters, drafted in the notebooks, involve the continuing cover-up of the fraud, while "over 80,000" visitors queue up to see the exhibition. "Eventually the whole cargo of false treasure, like the caravans of old, disappears once again into the heart of Africa." Lush Coldbreath inherits money, so Dolly Spiller marries her and sheds his mother, and they move to "a smart converted warehouse on Bermondsey river frontage." Mrs. Spiller sinks into alcoholism, getting her gin at different wine shops so that "no one will know how many bottles she buys." Len and Dousha have a baby girl called Wilhelmina Coker: "Surely there must be a great future ahead for a girl with a name like that." Sir William has left Waring exactly enough money to pay off his mortgage. He leaves the museum and gets a job as a curator in "a small provincial museum on the Suffolk coast"—the setting of Fitzgerald's next novel. He, Len and Untermensch have a farewell evening in their usual Greek café, because they are all going their different ways. It is a touching scene.

> Then the Professor leant forward and kissed both the young men on both cheeks.
> —Many thanks for your hospitality, he said to Len. If you and your wife and the little one should ever need somewhere to go, under my roof you will find shelter.
> —But where is your roof? Len asked.
> —I cannot say. But wherever it is you are welcome. And then turning to Waring:
> —And you too are my friend for life. Always! Always!
> Len also prepared to go.
> See you around, he said.

Waring's wife has not come back yet: she never appears in the novel. But "Waring hopes she will soon join him at Grimesborough. The air is very good there. And if it is true that all is not gold that glitters, it is also true that the falling out of friends is the renewal of love." That appears to be the ending as originally planned. But in the notebooks, the existing last scene—"It looks almost new"—is also underlined in red as: "End." Which ending did she really want? It is an enigma.

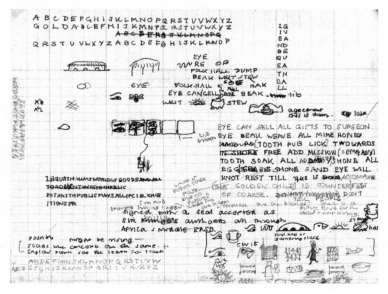

ᴊᴏ

The publisher who told her to cut *The Golden Child* "because readers like short novels" was Colin Haycraft, with whom Fitzgerald had a brief and rocky publishing relationship. Since she had shed Michael Joseph because they did not want *The Knox Brothers,* and *The Golden Child* was not going to suit Macmillan, she was now on to her third publisher for her third book, in two years. She always said that she got Haycraft's name out of the *Writers' and Artists' Yearbook.* This may have been one of those half-joking simplifications she liked to make in interviews, or it might be true. But she could have made contact with Haycraft through other writers she knew from *World Review* days, Stevie Smith or Neville Braybrooke, or through her *Burne-Jones* editor Raleigh Trevelyan. Trevelyan and Haycraft came of similar Empire-serving stock. Their fathers were in the same battalions in the Indian Army. Colin Haycraft's father was shot by one of his Sikh sepoys and Haycraft's mother had a breakdown. Trevelyan and Haycraft became friends and used to eat tapioca pudding together at the Travellers' Club. Trevelyan found Haycraft likeable and amusing. So did most people.

Duckworth & Co. had been founded by Virginia Woolf's half-brother Gerald Duckworth, who published her first two novels in the 1910s. Colin Haycraft, who took it over in 1968 from an eccentric character called Mervyn Horder, was a brilliant classicist with a passion for classics, philosophy, real tennis, Oxford, the eighteenth century and recondite information. He was also charming, funny, rude, unconventional, argumentative and expansive: "He lived on wit, adrenalin, too much coffee, strong drink, small cigars, flexed nerves and a ready laugh."[4] In 1956 he married Anna Lindholm, a Welsh, Russian-Finnish, Liverpool Catholic, a beautiful, sharp-witted, idiosyncratic bohemian, and a depressive. They bought a large terraced house in Gloucester Crescent, in north London, and ran the publishing house in the Old Piano Factory at the other end of the street, in Oval Road. They had several children, though one died young and one had a tragic accidental death in 1978. Haycraft published classical and philosophical books, and they also published fiction, mainly edited by Anna, who, under the name of Alice Thomas Ellis, published her own novels, short, satirical, black family comedies loaded with Catholic guilt. Her closest friend, who lived nearby, was Beryl Bainbridge, also a Liverpool Catholic writer in London, also strikingly eccentric, but a much more brilliant, versatile and long-lasting writer. Anna, Beryl and Colin were a close and in some ways toxic trio. The style of Ellis's fiction and of Bainbridge's early novels, and of other authors they published, like Caroline Blackwood, created a minor, recognisable genre, with which Fitzgerald was briefly identified. An appreciative 1980 review by Frank Kermode of *Human Voices* and Beryl Bainbridge's *Winter Garden* in the *London Review of Books* was headed "The Duckworth School of Writers."[5]

The Duckworth/Haycraft parties, spilling out of the large house into their overgrown garden, were numerous and legendary. Anna presided wittily over the Aga; Colin, on one memorable occasion, recited the end of *The Decline and Fall of the Roman Empire* on the balcony, in celebration of Gibbon's finishing the work two hundred years before. There would be Catholic priests under the table, Beryl lying the worse for wear in a skip, and a whole colony of London writers, artists, musicians and intellectuals—Jonathan Miller, Alan Bennett, Oliver Sacks, A. J. Ayer, Francis King, Brian McGuinness, the young A. N. Wilson, the Tomalins, the Vaughan-Williamses. Whisky, Angostura bitters, wine and Cointreau flowed extremely freely. "Colin's Killers" were a mixture of fizzy white wine, Cointreau, a sugar cube and a maraschino cherry. Penelope went to some of the parties, and enjoyed herself (A. N. Wilson observed that "she saw the point of a drink"), but she was not going to be trapped under the "Duckworth School" label for very long.

Colin's attitude to women novelists, including his wife, was notoriously dismissive. His real interest was in his classics list, and he called the fiction list "the distaff side of the business," or "a branch of gynaecology." Anna saw herself as the fiction editor, but authors sometimes weren't sure whether they were dealing with her or with Colin, or whether they had become pawns in a complicated marital game. They also weren't sure whether they would ever get their royalties. Haycraft was notorious for shortchanging his authors. All of them complained, but many stayed on because it seemed "a small price to pay for the honour of being published by a man we adored." Beryl Bainbridge's writing life and her reputation were transformed when she left Duckworth after years of being underpaid, patronised and underpromoted.[6]

Fitzgerald realised more quickly than Bainbridge that the relationship was not going to work well for her, though, like everyone, she found Colin sympathetic and entertaining, and never spoke ill of him. Anna Haycraft's acceptance letter for *The Golden Child* was an ominous start: "The story would benefit from some changes. Would you be prepared to remove a few characters and add a little suspense?" She agreed, and a proposal followed from Colin: "I suggest an advance of £200. Does this seem acceptable?" Penelope wrote a note to herself on the letter: "No, but I haven't the courage to say so." The contract was duly drawn up, with the £200 advance, and a royalty of 10 per cent up to 3,000. Her first (and possibly only) royalty statement, for 1 January to 30 June, 1978, showed sales of 79 copies.[7]

As the messy production of *The Golden Child* staggered on, she became increasingly despondent. She wrote to Richard Garnett:

> I thought quite well of the book at first but it's now almost unintelligible, it was probably an improvement that the last chapters got lost, but then 4 characters & 1000s of words had to be cut to save paper, then the artwork got lost (by the printers this time) so we had to use my roughs and it looks pretty bad, but there you are, it doesn't matter, and no-one will notice, and Colin works so hard, I wouldn't be surprised to find him, sitting in the Old Piano Factory with a bottle of whisky doing all the packing and despatch himself.[8]

Still, she would sign two more contracts with Haycraft in 1978 before the parting of ways.

She was exhausted from Desmond's death and from finishing two books at once. She decided to give up teaching at Queen's Gate in 1977 and just to keep on at Westminster Tutors. When *The Knox Brothers* was delivered to Macmillan in January 1977, Valpy wrote (evidently in response to her having complained of feeling worn out): "I am glad you got your book off in time, and that SuperMac [Harold Macmillan] had a look at it . . . But I am worried that you might overstress yourself working so hard—I know it is all good money, but what is the point of it if you are too ill to enjoy it? Couldn't you perhaps write shorter pieces for magazines that wouldn't involve so much hard labour?"[9] He had not understood that she was a writer of books, and he was not alone in his attitude. Richard Garnett, that year, suggested she was not a real professional. She responded: "It worried me terribly when you told me I was only an amateur writer and I asked myself, how many books do you have to write and how many semi-colons do you have to discard before you lose amateur status?"[10] The issue rankled. She wrote to a new friend, the novelist Francis King, in 1978, about one of her new projects: "I'm not a professional writer, but only very anxious to write one or 2 things which interest me."[11]

❧

In her secret archive, however, many things were taking shape. Her debts were paid, she had a home, no one was depending on her and time was short: she was sixty. Her outpouring of ideas in the late 1970s was astonishingly energetic, rapid and profuse. Alongside the almost simultaneous publication of *The Golden Child* and *The Knox Brothers* in the autumn of 1977, Fitzgerald started at least five books: two novels, the book on Renaissance painting and flowers inspired by her work on Burne-Jones, and two biographies. None of these were ever finished, some would continue to be worked on for years, and some were recycled in her published work. She was working on several things at once.

Both the novels were to be thrillers featuring Professor Untermensch, so they clearly evolved in response to Haycraft's suggestion that she use her Beckettian-Viennese "superman" as her recurring detective. The idea for one book came out of a holiday in Turkey she and Desmond had taken in 1969. She was already thinking about the novel when he died. Jasmine Blakeway, whose husband, John, Desmond's old friend, was then Consul-General in Istanbul, saw the announcement in *The Times*. She said to her husband, "Desmond's gone and died." Though not a person to show his emotions, John Blakeway was extremely upset. He and Jasmine wrote a condolence letter to Penelope, who, in her reply, remarked: "I am very interested in Istanbul. I'm writing a book about the cast-iron church—have you seen it?"[12] The novel was to be called "The Iron Bridge."

It began: "The Golden Horn runs very deep under the Galata Bridge." A young man called Green—one of her bewildered, hopeful pilgrims—has been sent by his father to Istanbul, in 1975, as a business emissary from the Ipswich family firm, which makes and exports "Peerless Screws," to extract payment from the company involved in building a new, iron bridge, as a backup for the overcrowded Galata Bridge. Green has taken a business course, and there are notes on management-speak. Part of the pleasure of the novel was clearly going to be its many different languages. There is an escaped Russian novelist, Volodya, who will be the dramatic, seductive character. There is a childish Bulgarian girl called Bela, presumably to be the love-object and source of rivalry between Volodya and Green. There is a Turk with a part share in a nightclub whose music annoys the British consul next door: "But Nasreddin tells him that he is fortunate to have the music free when others must pay." There is a pianist, who is to play Beethoven's Trio in D Major, "The Ghost," with its "flickering" sudden chords in the last movement. (She makes more than one note of this piece of music, which mattered to her.) Dirty business over the iron and steel trade, for Professor Untermensch to sort out, is to be mixed with the stories of exiles and clashing cultures. There will be scenes in the Bulgarian cast-iron church, and in a "village of the dead" ("invented by me"), reached by a journey up the Bosphorus, "winding between the hills of Europe and Asia."

There are notes on Jews; on French, Russian and Greek inhabitants of Istanbul; on the British Council; on restaurants, bread, storks, Anatolian villages, carpets, bazaars, evening classes, cemeteries, djinns, churches and small businesses. She is going to compress all this homework, so that the reader will feel they know everything about life in Istanbul without being told. There are plot suggestions ("duel in a fish restaurant?") and there is a plan for the ending, which will be borne in mind for *Offshore:* "Volodya shot. Green tries to row, freak current, swept backward, although a good oarsman usually, rescued by Prof with freighter full of steel parts." There are phrases jotted down: "Pity is a disease, one must cure oneself." "Such moments must be treasured, and will see us through a certain number of dark hours." "The whole art of happiness consists in staying in one place."[13]

Mixed up with these notes is a jotting for a short story. "A search for some small beautiful bird in the jungle. Structuralists, anthropologists, etc. Bird important (50 Australian dollars for a bluebird plume in New Guinea) but the bird is still not found." "The Iron Bridge" came to nothing. But the idea of setting a novel in Turkey stayed with her; and so did the search for some rare blue object of value, "still not found."

The other unfinished novel was called "Sale or Return," and was inspired—as *The Golden Child* had been by the Tutankhamun exhibition— by the sale of Lord Rosebery's treasures at Mentmore Towers in August 1977. This was a state-of-England novel, a satire on the art trade, on government and the upper classes, masquerading as a thriller. The material about arts funding and the Civil Service that she cut out of *The Golden Child* is recycled, and she has to keep reminding herself in her notes what she had already used ("Is that in *The Golden Child*? YES IT IS YOU CLOT.")

Mentmore, the vast Victorian Buckinghamshire mansion built and owned by the Rothschilds and, later, the Earls of Rosebery, was in the news in the mid-1970s because of the Labour government's refusal, on the death of the 6th Earl of Rosebery, to accept its cornucopia of art treasures in lieu of inheritance tax. This decision created a storm of debate, which Fitzgerald followed with interest. In the end the entire contents of Mentmore—Tiepolos, Gainsboroughs, Reynoldses, Chippendale furniture, Limoges enamels, Russian silver—were auctioned by Sotheby's for over £6 million. The sale made headline news for weeks.

"Sale or Return" centres on the sale of treasures from an English stately home in remote West Sussex. The old Earl, "Lord Bolter," mysteriously disappeared seven years ago, and the estate has been "frozen" since then. The onstage cast includes the surviving family, with one of her usual spoilt girls, who stands to inherit millions; Harrison, the local auctioneer "who has lived for so long in an acquisitive & competitive world that he sometimes felt confused as to who he liked & who he didn't"; and the powerful, ambiguous figure of the art dealer Peter Spekulans, English-Viennese, who may in the past have "picked up little bits & pieces from the ruins of Europe" but is now known as "totally honest & knowledgeable." There is a PR firm which seems to be called "More's The Pity," and a mad elderly General Failing, "a queer old perpetual visitor to the house," a try-out for General Gamart in *The Bookshop*. ("'I think I must have been 20 once,' said [the General] quietly. The chill of evening fell over the long-inhabited house. He raised his almost transparent hands to warm them at the steam of the soup.") Untermensch appears in one scene, waving his arms wildly outside the window, trying to get into the auction, like the prophet in her poem about the bus stop ("We in you out"). There are corrupt or ineffectual politicians, special advisers on culture ("a shoddy crew"), village folk, and a dull country solicitor, who will also be reworked in *The Bookshop*. The "missing" Earl—or possibly the mad General—is meant to blow up the house, and the story will end with the words: "the hammer falls." As if by magic, the sleeping spoils are transformed into public treasures.

True artists, craftsmen, teachers, writers and poets do not have heaped-up inherited spoils or political influence, nor should they. That is Fitzgerald's life's view, and it comes through strongly in these "early" books, both finished and unfinished, from *Burne-Jones* to *The Bookshop*. Her love of small, heartfelt, unworldly and usually failing enterprises, as opposed to big, well-endowed, showy successes, is a strong repeated theme.

While the Untermensch thrillers were being drafted and discarded in the mid-1970s, two nonfiction ideas were gestating, which would rumble on for years. One was for a book about the Poetry Bookshop. The other was a biography of the novelist Leslie Hartley. This, sadly, came to nothing.

Leslie Hartley was a friend. He belonged to the generation just before her (born in 1895, first published in 1924), which created an attractive balance for her of distance and closeness. The Joseph Losey/Harold Pinter film of *The Go-Between* in 1970 had created renewed interest in him, and he had died in 1972, so he was a subject ripe for biographical treatment. They had met in the early 1950s, when he contributed stories to the *World Review,* and had kept up since then, though whatever letters he wrote her were "all at the bottom of the Thames." He had occasionally invited her out to dinner (with the "exceedingly nice Veronica Wedgwood," she remembered), he had been part of her short-lived literary life in Chestnut Lodge, and she and Desmond had visited him now and then in his large riverside house, Avondale, at Bathford—his name and address were in Desmond's 1968 diary. When she saw it again, long after Hartley's death, "now transformed into the Misty Waters Grade 2 Hotel and Canoeing Centre," her heart sank. He was a generous friend who at one point, probably in the 1960s, offered her money, as he did to others in need, "so that they wouldn't have to work too hard." ("But no-one accepted it . . . because it would be a destructive thing from the point of view of friendship.") He confided in her about his work: that *Eustace and Hilda* was "meant to be my own tragedy"; that the model for the main character in *The Hireling* was "the proprietor of Jack's Car Hire of Brixton." They shared some literary enthusiasms, as for the novelist L. H. Myers, in their view an under-regarded genius.[14]

Her feelings about Hartley's work were mixed. In his seventies, he wrote too much and not well, and she thought most of his late books "irredeemably bad, in a quite distinctive way." But she admired the *Eustace and Hilda* trilogy, *The Go-Between,* and painfully autobiographical novels such as *The Hireling* and, very late, *The Harness Room.* She liked him as a writer of ghost stories. She understood his feeling for childhood, English class relations and unhappy, awkward relationships. In her annotations to his novels—which include lists of the real models for his fictional characters—her sympathy is clear, especially for *The Go-Between:* "We can't decide between good & evil, only perhaps reconcile them." In her letters to their mutual friend Francis King, she wrote: "LPH told me and I'm sure many others . . . that it is the supreme experiences which make life worthwhile, but they are <u>always</u> destructive . . . No-one who is brought up an evangelical can quite learn to trust earthly happiness, it must destroy you somehow."[15]

Trying to write a life of a person one had liked was moving, and could be upsetting. When she went to Leslie's childhood home, Fletton Tower, where his redoubtable younger sister Norah still lived, "and saw LPH's desk and the cyclamen transplanted from Avondale in one of the flowerbeds . . . I felt like crying, he was such a good friend." She felt that the best possible kind of life was "a primary biography by people who know the subject and are really fond of him"; that kind of biography, she thought, was "a protection." Richard Ollard at Collins, proposing the book to his firm in January 1979, said: "She was very fond of him and much admired him." But, the memo ended ominously: "Suffice it to say there are problems."[16]

When she first embarked on the project in the spring of 1977, encouraged by Colin Haycraft—"It was you who asked for it," she would remind him, when they agreed an advance for £500 in 1978—she had no idea quite how many problems there would be. But they soon became apparent. L. P. Hartley had a comfortable, stifling childhood (his father was a wealthy Northamptonshire Methodist brickworks manager) in the vast Victorian house in Peterborough, which Penelope described in 1978 as utterly unchanged, down to "the tablecloth presses and brass light-fittings and glass shades." His possessive mother and domineering older sister swamped his life—as in *The Shrimp and the Anemone*. At school and at Oxford, he escaped into close male friendships, most intensely with the young David Cecil, whose marriage left him bereft. He had a "passion for grandes dames" and became a fixture in the houses of "the beautiful people"—her phrase—Ottoline Morrell at Garsington, Cynthia Asquith at Mells (where he would have constantly encountered Ronnie Knox), the Sitwells and the Aberconways. He spent a great deal of time in Venice, hobnobbing with princesses. All this was not to Penelope's taste: "He loved to be given orders by the imperious and to do errands for people who had everything." For years, he was a hard-working critic and reviewer and an active member of PEN; success as a novelist came to him late. He was a generous friend. But he was also an alcoholic with a messy private life. There were affairs with servants, gondoliers, chauffeurs and assorted rough trade, one of whom tried to murder him: "young men," she wrote tolerantly but drily, "who amused him more than they amused his visitors." In old age the boozing got completely out of control—his "grande dame" Venetian friends tried to stop him having his first drink at 10 a.m., but it was hopeless. He became wildly reactionary and aberrant, notoriously poisoning the swans on the Avon which got in the way of his boat. He had a strong constitution, however, and "only drank himself to death with the greatest difficulty."[17]

The legacy of all this was confused. Norah Hartley at Fletton Tower, surrounded by his papers and the giant deerhounds she bred and showed, was the executor. She and Penelope got on excellently—in fact, Penelope came to find Norah more interesting than Leslie—but it was clear that Norah would never give permission for anything to be published that would expose Leslie's homosexuality or his alcoholism. It also transpired that there was an unresolved legal dispute with one Sybil Dreda-Owen, possibly an illegitimate child (though Hartley's doctor said Leslie was sterile), who maintained she had a claim on the estate. The critic Walter Allen was supposed to be the literary executor, but had retired "stricken." Norah was in thrall to Lord David Cecil, who, when approached by Penelope, of whom he had never heard, wrote off-puttingly: "I see no point in our meeting—I am firmly opposed to any biography of him being written for many years to come and am prepared to do nothing that could assist such a project."[18] Presumably he was protecting the secrets of his own past, as well as the posthumous life of his friend.

Nevertheless, she persisted, with encouragement from Francis King. Colin Haycraft (who grew up with Francis, having been taken in by the King family after his father's assassination) was the link between Penelope and Francis. Francis was gregarious, knowledgeable, gay, gossipy, and an interesting poet and novelist. He thought that writers should be socially responsible, and was for years a leading figure at PEN, where he introduced Penelope. He had excellent taste, read hugely and knew everybody. He had written for the *World Review,* and remembered visiting Avondale at the same time as Penelope. He had the impression on that occasion that she was "half in love with" Hartley, and was busy bustling around, doing things for him.

Francis helped her greatly with Hartley. He opened all the right doors and responded kindly to her difficulties: "You must write it even if not for years & years."[19] He introduced her to Norah, and to other key figures in Hartley's life: Anthony Powell, Hamish Hamilton, Francis Wyndham, Paul Bloomfield, Princess Clary from Venice. Between 1979 and the early 1980s, she recorded this series of encounters in her notebooks, with sharp comic zest. She liked Francis Wyndham, who was worried by her assumption that Leslie was a terrible snob, and privately thought this a bad basis for writing about him. Hamish Hamilton was a master of suavity and blandness— "I now see all the charm with which he conned lady authors & got world rights etc." From the splendid Princess Clary, who reminded her of Proust's Duchesse de Guermantes, she got stories about gondoliers and Venetian hostesses, and a wonderful detail, nothing to do with Hartley, which she would save up for *Innocence:* "She did go to Fortuny [the great Italian dress designer] but Fortuny would not let her buy the finely pleated chiffon she wanted—said she hadn't the figure for it—she was too short."

Her visit to Anthony and Violet Powell got off to a bad start, as the taxi driver taking her to the house asked if she had "come down for a housekeeper's job, which made me wonder if I'm wearing the right clothes." But Powell, handsome in tweeds in his lovely country house with five thousand books "none of which AP says he feels like reading," was funny, forthcoming and helpfully free with anecdotes, like one about a servant-boyfriend "lying naked on the bed while LPH read to him from the Bible." Powell at once got in touch with David Cecil and told him to "come off it, as Leslie's biography was sure to be written some time." So Antonia Southern, her colleague at Westminster Tutors, drove her to Red Lion House in Cranborne. Penelope took note of Lord David's vague, shabby, charming ways, his dependency on his wife for all practical matters, his knocking back the sherry, his piles of yellowing papers he wouldn't let her look at, his disapproval of things he thought "common" (the TV version of *Eustace and Hilda,* the film of *The Go-Between*), his refusal to be drawn on Leslie's reaction to his marriage and his bewilderment at any suggestion that Leslie's life might have been dark or difficult. "Lord D clearly wants to present a happy blameless life . . . [he] is like the sun coming out & saying 'What's all this about darkness? I don't see any.' "[20]

The work carried on, and she continued to ask herself the essential questions about it: "<u>What</u> is the situation which every writer reverts to when he is alone with his thoughts?"[21] She went for a week in April 1979 to the Harry Ransom archive in Austin, Texas, to do research on the Poetry Bookshop and to read Hartley's papers. But her letters increasingly noted the frustrations of the task. "It's proving a bit beyond me . . ." "There is a Quest for Corvo atmosphere about the whole undertaking I'm afraid."[22] As she became increasingly discouraged, she even thought of leaving all the materials she had amassed to Francis in her will, so that *he* could write it. She gave various reasons for giving up: Norah's censorship, Lord David's controlling hand, the ongoing lawsuit, the difficulty of accessing some of the materials.[23] Other writers (Alan Hollinghurst, Miranda Seymour) began to enquire whether she was still doing it, and if not whether they might.[24] Eventually, Norah gave permission to Adrian Wright, who published his biography in 1996, after her death. Perhaps there were other reasons, too, for this failure. It may be that Francis Wyndham was right, and that Fitzgerald found, in the end, she didn't like Hartley enough. It may be she couldn't face the prospect of writing about the years of his life lost to drink. It may be that she did not want to betray him, as her comments on Wright's rather timid biography suggest:

What is certain is that Hartley himself wouldn't have welcomed any investigation that went further than this book. Although he admitted that "Freud was in the air the writer breathes," he objected strongly to the idea of Freudian analysis. This is clear enough from one of his most disturbing short stories, "A Tonic." A tonic is all that the patient, Mr. Amber, wants or needs; but, while Mr. Amber is unconscious, the famous specialist conducts a complete examination, "which in his waking moments he had so passionately withstood."[25]

The idea for a book on the Poetry Bookshop went back much further than her friendship for L. P. Hartley, and was tinged, like *The Knox Brothers,* with a strong feeling of nostalgia. It grew out of her Georgian childhood: the rhyme sheets on her bedroom walls, the visits to the Bookshop in Bloomsbury, the sightings of Walter de la Mare and Eleanor Farjeon, Harold and Alida Monro. She had been trying to collect Poetry Bookshop rhyme sheets, lost since childhood, for years. The Poetry Bookshop connected with her feelings for Morris and Burne-Jones and her Ruskinian passion for the useful arts. Like *The Knox Brothers,* it was a "group" subject, structured within a small-scale community, with no outstanding hero-figure. The idea for the book came out of a fascination with Harold Monro, and led eventually to a life of Charlotte Mew, both sad, even tragic, figures. An atmosphere of aspiration, melancholy and disappointment hung over their lives. So there was a strong link between "The Poetry Bookshop," a book that was never written, and *The Bookshop,* the novel about a failed literary endeavour, which overtook it.

As she researched it, characters she had glimpsed and read in her youth came into focus. She went to see the sad old poet Patric Dickinson in Rye ("says his life has been devoted to poetry but not a word of his poetry is read & never will be"). She took copious notes on the writers that Monro published, edited, promoted and befriended, in his pioneering magazines, *Poetry Review, Poetry and Drama, Georgian Poetry,* and at the Bookshop, with its regular readings. Of the network that converged on the Bookshop before, during and after the Great War—Hulme, Aldington, Edward Thomas, the craftsman Romney Green, Lawrence, Anna Wickham—she was especially interested in F. S. Flint, and wrote pages of notes about him. But all that was compressed into a short paragraph in a 1988 piece on the Poetry Bookshop, written as an introduction for a bibliography compiled by the American scholar Howard Woolmer. She and Woolmer found that they shared a lifelong enthusiasm for tracking down the rhyme sheets, and

RHYME SHEET: [Second Series]

THERE IS A LADY SWEET AND KIND

There is a Lady sweet and kind,
Was never face so pleased my mind,
I did but see her passing by,
And yet I love her till I die.

Her gesture, motion, and her smiles,
Her wit, her voice my heart beguiles,
Beguiles my heart, I know not why,
And yet I love her till I die.

Cupid is wingèd and doth range,
Her country so my love doth change:
But change she earth, or change she sky,
Yet will I love her till I die.

Decorations by C. Lovat Fraser

The Poetry Bookshop
35 Devonshire Street
W.C.1

[No. 4]
Third Thousand

[Poem, Anonymous]

exchanged many letters about their quest.[26] He understood her feelings: "If only I could return to childhood just for a day and get all my rhymesheets back!" But, as she said wistfully, they were meant to be ephemeral, "literally blown away with the wind." The thought of them evoked her most plangent tone:

> The sheets were meant to be pinned up and replaced at will, but the memory would retain the song and the last word would belong, not to time, but to joy, a memory which would last when the sheets were thrown away with the rubbish or blown with the wind.[27]

In her outpouring of energies into all these ideas for new books, she was encouraged by some respectful and interested reviews of *The Knox Brothers*. J. C. Trewin was appreciative in *The Times,* and Muggeridge, stifling his private feelings about Evoe, was generous in the *TLS* ("a memorable and delightful book") and chose it for his *Observer* Book of the Year for 1977. Even *The Golden Child,* marketed by Duckworth as "mystery first novel about hanky-panky in the British Museum," got some nice brief notices from regular crime-writing reviewers like T. J. Binyon and H. R. F. Keating.[28] In the aftermath of the publication of the two books, and with the rest of the advance from *The Knox Brothers* in her pocket, she decided to treat herself to an adventure. She wrote to Richard Garnett at Macmillan: "As soon as you sent the money I took the opportunity to go to China, as I've wanted all my life to see the Great Wall under snow."[29]

Newly vaccinated against smallpox and cholera, she went on a Thompson's package tour to Peking and Shanghai, from 3 to 14 December. It was a long journey, via Bucharest and Karachi, her first holiday abroad since Desmond's death. Her diary of the trip could have been the basis for another lost novel. Probably her fellow passengers were unaware that the short, stocky, unglamorous widow-lady, always carrying a small red notebook, was a sharp observer of them and their journey. She felt herself to be unprepossessing and lonely, with "my shabby luggage. My sweaters and trousers much too hot. My fringe scanty. Am I going bald?" But she was just as ruthless about her tourist companions, dear Miss How, a missionary, with her "primus stove & tea-bags & spare bath-plugs," forever making tea in their room, and with a horror of chopsticks and Chinese breakfasts, "which nearly make her weep." There was also "Knightsbridgey" Mrs. Handley-Page ("Persian lamb coat"), who thought "dear Lord David is so clever and Msgr Knox was a genius," Mr. Hall the Norfolk builder, eager to tell everyone that he was "a rolling stone who went to sea before his 15th birthday," Mr. Ross the Newcastle manufacturer who got tiddly at a banquet on rice wine and "made a speech from the heart of my bottom, oh I beg your pardon," and mad Mr. Holford: "Explains that when he says 'all aboard' it is a jest, pretending momentarily that the bus is a boat." The only person she warmed to was their Peking tour guide, little Mrs. Sun, who told her her life story.

She is acerbic about the tourists' compulsive shopping—they have all "gone berserk," as far as she can see, and keep having to buy more bags to hold more "trash." But she gives way herself, and buys a padded baby's jacket for her first grandson, "which I daresay won't ever be wanted," and a large enamel dish "which I expect you can get in a Brixton market."

She was in China in the last phase of its inward, repressed, moribund period—Shanghai seems to her decadent and decrepit—and they are taken to many official, obligatory sights: the pandas at the zoo ("10 minutes only thank heaven"), the Great Wall ("just as I expected"), a commune ("I ask about publishing, translations of Western titles, [&] say there should be a Peking Book Fair"), the Chinese opera (propaganda, spectacle, flummoxed interpreters), a factory, the Temple of Heaven ("strange and impressive beyond belief") and the Forbidden City ("much more atmosphere than Versailles, something terrifying"). One of the high points is the Revolutionary Street Committee Kindergarten performance:

> Children execute dance representing Pulling up the Turnip in the spirit of the 11th Chinese Communist Party Convention (ie all pulling together). Child doing the turnip has a crown of green leaves. Mrs. Sun smiles & laughs—it seems she danced as a turnip in her day.
>
> As we left, they all turned out waving their red scarves & shouting "Good bye, Aunt & Uncle Thompson" as the blue dusk fell, which touched the heart, & how I wish D. was alive to hear this tribute to Thompsons travel.[30]

Waking in the early mornings in China, and not wanting to disturb her roommate, Miss How, she turned "My China Diary" upside down, and, at the back of it, began to write *The Bookshop*.[31] The first scene is rapidly and quite fully sketched in, as if springing onto the page. The rest of the novel was written fast, once she got home, over the next few weeks. The draft begins with this sentence:

Experiences aren't given us to be "got over," otherwise they would hardly be experiences.

CHAPTER TWELVE

The Prize

I know I was an outsider.[1]

The Bookshop, her fourth published book, written at the age of sixty-one, was the first of the novels in which Fitzgerald drew directly on her own past. Given permission by Desmond's death, she felt her way back into late 1950s Suffolk and into the painful emotions of twenty years before. She intensely reimagined the place, the people and the time. She turned that difficult part of her life into a perfectly controlled short novel, funny and profoundly sad. The modest midlife success of her two biographies and her quirky thriller, which, under cover, expressed the values in life she most cared about, cleared the way for her distinctive style of fiction writing, in which she both kept herself concealed and gave herself away. Later novels would be more strange, daring and formally original. But the voice was now forged, and began to be recognised. She was doing exactly what she had always wanted to do, and she had rich and copious resources of material to draw on. There was no reason to hold back. In the four years between 1978 and 1982 she published four novels, which followed, in different ways, the blueprint of *The Bookshop,* subtly and flexibly transforming her own experiences into dark comedies, each of which evoked an entire historical world in a contained space.

At the same time she was working on her never-finished biographies, and she thought a lot, then and later, about the different challenges of biography and fiction. Sometimes this just took the form of a joke: "On the whole I think biographers are madder than novelists," she told Francis King in 1978.[2] On the dust jacket of *The Bookshop* she quoted some advice once given to her by Ronald Knox, that "biographies should be written about people you love and novels about characters you dislike." Over time, she appropriated and recycled the saying: "On the whole I think you should write biographies of those you admire and respect, and novels about human beings who you think are sadly mistaken."[3] To some interviewers she would say that biography was easier than fiction, "because you've got to do a lot of research . . . and while you're doing that, you feel that you're working hard and it's quite fun to do . . . with fiction, you're really out on your own."[4] To others she sometimes said that she started writing fiction in order to pay for writing biography. In the 1980s and '90s she would regularly review biographies and maintain her admiration for and interest in the genre. In the early 1980s, she and Michael Holroyd argued on the Arts Council Literature Panel for biography to be recognised as an art form in its own right alongside poetry and fiction.[5] For herself, as time went on, she would say that she lacked the stomach, the "true grit," the "energy and resilience" needed for writing biography.[6] Besides, the wonderful advantage of fiction over biography was dialogue: "I am very interested in dialogue because the reader has to learn to listen to the voices and to identify the character without the author's interjection. Also, it covers a lot of space on the page."[7]

Such quizzical pronouncements were some way off. Through 1978 and 1979, at the same time as writing fiction, she went on working on the life of Hartley and on the Poetry Bookshop, complaining to family, friends and publishers about the difficulties of the tasks. Meanwhile, pernickety complaints trickled in about errors of fact in *The Knox Brothers,* which was published in the United States in March 1978. "My correspondents now say that *it is impossible for a magpie to nest in a chimney.*"[8]

She got little encouragement from Colin Haycraft about the Hartley book, in spite of their contract, and there was never much enthusiasm from Richard Ollard for the Poetry Bookshop as a "group" subject. Gradually—certainly by 1980—that book began to shape-shift into a biography of Charlotte Mew. Hartley was not finally laid to rest until a few years later, with many apologies and self-recriminations to those who had helped her. But her research into these life stories, her interest in the historical context and the peripheral characters, the questions she asked herself about how to enter into another person's life, the melancholy and mess of the lives she was drawn to, all fuelled her novel writing, the more so as fictions of history replaced autobiographical fictions. As she said of *The Golden Child,* "All novels, in fact, are historical." Eventually, in the words of Novalis, she took this idea to its conclusion: "Novels arise out of the shortcomings of history."[9]

Conditions were good for writing. She was only doing two days' teaching a week. Almeric Road suited her well. The street was shabby and run-down—Clapham had not yet been gentrified—with multi-occupied houses, old south London ladies rubbing shoulders with newly arrived immigrant families and Tesco lorries delivering noisily at the Battersea Rise end of the road. At that end, there was "a notice board of the Tulipean Brethren, a religious sect—don't go in there," she told Francis. Not far away, where her Number 49 bus stopped, there was "Arding and Hobbs, the Mecca of South London." Once upon a time the district had been for lavender growing—there is a "Lavender Walk" and a "Lavender Hill" nearby—and she liked to imagine what it would have been like when it was all lavender fields.[10]

Life at 25 Almeric Road was less of a struggle for her than at Poynders Gardens, only a mile or so away on the other side of Clapham Common. She lived in the downstairs rooms: the back bedroom, where Desmond had died, with French windows onto the small garden, and her front sitting room, which she painted dark green, with a grapefruit tree in the bay window, and a laurel hedge outside. The old outdoor lavatory was in a cubicle at the side. At the back was a narrow dining room and a kitchen, where she wrote at a pine table. She transformed the garden, building a brick terrace to catch the sun, breaking up the old concrete with vinegar, and cramming in a mass of shrubs and flowers and climbers. At last she could plant things and watch them grow, something she had always longed for. Tina and Terence, on the two floors upstairs, went about their lives, teaching, having friends round, going out to films and plays and the theatre, getting home exhausted. They were both language teachers and had both been promoted young to heads of department, Terence at the Convent of Jesus and Mary High School in Harlesden, Tina at Lady Margaret School, a small girls' Church of England comprehensive in Parsons Green, after a short stint alongside Penelope at Westminster Tutors. The house filled up with secondhand books, Terence's passion. Penelope saw them all the time, but mostly ate separately. They would talk about domestic, everyday matters, rather than about her work. She paid them, irregularly, for some of her expenses. By the phone she kept a book, listing her calls. Desmond had made his own entries in it, too. After his death, she drew a line in the book, and wrote: "End of poor Desmond's calls."

She was not lonely. Maria and John were living round the corner in a flat in Clapham, and dropped in all the time. Friends and relatives came to see her—Francis King, Tony and Sylvia Peck, and Mary Knox, who saw a great deal of Penelope at this time. She went off on her travels, on interviewing forays for L. P. Hartley, on short holidays—in August 1977 to Scotland with Maria and John, in July 1978 to stay with Willie and Mike Conder on Alderney. At home she was writing every day, sitting up in her bed early, or at her little wooden table by the garden window, writing fast into her notebooks.

The Bookshop was finished by the summer of 1978; "written in rather a few weeks," she told Colin Haycraft. He told her it was "very sad," and thought it "seemed a pity that Mr. Brandesh's [he meant Brundish] real intentions are never known to the heroine, but I suppose that is part of the plot." On this note, she scribbled to herself, only half forgivingly: "Doesn't even know names of characters! But this has been a rotten year for him." (His son had had a fatal accident.) She approved the cover, a line drawing of a woman in a headscarf gazing at an estuary, which she thought gave "a very good idea of Southwold Common looking towards Blyth." She wrote an evasive author note, which said she was the niece of Ronald Knox and author of two biographies, and dedicated it "to an old friend": Phyllis Neame, the bookshop owner. When Mrs. Neame read the novel, she wrote a friendly letter, saying how well she remembered the poltergeist, but disputing the fictional version of the Southwold bookshop and saying how nice everyone had been to her when she bought it.[11]

By the time advance copies arrived from Duckworth in October, she had started writing *Offshore,* plunging back into her rough, harassed, scavenging life on the river of seventeen years before. It was a matter of joy to her that Maria, the daughter whom she was, at that very time, turning into the wild little character of Tilda in the novel, was married to her long-term partner, John Lake, on 14 October 1978. Tina organised everything, and after the ceremony in Brixton registry office, there was lunch in the upstairs part of the Almeric Road house for Maria, in her new Laura Ashley dress, John and his parents, Valpy and Angelines and their little boys, come from Cambridge, Terence and Tina, and Mops. It was all simple and happy and inexpensive, and everyone behaved well. Desmond was acutely missed.

That was one of two major events of the autumn. The other was that, while *The Bookshop* was still being reviewed, it was short-listed for the Booker Prize. This was a great surprise, since the reviews were mostly condescending. The *Times* (male) reviewer called it "a harmless, conventional little anecdote, charming enough, well-tailored but uninvolving," about "an elderly lady failing to make a go of a bookshop in a little seaside town." A bemused Canadian reviewer in the *Toronto Globe and Mail,* under the heading "Signs of Malaise in the State of BritLit," puzzled over why on earth this novel should be short-listed for "the most important annual prize for fiction in Britain." Though "author Fitzgerald has a nice sense of irony and satire, and a gift for evoking a strong sense of place," "in Canada it would hardly be given a second look." "Maybe it was just an off year," he muses, or maybe Canadian readers just don't get "the class structure in the kind of provincial society" that the novel deals with. Under the heading "Women's Novels," in the *Guardian,* Norman Shrapnel batched it with Michèle Roberts's first book and a novel by Françoise Sagan, as a quiet and "disquieting" novel about "really nasty people living in a really nice little coastal town." Valentine Cunningham praised it in the *Times Literary Supplement* as a "fetchingly orchestrated," "marvellously piercing" book, while labelling it as an example of "the Beryl Bainbridge school of anguished women's fiction." Auberon Waugh advised her, in his review for the *Evening Standard,* to write longer books. ("I do not think I have ever before advised a female novelist to write at greater length.") A few readers understood her at once: Richard Mayne, on BBC Radio 3's *Critics' Forum,* was struck by "the wonderful precision, economy and certainty of the writer: it was as if she knew exactly what she was going to do." But no one flagged it up as a likely candidate for a major literary prize. When Colin Haycraft sent her the news on 17 October she was "staggered," and thought he must have made a mistake, "only it's not the sort of mistake he makes."[12]

The Booker was not such a high-profile affair in 1978 as it became in the 1980s, after Burgess and Golding's rivalry and the start of the prize's television coverage. Fitzgerald was very pleased to be short-listed—"I am delighted to be there with such a simple story"—but her tone about the whole event was laconic. Being short-listed, she wrote in 1989, "raised the problem of evening dress, because the Booker dinner is a formal occasion. Still, it isn't difficult to make a long skirt, and I was advised to wear earrings and not take off my shoes under the table, because at some point each writer would have to go up separately and shake hands with the chairman. For the same reason, I ought to make sure that I looked all right from behind. This advice has taken me through three Booker dinners."[13]

The judges that year were the philosopher A. J. Ayer, the novelists Clare Boylan and Angela Huth, the *Listener's* literary editor Derwent May, and P. H. Newby, who had won the prize in its first year, in 1969. Howard Newby had been published in the *World Review,* and, she would later discover, was the judge who had voted for her.[14] The other short-listed books were Iris Murdoch's *The Sea, the Sea,* Kingsley Amis's *Jake's Thing,* André Brink's *Rumours of Rain,* Jane Gardam's *God on the Rocks* and *A Five Year Sentence* by Bernice Rubens (who had won before, in 1970). Iris Murdoch won.

Colin Haycraft did not attend, on the pretext that he didn't have a dinner jacket, but gave his seat to Anna, who brought Caroline Blackwood.

Tina hired a car and drove with Penelope to pick them up from Gloucester Crescent. They were late getting ready, and unfriendly to Penelope and Tina, whom they treated throughout the evening as outsiders. There may have been some jealousy. Penelope told Francis they were both "sunk in gloom": this was possibly a euphemism. She enjoyed the dinner "because I hardly ever go to such things," even though the short-listed authors "had to file up just like the school prize-giving," and spent the evening trying to cheer up her unhelpful table companions.[15]

Haycraft told the Booker Prize administrators, to no effect, that the runners-up should get something, "like the Miss World contest (£200 and a package holiday in Bulgaria)." In his view, Iris Murdoch "didn't need the money." "It's hard for me to imagine anyone who doesn't need £10,000," Penelope mused. As a consolation prize, he sent her a box of chocolates. This casual treatment of her short-listing did not help with what was already an unsatisfactory relationship. When the list was announced, she wrote him a vulnerable letter. "If I could ask for a word of advice: do you think it would be a good idea to write another novel or not, as I'm never likely to do much better than this?"[16] This was somewhat disingenuous, since she was already well under way with *Offshore*. What she meant was, would Duckworth take her seriously as a novelist, not a writer of thrillers? Haycraft's response, over lunch, was profoundly disappointing to her. He seems to have said that he and, particularly, Anna could not see their way to publishing any more of her novels, that no one else but them would have published her in the first place, that only thrillers would make money and that they already had too many short novels on their list. Or that, at least, was how she read their conversation. Proud, hurt and insulted, she confided in Francis King, to whom she had already said, just after the short-listing, that "after 3 years" of being in the "literary world," she found it "most harassing and puzzling."[17] Francis advised her to change publishers, meanwhile giving the full flavour of events to another mutual friend, the novelist June Braybrooke. June wrote under the pen name Isobel English, was good friends with Stevie Smith and co-authored a life of Olivia Manning with her husband, Neville Braybrooke, who completed it after her death. Both June and Neville were familiar with the "Dance of Death," as June called it, that was always going on between Colin, Anna and their authors. June wrote to Francis:

Wow! That is certainly some story about Penelope Fitzgerald. But it all fits together doesn't it? [She continued with other examples of authors who had been insultingly treated by the Haycrafts.] I do feel sorry for Penelope, whom I have never met. She must keep faith with herself and hold on tight to the knowledge of the very real success she has had by being a Booker runner-up. The extraordinary message given to her over lunch by Colin from Anna, may well be part of their game—Colin's and Anna's—and nothing to do with Penelope *or* her novels. For instance: suppose that Penelope were to run into Anna and say how distressed she had been by Colin's message. The chances are very high that Anna would speak thus: "Oh God! Why does he do it? Why can't he leave the fiction list alone? He has to put his bloody finger in everything. Look Peaches, come and see me tomorrow. Come for lunch. Colin won't be there. He's in Oxford. Oh darling! If only *I* had spoken to you *first*, we could have sorted it all out beautifully . . ." and so on. I could go on forever; but must not.[18]

Penelope wrote to Willie Conder: "Long melodrama at Duckworths which I feel I'm much too old for, so now I have to find yet another publisher! However I quite enjoy it, it's like weaving, I suppose, it keeps you busy. I am trying to write a novel about the houseboats on Battersea Reach, where we used to live." She found plenty of time in this letter to talk about family matters and to go off on one of her comic riffs:

I loved the story of . . . the church decorations—but am worried about the lampshades constructed out of lollipop sticks. I consider the scheme madness. I know some people who construct dolls' rocking-chairs entirely out of split clothes-pegs, and they are going mad. It's the snow, you'll emerge at the end of winter like the woodcutters of the Tyrol having carved and fashioned many things but gibbering and staring wildly at each other.

She, by contrast, was not a loopy, homespun amateur, and was not going to be treated like one. On 19 January 1979, she wrote two firm letters. One was to Francis. "I've followed the advice you kindly gave me (after all it's not much use asking for advice if you don't take it) and changed publishers . . . I'm sure Colin will be glad to get rid of me, I'm only causing embarrassment there, for some reason."[19] The other was to Colin:

Dear Colin—Thankyou very much for the notices of the *Bookshop*—I'd just like to say, having taken the advice, not to say instructions, you gave me to find another publisher for these novels, that I'm very grateful for the start which you and Anna gave me. I'm sure you were right in saying no-one else would have taken them, and I was happy at Duckworths and very much admired the firm for its spirited conduct of the war on every front.—Best wishes and I hope you and Anna have nothing but happy years ahead.—Penelope.[20]

Colin, very taken aback, at once rang her up, and they had a confused conversation, after which he wrote her a letter:

For the record, I feel that I must answer your letter of the 19th, even though we have spoken about it on the telephone. I was shocked to receive the letter and it took me completely by surprise.

It is simply not true that I "advised" or "instructed" you to find another publisher. If so, why am I now so disappointed?

Nor is it true that I said "no one else would have taken your first two novels." Many publishers would have taken them and we were delighted that you offered them to us. What I remember is a general conversation about publishing, in which at one point I said that large publishers were usually, though not always, able to sell more copies of books than small publishers [so] . . . tended to avoid first novels or novels by novelists not yet established. That is quite a different thing.

If you wish now to go to a large publisher, you are of course perfectly entitled to do so. We don't have option clauses in our contracts, because we don't want to keep any author who wants to go elsewhere, even though we may have launched him [*sic*]. All I ask is that you should not say what is simply not true, that I wished, or told, you to go elsewhere.

You said on the telephone that this was the "impression" you got. If so, I cannot understand how. In any case, in view of the admiration I have always expressed for your books and the surprising nature therefore of what you say you thought you obliquely heard, it is very odd, and a pity for me, that you did not check that your "impression" was right before taking an irrevocable step.

With all good wishes, Yours, Colin.[21]

She replied the next day.

Dear Colin, I'm terribly distressed at having done the wrong thing and caused trouble when I meant to remove it. That is, I'd thought the most helpful thing to do would be to take myself off without making a fuss. You did tell me, you know, that if I went on writing novels you didn't want it blamed on you and that Anna thought I should do detective stories and also, by the way, that you had too many short novels with sad endings on your hands, and I thought, well, he's getting rid of me, but in a very nice way. I don't at all expect you to remember everything you say to 32 authors, but the trouble is we take all these remarks seriously and ourselves too seriously as well, I expect.

I would have liked to stay, because I'm not the sort of person who ever has any money anyway, and I admire the firm so much and then you were always so clever and funny that everyone else seemed exceedingly slow by comparison. However having made this mistake, and I'd rather be taken for an idiot than a liar, I'll be careful to make it clear that it *was* my mistake, which is what you want, I think.[22]

She bore him no ill will, and in April told Francis that she missed Colin very much, though there was an edge to her fond description of him. "He was so clever, and always knew what you were going to say before you said it, so it wasn't necessary to finish the sentence . . . he was also so persuasive that after half an hour on the telephone I was almost persuaded I had been in the wrong—e pur si muove—or rather he certainly did tell me to move on, and I was somewhat disappointed as I thought I could write a rather better novel next time—but I suppose everyone always thinks this! However, he's quite certainly forgotten about the whole matter by now, he has a most enviable ability to do this, necessary, as he told me, if you're an optimist married to a pessimist."[23]

She was irritated with him when a media company approached her in 1979 about the possibility of a film of *The Bookshop* with Anna Massey; she noted on the bottom of their letter that "Colin was very abrupt & unhelpful [&] seemed to show little interest in the matter."[24] But she kept in touch with him about the Hartley biography, for instance, in February 1979: "I've been going on doggedly . . . and got quite a long way with it."[25] She told Francis in April 1979: "If I really get anywhere near finishing LPH I shall have to ask him if he still wants the book, and brace myself for a possible cutting reply, or none at all."[26] But it never came to that.

A dozen years later, when Haycraft was giving his farewell party at the Old Piano Factory, Duckworth having fallen on hard times and the office about to move to Hoxton, she went back to find that "it was just the same as in the old days, everyone introduced as geniuses and Beryl loyal as ever, only asking to be stopped getting too drunk to take a taxi to the airport—but as all the furniture was gone the refreshments had to be put on the floor and the authors' coats (most of them had come from Oxford and Cambridge in their best sherry-party clothes) had to go in what were once the packing rooms and were thick with dust and bits of paper. I hated to see it all go, and was glad to be able to wish him luck."[27] Three years after that move, in 1994, Colin Haycraft died suddenly at the age of sixty-five.

The publisher she left him for was a much better match. Richard Ollard was the Yorkshire-born son of an Anglican clergyman and church historian. He was a brilliant classicist and seventeenth-century historian, a scholarly intellectual who had taught history for a time at the Royal Naval College at Greenwich, and joined the firm of Collins in 1960, when he was thirty-seven. He had been friends at Eton with Oliver Knox, whose novels he was publishing. It was Oliver who "sent" Penelope to him. He was also friendly with Raleigh Trevelyan.

His writing was as important to him as his publishing, and he kept a day a week free for his own work. He wrote on Charles II, the Civil War, the Restoration navy, Pepys and Clarendon, and, in his retirement, a frank biography of A. L. Rowse, whom he criticised but admired. Penelope respected his writing; of the Civil War book, *This War Without an Enemy*, she said: "All your books make up a continuous argument in favour of friendship, loyalty, and decent moderation."[28]

They had like-minded attitudes to religion, literature and life. At first encounter Ollard seemed donnish and austere, with the laconic, ironical manner of an Oxford academic of that generation and class. But with his friends and chosen authors he was funny, gossipy, warm, impeccably courteous and always interesting.[29] She became extremely fond of him and of his wife, Mary, and their children, and went to visit them often, first in Blackheath and then in their remote house near Bridport in Dorset, comfortable and friendly, bulging with classical and historical books, where Richard and Penelope would go together to the village church, Whitchurch Canonicorum, for the 8 a.m. Sunday service. As with all her male publishers, she wanted him to look after her, as if he were her agent, as well as her publisher and her friend. In this case, she had an unswerving professional ally.

Collins was then dominated by its proprietor, Billy Collins, a formidable, hardheaded salesman who made a famously profitable general list out of Bibles, and natural history books (and dictionaries, which came later, under his son, Jan Collins). But he also surrounded himself with a group of urbane, intellectually sophisticated young men, all writers themselves, Mark Bonham Carter, Philip Ziegler and Ollard, who commissioned some distinguished nonfiction books. Ollard had an excellent history list, which included Veronica Wedgwood, and J. H. Plumb as the general editor of the Fontana History of Europe series. And he published a few outstanding fiction writers, notably Patrick O'Brian, Sybille Bedford and the young Michael Frayn.

He was an editor of "extraordinary discernment and high standards." As his successor Stuart Proffitt said, "he had an unerring eye for a straight alpha." He wouldn't publish an author he didn't like, and he would never say to an author "you must." Oliver Knox's son Tim described him as "inordinately particular and accurate." He was punctilious and sympathetic, but intolerant of authorial vanity, missed deadlines and inaccuracy.

The moment Penelope Fitzgerald came his way, he saw the point of her completely. He worked with her for four vital years, from 1979 to 1983, when he retired, passing her into the hands of Stuart Proffitt but continuing to give her advice. Because of him, and then Stuart, she would never dream of leaving the firm. His first business letter to her, on 15 January 1979, three days after she had sent him the typescript of *Offshore,* and three days before she wrote her parting letter to Haycraft, set the tone promisingly: "Do you want as much money as possible as soon as possible?"[30] The contract was signed on 24 January, for an advance of £2,000, with 12.5 per cent up to 5,000 copies sold, and 15 per cent thereafter: quite a difference from the Duckworth contract of a £200 advance for *The Bookshop.* (Though, acting fairly, she told Ollard she would not give Collins an option on nonfiction in case Duckworth were still interested in the Hartley biography.)[31]

Ollard's in-house memos about Fitzgerald were perceptive and enthusiastic. His first introduction of her to the firm, just after he had accepted *Offshore,* laid out the various possibilities he had discussed with her— the biography of Hartley, the Poetry Bookshop book, the Flower book, and something else he liked even more, presumably her next idea for a novel. Whatever she decided on, "I have a healthy respect for her intelligence." Of *Offshore,* he wrote to his colleagues: "This book is funny and serious, tender and harsh, in the true tradition of the English novel . . . This is that rarest of all things, a novel of first-class literary quality which also has warmth, humanity, and a strong astringent moral sense."[32] For her part, she decided to trust him completely, and wrote to him very fully about what was on her mind. If he told her Charles Monteith at Faber was "not <u>very</u> nice," she decided never to approach him. If he went with her to a literary party, she felt much better ("I should never have had the resolution to go otherwise"). If she had a complaint about a cover, she knew she could tell him: "I know you're tolerant about such things, indeed about everything." If the PR man at Collins despaired of her, she knew that Ollard would understand when she said: "It's no good pretending to be what you're not."[33] Nevertheless, with all this apparent mildness, anxiety and dependency, he could see very well that she was also sharp-eyed and resolute, and would not put up with anything she did not like.

Offshore was written fast, in a few months in 1978, and sent to Richard Ollard in January 1979. In April, Collins advertised it in their list for that year, and the *Bookseller* commented: "Duckworth's loss is Collins's gain."[34] Then she flew off to Austin, Texas, to work on Poetry Bookshop papers at the Harry Ransom Research Center, an adventure she greatly enjoyed. She was also helping her brother with his nicely illustrated book about Kipper, *The Work of E. H. Shepard,* published in 1979 for his centenary, three years after his death. Penelope contributed a chapter on his early drawings, invoking the late-nineteenth-century world of art students and illustrators, all energised by "the Victorian value of hard work." She wrote eloquently of the air and movement in Shepard's drawings, which "would blow across the white spaces of a text from one page to another." For Mary's sake, Rawle censored out the trouble between Kipper and Evoe, when Evoe, his friend and contemporary, married his daughter. But he was frank about Kipper's ruthlessness and repressed emotions—the sort of behaviour Rawle knew all about: "His immediate outward reaction to grief was to ignore it completely. That was how he had been brought up to behave." The book also noted the rising prices, in the 1960s, for Shepard's original drawings for the *Winnie-the-Pooh* books, buoyed by the Disney film and the growing cult of Pooh. But the Fitzgerald family reaped no benefits from this legacy.[35]

The book brought Rawle and Penelope back in closer touch. Rawle's daughter Belinda was married in October, and Penelope sent her a wistful congratulatory note: "Rawle and I sigh and say All Our Chicks have now left the Nest but Valpy says You Can sit back Now We Are All Off Your Hands. Perhaps neither is very relevant."[36]

All through 1979 she was working on *Human Voices,* which at first was called "Ten Seconds from Now." Meanwhile, copies of *Offshore* arrived in August, and she provided what would become her standard, quizzical author note:

> Penelope Fitzgerald is an Oxford graduate and has worked in journalism, the Ministry of Food, the BBC, an all-night coffee stall, a bookshop, and various schools, including a theatrical school. She has three grown-up children, an economist, a Spanish teacher, and a physiologist. The family used to live on a Thames barge, which sank, but are now settled in London and Cambridge.[37]

The novel was published on 3 September, and some attention was paid. Thomas Hinde wrote in the *Sunday Telegraph:* "The deft handling of every tiny incident . . . makes a summary entirely inadequate since the book perfectly conveys the sadness which lies below its characters' comic misfortunes." Bernard Levin, at the time the *Sunday Times*'s most influential reviewer, wrote: "This is an astonishing book. Hardly more than 50,000 words, it is written with a manic economy that makes it seem even shorter, and with a tamped-down force that continually explodes in a series of exactly controlled detonations . . . a marvellous achievement: strong, supple, human, ripe, generous and graceful." Victoria Glendinning, in the *Times Literary Supplement,* observed that "Mrs. Fitzgerald has evolved a way of writing about people that compresses and therefore intensifies expression . . . It is a book of peculiar interest and excellence." Other reviewers were not so kind. Ollard wrote to cheer her up, and she thanked him: "It's good of you to take time to console your easily depressed authors."[38] Depression lifted when *Offshore* was short-listed for the Booker Prize.

The reviewer she minded the most about was Frank Kermode, who wrote a long piece on the Booker Prize for the *London Review of Books,* which contained the most searching account of her work she had yet received. He wrote:

> *Offshore,* though admirable, strikes me as decidedly inferior to *The Bookshop*. The earlier book was defter, more resonant, and more complete. Penelope Fitzgerald is a writer who came late to the novel, bringing with her a powerful, slightly unorthodox intelligence and a remarkable habit of accuracy, which shows not only in the wit of the book but in the provision, by apparently casual means, of a deep surface polish, an illusion of total specification . . .

She writes a kind of fiction in which perfection is almost to be hoped for, unostentatious as true virtuosity can make it, its texture a pure pleasure.

Offshore, like its predecessor set in the early Sixties . . . deals with . . . a community as tight as that of the isolated East Anglian town of *The Bookshop* . . . What is admirable is the economical strength with which the conditions of life are specified. But the book seems, by comparison, anecdotal. Some of the anecdotes are very good . . . But the apocalyptic flood of the ending doesn't hold everything together. The book is excellent on water, on kindness, courage, loneliness. If it wins, though, it should be understood as standing in for *The Bookshop*.[39]

She wrote in some distress to Richard: "He is the only critic . . . whose opinion I value since Lionel Trilling, and indeed I don't think I could teach anyone anything about the novel at all if it hadn't been for his The Sense of An Ending. What worries me is [not] that he doesn't think too well of Offshore—(in fact I'm very pleased that he should say anything about me at all), but that I get the feeling that he's saying I can write a single-consciousness novel (which anyone can do if they can find a pen and a bit of paper) but I'm not up to multiple-consciousness, then I just fall into bits, and that depresses me."[40]

Kermode was right about what made Fitzgerald a fine novelist, but wrong about the decision of the Booker Prize judges on 23 October 1979. Asa Briggs, with Michael Ratcliffe, Hilary Spurling, Paul Theroux and Benny Green, had discarded some of the heavyweight books of that year (Nadine Gordimer's *Burger's Daughter,* William Golding's *Darkness Visible*) and were choosing between Thomas Keneally's Civil War epic *Confederates,* V. S. Naipaul's African novel *A Bend in the River* (he had won in 1971 with *In a Free State*), *Joseph* by Julian Rathbone, a picaresque Spanish historical novel set in the time of Goya, Fay Weldon's *Praxis,* a sharp, mischievous satire on gender politics, and *Offshore.* Unusually, they ended up with a short-list of only five books, because Patrick White withdrew *The Twyborn Affair,* saying that he had told his publishers not to enter it. André Brink, another possible contender with *Dry White Season,* had not been entered in time. The general assumption was that Naipaul would win.

The Booker McConnell people issued the authors with their instructions. Penelope was "harangued" by them before the event about the need for her to "get an agent to sell the TV rights of *Offshore*": " 'You cannot expect the publisher to do this for you,' they said reprovingly." All the authors and their publishers were bidden to the dinner at the Stationers' Hall (Naipaul did not appear) and put through the usual ordeal of management speeches, public eating (artichoke soup, mackerel pâté, duck and chestnut soufflé), drinking, smiling and horrible waiting. Penelope, who took Maria with her for support, had bought a pretty, flowered long dress—she asked advice about this from all her colleagues at Westminster Tutors—and combed her hair. As she didn't have an evening bag, she took a sponge bag. She looked unglamorous, youthful and old-fashioned. In his chairman's speech, Asa Briggs called *Offshore* "wholly original . . . A supremely honest novel . . . which presents a beautifully defined world, and with a perpetual element of surprise." Nobody, however, except perhaps its author, really expected it to win the £10,000 prize. At the moment of the announcement, she knew, with keen pleasure, "that some of the people who read it must have understood it." She took her cheque demurely and made a brief speech, in which she spoke for all those readers who never travel without a novel on bus, tube or train, picking up each morning where they left off the night before and showing no relief at the end of a book, only anxiety to get lost in yet another novel.[41]

What followed was not exactly gratifying. She described it all to Francis King:

In the stories I used to read when I was a little girl cab-horses used to win the National and everyone seemed to cheer, but you can't expect this in real life, and I know I was an outsider—however Asa Briggs explained to me that they'd ruled out novels evidently written with one eye on the film rights as they'd been looking for *le roman pur,* and I naturally agreed with him.—When I got to the Book Programme, soaking wet because I'd had to be photographed on a bale of rope on the Embankment, R[obert] Robinson was in a very bad temper and complained to his programme executive "who are these people, you promised me they were going to be the losers."—I couldn't help enjoying the dinner, though the Evening Standard man told me frankly that they'd all written their pieces about Naipaul and felt they were free to get drunk, wh: he certainly was . . . the best [moment] was when the editor of the Financial Times, who was at my table, looked at the cheque and said to the Booker McC Chairman "Hmph, I see you've changed your chief cashier." Both their faces were alight with interest.—I'm afraid

Booker Mc rather wish they'd decided to patronise show-jumping, or snooker—the novelists are so difficult and odd, not appreciating their surprise.[42]

The BBC *Book Programme* about the Booker Prize, recorded and aired on 24 October, was breathtakingly condescending and ill-judged. All the participants had dressed up for TV in the styles of the time: Robert Robinson in suit, striped tie, square glasses and comb-over, Fay Weldon opulent in a flowing gold dress, Susan Hill (brought in as Booker expert, both as ex-judge and previously short-listed novelist) sharp-edged and bright in a lime-green waistcoat and pink shirt, Julian Rathbone in cream suit, matching shoes and wide paisley tie. Penelope wore a neat, dark green, white-spotted long-sleeved frock, done up to the throat, and low-heeled black shoes, and sat with legs crossed and hands folded in her lap. Her hair looked tousled and she had no make-up.

Robinson, evidently thrown by not having the big beasts he had expected, and by being presented with a winner he had clearly never heard of, or read, steers the conversation, in his best patrician manner, with many jokey remarks about the betting at Ladbrokes and the tax-free cheque, into a general discussion about literary prizes. He begins by proposing to everyone, including "Mrs. Fitzgerald," that "the Booker judges had made the wrong choice" and "the best book didn't win." Susan Hill eagerly agrees: "I know it's an appalling thing to say and I don't want to discomfort her, but I wouldn't have chosen it." (In later years, though, she would become a devoted admirer.) Julian Rathbone says that a prize of this stature should go to a novel that makes "statements of some importance about the world and the society we live in." Fay Weldon makes vague, kindly, lightly barbed noises about horse races and lotteries and authors as "sacrificial victims." Turning at last to the winner, Robinson asks her if she was surprised. "I felt as though something had hit me very hard on the head," she replies. And that is rather how she appears throughout.

Robinson, Hill and Weldon dominate the proceedings, animatedly discussing the process of judging ("skulduggery," says Susan Hill darkly), the effect on sales, the Booker compared with the Goncourt Prize and so on. Nothing is said about *Offshore*. Occasionally, with a marked effort, Robinson says he would like to ask Mrs. Fitzgerald another question. Would she like to be a judge? "Oh yes, I'd like the tranquillity of mind." Did she think there were other books that should have been short-listed? "I really didn't give the whole thing enough thought, I can see that." Did she have a view of what the novel should be? "That's the scandal about novels, isn't it?" she replies. "That they don't have any classical models. But I would say it started as soon as people realised that it was dark as night—that it was dark outside. And they felt that they would like a story told them. And that's what novels are for." Blankly uncomprehending, Robinson lumbers on: "But don't you think it must deliver something of importance to everyone?" "No, I don't," she answers, just for a moment allowing sharpness through. "I think it's that, for the time being, you forget that it's dark outside." Robinson quickly goes back to talking to Susan Hill about her books, and concludes by reading out a list of funny foreign names—authors who once won the Nobel Prize. "Not that I wish to bring a cloud over the head of Mrs. Fitzgerald," he quips, "but which of us have read Bjørnstjerne Bjørnson?" Off-camera, her voice, at once drowned out, is heard saying: "I shall go and read him at once."[43]

Snide pieces appeared that day in the London papers, describing the winner as "Shy Penelope," author of "a whimsical family drama," "the 10-to-1 outsider." W. L. Webb, in the *Guardian,* wondered whether the judges had deliberately given the prize to a dark horse "to secure secrecy." One of the judges, Hilary Spurling, defended their decision, reached in "the civil but charged atmosphere of a literary seminar," as a vote for "something sober, lucid, subtle rather than showy . . . and conventional."[44]

Richard Ollard was furious about her treatment. He told Bernard Levin that his review was "a good deed in a naughty world." In his experience of publishing, he had not come across "so unpleasant a demonstration of naked spite, diaphanously robed in the pretensions of social conscience." The *Book Programme,* he said, had been set up "on the assumption that V. S. Naipaul was to be the winner and all the runners-up were gathered together to grind their teeth in front of the cameras. The fact that those present included the winner did not lead Mr. Robinson to alter his scenario in any particular and the result was to say the least unedifying." Though she spoke of it lightly, Fitzgerald, too, was upset: "I'll never forget the *Book Programme,*" she told Ollard a few months later. "I still get letters about it." She came to think of it as "this trouble-creating Booker Prize." And, in spite of the prize, she was still being described as "of the school of Beryl Bainbridge which is a good corrective to vanity, I expect." "You are in [Barbara Pym]'s group someone said to me firmly the other day you either have to be in hers or Beryl's." She admired Barbara Pym—more than she admired Beryl Bainbridge—but she did not want to be in anyone's group.[45]

In interviews, she played the role which she would now adopt as a useful camouflage. Glenys Roberts in the *Evening News* completely fell for it. Her piece was titled "The Original Boat Person: The Lady Who Sailed Away with £10,000."[46] "At 62 Mrs. Fitzgerald is that wonderfully dotty and endearing sort of lady other people always seem to have as a favourite aunt." How had she felt on the night? "I felt faint when they announced it, the way one does, you know." What would she spend the prize money on? "I told them I was going to buy an iron and a typewriter with the prize money. They wouldn't believe me, but I do think the domestic sort of things are very important in life, don't you? . . . I have a tiny portable which everybody laughs at . . . It's important to have an electric one, you see, with a self-threading ribbon so you don't get your fingers dirty." After describing life on the barge, "she speaks dreamily of electric heaters and fridges and proper loos which you can flush without having to wait for the falling tide." "Today Mrs. Fitzgerald lives in a neat terraced house in Clapham with her married daughter and a lot of plants, books and rose petal pot pourri." Her literary lineage is then respectfully cited, and for a moment the interviewer seems to realise that she is being hoodwinked. "In the modest manner of actual intellectuals she is more informed and less vague than she appears on first sight." And then play resumes. When does she write? "Well, not very often actually . . . A woman is a sitting target for interruption." On she goes ("perhaps I'll use the prize to go to China again—I really liked it. I'll ask the children"), leaving her interviewer charmed and baffled.

Among family and friends, ex-students and colleagues, there was great delight and some amazement. Telegrams and letters poured in, as from Tina: "He He clever old Ma love Tina," or from Rawle and Helen: "Hooray for You Hooray Hooray." She wrote thank-you letters to everyone. To her niece Belinda (on a postcard of one of her favourite paintings, Vincenzo Foppa's *The Young Cicero Reading*) she said: "I was a rank outsider, I wish I'd backed myself at 20 to 1—but I can't help being thrilled—love Mops."[47]

In publishing terms, the results were excellent. Though Ollard could not find an American publisher for *Offshore,* he immediately got a paperback deal with Magnum, a branch of Methuen, for a £4,000 advance, and the novel reprinted at once: 3,000 copies on 1 November.[48] She began to go on the circuit of festivals and readings, which was just getting into its stride in the late 1970s, dutifully if not always happily doing what was asked of her. With her publishers she was helpful and tireless; with her interviewers and fellow writers she presented an unpredictable and disconcerting mixture of obedient-seeming attentiveness, evasiveness and sharp wit. She was not as kind as she looked. "I've got to go to Brighton—to discuss Men As Women Writers See Them with Susan Hill and Jacky Gillott, pity me."[49] Thanks to Francis King, she became a member of PEN at this time, and began to cast her sharp eye on the always very "strange" PEN meetings. She became a regular at Book House in Wandsworth (a building "so much more suitable for a seaside hotel"), the new home of the National Book League, recently renamed Book Trust by its director Martyn Goff, and trekked out there to listen to lectures on modern fiction and to Goff's "supremely tactless" speeches.[50] She was asked to join the Arts Council Literature Panel and continued to be a faithful member of the William Morris Society. She became, very rapidly, a sought-after, active and visible figure in the literary world.

She spent her Booker money, not on an iron, but on a trip to New York with Tina and Terence in April 1980, a package deal with flight and hotel. They stayed at the Tudor Hotel on East 42nd, and went to all the sights and museums. She insisted on a horse-and-carriage ride round Central Park. She also used the trip to meet the Poetry Bookshop expert Howard Woolmer, who lived in Revere, Pennsylvania: intrepidly, she took the bus from Port Authority. He gave her a few precious Poetry Bookshop items. "It's wonderful to find someone who cares about the same material as you do yourself, and I felt really happy at seeing your collection," she wrote to him gratefully. "In fact I was thinking about it while I walked back from the bus station and scarcely noticed the distance from W.41 to E.42." Probably no one else but Penelope Fitzgerald has walked that route immersed in thinking about Poetry Bookshop rhyme sheets. She went on thinking about the book when she got home. But Ollard repeatedly said no, and by the end of 1980 she was channelling the work into a biography of Charlotte Mew.[51] She still could not quite give up on Hartley: "It's just a kind of feeble obstinacy that keeps me going on," she told Francis. " 'Call it going, call it on' as Beckett says."

The prize created a slight pressure from Collins that she should now write longer novels. But, as she said to Francis, "I deeply believe that less is more." She knew that it was not in her nature to be "spectacular or panoramic."[52] By February 1980 she had a typescript of *Human Voices* for Ollard. She sent him a note of instructions for the blurb, which shows how much she trusted his judgement. "Do you think," she wrote, "it would be possible to make this book sound a little bit less like a historical study and more like a novel? It is really about the love-hate relationship between 2 of the eccentrics on whom the BBC depended, and about love, jealousy, death, childbirth in Broadcasting House and the crises that go on behind the microphone to produce the 9 o'clock news on which the whole nation relied during the war years, heartbreak etc, and also about this truth telling business."

Ollard circulated a memo enthusiastically talking up "this marvellously witty book," which "will consolidate and extend her reputation as a novelist of outstanding quality who can sell across the board." "She can only be so funny because she is extremely clever." The contract, signed in April, gave her a £2,000 advance and royalties of 12.5 per cent up to sales of 5,000, thereafter 15 per cent. It was the same as the *Offshore* contract: winning the prize had not increased her advance. Publication was scheduled for 25 September 1980. The novel, with its vivid fictional version of Evoe, was dedicated to Mary Knox.[53]

The three novels drawing on her past—*The Bookshop, Offshore, Human Voices*—had been written at concentrated speed between the end of 1977 and the beginning of 1980, one started as soon as the other was finished, as if they had been waiting to be written. Now, after handing in *Human Voices,* she cast around a little, beginning to move towards subjects that went beyond her own life. She made some notes for a novel set in Italy after the war, which she thought of calling "The Same Mistake," or "Happiness." She returned to two ideas which had long haunted her: the novel set in Turkey, and the family of Burne-Jones's lover Maria Zambaco. In her Burne-Jones research, she had noted the family tree of the Zambacos and the Ionides, "the leading family in the Greek community of Victorian England," whose property in Constantinople had been seized by the Turks. A notebook called "Dimmie," from the early 1980s, sketches a plot about a young painter called Demetrius, trained by G. F. Watts, who is sent in 1876 by his father Ionides Constantinopoulos, a wealthy cotton importer and art patron, to the family office in Istanbul, to paint a portrait of his aunt and to meet his cousin Eugenia, a possible wife. The quest is dogged by mishaps and misunderstandings. His aunt thinks that it will bring down the evil eye to have her portrait painted, and he is wary of his cousin. Eventually, this was turned into a pared-down, inconclusive, comical story called "The Likeness."[54] But by the time *Human Voices* was published in September, she had abandoned her Turkish novel and set aside her Italian novel, and had started to work on *At Freddie's.*

After the mixed reaction to *Offshore* as a Booker winner, she was sensitive about the reception of *Human Voices*. She thanked Richard for letting her know that it would be reviewed on *Kaleidoscope* and *Critics' Forum*. "I shan't listen as they were so unpleasant last time and I find I get less and less resilient as time goes on." In fact, her reviews were largely respect- ful. Howard Newby, in the *Listener,* liked it less than *Offshore,* but she thought his remarks were "just": "I couldn't quite get *Human Voices* to hang together," she told Ollard self-critically, "but it was the best I could do." Bernard Levin said that all the critics who were so enraged by her win- ning the Booker Prize that they decided "to behave as though [the award] had not been made" should now eat their words. "Beneath the cool wit of the surface there is something remarkably like passion and something even more like truth . . . *Human Voices* is funny and touching and authentic, but it is more. It is affirmative in the best and most important sense . . . It will last." Francis King, reviewing her warmly in the *Spectator,* urged her to have more "hubris," to take on more: "She might crash; but I have sufficient faith in her abilities to believe that it is much more likely that she would soar." Kermode, still labelling her as part of "The Duckworth School," celebrated again her "assured elegance of workmanship as well as the ability to surprise." He picked out the flashback to Annie Asra and her piano-tuner father in Birmingham as the best thing she had done yet. The novel, he concludes, "has a cool tenderness that lingers in the memory," and "extraordinary self-assurance."[55]

Human Voices, the work of an established and well-known writer, with a voice now recognised as "unmistakably hers," filled the reader's ear with sounds. It is a novel of voices and music, and also of silences. She always hears, in her inner ear, when she is writing, the voices of the characters, and needs the reader to hear them. "Of course you want to hear their voices." She also hears, and leads us to hear, things unsaid in the spaces between the voices. "One of the privileges of dialogue is silence."[56]

The voices in the air of the wartime BBC were replaced in her mind's ear by the voices of Freddie and her child actors, ventriloquists and imper- sonators all, suspended, like the characters of *Human Voices,* in the time bubble she lightly spun around them. She delivered *At Freddie's* by July 1981 and told Richard Ollard what she wanted for the jacket—a high wall with a broken basket of fruit at the bottom, because "I did think of the stage children as . . . expendable products, like the fruit." In the end she got a less subtle image of a fallen child.[57] Ollard's in-house memo recommended publication ("Emphatically, yes") and is particularly enthusiastic about her treatment of children: "loving them but not being taken in by them." In his blurb, he wrote: "Penelope Fitzgerald has emerged as the most original novelist of the decade . . . What is extraordinary is her combination of sharpness with generosity in her observation of people."[58]

The contract gave her an advance of £2,500, for an initial printing of 5,000 copies, with 10 per cent royalties up to sales of 3,000. This was her first novel to find an American publisher, Godine, who came up with a £750 advance. She wanted it to come out as soon as possible: "I just feel I shall lose heart if it's got to wait till next autumn." It was published on 29 March 1982, to mixed reviews. Paul Bailey said she had plundered a biography of Lilian Baylis, John Sutherland in the *London Review of Books* found it "hard to see why it was undertaken and hard to forgive its broad sentimentality," the *Sunday Times* called it "a mere pot-pourri of nostalgic anecdote." Light praise came from other reviewers, including Anthony Thwaite: "She moves at speed, is full of sharp observations and inventions, and at her best is very funny." She was downhearted: "I do feel rather daunted and wonder if it's a good idea to go on, if the going is to be quite so hard." Ollard encouraged her—he loved the novel, and he had no doubts.[59]

At Freddie's was the last novel she wrote based closely on her own past. Her life's subjects—hopefulness, innocence, misfortune, failure, stoicism—would persist, but she would find different embodiments for them from now on. But the child actors and their impersonations, and the childlike adults at odds with the real world, continued to haunt her.

Our kitten is now nearly a cat

CHAPTER THIRTEEN

The Ventriloquist

Such an improbable, inhibited, tantalizing but touching story,
once again an entire life's emotional history in a short space.[1]

The publication of *At Freddie's* in 1982 coincided with a time of disruption and grief, which shadowed the mood of her next book, a quiet, dark masterpiece. She was happily settled at Almeric Road, and enjoying her life as a writer in demand. The family was doing well. Valpy, at thirty-two, had left Cambridge for a professorship in development economics at the Institute of Social Studies in The Hague. She had gone to his inaugural lecture in November 1980. Maria's academic career in neurobiology was taking shape, and John Lake had decided to give up mathematics and take his skills to the City, selling gilts, with great success. Tina and Terence both had busy teaching jobs. Now Tina became pregnant. The Dooleys could see at once they would have to leave Almeric Road. There was nowhere to hang wet nappies; the pram would have to go through Penelope's room every time they wanted to take the baby out into the garden; the garden was much too small. They started to house-hunt in Chiswick, but every house Tina looked at with her mother seemed to have something wrong with it. There were no arguments, but Penelope, at her most obstructive, was vetoing every possibility. She did not want to move, and was miserable at the thought of it.

All of a sudden, breaking through this impasse, the Dooleys decided to give up teaching and go to the country. Towards the end of 1980, they started to look for houses, first in Norfolk, then in Somerset, while Penelope kept protesting that she didn't want to leave London. Nevertheless, they found a house which came with a post office and shop, in Theale, a small village in Somerset. They were going to be village postmasters, and Penelope would have to make her plans accordingly. She wrote, crossly, to Richard Ollard: "I feel rather under pressure as my daughter and son-in-law (baby due in 5 weeks) have suddenly decided they . . . would like to keep a small post-office in the depths of the country and they've kindly asked me to go with them to dig the vegetable patch—it is very good of them and indeed I've no option . . . I personally can <u>only</u> write in London, I love the noise and squalor and the perpetual distractions and the temptation to take an aircraft somewhere else."[2]

Very soon after the decision had been made, Fergus Dooley was born, on 15 May 1981. It quickly became apparent that all was not well. Jini Fiennes (who had had six children herself), by then living in Wandsworth, told Tina, to whom she was close, a few weeks after the birth, that she thought there was something wrong with the baby. Penelope went, in June, to teach her first Arvon writing course at Lumb Bank, at Heptonstall in Yorkshire, where Terence's sister Maura and her partner, David, were the administrators. She came back full of excitement, wanting to tell her stories, to find Tina and Terence in shock. Fergus had been diagnosed with congenital spinal muscular atrophy. The prognosis was not good.

By August, the Dooleys had resigned their teaching jobs and moved, with their sick baby, to Theale. Penelope went with them, but was to have a base in London—she was still teaching two days a week—and to travel up and down. Her bits and pieces of furniture and most of her books went to Theale and sat about in boxes, waiting to be unpacked. "I'm irreparably divided in 2 and don't know where everything is, including my typewriter." "I can't find <u>anything</u> . . . it's not like an ordinary move because the shop had to open straight away to keep the goodwill of the village, so we haven't got anything sorted out and I wonder if we ever will."[3]

Theale was a tiny village in beautiful farming country, on the Somerset Levels, "the very depths of the cow and cider-apple country," as she described it. The house and shop, on the main road from Wells to Wedmore, with little traffic then, had been a row of old terraced cottages—"the kind of stone-built cottage with low doors where tall people hit their heads." It was painted a creamy-yellow colour with a slate roof, very picturesque. The Dooleys at once became part of village life. The farmers left their lists of requirements in a red notebook on a Monday and they took the orders round to the farms once a week. People came to the post office to use the phone, there were telegrams to deliver, village children bought sweets by the ounce. "The locals come in for their morning paper, leaving all their cows outside in the road, and they peer through the window."[4] Tina and Terence got to know everyone, and they had lots of visitors.

Penelope had the main front room on the first floor, a large bed-sitting room with a little kitchen off it. (They all shared the bathroom.) As usual she painted it dark blue and green and put her mark on it. At one

point, busily DIY-ing, she fell off a ladder, and had to be stitched up "like
a bit of craft patchwork." "The hospital did not believe in the ladder, and
clearly thinks we're a gypsy family who've been having a 'disagreement.'"
She was keen to start work on the big walled jungle of "eight foot high"
nettles and overgrown fruit trees, and eventually turned it into the garden
she had always wanted, with a greenhouse, fruit and vegetables, a wild
asparagus bed, a lawn with wonderful cottage-garden borders, and swathes
of lavender which she sent to her friends with their birthday and Christmas
cards. She made wine and redcurrant jelly, she kept bantams. Her Theale
letters were full of rural business: "I must now go and negotiate to borrow a goat, to eat down the nettles on the verge of the road." "All the broad
beans have come up—but the hens keep getting out, nothing, it seems,
will keep them in."[5]

But at first things were difficult. The journey from London to Theale
and back, twice a week, was long and arduous: by train to Bath, then by
bus to Wells, then in the car to the village. She felt unsettled and upset.
And she was not good at dealing with the tension and wretchedness over
Fergus's condition. She did her share of watching and praying: "I'm sitting
in a cubicle at the Bristol Hospital for sick babies, among plastic mobiles
and blue elephants."[6] But she could not take charge, or console. When the
children were young and Desmond was incapacitated, she had been the
person who kept everything going. Now it was she, her daughters felt, who
required looking after. Fergus died in March 1982, aged ten months. Penelope, profoundly distressed, could barely speak of it, and was unable to give
Tina any comfort. Others in the family, friends and villagers were more help

to the Dooleys. Penelope wrote to Mary Lago: "He was born very delicate, but battled on gamely, then he became too weak to go on breathing, and we buried him in the churchyard at Theale, a lovely country place where primroses grow wild. They're carrying on with the shop, and they're still young, but it was a very heavy loss."[7] Later that year, she told her niece Belinda: "T & T still gallantly keeping the shop, with dogs, cats, hens, villagers & oldest inhabitants. Having a lot to do is the best thing, I'm sure they're right about that."[8] Silent though she was at the time, every year on Fergus's birthday, without fail, she would send Tina a card and a message. The following August, Tina's second child, Luke, was born. All was well, and Luke, who grew up into an imaginative and articulate boy, became Penelope's great friend, the first grandchild with whom she had a close relationship. But the lost child remained forever in her memory and in her mind.

For a short time, she found a London base, thanks to Jean Talbot, in rooms in the Inner Temple, but this was a stopgap. She asked around, and through mutual friends she was put in touch with Joan Mathew, a relative of Penelope's old friend Mary Bennett. Joan rented rooms in her house in St. John's Wood. As Joan Young, daughter of the baronet George Young, descendant of a long line of classicists and administrators, she had been at Somerville College, reading Modern Languages, a little before Penelope. She was a widow; her husband, a Catholic lawyer, died young and left her with two children, Perdita and Theo, and very little money. Hence, "paying guests," all of whom were friends of friends. Antonia Southern had rented a room in her house in the 1950s. A friend of Theo's, Desmond Maxwell, was in the basement, the children and Joan were in the main part of the house, and Penelope rented the furnished attic flat—bedroom, living room, bathroom.

Number 76 Clifton Hill, a tall, narrow Victorian house off Abbey Road, in a quiet tree-lined side street (but within reach of the 159 bus), was shabby-grand, with fine pieces of furniture all falling to bits. There were bullet holes from Indian skirmishes in the pictures in the hall. Nothing—taps, heating, baths, lights—quite worked as it should. Penelope described her quarters to friends with amused pleasure: "This is a kind of attic, overlooking the tree-tops, with gold wallpaper. It's rather <u>strange</u>. I was moving an arm-chair wh: had no bottom, so people fell through it, and found some valuable jewellery wh: had been lost for 25 years." "2 strange little rooms (but they suit me) at the top of a house." "The house is falling to bits and the banister is broken . . . I'm very fond of the person the house belongs to and don't like to say anything about the banister, because I'm sure she hasn't noticed."[9]

Joan had been a glamorous woman, and in her seventies was still funny and resourceful and sharp-tongued, slim and striking, always with a slash of red lipstick, inventively coloured hair and an air of adventure. Perdita, her daughter, thought of Penelope as a kind of White Queen in a cardigan, "gentle and faintly woolly." Theo, the difficult son, was kept awake by Penelope in the room above him coughing "like a sheep," "padding about at night" and getting up "at the screech of dawn" to work. Desmond Maxwell occasionally passed her on the stairs, and had the impression she had come there to write, was busy and not at all lonely. Penelope thought Joan was splendid, and Theo a lazy slob who made his mother do all the work. Tina and Maria and Valpy thought of Clifton Hill as a makeshift, not a proper home, with an eccentric châtelaine. But Antonia Southern, who saw a good deal of Penelope in the 1980s, recognised that, though she relied on her daughters and on being part of their families, this was a congenial setting for her and represented a kind of late freedom. In the Clifton Hill attic, for the first time in about forty years, she was not dependent on anyone else, and had no one depending on her. London was at her disposal, and she could suit herself. She lived there for seven years, through her late sixties and early seventies.[10]

She went to Theale less often as those years passed. In 1986, the Dooleys gave up the village shop for lack of income, and moved around the country, going back to teaching. They lived in a series of impractical and beautiful locations, with (by 1988) three small children and very little money, almost as though re-enacting Tina's childhood in Southwold and on the barge. There was a big dilapidated Victorian seaside house with holes in the roof in Weston-super-Mare, then an unrestored Georgian terraced house overlooking a fishing harbour in Watchet, Somerset, with a steam train at the bottom of the garden, then a too-small cottage on the green in Milton Abbot, near Tavistock, on the edge of Dartmoor, in west Devon (which Penelope loved), and last, in the mid-1990s, a house in a small isolated village on the north coast of Cornwall, near Boscastle.[11] She followed them everywhere, helping with their gardens, attentive to her grandchildren, and, as she became more well-off, stocking up with a week's shopping at Sainsbury's when Tina met her off the train, always including a bottle of dry Martini for herself. But after the early years at Theale she did not live with them again. Maria and John, with their children, settled into a big house in Highgate in the late 1980s, and that, in the end, became her home.

Just after *At Freddie's* came out, Fitzgerald published two short stories, also with parts for children. In one, "The Prescription," the last trace of her unwritten Turkish novel, a Greek widower sends his son Alecco to work as an odd-job boy for a wealthy Turkish doctor. The boy is sharp and quick, and rapidly learns how the practice works. The doctor resents his talent. He finds Alecco, one night, teaching himself to make up prescriptions, and, in a startling act of violence, forces him to drink down what he hopes will be a lethal potion. Alecco escapes to England, and ten years later returns as a qualified doctor with an interest in new, psychotherapeutic treatments. But the old Turk, meeting him again, still gets the better of him. It is a story about cruelty, power and surviving against the odds.

The other, slight but touching, story of 1983, "Worlds Apart," is a love story, though the word "love" is not mentioned. Really it is a story about home. Hester, whose husband has left her, and who has a six-year-old daughter, Tilly, takes in a Polish lodger, who works with refugees, in her spare room. He is punctilious, lonely and neat. Hester, otherwise a sensible woman, is incapable of speaking her feelings, "saying something kind" or acting as she would like to. She finds herself "wanting to sleep and wake in the dark beside his darkness," but can say nothing to him. Tilly, who is intrepid and severe (the relationship is like Nenna's with her girls in *Off-shore*), sorts things out, and, surprisingly, there is a happy ending: the two, who started worlds apart, will be "home" together.[12]

In the early 1980s, Fitzgerald began to be in demand as a reviewer, and was always pleased to be asked, partly out of interest, partly, as she would say, for "£££." As a reviewer she was appreciative, decisive, knowledgeable, brilliant at succinctly invoking a whole life story and usually, though not always, benign. The earliest pieces she did were for the *London Review of Books*. Her editor there, Susannah Clapp, said that her copy was always "crystal-clear" and required very little alteration.[13] She was asked at first to write on subjects that connected back to Burne-Jones: Morris, Christina Rossetti, Charles Ashbee, founder of the Guild of Handicraft (a biography by Fiona MacCarthy, kindly reviewed). She wrote on the novelist Ada Leverson, "marvellously skilful . . . with non-events, or anti-events," and on Sylvia Townsend Warner, whom she admired for her quiet attention to daily life ("Few people can ever have described a teapot as well as STW"), her sympathy with other lives and her strong sense of the potential for "disorder" in life.[14]

Her piece on Rossetti compared her with Charlotte Mew. This remarkable lyric poet, a Georgian writer born in 1869, wrote a few stories for *The Yellow Book* and had two lean books of poems published by the Poetry Bookshop, *The Farmer's Bride* in 1916 (reissued with additions in 1923), and, posthumously, *The Rambling Sailor* in 1929. She was intensely admired, in her lifetime and afterwards, by a small number of readers. In 1982, Fitzgerald reviewed Val Warner's Virago edition of Charlotte Mew's *Collected Poems and Prose,* and called Mew "a writer who was completely successful perhaps only two or three times (though that's enough for a lyric poet) and whose sad life . . . refuses to be quite explained."[15]

But she wanted to explain her. Mew's sad and enigmatic character increasingly compelled her imagination, as she turned, in the early 1980s, from the Poetry Bookshop project to the idea of writing her biography. She took a sardonic view of Collins's reluctance to take on the Poetry Bookshop, writing to her fellow aficionado Howard Woolmer: "All the publishers (though you wouldn't guess it from their appearance) say they are so poor they can scarcely carry on for another week, and in any case couldn't reproduce the broadsheets and chapbook covers in colour, which was what I wanted." (They may also have demurred because a book on Harold Monro and the Poetry Bookshop had come out in 1967.) Ollard responded to her Charlotte Mew proposal, however, with "intense inter-est." In July 1982 she sent him her review of the Virago edition "as one more (the 7th) attempt by me to get you to think about a biography of CM." But, she added hastily, even though Carmen Callil had written her an enthusiastic letter, "DON'T tell me to go to Virago, as they are so close about the £££." A few days later: "I've just sent you another letter about Charlotte Mew, I can't help it, it keeps coming over me as they say. I still feel her life is interesting in its way." And again: "The interest is, to me, that she's a divided personality who had to produce so many versions of herself at the same time. Perhaps we all do."[16]

What drew her so to writing that life? It was not just a way of deploy-ing all the work she had done on the Poetry Bookshop, though it may have started out as that. It was not, presumably, in the hopes of "£££," since Mew was not, and never has been, seen as a major cultural figure in the way Burne-Jones was. A life of L. P. Hartley—which she now, finally, admitted she was never going to write—might have had more readers.[17] It was not a sentimental matter of identification: Mew and Fitzgerald were not alike, though there are some intriguing affinities. But clearly she had a fascina-tion with this reclusive and magnetic personality, and for her few, intense, disturbing poems. She would often talk about "my poor Charlotte" or "my little poetess," of whom "I have become very fond."[18] Pity is an unusual motive for a biographer. But it sets the tone for a book which enters with sympathy and tender humour into a tragic and peculiar life.

Charlotte Mew was "an incurable Londoner." She lived all her life in shabby-genteel poverty in Bloomsbury (Doughty Street, Gordon Street) and Camden. This is a book full of street scenes and London characters, written just after Fitzgerald had had to leave her London home and find a new base. She deeply understands Charlotte's love of the city: "She wanted company, even when she was declaring she didn't, she loved hurrying from one appointment to another, and feeling all round her the pressure of a million unknown lives." Fitzgerald had often used London settings—in *Burne-Jones, The Golden Child, Offshore, Human Voices, At Freddie's*—but this would be the last London book.

There was another landscape, though, that mattered to Charlotte. Her father, an unsuccessful architect, grew up on the Isle of Wight. Lotti's childhood holidays there stayed with her always—like the Knox family's memories of Kibworth, or her own of Balcombe. Fitzgerald edges into poetry herself, describing this. "But Lotti's was the summer and early autumn sea, and the phosphorescent darkness of the summer beach at night." Family life, however, was grim. Fred Mew had married his boss's daughter, unforgivingly described as "a tiny, pretty, silly young woman who grew, in time, to be a very silly old one." Her family treated him as an interloper. He lost heart, lost money and suffered from depression. His failure is done with sympathy: "By and large, he had not had much of a life of it." While Lotti was growing up, three of her little brothers died. There was "mental weakness" on the mother's side of the family. The eldest son, and then the liveliest younger sister, developed schizophrenia and were confined in mental hospitals—the girl on the Isle of Wight, which would darken Lotti's childhood memories of the place.

"What would be surprising, if we didn't know that the life of children is conducted on a totally different system from that of adults, is that Charlotte Mew always spoke of her childhood as a time of intense, but lost, happiness." Lotti was "brilliant, irresistible and defiant," hair-tossing and excitable (she once snapped in half a parasol which had been used to rap her over the knuckles), a literate, musical, "noticing" child, but given to "sudden withdrawals." She was tiny, and never grew much over five foot. She became an adult who looked like a strange child and sounded like a hoarse boy, with huge questioning eyes, a sardonic surprised look, "as though she thought that if life is a joke it is not a very good one," "a clear, pale, unlined skin and tiny hands and feet, shod in doll's boots." Fitzgerald wants us to think of her as never at home in the adult world. She greatly admires Mew's poem of 1912, "The Changeling," in which the poet imagines herself (as many gifted children do) not as her own parents' child but an imposter, deposited on them by fairy creatures from "the wet, wild wood," and finally escaping back into the dark, like the "little pale brother" she loved, who was also called away:

> I shall grow up, but never grow old,
> I shall always, always be very cold,
> I shall never come back again![19]

Fitzgerald calls these "verses for children": "Charlotte used to read them aloud . . . to children of her acquaintance, giving no explanation, because she believed (quite rightly) that none would be needed. They understood her at once." She had an uncanny affinity with them: the poems are full of children's games, fantasies, cruelties and language. Fitzgerald calls Mew herself a "changeling."

The changeling child in the poem is her parents' "disgrace," always being sent upstairs for bad behaviour. Lotti's childhood, too, was marked by a dark sense of "disgrace." Fitzgerald makes much of the Nonconformist nurse, Elizabeth Goodman, who ruled over her early life, loved and feared. Her "stern economies," her Bible readings and her punitive regime taught Charlotte a lifelong sense of guilt. As a child she would often feel that all of nature was watching and judging her, in what she called "a day of eyes." She suffered from "the spiritual nausea of belief and unbelief." Fitzgerald comments: "Guilt of this nature can never be eradicated, a lifetime is not long enough." She has to turn these emotions into images or they "would have broken her." This echoes Fitzgerald's view of Burne-Jones's obsessions; she imagines him saying: "If I had left these images hidden in my emotions, they might have torn me in pieces."

When Charlotte fell in love, as she did first at school with her inspiring, neurotic teacher Lucy Harrison, it was always humiliating and disastrous. She was haunted by a feeling of worthlessness, and lived "in a purgatory of her own, the circle of self-punishers." "The whole of Charlotte Mew's upbringing and her whole emotional experience had made it plain to her that there is a 'score' for human happiness and that we have no right to avoid payment." This is one of many moments in the biography—as in *Burne-Jones* and *The Knox Brothers*—where Fitzgerald's own feelings come through. So, when Mew writes on the death of a child: "She never suggested that writing the poems made the grief any less." Or: "Writers are not rational on the subject of their favourite work." "Terminal illness is a great simplifier of daily life, everything being reduced to the same point of hope against hope." She can speak as herself through the mask of writing another person's life.

Fred Mew died when Charlotte was twenty-nine, and her schizophrenic brother died soon after, in his thirties: this came as a terrible shock. The residual family consisted of Charlotte, her sister, Anne (biddable and pretty, with a talent for decoration), and their fussy dependent mother, with her bad-tempered parrot, Wek, a notable figure in the biography. The three women, like characters in a troubling fairy tale, lived together for years. They were extremely poor, and poverty is one of the strong themes of the book. Fitzgerald worries away at their accounts, their pitiful income and their expenditure, as though she herself were trying to make ends meet for them ("What could Charlotte and Anne not do without?"). They both had to make a living. Anne had a "ladylike—meaning badly paid—job with a guild of decorative artists," for which she took a studio. Charlotte, who had her "businesslike" side, determinedly set out on a writer's career, "partly to show herself what she could do, partly to earn money. Without money free will means very little." So that they could keep their "good address" at Gordon Street, they took in lodgers, but Ma had to be spared the "terrible humiliation" of collecting the rent. They had one maid-of-all-work, with a habit of bouncing in while Charlotte was writing to ask her domestic questions, "pitying her, as the brisk and efficient always pity a writer." Charlotte and the maid did all the housework together, and the house "made work."

A need to maintain appearances and keep the family secrets hidden was one of the "curious and pathetic" features of Charlotte's nature. Fitzgerald's theory is that she was split between two "irreconcilable" selves, and that "one side of her treated the other cruelly," with "fierce self-suppression." One side was "Miss Lotti," ladylike, genteel, moral. The other was "Charlotte," the "savage who threatened her from within," answerable to no one, capable of wild comic performances and overwhelming emotions which she exposed in her writing. This theory of the split self runs through the whole book, perhaps a bit too insistently.[20] The split self made her a "double-dealer," presenting "edited versions of herself." Fitzgerald, adept herself at evasions and self-editing, understands this performance well. She also sees it as self-punishing. It made Mew not only "one of society's outsiders," but "an outsider even to herself."

One of the secrets that Charlotte concealed even from her close friends was the madness in the family. She did not talk about it, though she let it out, "at a distance of time from the . . . experience," as a subject for a few poems, "Ken," "On the Asylum Road" and "In Nunhead Cemetery," beautifully invoked by Fitzgerald. But it shaped her whole life. Her siblings' mental illness coincided, "as ill-fortune would have it," with the dominance of the "science" of eugenics, which argued that "morbid inheritance" led to the gradual degeneration of society. People with mental illness in their families had a moral duty not to reproduce. Because of this, both sisters felt they should never marry or have children. Charlotte, in any case, came to feel that "all passion was destructive."

When Charlotte ventured out into the literary marketplace of the 1890s (Fitzgerald has fun with this), trying to place stories and essays in the many magazines of the time, and being taken up by *The Yellow Book,* she seemed to turn herself into the perfect "New Woman." She developed the look and the manner, with her velvet jacket, tweed skirt and cravat, her little boots and red stockings, her cropped hair, her big rolled umbrella carried like a weapon, her self-rolled cigarettes, gruff voice and (surprisingly) rough language. On her frequent trips to northern France she was capable of dancing a can-can "in her boots and silk directoire knickers," or of "quay-loafing" in the fishermen's quarter in Boulogne or Dieppe. But her mannish look, her Francophilia, her flâneuring, and her literary interest in lowlife and prostitutes didn't really make her a New Woman. Fitzgerald does not read her as a feminist, as some other writers on Mew have done.[21] When the Oscar Wilde scandal hit *The Yellow Book,* she backed off at once—to her own professional disadvantage. She was not a suffragist, she never even registered for the vote, and she was not "politically minded."

Her sexual desires did not make her happy. Fitzgerald describes her hopeless passions with poignancy. She fell in love with the "rash and generous," thoroughly heterosexual Ella D'Arcy, one of *The Yellow Book's* most vigorous female contributors, and pursued her to Paris in 1902, "in a state of passionate agitation." But Ella could not understand Charlotte's "self-tormenting self-doubting temperament," or the perversity in a nervous lover (something Fitzgerald recognises and often writes about), "which backs away from what it most wants." The episode ended in humiliation. Ten years later the pattern repeated itself, even more mortifyingly, with May Sinclair, the psychological novelist, whom Fitzgerald dislikes. Sinclair found Charlotte intriguing, but was aghast when she hurled herself at her. "It seems rather unlucky—but Charlotte was hardly ever lucky—that this incident . . . has only been recorded in terms of farce." The story went round, via Rebecca West, that a "lesbian poetess" had chased Sinclair into her bedroom and jumped over the bed at her. "Was it necessary for May

Sinclair to tell so many people about it?" Whatever really happened, it was clearly "an uncontrolled physical confession of furious longing . . . which terrified May, and perhaps also terrified Miss Lotti." Fitzgerald regards Mew's lesbianism as an ingrained part of her, not, as Simone de Beauvoir would have it, "a choice of life." She treats it matter-of-factly, as an essential element in her nature, but also as one of the things that made her life difficult and confirmed her sense of herself as an outsider.

People who tried to befriend Charlotte Mew had their work cut out, but she did have her guardian angels. (Ottoline Morrell's swooping attempts at patronage, however, were rebuffed, somewhat to the biographer's satisfaction. She does not like "Bloomsbury," right next door to, and a world away from, Charlotte's Bloomsbury.) Henry Harland, the genial editor of *The Yellow Book,* wisely advised her "that poignant subjects were best treated lightly and easily, and allowed to speak for themselves." Once she started publishing poems, in her early forties, she acquired one very determined helper. This was the strong-minded Amy Dawson Scott, known to all as Mrs. Sappho—not because she was gay but because she had written a poem called *Sappho*. She was the founder of International PEN, the bossy befriender of artists and writers and tireless cultural networker. It was she who brought Mew together with May Sinclair. "It is easy to criticize such people, difficult to do without them." Dawson Scott, fascinated by little Charlotte Mew, lured her to read her poems to select audiences, with astonishing effect. Her husband, however, was not so impressed. Fitzgerald did her own index, as usual, to her biography, and the entry for Dr. Scott reads: "Avoids wife's literary friends; thinks CM mad." Charlotte, biting the hand that fed, dropped Mrs. Sappho after the Sinclair imbroglio, which her patron heard about and was baffled by: "Charlotte is evidently a pervert," she wrote in her diary.[22]

Fitzgerald is equally ironical about Mew's later patron, Sydney Cockerell, another of life's great fixers and collectors. In youth he had been William Morris's secretary, so he links back to the world of Burne-Jones. Now he was Director of the Fitzwilliam Museum in Cambridge, from where "he spun his tireless web." Cockerell, an officious busybody, had a naive enthusiasm for great art and liked acting as "a knight-errant." Fitzgerald describes him in a letter to Ollard as "an old shit who was charming when he wanted to be a fairy godmother or cultivate famous people." But he took Charlotte under his wing. He introduced her to Thomas Hardy, to whom she had been compared, and who greatly liked her poems. Florence Hardy became her good friend. He sent her poems to Siegfried Sassoon, who became a lifelong admirer. He took her out for treats (they went to see a Charlie Chaplin film together) and invited her to his house in Cambridge, where he showed her his treasures, like a lock of Lizzie Siddal's hair. She became fond of his shy, invalid wife. "Shyness can only be cured by someone more shy." Best of all, when she and Anne were on the edge of penury in 1923, he fixed a small Civil List pension for her.[23] Cockerell came in touch with Mew because he read, and fell in love with, the only book of poems she published in her lifetime, *The Farmer's Bride*. It was published by the Poetry Bookshop, and it was Harold and Alida Monro who were Charlotte's best guardian angels.

All Fitzgerald's writing distils a mass of knowledge and research into a concentrated narrative. Her warmly affectionate chapters on the Poetry Bookshop are a good example of this process. She called her biography *Charlotte Mew and Her Friends,* because an outsider can only be understood by being set in a context, and because she wanted to show how the Poetry Bookshop changed her life. It was the one place "where she could venture to feel welcome without being altogether ridiculous."

Fitzgerald describes it with intense pleasure, remembering (though not alluding to) her own childhood visits to the dilapidated eighteenth-century house in the squalid Bloomsbury backstreet, with its wooden furniture, curtains of sacking, coloured cushions, coal fire, the cat leaping about on the books, the rhyme sheets on the walls, the long tables covered with slim volumes, chapbooks and magazines. Steep stairs led up to the dimly lit attic, where the famous twice-weekly evening readings took place. "Poets arriving in London, or even in England, made their way there as though by instinct."[24] Impoverished writers and artists needing somewhere to stay rented a cheap bed in the attic. From 1913 through the 1920s, hundreds of poets read there, including Yeats, Lawrence, Wilfred Owen, F. S. Flint, Ford Madox Ford, Edith Sitwell, Anna Wickham, W. H. Davies, Richard Aldington, Lascelles Abercrombie, John Drinkwater, Rupert Brooke, Marinetti, Eleanor Farjeon and Walter de la Mare.

The Poetry Bookshop comes into many memoirs of the generation who began publishing in the 1920s and '30s. John Lehmann spoke of "the magnet-pull of the Poetry Bookshop under Harold Monro," William Plomer of the "temple-like atmosphere and its polychromatic lining of 'slim volumes.'" Elizabeth Bowen remembered listening "after dark, in a barn-like room, to Ezra Pound reading aloud what was hypnotically unintelligible to me by the light of one candle." Rose Macaulay, friend of the Knoxes, often went to the readings: "De la Mare read his poetry deplorably,

Yeats had his own incantatory manner, fascinating, peculiar, and eventually soporific." A kind of "poetry-intoxication" emanated from the Bookshop, she thought. All remembered the sound of hammers from the gold-beaters' workshops in the district, the kipper bones and banana skins thrown from the slum houses, the nearby pubs and coffeehouses.[25]

For Fitzgerald, it embodied the values she most respected, and a time in history—she had written about it in *The Knox Brothers* and would again in *The Gate of Angels*—of hopefulness and possibility. The fact that it is a story with an unhappy ending made it all the more appealing to her. The Poetry Bookshop's open, democratic, not-for-profit ethos is her ideal: "Everything was for anyone to sit down and read." She loved Monro's contradictions: a poet who looked like a conventional businessman, a "dour, practical Scot" financed by "his family's private lunatic asylum" who was also a "romantic idealist." For Monro, "poetry was life." Unlike most poetry publishers of the time, he did not charge his poets for producing their books, though the Bookshop was always in financial difficulties. He took endless pains with his complaining and egocentric writers: "The amount of abuse he put up with, even in the long history of poets and their publishers, is quite astounding." She feels for his depressiveness, his alcoholism, his unhappy sexuality and his troubled dependency on his wife, Fitzgerald's heroine. Devoted, hard-working Alida Monro, "a beautiful girl from a Hampstead-Polish refugee family," dedicated her life to the homosexual Monro, and to the Bookshop, even after its move from Devonshire Street in 1926 and after Monro's death from alcoholism in 1932. She often read the poems aloud, as well as befriending the poets. She was a person of courage and "noble loyalty," and "when she gave her friendship (or, it must be said, her dislike) she put her whole heart in it."

Monro teamed up with the more conservative Edward Marsh to publish the *Georgian Poetry* anthologies—what Fitzgerald, showing her hand, calls "the last body of English poetry to be actually read by ordinary people, for pleasure." These were hugely successful. But Monro did not want to be identified only with Georgian poetry; he was an adventurous editor, interested in experimental work. He made some mistakes, turning down Edward Thomas and T. S. Eliot. But he published Pound's *Des Imagistes,* Aldington and F. S. Flint, Robert Graves's first book—and Charlotte Mew.

When Alida, who loved "The Farmer's Bride" and "The Changeling," invited Mew, in November 1915, to come and hear her read those poems at one of the evening sessions, they had not yet met. Into the Bookshop, out of the London fog, stepped "a tiny figure, apparently a maiden aunt, dressed in a hard felt hat and a small-sized man's overcoat." "She was asked, 'Are you Charlotte Mew?' and replied, with a slight smile, 'I am sorry to say I am.'" But the Bookshop did what it could for her. Alida and Charlotte became close friends, though not close enough for Charlotte to tell her her secrets. They worked together colouring the first series of rhyme sheets and some of the chapbook covers. But Alida was not allowed to look inside Charlotte's two large, mysterious trunks: "Possibly they were full of unread or rejected manuscripts; no-one could say."

Monro encouraged her to put her poems together for a collection, dealt patiently with her troublesome demands—she insisted on a special quarto format to get her long lines printed across the full width of the page—and consoled her for the slow sales. He placed a short, beautiful poem of hers, "Sea Love," in prime position at the end of his new *Monthly Chapbook* in July 1919.[26] He produced a second edition of *The Farmer's Bride* in 1921, with more poems, published in America as *Saturday Market.* He brought her recognition, most notably from Hardy ("she is far and away the best living woman poet, who will be read when others are forgotten") and Virginia Woolf: "I think her very good and very interesting and unlike anyone else."

For a short time, even in the war years, there were moments of "humorous serenity" in Charlotte Mew's life. But the need to leave Gordon Street (the lease was up) for Delancey Street in Camden, and the death of Ma, which should have been a blessing but came as a "stupefying blow," were hard for her. In 1926 her sister, Anne, from whom she had been inseparable for fifty years, fell ill with cancer. For a year, Charlotte nursed her, giving up Delancey Street to pay the medical bills and living with her in Anne's cold and uncomfortable studio. Anne died a slow and awful death at the age of fifty-four; "and now," Charlotte wrote to Cockerell, in June 1927, "she can never be old, or not properly taken care of, or alone." She plunged into a condition of morbid survivor's guilt and profound depression. Fitzgerald tells the story of Mew's last days simply and unflinchingly. She began to believe that she had buried her sister alive, or that Anne had been infected by the black specks (of soot) in the studio. She would not go into an asylum, but went to a dreary nursing home near Baker Street station. Friends—Sydney, Alida—visited her and were appalled at her state. On 24 March 1928 she bought a bottle of Lysol, a household disinfectant "with a violent corrosive action," which she drank. She was found in great pain, "foaming at the mouth." "For a short while she recovered consciousness, and said, 'Don't keep me, let me go.' This was her last attempt to speak to anyone, this side of silence."

This is how Fitzgerald ends her biography, choosing not to take the story on to the reports of the suicide in the local paper that described her as "Charlotte New, said to be a writer," to the posthumous publication of a second volume, *The Rambling Sailor,* in 1929, with a memoir by Alida, and to her small but lasting reputation, movingly commented on by Siegfried Sassoon to Cockerell, in 1932: "Time is the only agent, and many will be on the rubbish heap when Charlotte's star is at the zenith, where it will remain."[27] She does not follow through to the afterlife because she does not want to soften the blow of the death, whose tragedy confirms her view of a guilt-haunted character and a poetry of death, insanity and self-haunting. Like Emily Dickinson, Mew "felt her life closing before its close," and had often imagined her own death:

Some day I *shall* not think; I shall not *be*!

That is the last line of "The Quiet House," a haunting poem of a woman living on with her father after all the others in the family have died or gone away, in a dreary, autumnal London house, while "the world goes on the same outside."[28] She is waiting for someone who might come for her, but never does. Fitzgerald calls it a poem of "the guilt of wanting and not being wanted."

This biography is the only time she writes at length—and extremely well—about poetry, apart from a few cogent remarks, in reviews, about de la Mare, Edward Thomas, William Morris, Stevie Smith and Christina

Rossetti. She recognises that not all Mew's poems are equally good, but sees that the central impulse is always what Mew calls the "*cri de coeur,*" "the moment when the emotion unmistakably concentrates itself into a few words," something "extorted." She reads her strange, awkward, long colloquial utterances as "following line by line the impulses of the speaker, like jets of blood."[29]

The poem that made Mew famous was "The Farmer's Bride," spoken by the farmer who has married a wild, shy young girl who cannot bear to be touched. She runs away, he gets up a chase and brings her back to the house, but does not touch her. He is being driven mad by frustration as he thinks of her alone upstairs ("Oh! My God! The down, / The soft young down of her, the brown, / The brown of her—her eyes, her hair, her hair!"). Fitzgerald treats it as a short story: "Such an improbable, inhibited, tantalizing but touching story, once again an entire life's emotional history in a short space." She writes about "Madeleine in Church," a long dramatic monologue of a fallen woman, trying to pray to a distant Christ whose love she fears ("his arms are full of broken things"), as the voice of a person who "lets her life come back to her in fragments which her mind hardly wants to recognize." She has a particular fondness for a "small, unobtrusive poem" called "The Shade-Catchers," "as quiet as a passing remark on something just seen in the street." She likes it because it is about "children and their world of games which she observed with such respect," because it is a Londoner's poem, and because it is elusive, ambiguous and odd. "Charlotte Mew is a story-teller here as usual, and as usual 'not like anyone else.'"

> I think they were about as high
> As haycocks are. They went rushing by
> Catching bits of shade in the sunny street:
> "I've got one," cried sister to brother.
> "I've got two." "Now I've got another."
> But scudding away on their little bare feet,
> They left the shade in the sunny street.

Bits, fragments, broken things, voices, stories: these are what leap out at her from Mew's work and life. Fitzgerald is above all interested in her as an "impersonator," speaking in different voices. Her "mad" poems are "impersonations, written through, but not in, the first person. Mad people are described by a sane onlooker, but 'this I is not I' . . . the speaker, or spoken-through, is painfully indirect." "Why do poets impersonate?" she asks. They may do it "because they have a great deal to hide," or want to escape from the self. "To Charlotte Mew impersonation was necessary, rather than helpful." When Mew read her poems aloud, she seemed to go into a kind of trance, a state of possession. "She seemed not so much to be acting or reciting as a medium's body taken over by a distinct personality."

In a Fitzgerald notebook from the early 1980s, there are notes for a story she never wrote called "The Ventriloquist." This provides a strange and vital link between *At Freddie's*, *Charlotte Mew* and her next novels. The notes begin with the *OED* definition of ventriloquism: "The art or practice of speaking or producing sounds in such a manner that the voice appears to proceed from some person or object other than the speaker, and usu. at some distance from him." Then: "The important point for the performer is to make the imaginative effort of dividing himself into A (who puts the questions) and B who gives the response." Technical notes about how ventriloquists work lead into sketches for imaginary conversations between the actor and the voice which is apparently coming from his stomach. On one page, she writes a Beckettian speech of painful intensity, which looks as if it is meant for the ventriloquist's "voice" to utter:

If you wanted me last year why don't you want me this year. If you don't want me this year why didn't you say so. If you didn't want to say so then it must have been because you don't trust me. If you didn't trust me what reason have you not to. If there wasn't a reason not to trust me last year how could there be a reason this year. If you wanted me last year why don't you want me this year. If you don't want me this year why can't we sit down and talk it over. If we don't sit down and talk it over I shan't understand why you don't want me. If I could understand why you don't want me I could sit down and talk it over. If you want [another woman] not me, why does it have to be [a horrible little funperson] [not even a friend of mine but the daughter of someone else's], a little funperson with fun ear-rings. If you want a fun person with fun ear-rings why do you have to bring her back here. If you wanted to hurt me you could have taken her to [Majorca] Portugal. If you couldn't take her to Portugal why did you bring her back here. If you had to bring her back here why did it have to be on Wednesday. If it had to be on a Wednesday, why that one. [If you wanted me]—Laughter from audience should drown the end of the speech.

[Bravo! Bravo! Have at them all][30]

Also in this notebook is an idea for a story called "Fantasies," which centres on the thoughts of an old man called Higgs who lives in Theale. (He was, in real life, one of Theale's oldest inhabitants.) She tells herself what the shape and meaning of this story might be: "Novalis wrote: One can imagine stories which have no coherence, but only association of events, like dreams, or poems which at most have single verses which can be understood, like fragments of the most various objects."[31] This suggestive note connects to Mew's Madeleine, whose "life comes back to her in fragments which her mind hardly wants to recognise." And it points far forward, to *The Blue Flower*. Fitzgerald is musing to herself about writing as impersonation, and about a kind of writing, like a dream or a poem, which could be made of fragmentary associations. This, from now on, is increasingly how she will write, breaking away from the realist necessity of one-thing-after-another, creating big gaps and silences behind and around her vivid scenes and voices, explaining as little as possible. In *Charlotte Mew* itself, not a dense, long biography, certain scenes and moments stand out: Lotti breaking the parasol, Charlotte loafing with the fishing lads in Dieppe, Miss Mew arriving at the Poetry Bookshop. We are left with a powerful sense of her, and of the mystery and silence she left behind her.

Charlotte Mew is the crucial turning-point, the hinged door, between what, in another writer, you might call "early" and "late" work. And it stayed in her mind, too, because it had a vigorous afterlife. The work on the book, as with all her biographical work, involved masses of research, and all the pieces of good and bad luck that biographers get used to. She had "Charlotte-Mewing" sessions with fellow enthusiasts, like the novelist Lettice Cooper, Michael Holroyd at the Arts Council and Carmen Callil at Virago. Jonathan Barker, working at the Arts Council Poetry Library, helped her with research there, and was struck by her "self-effacement and her complete lack of pretension; I always felt that she was more interested in me than she felt I could possibly be in her." He detected, beneath that amiable surface, "a core of steel." Marjorie Watts, Amy Dawson Scott's elderly daughter, was difficult, and for years had refused to show her Mew letters to any potential biographers. Then, suddenly and abruptly, at a PEN meeting, she dropped a brown paper envelope into Penelope's lap, containing the whole correspondence. Meanwhile, there were ominous rumours that Robert Gittings was writing his own biography of Mew. The copyright was in a confused condition. Illustrations were hard to get hold of. "I'll never do a biography again!"

Collins were being infuriatingly obtuse about making the book look like a beautiful Poetry Bookshop chapbook. Stuart Proffitt, who arrived at Collins in January 1983, was given Fitzgerald to look after by Ollard, as he began to retire. At first Proffitt found her taxing. She "did not have an eye for detail." Typescript would arrive with little bits of paper, afterthoughts, stuck on with Bostik. There were inconsistencies and mistakes. As a result, the first edition of *Charlotte Mew* has "double tipping" (two copyright pages), because there had to be last-minute corrections. But the book, he had no doubt, was a masterpiece, and gradually he began to know and understand its author. He gave her a free hand with the blurb, whose keywords were reserve, secrets, melancholic, frustration, mystification, grief and tragic. The book was dedicated "To the Memory of the Poetry Bookshop."[32] There were excellent reviews by, among others, Victoria Glendinning, Peter Levi, Susannah Clapp, Hugh Haughton and John Gross, who called it "an admirable book, full of insight and sympathy and mellow humour . . . She supplies the context . . . but she doesn't try to explain the inexplicable."[33]

Throughout the 1980s, Charlotte Mew stayed with her. Of writing biography, she once said: "It's rather difficult to shake the people off when the book is written, and to return to yourself. They're not to be got rid of so easily." She had been given Mew's plain brass candlesticks ("I don't use them"), and there is a photograph of them, lit, at the end of the book. In 1985, the British Academy awarded her the Rose Mary Crawshay Prize (jointly with a book on Edmund Spenser), for her biography's "sympathetic interpretation of her shadowed and secretive life." She was moderately pleased: "It's all so completely typical, an award that no-one's ever heard of for 2 books which I fear not many people have heard of either."

In 1987, an intelligent and observant American editor, Chris Carduff, working at Addison-Wesley, who had read an enthusiastic review in the *New York Times,* wrote her a fan letter, and asked to publish *Charlotte Mew* in a new "Women's Radcliffe Biography Series," alongside books on Emily Dickinson, Margaret Fuller and Mary Cassatt. The rights were available from Collins, and Penelope was delighted to think of Charlotte in a series of "timeless women." She was offered $1,000. Over many letters and phone calls, a business communication—as so often with her—turned into a friendship. Carduff suggested printing a "chapbook" selection of Mew's poems at the back of the book, and she left the selection to him. He agreed to keep the illustrations "scattered" through the book, an important point for her: "I think they help to 'tell the story,' always a difficulty when you're trying to write about somebody who is not at all well known." There were excellent, long, serious reviews.[34]

In the late 1980s, both the British and the American editions went into paperback, and Fitzgerald wrote a long introduction to Howard Wool-mer's bibliography of the Poetry Bookshop. She continued to fly a flag for Mew, trying, unsuccessfully, to get Camden Council to put up a plaque in Delancey Street. In 1997, she wrote the *New Oxford Dictionary of National Biography* entry on Mew. "About her I've never changed my mind," she told Chris Carduff. "I still think that at least sometimes she was a great poet."[35]

CHAPTER FOURTEEN

Innocence

This is fiction, not history.[1]

After five novels and three biographies, Fitzgerald decided, in her late sixties, to stop writing fiction that drew directly on her own life. In interviews
she would talk about this decision as a means of escape, "a journey outside
myself."

> Most writers . . . feel the need to do something like this sooner or
> later. The temptation comes to take what seems almost like a vaca-
> tion in another country and above all in another time.[2]

> I didn't want to do anything more about things . . . that had hap-
> pened to me because I'm sure there are always some things in your
> life you don't want to write about, perhaps they're too sad. I think
> that happens a great deal with novelists: they finally have to leave
> their own experience. I thought I'd go to a different period, a com-
> pletely different field, different activities.[3]

What these statements omit are the ways in which her own experiences,
feelings and beliefs would, from now on, be metamorphosed into novels
set in 1950s Florence, Russia before the Revolution, Cambridge in the 1910s
and late-eighteenth-century Germany. The things that most matter to her
shaped these historical books just as much as they did her autobiographical
novels. Like Charlotte Mew's poetry, the late novels impersonate the lives
of others while speaking from Fitzgerald's "deepest convictions": "I mean
to the courage of those who are born to be defeated, the weaknesses of the
strong, and the tragedy of misunderstandings and missed opportunities
which I have done my best to treat as comedy, for otherwise how can we
manage to bear it?"[4]

Fitzgerald describes her books, when questioned about them, as "tragic
comedies," or "tragi-comedies." She says they are about the relationship

between mind and body, about failure, and about "exterminatees": "I think every period makes sacrifices of a certain kind of person. Those are the people that interest me."[5] "In my novels you have to settle for not very much in the end, for making do, for the possibility that two people might just be happy together. What else can you do but that?"[6] All this is as true of the later historical novels as it is of the earlier books. "I'm concerned with the difference between body & soul . . . and between those human beings who, however good their intentions, will always be defeated by the world as it is now, and those who will flourish, though perhaps not for ever . . . I would agree with whoever it was that said that twentieth century human beings have made themselves too unimportant to be tragic but too desperate to be comic. We have each other, however."[7]

One of the many working titles for *Innocence* (others included "The Same Mistake," "The Man Who Knew Too Little" and "The Fatal Gift of Beauty") was "Happiness." "*Unhappiness* would be better," she told Stuart Proffitt, but she thought it might put people off. "Really the book is about what a great mistake it is to try and make other people happy." The blurb notes: "Trying to make other people happy is not only difficult, but ruinous."[8] In her notebooks for *Innocence,* she has a paragraph ruminating on happiness:

> Happiness is a capacity like any other, very unequally shared among those who wake up every morning to find themselves likely to last through the following day. It is not a bad system for those to whom happiness is difficult to keep a record of their happy days. These are not likely to be complete days, but I count a day as anything more than six hours. The word happiness in itself suggests that it is short lived and has little to do with contentment. Happiness extended would not be contentment but insanity. Identifying the moments when one is happy is an art in itself, or I suppose a craft, which is the outcome of experience.[9]

Why did she choose post-war Italy as the setting for her novel about happiness—or unhappiness? Spain was the European country she knew best, and had visited most, yet, for whatever reasons, she did not choose to set a novel there. But Italy was also a country for which she had strong feelings. Desmond had fought there, and immediately after the war, in April 1949, they had their belated honeymoon in Rome. They published 1950s Italian writing in the *World Review,* and paid attention to post-war

Italian art, film and architecture. She would have seen the neo-realist films like *Bicycle Thieves* and, later, the 1950s and '60s movies by Fellini and Antonioni. All this made a strong impression on her. She was especially interested in Moravia's cold control and strangeness. One Italian novelist they published in the 1950s was Petroni, whose novel *The House Moves* Fitzgerald called "a tragic masterpiece." The silent Ugo Gattagni and his faithful housekeeper are waiting out the war in the big family house; eventually he dies, in silence and sadness, "a true Gattagni": "To know how to wait is the most difficult task." In *Innocence,* Cesare, who was to have been called Ugo, also knows how to wait. Cesare's looks are compared with his namesake's, Cesare Pavese. When her old editor Raleigh Trevelyan read *Innocence,* it seemed obvious to him from her "economy of style" that she had been reading the Italian novelists of the period. These writers—Pavese, Moravia, Ginzburg, Sciascia—were fluctuating between realism and experimentalism, localism and *europeismo.* Pavese had killed himself in 1950, but his posthumous work continued to come out. Pasolini wrote a long elegiac poem for Antonio Gramsci, the Marxist revolutionary leader and philosopher. Such literary styles and experiments infiltrate the mood of Fitzgerald's novel.[10]

She went more than once with Maria and Desmond to Italy in the 1960s, for instance, to Venice in 1961. When Desmond was dying, in the spring of 1976, she went alone to Florence, a journey full of intense emotion. He wanted her to go, and, some time after his death, she wrote at the front of her *Companion Guide to Florence:* "The year Desmond died. Ria said 'I don't know how you think you can afford the time.' But D got me the tickets & wanted me to go. Not forgotten for a moment."[11] She went back there in the summer of 1981, by which time she had started to think about a novel set in Italy, and was seen by her ex-student Jane Martineau walking down the Via Romana.[12] That may have been the same summer, or one of the summers, she visited Oliver and Patty Knox in their house in the Apennines, near Urbino, which they had lovingly "done out." An English couple who have renovated a Tuscan villa play a significant part in *Innocence,* and are not kindly treated.

In May 1983, she went on an International PEN conference to Venice (where she gave a talk about L. P. Hartley). After the conference there was a trip to Padua, organised by Francis King, and a visit to Petrarch's villa.[13] By then she was immersed in Italian research, while writing *Charlotte Mew:* as usual, she had two books on the go at once. She intended to give the novel a ten-year span from 1955: "It was supposed to end in the flood in Florence in 1966 but I gave up as all the characters would have got so old by that time."[14] All the reading she did on the great flood was set aside. In the end the book covered just over a year, from April 1955 to the summer of 1956.

A great mass of research lay under the novel, filtered through the process of distillation she had learned, in part, from writing her biographies. She made notes on villa building and design, on doctors, communists, social security, old people's homes, Mussolini, minestrone, vineyards, wild flowers, agriculture, police, roads, schools and taxes. For the doctor in the novel, she learned about neurology from Maria. From her *Companion Guide* (1966) she got some useful clues about Florentine character ("If you ask a Florentine how he is or how his work is going it is never *benissimo* or *splendido*. Extravagance, vagueness and sentimentality are looked on with suspicion"), about the cultivation of the vine and olive ("an art requiring talent, insight, patience, and great experience"), and about the state of farming gradually being replaced by tourism since the war. She studied Gramsci intensively for his appearance as a character in one crucial scene. Her notebooks are full of factual questions: "Is Fiat 1500 Sedan right for 1955?" "Are the vineyards all wrong?" "Are the children of a *conte* all *contessina*s?"[15]

Italy also took her back to Ruskin, Burne-Jones, Rossetti and the Pre-Raphaelite passion for Dante and Italian Renaissance art. Her imaginary sixteenth-century Florentine villa, the Ricordanza, is named—though she doesn't say so—after an Italian poem of Rossetti's. The apparently ancient inscription on its gates is a quotation from that poem, which asks if memory (*"ricordanza"*) is the most wretched of miseries, or the one flower of ease in the bitterest hell (*"amaro inferno"*). The feeling for Italian art and poetry which filled the Burne-Jones biography underlies *Innocence*. Chiara Ridolfi (it's an old Florentine surname) is compared to a Pontormo angel, and the cover illustration Fitzgerald asked for was a face—one of the unknown women accompanying Elizabeth—from Pontormo's painting *Visitation* at Carmignano. When Chiara wants to tell her closest friend how much in love she is, she quotes from Dante's *Vita Nuova*. But the Italy of *Innocence* is not an Italy of romance. Everyone in it has lived through the era of Fascism and the war; dead characters ring the action like shades; emotions are ranged on a scale from grief and rage to embarrassment and bewilderment.

Without explanation or lecturing, we are immersed in 1950s Italy—even if Fitzgerald gets one or two details wrong—and feel as if we are there.[16] As often, she picks a moment of possibility and hopefulness,

like the very start of the 1960s in *Offshore,* or, still to come, the period just
before the Russian Revolution in *The Beginning of Spring.* Mid-1950s Italy
is in the limbo between the aftermath of the war and the huge economic
boom which turned it from a mainly rural and agricultural country into an
industrialist powerhouse dominated by consumer values. Factories, business, tourism and museums were all taking off, to be boosted by the new
European Common Market in 1957—gloomily predicted by a character in
the novel who would prefer to see no changes. Quickly and deftly, she scat-
ters in the popular new names—Fiat 600s, Alfa Romeos, Vespas, Olivetti,
Fellini, Pasolini, Cinecittà.

Everything was changing, but everyone had a past that had to be faced,
or buried. Discredited Fascists, Nazi collaborators, ex–resistance fighters or
those who, under Mussolini, had settled for *attendismo,* wait-and-see-ism—
all had endured the war and the violent Liberation. *"Ricordanza"* was an
obligation and a necessity, but could also be a burden. Her characters live
on the edge of change, husbanding farms of olive trees that might soon
be abandoned because of the turn to cheaper cooking oils, or maintain-
ing dilapidated old villas being eyed for profit by the new Tourist Board,
or cherishing the values of the old left, overtaken by the post-war victory of the Christian Democrats. Yet tradition, always strong in Italy, persisted. Some things continued unchanged, particularly in Florence, that
most conservative of cities, and in the impoverished rural south, where the
economic "miracle" was slow to take effect. In Florence, in her novel, old
ladies went on visiting their dressmakers, the fashionable concert season
has resumed and good manners honed through "centuries of practice" continued to cover all social difficulties. "A dictatorship, a war and an occupation had not been sufficient to change them."

Her characters are individuals, not representative, but they cover
many aspects of Italian life. There are the impoverished Florentine aristocracy, their children now intermarrying with the children of southern
peasants. There are the defeated working-class revolutionaries, disciples of
Gramsci. There is the tradition-bound farmer and wine-grower. There is
the practitioner of a new medical science, professionalised out of his southern roots. There are the subtle Vatican bureaucrats, the incoming English
villa-owners, the old family retainers, the journalists, the novelists (gro-
tesquely caricatured), the art historians, the dressmakers and seamstresses,
the lawyers, the hospital administrators, the tourism managers. Some of
these only walk through the book for a moment; all are unerringly in
focus. They speak with a slight formality, as if in translation, with many

Italian words and phrases dropped in. The story moves from eye to eye, shifting as it is seen from different viewpoints.

All the places are vividly present, as in a film. *Innocence* begins by telling the ancient legend of the Ricordanza, high above the city on its southern edge. It is introduced to us by a voice which seems to know the place well: "Anyone can tell when they are passing the Ridolfi villa," it begins, and goes on to remind you of what you see there: stone statues of the "Dwarfs" gesturing against "the airy blue wash of the sky." Some of these gestures are welcoming, some, the voice notes warningly, "suggest quite the contrary." The legend is told with convincing simplicity and charm. Once upon a time the Ridolfis were dwarfs, or rather midgets. The only daughter of the house, a tenderhearted, sensitive girl, had to be surrounded by people of her own size so that she would never know she was different from the rest of the world. In the grounds of the villa can still be seen miniature grass and marble steps, specially built for her. A tiny playmate, a dumb girl called Gemma, is brought in to keep her company, but, to the daughter's distress, she starts to grow. Out of the kindness of her heart, and to prevent her dear friend from being treated as, or thinking of herself as, a monster, the daughter orders Gemma's eyes to be put out and her legs cut off at the knee.

Fitzgerald invents her legend with a cool relish for the violence, grotesquerie and drama of the Renaissance, a relish she shares with Italy-lovers of the past like Browning and Rossetti, both cited in the novel. She is at pains to distinguish her villa from the Villa Valmarana, with its famous "dwarf" statues, though this was clearly her inspiration. There were other sources, too. Francis King had told her a story about an "Italian family and their dwarves." Her notes for *Innocence* show that she was thinking about the figure of the dwarf (the same height as the little princess) in Velázquez's *Las Meninas*. She was fascinated by Walter de la Mare's *Memoirs of a Midget,* the story of a little person hopelessly in love with a full-size person. And her mind was full of Charlotte Mew, a tiny, childlike woman, not at home in the "normal" world.[17]

She gives the legend several things to do. It is a warning fable about the risks involved in trying to make another person happy. The sixteenth-century family doctor advised: "Don't be too concerned with the matter of happiness." The characters of the fable recur in modern guise, acting with the same rash kindheartedness, or becoming the victims of Ridolfi impetuousness. And the legend gets reworked. A Milanese communist cinéaste wants to turn it into a film about "the mutilated child of the people."

Perhaps, the family's contact at the Vatican hopes, this can be given "a Christian colouring, in the manner of Pasolini." When the Tourist Board requires the villa to be opened to the public, the story "as it stands won't do at all." A smart woman journalist provides a happy ending, in which Gemma escapes over the wall, at a spot convenient for tourists to take photographs. As the Tourist Board director says to the current head of the Ridolfis, "This is fiction, not history."

The jump from the legend to the modern Ridolfi story has the brilliant effect of making the 1950s story feel like history, not fiction. In wartime, the Villa Ricordanza has been requisitioned three times. After the Liberation, there was "the gradual withdrawal of evacuees, refugees and partisans from the various rooms, the removal of the corpses in the rose-hedge and the digging up of barrels of oil under the graves in the chapel." Now the villa stands unlived in, its furniture draped, its shutters half closed, looked after by the gardener and his wife. The current owner, Count Giancarlo Ridolfi, in his mid-sixties, is a figure from the past, and knows it. He has decided to "outface the last part of his life . . . by not minding about anything very much." His marriage to a rich American has been a failure. His younger brother, who inherited the family farm at Valsassina ("little stone"), thirty kilometres outside Florence, was shot during the Allied advance, and his brother's wife also died, in 1943. Their orphaned son, Giancarlo's silent nephew Cesare, now runs the farm, with its olive trees and vines. He lives there quite alone, apart from a half-crazy old man and his old woman, who keep house, the *fattore* out on the farm and an old gun dog.

The Count did his cavalry service in the First World War, and spent the second under house arrest in the decrepit family town house in the "Piazza Limbo." (Throughout, she intersperses comical invented names, such as the Ugolino golf course, with real ones.) Here Giancarlo, his young daughter, Chiara, his eccentric old sister, Maddalena, and their faithful, suspicious cook, Annunziata, live in the second-floor flat of the *palazzo,* above the Arno, in a "salon full of marble statuary, as yellow as old teeth." There is no money. The ground floor is let out to a hairdresser's and other small businesses, the courtyard is full of Vespas and Fiats. The mixture of shabby grandeur and city life is immaculately done.

In spite of his ironical policy of *attendismo* and indifference, the Count is troubled about his sister and his daughter. Chiara is seventeen, an angelic but awkward beauty, eager and diffident, generous, "hopeful and shining." Half Italian, she has been educated in an English convent school, where her best friend, the huge, decisive Barney, alias the Hon. Lavinia Gore-Barnes, a comic foil to Chiara (and giantess to her miniature) is quick to tell her when she is being "weedy," which is often. Chiara's awkward relationship to Florentine sophistication is summed up in a humiliating scene in which her aunt Mad takes her for a fitting to the famous couturier Parenti (based on Fortuny), who refuses to make her a dress—a story Fitzgerald was told by one of L. P. Hartley's Venetian lady friends.

Chiara meets the entirely unsuitable Dr. Salvatore Rossi at a concert, under the eye of Florence's high society. They fall immediately in love. The novel's farcical and agonising momentum comes from the clash of their histories, class and temperaments. As the 1950s section begins, Giancarlo is setting out for Valsassina to ask his nephew's advice. Could the wedding possibly take place at the farm?

The counterpoint to the history of the Ridolfi family, the old aristocracy accommodating to the post-war world, is the story of Salvatore's working-class childhood in the poorest part of the south. In the unpicturesque village of Mazzata, in Campania, there is nothing except an abandoned tomato-sauce cannery, built under Mussolini. Other features are some goats, a musty café, a grocery store with the only public telephone, a shoemaker's, a church (much frequented by Salvatore's conservative and superstitious mother) and a tricycle in the main piazza "supporting a glass case which contained biscuits of great age and packets of sweets," a feature of Salvatore's childhood which is still there when he returns.

Like so many workers from the south, Salvatore's father, Domenico, a communist bicycle-mechanic, and his best friend, the book-keeper Sannazzaro (like Len Coker in *The Golden Child*, an extreme revolutionary with a heart of gold), went north in the 1920s, to work in Turin. They are passionate followers of Gramsci, and believe in his hope for "a possible Italy, without poverty, favours or bribery." The intellectuals would "stay in their own communities and organize them." As a result "the south would be as prosperous as the north." "When the concept of property was abolished the struggle would be unnecessary." But, as the narrator's tone implies, and as we know, none of this will come to pass. There are no utopias. Gramsci is imprisoned, and his disciples join in the unsuccessful factory strikes, lose their jobs and walk back to their village as failures, like characters out of *Bicycle Thieves* or *La Strada*.

The novel's most startling scene is the visit Domenico makes with his son, in 1936, to visit the terminally ill and long-imprisoned Gramsci in hospital in Rome. (Gramsci died the following year.) Fitzgerald has, before this, brought historical characters vividly to life in her biographies. But this is the first time (apart from offstage appearances by Lilian Baylis and Noël Coward in *At Freddie's*) that she has thickened the feeling of authenticity by mixing a real person with her fictional lives. From now on she would do this in every novel, until at the last history and fiction would entirely blur.

In this case, the effect is bitterly ironic. The hero-worshipping Domenico wants his son to learn the great lesson of life from his Marxist hero, so that he will become "an intellectual for the people." But the dying Gramsci tells him grimly, "Don't try to make me infallible." And the boy, far from learning a political lesson, is horrified and revolted by the sight of a stunted, crippled hunchback, foul-smelling, contorted, like an ugly animal, oozing with blood. Aghast, he makes some instant resolutions. He says to himself (in an example of how she moves in and out of her characters' voices, impersonating them): "I will never concern myself with politics, I will never risk imprisonment for the sake of my principles, I will never give my health, still less my life, for my beliefs. He also resolved to be a doctor. In the end we shall all of us be at the mercy of our own bodies, but at least let me understand what is happening to them."

Salvatore at thirty is "not a temperate person." He is ferociously determined to be "independent and unclassifiable." "Any behaviour that is expected of you makes you less of an individual." He will never be condescended to, he will separate himself from everything that binds him—the south, his family, superstition, religion, politics. He perversely involves himself with unpopular causes and offends his superiors at the hospital. He is furious with himself, above all, for having fallen in love with the beautiful daughter of an aristocratic Florentine family. As a neurologist, he is exemplary—observant, reassuring, efficient. As a human being he is a raging torrent of contradictions.

Moving backwards and forwards as if in cinematic flashbacks (with many allusions to the popular cinema of the time), *Innocence* tracks the story of Chiara and Salvatore from their first meeting to their coming together, through a farcical series of accidents and confusion, at the Ricordanza (a sexual encounter of intense happiness, described indirectly, as always in her work) and their wedding at Valsassina, early in 1956. The wedding is only the middle of the story, not its happy ending. They launch into marriage as strangers to each other, and set up home in a tiny suburban flat. Chiara becomes pregnant, but the baby is "a fainthearted pioneer awash in strange seas" whose "doubtful experiment came to nothing." Salvatore fails to get a mortgage from the hospital, because he has affronted all the senior people. They quarrel about everything, in private and public. ("Come back! I'm saying what I don't mean!") They are helplessly "true to their own system of misunderstanding." Yet "they loved each other to the point of pain and could hardly bear to separate each morning." Each would give their life to make the other happy; each makes the other suffer. "What is all this about happiness?" Salvatore asks himself. "We never talked about it in Mazzata."

Caught up in their tragicomedy are all the other characters. Chiara's Aunt Mad, a reckless optimist with a crazy charity for old ladies and orphan babies, constantly muddies the waters. The brother of Cesare's late mother, suave Monsignor Gondi at the Vatican, one of Fitzgerald's "fixers," whose religion is "the bureaucratic faith," and who, at the mention of any name, "frowns a little, turning over the index cards of his mind," interferes unhelpfully. Salvatore's loyal, patient colleague Gentilini shows him the burdens of family life (touchingly done, especially a difficult small boy who hurtles through the edges of the novel). Salvatore has a mistress, a practical, sexually obliging dressmaker, whom he must get rid of once he has met Chiara. He rehearses to himself the rational, self-deceiving speech he will make to her, blurts out something quite different, and is utterly taken aback by her matter-of-fact reaction. It is a surprising scene for Fitzgerald, that shows how European and un-English she can be.

Gigantic, endearing Barney is there (like the unfortunate Harringtons, the ridiculous and bewildered Anglo-Tuscan villa-owners) to give an English viewpoint on Italy. When she first sets eyes on Salvatore, she exclaims: "God, he's Italian-looking," and the Harringtons know just what she means. She tells Chiara that her love affair could be called "'The Happiness of Dr. Rossi' . . . Film neorealistico, con Marcello Mastroianni e Maria Schell." Her conversations with the Count are a comedy of mutual bafflement. But Barney is touching, too, falling for everyone she meets and finally making a disappointing choice. The end of the friendship between the two girls comes as a muted moment of deep sadness.

One of Barney's most unhopeful love-objects is Chiara's cousin Cesare Ridolfi, who silently observes all that passes, and "never said anything unless the situation absolutely required it." Cesare's preoccupations are the state of his vines and his olive trees and the perpetually frustrating issue of the boundary line (drawn up in 1932) between the Chianti Classico area and the Ridolfi vineyards. We do not know his feelings about the killing of his father, except that we see he is keeping the farm going at all costs. His mother left a note for him when she was dying, but we never know what it says, or whether he ever reads it. It becomes apparent to us that he is deeply, silently in love with Chiara, who barely notices him, like an old table she has sat at since childhood. At one point, he buys writing paper and an envelope to write a long letter to her, which he tears up. We are not told what is in it. " 'At least that's something I haven't done,' he said aloud. It was irritating, though, to be left with the unused envelope."

Cesare's silence—in contrast with Salvatore's extravagant temper and Chiara's impulsive tactlessness—is in tune with the narrator's obliqueness. *Innocence* is her most complicated narrative. There are time-shifts, puzzles, tiny clues to unexplained events. A story which begins in April 1955 and ends in the summer of 1956 is told, for its first half, back to front, so that we don't understand the implications of the conversation the Count has with Cesare at the farm, at the start of the novel, until very many pages later. The wedding party, a beautiful set-piece which cuts from face to face, scene to scene, conversation to conversation, depends on our having paid attention to every detail. So does a later comic scene at an Anglo-Florentine modernist villa, the Hodgkiss Foundation at Bellosguardo (loosely based on I Tatti) on the hills outside Florence, looking onto "one of the most stupendous and banal views on earth," complete with young English art historian on the make ("he had the touchiness of those who are learning to put the great masters in their place"), and a heroically dedicated Italian museum curator. Here Salvatore and Chiara have one of their drastic public quarrels.

The narrative mesh reflects the muddle of people's lives. It requires the reader's close attention, as life should. It calls into question novelistic expectations, for instance, that love at first sight will lead to a happy marriage. And it shows how *"ricordanza"*—memory and memorialising—works in odd bits and pieces, not in a straight line. Occasionally we see the characters as if they are part of an old story, viewed in retrospect many years later. The live movement of the wedding party suddenly freezes into a snapshot: "Looking at the photographs of a wedding taken nearly thirty years ago one can't believe that so many, who now look as they do, once looked like *that*." Chiara is momentarily glimpsed "during the later stages of her life, at times when things were not going well for her." That is all we ever learn about the future.

Small details make the narrative read like life. Every encounter is set in the middle of the ordinary working day. The Count's visit to Cesare, for instance, is punctuated by the arrival and departure of the farm manager.

The fattore . . . wished everyone in general good morning, and retreated down the slope. At the bottom he got onto his bicycle, adjusting a sheet of corrugated iron which he had been carrying on the handlebars, and pedalled slowly away. The wind caught the flapping edge of the iron with a metallic note, repeated again and again, fainter and fainter . . .

When Chiara takes Salvatore by surprise at his clinic, we hear the hand printing press in the basement of his office building, "cranking away as it did every evening after office hours," unnoticed by them as they confront each other on the stairs. In the middle of Salvatore's parting scene with Marta the dressmaker, the coffeepot on her gas ring springs into life—its "tin lid had begun to clink slightly as it rose with the steam." Objects have their own lives to get on with.

And nature carries on all around (as in the Suffolk scenes in *The Bookshop,* or like the river in *Offshore*), with its own steady, self-propagating life. At the Ricordanza, "the lemon trees in their terracotta jars, each balanced on an empty one turned upside down, dispensed their bitter green smell: their dark green leaves were startlingly fresh against the blank, bleached, cracked and faded house." On the farm, the huge viburnum, like a character in its own right, flowers in September:

> On the north wall of the front yard the climbing viburnum reached serenely outwards to the farthest corners, unperturbed by shadow or sun, and covered with many thousands of flowers, a population of white flowers which looked as though they could never grow less . . . To catch the viburnum's scent you had to wait until dusk, until the moment when the greenish-white flowers of the garden release their fragrance and only the shapes of white things are visible. The years when the viburnum flowered repeatedly like this were supposed to be lucky.

Animals have their own concerns, like the doomed, happy rabbits and doves in their little stone columbarium on the farm, living inside "a semi-darkness peacefully reeking of birds and animals," or Cesare's old dog, "of the old-fashioned rough-haired Italian breed," always alert to any deviation from her lifelong habits. When she shakes and stretches herself "as a preparation for going out," "it was like the action of wringing a dish-mop."

No one we care for in *Innocence* talks about God or religion, but above and around the lives of humans is an arena which might be seen as consoling if anyone paid attention to it. Above the villa is "the airy blue wash of the sky." Outside the Count's window is the River Arno, reflecting "the yellowish light in its yellowish water" and throwing "over the nearby buildings a curious transparency, like a painting on glass. Giancarlo had seen this so often that he no longer noticed it."

How can nature be turned into an authentic art? The Count has a funny conversation with Chiara and Barney about Florentine painting, during which he observes that in his view, art-history courses give too much attention "to the great men. There are many delightful things by quite unknown artists, little country things." In a farcical scene in Rome when he is presented by Monsignor Gondi to a group of modern novelists, all quarrelling about the meaning of art, the Count picks up a little, simple terra-cotta statue, made by a great artist who was brought up as a poor boy in a monastery. In his hand, the small, quiet, "dignified" object grows warm, as though alive. The object reminds us of what true art is: something as close as can be to nature, which "has implanted in everything a hidden energy." The terra-cotta statuette expresses itself. Fiction, unlike sculpture, must use words, but can, without bullying or overexplaining, come as close as can be to the organic, energetic forms of nature.

In some of her unused notes for the novel, the Count owns a Renaissance herbal, with drawings of all the plants that are remedies for wounds. One of these is the gentian, which also features in Botticelli's *Primavera*: "The gentian is one of the flowers issuing from the mouth of the nymph on the right, who is being blown into life by the south wind. She blows first cold then warm, and the first flower that issues from her mouth is the blue gentian, as though it had just emerged from the snows. The gentian is strikingly accurate."[18] That accuracy of representation of the blue flower, as though blown into life by nature, is what she thinks of as true art.

For his part, Salvatore the nerve doctor thinks of art as a form of release, or therapy. "If art is of any use at all it must be to get rid of surplus emotion. In that way it functioned much like a dream. He had known hospital patients so heavily medicated that they were unable to dream, and compensated with hideous delusions by day." This is consistent with Fitzgerald's view that artists who retain within their system the images that haunt them are destroyed by them. So writing might work as a form of dreaming.

The mastery of the emotions—or its impossibility—is one of the subjects of the book. Salvatore's emotions are painful to him. The old communist Sannazzaro, who has "all the nobility of life's authentic losers," and speaks as if he is the ghost of Gramsci ("Every man survives in his useful and necessary actions"), tells Salvatore he should go back to the south. He rouses in Salvatore an emotion he painfully resents: "The old conscience, the old consciousness." Like many of Fitzgerald's characters, Salvatore finds himself on trial in his own mind, "found guilty again, before a court he had never been asked to recognize." Count Ridolfi, by contrast, has deflected his emotions through irony and fatalism. Chiara's emotions rush into her face, like blood: that is a mark of her innocence, so dangerous to others. One of the most uncomfortable of uncontrollable emotions is embarrassment, which runs through the book like a minor tune. It is out of a desire for her dear friend not to be embarrassed by her size that the Ridolfi girl in the legend cuts off her growth. Salvatore's extreme behaviour is an embarrassment to others. At the Vatican, the Count, faced with a roomful of modern writers, feels a sense of embarrassment "so strong that it resembled fear."

Cesare Rodolfi seems entirely free of such weaknesses. Like his namesake, Cesare Pavese, who committed himself to a solitary, reclusive, simple life and wrote in praise of isolation and monotony, Cesare has a philosophy for mastering the emotions, not explained but implied. It is a form of quietism, very important and attractive to Fitzgerald. (She learned it, in part, from Wilfred Knox.) In a crisis, Cesare will say: "You must think of what she wants"; "Let her be"; "Do nothing." This is not passivity, but a form of resistance, or endurance. At one point the Count is told that patience is the same as resignation. "Surely not," he replies. "Patience is passive, resignation is active." The trouble with this form of negative action, however, is that it usually involves not getting what you want.

In the original draft, the novel goes on into the 1960s, Cesare is called Ugo (like the character in the story by Petroni she so admired) and at the end he does get his heart's desire. Chiara and Salvatore separate, and the doctor returns to the south to fulfil his Gramscian obligation to his home-town. Chiara visits her cousin to tell him that she is going to run off with someone else. Why? he asks. The scene is written in note form:

> Because she wants to make at least one human being happy.
>   If that's all that's wanted, says Ugo, there is another solution. [He t]akes her, firmly but not particularly gently, by the arm[;] they go out at the back where they can see the vineyards and the patient doomed olive trees marching in their appointed order up to the pure sky, blue shading down through all its shades to white. A delicious day, possibly the real spring. They walked together.

The old dog came out with them a little way and lay down on the earth, because for the first time that year it was warm enough to lie on. It is worthwhile looking for such indications and indeed we [dis]regard them at our peril.[19]

In the final version of the novel, there is no such indication of a happy ending, though there is a suggestion that even in despair there might be some way of remaining hopeful. The superbly inconclusive last scene maintains her fine balance between tragedy and comedy. It draws some of its depth from deep-buried allusions to two of her favourite novels, with which *Innocence* stands comparison, Ford's *The Good Soldier* (where Dowell, the narrator, passively enables Edward Ashburnham to commit suicide) and Turgenev's *Fathers and Sons,* in which Bazarov self-destructively thinks of himself as a "superfluous man." The distraught Salvatore (who thinks, mistakenly, that Chiara has been complaining about his poverty to her family and asking them for help) goes out to the farm in the warm summer night to ask advice from Cesare, in his view the only reasonable member of the Ridolfi family. He presents himself as an expendable, useless person who would be better off dead. Cesare, true to his philosophy of resignation, is on the verge of allowing this to happen, when Chiara accidentally, unwittingly, intervenes. The novel ends with Salvatore rushing off to find her, throwing a last word to Cesare:

"What's to become of us? We can't go on like this."

"Yes, we can go on like this," said Cesare. "We can go on exactly like this for the rest of our lives."

The production of *Innocence* went smoothly, under Stuart Proffitt's attentive eye. He dissuaded her from calling it "The Same Mistake" or "The Villa of the Dwarfs." A clever new young designer ("with a pigtail") turned the Pontormo face she wanted for the cover, and which she had found in the *Companion Guide,* into a striking image, with the edges torn away, like a relic or a fragment. She was sardonic with Stuart about being asked to distribute promotion cards for the novel, with that image on it, to "influential people," "as I don't know any, however I could send them to <u>people</u>." And if there were any left over, she could "sell them in the character of an old gypsy woman at Green Park Station." She was very particular about the layout of the dialogue; but many of the Italian terms had to be corrected in proof. The contract with Collins was for an advance of £5,000 with 10 per cent royalties up to 3,000 sales, 12.5 per cent up to 7,000, and thereafter 15 per cent. The book was sold to Henry Holt, in the States, in August 1986, after what the Collins rights manager, Juliet Annan, described as "a lively auction," for an advance of $18,000.[20]

She still got a few reviews that were condescending or dismissive. Philip Howard in *The Times* said it had "the sort of whimsical perceptions you would expect." Valentine Cunningham in the *Observer*, who liked it, said that it "bustled along most agreeably." Christopher Hawtree, in the *Telegraph*, accused it of being "lifeless" and written in "careless" and "slapdash" prose. "One is not much troubled" about the characters, he added. But the attentive, large-scale reviews were now taking a different tone about Fitzgerald. John Gross, who reviewed the American edition with great enthusiasm in the *New York Times*, called her "an attractive writer with a fine sense of irony and an unostentatious sense of style . . . *Innocence* shows her in full command of her powers." Anne Duchêne, in the *TLS*, described it as "by far the fullest and richest" of her novels. "Her writing, as ever, has a natural authority, is very funny, warm, and gently ironic, and full of tenderness towards human beings and their bravery in living," with "a sense of tremendous physical presence in the writing, in surface-textures and sensuousness." In the *London Review of Books*, C. K. Stead wrote: "One has a sense that nothing we are told is insignificant. It has, not opacity, but density. It is a book that never seems to settle back . . . into a conventional exercise." And, like many of Fitzgerald's readers, he kept asking himself, with wonder and admiration: "How is it done?"[21]

CHAPTER FIFTEEN

The Beginning of Spring

Because I don't believe in this, Frank thought,
that doesn't mean it's not true.[1]

By the mid-1980s Fitzgerald was a well-known literary figure. She reviewed regularly, mainly for the *London Review of Books,* and, later, for the *Evening Standard, Prospect,* and the *Tablet,* sending in immaculately handwritten copy, always on time. She was an obedient servant to her publishers, willingly appearing at literary festivals and doing interviews—though she did tell Stuart Proffitt, now becoming a friend, that it had taken her a while to recover from her first Collins PR man, who had told her "that if I couldn't drink gin in the afternoons there was no hope for me."[2] She carried on with PEN and the William Morris Society. She went to the Arvon Foundation to teach creative writing ("but what is that, I often wonder?").[3] In the late 1980s she began to be called on as a dependable and perceptive judge for literary prizes. In 1988 she would be elected a Fellow of the Royal Society of Literature, a distinction which hugely pleased her.

She was, as she would say, regretfully, "an old writer who has never been a young one."[4] People took for granted the stocky, ruddy-cheeked, now white-haired figure, just off the bus or the train, with her Marks & Spencer's coats, her buttoned-up blouses, wide skirts and sensible shoes, carrying her capacious William Morris bags, giving an impression at once neat and shabby. The unwary continued to be taken in by her mild-voiced, scatty-seeming persona. In the Thatcher years, she was a spirited defender of public libraries—and a dogged opponent of the move of the British Library from the old round Reading Room (where she always liked to sit at the same desk) to the new building at St. Pancras. In one discussion at the Royal Society of Literature, a panel chaired by Melvyn Bragg on the future of libraries, a supremely confident representative from the right-wing Adam Smith Institute, there to argue the pointlessness of state funding for libraries, took one look at her and clearly thought she would be easy meat. He was startled to find her savaging him with a ferociously well-argued attack. (But she was always a supporter of lost causes, and his view has since prevailed.)[5]

She met and came to know many people in the literary world, but only a few of them got close to her. The people she kept in touch with most were, of course, family and old childhood friends, and those she had valued and trusted for years, like Francis King, Richard and Mary Ollard, J. L. Carr, Antonia Southern, Mary Bennett and Mary Lago. But a few new friendships did take shape out of her late literary life—with the novelist and short-story writer A. L. Barker (known to her friends as Pat), Sybille Bedford, Fiona MacCarthy, Carmen Callil. Such newer friends were added to the list of those who received her hand-painted Christmas cards, her careful thank-you letters and her occasional visits, always marked by some moment of comic oddity. They might hear about the Knoxes, about her daughters and her grandchildren, and about selected bits of her history, but very little, if anything, about past events concerning Desmond, or about Valpy. All would be struck by how much she preferred to talk about their concerns, or life in general, than about her own work.

One of these newer friends was the novelist Penelope Lively: she enjoyed the symmetry of writing "Dear Penelope . . . Love, Penelope." Lively knew that she had made an "extraordinary" friend. They taught together at Arvon in 1981, and before that, Penelope Fitzgerald went to stay with the Livelys at their house in Great Rollright, in Oxfordshire, a comfortable and welcoming place. Penelope particularly liked Jack Lively's habit of asking guests what music they would like to hear after dinner. She made wistful remarks there about never having had a house, or a study, of her own. Lively detected in her something self-deprecating—and also competitive. She thought her, not shy, but reserved. She was a funny house guest. It was snowing, unexpectedly, on her visit (in April 1981), and as they sat indoors, Lively, who had just been to New England, was tearing up old bits of fabric to make rag rugs. Penelope, with a glint in her eye, kept looking around: "Now, what could we tear up next?" She told comical stories about herself: how she had once fallen asleep on a bus to Cheltenham and woke up in the bus terminal at midnight, with no money on her, as she had been going to stay with friends. They closed the bus terminal and sent her to the police station, "like a bag lady," where she was put in a cell for the night with the door open.

Having no money was a regular theme. "I'm really quite well known," she said to Lively, "but I barely make enough money to live on." She minded her bad reviews, and talked about them, though not about her work-in-progress. She never forgot being criticised, and she could be snooty, obstinate (for instance, in her dislike of the new British Library building, which Lively supported) and extremely sharp about other writers. It was always a surprise, Lively said, to hear such dangerously pointed remarks uttered in that mild, soft voice.

In the mid-1980s, Penelope would sometimes see the Livelys in their London house in Cloudesley Road, Islington, because, by coincidence, Maria and John moved to the house next door. On 17 January 1985, Lively noted in her diary: "Penelope Fitz dropped in for a drink . . . and sat there in a red anorak which she would not remove and wellies making funny throwaway remarks—as sharp as a knife is old Penelope, and goes to great lengths to pretend not to be." On another occasion, the Livelys came out of their house to find Maria with a distraught Penelope, who had just had her bag snatched with everything in it.

She could be frustrating to talk to. "You could never have a conversation with her when one person says something and the other person replied; it always went off at a dog's leg. She didn't like to give information, and was evasive, or rather *elusive* . . . You kept wanting to yank her back on course, and couldn't." On literary panels she could create mayhem. Lively remembered her mischievously sabotaging a panel discussion at the Dartington Ways with Words festival, and turning it into a spectator sport. The chairman was completely unable to control her. Asked a direct question, she would start to answer it, then go off at wild tangents. At one PEN meeting, Lively sat behind Penelope, looking at the back of her dress, "curiously constructed I think out of curtains," while she made her usual leap-frogging, allusive remarks.[6]

Penelope Fitzgerald's letters to Penelope Lively are sympathetic and candid. Just after they had taught together at Arvon, she told her about Fergus's condition, which she had learned about on her return: "It's strange (anyway I feel it strange after all these years) how the world can darken over in just a few moments." She wrote warm thank-you letters: "I don't know how you manage to make it <u>seem</u> as though there was nothing to be done, and the meals, so to speak, got themselves—there's a very great art in that, perhaps you have to be born with it." She gave comical details of the places she was writing from—Almeric Road, the post office at Theale. "Water is leaking through the ceiling from the upstairs bathroom and pouring on to my prized new typewriter, which will probably end all this nonsense about literary aspirations." She was professionally careful and respectful to her as a fellow novelist, as when inviting her to speak at the Highgate Literary Institute, of which Penelope became a stalwart member in the 1990s: "Last time you gave a talk on the Novelist's Responsibilities, wh. you referred to as 'one of my two talks,' but I knew better." She wrote generously to her about her work, praising a reading Lively gave from her childhood memoir, *Oleander, Jacaranda,* in 1994: "I thought the Muswell Hill bookshop might have tested the mike, removed people liable to faint, etc, in advance, but it made no difference and your reading was an immense success . . . The only thing I would dissent from is 'alien'—I agree your childhood is something apart, possibly speaks a different language, but alien, never." When Lively was researching Russia for a piece of writing in the late 1990s, Penelope wrote at length to tell her what she had found useful for *The Beginning of Spring*.

They shared a common interest in daughters and grandchildren: "No! I don't think of the calm life of the childless and I don't believe you could do with it for a single day. Other substitute worries have to be found, and then there is the possibility of loneliness inconceivable if you haven't children, no matter how irritating they find you. The childless, after all, are also grand-childless." She wrote with great tact and sympathy about Jack Lively's death, and his memorial service, in 1998: "Do look after yourself, grief and loss are such hard work."[7]

As usual with her, she turned her publishers into her friends. Her team at Collins became devoted to her, though in the firm as a whole she was undervalued. The marketing people at Collins did not understand what they had in her: Fitzgerald was not one of their big popular names, like Patrick O'Brian. Because she never had an agent, it is probable that her publishers never paid her what she was worth, however well her individual editors treated her. Still, those who worked closely with her felt privileged and proud, wanted to do their best by her and came—it is not too strong a word—to love her. Stuart Proffitt, and later Philip Gwyn Jones, who took over at Collins after Proffitt left in 1998, Karen Duffy, her publicist, and Mandy Kirkby, her last editor at Flamingo, all recognised her worth, found her undemanding, modest, stoical, funny and warm, and were dedicated to her interests. Proffitt wanted her to be recognised and marketed by the firm as something special: he told his colleagues they needed to "develop another style for Fitzgerald."[8]

It took a little while for her to decide to trust him, and for him to get to know her: "She revealed herself very slowly." Once she did, you were hers for life. Her reticence and indirection were not strategic, in his view, but part of the assumptions of her class and background, where it "isn't done" to talk openly about one's emotions. When direct expressions of emotion *were* made, the effect was all the stronger.

Gradually, Proffitt began to understand her. At first he found her exasperatingly indecisive about specific enquiries; she seemed to be "hopeless with money."

> I *could* not get her to attend to any aspect of the business side of things . . . Penelope, what do you want on the jacket? I am sure you know best . . . What should we call this book? Oh, here are some possibilities, you choose . . . I remember writing to her with some exasperation on one occasion along the lines, Dear Penelope, would you like me to send you a contract for a new book and what would you like the advance to be? I should have known better. She wrote back, "We went up to Wales this weekend to John and Maria's new house, they have bought the children starter-kits—one bed roll, one spoon, one fork, etc. Alfie was so excited he couldn't sleep."

Eventually, he realised "what she was up to."

> Like her heroes Ruskin and Morris, Penelope believed that money was a despicable method of organising relations between individuals, even between herself and her publisher, and she would have none of it . . . She simply trusted that side of things would be taken care of. And so I hope it was.

This retrospective tribute (delivered at her memorial) somewhat romanticised her idealistic unworldliness—after all, she *did* mind about money and dust jackets and titles—but it expresses the heart of his feeling about her: that she valued integrity and trust above anything else.[9]

She needed encouragement. A postcard in 1989 thanked him for the American notices he had sent. "How is it that I always wake up in the small hours thinking about the bad ones, and feel that the good ones must be a mistake—I'm quite sure, however, that all on your list, indeed every single writer who's ever inhabited this earth, feels the same way."[10] In between *Innocence* and *The Beginning of Spring* she had a drop in confidence, and he provided reassurance. "I'm not quite sure," she wrote to him in November 1986, "about asking for an advance on a notional or half-notional novel. I know quite a few people who go round for an advance (not at Collins) the moment they finish one book, so that they can start another, they have so much energy and confidence, but I haven't much of either."[11] Stuart replied: "We should be delighted to sign you up however notional the novel is at present—I do assure you that authors are frequently signed up for books far less concrete than yours is—and indeed I hope that it might give you the energy and confidence that you need to begin writing it. In fact, I can think of fewer things that would give me more pleasure than to know that another of your novels, which I love and admire so much, was getting officially underway."[12] She wrote back: "You mention *energy and confidence*—I've almost forgotten what they are, if I ever knew, although I keep recommending them to those I teach. However, I *would* like to write another novel, in spite of everything, so if you think it would be possible to arrange a contract, please do so."[13]

His reply was strong: "If you ever feel that you want a boost of either energy or confidence, do please come in here and let me introduce you to eight or nine floors of your admirers . . . I cannot tell you how much we are all looking forward to a new novel from you; people come in or ring up most days to ask if there is another coming. If you knew how much confidence everyone here feels in your ability to produce a string of master-pieces, even Weston-super-Mare [she had been telling him about the Doo-leys' move from Theale] might be a little brighter." He went straight on to offer her a contract for the next novel, "whatever it is," with an advance of £7,000. "Let me know if this would suit you, and if there is anything at all I can do to bring the elusive 'e & c' back on board."[14] As well as an encourager, he was a good reader, though not always as quick to respond as she would have liked. He would say to her, of a new book, that "the only parallel I could make to the effect it had on me was to that of music, that I had felt physically better after reading it."[15]

Over the time they worked together, Penelope sent Stuart many let-ters, little hand-painted cards, greetings and thank-yous, as well as instruc-tions, queries and some mild complaints. She always wrote to thank him, at publication time, for the care he had taken over her novel. Sometimes she just wrote out of friendship, to ask how he was getting on. One post-card was a painting of the beach at Penzance, *The Rain It Raineth Every Day* by Norman Garstin. "Now this I do think is a good picture," Penelope remarked. "Specially the right top hand corner." This consists of a blank section of empty, clouded, rainy sky.

✺

Those who did not like Penelope Fitzgerald found her reserved, perverse, stubborn, mischievous, wilful and sharp-tongued. Those who did like her found her kind, wise, stoical, funny, reticent, brilliant and generous. But those two people were one person. The double effect she produced is well illustrated by her students' reactions to her at the Arvon Foundation, the centre for writers at Lumb Bank, Heptonstall, in West Yorkshire, founded by Ted and Carol Hughes, run in the 1980s by Maura Dooley and David Hunter. The students were would-be writers, or already published writers, mainly women, taking a week out of their busy lives to get some inspiration and guidance from a pair of established authors. Students and tutors lived, ate and worked together for a week, in the big stone house up on the hillside above Todmorden. Penelope taught there several times, with Penelope Lively, A. L. Barker, Thomas Hinde, J. L. Carr and Edward Blishen. Maura Dooley noted that she was "generous, exacting, and utterly brilliant in her analysis and her encouragement." There was a guest reader at every Arvon week, and Penelope always asked for "someone young and unexpected, to stir things up a bit."[16]

Blishen, in advance of their week in the summer of 1984, wrote, clearly in answer to an anxious letter from her: "Please don't worry about Lumb Bank. If you're schoolteacherly, what am I?" "The tutor's role," in his view, "is somehow neither to over-encourage or to under-encourage, but if possible to encourage."[17] Their week together went well. Teaching with J. L. Carr, known as Jim, was also a pleasure. She liked his quiet but "totally uncompromising" attitude to the literary life; she enjoyed the evocative, contained quality of *A Month in the Country* and his other novels; and she loved the little books he published on his Quince Tree Press, which he gave out to the Arvon students "as though they were sweets." As a writing teacher, she said, "he had a genius for listening."[18]

One of the students, who had signed up for the Arvon course because she admired *Offshore* and *The Bookshop,* found Penelope "quietly cheerful and pleasant to work with," with an amazing "capacity for reading and retaining the content and detail. She would take away great chunks of our work after the evening workshop and the very next day give us feedback, really good feedback." She told the students about one of her own problems while writing *Innocence:* "When writing Italian dialogue she didn't really want to follow it straight away with the English translation and hadn't worked out alternative solutions—how to get around that one?" Another budding writer, though, was not enthused: "She could be quite brusque . . . and of course people who are in the early stages of trying to write are very vulnerable . . . It wasn't a very constructive brusque-ness . . . I suspect that she was not really all that interested in novice writers . . . But . . . I did like her, in spite of the brusqueness . . . Was it the contrast between her impressive literary and academic credentials and the obviously rather hard life she'd had to lead? When we weren't talking about writing, she was friendly and unpretentious."[19] She kept an eye on Maura, who was trying to write poetry while running Lumb Bank, and gave her some advice: "I hope you'll be completely ruthless, take the best typewriter for yourself, neglect all the friends who come to stay, the hens, the course members, etc, in favour of the writing, otherwise it's not possible to get it done."[20]

In the 1980s, her public activities centred on PEN. She invited people she knew to give talks, for instance, Mavis Batey on Dillwyn and Bletchley's Room 40.[21] She attended the PEN Writers' Days faithfully, and reported sharply on what took place: "Doris Lessing spoke, and rather unexpectedly said that the novel of the future would be in computer language—not the language computers use to each other, but the language computer opera-tors use to each other, which she said could be 'blackly satirical.' "[22] She sat on PEN committees, where she was quiet but tough-minded.[23] She stoi-cally showed up at PEN demonstrations in support of imprisoned writers, and went on PEN excursions, for instance, to Rodmell: "Some of the PEN members were very disappointed, feeling that V. Woolf 'couldn't have done very well.' They expected it to be a house like Barbara Cartland's."[24]

Those who observed her there most closely were Francis King and his friend Josephine Pullein-Thompson, a PEN stalwart and president of the organisation in the 1990s.[25] Josephine's partner was Anthony Babington, who, by coincidence, had been a colleague of Desmond's in his Chambers and knew about his disgrace. Josephine felt that once "she realised I knew all about her," Penelope held her at bay. Both Francis and Josephine noted that, in spite of her literary success, Penelope always seemed to be short of money. This sometimes led to embarrassment. There were, for instance, some difficult moments at the PEN International Conference in Venice in May 1983.

The conference (on "Venice in Literary Sensibility") was held at the Fondazione Cini on the island of San Giorgio Maggiore, with many treats laid on, like a cocktail party at the Palazzo Donà delle Rose and excur-sions to Torcello and Murano. Josephine had arranged to meet Penelope at Heathrow for the flight, but, as she thought of her as vague and scatty, she was worried she might not show up in time. "You needn't worry," another

PEN member (and William Morris expert), Ray Watkinson, reassured her. "I'm sure God will get her there."[26]

Penelope had been asked to talk about L. P. Hartley and Venice. She had just begun to read an excellent paper, when the famous Bassani, author of *The Garden of the Finzi-Continis*, made a late and noisy appearance. He saw the President of PEN and greeted him loudly, and went up to Francis King and greeted him, while Penelope was trying to speak. She put down her papers and stared out. "I am not continuing till all this stops," she said; and she quelled the disturbance. The Italians thought it a disgraceful way for her to behave; the English thought she was impressive, and that it was Bassani who was disgraceful. He continued to be disruptive throughout. On the platform with Stephen Spender, who was reading Browning's "A Toccata of Galuppi's," he got up from his seat and peered over Spender's shoulder while he was reading. Spender took no notice.[27]

In Venice, Penelope shared a room at one of the cheaper hotels with Pullein-Thompson. In the first room they were offered, there was only a shower, and Penelope insisted on a bath. "She couldn't possibly have a *shower,*" Josephine mimicked her. "Total uproar" ensued. They were moved to a smaller room with a day-bed, on which Penelope slept. She reminisced to Josephine about the family holidays, years ago, when they had no money for restaurants.

Some of the PEN travellers went on to Padua from Venice. On one night, Francis offered to pay for her dinner. Penelope declined, and went to eat elsewhere, with a fellow PEN member; but then they came back to the restaurant where Francis was in the middle of his main course, and hung over his table: "We wanted to see what you were eating," she said. As in Venice, she was sharing a room at a cheaper hotel with Josephine, and again there was trouble. According to Josephine, the room "had about nine notices in different languages saying DON'T OPEN THE WINDOW." As soon as they walked in, Penelope threw open the windows. Of course the mosquitoes came in. But she wanted the window open so she could hang up her washing line, which she carried around everywhere in her bag.

This was not the only problem. Some of the women on the PEN trip had been complaining that their scarves were disappearing from the ladies' cloakroom. Items of Josephine's underwear went missing, too: perhaps the maid was stealing them? Getting ready for dinner, Josephine laid out black tights and a dress on the bed, while she had a bath; when she came back, the tights had gone. She went round the room looking for them; Penelope opened her bag and tossed them at her, saying: "Oh, *there* you are then." After that, while Penelope was out of the room, Josephine went through her bag, found a few more of her things, and took them back. Nothing was said; and the scarf thefts stopped.

What is to be made of this story, evidently much relished, and perhaps mischievously embellished, by the sole witness? Penelope's daughters, when told of it, found it incredible and entirely out of character. Yet it does tie in with anecdotes of how difficult she could be on foreign travels. And it does point to the long-lasting effects of years of deep anxiety about money, years which Penelope was recalling while she was in Italy.

There was money coming in now. She gave up Westminster Tutors, at long last, in 1987. It had fallen on hard times in the 1980s, when Oxbridge entrance exams ended, and it then tutored only A-level students. In the end it was bought up by another teaching organisation and renamed Westminster Sixth Form College. Penelope's old adversary there, Jane Darwin, felt that she was unsympathetic during these struggles. Antonia Southern, however, who was in charge during the rocky years, never had a word of criticism, and quite understood why Penelope would want to stop. She had been teaching for twenty-six years and she was seventy.

She could just about live on her writing and reviewing (and her government, and widow's, pensions). As well as the advance of £7,000 which Stuart Proffitt promised her in November 1986 for her next novel, which became *The Beginning of Spring,* the paperback branch of Collins, Flamingo, was bringing out *Offshore, Human Voices* and *At Freddie's*—and subsequently all the other fiction titles. Meanwhile, in the States, Holt were offering $3,500 for *Offshore,* and wanted to publish the rest of the backlist, and Chris Carduff at Addison-Wesley had paid a $6,000 advance for *Charlotte Mew.* By the time *The Beginning of Spring* was delivered in 1988, the advance had gone up to £12,000.[28]

In the family, grandchildren came thick and fast. Tina had Luke in 1983; Maria's first child, Thomas, was born in 1984; Valpy's third son, Camilo, in 1985. Valpy was working in The Hague, with frequent trips to Nicaragua, so she did not see much of his children. Paschal Dooley was born in 1986. Penelope marked this event in her appointments diary: "Baby! <u>Also</u> go to Arvon."[29] Every detail of the family's lives was of interest to her. She saw Maria (now lecturing at UCL) and John all the time in London, often lunching with Maria at the Habitat café in Tottenham Court Road. Regular, affectionate missives went off from St. John's Wood to Holland, and to the Dooleys in Weston-super-Mare, making stories out of every ordinary detail of her life. When she and the children got together, they would talk about the present and the past, as she describes in a 1980s note for a story to be called "Cuisine de Marché." It begins: "At one time—so this story could be classed as historical fiction—I had nowhere to live with my 3 children and had to apply to the local rehousing dept. At the present moment I have nowhere to live but the children have grown up and do have somewhere to live . . . I see them on Sundays. On Sundays we recall together, if the children feel like it, what it was like when we applied to the local rehousing department."[30]

She kept in touch with others in the family, too: Rawle and Helen and their grown-up children William Knox and Belinda Hunt, Oliver and Patty Knox and their children, the eccentric Prehen branch of the family, where Julian Peck still lived. Her closest family friend was, still, the increasingly frail Mary Knox, whom she saw and wrote to all the time. They went to Winchester together on the train in November 1986 to see an exhibition of her niece Belinda's artwork, and Penelope wrote to Mary, making the arrangements: "I don't think it was hard work that made you ill, Mary (though you do work hard, of course), I think it was worry, old worries and unhappiness that came up into the forefront of the mind, as such things will. But they're all gone now, and I think you're managing so well, knocking off the prescription slowly and getting really better at your own pace."[31] It was just one of many letters of encouragement and sympathy that passed between them, over many years.

Other old friendships were sustained or renewed. She went regularly to visit the Conders and the Talbots.[32] "Ham," Hugh Lee, her old friend from Oxford, had got in touch with her in 1978 and invited her to visit him and his wife in the Vineyard in Richmond; a friendly correspondence ensued. But there were things she would not talk about. Walking down Church Road in Richmond, seeing her to the train, he asked her what had happened to Desmond. She said: "He just died."[33]

Her friendship with Jasmine Blakeway was also reinvigorated. Penelope had visited her and John Blakeway after they retired to Warminster in Dorset in the 1970s, and they would go on little forays, for instance, to Thomas Hardy's house in Lower Bockhampton. After John's death, Jasmine moved to Salisbury, and Penelope often went to stay with her. They talked about the past, but Penelope never mentioned Desmond. Whatever the gaps and silences, it was a relationship Jasmine greatly valued: "She was a great great dear and she wanted to be a dear . . . It was lovely to be her friend."[34]

Even at times when "energy and confidence" dropped, she worked hard. "Get on with it!" read one entry in her appointments diary for 1988.[35] In the mid- to late 1980s, she poured out essays, introductions and reviews— for money, and out of interest. Some pieces built on past reading, like her introduction to Howard Woolmer's bibliography of *The Poetry Bookshop,* or to the Oxford University Press edition of L. H. Myers's visionary historical trilogy *The Root and the Flower,* a "strange masterpiece" which she had long admired.[36] In all of her reviews she is fascinated by life stories, especially of passionate effort and ultimate failure. Even when reviewing a life for which she did not feel much sympathy, her curiosity would be roused. So Victoria Glendinning's life of Rebecca West, that passionate, romantic "natural fighter," raises questions for Fitzgerald about how closely the work reflected the life: "the correspondence of what Browning called House and Shop."[37]

Some reviews revealed strong affinities. One of her first pieces for the *London Review of Books,* on Barbara Pym's last novel, *A Few Green Leaves,* pays tribute to a fellow spirit, who shows "a sense of pity for lost opportunities," a "brilliant comic writer" writing about issues which "are not comic at all." Pym, she thinks, is particularly good at male self-deception, "guards against sentimentality" and "understands her characters so well [that] the least she can do is to forgive them." "We have to keep alert, because she will never say exactly what we expect." Remarks in letters confirm her views: "I do like her very much, the incidents look so trivial that there's nothing in them and then you suddenly realise how much she's said."[38]

Other reviews show a strong attraction to the un-English. A review of new biographies and editions of Alain-Fournier allowed her to write about "the oddness and the great beauty" of *Le Grand Meaulnes.* What she loves is the coexistence of the "reassuringly familiar French village" and its everyday realities, with the dream world of romance. The two are inextricable: "Gradually it appears that the mysterious Domain is within easy distance of Nançay, where Seurel's uncle keeps a large grocery store. It could always have been found (as in the end it is) without difficulty." Olive Schreiner's *Letters,* painful, awkward, neurotic, admirable, aroused her thoughts about "that very strange book" *The Story of an African Farm:* "More than anything it is a book of dreams, and specifically the dreams of children . . . Waldo, the son of the farm overseer, represents another side of Olive . . . A stranger who rides in from the Karoo tells him a story—'The Search for the Bird of Truth.' But Waldo, though he understands the allegory, dies without getting his opportunity. 'In after years,' Olive wrote, 'we cry to Fate, "Now, deal us your hardest blow, give us what you will, but let us never again suffer as we suffered when we were children." ' "[39] The novel would haunt her when she came to write *The Blue Flower*.

Virago's 1980s reissues of neglected women writers gave her the chance to revisit some of her old favourites, like Ada Leverson; she relished her comedy and her sympathy for "the absurdity of human beings in a trap of their own making."[40] She wrote introductions to Margaret Oliphant's 1860s Carlingford novels, commissioned by Carmen Callil, who swept Fitzgerald up into Virago publicity and events. These made her feel a little weak. She told Richard Ollard: "The truth is I can't manage the publishing world. Addressing the Virago, Hogarth, Chatto etc sales reps at the Drury Lane Hotel at 8:15 in the morning laid me out completely, and then Carmen goes on all day and takes these dreadful people out to a dinner dance in the evening. How can she?"[41] But she enjoyed writing about Mrs. Oliphant. She liked novels like *Salem Chapel,* of religious anxieties, strong women, weak men and a "sympathetic relish for contradictions." She liked her tone: "Then there is the terribly ugly, but perfectly good carpet left behind by the last Rector. Mrs. Morgan detests this carpet. But she tells herself, with hard-won self-control, 'It would not look like Christ's work . . . if we had it all our own way.' She cannot afford to complain. Time has robbed her of the luxury of ingratitude."[42] Some years later she wrote to Carmen that she still thought Oliphant's *The Doctor's Wife* was "wonderfully suited for TV, but I've come to accept that not everything I believe in is going to come true."[43]

The work that went into these essays was as nothing to the research buried under her concentrated historical novels. The second of these, worked on through 1986 and 1987 and published in 1988, *The Beginning of Spring,* took her back to a country and a literature which had always fired her imagination.

The first idea for it had come from her old friend Mary Chamot, the art curator she got to know in the early 1970s and who helped her with *Burne-Jones.* Her family had had a greenhouse business in Moscow from the mid-nineteenth century and, unlike most of the foreign business community, had stayed on for a few years after the Revolution.[44] The novel was to have been called "The Greenhouse," and though the greenhouse disappeared in the final version, it still shadowed the book. She commented on this process in a later talk, here in note form:

A strange thing . . . is that in the process of writing[,] this original image, or original idea, can disappear altogether, even though I believe it always stays so to speak latent, within the novel when it's finished. This happened to a novel I wrote in 1988 about Russia as it was just before the First World War. The idea first came to me from a friend of mine who was Swiss but had been brought up in Russia . . . they had a greenhouse and stayed in Moscow all through the 1st world war, the Bolshevik Revolution, arrival of Lenin, defeat of White Russian army in 1920, and all this time allowed fuel for greenhouse (coal, wood, birchbark, newspaper) because Russian officials have passion for flowers. But greenhouse dropped out . . . I can't tell what relationship, if any, these images have to any other hallucinations. They're not hallucinations, writers know that, because they're not deceptive. I can only say that they seem to me close to the mysterious individual life of the novel which you can recognise whether you're reading it or writing it.

She adds: "A sort of noble absurdity in carrying on in unlikely circumstances—that was what the image meant to me."[45]

The idea had stayed with her for years, long after her Russian-language classes in the 1960s, or her one trip there in 1975, from which she so vividly remembered her visit to Tolstoy's house and to a dacha in the middle of birch woods. Waring's alarming experience of Russia in *The Golden Child* was a comic try-out for turning that visit into fiction. In her notes for *The Beginning of Spring,* she reminds herself that she has used the phrase "sluggish, secretive power" to describe Moscow in *The Golden Child*—so she is evidently going back to it. All her adult life, she read the great Russians, mostly in the Garnett translations, Tolstoy, Dostoevsky, Turgenev, Chekhov, Ostrovsky, Pasternak, Solzhenitsyn.

She regularly said that, at a certain point in her writing, she wanted to get away from her own experiences. But she also wanted not to be defined by Englishness. This was not just a matter of moving her subject matter outside England. Her strategies for making a fictional world out of scenes, images, fragments, moments, with a light yoking of plot and a strong feeling of things not said, created a feeling of strangeness in what could be superficially read as lightweight comedies of manners. (She disliked being called a *light* novelist.)[46] These strategies made her more like Turgenev than like Barbara Pym. Always evasive, she enjoyed camouflaging herself in foreign colours.

The camouflage required the creation of a sense of otherness. We feel in these novels that we are living in another world, listening to people speaking in another language, walking through places where we are not at home yet which seem very familiar to us, as in a dream. In *Innocence* and *The Beginning of Spring* the effect is underpinned by the viewpoint of English characters observing a foreign country. In *Innocence* this is a comic subplot; in *The Beginning of Spring* it is at the centre of the story; in *The Blue Flower* she will, daringly, dispense with it altogether.

The story of the English family in Russia is, typically, poised at a moment just before cataclysmic changes. She would comment on her liking for such moments, here, in notes for a talk, linking *The Beginning of Spring* with her next novel, *The Gate of Angels:*

> BS and GA . . . both set in a definite period, 1912 to 13-ish, immediately before the First World War, a time that's always interested me very much. Time of very great hope. The hopefulness of the coming 20th century, hopes of a New Life, a new world, the New Woman, a new relationship between the artist and the craftsman—then came 1914. The Beginning of Spring was a title which I hope suggested this, and it's set in Moscow at a time when Russia was on the verge of modernization . . . At the same time the various revolutionary and activist movements were pressing urgently from below. You've got an English family living in Moscow, loving the country which is the only home they've ever known, but uneasy, and it's an uneasy season, late winter with Russia's ice just about to crack and release the long awaited torrents of spring.[47]

These notes break off as she is about to tell the story of the novel—a story, which is, essentially, quite a simple one, though it comes at us through indirection and flashbacks. Frank Reid, an Englishman whose family originally came from Salford, was born and grew up in Moscow, and has inherited his father Albert's printing business, set up in the 1870s. Frank was sent back to England to train for the business, and while getting experience with "more up-to-date" printing machines in Norbury, meets and marries a determined twenty-six-year-old teacher, Nellie Cooper, who is living with her brother and his wife, and longing to get out of Norbury. (The whole Edwardian provincial setting, with choral performances of *Hiawatha*, stained-glass panels in the entrance doors, damp lodgings with not enough food, is perfectly done.) They go to live in Frankfurt for three years, while Frank works with a German printing firm. Nellie has a miscarriage. After that they have two children, Dolly and Ben, and then, in 1905, the year of Russia's strikes and revolution, Albert Reid dies, followed quickly by his wife. Frank and his family go to live in Moscow, and he takes over the printing works. Nellie has another child, Annushka, in 1911. At the start of the novel, in March 1913, Dolly is ten, Ben is nine, and Annushka is two. And Nellie has suddenly left Frank, got on a train, sent the children home without her and gone to England. So a novel set in Moscow starts, paradoxically, with someone leaving it.

Frank, whose deep distress and bewilderment at Nellie's disappearance is kept muted, but is felt in everything he says and does, must carry on running his printing works, with the help—or hindrance—of his accountant, an eccentric Tolstoyan Englishman, Selwyn Crane. He must also make sure that his children are looked after while he is at work. He makes a catastrophic attempt to leave them with a neighbouring Russian merchant's family, and avoids hiring a dreary governess whom the English Chaplain's beady wife tries to foist on him. Then Selwyn recommends a village girl he has met working on the handkerchief counter of Muir & Merrilees. Lisa Ivanovna arrives, calm, blonde, bovine, silent and enigmatic ("she had the pale, broad, patient, dreaming Russian face"), and everyone is transfixed by her. Frank falls, as people in Fitzgerald novels fall, at once, silently and impossibly, in love with her.

Waiting to see if Nellie will return, waiting for the end of winter, the story seems to hold its breath, punctuated by surprises, dramas and comedies. There is a break-in at the press by an apparent student revolutionary who turns out also to be in love with Lisa, and who commits a violent and destructive act which prefigures the future. There is a splendid comical visit from Nellie's brother Charlie—a "Mr. Pooter Goes to Moscow" episode. There is a winter journey taken by Lisa and the children to the Reids' dacha, and, at the secret heart of the novel, a mysterious encounter in birch woods outside the city. Frank begins to feel mounting pressure from the Russian authorities (part comic, part sinister) to make him leave Moscow. There are clues and signs everywhere that a change is coming. Lisa, who is not what she seems, vanishes as quietly and suddenly as she has arrived. On the last page, spring bursts in, and Frank's life changes again. We do not know what will happen next to all these people. We suppose the Reids will have to get out of Russia and leave their home and their work behind. But we are held in the moment of the book.

Digging back into Fitzgerald's source materials for this story cannot unlock the secret of her gift for creating a completely known, yet strange, world in an intensely compressed, though spacious-seeming, novel. But tracking her sources does show how deftly she works. On every page there is a light scattering of taken-for-granted facts and names, put in whenever the characters need to make use of them. The characters' speech moves fluidly between English and Russian, rendered in a light "translationese," with Russian words dropped in everywhere: "*podvipevchye*—with just a dear little touch of drunkenness," "the *nachalnik* is in his office." She wants us hardly to notice what she is doing, to make it all seem easy, natural and real.

In a letter of 1999 to Penelope Lively (who was then doing some Russian research), she tells her about Mary Chamot and the greenhouse, and about what else she has found useful:

> My [main source] . . . is the Baedeker's Russia 1914 . . . and the Russian Supplements of The Times which were published (in English, of course) up to the beginning of World War I in the (mistaken) idea that Russia was going to be our great trading partner . . . you have to trail up to the BL Newspaper Library in Colindale Avenue . . . The great expert is Harvey Pitcher . . . He wrote a book on Muir & Merrilees, the great Scottish department store in Moscow, and another one on English governesses in Russia . . . Then there is Eugenie Fraser's *The House by the Dvina* . . . just the right period and a wonderful memoir . . . Of course, what you want are the real facts, not the atmosphere, which is a very different thing. I had to make up all the part about the printing-works, but then I think in a novel you must be allowed to make up something.[48]

In fact, there is a great deal of homework in her notebooks on printing works, alongside notes on merchants, railway stations, ministries, churches, birch trees, dachas and mushrooms. She is reliable and exact on the machinery and tools and methods of the press, on changes in production methods, on guilds and unions, and on the personnel of a small printing house in turn-of-the-century Moscow: "three hand-compositors and their two apprentices, the pressmen, the readers, the three machine-men, the putting-on and taking-off boys, the gatherers, the folders, the deliverers, the storekeeper, the warehouseman . . . the paper-wetting boys, the errand-boys, the doorman and Agafya [the tea-lady] and her assistant."

There are pages of notes from Harvey Pitcher's books on the British in Moscow, and from Ronald Hingley on Russian writers and society. She did some research on Aylmer Maude, who went to live in Moscow at sixteen, became a tutor, a businessman and an active member of the Moscow British community, fell under Tolstoy's spell in the 1890s, gave up business and returned to England, where he was involved in Tolstoyan communities. He spent the rest of his life translating and editing Tolstoy and writing his biography, which throbs with utopian rhetoric: "Tolstoy's passionate ardour . . . caused his words to change the lives of many men . . . [his] message . . . can . . . give them universal welfare."[49]

The Beginning of Spring starts with this sentence: "In 1913 the journey from Moscow to Charing Cross, changing at Warsaw, cost fourteen pounds, six shillings and threepence and took two and a half days." Sure enough, *Baedeker's Russia* for 1914 informs you that the train—going the other way from Charing Cross to Moscow via Warsaw—takes two and a half days and costs £14 6s. 3d. Baedeker gave her everything she needed by way of maps, place-names, shops, markets, restaurants, parks, churches, stations, concert halls, passport requirements, rules and regulations for non-Russians, the contents of picture galleries (including a painting by one Yendoghrov called *Beginning of Spring*) and general thoughts on the city's atmosphere: "If ever a city expressed the characteristics and peculiarities of its inhabitants, that city is Moscow."

One example shows how closely she studied the 1914 guidebook. When Dolly bossily takes her uncle Charlie shopping for souvenirs on his last day in Moscow, they go to the Trading Rows (where Penelope had been shopping with Maria in 1975, and bought an abacus). "They climbed to the Upper Rows, the top storey of the great market, intersected in each direction by glass-covered corridors from which the moving mass of shoppers, also under glass, could be seen swarming back and forth." After their shopping, they try to get a cup of tea in the crowded restaurant "in the basement of one of the sandstone towers." Baedeker notes that "the Upper Rows [are] intersected in each direction by three glass-covered corridors," that the towers are made of sandstone and the restaurant is in the basement.[50]

Ronald Hingley also provided factual details, like the use of abacuses for accounting, or the dates of the old-style Russian calendar. Like Baedeker, Hingley characterised early-twentieth-century Moscow as more village-like, inert and inward-looking than Europeanised St. Petersburg. It was "a sprawling, ramshackle settlement, more an overgrown village than a town . . . It looked to Russia's past . . . a place of priests and merchants . . . churches and tumbledown log cabins."[51] In *The Beginning of Spring,* this inspires a tour de force in one sentence, demonstrating Frank's deep affection for the city:

> Dear, slovenly, mother Moscow, bemused with the bells of its four times forty churches, indifferently sheltering factories, whore-houses and golden domes, impeded by Greeks and Persians and bewildered villagers and seminarists straying on to the tram-lines, centred on its holy citadel, but reaching outwards with a frowsty leap across the boulevards to the circle of workers' dormitories and railheads, where the monasteries still prayed, and at last to a circle of pigsties, cabbage-patches, earth roads, earth closets, where Moscow sank back, seemingly with relief, into a village.

The central characters are the English, and the Russian characters are seen through their eyes. Silent, beautiful Lisa is the least understood, because she must be kept mysterious. But others are solidly in focus: Tvyordov, the composer at the press, a man of absolute dedication, regularity and very few words; Volodya, the pale, reproachful, emotional student; Bernov, the sharp-eyed humourless costing accountant. As always in Fitzgerald, "background" figures, the people who are going about their daily life and doing their everyday tasks, jump off the page. As Frank goes to fetch his abandoned children from the Alexander station, he sees in the snow-covered freight yard two men unloading a consignment from a factory of "small metal crosses," "painstakingly" checking their numbers in their "woven straw baskets." Work goes on.

Kuriatin the timber merchant is the most sensational of the Russian characters, a terrific mixture of the barbaric and the brash, of old and new Russia. He has "an absurdly old-fashioned counting-house," but imports one of the few powerful cars to be seen in Moscow, which is as unreliable as he is. He owns a huge house with no telephone and no electricity. Its vast salon is closed up except when he entertains, with lavish ostentation, his table laden with vodka and champagne, clinking and clashing "with imported silver and glass," and doormen dressed up as waiters. The real life of the house is at the back, where the womenfolk, always at home, dispensing superstition, folklore and emotion, are cooped up in "two low-ceilinged smoky rooms." In his business dealings, which he likes to carry out at the top of his voice in lurid, noisy restaurants, Kuriatin veers wildly between cruel jokes, aggression and guile, and tearful outbursts of generosity and remorse. He speaks only Russian, wears a black kaftan and (like Lopakhin in *The Cherry Orchard*) is obsessed with cutting down trees.

All this seems larger than life, but also alarmingly lifelike. Kuriatin's "half-savage" household is seen in action when he gives his spoilt son Mitya—treated like a Crown Prince by the women—a tame bear cub ("or perhaps not tamed"). The animal is teased, tortured and made drunk on vodka by the uncontrolled boy, while the English children look on, aghast. The bear runs pitifully amok all over the house, tearing down and breaking all the bottles and glasses from the table in the big salon, and is finally set on fire: "The bear screamed, its screams being like that of a human child. Already alight, it tried to protect its face with its front paws. Mitya was already doubled up with laughter when from the passage outside could be heard the roar of Kuriatin."

It might be possible to criticise this scene as an exaggerated caricature of barbaric "Russianness." Embedded as it is, though, in her minute, carefully planted historical details, and seen through the eyes of the English family, it reads with startling convincingness. And the sources she draws on confirm its plausibility.

According to Ronald Hingley, the merchants of the time wore huge beards and long coats, only spoke Russian, were often illiterate, kept their women and daughters at home, and loved to entertain with vast banquets in rooms kept mainly for show, while domestic life "went on in poky little rooms in some corner of the house."[52] Harvey Pitcher gives a specific example of the type. *The Smiths in Moscow* (1984) tells the story of a member of the Moscow British community, a story very like that of the Reids. The Scottish Richard Smith set up a boiler-works business in Moscow in the 1850s; his son, Harry, took it over. Pitcher describes their life in Moscow in the years before the Revolution (with a useful map of the city in 1914, closely annotated in her copy by Fitzgerald). Like Frank Reid, Harry Smith was completely accepted by the Muscovites, and one of his closest friends was the business magnate Savva Mozorov. He was a wealthy Tartar factory owner who lived in a huge neo-Gothic place full of costly objects. Pitcher describes him as phenomenally energetic, genial and impatient—much like Kuriatin. He also tells an anecdote of a bear cub named Mishka given by one of the Smiths to another Russian friend:

> They had lots of fun with Mishka and hit upon the idea of giving him vodka to drink . . . they rocked with laughter to see him on

his hind legs reeling and swaying like a drunken old man. One day they were about to give a big dinner party . . . Silver and crystal sparkled on the table . . . Mishka . . . seeing all the bottles on the table thought he would like a drink, so he dug his claws into the tablecloth and started to clamber up. There was an almighty crash and Mishka found himself on the floor with tablecloth, bottles, glass, silver and everything on top of him! [The bear was sent away after that to a circus.][53]

Fitzgerald wrote to Harvey Pitcher when *The Beginning of Spring* was about to come out, to ask if she could use his story of the bear who ran riot in the drawing room, "though not with the ending which you give it in your book, because that was truth, and mine is only fiction."[54] He was happy to oblige, and a friendly correspondence ensued. He would have noticed many other links, too, between *The Smiths of Moscow* and *The Beginning of Spring:* the English families' dachas outside Moscow, set in woods of silver birches, the corruption and obstructiveness of government and police, the assimilation of the English children, all of whom spoke perfect Russian and felt completely at home in Moscow. Fitzgerald raided Smith, too, for the English chaplaincy, the English governess, and the big Scottish department store, Muir & Merrilees.

The novel's second chapter begins:

Up till a few years ago the first sound in the morning in Moscow had been the cows coming out of the side-streets, where they were kept in stalls and backyards, and making their own way among the horse-trams to their meeting-point at the edge of the Khamovniki, where they were taken by the municipal cowman to their pasture, or, in winter, through the darkness, to the suburban stores of hay. Since the tram-lines were electrified, the cows had disappeared.

This beautiful passage has its origins in Pitcher's account of the changing Moscow streets: "In the early morning the cows are let out, and make their way to a barrier of the city: others join, and when they all arrive, there are a goodly number; at the barrier they meet a man with a horn, who drives them in a body to pasture, and collects them again in the evening." But after 1900, the horse-drawn trams were replaced by electric ones, and "no longer were the cows driven to their pasture."[55]

The memoir which Fitzgerald mentioned to Penelope Lively, Eugenie

Fraser's *The House by the Dvina,* was also a rich source. It begins with the author, as a little girl, going on a night journey alone by train from St. Petersburg to Archangel, to join her Russian-Scottish parents. Eugenie Fraser's mother had never been out of Dundee before she married; her name was Nellie. *The House by the Dvina* is full of food and cooking, religious rituals and domestic details: the window frames being brought down from the garrets and put up all over the house at the onset of winter, the tradition of sitting down silently together before setting out on a journey. Like many other writers of Russia, Fraser dwells on the moment when spring returns, the ice breaks up and the rivers start to flow in torrents. At one point the children make a mysterious trip to a clearing in a birch wood, where they find a dark secret. A young woman called Marusya comes to work in the house, whose large eyes "held a serenity seen often in the eyes of grazing cows," and whose slow walk was "sexually provocative." Maruysa is too seductive, gets into trouble, takes her passport and leaves: "After gathering her few belongings, she vanished like the snows in spring and was never seen again." Eventually the family must also leave, and abandon their Russian home; those who don't escape before the onset of the Revolution come to a terrible end.[56]

Wherever Fitzgerald finds something that will work for the novel, she takes it. After the student breaks into the printing works and causes havoc, Frank, or the narrator (they are often interchangeable), says to himself: "Open the doors, the Russians say, here comes trouble." Fraser's memoir records an old Russian saying: "Open wide the gates—here comes trouble."[57] At the start of the haunting scene at the dacha, where Dolly follows Lisa into the snowy birch wood at night, there is a strange moment, like a shift from reality into a dream world: "Sleep walks along the benches, according to the Russian lullaby, and says, 'I am sleepy.' Drowsiness says 'I am drowsy.' On the third night, Dolly woke, and knew she had been woken, by the slight noise of a door opening, the door on to the veranda." In the dry, factual pages of the *Times*'s Russian Supplement for 1911, Fitzgerald must have found an entry on "Russian Folk Songs: The Songs of the Peasants," which gave some translated examples of cradle songs: "Sleep creeps along the bench / Drowsiness about the hut. Sleep says: / 'I am sleepy.' / Drowsiness says: / 'I am drowsy.' / They creep / Over the floor and benches. / They peep in at John / In his cradle. / They peep at him: / They make him sleep."[58]

To excavate these sources is not to diminish Fitzgerald's imaginative brilliance, but, on the contrary, to show how, while using them closely and freely, she gives the appearance of having done no homework at all, and makes her fictive world seem real. And her knowledge of the terrain meant that she was not in danger of producing untested clichés about the Russian character. She is, indeed, extremely careful to draw fine distinctions between different types of Muscovite. In a comical episode, Uncle Charlie, Kuriatin and Frank's new accountant, Bernov, a forward-looking urbanite, take a disastrous motor trip together (intended as a Russian version of *Three Men in a Boat*). Charlie, who speaks no Russian, asks Bernov to translate Kuriatin's outbursts:

> "What's he saying now?"
> "He's saying that a man who has drunk vodka is like a child: what is in his heart comes straight to his lips."
> "Is that a traditional saying?"
> "It may be," said Bernov, "I've never lived in a village and I'm not familiar with traditional sayings."

Frank Reid, though a quiet and undemonstrative man by nature, knows that "there were times when his life had to be acted out, as though on a stage." Much of the comic energy of the novel comes from the awkward entanglement between reserved English and extravagant Russian ways of behaving. At the start of the novel, when Frank reads Nellie's farewell note, he tells his household in Lipka Street that she has gone. In fact, they already know—everyone in Moscow always seems to know Frank's business. "The women began to cry. They must have helped Nellie to pack, and been the recipients of the winter clothes which wouldn't go into the trunks, but these were real tears, true grief." The scene in the stationmaster's house, where the children have been left, is a whole Russian novel in two pages, with everyone crowding in, shouting and hammering on the doors, life stories exchanged, tea and cherry jam, memories of childhood, laments at overwork, friendships plighted for life. When Frank gets the children back to Lipka Street, "they might have been away several years." The whole household is laughing and crying. It feels like a "carnival."

The most absurd performance in the novel's carnival is English, not Russian. Selwyn Crane, her Aylmer Maude–ish Tolstoyan, is the cross Frank has to bear: "Selwyn to be the eternal irritant," she noted in her plans for the novel.[59] He looks like a crane, tall, lean, "kindly smiling, earnestly questing, not quite sane-looking," wearing a motley mix of peasant blouse, English tweed trousers, black frock coat and leather boots or birch-bark sandals. His "large hazel eyes" are "alight with tender curiosity and goodwill."

He is a maddening combination of passivity and interference, busily seeking out misfortunes "with the terrible aimlessness of the benevolent," while "the current of history" carries him gently along. Vegetarian, musical, philosophical, poetic, he lives in a deprived area of the city, because, as Dolly explains, "he likes to walk about at night among the unfortunate." From here he dispenses "spiritual advice" and, instead of tea, "an infusion of the nine herbs of healing." His little book of poems, *Birch Tree Thoughts,* which Reid's is printing on its handpress, is his pride and joy.

> "Dost feel the cold, silver birch?"
> "No, Brother Snow,
> I feel it not." "What, not?" "No, not!"

Selwyn is more than just a joke, however. He turns out to be weak and cowardly, as well as benign, and has more to do with Nellie's disappearance than Frank knows. (That Nellie would take an interest in Selwyn or join a Tolstoyan community is the weakest ingredient in the plot, though it is prepared for by her boldness, her interest in the Arts and Crafts movement and her "unaccountable" character.) We are meant to find Selwyn's naive utopianism absurd, as in this exchange: " 'Poverty isn't a matter for regret, but for rejoicing.' 'No, Selwyn, it's not,' said Frank." But he does throw down a challenge. He makes everyone else feel guilty, he "acts like a reproach."

Behind him looms the figure of his hero Tolstoy, who does not appear as an onstage character, as Gramsci does in *Innocence,* but whose presence is strongly felt. *Resurrection,* that mighty spiritual epic of self-discovery, is cited, with its outburst of spring on the first page, and its belief that (as Frank puts it) "the resurrection, for those who understand how to change their lives, takes place on this earth." And Selwyn's Tolstoyan belief that "the spiritual and the material" should be indivisible has to be considered.

Frank is a practical person, fundamentally optimistic and good-natured: "He always did everything quickly and neatly, without making a business of it." He is kind, and this gets him into trouble. As in her other novels, we see the hopeless results of trying to help other people. Frank is quiet and self-denying, like Cesare in *Innocence.* But he is not passive. He gets angry with Selwyn, he resists the dreadful governess Miss Kinsman and the prying English Chaplain's wife, he takes firm action when it is required. He is one of her bewildered, likeable men, who is trying to do the right thing under puzzling circumstances. Her notes to herself about him read: "Don't make him too repressed . . . Frank mustn't always go under."[60] But how is he best to survive?

Under its comic brio, the novel considers how we survive and endure catastrophe. Work is a great resource, and the silent hero of the book is the man who, at all costs, does his work well. Tvyordov the compositor's regularity in the workplace is "indescribably soothing" and reassuring. His tragedy—the wrecking of his frame, the end of his working routine—presages the end of a whole way of life. The most regular habits in the world cannot protect you from the unforeseen. How was Frank to know Nellie would leave and Lisa would arrive? "Open the doors, here comes trouble."

Volodya the student's message to Lisa—"You're alive. I too am alive"— is a loud call for a free life of the emotions. Fitzgerald does not give her characters long passages of self-analysis. But we see that Frank has fallen deeply, sexually in love for the first time in his life, that he is in love with two people at once, and that there is no solution to this predicament. *The Beginning of Spring* places its puzzled hero between a wife who has chosen to leave her husband and children, and a young woman who may be the leader of an underground revolutionary group. Running all through, implicitly, is a consideration of the position of women: how much better they are treated in England than in Russia, and how the beginning of the twentieth century is also the beginning of their emancipation. The women in the novel are the stronger characters, which is true of most of her books.

The children, too, are at the beginning of their "spring." As with the girls in *Offshore* or the actors in *At Freddie's,* the Reid children's absorption in the world they have grown up in is completely convincing. Nine-year-old Ben, with his definitive knowledge of cars, trains, garages and regulations for horse-drawn cabs, and the baby Annushka, ingesting whatever she hears around her like a sponge, her character done in one stroke ("born to take life in the way easiest to herself and to extract from any situation only the aspect which did her most credit"), are unsentimentally solid. The oldest child, Dolly, is impressive and touching, standing in for her absent mother. She is English and Russian ("I can only write properly in Russian, in any case"), a child and an adult, outspoken but undemonstrative: "He would rather have liked Dolly to give him a hug . . . [but] all that Dolly gave him was a fearless, affectionate glance."

Uncle Charlie, who sees everything in English terms, compares the "kiddies" to the Lost Boys in *Peter Pan,* waiting for their mother to return. Charlie is a dope, but he is right. Like *Peter Pan,* this is a story about having to grow up and lose innocence. The most poignant moment comes when Lisa has vanished and Dolly, doubly abandoned, clings to her father, pale and distraught, and will not leave him. We see that Dolly as an adult will always look back on this time, during her Russian childhood, when her mother left and Lisa came and went. The novel is her story. As Lisa says to the silent listeners in the birch wood: "If she remembers it, she'll understand in time what she's seen."

Frank and his family are realists. Their main aim in life is to deal with things as they are. In that sense they act as counterweights to Selwyn's utopianism and Lisa's mystery. This is, it turns out, a novel about belief and the soul. Fitzgerald's last three books, written in her seventies, are more explicitly about the relation between spiritual and material life than her earlier work, though this had always been her concern. In this novel, she projects her own feeling for religion on to the rituals of the Russian Holy Year and the traditional beliefs of her Muscovites. The book is marked out with a series of rituals, and "the vast reverberations" of Moscow's great bells ring out through the book.

Frank's own beliefs are in limbo. Talking to the children at supper about religion, he realises that he does not know what he believes. "Lukewarm, but not quite cold, unbelieving, but not quite disbelieving, he had fallen into the habit of not asking himself what he thought." The English Chaplain waves him a friendly, ironic invitation to go to the evening service, but it leaves him uneasy, and he goes off "into the darkness."

But sometimes—as when reading a novel—disbelief needs to be suspended. Frank takes part in the blessing of the icon at the press and, with his entire workforce, listens to the priest's all-encompassing prayers. "Because I don't believe in this, Frank thought, that doesn't mean it's not true." "Perhaps," he thinks, "I have faith, even if I have no beliefs." There is an eloquent use of "perhaps" all through the novel, as though the novelist herself does not know everything about her creation: "Mrs. Reid, perhaps, really did die of grief"; "Selwyn seemed to be murmuring something, perhaps a blessing." Sometimes, she appears to be saying, we have to rest in uncertainties.

In this context, Lisa Ivanovna's mysteriousness works well. From the start we are as unsure about her as Frank is. "Her self-possession produced a curious effect, as though, in spite of the politeness, she was listening to something else a little beyond his range." We know very little about her. It is never clear, for instance, whether she secretly understands English, and whether, when Frank says, in the middle of another conversation, in English, "Stay here, I'm in love with you," she knows what he has said. We do not know why she sleeps with Frank—in their one, unwitnessed night together—and whether she, too, has fallen in love. We do see that she is fatal: everyone she meets is magnetised by her, including the children. But, in the end, "heaven knows what" she is.

Towards the end of the novel, Lisa and the three children go to stay in the dacha in the woods. The dacha is brought to life, as usual, with practical details (how to reach it from the branch line, how the food is stored, how the bathhouse works), but the birch trees, giving out "the true scent of wild and lonely places," are described with a passionate lyricism not quite like anything else in the book. All is seen through Dolly's eyes. In the moonlit night, she hears Lisa going out, and follows her through the trees to a clearing in the forest. There are people there (are they people?) standing by the trees. "Dolly began to see on each side of her, among the thronging stems of the birch trees, what looked like human hands, moving to touch each other across the whiteness and the blackness." Lisa tells them she knows they have come from far to meet her, but she cannot stay, because of the child. "No-one answered her, no-one spoke." She turns and goes back to the dacha, and Dolly follows. It is like a dream. It is also like a poem Fitzgerald had known since she was a child, Walter de la Mare's "The Listeners," with its "host of phantom listeners," silent in the dark forest. ("Is there anybody there?" said the Traveller / Knocking on the moonlit door.")

The scene is not explained. In Fitzgerald's notes to herself, it is clear that Dolly was not dreaming but has witnessed a gathering of revolutionary conspirators: "Lisa to impress on Dolly that she's seen people who are prepared to give their lives. Serious. Not too much." That "Not too much" is the keynote of a writer who knows exactly what she is doing, and how to do it. The dream-like ghostliness of the scene is part of what makes, in the phrase she uses of Le Grand Meaulnes, "the oddness and the great beauty" of this novel.[61]

In her notes on birch trees, she tells herself that they should be Lawrentian, feminine, with a "queer DHL-like power."[62] Her intense account of their whole life cycle seems to turn them into characters in the novel (like the Tuscan viburnum in Innocence, or the River Thames in Offshore). This works in a novel where, under the squalid, ramshackle, messy life of the vast dilapidated city, nature is powerfully felt. Everything moves towards the beginning of spring.

As the ice melts and "the voice of the water" begins to be heard, there is an acute underlying sense of future change. Frank feels keenly what it would mean to leave Russia, "the magnificent and ramshackle country" that is his home and that he loves. But all is moving, like the mighty river, carrying the past away. The novel ends with windows of the house being thrown open. Is it a moment of hope? Perhaps.

> Throughout the winter the house had been deaf, turned inwards, able to listen only to itself. Now the sounds of Moscow broke in, the bells and voices, the cabs and taxis which had gone by all winter unheard like ghosts of themselves, and with the noise came the spring wind, fresher than it felt in the street, blowing in uninterrupted from the northern regions where the frost still lay.

჻

Stuart Proffit dissuaded her from calling the novel "Nellie and Lisa," and suggested "something like 'the coming of spring,'" which she liked, and improved on.[63] The novel came out to glowing reviews: a "tour de force," a "flawless," "marvellous, intelligent, beautifully crafted book." Jan Morris, asking "How is it done?," called it "one of the most skilful and utterly fascinating novels I have read for years." Anita Brookner, by now a dedicated fan, called it "a real Russian comedy, at once crafty and scatty": "She has written something remarkable, part novel, part evocation, and done so in prose that never puts a foot wrong. She is so unostentatious a writer that she needs to be read several times. What is impressive is the calm confidence behind the apparent simplicity of utterance." "She is the mistress of the hint of the sublime," Andrew Sinclair wrote. Experts on Russia thought it a masterpiece. She told some people that she had been often to Russia, others that she had never been there in her life.[64]

The Beginning of Spring was short-listed for the Booker Prize that autumn. It was her third appearance on the Booker short list, in a strong and dramatic year for the prize. The other books were Peter Carey's *Oscar and Lucinda,* which won, Bruce Chatwin's *Utz,* David Lodge's *Nice Work,* Salman Rushdie's *The Satanic Verses,* and Marina Warner's *The Lost Father.* The judges were Sebastian Faulks, Philip French, Blake Morrison and Rose Tremain, chaired by Michael Foot, who "drifted alarmingly in his (supposedly) summing-up speech." Fitzgerald had nothing to say about the winner, but made some cool remarks about the Rushdie crisis: "The stately corridors of the Guildhall were lined with police, as Salman R claimed that a threat had been made against his life and he was in imminent danger; still there were plenty of people there and Ria and I enjoyed ourselves very much and were taken about in a car from the Collins fleet."[65] This was some months before the fatwa had been pronounced. When it was, she was not much more sympathetic: "Poor S. Rushdie, or rich S. Rushdie, whichever you like, that was a publicity campaign that went dreadfully wrong. I don't think he ought to go into hiding, though. My local Patel grocery on the corner tells me that it is not a dignified act."[66]

The Beginning of Spring, she would say from then on, was her favourite of her books. And the interest in Russia which fired it never diminished. In the 1990s she wrote several more reviews of Russian writers—Tatyana Tolstaya, Ratushinskaya, Baklanov and Popov.[67] Asked at the turn of the century by the *Moscow Times* (which called her "an ardent Russophile") to name the greatest Russian book of the millennium, she said that if she had been asked ten years before, in 1989, she would have said Tolstoy's *Resurrection,* Turgenev's *Fathers and Sons* and the stories of Tatyana Tolstaya, "in particular 'A Clean Sheet' (if only for the sentence 'Ignatiev did not know how to cry, so he smoked')."[68] But now she chose Andrei Platonov's story

"The Return," translated by Robert Chandler. This is how she described it, in a tone reminiscent of *The Beginning of Spring:*

> In "The Return," everything happens naturally, but by chance. At the very beginning Ivanov has received his demobilization papers and is ready to go home to his wife and children. His unit gives him a send-off party. But there is no train at the station and he has to go back to the barracks for the night. The next evening there is another, much less enthusiastic, party and, once again, no train. Ivanov can't face his mates again, and prepares to spend the night on the platform; that is how he comes to meet Masha, with whom he half falls in love. Then, at the end, when he takes the train again, this time in search of Masha, he looks out of the window, just to see how far it is to the crossing, and catches sight of his own two children stumbling along in a vain attempt to intercept him. Ivanov has not been getting on at all well with his son Petya—but still, these are his children. He throws his bag out of the window and climbs down from the carriage. One might think "how Russian," but that is another way of saying that Russian writers above all acknowledge the tragicomedy of chance and at the same time the moment when (as Ivanov puts it) a human being "touches another life with his naked heart."[69]

CHAPTER SIXTEEN

The Gate of Angels

What he was offering her was the best of himself, keeping nothing back,
the best, then, that one human being can offer to another.[1]

In the summer of 1988, just before *The Beginning of Spring* was published,
Penelope moved to live with Maria and John. She was seventy-two, and
was beginning to have problems with her health. Living alone in the attic
rooms in St. John's Wood was no longer such a pleasure. Maria and John
had talked to Tina and Terence about her moving; they felt it was their
turn, and they wanted her with them. John Lake had been doing well in
the City, Maria was a Lecturer in Neuroscience at University College London, to be promoted to a Reader in 1990 and a Professor in 1995, and they
had started their family. In 1986 they had bought a house in Bishops Road,
a quiet leafy side street in Highgate, off the Archway Road, just opposite
the entrance to Highgate Woods, with a magistrates' court at the corner of
the main road. Number 27 had literary form: the last inhabitant had been
Arnold Wesker. Penelope described it as "a nice friendly place." It is a large,
attractive grey gault-brick Victorian house with a welcoming look, pretty
details ("wonderful ridge-tiles and finials"), a small front garden, a big
entrance porch, spacious, solid rooms and a wide back garden. At the side
was a former coach house, which the Lakes turned into a small flat with its
own entrance. Penelope would refer to it as "Arnold Wesker's wash-room."
The flat, 27A, had a kitchen looking out onto the street, a narrow corridor
with just enough room for bookshelves, a bathroom and separate lavatory
off the corridor, and a small bedsitting room painted green, with a window
over the back garden.

This was where Penelope lived, from 11 June 1988, for the rest of her
life, and where she would write two more novels. It suited her very well.
She had her books in the corridor and in her room, on the old wooden
bookshelves she had picked up secondhand, a sofa and a bed, her little
wooden writing table by the garden window, and her few treasures on the
walls: framed rhyme sheets, like Lovat Fraser's "The Wind," small objects

from Russia and Mexico, a few of her own hand-painted drawings and cards, an antique clock.[2]

The move meant downsizing. "I am a very slow, inefficient and tearful mover." There were all kinds of things she couldn't bear to part with but which had to be thrown away, like "old envelopes, jam-jars and bits of string." And there were great heaps of papers. It would not have occurred to her that anyone might want these, but her American book-dealer friend and fellow Poetry Bookshop enthusiast, Howard Woolmer, suggested that she use him as a go-between to sell her archive to the Harry Ransom Center at Austin, Texas, where she had worked on the Poetry Bookshop in 1979. He persuaded the Center to buy the papers—there was some resistance, as she was not felt to be sufficiently well known—and negotiated a "fair price" on her behalf. (The payment for a second tranche of papers, sold through Woolmer in 1996, was £1,860.) As soon as she was in Bishops Road, she started sorting and packing up the papers. "I suppose selling your papers is a ritual stage in a writer's life—a very late one," she wrote to Mary Lago. She was dubious about their value: "A high proportion . . . seem to be yellowing newspaper-clippings and letters of the perhaps-we-could-meet-for-a-drink-at-6:30-variety." She made a careful cull, keeping back everything related to L. P. Hartley, and as far as possible all personal materials—though one or two things accidentally slipped through her net. There was a worrying moment when all the boxes went astray en route to Texas. But they arrived in the end, and the sale gave her enough room in the cupboards of her new home "to put my shoes."[3]

Her routine in her "little green room" was the same as at Almeric Road. She got up very early to write, going into town on some days to work in the British Library or attend meetings or see friends. There were no rules, but some negotiations, over how much time she spent with the family. She would drop in on them in the evenings (though not every evening) and at weekends she would, in Maria's phrase, "potter through" to the main house, usually for tea and a chat. If she had visitors she wanted to entertain more grandly, she would ask to use the big sitting room. She cooked for herself, though John picked up the heavy items for her—oranges and potatoes. She was part of the family, keenly interested in and involved with their doings. Maria often went with her to literary events, or to the theatre or the ballet. John paid all the household bills and there was, of course, no rent. So, apart from clothes (never a great outlay for her), food and other expenses, she had few outgoings now—and more money coming in than ever before. But she did not have the habit of spending.

Maria found her a secretary in her department to type her manuscripts, a service which Penelope paid for. She would get irritated if the
typist altered the layout of lines or the spaces between paragraphs ("that
means a passage of time"), and on one occasion refused to pay her again
for having a section retyped. When she gave Maria the manuscripts to take
into work, she would ask her not to read them. Though they were living
together, and were very close, they never discussed her work-in-progress.

She became a familiar figure in the neighbourhood. She liked Highgate Woods (the birch trees were like Russia, she thought) and often
walked there. She was regularly to be seen on her way up the Archway
Road from Highgate tube station in a red anorak, or shopping for herself
in the butcher's and the greengrocer's, stopping to talk to people she knew.
She joined the Highgate Literary and Scientific Institute, a venerable cultural organisation full of energetic book-lovers. She became a regular at
her local church, All Saints, and always went to the early Sunday morning
service. Thomas Lake, who was four when his grandmother moved in,
remembered the smell of her breakfast fry-ups from her kitchen after she
got back from church.

At the start of 1988, the year of the house move and of *The Beginning
of Spring,* she went, with some trepidation, to the Toronto Harbourfront
Festival. The organiser, the "affable" Greg Gatenby, had told her that there
were "two dozen international poets and fictioneers coming, so perhaps I
can largely escape notice." In the end she enjoyed the "Olympian Writers"
Week ('Olympian' referring to the Winter Olympics, <u>not</u> the writers)."[4]

More important events for her that year were the births of two
grandchildren, Maria's second child, Sophie, in February and Tina's daughter Jemima in May. These two little girls became very dear to her. Her
appointment diaries, which she got from the Museum Association, usually
choosing the series called "Children in Art," each month marked with a
jungle of blue circles and arrows, were a tangled mixture of professional and
domestic events. "Get new gas cooker, write piece on RAK[nox]." "Borrow bathroom scales, Oxford and Cambridge Club, Pen AGM, Tommy
carols." For one specimen month, the entries read: "Get hair cut. Insti
[Highgate Institute] committee meeting. Antonia Byatt [Jr] Arts Council
meeting. Pen, The 2 Cultures. T & T to London. Wm Morris (no). Make
cake. Sophie's Birthday. Doctor."[5]

Being a grandmother was an occupation. Thomas and Sophie Lake
were growing up under her eyes, and she went to all their school events and
kept an observant eye on them. Her last grandchild, Maria's second son,

Alfie, was born in August 1992, which meant, as she habitually and proudly said in her letters, that she had nine.

She saw Valpy's children less than she did her other grandchildren. Through the 1980s, Valpy and Angelines were in The Hague, from where he was sent as economic adviser to the government of Nicaragua, and spent long periods there, with his family, during the Sandinista revolution, often in dangerous conditions. In 1993 he moved to Oxford, to St. Antony's College and the Department of Development Economics. His life was a professional success story. But after a series of acute anxiety attacks in the early 1990s, a course of cognitive behavioural therapy led him to understand that the source of these attacks was a fear of being seen as a failure in his mother's eyes.[6]

Visits to The Hague were not a great success—relations with Angelines had never warmed. But Valpy and Angelines's children liked their English grandmother. The eldest son, Valpy Gregory, twenty in 1993, thought she was "really cool," though "not a sharp dresser." He remembered from childhood what a cunning games-player she was, how she required a certain standard of behaviour—you wouldn't swear in front of her or tell blue jokes—and that he never saw her angry or grumpy. As a young man in London, he would seek her out occasionally and talk to her about books. He would have liked to hear more about his grandfather, whose war sounded exciting and heroic to him, but she never spoke of him. Still, it seemed to him that the grandmother he got to know was not the person his mother had been describing to him all his life.[7]

She was much closer to Tina's and Maria's children. There were childhood problems for Paschal Dooley, who had Asperger's, and did not learn to speak until he was seven. As with the dark times of Desmond's illness and of the death of baby Fergus, Penelope was awkward at dealing with this face-to-face, but wrote encouragingly to Tina about it when she was away: "You said to me 'Paschal will talk' and of course he will . . . P. manages very well considering his intelligence is so very much all there but doesn't get the supplies (yet) that other children do and he has to rely to a great extent on his own inner world." To friends who knew the family she wrote wisely: "It's painful to see how puzzled [Paschal] is. He's 2-and-a-half, and the doctors are doing this, that and the other thing . . . Meanwhile he's invented a sign language of his own which is quite adequate for day-to-day purposes, and probably wonders what we're making such a fuss about . . . He's very well able to make people understand what he doesn't want."[8]

Terence moved jobs, frustrated by the school where he was teaching, and the Dooleys' lives, during Paschal's early childhood, when they were moving from Weston to Watchet to Milton Abbot, were not easy. Dating from those years, a routine of mutual help grew up between Tina and Penelope. Every Sunday, at eleven o'clock, Penelope would ring her daughter for a long talk, while Terence was at church with the children. An hour and a half later, when they came back, Tina would still be on the phone. Much of the conversation consisted of Penelope's worries, but not all. It was an intimate flow of chatter and confidences. When she went to stay with them, she would set to in their garden straight away, yanking out weeds, pruning and planting. From 1990 onwards, she took them all on a two-week holiday every year, the first time in Devon and after that in mainland Europe. It was her main annual expenditure, a gesture of gratitude and a way of making their lives easier. Tina made all the arrangements, and Penelope paid for everything. They would rent a large holiday house with a pool, and hired two cars. In this style, over nine years, they visited the Cherbourg peninsula, the Costa Brava, southern Italy near Paestum, Asturias, Grasse, the Italian lakes, Montejaque in Andalusia, Salobreña near Granada, and Menorca.

On these holidays she got to know her Dooley grandchildren well. When it was fine they went on expeditions or sat by the pool or went to the beach. "Forward the shrimping party," she would say. When it rained they played games and read. The children remembered her pulling endless supplies for them out of her enormous bag, cheating at games (playing Picture Lotto with Luke, aged three, she would change the cards when he wasn't looking) and having long, absorbed conversations. Luke was aware from early on that she was interested in words and in his use of them. She sent them all little drawings and letters and poems. One typical note to Luke read: "It was very nice to see you. Now I am in London, and I miss you very much. I am so sorry we did not mow the lawn. If the grass grows much longer, it will be as tall as you are. I shan't be able to find you, and I shall say 'Where's Luke?' All my love from Granny." And she drew a picture of Luke, in among the long grasses.[9] She did not cuddle them, but she might call them "dearie," and she liked them to call her "Granny." If one of them was walking along with her, and was upset, she would take their hand in hers and tap joined hands gently against their side. She liked being quiet with them, smiling, holding back and letting them talk. Luke recognised in her a preference for order, manners and "social grace." As an adult, pondering her chief quality, he called it "spirituality."

✒

What part does "spirituality" play in practical everyday life? *The Gate of Angels* masquerades as a light, comical love story set in Edwardian times, centring on the simple and traditional plot of a young man's search for a young woman: "I can't get over the conviction that this is the most important subject, not only for novelists."[10] But it also stirs up questions about the nature of belief, reality and truth, while making no grand claims or conclusions, and leaving us to work things out for ourselves. As she often said, she did not like to explain too much. "I try to make everything quite clear, but then I think, this is an insult to the reader, I don't need to explain all this, I shouldn't like to have all this explained to me, and so I begin to cut out, whole chapters go, and perhaps as a result things get hard to follow. But I'm frightened of over-explanation. Lawrence said that if you try to nail anything down in the novel, either it kills the novel, or the novel gets up and walks away with the nail."[11] She would also say that in order to start writing she needed the title, the last sentence and the first paragraph. *The Gate of Angels* took off (as with the greenhouse which eventually disappeared from *The Beginning of Spring*) from a single image:

> It was something I saw on a visit to Cambridge, through the window of a bus, somewhere near Newnham. It was a tremendously windy day, and on one of Cambridge's unexpected patches of green land there were cows moving about under the willow trees. The wind had torn great wreaths and branches off the willows and thrown them down to the ground. The cows were ecstatic—they were prancing, almost dancing—they'd hoped all their lives to get at the trees and now at last they could—and it struck me that in this orderly University city, the headquarters of rational and scientific thinking, things had suddenly turned upside down, reason had given way to imagination.[12]

This is what she does with that image at the start of the novel.

> How could the wind be so strong . . . ? . . . The cows had gone mad, tossing up the silvery weeping leaves which were suddenly, quite contrary to all their experience, everywhere within reach. Their horns were festooned with willow boughs. Not being able to see properly, they tripped and fell. Two or three of them were wallowing on their backs, idiotically, exhibiting vast pale bellies intended by nature to be always hidden. They were still munch-

ing. A scene of disorder, tree-tops on the earth, legs in the air, in a university city devoted to logic and reason.

It is a little like the moment in Ford Madox Ford's *The Good Soldier* when Dowell, the narrator, laughs at the absurd sight, seen from the window of a train, of one cow tipping another one over into a stream. In her copy of the novel, she annotated this as an example of "D's love of violence." And the scene of brute disorder, in both novels, is a harbinger of what is soon to come in the world. Her story of a world turned upside down is set in Cambridge and London in 1912, the period she most liked to write about, full of possibility. It is the only English novel of her four late books, but it is intercut with a brief slice of Spanish history, her one fictional glimpse of the country she knew so well.

The young man who is bicycling along in the high wind is twenty-five-year-old Fred Fairly (his surname tells us he is one of her kindhearted "decent sorts"),[13] a highly intelligent, poor rector's son from the country. He is working as a Lecturer in Practical Physics at the Cavendish Laboratory in Cambridge, in the early days of atomic research, a time of great scientific excitement and new discoveries. The pioneering physicists of the day are like gods to Fred. He believes that "if it works, it must be true," that "as soon as something's completely described, it's explained." He used to believe in religion; now he believes in the new science.

He is also, in this novel full of contradictions and absurdities, a junior member of an extremely old-fashioned Cambridge college, St. Angelicus, or "Angels." Unlike the Cavendish Laboratory, this is an imaginary institution, but described with minute plausibility. It is the smallest college in the city, with no room for students to live in, and only six fellows, all of them scientists or mathematicians. It was founded by the (real) fourteenth-century Spanish pope Benedict XIII, an Aragonese of extreme stubbornness who refused to accept his dethroning as pope and maintained an alternative papacy for decades, withdrawing finally to a castle on the jagged island rock of Peñiscola, a place Fitzgerald knew. His Spanish motto, over the college gate (a more forbidding motto than the Ricordanza's) "is translated as 'I have not changed my mind,' but 'nothing doing' might be nearer." The college is headed by a blind Master, a stickler for absolute truth and a perfectly adapted Cambridge character, aware of every movement in his college, and given to utterances such as: "Now, tell me, have you made up your mind on the most important question of all?" or "I hope you weren't unwise enough to go to hospital?" The college allows no "female animals capable of reproduction" into its sheltered grounds, "though starlings couldn't altogether be regulated." In its tiny, chilly, dark, damp, fortress-like precincts, lit only by candles, with an ancient walnut tree at its centre, there is one mysterious narrow door, "a strangely tall and narrow gate," which has only been found opened twice, once at the death of Pope Benedict and once when women were admitted to Cambridge. In short, St. Angelicus is the home of stubbornly maintained traditions and lost causes.

A frequent, amused visitor to the college is Dr. Matthews, Provost of St. James's, "a medievalist and palaeographer, who, as a form of relaxation, wrote ghost stories." Dr. Matthews, a faintly sinister character, thinks the scientific beliefs of the Fellows of St. Angelicus lead them nowhere, "and quite conceivably backwards." In his view, there is much more to life, and death, than what can be rationally argued or proved, and his terrifying stories (of which we get a fine example) illustrate his point. Like Sir William, the old archaeologist of *The Golden Child,* he warns Fred of the "many things" that "walk when they seem to be buried safely enough," of the places on or under the earth which "cannot be disturbed" except with dire consequences.

Fred Fairly is also a member of the Disobligers' Society, where all speakers in debates must argue against what they believe, and eat food which they do not enjoy. As he bicycles along in the high wind at the start of the novel, he is called out to by a fellow cyclist and Disobliger, with the words "Thought is blood." This is the topic of their next debate. Against his own conviction that "we have no supernatural protectors or supernatural enemies," he has to argue that "everything in life can't be referred back to physical causes." If, as everyday experience can prove, "the body has a mind of its own," then it follows that "the Mind has a body of its own, even if it's like nothing that we can see around us, or have ever seen." And so it could be argued that the body's mind might survive after death, and might then be called the soul. The childish solemnity and absurdity of these young male Cambridge philosopher-scientists, puffing on their pipes and forcing Health Biscuits on one another, is tenderly ridiculed; but their topsy-turvy argument is essential to the novel.

One other set of beliefs calls out to Fred: those he has been brought up with. He has to go back to the rectory to tell his father he has lost his childhood faith, a conversation he is dreading, and which, like all prepared confrontations in Fitzgerald's novels, does not go according to plan. He is going to tell his father, reasonably, that "he was an unbeliever, but his unbelief was conditional. He had no acceptable evidence that Christianity was true." At the family home, a jumble of rain-faded notices, old mangles and broken hymn-boards—"nothing was got rid of at the Rectory"—Fred finds his mother and sisters, new recruits to the suffrage cause, busily making banners, and his father, as usual, staring out of the window, waiting for parishioners to call. He blurts out some "broken phrases," but his father would rather Fred did not talk to him about "having no further use for the soul." Sadly, he asks Fred whether he knows what to do with the "left-overs" that have been set aside for them for lunch. Fred replies: "You don't have to do anything with them. They're left over from whatever was done to them before."

But Fred is currently distracted from leftover faiths and family allegiances, scientific research, his college and the Disobligers' Society, because he is trying to find a young woman called Daisy Saunders, whom he has met only once, under unusual circumstances. He has recently been in an accident on the outskirts of Cambridge, when he was knocked off his bike by a horse-driven farm cart with no lights, suddenly appearing in the dark out of a side road. He fell onto the young woman, who was cycling along next to a third person who then disappeared—as did the driver of the cart. They were picked up unconscious, and put to bed together in the suburban house of a dreadful Cambridge don and his wife (excellent, horrifying caricatures), who thought they were a married couple. Since then Fred has lost track of Daisy, but he must find her, because he has fallen in love with her.

Daisy's life story, told, like Fred's, through a series of short, evocative scenes, is in strong contrast to his. Like Chiara and Salvatore in *Innocence*, they come from utterly different worlds within one country. She is just as intelligent as he is, but her background is urban and tough, the other end of the English spectrum from Cambridge's protected environment. She is one of the "kept-outs," but she is also a "fearless survivor," like Annie Asra in *Human Voices* or Nellie in *The Beginning of Spring*. She is not interested in scientific theories or abstract ideas, but in bodily life. She is also, though, a firm believer, and we see her go into a church to pray. In her notes for the novel Fitzgerald asks herself, "Must I explain this?," and crosses out a passage about Daisy being a "naturally religious soul": "She knew that all prayers are answered. You just have to make the best you can of the answer."[14]

Daisy grew up on crowded south London pavements, "with the smells of vinegar, gin, coal smoke, paraffin, sulphur, horse-dung from backyard stables, chloride of lime from backstreet factories, and baking bread every morning." Her mother, who works as a bottle-capper at the brewery, buys cow-heels from the market stalls to boil down for broth and sells the bones to the glue factories. They move from lodging to lodging, with the help of the men with barrows who do night-time flits. Daisy starts work at fifteen as a "clerical," crossing the river with thousands of other south London commuters, fighting their way onto the trams "like a dark swarm of bees." Sexual threats are all part of the daily struggle. The men in the trams cover their genitals, the girls wear wedding rings, corsets and hatpins and fight off the gropers. The shop downstairs sells herbs for "bringing it on" and "bringing it off." The men at "Sedley's Cartons" think it's their right to have a go at her.

But Daisy is robust: "Life would get a lot of work out of her." She arrives at her dreary job with "the irrepressible readiness to please, as though on creation's first morning, which is one of the earth's great spectacles of wasted force." Always the disabused voice of the narrator shadows her character's joyful ebullience. She is the apple of her mother's eye (the father is long vanished), but the mother, proud defences up, will never tell her this. Mrs. Saunders is not well when they go together to the grand opening of the magnificent new Selfridges, and dies a few days later. Daisy "felt the loss through and through." The unexpressed love between mother and daughter, and the loss, is the more moving, as always in Fitzgerald, for being so quiet.

Alone and penniless, but hopeful, Daisy goes to the Blackfriars Hospital for an interview with a daunting Matron. Fitzgerald would use their combative conversation to illustrate how her writing worked, as "a confrontation where the reader is asked to have some sympathy at least with both sides," where it is seen that "no-one ever gets the better of Daisy except herself." "As I'm a hopelessly addicted writer of short books I have to try to see to it that every confrontation and every dialogue has some reference to what I hope will be understood as the heart of the novel . . . [It is] about body, mind and spirit."[15]

Daisy wants to know "how the human body works and what has to be done to it when it doesn't work." She finds this out at the hospital, done with immaculate comic realism: "In the wards the kidney sufferers, waiting to sweat into their thick flared night-shirts, were dosed with nitre, squill and broom. Fever cases had a drop of aconite in a teaspoonful of water every fifteen minutes, then antimony every quarter of an hour. Babies with enteritis had tar-water and brandy." She also encounters the explosive Dr. Sage, the alienist, who believes in the human rights of mental patients. He is as indulged by "the protected world of the hospital" as the blind Master is at St. Angelicus. In the world-turned-upside-down of the novel, it seems probable that a wildly eccentric doctor should be treating the insane.

Daisy thrives at her work, but she has an unfortunate tendency to do things for other people, "not knowing how dangerous generosity is to the giver." This goes with her habit of finding it "so much more easy to give than to take," which makes her a difficult person to propose marriage to. She helps out an incompetent fellow nurse, and a needy Spanish woman working in the laundry, and a deluded patient who has tried to jump in the river and wants a notice put in the papers so that the woman he loves will see it. Daisy reproves him for talking about taking his own life: "It's not your own life," said Daisy. "How did you get that idea?" But she takes his story to a local paper, which puts her in the power of a seedy journalist, Thomas Kelly, and loses her her job.

The landscape of Edwardian London which Kelly and Daisy inhabit— the shabby newspaper office, the ABC teashop, the borough library with the public wash-house next door, the tea stall next to the car park, the barges on the river—is as vividly seen as Charlotte Mew's Fitzrovia or Evoe Knox's Fleet Street. Kelly is an unusual character in Fitzgerald's novels, dingy and jaunty like a music-hall comic, a lowlife socialist enraged by religion and the class system, brutally cynical about sex: "It's nothing. You just want to take a couple of whiskies." He is the only person in the novel who sees the war coming: "I'll have to go and be shot . . . I'm a Territorial." (At Cambridge the young men hardly notice "a lecturer in Propellant Explosives being suddenly recalled to Germany.") But every time Kelly appears he seems more "ill and savage," by the end verging on the demonic, giving off a "physical sensation . . . of guilt and danger."

Daisy feels brought down by being with Kelly. By contrast, in her scenes with Fred (who does manage to find her), "her capacity for enjoying herself and being pleased," her energy, her radiance, her curiosity and her sense of humour bubble up. On a walk in the country together, they go inside a sad empty house, which "like all houses which have stood vacant for any length of time, seemed full of bits of paper." Together they look at the scraps of letters and inside the drawers, and Daisy imagines the life of the person who once lived there. "All by himself, I suppose, you have to be sorry for him." Her "ready sympathy" makes her understand what Fred wants to give her. "What he was offering her was the best of himself, keeping nothing back, the best, then, that one human being can offer to another." But they will lose each other again.

Fred's quest for Daisy provides the movement of the novel. "I think it is very important when you are writing to lay down the movement, no matter what kind of novel it is. The movement should be what readers want to happen . . . You should hope, if you read this book, that Fred and Daisy would end up happily."[16] Playing across that movement are the arguments about science, the family life at the rectory, Dr. Matthew's ghost story, the dreadful don and his put-upon wife—strands which culminate, rapidly, in a court case, a fight, the disposal of an inert body and a quarrel. Daisy and Fred find themselves in the disastrous situation of many of Fitzgerald's couples, "by which they were obliged to say to each other what they did not mean and to attack what they wished to defend." It is a Disobligers' Society of two. There follows a rescue, and a miraculous coincidence—or, as Fred would see it, a terrific piece of luck. Pace and suspense are kept up in what is a very short novel (the shortest of her last four), which covers only a few weeks in early spring, starting in March 1912,[17] and which works through her perfected method of short scenes, plain dialogue and strong images.

The cyclists and cows in the high wind, Daisy with her mother at the opening of Selfridges, the blind Master fallen under the walnut tree in the college—such moments stay in the mind like scenes from a film, or a dream. As always in her novels, characters who only appear once are completely realised, like the manageress of a little café who asks if she should light the gas, and in whose voice Fred "recognised the note, universal as the voice of the sea, of worry about money," or the Tutor of Angels who is "a volunteer with the East Anglian Territorial Bicycle Corps, and, largely for reasons of vanity, rode at all times his specially adapted safety machine with its leather case for signal flags, rifle rest and spare water barrel."

The words "obligation," "continuity," "observable," "mind," "blood" and "body" are struck like repeated notes. Images of water flow through a novel in which truth is unstable and fluid and beliefs are ebbing. Fred "makes landfall" out of the storm, Daisy (like the characters in *Offshore*) knows "the many voices, not all of them friendly" of the River Thames. She remembers a childhood trip to Southend on a boat at night with Japanese lanterns and a band on shore, when "the music travelled across the water as though it was going to settle there." Fred takes Daisy past the flooded meadows of the Fens, "these shining fields." The cart that comes to rescue her at the end of the novel rocks "like a ship at sea."

The short chapters have perky, anecdotal titles ("How Fred Got This Job in the First Place," "No Mystery About Daisy's Movements"), as in Jerome K. Jerome, or Forster's *A Room with a View*. The novel is full of

Edwardian sources and allusions, all securely bedded down. Fitzgerald drew on books about the Edwardian urban underclass, like George Gissing's *The Nether World,* or C. F. G. Masterman's *The Condition of England.* She looked at books on nursing—Eva Luckes on *Hospital Sisters and Their Duties* (1912) and Honnor Morten on *How to Become a Nurse* (1892). Dr. Sloane has a touch of the pioneering mind-doctor Henry Maudsley, whose *Body and Mind* she read. Daisy and Fred's outings invoke Edwardian comedies like the Grossmiths' *Diary of a Nobody,* or Barry Pain's *Eliza* (a book she was fond of, and once tried to adapt for TV), or the novels of W. W. Jacobs. These books all have the kind of "independent sharp-tongued young women" "who could take on all the world." "Men don't disconcert these girls, nor do the regulations and prohibitions men make." Theatrical productions also come in useful. Fred and Daisy go to see a Cambridge performance of Sullivan's *Cox and Box* (which Daisy prefers to Rupert Brooke as Mephistopheles in *Doctor Faustus*). It is a little private joke: the comedy's offstage object of desire is called Penelope, and she marries a Mr. Knox.[18]

As usual, so that she can invent freely on the back of factual certainties, every detail is researched. In her notebooks there are lists of telephone charges in the 1900s, cockney rhyming slang (her seedy Londoners say "You can stick that up your Khyber" or "I give you my dicky-bird"), and notes on college regulations, academic dress, dining habits, maps and architecture.[19] "I calculated there would just be room for St. Angelicus," she told a correspondent, "if I made its back wall run down Jesus Lane, and kept it very small."[20]

Fred's 1910s Cambridge was well known to her because it was Dillwyn Knox's world. Of course she read up on it, using, among many other sources, the writings of G. E. Moore, the fastidious, depressive diaries of A. C. Benson, Master of Magdalene College, and the memoirs of M. R. James. But she also went back to *The Knox Brothers,* which was being reissued by Collins in the same year as *The Gate of Angels.* The novel's affectionate tone derives from her feeling about Dillwyn and her family. Her own beliefs and experiences, as in all her "historical" novels, deeply colour *The Gate of Angels.*

Dillwyn Knox was a classical scholar, not a physicist, but his passionate attention to exact detail and conclusive proofs, both as a classical editor and at Bletchley, resembles Fred's work at the Cavendish Laboratory. Fred's loss of religious belief recalls Dillwyn's abandoning of the faith "which had been interwoven since childhood with his daily life," and his postponement of the confrontation with his father, Bishop Knox, not through fear, but "the fear of giving pain." Dilly's unresolved conflict between reason and emotion, and the Knox family preference for not talking about difficult feelings, is echoed in the Fairly family. Dillwyn's Cambridge, dedicated, as she says in *The Knox Brothers,* "to the exposure of truth at all costs . . . under the remorseless light and in the cold winds of the Fen country," is the inspiration for the novel. The Disobligers' Society gets its name from one of Dilly's absurd college debating groups, "The As It Were In Contradistinction Society," and its atmosphere from the Apostles. Dillwyn was a student, and later a Fellow, of King's, where the Fellows were rationalists and atheists.[21] There was one exception, however, and that was the Provost of King's in Dillwyn's time, M. R. James.

"Monty" James interested Fitzgerald, though she didn't think anyone would have heard of him in the 1990s. Like Dr. Matthews in the novel, he was affable, learned, conservative and odd, a medievalist palaeographer who wrote ghost stories. She describes him with relish both in *The Knox Brothers* and in a much later introduction to his stories, one of the last things she wrote. (She once told the biographer Richard Holmes that it was an essay of his on M. R. James which made her start to write.)[22] James detested science, mathematics and philosophy. At dinner, overhearing "two undergraduates disputing a problematic point . . . he rapped on the table sharply with his pipe and called out, 'No thinking, gentlemen, please!' " In his ghost stories, she says, there are "dreams that wonderfully suggest the feeling of suffocation and powerlessness that comes with 'dreaming true.' " His protagonists are rationalists who don't believe in ghosts, and they get a horrible comeuppance. "Faced by the obstinate disbeliever, Monty takes his not-so-mild revenge."[23]

Like all the real historical characters in her novels, M. R. James is there for a purpose. "I set my novel in the Cambridge of 1912 because that was the height of the so-called 'body/mind controversy,' with the scientists of the Cavendish in controversy with professing Christians, championed by James . . . [who] made an unforgettable comment on the situation in his ghost story 'Oh Whistle and I'll Come to You, My Lad.' "[24] "The ghost story is there to give atmosphere to the anti-materialists of Cambridge, who don't believe that physics can explain everything."[25]

Many Cambridge dons in the early twentieth century, like M. R. James and A. C. Benson, disapproved of, and knew little about, the scientific research being done under their noses. (C. P. Snow expostulated, in 1959, on the amazing ignorance of humanists about basic science, in *Two Cultures,* which Fitzgerald reread for her novel.) But, though such individuals—like the fourteenth-century Spanish founder of St. Angelicus—were stubbornly resistant to new ideas, the air around them was full of change. Fitzgerald would give a humorous account of her interest in this period when talking about her novel, which she said originated in curiosity about the Austrian physicist-philosopher Ernst Mach—as well as in the sight of the upside-down cows:

> Mach was an opponent of Rutherford and the early atomic physicists because he considered that atoms were only a provisional idea; they were unobservables, and science shouldn't be based on the unobservable, otherwise it was no better off than metaphysics, which asks us to speculate about the unseeable. While I was trying to think about this . . . a novel suggested itself, turning on the problem of body and soul. The title would be *The Unobservables*. But the publishers . . . rejected this immediately as lacking not only in sex but in human appeal of any kind. I changed it to *Mistakes made by Scientists*, which I liked almost as much, but I was told, quite correctly, that it wouldn't fit on the jacket and didn't sound like a novel anyway.[26]

She set her novel in the 1910s so as to coincide with the transformatory period in physics, when theories of relativity and the beginnings of quantum theory were changing the reading of the universe. Classical physicists were being challenged by theorists like Einstein and Max Planck. The atomic theory of matter, and conclusive experimental evidence for the atom, were being developed. Theoretical physicists were beginning to construct atomic models to account for the observed properties of matter. These were radical discoveries, causing great upheaval.

Much of this was happening in Cambridge. The Cavendish Laboratory, which opened there in 1874, was the greatest centre in the world for experimental physics. But there had been a great deal of resistance in the university to its setting up. Colleges had to be persuaded that the teaching of "practical physics" and the presence of scientific researchers in the university was all part of a liberal education. *The Gate of Angels* captures the pioneering, ramshackle, unconventional atmosphere of the Cavendish in the early twentieth century, where overcrowded and squalid conditions were producing "indisputable greatness."

Ernest Rutherford, one of Fred's heroes, the Nobel Prize–winning experimental physicist and discoverer of the nuclear atom, who, with his team, provided the basic view of atomic theory that has been in use ever since, started working at the Cavendish in 1896 on X-rays and radioactivity. He was a research assistant to J. J. Thomson, who discovered the electron and isolated it as a particle. Rutherford spent the rest of his life working on the structure of the atom, at Manchester and, after the war, from 1919, as director of the Cavendish. Niels Bohr ("whose almost inaudible lectures" Fred has attended) went to Cambridge in 1911 to work with Thomson on atomic research, but moved to Manchester to work with Rutherford. C. T. R. Wilson, Fred's research director, showed, in 1911, how to photograph the paths of charged particles in his famous cloud chamber. These are Fred's gurus.

But for many classical physicists, the atomic concept was incomprehensible and unacceptable. Ernst Mach considered unobservable entities like atoms as having no role to play in causal explanations in physics. He and his followers maintained that all the correct results in atomic theory would be obtainable by theories only involving observable entities. It was a view that was losing ground. Mach's extreme empiricism ("sense impressions were the only things we could know of the world"), and his preference for tentativeness in science rather than overweening certainty, was, as it transpired, a lost cause, which is why he appeals to Fitzgerald.

The debates between the great scientists of the early twentieth century—Einstein, Planck, Bohr, Heisenberg, Mach—were essentially over reality. How did quantum theory deal with the reality of the physical world? Were atoms real? Does anything have reality that cannot be observed or measured? The argument over whether atoms literally existed had to do, as Fitzgerald says, with observables. Scientific "realists" believed that "the aim of science was to give a true description of the world." Scientific "anti-realists" believed that "the aim of science was to provide a true description of a certain *part* of the world—the 'observable' part."[27] For how can the unobservable be real? These philosophical debates resemble arguments between agnostics and believers over the existence of God and the soul, and that parallel runs through *The Gate of Angels*.

In the novel, Fred is passionately dedicated to the work being done at the Cavendish. But his mentor, Professor Flowerdew, is out of sympathy with the new developments in quantum theory, and agrees with Mach, whose spokesman he is. Like Mach he is supporting a lost cause, and will never change his mind. "Go back to what can be known through the senses," he tells Fred. "To base one's calculations on unobservables—such as God, such as the soul, such as the atom, such as the elementary particle—was nothing more than a comforting weakness." He mocks Fred's work with C. T. R. Wilson on what Flowerdew calls photographing the "alleged" tracks of ionising particles, and Fred turns red. Flowerdew foretells a future of disorder and chaos, though he does not foresee, and nor does anyone in the novel, the rush of the Cavendish students in 1914 to put their physics to work for the war effort, or the later discovery of the atom bomb.

Fitzgerald gives a convincing and informed account of the scientific arguments of the day. But of course she takes the liberties she needs, for instance, making Flowerdew a Professor of "Observable Experimental Physics" (when the term "observable" would not have been used), or giving Fred a heartfelt speech to his students about the need for scientists not to think of themselves as extraordinary or believe that their ideas are superior to those of nonscientists. "It's very good for an idea to be commonplace." And "scientists are not dispassionate."[28]

At a moment like that, we seem to hear her own views coming through. But she does not propose a simple opposition between the observable and the invisible, or unprovable. There are contradictions throughout. Writing about the treatment of mental patients, for instance, something which has always intrigued her (it also gets into *Innocence* and her story "The Prescription"), she does not decide whether mental illness should or can be treated by physiological methods, though she clearly thinks there is an inextricable connection between states of mind and the life of the body. Nor does the novel come to a conclusion about the relation between reason and emotion. As she says elsewhere: "I have grown old, but I haven't solved the problem of being brought up to believe that reason is the highest human faculty and we should rely on it, and yet finding that when we get to life's most difficult moments, we can't and don't."[29]

The main contrast in the novel is between Fred and Daisy. They stand for the opposition between mind and body, unobservables and observables, scientific truth and pragmatism: "There is no absolute truth for Daisy and it may be said that she quite often tells lies. Can these two people ever get together?"[30]

Daisy's world of bodily observables is particularly associated with women's lives. *The Gate of Angels* is the most feminist of all Fitzgerald's novels, even though she avoids that categorisation. She has always had tough, solitary heroines who have had to make their own way. She has always been sardonic about male privilege and exploitation—sexual predators at the BBC, spoilt tyrants in museums, lawyers, bankers and doctors browbeating women. But this novel in particular is about women's struggles, the abuses against them and their need for solidarity. This is her *Jacob's Room* or *A Room of One's Own,* a novel about the history of female, as well as class, exclusion from the world of the male elite. The Fairly women making their suffrage banners (as Christina Hicks once did), or the dreary life of the don's wife, Mrs. Wrayburn, whose spoilt, pompous husband has prevented her from having a life of her own, are lightly done, but are meant seriously.

Women, especially poor women, often don't have the luxury of thinking about abstractions. They have to cope with what's there. The novel loves to name and list observable things, things that women deal with every day, like the items Mrs. Wrayburn has to get out for her husband's lunch:

> Like most of her friends, she had prayed not to marry a clergyman, a general practitioner, or a university lecturer without a fellowship. All these . . . were professions that meant luncheon at home, so that every day (in addition to cups, plates and dishes) demanded toast-racks, egg-cups, egg-cosies, hot water jugs, hot milk strainers, tea-strainers, coffee-strainers, bone egg-spoons, sugar-tongs, mustard-pots . . . silver fruit knives . . . napkins with differently coloured rings for each person at table, vegetable dishes with handles in the shape of artichokes, gravy boats, dishcovers, fish-forks with which it was difficult to eat fish (but fish-knives were only for vulgarians), muffin-dishes which had to be filled with boiling water to keep the muffins at their correct temperature . . . cut-glass blancmange dishes, knife-rests for knives, fork-rests for forks, cheese dishes with lids the shape of a piece of cheese, compotiers, ramekins, pipkins, cruets, pots.

But, paradoxically, women are also associated with magic, the irrational, the supernatural. From a male point of view, this can be baleful or alarming. Dr. Matthews's ghost story gives a horrifying account of an archaeologist who becomes haunted by what happened at the site he is researching, a medieval nunnery where the few remaining inhabitants were to be evicted by a bishop's commissioner, who is tortured and horribly killed by three horrible old women—nuns, or witches?—in a scene that the unfortunate archaeologist is doomed to re-enact.

Women have benign magical associations, too. Daisy, although the most physical and robust of characters, has something miraculous about her. Good and bad female angels, demons and protectors, are placed in her path. Mrs. Martinez, the dark Spanish woman at the hospital, betrays her. The cloaked woman who rescues her in the farm cart at the end of the novel seems to be something more than a farmer's wife.

> "You looked as if you'd lost something, that's why I stopped for you."
>   Daisy hesitated. "You don't know who I am."
>   "Yes, I do," said Mrs. Turner.

Daisy herself is a kind of ministering angel (and it takes the demonic Kelly to spot it). Though she is one of the kept-outs because of her class, her education, her poverty and her gender, she can also make things change. At the end of the novel, she walks through the gate of angels, which has mysteriously opened to let her in, so as to act as a nurse to the old blind Master, lying under the walnut tree, while cries of "animal terror" go up at the invasion of a female presence into the hallowed college grounds. Thanks to this miraculous chance, or miracle, Daisy finds and is found by the person who loves her.

Reviewers of *The Gate of Angels,* in long, enthusiastic pieces, sought for the perfect phrase to describe a Fitzgerald novel. John Bayley spoke of her "mesmeric insouciance." Sebastian Faulks said it was like being taken for a ride in "a peculiar kind of car," where everything works beautifully but, halfway through, "someone throws the steering-wheel out of the window," with exhilarating results.[31] The novel was short-listed for the Irish Times/ Aer Lingus Prize ("I don't see how it can do much against J. Updike," she said to Stuart Proffitt)[32] and for the Booker. The judges—Denis Forman as chairman, Walton Litz, Hilary Mantel, Kate Saunders and Susannah Clapp—chose Fitzgerald, Bainbridge (*An Awfully Big Adventure*), John McGahern (*Amongst Women*), Brian Moore (*Lies of Silence*), Mordecai Richler (*Solomon Gursky Was Here*) and A. S. Byatt (*Possession*). This admirable list was generally held to give off "a whiff of mustiness, of déjà vu." There were headlines like "Booker Judges Favour Safe Read from Old Literary Lions." The journalist John Walsh remarked: "This is septuagenarian Fitzgerald's fourth go. Soon they'll have to give her a season ticket."[33] She went along, to see A. S. Byatt, her old colleague from Westminster Tutors, claiming the prize. As in other years when another novel won the prize, she was self-contained and dignified in defeat. Stuart Proffitt, on this occasion, congratulated her on her calmness. "I enjoyed [it] really, and so did Ria," she told him, "and it was worth going even if it was only to hear the round of applause when Shakespeare was mentioned."[34] All the same, in her humorous, rueful way, she minded passionately about her successes, did not like to be defeated and was to be heard, on at least one occasion, making sharp remarks about the judges.

There was much more publicity for *The Gate of Angels* than for her previous novels. She was photographed by the *Observer*'s Jane Bown (surely a kindred spirit). There were a lot of festival appearances and interviews, in which she ran through her usual formulas and batted away personal questions. Occasionally there would be a revealing moment: "Happiness is very difficult to write about—it's the English temperament. Certainly we are depressive. Contentment is impossible to write about." Asked by one newspaper what she was currently reading, she replied: "I have *Teach Yourself Chinese Martial Arts* by the bed, because my grandson [Luke], who is nearly six, says it will do me good, and it does have a picture of someone of 94 wielding a kind of sword. I can do a bit of the shadow-boxing for old people. And I'm reading *The Trick Is to Keep Breathing* by Janice Galloway, a very funny and sad novel . . . and Claire Tomalin's *The Invisible Woman: The Story of Dickens and Nelly Ternan*. I'm interested in the point of view of someone who had effectively disappeared."[35]

The first printing of *The Gate of Angels* was for 5,000 copies. The Flamingo paperback editions of her backlist were doing well. Her name was still to be made, though, in the States. Stuart Proffitt felt that Holt had done a poor job with her titles, and *The Gate of Angels* went to the formidable Nan Talese, who had recently moved from Houghton Mifflin to set up her own list at Doubleday. This turned out not to be a match made in heaven, though Doubleday did a reasonable job on the novel. Fitzgerald found Talese bullying. She didn't like the cover chosen for *The Gate of Angels*, but "what's the use of arguing with her." The American paperback was published by Carroll & Graf, who had also paperbacked *Innocence, Offshore* and *The Beginning of Spring*. Chris Carduff, who had published *Charlotte Mew* with Addison-Wesley in 1988, went on to be a magazine editor at the *New Criterion*, and invited her in 1992 to write for him about the demise of *Punch*, an event which saddened her. She wrote him a funny, tender reminiscence. Carduff moved on to Houghton Mifflin, with good results for Fitzgerald.[36]

Gale Research, an American educational publisher, offered her $1,000 for an account of her life in their Contemporary Authors series. A touching and evasive "Curriculum Vitae" resulted. It was oblique about the Knox family characteristics, her mother's death, her falling in love at the BBC, her married life (Desmond was as ever described as "an Irish soldier"), her children and the pattern of her writing life. But it beautifully evoked some of her places, the inspirations for her early books and her life's beliefs.[37]

She worked up a talk on fiction writing, which she took around, with variants, to Somerville College, various festivals and a British Council literary congress in Alcalá, Spain, in August 1992. She published a short version of it in Maura Dooley's anthology, *How Novelists Work*. The talk was rueful about her attitude to her work. She found it "very difficult to write anything at all," she said (as she often did in late interviews). "At no point when I'm writing a book am I anything less than miserable, and I would take any possible excuse to break off and do something different." But it also went seriously into the origins of works of fiction, her own and other writers': Henry James, Conrad, George Eliot, Joyce, Beckett, Tolstoy, Hardy, Mary Shelley and Lawrence, who interested her greatly. A novel might originate in a story the writer has been told, or read; in a childhood memory; in a haunting image that might eventually disappear. How can these origins be accounted for? "To describe what's actually going on here I think you might have to go back to a very ancient definition of the imagination, as a messenger between the sense and the mind, but a messenger who has an authority of his own because when his time comes he may also rule in his turn."[38]

In the 1990s, her novels were beginning to be translated. She was published by Stock in France, by Insel in Germany, by Grijalbo Mondadori in Spain and by Sellerio Editore in Italy. Some of her titles were also translated into Serbo-Croat, Japanese, Russian, Hungarian, Slovak, Czech, Greek and Portuguese. She wasn't sure how they went down. "I have no idea what kind of people read them . . . I imagine, people who are not so fond of blockbusters, and who are ready to listen to a quiet voice."[39]

In 1992, she began to keep a regular (if idiosyncratic) account of her earnings in a notebook called "My Takings." For the HarperCollins paperback reprint of *The Knox Brothers* in 1990, she had received an advance of £1,000, exactly the same as for its first publication by Macmillan in 1979. But her takings, in other areas, had risen hugely since her early publishing days. By June 1992 she had £102,593 in her savings account and £7,337 in her current account. Part of her income was from reviewing, prize judging and literary festival appearances. On average, she would get

£180 for a piece for *The Times*, £200 from the *Observer*, between £150 and £370, depending on length, from the *Evening Standard*, £85 from the *Times Literary Supplement*, £100 from the *London Review of Books* and £200 from the *New York Times*. Every so often these sums are annotated: "I've no idea what this is for," or, "Oh dear where is The Observer [cheque]? I'VE LOST IT."

Her royalties from HarperCollins were—as an example—£8,889 for the six months ending in December 1990, and £1,459 for the six months ending in March 1994. For the period ending in April 1992 she noted that they were £14,855, and then asked herself, "Is this right?" Perhaps she couldn't believe it, or perhaps she had put the comma in the wrong place. Her Public Lending Right payments were £1,588 in February 1992, £1,335 in January 1993 and £1,301 in December 1995. For the publication of a single story ("The Means of Escape") in a Random House anthology in 1993, she was paid £500. Her advance for *The Blue Flower*, paid in two tranches in 1994 and 1995, was £35,000.

Prize judging added to her savings, and also interested her. She frequently complained about the huge piles of prize books mounting up to be read in her little green room, but she had an appetite for the work. She judged the Booker Prize twice, in 1991 and in 1998. The first was a difficult year for the prize. The novelist Nicholas Mosley walked out on the proceedings because the novel he wanted (by Allan Massie) was being ignored by the other judges, Jonathan Keates, Ann Schlee, Penelope and Jeremy Treglown, the Chair. Jonathan Keates, writer and teacher, was entranced by Penelope, from the moment she arrived, with her bags and hats and air of "complete authenticity," yet with something "buccaneering" and "dashing" about her, too. She was nice to him about his teaching, and he felt at once she was someone whose good opinion he wanted to earn. He liked her ruthless candour. "Goodness, why bother?" she would say of a book, or "Pointless portentousness." "She never said more than she absolutely needed to, either in dispraise or commendation. Words weren't things to be wasted." She was amused by and scornful of Nicholas Mosley's walkout. Her own favourite book, Roddy Doyle's *The Van*, which she enjoyed for its "effrontery, its air of shamelessness and the uses it made of modern Irish demotic," did not win, but she "made the best of it" and accepted the final decision, which was for Ben Okri's *The Famished Road*.[40]

A very different account of what it was like to be her fellow judge a few years later was given by the academic Valentine Cunningham, who found her irritable, perverse and ungenerous. She snapped at him in one meeting for his habit of calling writers' work their "stuff " ("They're not *stuff*!"), which stung him, "especially as I regarded myself as one of the reviewers who helped put her on the map as a novelist." But, worse than that, she took every opportunity to wreck Beryl Bainbridge's chances with *Master Georgie,* while referring to her as "my old friend Beryl." She backed *The Restraint of Beasts* by Magnus Mills, a curious, semi-allegorical first novel about Scottish fence-makers (also much admired by Thomas Pynchon) which no one else had liked. The eventual winner was Ian McEwan's *Amsterdam.* Her own view of the proceedings was equally unhappy: "It's always the same, you make up your mind to remain calm, dispassionate and civilised and then as the meetings go on you become increasingly heated and quarrelsome. The book I wanted to win . . . didn't win, and I felt like weeping. And everyone complained, as they always do, that the judges must have lost their wits anyway."[41]

Even if they made her weep, she judged many other prizes. In 1990, she was a judge on the Whitbread Prize, won, ironically, by Nicholas Mosley's *Hopeful Monsters,* and the Commonwealth Prize, won by Mordecai Richler. She relished a story which she heard at the first Whitbread meeting, about Segovia judging a young guitarists' competition. When asked how long each competitor was to play for, Segovia replied: "For one minute only, that is sufficient." She judged the John Llewellyn Rhys Prize in 1992 (given to Ray Monk's biography of Wittgenstein, which she greatly admired), the Forward Prize for poetry in 1996 and, in 1999, two prizes for the Royal Society of Literature. The Heinemann Prize for nonfiction went to Geoffrey Hill for *The Triumph of Love,* of which she noted: "Sees himself as irascible unwanted old man, clinging to outdated truths. Shocked by holocaust, corruption of church, war. Wants to forgive but can't yet, can't even forgive himself." The Winifred Holtby Memorial Prize for a novel with local interest went to Andrew O'Hagan's *Our Fathers.* She also judged the Encore Award for short stories, and the Arts Council bursary applications, in 1990, of which she noted shamelessly: "32 novels to read, but might be able to get something for some crony."[42]

In 1995 she gave the Cheltenham Prize, which is awarded by a single judge at the Literature Festival, to Kazuo Ishiguro.[43] Ishiguro was signing copies of *The Unconsoled* in the Muswell Hill Bookshop, and a woman in the line said something nice to him about the book, asked him just to write "To Penelope" and quietly went away. After she had gone, someone else said to him, "You just signed a book for Penelope Fitzgerald." A few weeks later, he heard she was going to give him the Cheltenham Prize. Because he couldn't go to the Festival, they recorded an interview at Bishops Road. She seemed to him gentle, modest, open and interested in the world, supportive to young writers, looking outward, with a kind of freshness. "She was lovely." And she found his work intensely appealing. She liked the dream-like strangeness of *The Unconsoled,* but her favourite was *A Pale View of Hills:* "You couldn't get a better example of saying things by leaving them unsaid."[44]

However perverse or ruthless she could be, she had adventurous, bold tastes in modern writing. She liked daring new fiction which used language strongly, inhabited unusual worlds or dealt with characters not usually given a voice. As well as Mills, Doyle and Ishiguro, she gave early praise to Esther Freud, Claire Messud and Carol Shields. In her jumbled little notebooks on her prize judgings, there are plenty of caustic notes. Of a book on the magician John Dee, she noted: "Like all books on Dee, writer more interested than reader." Of a book about how men like to kill: "Academic, apparently mad, marshals tedious amount of evidence on her side only." But there are many traces of her perceptive enthusiasms, too. Of Colm Tóibín's *The South:* "superior writing, lyrical"; of Helen Simpson's *Four Bare Legs in a Bed:* "lively, good dialogue, terrible funny stories of pre-natal." Generously, she enjoyed and praised writers who were quite unlike her.[45] Praise came to her, too, from old and new admirers. J. L. Carr wrote to her in 1993, two months before his death, to say: "Keep it up Penelope—you are an adornment to the literary scene. We old timers didn't do so badly after all, did we?"[46]

She did a lot of reviewing in the early to mid-1990s, on a wide range of subjects—biographies of Emily Tennyson, Ford, Waugh, C. S. Lewis and Carrington ("Reading a good biographer means thinking of unfulfilled conditionals"); letters of Yeats, Larkin and Edward Thomas; stories by McGahern (highly praised as "a realist who writes . . . as a poet") and William Trevor's memoirs, with their "magical sense of time passing, and his own life passing with it, as his perspective alters."[47]

She was also doing some media work (a BBC Radio 4 programme in a series called "Visiting Lives," with Ann Thwaite, in 1989). She was busily involved in her usual societies, and with the campaign against the move to the new British Library. A lot of her energies went into the Highgate "Insti," as she called it. In her diary for 18 April 1991 she reminded herself to make twelve rounds of egg sandwiches by 5:45 that evening for their theatre trip. As chief "inviter" of speakers, her filing system was to keep a record of acceptances and dates on the front of a manila file, inside which she kept the correspondence. She would write on the file cover: "J. Gardam *can't* come! Tim Hilton *won't* come! Nina Bawden *can* come!" Julian Barnes was invited in March 1993, for January 1994. He replied politely, asking if she was *the* Penelope Fitzgerald, and telling her that he greatly admired *The Beginning of Spring*. He didn't like to be asked "9½ months ahead," and he might be in Argentina, but otherwise he would accept. Yes, she replied, "I admit I'm the one, or one of the ones, that writes novels." She would pencil him in for 18 January 1994, she added with quiet persistence, and would write again: "If it doesn't suit, it will be my fault and no-one else's." On her folder, she wrote: "He says yes, if he doesn't have to go to the Argentines." He did come, and she introduced him by saying that *Metroland* was her favourite of his novels, "because it is lighthearted in the way you only can be once in life," and that although English readers are supposed not to like very clever writers, "and he is very clever, let's face it," "still he is, if he doesn't mind my saying so, much loved."[48]

Her colleagues at the Highgate Institute noted that she was not always kind about her fellow writers. She feared that a well-known but short comic novelist might not be able to see over the lectern: perhaps a good reason for not inviting him. After a talk by Joanna Trollope, Penelope only remarked: "I loved her little suede bootees." Her letters, as everyone's private letters can be, are full of sharp things. Her literary peers sometimes filled her with despair, both en masse—"and now the dreaded [PEN] Writer's Day is coming round—terrible to see so many writers in one place"—and individually. "I don't see how a life of Dickens written by someone [Peter Ackroyd] who has no sense of humour whatever can be a success." Richard Holmes "talked with such Coleridge-like profuseness and charm" at a dinner party that she couldn't hear what anyone else was saying. At an Edinburgh Festival interview in 1989, "Hermione Lee was very kind, although she clearly thinks I am hopeless about feminism, and says this is the generation gap." To Tina, wickedly: "I think I'll *have* to resign from the Royal Soc Lit committee, as Maggie Gee is due to come on to it." The "dread" Malcolm Bradbury, who did not like her work, always came off badly: "I realise now that you can't get hold of Malcolm Bradbury, he seems to be made of some plastic or semi-fluid substance which gives way or changes in your hands." But her jokes could be admiring, too. A letter to Oliver and Patty Knox in 1991 sang the praises of Stuart Proffitt and his endless energy and resourcefulness. "He just doesn't mind <u>what</u> he does. I'll never forget him offering to teach Anita Brookner to drive. 'Many have offered to teach me to drive,' she answered superbly."[49]

By the early 1990s Proffitt was deep in the challenges of the new regime at HarperCollins. Rupert Murdoch took over in 1989 and the firm moved to a vast new building in Hammersmith, which Fitzgerald regarded—as she regarded everything to do with Rupert Murdoch—with dread and suspicion. What she called the new "palace of glass" in Fulham Palace Road seemed designed to be daunting to writers.[50] Still, she was being looked after. She was given a young publicist, Karen Duffy, twenty-four years old, fresh from an English degree. They travelled together to all Fitzgerald's events, and forged a warm friendship. Karen was impressed with her elderly author's punctiliousness, stamina and modesty. Whenever she went to pick her up from Bishops Road, she would always be ready, waiting with her William Morris bag and her keys. She would talk to Karen about other writers she admired, like Leslie Hartley or J. L. Carr, about daughters and grandchildren—but not about her son, or her late husband, or her work-in-progress—and about topics that interested her. On a trip to the Edinburgh Festival they went to an exhibition of Russian art, and Karen was awed by how much Penelope knew. Penelope would send Karen characteristic postcards reporting on her progress, as on the way home on the plane from the Edinburgh Festival ("I sat next to an old priest who recited the rosary twice during the trip but could not open his butter or milk so I did it for him, & hope that shows my character is getting stronger") or after a reading at Northampton: "I nearly went to Nottingham, as I'd lost the relevant file, but remembered at the last moment." She put up with late trains and slow journeys, and was always thoughtful, though not exactly motherly. "Are you getting enough sleep," she would say. "Karen, you've had that cold a long time." Karen became deeply attached to her, and felt that Collins, who preferred their big flashy names like Jack Higgins, did not make enough of her.[51]

She went on her own, though, to Sydney and Tasmania, to speak at the Hobart Literary Festival in November 1991. In advance of the long journey, she put in her diary: "Free week in Tasmania: What the hell am I supposed to do?" To Willie Conder, she said that the organiser of the Festival had told her to bring only light clothing, so she would have to save up her "new pink jersey from Jumpers" till she got back:

> It's terrible, Willie, I'm always giving myself little rewards and prohibitions, as if I were 3 years old, and I suppose, in fact, it's a sign of second childhood. Now I'm telling myself that the pink jersey . . . will be something to think about and keep me going while I'm giving dreary talks . . . on the Hobart waterfront. It's a disgrace.[52]

Once there, she enjoyed it, took careful note of everything around her, and gave a generous interview to a Tasmanian literary magazine, *Island,* which put her picture on its cover. But it was a very long way, and, for all her energy and stamina, she tired more easily now. She did take another long journey, though, in April 1992, one which she had long promised herself. This was a trip to the "Holy Land." She went with a Methodist group called Inter-Church Travel. Her main ambitions were to see the flowers, and to be rebaptised in the Jordan. (Though they did not talk about religion, Stuart Proffitt saw how important this was to her.) From her *Flowers of the Mediterranean,* she learned that there were "a thousand different flowering plants within a five-mile radius of Jerusalem." "I hesitated to ring up the travel agency to ask them how many would be out at the beginning of April, because I didn't want to sound like what I was, an elderly English female traveller. In the end, I did ring up. It turned out that everyone else had asked the same thing. And although it had been snowing the day before we arrived, the lilies of the field were out in their myriads."[53]

They were taken to all the sites in Palestine where visitors were taken at that time—the Church of the Holy Sepulchre ("a nightmare"), the Western Wall, the Temple Mount, the Dome of the Rock, the Shepherds' Fields, the "bewildering" Church of the Nativity in Bethlehem, Masada, the obligatory bathe in the Dead Sea, the Mount of Olives, the house of Lazarus, Herod's Palace, a kibbutz, Cana, the River Jordan and the shore of Lake Galilee. She had the sense of confusion, dismay and stress that all travellers in search of "tranquillity" in the Holy Land find themselves experiencing. "You have to take yourself to one side and remind yourself that you know, or have been warned, that almost all the churches have been rebuilt, that there is scarcely any proof that anything's what it's traditionally said to be." Still, on Palm Sunday, on the north-west shore of the clear waters of the Galilee, taking outdoor communion at St. Peter's Chapel, she did find something resembling tranquillity, and took a perfectly flat, smooth, pale red pebble home to remind herself of it. "I think it may have some jasper in it, and it shines a little in a good light."[54]

All this activity kept pace with the writing of her next novel, *The Blue Flower.* But the gap between books was now the longest since she had started publishing, twenty years before. She had been thinking about the subject of *The Blue Flower* for years, and she began to research it in 1991. It took her four years to write. One of the reasons she made slow progress was her health. From her mid-seventies, she began to suffer from illnesses which damaged her strength and caused her pain. She was stoical and resilient, but the quality of her life was diminished. Like her father and her son, she had always suffered from asthma, and from severe hay fever in the summers. In the early 1990s she developed arrhythmia and high blood pressure. She also had increasingly bad arthritis, in her back, her shoulders and her hands. She was often in pain; Tina remembered her sitting with her back against the radiator when she went to visit, to ease it. She was short of breath and found going uphill and long walks hard. Walking with someone she didn't know well, she would pretend to stop to look in a window or at the view, or to find something in her bag, to avoid giving herself away or having to complain.

Her diary in the early 1990s is punctuated by visits to doctors at the Whittington Hospital in Highgate. "I've got a much nicer heart specialist at the Whittington now," she told Richard and Mary Ollard in January 1993, "who doesn't keep menacing me with warfarin as he knows I don't like the idea of it (the idea of rat-poison I mean) and so I am hoping to get into better condition. It comes and goes rather." But a year or so later she was telling Rachel Hichens and her daughter Lis that the pills she was being given all "make me feel ill in different ways" and "none of them seem to make my heart any better." "The registrar at the Whittington . . . a harassed little Sri Lankan, rejects my complaints and says 'you are elderly and must take these substances.'" She developed a characteristically rueful and laconic way of talking about "my old enemies, My Back and My Heart": "I can't breathe very well, which is inconvenient"; "I am writing in rather a decrepit state as my heart seems to be beating too fast and I can't get my cough to clear up, rather like La Traviata." She sometimes had to cancel appointments and turn down events. Telling Willie Conder in 1994 about "this tiresome irregular heart-beat and breathlessness and general inability to walk anywhere much," she said, plaintively: "I don't quite know what to do—whether to cancel the thing I'm supposed to be doing for the *whole* of the year, or hope for the best (which isn't ordinarily something I ever do)." But she hated to let people down, or to sit idle. "My heart is still not going at the right pace so I thought I'd see what a day's absolute laziness . . . would do for it. But the laziness makes me feel guilty for that is how I was brought up."[55]

She made her will in May 1993, when she was seventy-six. But though her body was starting to weaken, she was in powerful control of her life and her mind, unlike her two oldest and longest-known relatives, whose condition was pitiable. From the early 1990s, Penelope had to watch her stepmother, Mary Knox, who had been her close friend for over fifty years, succumb to dementia. The flat she had moved into in Frognal Mansions twenty years before, after Evoe's death, was in an appalling condition, and in 1994 she was moved into a home in Hampstead. Penelope, often with Tina or Maria and her children, would visit her regularly, but Mary no longer recognised her, or anyone. It was a long-drawn-out process; in the end, Mary would outlive her stepdaughter by a few months, and die at the age of ninety-one.

Rawle, too, was very unwell. He had had Parkinson's for some years, and at his eightieth birthday celebrations in July 1993 he was extremely frail. He died less than a year later, on 5 June 1994. His life had been wretched for a long time, and for Helen, Belinda and William it was something of a relief. Letters of condolence came from Hicks and Peck and Knox relations. Her old friend Rachel Hichens wrote understandingly: "What an awful time he must have had. No-one would want him to suffer more, but what a gap in your life after so many years." His *Times* obituary noted his POW experiences, his family pedigree, his journalism, his mastery of Far Eastern affairs, his stammer and his genial nature. At his funeral on 14 June, thanks were given for "his gentle charm, humour, intelligence, and the affection he evoked in so many." One of the readings, by Belinda, was the old Knox favourite, "They told me, Heraclitus, they told me you were dead."

Penelope wrote a kind letter to Belinda and again to Helen after the memorial ceremony for the erecting of the tombstone, which read "writer, humanist and friend." There had always been difficulties and distance in her relationship with Rawle. Nevertheless, it was a momentous loss. The date of his death, in her diary, is blocked out with an ink mark, and a year later she noted it with a cross. To her dear old friend Willie Conder she wrote, "I'm the last of my family."[56]

CHAPTER SEVENTEEN

The Blue Flower

He added: "What is the meaning of the blue flower?"
Karoline saw that he was not going to answer this himself.[1]

The first chapter of *The Blue Flower* is called "Washday." This is how it begins:

> Jacob Dietmahler was not such a fool that he could not see that they had arrived at his friend's home on the washday. They should not have arrived anywhere, certainly not at this great house, the largest but two in Weissenfels, at such a time. Dietmahler's own mother supervised the washing three times a year, therefore the household had linen and white underwear for four months only. He himself possessed eighty-nine shirts, no more. But here, at the Hardenberg house in Kloster Gasse, he could tell from the great dingy snowfalls of sheets, pillow-cases, bolster-cases, vests, bodices, drawers, from the upper windows into the courtyard, where grave-looking servants, both men and women, were receiving them into giant baskets, that they washed only once a year. This might not mean wealth, in fact he knew that in this case it didn't, but it was certainly an indication of long standing. A numerous family, also. The underwear of children and young persons, as well as the larger sizes, fluttered through the blue air, as though the children themselves had taken to flight.
>
> "Fritz, I'm afraid you have brought me here at an inconvenient moment. You should have let me know. Here I am, a stranger to your honoured family, knee deep in your smallclothes."
>
> "How can I tell when they're going to wash?" said Fritz. "Anyway, you're a thousand times welcome at all times."

These are the first words of the main character, the subject, of the novel, Friedrich von Hardenberg. After that the two friends burst out into an imi-

tation of their university teacher (though we don't know what they are talking about at this point, nor will we for about thirty chapters, so it sounds
like nonsense), the family starts calling out and appearing in the courtyard,
and Jacob Dietmahler is swept up into the life and movement of the Hardenberg house. An author's note has told us that the novel is based on the
life of Friedrich von Hardenberg (1772–1801), "before he became famous
under the name Novalis." But we don't yet know anything about him, or
whether "Friedrich" is the same person as "Fritz." We quickly sense that the
two men are very young, hardly more than boys. Jacob (at once proud and
bashful about his eighty-nine shirts) is twenty-two, Fritz is twenty-three.
Very soon we will start to find out about Fritz's family and its surrounding
world. But in this entrancing first page we are already being told, with the
utmost tact and speed, a great deal about the inhabitants of this novel.

Those double negatives in the first sentence tell us to read with
attention, to be on the alert for mixed feelings and uncertainties. We see
at once that this is going to be a novel (like *The Gate of Angels*) greatly
concerned with observables. Details of housekeeping and everyday life are
going to matter—even if, as Fritz's first words suggests, they don't always
matter much to him. And these domestic details rapidly tell us that this is
a large, old family living in a big house, without much money. By plunging
us into the point of view of a character who immediately deduces all this,
rather than by telling us facts directly, she puts us there: we, too, at this
moment, are walking into the courtyard of an unfamiliar house.[2]

As well as the solid detail, there is also a feeling of strangeness. There is
something peculiar about the diction, which seems on the edge of being in
translation. The formality of "at such a time," "possessed," "no more," the
construction of "A numerous family, also," with the adverb at the end of
the phrase, the slight archaism of "your honoured family" and "a thousand
times welcome at all times" place us away from home and in the past—as
well as telling us that Jacob is polite and embarrassable and Fritz is impulsive and generous. The estrangement is not only linguistic. We think nothing of it at this point, but the arrival of a stranger at a house, an unexpected
visitor, is a theme that will enter Fritz's dream, or story, of the blue flower.
And there is something disconcerting about starting with the name and the
point of view of a person who is going, in fact, to be a minor character. We
will often see Fritz as others see him, rather than entering into his mind.
That, too, is a kind of estrangement. Although the scene is domestic, it
is unstable, even hallucinatory: those white shapes floating down, those
children's clothes fluttering "through the blue air," "as though the children
themselves had taken to flight." (Not "taken flight.") In a novel that will

be full of children, of dreams and visions, angels and early deaths, this first image will stay to haunt us.

The Blue Flower is a mysterious short book, as well as a very fully realised, complex, populated and realistic one. Part of its mystery is in its origins. There is no evidence that German Romanticism had been a life-long interest of Fitzgerald's. Nor had she been in the habit of writing novels about writers. Yet there are many scattered clues, going a long way back, pointing towards a fascination with Novalis.

In interviews about the novel, she would say that she had once heard, in a church in Bonn, a musical setting of Novalis's mystic poems, *Hymns to the Night,* and had then begun "to look into his life." That would have been in the early 1960s, when Rawle was working in Bonn and she went to visit him there. (Apart from a couple of later short holidays in Austria, that was her only time spent in German-speaking countries.)[3] Also in the 1960s, when she was living on the barge *Grace,* she used regularly to walk past the Moravian church and—as she described it in *Offshore*—the "peaceful garden where the faithful of the Moravian sect lie buried," standing upright so that "on Judgement Day they can rise straight upward." Novalis is educated by the Moravians, and their beliefs are referred to in *The Blue Flower*.

The story of the blue flower lies at the heart of Novalis's unfinished Romantic novel, *Heinrich von Ofterdingen*. Fitzgerald came at it through an indirect route, long before she started work on her own novel. She had always been a keen reader, and teacher, of D. H. Lawrence—she particularly liked his novellas—and her copy of his story "The Fox" is thickly annotated. In that powerful, strange story, two young women, March and Banford, living together in the country in wartime, and trying to make a living from chicken-farming, are threatened by the incursions of a fox. Then a young soldier turns up and stays with them. To March, the stronger girl, he is the embodiment of the fox. The young man fixes his sights on her, but the other girl—needy, neurotic—has to be brutally got rid of. March goes with the young man, but they can't be as one, because she must, in that unfortunate way that women have, go on with her own separate quest for happiness. And what is that? An "awful mistake," according to Lawrence. "The more you reached after the fatal flower of happiness, which trembles so blue and lovely in a crevice just beyond your grasp, the more fearfully you become aware of the ghastly and awful gulf of the precipice below you, into which you will inevitably plunge, as into the bottomless pit, if you reach any further. The flower itself—its calyx is a horrible gulf, it is the bottomless pit."[4]

Fitzgerald has nothing to say about Lawrence's ideas on sexuality and the will, but she admires him as "a flawless impersonator," and is very interested in his image for happiness. In notes for a talk on *The Blue Flower,* she writes: "The very first idea of this book came to me when I read DHL's The Fox, fatal flower of happiness." "I always wondered how did he know the flower was blue. He wrote The Fox in 1922, but it turned out that the <u>idea</u> of the blue flower came from the German Romantic poet Novalis." "Why does DHL say the flower is blue? Gentians? . . . Once you've seen . . . meconopsis bayleyí [baileyi], the blue poppy . . . you have to think of it as the supreme blue flower & it has what seems to me a very interesting history of its own, but I had to leave this when I realised that DHL didn't mean this by the blue flower. There are things you've always wanted to know about or find out about just as there are countries you've always wanted to see & then the point comes when you realise that time will run out or even is running out & I've always wanted to know about the blue flower." She adds: "But whatever flower, not meconopsis b., which [was] only brought here in 1911—seeds in 1924. I'm just left to wish that Novalis could have seen it."[5]

The allusion to *Meconopsis baileyi* would recur when she was asked why the image of the blue flower had tantalised her. "Well," she replied, "it's difficult to explain in any way that sounds sane, you know. But I've always had a very strong feeling for a certain blue flower . . . It's the Himalayan poppy. It's the most wonderful flower. It's like the black swan, you know, you just don't know what to say when you see it. But however this is not the blue poppy that inspired Novalis because it hadn't been discovered by western botanists then."[6]

This image had haunted her for a long time. Burne-Jones's work on the language of flowers absorbed her while she was writing his biography. Her work on Burne-Jones also led her to Novalis via his father-in-law, George MacDonald, a Novalis enthusiast and in her view "the only person who really understood him."[7] Her idea for a book on the language of Renaissance flowers stayed with her for years. At the end of *The Bookshop,* one of the two books Florence took away with her was Ruskin's *Unto This Last,* with a faded alpine gentian pressed between its pages. In notes for an unwritten part of *Innocence,* she alludes to the blue gentian, cold flower of the mountains, in Botticelli's *Primavera.*

The idea of a quest haunted her, and would take its final form in a very late short story, "Desideratus." Among her many ideas for stories in the late 1970s, there is one for "a search for some small beautiful [blue] bird in the jungle" which is never found. In a 1988 piece about Olive

Schreiner, she mentions the stranger in *The Story of an African Farm,* who turns up mysteriously and tells Waldo the story of "The Search for the Bird of Truth." Her notes for *The Blue Flower* had a subplot which was discarded, based on the lives of two nineteenth-century explorers, Frederick Marshman Bailey and Captain Henry Morshead, who are looking for the Tsangpo River Falls on the Tibetan border, and who find the Himalayan poppy. She intends them to discuss the blue flower.[8]

Her own quest for Novalis had started years before she began to write the novel. In *The Beginning of Spring,* Selwyn utters a rhapsodic speech about the blue stream flowing above our heads; it is an unattributed quotation from Novalis. There is a glimpse of him before that, too, in the notes written at the time of *Charlotte Mew,* imagining a new kind of storytelling, inspired by Novalis, made out of fragments and associations, like dreams.[9] This novel puts that kind of imagining into play.

Having become interested in Novalis, she settled down to do her homework, and spent about three years, between 1991 and 1993, reading his work and his letters, and, as usual, a great deal of historical background. She repeatedly told people that the book took her so long because her German was poor. Writing to Alberto Manguel, for instance, who loved the novel, she said: "It took me a long time to write because my German is so slow. I had Novalis's complete letters etc out from the London Library for two years, and they never asked for it back, much to their credit, I think."[10] She would also say, less plausibly, that it was because of her poor German that she chose to write a novel about him, and not a biography.

Novalis and his story of the blue flower was not an obscure subject—at least, not in Europe. It would be as if a German novelist had decided to write a novel based on Keats's Grecian Urn, or Coleridge's Kubla Khan. In Germany—and also in France—Novalis was one of the most famous of the German Romantics, a cult figure who had spawned a large industry of critical and biographical books. But he and his unfinished novel had remained mysterious, and that was one reason she was drawn to him. Novalis has been described as the creator of "the central Romantic symbol," and also as a notoriously hard nut to crack: "Mystical, fragmentary, allusive, paradoxical, abstruse, Novalis represents the first wave of German Romanticism at its most intractable." All the facts that are known about him "have a way of becoming myths."[11]

Friedrich von Hardenberg was born in 1772. His family (as his friend Jacob rightly deduces) was old, grand and impoverished. The Hardenbergs were aristocrats with town and country properties in Saxony and Thuringia, no money for their upkeep, and eleven children, only one of whom outlived both parents. The father was Director of the Salt Mines (the region's dominant industry), and a convert to the Moravian faith. Friedrich, the eldest son, had a serious illness at nine years old and thereafter became a prodigy. By his teens, he was reading Latin and Greek, Mathematics and Physiology, Theology and History. He was to be Assistant Director of the Salt Mines. He was educated by the pious, plain-living Moravian Brothers and by a home tutor, whom he soon outgrew. Between 1790 and 1794, he went to the universities of Jena, Leipzig and Wittenberg. He got a taste of a more worldly life from staying with his uncle in Brunswick, had some wild times as a student, and may have taken opium. Later, he also went to Freiburg, to learn more about geology and mining. He briefly thought of becoming a soldier, but, after university, was apprenticed to Coelestin Just, the supervisor of tax collection at Tennstedt, in Thuringia. In his work, he travelled all over this forested, inland region of south-eastern Germany, with its many rivers ("the Saale, the Unstrut, the Helme, the Elster, the Wipper"), known as the "golden hollow" of the Holy Roman Empire, on the southern edge of the Harz Mountains. But he never went far beyond it, and never travelled abroad. In *The Blue Flower,* this landscape is described with the imaginative eloquence, humorous attention to historical detail and tender empathy which make Fitzgerald's novel so beautiful and interesting.

> Scores of miles of rolling country, uncomplainingly bringing forth potatoes and turnips and the great whiteheart pickling cabbages which had to be sliced with a saw, lay between hometown and hometown, each with its own-ness, but also its welcome likeness to the last one. The hometowns were reassuring to the traveller, who fixed his sights from a distance on the wooden roof of the old church, the cupola of the new one, and came at length to the streets of small houses drawn up in order, each with its pig sty, its prune oven and bread oven and sometimes its wooden garden-house, where the master, in the cool of the evening, sat smoking in total blankness of mind, under a carved motto: ALL HAPPINESS IS HERE or CONTENTMENT IS WEALTH. Sometimes, though not often, a woman, also, found time to sit in the garden-house.

In December 1794, Friedrich met Sophie von Kühn, the young step-daughter of a large neighbouring family of the Justs, the Rockenthiens. He was twenty-two, she was twelve. (It is rather like Dante meeting Beatrice when she was eight.) He fell at once in love with her, and knew that he would wait to marry her when she was sixteen, the usual age for a girl to marry. Sophie seems to have been attractive, lovable, uneducated and dim, and none of his friends could understand his choice. But to him she was his "Absolute," his "Perfection," his "Philo-Sophie." They got engaged, but Sophie developed tuberculosis, and after a series of unsuccessful operations on a tumour, carried out without anaesthetic, she died, in horrible pain, shortly after her fifteenth birthday, in 1797.

Friedrich, consumed with grief, and longing for death himself, poured out poems and stories, including his *Hymns to the Night* (*Hymnen an die Nacht*). In 1798 he adopted the pen name "Novalis," derived from an ancestral family name and meaning "newly cleared ground." In 1799 he fell in love again, and got engaged to Julie von Charpentier. He was doing well in his profession, and writing copiously—including a book on the need for medieval Catholicism to be resuscitated so as to reunify modern Europe. In 1800 he began *Heinrich von Ofterdingen*. In March 1801 he died of consumption, aged twenty-nine. The unfinished novel was published posthumously in 1802.

At first, his work was neglected, though Coleridge knew of him. In the 1820s and '30s he was picked up by Heine and Carlyle. Later, the French Symbolist poets and the Belgian writer Maeterlinck idealised him, rather as Shelley was posthumously idealised as an aetherial spirit. Novalis's grave in Weissenfels, topped by a romantic sculpted bust with wide eyes and flow-ing hair, became a pilgrimage spot, like Oscar Wilde's in Paris or Keats's and Shelley's graves in Rome. In the early twentieth century Novalis was a Romantic hero for European critics such as Georg Lukács, who called him "the only true poet of the Romantic school." In the 1980s, his juvenilia was discovered, and that led to a revival and a new outpouring of biographies and critical works.

Novalis was seventeen when the Bastille fell, and grew up into the years of the French Revolution, the loss of influence of the Holy Roman Empire (the Reich), the tussles for power between Austria and Freder-ick II's Prussia, the struggle for nation-states like Saxony to maintain their independence, the catastrophic Austrian and Prussian defeats in the war with France, and Napoleon's apparently unstoppable rise to power. Like all his generation he was deeply affected by these dramatic revolutionary upheavals, which made the dream of a Golden Age seem conceivable. That sense of being on the brink of great changes, at a time of "uncertainty and expectancy," when everything is possible, is part of what attracted Fitzgerald to this historical moment, as she was attracted to the period before the Great War.

Fitzgerald spreads Novalis's beliefs and ideas lightly through the novel, like overheard music, or traces of colour. All are drawn from his writings, though with some licence: "He insists that the body is not flesh, but the same stuff as the soul." "He told me that the golden age would return, and that there was nothing evil in the world." "All human knowledge is one." "The spirit of the Revolution . . . could be transferred to the world of the imagination, and administered by poets." "The external world is the world of shadows. It throws its shadows into the kingdom of light. How different they will appear when this darkness is gone and the shadow-body has passed away. The universe, after all, is within us. The way leads inwards, always inwards."

These gnomic thoughts were peculiar to Novalis. But they were also of their time, and with her particular attentive historical curiosity Fitzgerald touches on the context of his thinking. He belonged to the Jena school of philosophy, a close-knit circle of young intellectuals centring on the university in the 1790s, all vying to define and voice a new kind of thinking, all moving away from Enlightenment rationalism to Romantic aestheticism. Their guru (who like all gurus also had to be rejected) was Johann Fichte, who taught Novalis philosophy. Fichte's students would get together after his lectures to *"Fichtisieren,"* and Novalis kept notes on his teaching, his *Fichte-Studien*. Fichte was steeped in Kant's ideas about the relation of the mind to the universe. An ardent nationalist and a transcendental idealist, Fichte proposed a doctrine of the infinite power of the will, the omnipotence of the ego (the "Ur-Ich," he called it, the Primeval Self) and the unreality of the external world. According to Fichte, objects do not exist as separate entities. The ego, the Self, has the freedom, and the moral agency, to perceive and create the only world there is.

Also teaching at Jena was the great playwright and historian Friedrich Schiller, from whom Novalis heard inspiring concepts of the moral beauty of the human soul, man's perfectibility and the possibility of an ideal relation between culture and nature. Schiller and Fichte were both in their thirties when they taught Novalis. The rest of the Jena circle were, like him, young writers in their twenties, as excited about making new art and thinking new thoughts as their contemporaries, the first generation of

Romantic poets in England. As with the English Romantics, women were crucial to the group dynamics. The brothers Friedrich Schlegel (the poet and critic) and August Schlegel (the linguist and translator), who between them founded an influential magazine, the *Athenäum,* wrote transcendental poetry, translated Shakespeare, and aspired to the unity of art, philosophy and religion; they lived with two brilliant women, Caroline, who would leave August Schlegel for another member of the group, the philosopher Friedrich Schelling, and Dorothea, daughter of Moses Mendelssohn. Also connected to the Jena circle, but not mentioned by Fitzgerald, were Novalis's first editor, the poet and dramatist Ludwig Tieck, Hegel and Hölderlin. Looming over them all was the presence of Goethe, a mighty influence and challenge.

Jena philosophy argued for the overthrowing of traditional hierarchies, the basing of creativity on autonomy and freedom, and the importance of originality. It also had a deep interest in the relation of science, nature and art. Experimental scientists like the Scottish doctor John Brown, who was investigating the use of laudanum to regulate the proper degree of "excitability" in organisms, or the physicist Johann Ritter, working on galvanism and electricity, were much discussed in the Jena circle.[12]

Novalis, like all true originals (Coleridge is another), took what he needed from everyone around him to feed his thought-processes. His ideas were never systematised; they were expressed in fragments, aphorisms, notes, symbols, poems, essays, unfinished stories. It is that fragmentariness Fitzgerald captures in the form and tone of *The Blue Flower.*

It was the piecemeal, inconclusive quality of his work which made Novalis so alluring as a Romantic prophet. Yet its underlying theme was unity. As her quotations from Novalis show, he believed in a universal language in which art, nature and science were all one. He thought of the arts as converging into a single art, with music as the purest of them all. He thought of matter and spirit as one, not as divided. He imagined death as a continuation of life, not a separation from it, and his death longings—as in *Hymns to the Night*—were expressions of spiritual and passionate yearning, rather than of morbid self-destructiveness. There was an optimism in Novalis's work, as well as sadness and darkness. He believed in the power of dreams and art to remake the universe.

Heinrich von Ofterdingen expressed all this in a strange, rambling, mythical fable. It is a mixture of *Bildungsroman* and fairy tale, dream and quest, the exotic and the real, in which characters and settings keep shape-shifting. The quest has to be started again and again and is never completed. It goes on in a magical landscape which seems to be an allegory for a journey into the inner self: "The way leads inwards, always inwards." It played a vital part in the long Romantic literary tradition of quests for the Holy Grail, magical journeys, dreams, transformations beyond death and searchings for an unattainable love-object.

Novalis wrote it while he was reading, and reacting against, Goethe's *Wilhelm Meister's Apprenticeship*. The young Romantics disliked *Wilhelm Meister* for tracing a journey out of dreams into reality. *Heinrich von Ofterdingen* moves in the opposite direction. There are two parts to the story, *Erwartung*, "Expectation," and *Erfüllung*, "Fulfilment." In the first part, a stranger appears who tells Heinrich the story of the blue flower, as in a dream. Heinrich's father compares it with a similar dream he has had, but says that "dreams are bubbles." Heinrich journeys with his mother to Augsburg, sees a mysterious book with pictures of his own life in another epoch and falls in love with Mathilde, the daughter of the poet Klingsohr, a magus-figure, who tells him a story of the return to the Golden Age through poetry. In the unfinished second part (Novalis dictated notes for its conclusion on his deathbed), Mathilde has drowned, and another young woman leads him on his quest. He reaches a fairy world in the mountains, finds the blue flower, which has the face of Mathilde within it, picks it, loses her again, finds her again . . . So it goes on. In the notes, a journey through Europe and the Orient, scenes of war and the dawning of the Golden Age are projected. Heinrich must be initiated into the art of poetry to bring about the redemption of the world. But the blue flower remains out of reach. It can never be found, it can only be sought. It is the embodiment of that untranslatable German Romantic concept *"Sehnsucht,"* an emotion of yearning which cannot be defined or fulfilled, but which is something like nostalgia or homesickness. Asked where Heinrich is going, Novalis replied: *"Immer nach Hause."* ("Home. All the time.")[13]

The sentence at the start of *Heinrich von Ofterdingen*, which sets the whole magical story in motion, reads: *"Aber die blaue Blume sehn'ich mich zu erblicken. Sie liegt mir unaufhörlich in Sinn, und ich kann nichts anders dichten und denken."* Fitzgerald translates it thus: "But I long to see the Blue Flower. It lies incessantly at my heart, and I can imagine and think about nothing else."

What Fitzgerald does with the life story of Novalis is the very opposite of a straightforward biographical account. She did have copious notes on

Moravians, salt mines, Jena, Goethe, opium, transcendental idealism, pig cheeks, laundries, Romanticism and the like. And she kept rousing herself up in her notebooks to get on with the necessary homework for the book: "Brace up and get down to life of Novalis from Encycl; Check German lives of N"; "YOU ASS GET OUT COLERIDGE'S NOTEBOOK."[14] But all this information is dropped in like facts about people we know in our own lives: in bits and pieces, through glimpses and conversations. The novel has fifty-five tiny chapters, like short songs in a song cycle, each with a fragment of speech for a title ("I Can't Comprehend," "What Is the Meaning?"). Each is made up, unpredictably, of encounters, thought processes, dialogue, journals, letters, gossip, dramas, description, scattered with German words and the names of people and places. But the chapters also give off a feeling of space, of moments caught outside time. They are like scenes in a play or a dream, coming at us with as little explanation as possible. The book ends with a broken half sentence, and a dash. This is the strangest and boldest example of Fitzgerald's method.

Historical characters have appeared in her novels before, and she has been thinking all her writing life about the relation between biography, history and fiction. Now she merges the genres to create a new kind of book, which she referred to, with her usual Knoxian understatement, as "a novel *of sorts*."[15] Her remarks about not writing a biography of Novalis because her German wasn't good enough were a typical smokescreen. She had no intention of writing a biography—she frequently said, after *Charlotte Mew,* that she no longer had the energy for it. "I didn't try to do a biography . . . I felt the enormous quantity of material[,] letters bills notebooks diaries reports about salt-mines and so on[,] would make it more difficult to tell the human story . . . this sounds like laziness but I'm asking you to understand that it's not, Novalis himself wrote that 'novels arise out of the shortcomings of history' and I've put that as the epigraph to the blue flower."[16] Novalis's own methods converged with hers.

She manipulated her biographical data so as to make history feel present. As in all her late novels, she takes a loop back in time from the starting-point (late summer 1795, though we don't find out the date until later), catches up with her beginning and carries on from there. Though she deals with Novalis's life only up to 1797, a brief "afterword" summarises the later facts of his life (and of all their lives) and ends by telling us that the ring he gave Sophie is in the Weissenfels museum. So characters who have become dear to us are finally and sadly sent far away into the historical distance.

Wars, revolutions, campaigns, peace treaties and foreign news are dropped in as and when they affect the characters. As usual, she takes some fictional liberties. Jacob Dietmahler is an invention. Fritz thinks of the story of the blue flower at the time he meets Sophie, though in fact he did not start writing his novel until about two years after her death, while he was falling in love with someone else. But who is to say he had not thought of the story earlier? After all, Fitzgerald had been thinking about it for years before she began to write *The Blue Flower*.

The major intellectual figures in Novalis's life, and in German philosophy, are sketched in on the edges. As with her Cambridge dons, museum curators or BBC administrators, they provide another gleeful opportunity for the mockery of elite coteries. Fichte is a mad professor, barking out his philosophical dictums ("Gentlemen! Withdraw into yourselves!"), championing "German philosophy" above all else, and much parodied by his students: "Let your thought be the washbasket!" What is wrong with his system, Fritz suddenly understands, is that "there is no place in it for love." Schiller appears as a sick man being looked after by his students ("Great men," says one woman observer, "are the most difficult to nurse") and dictating to them from his bed: "To what end does man study universal history?" The voices of the Jena circle are dominated by the women, Dorothea and Caroline, gossipy, warmhearted and garrulous, ready to "*fichtisieren* and symphilosophise and *sympoetisieren* until the dawn breaks." Goethe—known to the Jena women as "His Ancient and Divine Majesty"—makes a solemn appearance late in the book, as a stately visitor to Sophie's sickbed, after which he pontificates on young women as the source of love and happiness for a poet, but shows not the least interest in her as an individual.

Novalis—or rather Fritz—is affectionately portrayed as eager, curious, serious, lovable, fixing people with "his brilliant half-wild gaze," utterly wrapped up in himself and, above all, very young. He never stops talking. He swerves between visionary flights and practical curiosity. He is addicted to ideas, inventions, new thoughts, conversation. He has to tell everyone what he is thinking. He feels things intensely and at once, as when he arrives at the Just household in Tennstedt, and says to them: "'When I came into your home, everything, the wine-decanter, the tea, the sugar, the chairs, the dark green tablecloth with its abundant fringe, everything was illuminated' . . . He had seen not their everyday, but their spiritual selves. He could not tell when these transfigurations would come to him. When the moment came it was as the whole world would be when body at last became subservient to soul."

It is always within these ordinary domestic settings that Fritz has his visions. Like a Russian or an English nineteenth-century novel, *The Blue Flower* moves between the everyday lives of neighbouring provincial families. The Hardenbergs are reclusive and regimented. The father is old-fashioned, snobbish and pious, bitter about his lost inheritance and his derelict country properties. He browbeats his socially incompetent second wife, and keeps his gifted children on strict, narrow paths. They carry on a seething, mutinous life among themselves, which Fritz is part involved with, part separate from. The novel supposes what it would be like to have a young genius in the family, before he has been recognised.

Fritz's main audience, after his student days, are women. Though its hero is a brilliant young man, *The Blue Flower* vividly imagines the lives of women, usually relegated to the margins in books about Novalis. Fritz's brothers—his devoted, argumentative rival Erasmus, and the angelic Bernhard—are compelling characters. But the sister, fifteen-year-old Sidonie, is magnetic, "burning like a flame" with restlessness and resentment, hating her mother's incarcerated life, running the household in her place out of "pity and painful anxiety." The mother's terror at encountering guests, her silent devotion to Fritz, her fear of her husband and her utter lack of prospects ("she was forty-five, and she did not see how she was going to get through the rest of her life") are painfully felt.

At the house of Coelestin Just, Fritz finds a completely different atmosphere, childless and rational. Here he meets the novel's admirable, intelligent, unfortunate heroine, the niece, Karoline Just—a real historical figure, to whom Novalis wrote confiding letters. Fitzgerald reinvents her. Karoline falls in love with Fritz, with the hopeless, unending, silent love which occurs in so many of Fitzgerald's novels, which seems to have a deep and utterly secret connection to Fitzgerald's own life, and of which she had observed that "the human species no longer found it biologically useful."[17] To Fritz, Karoline is a great friend. He tells her his thoughts, gives her a nickname, "Justen," says they are thesis and antithesis, "like two watches set to the same time," and reads her the story of the blue flower.

"Have you read this to anyone else, Hardenberg?"
"Never to anyone else. How could I? It is only just written . . ."
He added: "What is the meaning of the blue flower?"
Karoline saw that he was not going to answer this himself . . .
[She] felt chilled with anxiety. She would rather cut off one of her hands than disappoint him, as he sat looking at her, trusting

and intent, with his large light-brown eyes, impatient for a sign of comprehension.

When Fritz tells Karoline he has fallen in love with the twelve-year-old Sophie von Kühn, she does not give herself away, but feels as if her "body had been hollowed out." He notices nothing, and continues to confide in her. In order to conceal her feelings, she invents for herself a thwarted passion for a secret admirer. Fritz's sympathy is immediate; his lack of perception about her is as total. From then on, Justen must live with this imaginary fourth person, and with her silent feelings. The language for her story is low-key, but anguished: "In her mouth was something bitter, that tasted like the waters of death." She looks at her neighbours, who greet her cheerfully every day, and thinks: "Many of these people would get up in Tennstedt, and go to bed again there at the end of the day, perhaps in all eighteen thousand or so times." We discover, in the notes at the end of the book, that she has married a cousin whom she does not like very much, a year after Fritz's death.

"How could he? How could he?" Karoline bursts out to Fritz's brother Erasmus, burying her head in her hands, as they discuss Fritz's inexplicable love for Sophie. She is just a "very noisy, very young girl," stupid and empty-headed, Erasmus thinks—before he, too, starts to fall under her artless spell. Sophie's naive lovability is one of the novel's triumphs, and is created partly through the impact of her family, the Rockenthiens. This huge, jolly, extravagant household, full of children and stepchildren, visitors, hangers-on, charity cases, dogs, caged birds, music, food, drink, laughter and chatter, pours onto the page. Unlike the Hardenberg house at Weissenfels, at Schloss Grüningen the doors are open to all comers, the lights are blazing, the tables are groaning. When there are "only twenty-six people left at home," Herr von Rockenthien feels that the house is deserted. When Sophie falls ill, his jollity vanishes, "as though a giant hand had closed over him, squeezing him clear of hope." An attempt to introduce a tutor for Sophie into the sickroom founders in the family hubbub. "The Magister Kegel closed his book. 'After all, these people were born for joy,' he thought."

The only organised member of the Rockenthien ménage is Sophie's older married sister Friedericke Mandelsloh, known as "the Mandelsloh," the person who takes responsibility for her as her illness gets worse and takes her to Jena for her appalling operations. She is the most impressive of the novel's strong women. Married at sixteen to a soldier, she has developed a "brusque semi-military manner." Watching her bringing Sophie home from her ordeal, Erasmus thinks of her as "a warrior saint, a strong angel of the battlefield." She is a realist: "Time given to wishing for what can't be is not only spent, but wasted, and for all that we waste we shall be accountable." Her practicality sets up a female challenge to Fritz's philosophising. He tells her that women have beautiful souls and can reach perfection where men can't, "in spite of the fact that they particularise, we generalise." " 'What is wrong with particulars?' she replies. 'Someone has to look after them.' "

The Mandelsloh, though still only twenty-two, seems more grown-up than any of the others. Sophie is a child, born for joy, with "a child's brightness." Seen objectively, she is "a decent, good-hearted Saxon girl, potato-fed, with the bloom of thirteen summers." She likes treats, music, dancing, wine, entertainment, shopping, little dogs, kittens, her family, stories. She likes cabbage soup and smoked eel and a pipe of tobacco. She has "the remorseless perseverance of the truly pleasure-loving." She wants to please and be pleased. She shrieks with laughter all the time. She is not well educated, and can't spell Fritz's surname.

Part of the novel's comedy comes from the difference between them, as when he tries to talk to her about the transmigration of souls. " 'Should you like to be born again?' Sophie considered a little. 'Yes, if I could have fair hair.' " Her diary and her letters are childish and simple. "Today we were again alone & nothing much happened . . . Today Hardenburch went away & I had nothing to amuse me." Many of these entries are translated from Sophie's German diaries, but Fitzgerald's tone is so secure that we cannot tell what is genuine and what is invented.

Fritz is as baffled by her as she is by him. "I love something that I do not understand." In his visionary scheme of things, she is his Absolute, his Perfection, his Wisdom. He thinks she looks like a self-portrait of Raphael. But he also knows her limitations: "She likes listening to stories . . . She doesn't want to be embarrassed by my love . . . She is cold through and through." Her hedonism chills him; he is shocked that she has no belief in life after death. However, when Sophie starts to endure the handling of the medical experts, when her beautiful hair falls out and she gets weaker and weaker, she acquires a kind of dignity. She knows her own limits; she endures her pain with courage. Her silly laughter becomes a form of heroism. "She is not such a fool," says one observer. By the end she becomes deeply touching, and she moves everyone, even grumpy old von Hardenberg.

To Sophie and her sister, the story of the blue flower which Fritz tells them seems to be "a story for children"—and none the worse for that, Sophie thinks. *The Blue Flower* is partly a novel about childhood. Children and very young people are in and out of the book all the time. Not all of them are endearing. Sophie's terrible little brother George is built only for fighting, swearing, shouting and cramming his face with pastry. By contrast, the golden boy of the Hardenbergs, "the Bernhard," about nine years old, is an entrancing phenomenon. He is first seen running out of the house to the river, with his red cap on his hair "fair as wheat": " 'I will never come back,' the Bernhard called." Odd, precocious, funny, he sings like an angel and is indeed known to be an Angel—or a changeling. The Bernhard imbibes all Fritz's beliefs. He is a juvenile revolutionary who knows that "in a republic there would be no possessions." He understands the story of the blue flower very well. It was "a matter of recognising your own fate and greeting it as familiar when it came." What might the Bernhard have become? Another genius, probably. He drowns—we are told at the end—when still very young.

The person we see dying is Sophie, and the account of her operation (taken in part, Fitzgerald says in her author's note, from Fanny Burney's account of her mastectomy without anaesthetic) is done quietly, concisely and with horrifying effect. The brilliant stroke is to tell us what is being done to her, not by describing it in any detail, but through the vicarious interest of the Jena landlady, the kind of person who is all too eager to be involved with illness and suffering, and through the formal dialogue between the male surgeon and his colleague.

> "Esteemed colleague, am I to make the incision? Is that what you would advise?"
>
> "Yes, Herr Professor, I advise it."
>
> "You would make two incisions, or one only?"
>
> "Two, Herr Professor."
>
> "So?"
>
> "So."
>
> Frau Winkler, waiting below on the bottom stair, had been able to hear nothing, but now her patience was rewarded.

Body and spirit are one, says Novalis. The life of the body, at its most excruciating in the accounts of Sophie's suffering, is vividly present to us. Fritz's visionary dreams are always running alongside the salt-mining business. Talking to Karoline, he switches between talking about nature's universal laws and "the boiling-points for cooking-salt and salt fertilisers." To him, all things are linked. He sees himself as an inventor, an engineer and a natural scientist, as well as a philosopher; at one point he has a good idea for inventing an automatic copying machine. Details about the tax office follow straight on from the story of the blue flower. Debunking romantic fervour with mundane interventions is an old strategy. Byron does it in *Don Juan,* Flaubert does it in *Madame Bovary*—two authors Fitzgerald admires. In her rough, drunken scene of student life (rather like miniatures of the student scenes in Flaubert's *L'Education sentimentale*), Fritz is involved in a duel in which one of the boys fighting has two fingers sliced off. Jacob Dietmahler, the medical student, tells Fritz to put them in his mouth to keep them warm, so he can sew them on again. "Fritz was not likely to forget" this physical sensation. (Fitzgerald was haunted, from childhood, by the boy she encountered on a skating rink who had had his finger sliced off, and asked her to help him look for it.) Physical "particulars" give the novel its life and its colour: the silent lives of horses, the smells of autumn city streets, a pig fair ("the ears, snout and strips of fat from the pig's neck boiled with peppermint schnaps"), how people talk when they are moving a piano ("Not up the front steps, you triple fool!— A little to the right.—It would be easier if we could take off the legs"). Karoline listens to Fritz after her day's housework: "sausage-making, beating flax for the winter spinning, killing the geese . . . for their third and last crop of down." Christmas comes to Weissenfels, and the local poor come to the house for charity, including "the girls with unwanted pregnancies, who could not afford the services of the Angel-maker, the back-street abortionist."

> Inside the library the myriad fiery shining points of light threw vast shadows of the fir branches onto the high walls and even across the ceiling. In the warmth the room breathed even more deeply, more resinously, more greenly. On the tables the light sparkled across gold-painted walnuts, birds in cages, dormice in their nests, dolls made of white bread twisted into shapes, hymnbooks, Fritz's needle-cases and little bottles of *Kölnischwasser,* Sidonie's embroidery, oddments made out of willow and birch, pocket-knives, scissors, pipes, wooden spoons with curious handles which made them almost unusable, religious prints mounted on brilliant sheets of tin.

Summer supper is served at Grüningen:

The servants had already brought in the soups, one made of
beer, sugar and eggs, one of rose-hips and onions, one of bread
and cabbage-water, one of cows' udders flavoured with nutmeg.
There was dough mixed with beech-nut oil, pickled herrings and
goose with treacle sauce, hard-boiled eggs, numerous dumplings.
It is dangerous—on this, at least, all Germany's physicians were
agreed—not to keep the stomach full at all times.
        Good appetite!

So the human lives of late-eighteenth-century Germany, in the prov-
inces, the small towns, the villages, are thickly, densely, realised, all within
these brief scenes. Every minor character, as always in Fitzgerald, has a
whole life furled inside them, even if only just glimpsed—the bookshop
owner who wants Fritz to be a poet, the bossy, know-all Hardenberg uncle,
poor Dietmahler, suffering from injured pride when Sidonie forgets his
name, a disgraced salt-mine inspector, prisoners working and begging on
the road, the Hardenbergs' pious servant. Abortionists, farmers, tax collectors and pig traders coexist with romantic philosophers.
    Fritz walks one misty evening in a graveyard where there are old spades
and dinner baskets lying about, weeds and stinging insects from the dung-
heaps. Suddenly through the mist he sees, as in a Romantic painting, the
figure of a pale young man, "as white, still and speechless as a memorial."
It is as strange a moment as the birch-tree scene in *The Beginning of Spring*.
Perhaps it is his own future tomb, or a spirit, we don't know. "The sight
was consoling to Fritz, who knew that the young man, although living, was
not human, but also that at the moment there was no boundary between
them."
    Even in the most homely of scenes, a note of longing or strangeness can
creep in, as when the family returns to one of their old, dilapidated country
houses, where there is "a diffused sense, in that misty valley, of relaxation,
of perpetual forgiveness, of coming home after having done one's best."
Or when a portrait painter, whom Fritz has hired, with unsatisfactory
results, to paint Sophie, tells him (as the stranger tells the farm boy in
Schreiner's *Story of an African Farm*) that every life, every organism, has
something to voice, even though it can't always be heard: "In every created thing . . . there is an attempt to communicate, even among the totally
silent. There is a question being asked, a different question for every entity,

which for the most part will never be put into words, even by those who can speak. It is asked incessantly, most of the time however hardly noticeably, even faintly, like a church bell heard across meadows and enclosures."

Music is of the utmost importance in the novel—as it was to Novalis. It is the passageway between the real and the dream worlds. Everyone sings, tunes are always being played or remembered, quotations from songs are scattered all through. When Sophie is lying ill in Jena, the students serenade her from the street. At the family party when Fritz's "Intended" arrives at Weissenfels, Anton, the most musical of the Hardenberg children, plays for the company. He wants to play a revolutionary song by Reichard, but his mother, in an anguish of anxiety, tells him to play "some religious music . . . *Wie sie so sanft ruhn*." (The phrase, not translated, is the first line of a hymn called "The Dead": "How they so softly rest / All they the holy ones / Unto whose dwelling place / Now doth my soul draw near.")[18] Then he plays a setting of Zinzendorf's hymns for the Moravian Brethren, and then something no one can identify: "And the, what was the piece that he played after that?—that very beautiful piece, I did not know it, could Anton have improvised it himself?" Lastly he plays Bach's *Capriccio on the Departure of His Most Beloved Brother,* and everyone sighs deeply. Her re-creation of the music and its audience is rather like Browning's *A Toccata of Galuppi's,* imagining the long-dead Venetian audience through the music of the time. Fitzgerald liked that poem, and annotated it in her copy: "Browning felt past cultures were best understood through music."

The tune Anton plays, which no one can quite name, is like the story of the blue flower. It is something you seem always to be on the edge of remembering or identifying. And it runs through the novel like a recurrent tune. This is its first appearance:

His father and mother were already in bed and asleep, the clock on the wall ticked with a monotonous beat, the wind whistled outside the rattling window-pane. From time to time the room grew brighter when the moonlight shone in. The young man lay restlessly on his bed and remembered the stranger and his stories. "It was not the thought of the treasure which stirred up such unspeakable longings in me," he said to himself. "I have no craving to be rich, but I long to see the blue flower. It lies incessantly at my heart, and I can imagine and think about nothing else. Never did I feel like this before. It is as if until now I had been dreaming, or as if sleep had carried me into another world. For in the world I used to live in, who would have troubled himself about flowers? Such a wild passion for a flower was never heard of there. But where could this stranger have come from? None of us had ever seen such a man before. And yet I don't know how it was that I alone was truly caught and held by what he told us. Everyone else heard what I did, yet none of them paid him serious attention.

The story recurs, sometimes in the same words, sometimes in different guises. Each time, the flower seems to have a different meaning. It means death, or mortality, or love, or immortality, or a universal language, or fate. Fritz himself does not know what it means.

"Please, Hardenberg, what is the name of the flower?" asked Sophie.

"He knew once," said Fritz. "He was told the name, but he has forgotten it. He would give his life to remember it."

. . .

"Certainly I should like to know what is going to happen," she said doubtfully.

He said, "If a story begins with finding, it must end with searching."

~

She made up that quotation, though it sounds just like Novalis, mysterious and suggestive. The blue flower, Fitzgerald explained in the talks she gave about the novel, means what you think it means. It is "what you think yourself, [it has] what significance you think it has. I don't only mean for Novalis but surely for everyone and even if there's no possibility of reaching it you must never give up."[19] Fitzgerald did not identify with Novalis. She was not a Romantic or a symbolist or an optimist. Like all the utopian characters in her novels, he is a little absurd. Nevertheless, his idea that "death is only a change in condition" strongly appealed to her. "What are your own feelings about this?" a sympathetic interviewer asked her, after *The Blue Flower* was published. There was a long pause. "I do believe it," she replied. "Was it easy to believe?" "I don't think you can believe by trying or learning to believe. It doesn't come that way. Nor can you prove it to anyone, I should think, because it's unobservable. I mean there's nothing that you can do about it. You either believe or you don't."[20]

The author of *The Blue Flower* is an imaginative genius writing about what "genius" is. She is an old person keeping her imagination fresh by writing about youth. And she is, also, an old person thinking about the end of life and the prospect of death. Speaking about *The Blue Flower,* and about her work as a whole, she asks whether she wants the novel to be a form of consolation.[21] Not if "consolation means something second best, to keep you quiet," as in "consolation prize." But yes, she does want it, "if consolation is to be made welcome in a different world, where the laws of time are suspended, and yet which is still my own."

CHAPTER EIGHTEEN

Last Words

As a biographer you're never satisfied. There can't be any last word on another person's life, except rest in peace.[1]

Penelope told Stuart Proffitt in April 1993 that she was writing something, but was "not sure if it's a novel or not." She sent him *The Blue Flower* in August 1994, when she got back from her family holiday in Spain. It took him nearly two months to respond, which annoyed her. "At last!" she annotated his letter of 27 October. But the letter was ecstatic. "I hardly know what to say about it," he wrote, "except that there came a moment some time after midnight last night when I couldn't stop but just had to continue, and finished with tears all over my cheeks. . . . It is so wonderfully funny and wise and understanding, as always; and there is the swell throughout of perpetual forgiveness, as you put it at one point, for all human beings."[2] Production went smoothly. He liked her title (for once), and she liked their jacket design, a rich, romantic and Pre-Raphaelite-looking portrait of a dark-haired young girl in profile in a blue dress, from a painting by Fernand Khnopff, against a collage of Novalis's letters.

HarperCollins published it in September 1995. The response to what she had been describing as a "not-quite-novel" or "a novel of sorts" was very strong.[3] Frank Kermode, among many enthusiastic reviewers, was particularly eloquent: "She has the gift of knowing, of seeming to know, everything necessary, and as it were knowing it from the inside . . . It is hard to see how the hopes and defeats of Romanticism, or the relation between inspiration and common life . . . could be more deftly rendered than they are in this admirable novel."[4] Philip Hensher wrote a celebratory piece on her work, and she thanked him in a letter, saying that she had written her novels and watched them disappear, that nothing seemed to last, but that she was grateful and surprised to have her work as a whole so well considered.[5] Ecstatic fan letters came in from other writers, including Carol Shields, Candia McWilliam and Alberto Manguel. McWilliam said that the novel had "an unbearable noticing fleetness of beauty at such a high pitch . . . it is also so funny . . . I do believe you are like no other writer . . . and I always use the word of you [I] really keep pretty much clear for Henry James, Mozart and other acts of God—ie genius."[6] Manguel told her he was "overwhelmed by the exquisite beauty of the book. Your reviewers, again and again, seem to ask 'How does she do it?' How indeed?" He asked to use a line of it as an epigram for his next book. And he told her that Borges had asked for Novalis's *Heinrich von Ofterdingen* to be read to him on his deathbed.

It was not their first exchange as fellow readers. Among Fitzgerald's books is Max Beerbohm's 1943 pamphlet-essay on Lytton Strachey. It is dedicated: "Daddy, Love from Mops, Christmas 1943." A pencil scrawl above, perhaps a bookseller's, notes: "To E.V. Knox from his daughter Penelope Fitzgerald." Tucked into the pamphlet is a postcard, dated 6 July 1998: "Dear Penelope Fitzgerald, Among the books chance puts in our hands are a few that were never meant for us: this one, of course, was meant to come back to you, and it gives me great pleasure to be able to redirect it. With all best wishes, Alberto Manguel." She thanked him for this gift at once: "I can't tell you how pleased I was . . . I remember giving it to my father. He came up to London as a young man before the first world war . . . and one of his ambitions was to meet the great Max Beerbohm." It was one of many reminders and revisitings of the distant past which coloured the last years of her life. A few months after that exchange, in reply to Manguel's praise of *The Blue Flower,* she wrote congratulating him on *his* book, *A History of Reading:* "At the end of your fine book you say that 'The history of reading has no end.' I treasure these words and can only pray that they're true."[7]

The Booker judges for 1995 (George Walden, Peter Kemp, Ruth Rendell, Kate Kellaway and Adam Mars-Jones) ignored *The Blue Flower*. From a short-list of Justin Cartwright, Salman Rushdie, Tim Winton and Barry Unsworth, they gave their prize to Pat Barker's *The Ghost Road*. But at the end of the year, twenty-five critics chose *The Blue Flower* as their Book of the Year. And in America, at the age of eighty, Fitzgerald now became a famous writer. Up till then, her publishing career there had been shaky. There had been years of respectful reviews and low sales. Henry Holt had published *The Beginning of Spring* and Nan Talese *The Gate of Angels* at Doubleday, but neither title sold more than 3,000 copies in hardback. Because of that, Talese turned down *The Blue Flower*. But Chris Carduff, who had published *Charlotte Mew* with Addison-Wesley in 1987, had now moved to Houghton Mifflin, and was starting a new paperback imprint there, Mariner Books. Talese relinquished the rights and Carduff made *The Blue Flower* his first fiction title in the new list. Penelope wished him luck with the new venture, quoting Thomas Hood's lines: "The stars are with the voyager wherever he may sail."[8]

In April 1997, Carduff shrewdly published *The Blue Flower* as a paperback original, talked it up, made sure of big coverage by alerting all those who had ever shown an interest in her work and helped to transform her reputation in the States. He followed this six months later with a Mariner paperback reissue of *The Bookshop*—a great success, and a particularly popular choice for the many reading groups springing up all over the country—and then with a uniform paperback edition of all the novels. *Offshore, The Gate of Angels, Innocence* and *The Beginning of Spring* came out in 1997; *At Freddie's, Human Voices* and *The Golden Child,* in 1998. Stuart Proffitt negotiated a $10,000 advance for each book, of which she got 85 per cent, which, at 1997 exchange rates, meant a lump sum of about £20,000.[9] Sales did well for a time; and then tailed off. Carduff was forced out of Houghton Mifflin by new management, went to Counterpoint Press, and published new editions there of *Charlotte Mew* and *The Knox Brothers.* That was the last book of Fitzgerald's published in her lifetime, and, in financial terms, it marked the trajectory of writing life: Macmillan had paid her £1,000 for it in 1975; Counterpoint paid her $10,000 for it in 2000.

She was extremely grateful to Chris Carduff, who called his cat Charlotte Mew, and whom she thought of as a high-minded character, vulnerable in the jungle of American publishing. She wrote to him often and affectionately: "Thank you so much for all you did for me, Chris, you can be sure I never look at one of my books without thinking about you." They only met once, when he went to lunch with her at Bishops Road in February 2000, sitting by the garden window with a green tablecloth on the table. They talked about their families, self-publishing, Bloomsbury versus the Georgians. She made him chicken and rice and they drank a lot of white wine. There was olive bread: "If you don't like the olives you can pick them out," she said. He was entranced and baffled by her, as he had been from the first: "When our correspondence began, she was a charming mystery to me. With each passing year . . . and each new book, the charm and the mystery only deepened."[10]

She had cause to be grateful to him. The publication of *The Blue Flower* in America was a "perfect storm." The novel caught fire; it became, that year, the book everyone wanted to read. And that, as Carduff pointed out, was not just because it was a work of genius, it was also because it was a paperback selling for "twelve bucks," not a $24.95 hardback. The *New York Times* gave it a front-page review by Michael Hofmann, the poet and translator of German literature, who called it "a quite astonishing book, a masterpiece," a "luminous and authentic . . . piece of imaginative writing about a writer . . . a wholly convincing account of that very difficult subject, genius." (He was not the only German expert who admired it. Gerhard Schulz, Novalis's leading scholar, wrote to tell her it was marvellous.) *The Times* made it an "editor's choice," calling it "an interrogation of life," its economy "miraculous," its language "an enchantment."[11] Richard Holmes, writing at length in the *New York Review of Books*, said it was "the book that Fitzgerald was born to write," whose "swift and constant play of extremities and incongruities, of light and dark, love and misunderstanding, imagination and foolishness, idealism and gross physicality, gives [it] its distinctive power and narrative conviction."[12] She began to be called "the finest British writer alive."[13]

In March 1998, the judges of the National Book Critics Circle award gave *The Blue Flower* the prize in the fiction category for books published in 1997. The prize, judged by a large, rotating panel of twenty-four readers, had just been opened up to non-U.S. writers. *The Blue Flower* was up against Don DeLillo's *Underworld,* Philip Roth's *American Pastoral* and Charles Frazier's *Cold Mountain.* Not surprisingly, the judges were extremely divided. The writer and translator James Marcus, one of *The Blue Flower*'s passionate advocates on the panel, defended the choice at the time and years later. He was offended by suggestions that "we threw some old bag the prize because we were rent asunder by Phil and Don . . . [*The Blue Flower* is] a masterpiece, and deserved the prize as richly as any novel in the organization's history." Accepting on her behalf, Chris Carduff said she had considered getting the prize "improbable." Headlines appeared reading "British Author Beats Heavyweights for Book Award." With interviewers, she played her usual game: "I was so unprepared to win the award that I hadn't even planned a celebration. I certainly shan't do any ironing today." To Carduff, she wrote drily: "I see that a lot of people felt that I shouldn't have been awarded this prize." She played it down to her friends, telling Willie Conder that she was having "a mild success" in America. Nevertheless, it transformed her bank balance and her reputation. In 1992–94 her royalty statement from HarperCollins, neatly recorded in her account book, averaged £3,000. In 1999 and 2000 the royalties from Houghton Mifflin, paid to her via HarperCollins, were edging up towards £30,000, a year and her HarperCollins royalties were about £18,000. Janet Silver, editor-in-chief at Houghton Mifflin, wrote to her: "In terms of American commercialism, you are now officially a 'brand' name." Penelope told Willie: "The Blue Flower sold so well that I actually have a bit of money and now don't feel impelled to write anything at all."[14]

In Britain, the Flamingo paperbacks on the backlist were selling steadily even before the success of *The Blue Flower. The Beginning of Spring,* for instance, the title which did best, published in Flamingo paperback in 1989, had sold 37,500 copies by 1996.[15] *The Blue Flower* was short-listed for the Irish Times International Fiction prize. And she was awarded two prizes for her lifetime's work. In June 1996 she was given the £10,000 Heywood Hill Literary Prize, named after a venerable London bookshop in Curzon Street, launched by the bookshop's owner John Saumarez Smith and its patron, the Duke of Devonshire, and judged by Saumarez-Smith, Victoria Glendinning and Mark Amory. The prize had been set up in 1994 to honour "bookmanship" and "a life-time's contribution to the enjoyment of books," in reaction to James Kelman's winning the Booker Prize for his tough Glasgow novel. It was known by some as the "toffs' prize." Really, she told Mary Lago, it was "fairy gold . . . because I'd never heard of it, nor I think had anyone else." It was awarded by the Duke at Chatsworth House. Penelope, who was not feeling well, went up on the train with Karen Duffy and her new Flamingo editor, Mandy Kirkby, and told them she couldn't have managed it without them. And, she told Oliver Knox, "everyone kept telling me what a touching few words P[atrick] O'Brian had said last year, and you know how discouraging <u>that</u> is." But the great house was resplendent "in all its summer glory," she was shown round the library by the "sensitive and suffering" librarian, Noel Annan made a kind speech, Richard and Mary Ollard showed up, and to her delight there were brass bands and the local mayors wearing their chains.[16]

In March 1999, at the PEN International Writers' Day, with Maria as always in attendance for support, she was given the Golden PEN Award "for my (alleged) services to literature." This was not such a joyous occasion. The gold pen was "only gold-plated, I fear"; the Café Royal, where the ceremony took place, was looking "tarnished and worn-out"; and the lunch was horrible, "with <u>hard</u> roast chicken which you could scarcely bite into." All the same, she was pleased.[17]

These accolades clustered around her eightieth birthday, which she celebrated, twice, in 1996. The two parties cost her £3,000. (Her other great expenditure was a Mont Blanc pen.) A great deal of thought went into the two parties. The first, larger event, was held at Bishops Road on Saturday, 7 September, at 12:30 for about fifty people. "PARTY TIME!" she wrote in her diary. Though hosted by Maria and John, this was not a family gathering, so the Dooleys were not invited, and were a little put out. It was meant as an expression of gratitude to all her literary friends and contacts. Maura Dooley and her partner, Dave Hunter, were there, but because of their work at Arvon, not as in-laws. Her publishers all came—Mandy, Karen, Philip Gwyn Jones (Stuart's eventual successor at Collins) and Stuart, who would lovingly remember a happy sunny day, with people drifting out into the garden. Mary Bennett from long-ago Oxford, Penelope Lively, the Highgate Institute people (Anne Riddell, Hilary Laurie), Josephine Pullein-Thompson from PEN, people from the Royal Society of Literature and the William Morris Society, her old publisher Raleigh Trevelyan, and Francis King and his partner were among the guests. She insisted there should be hot soup, and chairs for everyone to sit on, given the general age of the party. Maria observed that she was unfussed, organised and enjoying herself greatly.

The other birthday celebration was a large family party, held at Café Rouge in Highgate, next door to the Institute on Saturday, 28 December. Here she was not Penelope Fitzgerald, she was Mops, Ma or Granny. There were lots of presents, and everyone came: Valpy and Angelines with Valpy Gregory (the oldest grandchild, now twenty-three, and soon to be married), Laurence and Camilo; Terence and Tina with Luke (now thirteen), Paschal and Jemima; Maria and John with John's parents and with Thomas (twelve), Sophie (eight) and Alfred (at four, the youngest grandchild there). Rawle's widow, Helen, came with her children, William Knox's first wife with their two children, and Belinda with her husband, Robert Hunt. Belinda thought her famous aunt, at her birthday party, seemed "demure" and contented. Oliver Knox came without Patty or his children, and was garrulous and offhand. Mary Knox, now in a home and barely recognising anyone, was too ill to come. Valpy made a proud and affectionate speech, and they all went back to Bishops Road for tea.

She kept a keen eye on family life, whether that was Maria giving her inaugural professorial lecture at University College London in May 1996 (on "Painful Beginnings: Studies in Foetal and Infant Sensation"), or Maria and John acquiring and doing up a holiday cottage in Wales, or the wedding of Valpy's oldest son to Lidia in Córdoba in 1999 (she wasn't well enough to go, but noted drily that Lidia and Angelines had developed "an old-fashioned Spanish mother-and-daughter-in-law relationship"), or

Luke Dooley taking his GCSEs, or her nephew William Knox getting married again at a St. Albans registry office. She did go to that, with Belinda, who travelled back with her on a hot day from St. Albans to London on the Thameslink train, and then left her outside a pub near the station to go and find her a taxi. As she came back in the cab, she saw her aunt, standing quietly and very still, patiently waiting and absorbed in her own thoughts, a small, inconspicuous old lady on a London street, and thought to herself: "If you but knew what's in her head!"[18]

There were funerals and memorial services, as well as marriages and remarriages. Joan Mathew, her old landlady in St. John's Wood, died. Her friend J. L. Carr had died in 1994. Edward Blishen, whom she had taught with at Arvon, died in 1996, and she went to the memorial service in East Finchley. Meanwhile, she "GOT ON WITH IT" (as she urged herself in her appointment diary): got on with judging prizes, going to PEN meetings, reviewing books, doing interviews, travelling to conferences and festivals, speaking on the radio, writing letters, accepting invitations.

Philip Hensher encountered her at the unveiling of A. S. Byatt's portrait by Patrick Heron at the National Portrait Gallery in 1998. "She was dressed without any concession to the party," he recalled, "in a raincoat and carrying two plastic bags. She reminded me instantly, as she reminded many people, of the White Queen in Alice. I asked her if she was writing another novel, and I had her full, not unkind, but wary assessment. She said she was not, and it would not come. I said that it would surely come with patience. She gave me that strong, warning look, and I was warned. She seemed to have complete indifference to her surroundings, and to be not exactly slow, but weighted down; she also gave the very strong impression of having come out for a particular purpose, and, having fulfilled it, would go home. I also thought that her impatience was very near the surface—not easily voiced, but easily perceptible."[19] A young Oxford academic at a London wedding party found herself on the receiving end of that impatience. Penelope, placed next to her, at once began to berate her about "literary theory." How could literature be understood by students if all they were taught was "literary theory"? Attempts by the young woman to say that she herself was much keener on literature than on theory were overridden. At last, trying to change the subject, she said: "Are you working on a new novel now?" And was met with a grim look, and silence.

In 1997, she went to York University for a panel called "Writers at Work," with Helen Dunmore, Edmund White and Julian Barnes, where she talked about *The Blue Flower*. Julian Barnes, a great admirer of her work, described her as comporting herself as "some harmless jam-making grandmother who scarcely knew her way in the world." He gave an account of their journey back together from York, a journey for which he had been offered a first-class ticket in lieu of a speaking fee, while she had agreed to a fee and a standard-class ticket. Of course he travelled with her.

> At King's Cross I suggested that we share a cab, since we both lived in the same part of north London. Oh no, she replied, she would take the Underground—after all, she had been given this splendid free travel-pass by the Mayor of London (she made it sound like a personal gift, rather than something every pensioner got). Assuming she must be feeling the day even longer than I did, I pressed again for the taxi option, but she was quietly obstinate, and came up with the clinching argument: she had to pick up a pint of milk on the way from the Underground station, and if she went home by cab it would mean having to go out again later. I ploddingly speculated that we could very easily stop the taxi outside the shop and have it wait while she bought her milk. "I hadn't thought of that," she said. But no, I still hadn't convinced her: she had decided to take the Underground and that was that. So I waited beside her on the concourse while she looked for her free pass in the tumult of her carrier bag. It must be there, surely, but no, after much dredging, it didn't seem to be findable. I was by this point feeling—and perhaps exhibiting—a certain impatience, so I marched us to the ticket machine, bought our tickets, and squired her down the escalator to the Northern Line. As we waited for the train, she turned to me with an expression of gentle concern. "Oh dear," she said, "I do seem to have involved you in some low forms of transport."[20]

In 1997, she was made an Honorary Fellow of her, and her mother's, old college, Somerville, and joined the Council of the Royal Society of Literature. John Mortimer was chairing the council, and the meetings, at the shabby-grand premises at Hyde Park Gardens, were often hilarious and eccentric. Maggie Fergusson, the RSL's administrator, who became friendly with Penelope, remembered her as silent but "watchful," moving in on the discussion sideways, "in her gentle slightly warbly voice, with views that could be quite surprising and strong. She wasn't afraid to upset the apple cart." When Maggie had her first child, Penelope sent her a baby book, suggesting that she keep a diary of Flora's early days.[21]

Just at a time when most writers would want to be settled, the apple cart was being seriously upset at her publishing house. Early in 1998, Rupert Murdoch, the proprietor of HarperCollins, blocked the publication of Chris Patten's book on the Chinese takeover of Hong Kong. Murdoch thought that the book, which was critical of Chinese communism, would adversely affect his growing satellite-television interests in China. He put pressure on the managers and editors. They were to tell Michael Sissons, Patten's agent, that the book was being turned down because it was substandard and "boring." Stuart Proffitt, who by then had been at the firm for fifteen years and risen to be in charge of the trade division, was Chris Patten's editor, and had already written to tell him how good he thought the first section of the book was. He refused to lie, was sacked, published his account of events and proceeded to sue for constructive dismissal. Patten published his book in the States and with Macmillan in England, sued for breach of contract, and got an apology from Murdoch and a financial settlement.

Many HarperCollins authors voiced their support for Proffitt. Fitzgerald was one of these. The *Daily Telegraph,* which was running the story throughout February and March 1998 on its front pages (while *The Times* was playing it down), headed its 28 February story "Authors in Revolt over Murdoch." Doris Lessing said she was "extremely angry." Alan Bullock said it was "monstrous." Patrick O'Brian said he would follow Stuart Proffitt wherever he went. Fitzgerald was quoted as saying: "One is appalled to think that someone can buy a publisher like a soap factory and then scrap the part they don't want. Evidently this is his idea of the relationship between the proprietor and the publishing firm—that it is there to suit his ends." In private, to Willie Conder, she lamented, and lucidly summed up, the upheaval. "My dearly-loved English publisher, Stuart, has left Harper-Collins on a point of principle . . . I feel I must leave HarperCollins and go wherever he goes. What a nuisance, I don't like these upsets, I like everything to go on just the same from day to day. My cup of tea at 7:30, my little walk to the shop to get the *Evening Standard*—it's dreadful, really, but Willie, we're survivors, so we might as well revel in it."[22]

Stuart started a new job at Penguin in 1998. He took her out to lunch to ask her if she would go with him. She replied: "Of course I will—but I haven't written a book." It was a painful dilemma for her. Before his ousting, he had made a good contract for her for an "Untitled Novel," paying her a big advance of £35,000, after the success of *The Blue Flower.* But she could not find an idea for a new book, and she was not well. She did, however, have some short stories, and was writing more. Her new editors at HarperCollins, Mandy Kirkby and Philip Gwyn Jones, wanted to help her. Like almost all her publishers, they became her friends and protectors. Mandy, who worked with her on *The Blue Flower* and on her stories, felt that Penelope did not fit at all with the harsh new corporate tone of HarperCollins: "You couldn't jazz her up." She thought that the firm undervalued, and underpaid, her. She recognised the strong opinions under the gentle manner, her clear sense of her own worth, her refusal ever to make a fuss: you had to work out what she wanted from what she *didn't* say. Both Mandy and Philip could see that Penelope felt badly about not having another novel to offer. They transferred the advance to a volume of short stories. These would not be published until after her death, in the Flamingo paperback imprint of the firm, and by Houghton Mifflin in America. She never went to Penguin, and HarperCollins remains her British publisher to this day. [23]

The stories in *The Means of Escape* date from the 1970s to the late 1990s. (She would have preferred the volume title to be "Not Shown," but her American editor, Janet Silver, "steam-rollered" her.)[24] They included her first publication, "The Axe," the early undated story which came out of her Mexican journey, "Our Lives Are Only Lent to Us," two 1980s stories ("The Prescription" and "The Likeness") linked to her unwritten Istanbul novel, "The Iron Bridge," the three stories published in the early 1990s while she was working on *The Blue Flower,* and three very late stories.

"Not Shown," first published in 1993, is a grotesque black comedy. An obscure caretaker with something "not quite right about him"—one of her lonely "exterminatees"—is put in charge, by the bossy Lady P, of showing visitors round an Arts and Crafts farmhouse built by Philip Webb (based on Standen, in West Sussex, a house she loved). But his quiet niche is stampeded into by the aggressive and vulgar Mrs. Horrabin, who seems to know all about his past, and wants to take his job, his body and his peace of mind. There is no plot to speak of, but there is an emotion, familiar to readers of Fitzgerald:

> She belonged to the tribe of torturers. Why pretend they don't exist?
> "You have it in mind," he said, "to take away my last chance."

The other two stories of the early 1990s are like elliptical, haunting short novels. Both are set in the nineteenth century, and are concerned with the lives of obscure, ordinary colonists trying to survive far from home. In both she creates her powerful sense of a large history condensed into a small space. "The Means of Escape" is set in 1850s Hobart: clearly she had paid close attention to Tasmania in her two weeks there in 1991. The Rector's daughter, Alice, plays the "seraphine" in St. George's Church (an angelic link to *The Gate of Angels,* written just before this story). She is ambushed one evening in the darkening church by an escaped convict from Port Arthur. He is wearing a sack with eyeholes over his head "like a butchered animal," and gives off a "rancid stench." He calls himself Savage, but turns out to be an educated man. The sudden encounter, with its threat of violence, like the beginning of *Great Expectations,* is an adventure for Alice. But her plan to help the convict escape to England, and to join him there, is sabotaged by the rectory's silent housekeeper, Mrs. Watson, a ticket-of-leave woman with an appalling past, who is passionately devoted to Alice but takes her chance away from her. The story ends (as in the coda to *The Blue Flower*) with a document in the National Library of Tasmania, sending the characters away from us into distant history. But documents do not explain the obscurity of people's lives. Mrs. Watson's "motives for doing what she did . . . were never set down, and can only be guessed at."

"At Hiruharama" has a more remote setting, a tiny homestead on the North Island of New Zealand. She heard the story from a New Zealander on her trip to the Holy Land, while they were both being baptised in the River Jordan.[25] It concerns the grandparents of a Mr. Tanner, and of the preparations made by the grandfather, living in remote isolation, when his wife becomes pregnant. The story seems to be told by someone talking to us and interrupting themselves: "But wait a minute, surely he couldn't read or write?" We are taken in, through this voice, to these long-vanished lives. We hear Tanner's wife, from the room next door, in childbirth—sounds that Tanner has never heard before, "not in a shipwreck—and he had been in a wreck—and not in a slaughterhouse." Meanwhile, the nearest neighbour, the bachelor Mr. Brinkman, who has come eight miles for his half-yearly visit, is sitting smoking his pipe, hoping to get some dinner eventually. He is pleased when twin girls are born. "Two more women born into the world! It must have seemed to him that if this sort of thing went on there should be a good chance, in the end, for him to acquire one for himself." But Tanner has nearly thrown the second girl baby out into the trash, thinking it was the afterbirth.

Such brutal facts coexist with tender small details. Tanner has bought a pair of racing pigeons so as to send them back as messengers to the nearest town, Awanui, when the doctor is needed. He takes them home, "still shifting about and conferring in their wicker basket," and when the time comes for their life-or-death mission, releases them into the air. "How to toss a pigeon he had no idea. He opened the basket, and before he could think what to do next they were out and up into the blue. He watched in terror as after reaching a certain height they began turning round in tight circles as though puzzled or lost. Then, apparently sighting something on the horizon that they knew, they set off strongly towards Awanui."

The last three stories she wrote date from the late 1990s. "Beehernz" was first published in *BBC Music Magazine* in October 1997. "Desideratus" came out in the 1997 volume of the British Council's *New Writing*. "The Red-Haired Girl" was published in the *TLS* in 1998, her last fictional publication in her lifetime. All three late stories are about different kinds of silence and obscurity. A conundrum, something unsaid, is at the heart of most of the stories in *The Means of Escape*, but especially these three.

"The Red-Haired Girl" grew out of a summer holiday with the Dooleys on the Cherbourg peninsula in 1991, her memory of Charlotte Mew watching the "fisher-folk" in Dieppe and her long-ago work on the young artists in Rossetti's studio. A group of young English artists, studying in Paris with the reactionary old Bonvin, go to paint in Brittany. Bonvin believes in studio work, but these are the next generation who want to paint from nature in "plein air." Hackett writes home to his "Intended" about his improvised quarters in the hotel in "Palourde" (it's the word for a Brittany clam), and his search for a young female model. All this is done lightly, affectionately, absurdly. A model turns up, in the substantial shape of the redheaded girl with "a blank expression." Her name is Annik, but he renames her Anny, tells her to come to be painted at a specific time (but she has no watch) and to wear a red shawl. He knows nothing about her harsh, dull life in the fishing village. She bursts out at him: "You don't know what I want, and you don't know what I feel."

Old Bonvin arrives, and lectures them about their ridiculous attempts to paint from nature. They should paint in the studio, paint "the experiences of the heart." Hackett realises that he knows nothing of the experiences of Anny's heart. But it is too late, she has vanished. Could she have killed herself? "The question reared up in his mind, like a savage dog getting up from his sleep." A "withering sense of insignificance" can "bring one as low as grief." The light story has darkened terribly. But it turns out she has been dismissed; a watch has gone missing. So the story ends, with the redheaded girl vanishing in time, unattended to. All her life Fitzgerald paid attention to such people.

"Beehernz" is set on a tiny, remote island off Iona called Reilig (but it is not on any map) and draws eloquently on her long-ago visits to the retreat on Iona. Hopkins, the artistic director of a music festival, is not in tune with this setting. He is a managerial type (like the bustling employer in "The Axe" or the bullying Mrs. Horrabin in "Not Shown"), whose aim is to bring back a very old maestro from his seclusion to conduct one last big Mahler concert. Most people think that Beehernz is dead (Reilig means "graveyard"), but Hopkins has tracked him down. Forty years before, in 1960, Beehernz was booked to conduct Mahler's Eighth Symphony, but in the end preferred not to. What is your objection to it? he was asked. "It is too noisy."

Hopkins now sets himself, with the help of a young woman singer and his assistant, to cajole Beehernz into making a comeback. The old house looks abandoned. Inside there is "no electricity, no radio, a single bed covered with a plaid, an armchair, no books, no bookcase, no scores, no manuscripts." There is a rotting old piano, which turns out to be a silent one. The "little, light old man" is a wonderfully obstructive and enigmatic character, more interested in his potato patch than in Mahler. His utterances are simple and cryptic. Hopkins tries to interest him in a contract, but Beehernz (like Cesare in *Innocence*) puts both hands down flat on the papers, "as if to eliminate them from his sight." He is the last of those powerfully contemplative figures who appear all through her work.

The young singer, Mary, goes into the kitchen to make tea, singing to herself a few bars of German lieder. The song, not identified or translated in the story, is Goethe's "Gefunden" ("Found"). It takes us back to *The Blue Flower*. The poet is walking alone through a forest. He notices a little blue flower, a *"Blümchen,"* shining at him, and is about to pick it, when the flower speaks: "Shall I be gathered only to fade?" Instead of picking it, the poet digs up its roots and replants it in his garden, where it still blooms.[26] Beehernz, too, has been "found." He had said he would not leave his island. But in the morning the old man has changed his mind, and is ready to leave for the mainland. "I should like to hear her sing again. You see, it is so long since I heard music."

In "Desideratus," a poor country boy, Jack Digby, is given a precious medal by his godmother on his birthday in 1663. On it is an angel, and an inscription, which is the story's title. He loses it on the hill outside his village, in winter. "Anything you carry about in your pockets you are bound to lose sooner or later." He goes back to look for it, and finds it shining in a hole covered in green ice. The ice melts, and the water—with his medal—runs down to the big house. In trepidation, the boy goes to seek for it there. The servants in the big house send him to the master, Mr. Jonas, who suggests he might prefer to have some money rather than the thing he came for, but then tells him to go upstairs. " 'I think, sir, I won't go any further. What I lost can't be here.' 'It's poor-spirited to say "I won't go any further," ' said Mr. Jonas." Jack Digby has to take courage. Upstairs is a sick redheaded boy lying in bed, with the medal in his outstretched hand. It is like a fairy story, or a dream. He must take the medal from the other boy's hand. "I am very far from home," he thinks. Afterwards, Jack often wonders how much money Mr. Jonas might have given him instead. "Anyone who has ever been poor . . . will sympathize with him in this matter."

These mysterious stories, about truthfulness, resistance, integrity and courage, are full of Fitzgerald's unprivileged, vulnerable people, making their way in the world with some bewilderment, who may never have the chance to tell their stories, or who are bullied or exploited by what she calls "the tribe of torturers." Cruelty, indifference, violence and the exercise of power are the realities of life. But the stories are also coloured with her characteristic tender, funny alertness to human oddity and ordinariness, moments of good luck or hopefulness, something found or desired shining through the darkness. Just occasionally, in her luminous, dark, unflinching world, people do find their way home, or their longed-for "Desideratus," or their means of escape.

She was writing a great many other things, too, in her old age—too many, as she complained to Tina in 1999:

> I have at the moment 2 pieces for the LRB to do (but have written to get out of one of them), an intro. for Folio Society for Middle-march, an intro for J. L. Carr's A Month in the Country for Stuart, a serious piece for the New York Times on Vol 2 of Richard Holmes's Coleridge and a vexatious piece which I'm also trying to get out of, for the New York Times magazine on the Best Idea of the Past Millennium, an absurd subject.[27]

A slightly earlier piece called "Last Words," written in 1988 for Maura Dooley, for a collection called *End Games,* set the tone for many of her late reviews. It begins with a quotation from one of her favourite authors:

"Old end-game lost of old," Beckett calls it, "play and lose and have done with losing." A human being is old when he has survived long enough to name, with absolute confidence, a year, one of the next thirty, which he won't be there to see. Clinically speaking, during these last stages, he is likely to lose his memory for recent events, his skill at problem solving, his power of abstract reasoning, and his ability to work with new and unfamiliar systems. (This will be partly because he can't adapt to them, but just as much because he doesn't admit the need for them.) What survives, if his body doesn't let him down completely, will be word fluency, understanding, enthusiasm, memory of long past events.

He—or she—will not necessarily be benign.

An old writer is even less likely than any other old person to be serene, mellow, and so forth. More probable are a vast irritation with human perversity, sometimes with fame itself, and an obstinate sense, against all odds, of the right direction for the future.

She goes on to consider how Tolstoy, Hardy, William Morris, Joyce and Woolf treat, and write in, old age—often with "a note of leave-taking." She pauses on that note in *Finnegans Wake:* "Quiet takes back her folded fields. Tranquille thanks. Adew." And she ends with Woolf's last writer-character, Miss La Trobe in *Between the Acts,* frustrated by her audience's inability to understand her play, but already, as "she takes her voyage away from the shore," thinking of her next work:

> Miss La Trobe is already possessed by a new idea. She has "heard the first words." These are words that other characters in the book will speak, but have not yet spoken. In fact, we never know what they are. But Miss La Trobe does know.[28]

Thoughts about old age and last words run like a tune through her late reviews. Of Saul Bellow's last novel, *Ravelstein,* she says: "Old age, on the whole, is not a time to be recommended, but very old novelists are allowed to write about what they like." A warm review of the second volume of Richard Holmes's *Coleridge* ends by quoting Holmes: " 'There is a particular kind of silence which falls after a life like Coleridge's . . . and perhaps it should be observed.' " A piece on Victor Klemperer's harrowing diaries of life under Hitler notes the need "to bear witness to the very last." Her affectionate preface to J. L. Carr's *A Month in the Country* dwells on memory, and, odder than memory, "nostalgia for something we have never had." Her 1999 introduction to *Middlemarch* emphasises George Eliot's "meliorist" creed, her feelings for her lost pastoral childhood, her awareness of the "paths not taken" for all her characters and her shaping of her big, complex story as it reaches its end with the passage on Dorothea's obscure, but not wasted, life:

> This is part of the book's great diminuendo, not tragic but majestic, drawing back, after all its vast complications, into itself, the characters' prospects narrowing as the story closes. But we have actually seen the effect of Dorothea's being on those around her . . . On these "unhistoric acts" in an undistinguished ribbon-manufacturing town in the midlands, the growing good of the world may partly depend. We must believe this, if we can.[29]

Not all her last essays are as contemplative as these. Her splendidly bad-tempered essay for the *New York Times*'s "absurd" series on "Best Ideas of the Past Millennium" describes the nineteenth-century philanthropist Octavia Hill's founding of the National Trust. It was meant to preserve "certain sources of happiness," like open space and footpaths, "exactly as they were," but it turned into the buying-up of grand houses for thousands of visitors to tramp through. Perhaps the best thing Octavia could have done with her idea was "never to put it into practice." The bewildered American editor wanted her to change the ending: "I do feel you were working towards a conclusion less cynical than this."[30]

The last thing she wrote for publication was an additional paragraph to her "foreword" to *The Knox Brothers,* for the Counterpoint and Flamingo paperback reissues, which had a sympathetic introduction by Richard Holmes. She wrote it in March 2000, a few weeks before her death. It imagined the brothers reborn into the twenty-first century, recalled the memorable things they said to her and ended: "I miss them all more than I can say."[31]

જી.

Old writers are expected to reminisce and sum up. Since the millennium was approaching—it would coincide, more or less, with her eighty-third birthday on 17 December 1999, and was celebrated with a big family dinner at Bishops Road and a walk up to Hampstead Heath to see the fireworks—she kept being asked for her favourite books of the century, or of the decade, or of her lifetime's reading. Her answers would vary depending on her mood. One list of contemporary favourites was Ishiguro's *A Pale View of Hills,* Christopher Hope's *Kruger's Alp,* Anita Brookner's *Hotel du Lac,* Roddy Doyle's *The Snapper* and Magnus Mills's *The Restraint of Beasts.* For the "books that have made the greatest impression on me," she offered the New Testament (she first remembered listening to her mother reading it), Joyce's *Portrait of the Artist as a Young Man* (because her students always said it described their own feelings) and Turgenev's *Fathers and Sons:* "I still feel close to weeping when I get to the end and the old Bazarovs, resigned to their loss, are left side by side, their heads dropping like those of two sheep at mid-day." She loved the novel because of the "great tenderness" it showed to both the young and the old and "the impossibility of their ever being able to understand each other." Her other "best books of the century" were Conrad's *The Secret Agent,* Somerville and Ross's *The Real Charlotte* (in fact published in 1894), Alain-Fournier's *Le Grand Meaulnes,* Kafka's *The Trial* and Italo Svevo's *Confessions of Zeno.* Asked for the best-known book she had never read, she chose Darwin's *Origin of Species:* "Wild life programmes on TV make me rather guilty about this." Asked which of her books she would take to a desert island (not that she was ever asked to do *Desert Island Discs*), she picked *Gerard's Herbal,* the 1633 edition.[32]

The striking un-Englishness of most of her choices links to a theme that ran through her late interviews. She often described herself as a typically English novelist, typical because English wit is a matter of "self-concealment, meiosis, [and] self-deprecation," because most English people think "life not important enough to be tragic and too serious to be comic," because if you are English you feel "you shouldn't make a fuss" and because English humorists are also great depressives. She calls herself "a depressive humorist—or depressed, what's the difference." "I think in general everything goes wrong and is disappointing." Yet she identifies much more with European writers, often speaking of her love of the European novella (Mann's *Death in Venice,* Tolstoy's *Master and Man,* Balzac's short novels). She is—and she knows it—a very un-English English novelist, more to be compared with writers such as Beckett, Turgenev, Alain-Fournier or Pavese than with English counterparts like Stevie Smith, Barbara Pym, Beryl Bainbridge or J. L. Carr.

She often says, too, that she feels alienated from late-twentieth-century

English politics, that "her" Liberal Party, which she identifies as the defeated pacifist George Lansbury's party, has vanished. To her young Chinese interviewer Lian Lu, who was writing a thesis on her, and to whom she wrote helpfully between 1994 and 1999, she gave the *Fontana Dictionary of Modern Thought* definition of liberalism as springing "from a vision of society as composed of individuals . . . and of their liberty as the primary social good. This liberty is to be defended in such rights as those to free political institutions, religious practices, intellectual and artistic expression." And she adds: "My characters only demand a modest degree of freedom, but that degree is a necessity to them." Yet, though British politics no longer engaged her, she told Lian Lu that "I love my country and don't want to live anywhere else for more than a short time. England has changed, but it's still a place of understatement, irony, green fields, water-colour painting, obstinacy and unexpected courage."

She repeatedly spoke of failure as a theme both of her work and her life. Her characters were "exterminatees" and she felt she was one herself. Her feelings went out always to "decent chaps" who struggled and did not succeed, to women who were always interrupted, to vulnerable children, to people who loved silently and without much hope. She was deeply pessimistic and found it hard to write happy endings. Because life is sad, the writer's task, all the more, is sympathy and understanding. Her own subject was "fortitude in the face of the world's difficulties." And what she looked for in other writers was "the quality of pity and kindness. I don't see how this world is to be managed if we don't pity each other."

She talked about her own work in terms of regret and inadequacy. She would repeatedly tell the story about her first publisher cutting the last eight chapters of her first book, and make her jokes about librarians not liking short books and writers not wanting to be called "light." She would say that she felt it insulted the reader to explain too much. She told interviewers that she was miserable when she was writing and much preferred to paint or make things. She always said she was attracted to periods of time when there were "prohibitions": "It's easier to write about earlier periods because there's much more reason for people *not* to do things." Above all she spoke of her regret at not having been more explicit in her novels about her religious beliefs, and accused herself of cowardice. She never looked back on her own work with pleasure. "One always feels one ought to have done things differently."

Interviewers regularly reported on how "maddeningly elusive" she was. All arrived at the door of Bishops Road or at the recording studio fully intending to get to the secrets beneath; all retired baffled. Sometimes she would fend them off with a poker-faced joke: tired of being asked how she researched *The Blue Flower,* she told one interviewer brightly: "I found it all on the internet!" She was extremely cagey about her past, though with particularly attentive interviewers such as Eleanor Wachtel, Sylvia Brownrigg or Joan Acocella, she let some glimpses out: her feeling that an Evangelical upbringing could "never, never, ever" be escaped from, her wretchedness when she went up to Oxford after her mother's death, the drama of the sinking of the barge, her memory of hearing Yeats on the radio when she was a child, reading "I knew a phoenix in my youth . . ." She frequently told her interviewers how secretive she was about her work, and she was evasive when asked what she was working on after *The Blue Flower*. To one interviewer, who should have known better than to ask, she burst out with mild indignation: "I'm surprised to hear you ask that, because it's a very unlucky question."[33]

Her reticence was ingrained, but it also arose from her struggle to find a subject for a new novel and the energy to write it. Casting around, she went back to early memories. Her notes towards the late stories are mixed in with sketches for her never-to-be-written Oxford novel, "Why (or 'How') We Were Very Young," in which she mapped out glimpses of her time as a student in the 1930s and some passages on Tolkien and C. S. Lewis. But alongside those drafts, which came to nothing, is another idea, not at all nostalgic, about grandmothers, written in a wry, melancholy tone:

> A grandmother clock is smaller than a grandfather clock and, by inference, weaker . . . A granny knot is one that comes undone at once, granny bonds are or were a saving scheme which was simple enough for even the densest to understand, a granny flat is a subsection of the main house where the damage granny may do through absent-mindedness will be under kindly control. Grannies lose things, which they call not knowing where they've put them . . . I suppose the expression "Teach your grandmother to suck eggs" implies that grannies know how to do <u>something</u>, but not anything of any practical use.[34]

In her real life as a grandmother, she continued to be involved and valued. She sometimes wished, wistfully, that she had been a different kind of granny, the smart, rich kind. A letter to Tina said sadly: "Don't thank me, indeed I feel you shouldn't, as I have failed to produce the fur coat, the crocodile bag, the little freehold property in good condition, all the things I dreamed of. Instead of that, you know I'll help if I can."[35] One touching relic of her relationships with her grandchildren is a birthday poem which she wrote in 1999 for her eleven-year-old granddaughter, Sophie Lake, inside a card on which she had gummed a flower and drawn a picture of a vase.

> This is a bunch of edelweiss
> Which must have lived with snow and ice—
> The edelweiss grows very high,
> But you can get there if you try—
> I know you will, I know you can—
> With love and confidence from Gran.[36]

She was imagining her grandchildren into their future lives, with a squeeze of the hand.

By 1998 she was becoming very ill. The painful arthritis which had begun to develop in the early 1990s, the irregular heartbeat and shortness of breath, the high blood pressure, were all getting worse. On her last holiday with the Dooleys, in Menorca, she used a wheelchair at the airport. Her 1999 diary is scattered with appointments at the Whittington Cardiology and Rheumatology clinics—which she often cancelled. Her heart disease and her rheumatoid arthritis were by now severe. She was on steroids, as a result of which, she thought, she developed chronic gout. She found it hard to type or hold a pen or pick things up.

She felt she should battle on ("Call it going, call it on") and was still taking on major tasks, like judging the Booker Prize in 1998. She tried to play down her condition to her publishers ("I've been ill on and off, but never mind that," she told Stuart in March 1999). But they noticed her tiredness: Mandy Kirkby often observed that she would start a sentence and give up halfway through—"Oh, it doesn't matter." And she was increasingly, reluctantly, having to cancel trips and appearances. She told Karen, for instance, in 1998, that she couldn't face going by train to Birmingham and Leicester, where she was booked to share a platform with Hilary Mantel: "She is a very good speaker and can manage very well without me." Stuart sent her anxious letters: "I am very concerned that you should be getting proper medical attention . . . Although I do not want to interfere . . . I would, if you would allow me, like to organise some second opinions." She wrote to Michael Holroyd apologetically resigning from the Council of the RSL, but gallantly agreeing to judge the prizes as she had promised.[37]

She found her regular forays to the Archway Road more trying. "Expeditions to the shops getting rather painful and I always drop some money and feel people are laughing at me," she told Tina. She had to miss the early morning Palm Sunday service at All Saints for the first time in the spring of 1999, but, as she said to Willie Conder, "I dread not being able to get up from a kneeling position—just think of it, Willie, the embarrassment, the vicar kindly putting out a helping hand, etc." She confided more in Willie, far away in Lancashire, than anyone. They had, after all, been friends for seventy years.

> I feel sorry for my heart which has made such an effort for so long (rather like the horse that comes in last on the Saturday afternoon racing on TV . . . and we're told "the distance was too much for poor old—."). I was supposed to be going on a tour of Europe . . . for the British Council, but have had to say I can't go.—I can just about walk down to the shops and back, or to the top of the hill where I can get a bus to go and see Mary (who is still in her nursing home and gives me a great welcome but alas! doesn't know who I am at all). The upshot of all this is . . . that I don't really feel up to a long journey, but I do so much want to see you and Mike—indeed, I caught myself sitting and thinking, shall I ever see Mike and Willie again in this life? but then told myself that this sort of thing wouldn't do.[38]

She wrote a reminder entry to herself at the end of her 1999 diary for March 2000: GET BUS PASS. On 29 March 2000, she wrote a letter to Chris Carduff about *The Knox Brothers* reissue, mentioning that Ria wanted to repaint the walls of her flat while she went on her annual holiday with the Dooleys in April: "I'd hoped they might last me out, but she says not." A few days later, she had a stroke, in the morning, and then another one shortly after. She was taken to the Whittington. At first, though weak and tired, she seemed her normal self. She picked a horse for the Grand National and admired Alfie's new Pokémon cards. Tina was reading William Maxwell's novella *So Long, See You Tomorrow,* and they talked about it, and about one of Penelope's essays, on L. H. Myers.

The family thought she would recover, and Terence took the Dooley children on their planned holiday in Spain. The others kept vigil through the April days. Valpy, at one point, asked her if she was afraid to die. She said that she was not afraid. She was ready to go, as she felt very tired, and was looking forward to a rest.

Maria and Tina sent notes out to the people closest to their mother, telling them what had happened, but saying "that they were all hoping for a good recovery eventually." A shoal of anxious letters poured in. On 20 April she had another stroke. Now she could barely speak, though she knew who everyone was. When Paschal, who had been a redhead (like her) as a little boy, came in, she said: "Red hair." She was having to be tube-fed, and had a breathing-mask. Maria, Tina and Valpy kept watch. There was a kind Filipina nurse, who called her "Pen." On 28 April, in the late afternoon, towards six o'clock, they told her they were going out for a cup of tea, kissed her, said "We're off now" and left her to herself. When they came back, she had died. They sat with her, and for a time nobody came, and they didn't know what to do. Finally a young woman doctor, new to them, came in, and certified the death. She looked at the name and said: "Penelope Fitzgerald. I love her books."

On 5 May, the Reverend David Hubbard conducted the funeral service at the Church of All Saints, Highgate, where she had been a regular. The coffin was heaped with spring flowers. Hubbard spoke of "the calm influence of a very gentle, gracious person," of her "deep loyalty to the Church of England," of her "quiet and unassuming modesty" and of the use she made of "her talents." Terence read one of her favourite poems, Christina Rossetti's "Does the road wind up-hill all the way?" ("Yes, to the very end.")

Rather than laying her to rest next to Desmond in Putney Vale Cemetery, her children decided to inter her ashes with Evoe's in the graveyard of Hampstead Parish Church, St. John's, in a shady corner by the columbarium. This took place on 1 July 2000. Penelope had often gone there to look after Evoe's grave, and she liked the noise of the children coming from the primary school playground next door. Below the upright grey slate reading "In loving memory E.V. Knox, 'Evoe,' 1881–1971, 'Still are thy pleasant voices, thy nightingales, awake,'" was a space for Mary. After Mary's death, in September of that year, at ninety, her ashes were interred there under a carved slate reading: "Mary Knox née Shepard, 1909–2000, Artist and devoted wife of Evoe," with an outline of a woman's hand holding a paintbrush. Below that is a grey slate reading: "Penelope Fitzgerald née Knox, 1916–2000. Writer and dearly loved mother," with an outline of a woman's hand holding a pen. Below all three, at the foot of the grave, is inscribed a line she had marked in her copy of Henry Vaughan's poems: "They are all gone into the world of light."[39]

In her will, drawn up in 1993, she had made John Lake her executor and Terence Dooley her literary executor. Small legacies were left to the William Morris Society, to PEN, to the Highgate Literary and Scientific Institute, and to All Saints. Stuart was left her copy of Ruskin's *The Seven Lamps of Architecture,* Willie her "little pottery cups" from Cana, Jean Talbot her "1917 crochet pin cushion." Maria was given all her jewellery and clothes and household goods, Tina was left all the books and manuscripts. She divided the rest of her estate equally between her three children.

On 10 October 2000, a packed memorial service was held at St. James's Church, Piccadilly. There were speeches by Barbara Craig, from Somerville, Francis King, Stuart Proffitt, A. N. Wilson, Christine Poulson, from the William Morris Society, and Tina. There were hymns ("My song is love unknown," "Thine be the glory, risen, conquering Son"). The Evening Prayer from *Hansel and Gretel* was sung, as it was by the two girls in *Offshore:* "*Abends wenn wir schlafen geh'n . . .*" "When I lay me down to sleep, fourteen angels watch do keep . . ."

MEMORIAL SERVICE

FOR THE LIFE AND WORK OF

PENELOPE FITZGERALD

1916–2000

10 OCTOBER 2000

ST JAMES'S CHURCH, PICCADILLY, LONDON W1
AT 3 PM.

A celebration of her life and work at the Royal Society of Literature followed a year later, with contributions by Sebastian Faulks, who read with gusto from *Human Voices,* Philip Hensher, Harriet Harvey Wood, Michèle Roberts and A. S. Byatt. Byatt spoke about science in *The Gate of Angels.* She expressed her enormous admiration for Fitzgerald, but also her bafflement. Her books are apparently precise, she said, yet "they cannot be grasped, or completely understood."[40]

Tina and Terence Dooley set to work, with her publishers, to nourish her posthumous life. *The Means of Escape* appeared in 2000, casting her readers a last, enigmatic look. A volume of her selected writings, *A House of Air,* edited by Terence, Mandy Kirkby and Chris Carduff, was published by Flamingo and Counterpoint in 2003. Terence's edition of the letters, *So I Have Thought of You,* was published by Fourth Estate (an imprint of HarperCollins) in 2008. All these were widely and seriously reviewed.

Some years after her death, Tina and Terence approached me to write Penelope Fitzgerald's biography. I had written the introduction to *A House of Air,* and they knew that I passionately admired her work. I had known her, though not well, since the 1980s. I remember her telling me, at a Royal Society of Literature evening, how Marjorie Watts had suddenly thrown into her lap, at a PEN meeting, a brown envelope of Charlotte Mew's letters to Watts's mother, and how, as a biographer, you never know what is going to turn up. In 1989 she sent me a copy of *Charlotte Mew,* as I had told her I was thinking of doing an anthology of women poets: "I want CM to be properly represented," she told Richard Ollard, referring to me as "Hermione the Inferior," as he had just had a granddaughter called Hermione.[41] I was on the platform with her at the RSL for the discussion about public libraries in October 1993 when she savaged the man from the Adam Smith Institute. In 1996, she gave my biography of Virginia Woolf a generous review, and came to my launch party, where she was very nice to my friends. I interviewed her several times, on platforms, in print and on the radio: an extract from one of these interviews was played, to my surprise, at her memorial service.[42] In May 1997 I chaired the "Writers at Work" day at York from which Julian Barnes travelled back with her on "low forms of transport." A few months before that, I went to Bishops Road to talk to her for a piece in a British Council *New Writing* volume. There were delays on the tube, and I arrived late and flustered. She was kind and patient, gave me tea and chocolate cake, and sat on the little sofa opposite me, hands obediently folded, looking obliging, waiting to be questioned. My attempts to elicit her life story and the secrets of her writing life were met, politely and affably, with well-trodden phrases from other interviews, short bursts of excitement and interest, enthusiastic considerations of other writers, and evasive deflections masquerading as changes of subject, all in her light, clear, melodious voice, interspersed with laughter, sighs and very long pauses.

At the time of these encounters, I had no idea that I would become her biographer. I greatly regret, of course, not having paid closer attention to everything she said when I met her and talked to her. But, perhaps self-deceivingly, I have felt while writing this book that she might not have disapproved of me as her biographer—if there must be a life—because she liked my book about Virginia Woolf, and had been kind to me when we met. Fiona MacCarthy, following her as Edward Burne-Jones's biographer, remembered that Penelope would say that writers of the past sometimes seemed to be encouraging her onwards with "a squeeze of the hand." I have allowed myself to think of that while writing this book.

But I have also had in mind her reticence, evasiveness and secrecy, and I am aware that I am working against those characteristics and those preferences. If, like her, I believed in ghosts, I would think of her looking on with reluctance as I trawled through her private papers, her annotations in her books, her notebooks and her manuscripts. Part of this archive belongs to the family, and, having decided they wanted a biography, they generously put it at my disposal. Part of my work was done at the Harry Ransom Humanities Research Center at Austin, Texas, where Fitzgerald had been before me.

Combing through her immaculately catalogued papers in that calm, orderly, air-conditioned environment, many miles from my home, and hers, I am acutely aware of two things. One is the enormous amount of work she did, and then compressed, for every book she wrote. The other is the speaking presence of the gaps and silences left in the metaphorical creases between the pages I am reading. There are many things she did not want anyone to know about her, and which no one will ever know. I find this frustrating, amusing, seductive and admirable.

When I get to the last documents of her life, I try to decipher her many crossings-out, scribbles and revisions, and all the suggestive, cryptic fragments she left behind. The last notebook, with many empty pages towards the end, has notes and drafts for her late reviews, for the book about grandmothers which she never wrote, and two mysterious beginnings of stories.

One is called "Tapper Hardy." A brother and sister are living in a village, and a mysterious stranger called Tapper Hardy holds a meeting in the village hall. They go to the meeting, and there is nobody else there. But he greets them: "Now you have come."

The other story fragment, which has no title, concerns two characters called Sandford and Merton. This was the title of a well-known late-eighteenth-century moral tale for children, the sort of book that would have sat in a Victorian bishop's household. She gave the names to the two family dogs at Fred's family rectory in *The Gate of Angels,* so she clearly associates the book with religious households of old times, like those of her Knox grandfather and her Hicks grandfather, remembered from childhood.

She has written one paragraph of the story, the last entry in the last notebook. Sandford receives a letter from someone called Merton. The letter says: "Come at once, for old times sake." The address on the letter is 194 Leaning Lane, with a north London postcode. "Sandford smoothed out the numerous creases in the much-folded piece of thin tissue paper." It strikes him he is like a man performing a conjuring trick, and he remembers a magician called Oswald Williams in the Edwardian conjuring show "Maskelyne's Mysteries," who told you how to make a piece of paper vanish by squeezing it.[43] "More urgently, who was Merton and what was meant by 'for old times sake'? . . . Sandford looked up this address in the A to Z and found that Leaning Lane was on the crease between two pages."

Acknowledgements

This book would not, and could not, have been written without the invitation, the patient encouragement and the generous help of Penelope Fitzgerald's daughter Tina Dooley and her husband, Terence Dooley, Fitzgerald's literary executor and the editor of her essays and letters. I cannot thank them enough. I am also profoundly grateful to Penelope Fitzgerald's daughter Maria, and to her son, Valpy Fitzgerald, for all their help, their time, their encouragement and their willingness to talk to me about their mother. I am greatly indebted, too, to other members of Fitzgerald's family: John Lake, Belinda Hunt, Angelines Fitzgerald and her and Valpy's son Valpy Gregory, Luke and Paschal Dooley, Thomas, Sophie and Alfred Lake, William Knox, Colin Peck, Sylvia Peck, Maura Dooley, Charlotte, Dilwyn and Tim Knox. I am especially grateful to Tim Hicks for his generous loan of Hicks family documents.

Friends of Penelope Fitzgerald have been unstintingly helpful. I owe a great deal, in particular to the late Hugh Lee and to Penny Lee, to Jasmine Blakeway (and her daughter Alyss Fennell), the late Mavis Batey (who worked with Dillwyn Knox at Bletchley), Elisabeth Barnett (Fitzgerald's god-daughter), Deborah Chorlton, Anne Conder (Willie Conder's daughter), Perdita Dawson (Joan Mathew's daughter), Judge Elisabeth Fisher (Jean Talbot's niece), Linda Hughes (Mary Lago's daughter), Penelope Lively, Fiona MacCarthy, Desmond Maxwell, Belinda Probert (Janet Probert's daughter), Howard J. Woolmer and Francesca Zawadzki.

Ex-students and colleagues of Fitzgerald's, and those who put me in touch with them, have been generous with their reminiscences. I am especially grateful to Antonia Southern, Penelope's colleague at Westminster Tutors for many years, to the novelist A. S. Byatt, who taught with her at Westminster Tutors, to her daughter Antonia Byatt, who was taught by her, and to Wanda Carter, Elizabeth Chandler, Joe Coughlan, Tiffany Daneff, Jane Darwin, Kay Dunbar, Katherine Duncan-Jones, Lucinda Evans, Rena Fogel, Jo Greenwell, Henrietta Heald, Eliza Manningham-Buller, Patrick Marber, Jane Martineau, Catherine Mulgan, Nesta Phillips, Edward St. Aubyn, Nicola-Rose Virgin, Lucy Wadham, Claire Wilson and Lucy Younger.

I am grateful for information from those who worked with Fitzgerald at the BBC, at PEN, the RSL, the William Morris Society, the Arts Council, the British Council, the Highgate Literary and Scientific Institute, at the *London Review of Books,* or on prize judgings or literary panels: Jonathan Barker, Alyson Barr, Susannah Clapp, Dorothy Coles, Valentine Cunningham, Maggie Fergusson, Ros Goulder (and her daughter Jill), Harriet Harvey Wood, Michael Holroyd, Jonathan Keates, the late Francis King, Hilary Laurie, Christine Poulson, Judy and Stanley Price, Josephine Pullein-Thompson and Anne Riddell.

I owe a great debt to Fitzgerald's publishers and editors and their relatives, in particular Stuart Proffitt and Chris Carduff, who have been enormously generous and helpful to me, and also Victoria Barnsley, Essie Cousins, Karen Duffy, Philip Gwyn Jones, David Jamieson, Mandy Kirkby, Richard Ollard's widow, Mary, and his son William, and Raleigh Trevelyan.

I am grateful to writers and academics who reviewed or wrote about Fitzgerald, and who have given me help: Joan Acocella, Sylvia Brownrigg, Robert Chandler, Ralph Erskine, Dean Flower and Linda Henchey, Philip Hensher, Richard Holmes, Kazuo Ishiguro, Lian Lu, Oliver Ready, Ann Thwaite, Eleanor Wachtel, Jackie Wullschlager and Francis Wyndham.

My thanks to the following: Brigid Allen for Somerville memories, Patricia Barr, Charles Bush and Stephen Forge at Oundle School, Harvey Brown for advice on physics, Philip Christensen for unpublished letters, Deirdre David for help with the Braybrookes, William Fiennes for information about the Fiennes family at Southwold, David Hubbard, vicar of All Saints, Highgate, David Kramer, Fitzgerald's accountant, Simon Loftus for Southwold information, Gina Mercer, editor of *Island,* Jamie Muir and Robyn Read for help with BBC archive materials, Michael Roberts for information about Port Washington, Fiona Stafford and Galen Strawson for anecdotes, Peter Straus for his work with Terence Dooley on the Fitzgerald estate, Charles Sturridge for help in interviewing Ros Goulder and Steve Uglow for legal advice.

I thank the archivists and librarians at the following institutions for their help and advice: Simon Armour (Academia Británica, Córdoba), Samantha Blake (BBC Written Archives Centre, Reading), Jonathan Seaman (Eastbourne Museums), Alla Barabtarlo (Rare Books and Special Collections, Ellis Library, University of Missouri), Bridget Howlett (London Metropolitan Archives), Patsy Williams (Gladstone's Library, Hawarden), Joanne Moye (Sir John Leman High School, ex–Beccles School, Southwold), Fran Baker (John Rylands Library, University of Manchester), Alice Millea and Colin Harris (Oxford University Archives, Bodleian Library), Nancy Fulford (Special Collections, University of Reading), Lorna Cahill (Royal Holloway College), Anne Manuel (Somerville College), Tina Cunningham (Wycombe Abbey School).

My deepest debt as a researcher is to all the staff, especially Patrice Fox and Richard Workman, at the Harry Ransom Humanities Research Center at the University of Texas at Austin.

I thank my agent, Caroline Dawnay, for her help and support, and I thank Zoe Pagnamenta. My late friend and agent Pat Kavanagh opened the discussions that led to this book, in the summer of 2008; I will always remember and be grateful.

Grateful thanks to my researchers, Edmund Gordon and Sumaya Partner, and to Vanessa Guignery for her kindness in helping me with research at the Harry Ransom Center.

I owe a great debt of thanks to the biographer Martin Stannard, who generously allowed me to make use of and to benefit from research he did on Penelope Fitzgerald between 2003 and 2004.

My warm thanks go to students and colleagues at Wolfson College and in the Oxford Centre for Life-Writing at Wolfson College, and in the English Faculty at Oxford University, for conversations about life-writing, and to Wolfson College for granting me a period of six months' leave in 2012 to finish the book.

I give my love and thanks to my friends and family, for many conversations and much help and advice: to Clio Barnard, Josie Barnard, Dinah Birch, Helen Brann, Michael Burden, Carmen Callil, Michael Fend, Roy Foster, Alex Harris, Hugh Haughton, Benjamin Lee, Amanda Lillie, Candia McWilliam, Bridget Patterson, Michèle Roberts and Faith Stewart-Gordon.

To Julian Barnes, a fellow admirer of Fitzgerald's, for his advice, encouragement and inspiration, and for helping this book on its way from start to finish, I owe a boundless debt.

To my superb editor and dear friend Jenny Uglow, I offer my life-long gratitude, admiration and love. My thanks to all, past and present, at Chatto & Windus and Random House who have helped in the making of the book, especially Clara Farmer, Alison Samuel, Parisa Ebrahimi and Suzanne Dean.

I thank, above all, my husband, John Barnard, to whom this book is dedicated.

Abbreviations

I. WORKS BY PENELOPE FITZGERALD

The following abbreviations and editions have been used. Date of first publication is followed by the edition(s) referred to in the endnotes.

Novels

AF   *At Freddie's*, Collins, 1982; Flamingo, 1989.

B   *The Bookshop*, Duckworth, 1978; Flamingo, 1989.

BF   *The Blue Flower*, Flamingo/HarperCollins, 1995; Flamingo, 1995, 2002.

BS   *The Beginning of Spring*, Collins, 1988; Flamingo, 1989.

GA   *The Gate of Angels*, Collins, 1990; Flamingo, 1991.

GC   *The Golden Child*, Duckworth, 1977; Flamingo, 1994.

HV   *Human Voices*, Collins, 1980; Flamingo, 1988.

I   *Innocence*, Collins, 1986; Flamingo, 1987.

O   *Offshore*, Collins, 1979; Magnum, 1980; Flamingo, 1988.

Biographies

CM   *Charlotte Mew & Her Friends*, Collins, 1984; as *Charlotte Mew and Her Friends*, Flamingo, 2002.

EBJ   *Edward Burne-Jones: A Biography*, Michael Joseph, 1975; Hamish Hamilton, 1989; Sutton Publishing, 2003.

KB   *The Knox Brothers*, Macmillan, 1977; Flamingo, 2000, 2002.

Short Stories

ME   *The Means of Escape*, Flamingo/HarperCollins, 2000; Flamingo, 2001.

Essays and Letters

HA   *A House of Air: Selected Writings*, edited by Terence Dooley with Mandy Kirkby and Chris Carduff, introduction by Hermione Lee, Flamingo/HarperCollins, 2003. [In the United States, with slight differences in content, as *The Afterlife: Essays and Criticism*, Counterpoint, 2003.]

L   *So I Have Thought of You: The Letters of Penelope Fitzgerald,* edited by Terence Dooley, preface by A. S. Byatt, Fourth Estate, 2008; Fourth Estate paperback, 2009.

Editing [with Desmond Fitzgerald]

WR   *World Review,* August 1950 to April–May 1953, Hulton Press.

For uncollected publications by PF, and other works consulted in the biography, see the endnotes.

2. ABBREVIATIONS IN ENDNOTES

Individuals

BH	Belinda Hunt
CC	Chris Carduff
CK	Christina Knox
DF	Desmond Fitzgerald
ELH	Edward Lee Hicks
EVK	Evoe Knox
FK	Francis King
HL	Hermione Lee
LPH	L. P. Hartley
Maria	Maria Fitzgerald
MK	Mary Knox
MS	Martin Stannard
PB	The Poetry Bookshop
PF	Penelope Fitzgerald [PK as Penelope Knox]
PL	Penelope Lively
RO	Richard Ollard
SP	Stuart Proffitt
TD	Terence Dooley
Tina	Tina Dooley
VF	Valpy Fitzgerald
WC	Willie Conder

Archives and Publications

BBC	BBC Written Archives Centre, Caversham Park, Reading.
HCA	HarperCollins Archive.
HR	Penelope Fitzgerald Papers, Harry Ransom Humanities Research Center, University of Texas at Austin.

   I: Penelope Fitzgerald Papers, 1912–1988.

   II: Penelope Fitzgerald, Additions to Her Papers, 1898–2001.

LRB   *London Review of Books.*

Lu   Lian Lu, *Beyond the Text: Direction of Literary Study from Studying the Fiction and Literary Career of Penelope Fitzgerald,* University of Fudan, 2005, revised from "The Fiction and Literary Career of Penelope Fitzgerald," PhD thesis, University of Glasgow, 1999.

NYRB   *New York Review of Books.*

OUP   Oxford University Press.

Somerville   Somerville College Archives, the Principal and Fellows, Somerville College, Oxford.

TLS   *Times Literary Supplement.*

TDA   Tina and Terence Dooley Archive.

THA   Tim Hicks Archive.

The term "to HL" used in the endnotes refers to interviews, emails, letters and phone calls from the interviewee named.

Notes

CHAPTER ONE
The Bishops' Granddaughter

1. All quotations in chapter 1 not otherwise identified are from *KB*.
2. Graham Neville, *Radical Churchman: Edward Lee Hicks and the New Liberalism,* Clarendon Press, 1998, 229. *The Diaries of ELH,* ed. Graham Neville (Lincoln Record Society, 1993), 15 May 1918, 224.
3. *HA,* 470–71.
4. *HA,* 74.
5. Graham Neville, "ELH: A Liberal Rector of Fenny Compton," *Warwickshire History,* vol. 9, no. 4 (Winter 1994–95).
6. Neville, *Radical Churchman,* 172.
7. J. H. Fowler, *The Life and Letters of ELH* (Christophers, 1922), 158–59.
8. *HA,* 468.
9. Letters from Catherine Hicks to Agnes Hicks, THA.
10. Tutors' records for Christina Hicks, 1904–6; Minutes of College Meetings, 1902–13, Somerville.
11. CK scrapbook, TDA.
12. Fowler, *Life of ELH,* 183, 184, 281.
13. Agnes Hicks to Ethel Knox, 16 June 1912, THA.
14. THA; Fowler, *Life of ELH,* 283.
15. Letters between CK and EVK, THA; TDA.
16. Eleanor Wachtel, interview with PF, *Writers & Company,* 21 April 1996.
17. William Knox to HL, 4 April 2010.
18. *HA,* 490.
19. *HA,* 469.
20. PL to J. L. Carr, 23 December [1993], *L,* 466.
21. Winifred Peck, *Home for the Holidays* (Faber, 1955), 101, 466.
22. Ibid., 38–39.
23. *HA,* 332.
24. Peck, *Home for the Holidays,* 164, 86.
25. *HA,* 469.
26. Ibid.
27. Robert Skidelsky treats the relationship as a passing schoolboy phase, "almost certainly sexual," in *Maynard Keynes* (Macmillan, 1983), 87. See also Donald Moggridge, *Keynes: An Economist's Biography* (Routledge, 1992).

28. Charlotte Knox to HL, 18 July 2010.
29. Wilfred Knox, *At a Great Price Obtained I This Freedom* (The Society of St. Peter & St. Paul, 1918).
30. On loving Herefordshire, PF to Hugh Lee ["Ham"], 29 June [1940], *L*, 10.
31. Wilfred Knox, *Meditation and Mental Prayer* (Alban Press, 1990), 20, 101, 137.
32. PF to Maria, 23 November [1974], *L*, 154.
33. PF to RO, 11 March [1981], *L*, 384.
34. PF ms., "Notes on Writing a Novel," notes for Somerville lecture, TDA, citing Ronald Knox, *Some Loose Stones* (Longmans, Green, 1913).
35. *HA*, 202; Peck, *Home for the Holidays*, 50.
36. Adrian Rushworth, reminiscence of EVK, April 1973, TDA.
37. J. L. Garvin to EVK, 2 April 1908, EVK to Mrs. Knox, 11 February 1910, TDA.
38. *HA*, 202.
39. MK to Mr. Gee, 9 October 1973, TDA. "PF, Evoe's daughter . . . has been commissioned to do a book about the four Knoxes . . . Penelope thinks that I could undertake a memoir [of Evoe]."
40. PF to CC, 15 March [2000], PF to Howard Woolmer, 15 January [1989], *L*, 517, 353.
41. PF to Oliver Knox, 15 August [1976], Charlotte Knox Archive.
42. PF to CC, 15 March [2000], *L*, 517.
43. Ibid.
44. William Knox to HL, 4 April 2010.
45. Charlotte Knox to HL, 18 July 2010.
46. BH to HL, 6 March 2010.
47. Jasmine Blakeway to HL, 17 March 2010.
48. *HA*, 471.

CHAPTER TWO
Learning to Read

1. "Schooldays," 1980, *HA*, 490.
2. *CM*, 187.
3. *KB*, 157.
4. EVK, *An Hour from Victoria* (Allen & Unwin, 1924); *KB*, 157–60.
5. For memories of Balcombe, *KB*, 157–60; "Curriculum Vitae," *HA*, 467–68; "Thinking of Balcombe," *HA*, 486–90, and draft typescript version, "A Country Childhood," TDA.
6. *HA*, 468, 485; EVK, *An Hour from Victoria*, 89.
7. EVK, "Priscilla Paints," "Priscilla Fails to Qualify," "Autumn and Priscilla," *Punch*, 7 July 1920, 13 October 1920, 8 December 1920; EVK, *An Hour from Victoria*, 92.
8. *HA*, 490.
9. In *HA*, 471, PF gives this date, correctly, as 1922; in *HA*, 490, she gives it as 1924.
10. Helen Knox, interview MS, 7 January 2004; *KB*, 160; *HA*, 471, 489–90; "A Country Childhood," typescript, TDA.
11. Helen Knox, interview MS.
12. *KB*, 170.
13. *KB*, 147.

14. *HA,* 277, 471, 481–86; *Buried in Hampstead: A Survey of Monuments at Saint-John-at-Hampstead* (Camden Historical Society, 1986), 2007.

15. *HA,* 471, 482; *KB,* 171.

16. *CM,* 146.

17. *HA,* 450, 184, 154–70; PF to Howard Woolmer, 28 September 1978, 2 July 1999, *L,* 330, 368.

18. CK, ed., *Pickwick Papers,* English Literature Series (Macmillan, 1931); *Don Quixote,* trans. Charles Jarvis (Macmillan, 1921).

19. *KB,* 176; *HA,* 482.

20. Helen Knox, interview MS.

21. *HA,* 497.

22. *HA,* 482, 495–98, 206.

23. *HA,* 491.

24. Deborah Chorlton to HL, 29 May 2010; PF to WC, 30 March [1995], *L,* 186–87; "Well Walk," 2004, *HA,* 484.

25. Deerhaddnn: Pike's *Directory of Eastbourne* for 1925; *HA,* 472, 491–92; PF to WC, 17 May [1999], *L,* 206.

26. AF ms., HR I, 5.11; *Island,* no. 52 (Spring 1992): 40; BBC script, *Woman's Hour,* PK, 1 November 1954, BBC.

27. *EBJ,* 5; *CM,* 10, 21, 25; *HA,* 186.

28. *AF,* 23; HV, 42; *I,* 168; *BF,* 11, 95; *ME,* 115.

29. Winifred Peck, *A Little Learning; or, A Victorian Childhood* (Faber, 1952), 113, 124, 118, 146; Elise Borderman, *Stands There a School* (Dolphin Press, 1965), 104; WC, interview MS, 20 February 2004.

30. Maria, interview MS, 13 February 2004.

31. PK, "Wicked Words," *Cherwell,* 10 June 1939, 129.

32. WC, interview MS, 20 February 2004; Elisabeth Fisher to HL, 10 August 2010, Anne Conder to HL, 2010; *Wycombe Abbey Gazette,* 8 December 1934, 213; 9 March 1935, 252; PF to CK, 10 March [1935], TDA.

33. Jean Fisher, interview MS, 8 January 2004; Elisabeth Fisher to HL, 10 August 2010; HL, interviews at Oundle School with Charles Bush and Stephen Forge, 7 September 2010.

34. *KB,* 192, 200, 204; J. M. Barrie to EVK, 14 November 1933, TDA. On EVK and Shepard, Rawle Knox, ed., *The Work of E. H. Shepard* (Methuen, 1979) [copy inscribed to PF, "With much, much, love—and thanks for all the help"], TDA.

35. *KB,* 172, 179, 191–92. *KB,* 1st edition, has "only defined by." Mavis Batey, "Dilly Knox— A Reminiscence," *Cryptologia,* no. 32 (2008): 104–30.

36. *KB,* 207–8, Jean Fisher, interview MS, 8 January 2004.

37. CK to "John," 21 November 1934, TDA.

38. Somerville College Association of Senior Members, 9th Annual Supplement to the Report of the College 1933–34, 9, Somerville.

39. RO, obituary of PF, *Independent,* 9 May 2000.

40. PK to CK, 10 February, 7, 10, 26 March [1935], TDA.

41. PF to WC, 7 May [1998], *L,* 199.

42. PK to CK and EVK from Le Perroux, May 1935, TDA.

43. Jean Fisher and WC, interviews MS.

44. *KB,* 208.
45. WC, interview MS.

CHAPTER THREE
The "Blonde Bombshell"

1. *Isis,* 19 May 1938.
2. 10th Annual Supplement, *Report of Somerville College,* 1934–35, 11, Somerville.
3. PF, interview with Joan Acocella, *New Yorker,* 7 February 2000, 82; Lu, 379.
4. *HA,* 353.
5. Lu, 377.
6. *KB,* 212.
7. Edward Whitley [quoting Iris Murdoch], *The Graduates* (Hamish Hamilton, 1986), 65, cited in Pauline Adams, *Somerville for Women* (OUP, 1996), 233.
8. Janet Probert, née Russell, to TD, 30 September and 10 October 2008.
9. Janet Probert to Hugh Lee, 18 February 2004.
10. Janet Probert to Hugh Lee, 7 July 2008, 14 July 2002, 14 August 2007.
11. Belinda Probert to HL, re her mother, Janet Probert, 27 September 2010; Anne Conder to HL, re WC, 2010; Barbara Craig, Jean Fisher, WC, interviews MS; 20 February, 9, 19 January, 2004; Somerville College, "Special Report for 1935," ed. Susan Hicklin, questionnaires from Janet Probert and Jean Fisher, Somerville.
12. Hope Rossitter to HL, June 2010.
13. Jean Talbot, née Fisher, interview MS, 8 January 2004; Janet Probert to Hugh Lee, 14 July 2002.
14. Sylvia Peck to HL, 7 February, 19 March, 28 July 2010.
15. *Isis,* 2 February 1938, 20 May 1937, 19 May 1938; *Cherwell,* 14 May 1938.
16. Sinclair Hood, letter to Hugh Lee, 3 March 2010.
17. Ibid.; Douglas Stuart to HL, 18 February 2010.
18. PF to Hugh Lee, 8, 20 July [1940], *L,* 12; Hugh Lee to HL, 15 January 2010.
19. Oliver Breakwell to Hugh Lee, December 1939, Hugh Lee archive.
20. Douglas Stuart to HL, 3, 18 February 2010.
21. Oliver Breakwell to Hugh Lee, 30 December 1939; PF to Hugh Lee, 1 January 1930, *L,* 8; Hugh Lee to HL, 25 February 2010.
22. VF to HL, 11 February 2010; *HA,* 354; "Why We Were Very Young," HR I, 2.2, II, 8.5; PF, interview with Humphrey Carpenter, BBC, 1998.
23. HR I, 2.2; II, 8.5.
24. *HA,* 84; Mavis Batey to HL, 19 March 2010.
25. Pauline Adams, *Somerville for Women: An Oxford College, 1879–1993* (OUP, 1996), 28, 208; Janet Probert to Hugh Lee, 28 July 2008; Whitley, *The Graduates,* 47; Dorothy Sayers, *Gaudy Night,* 1935, ch. 5.
26. Barbara Craig, interview MS, 20 February 2004.
27. Hope Rossitter to HL, June 2010; PF to RO, 8 May 1978, *L,* 244; "Notes on How Novels Work," ms., TDA.
28. Jane Aiken Hodge, "Penelope Knox Fitzgerald," *Somerville College Centenary Report and Supplement,* 1879–1979, 43, Somerville; Hope Rossitter to HL, June 2010.

29. PF, Questionnaire, "Special Report for 1935," Somerville.
30. Lu, 390.
31. *Milton's Poetical Works* (OUP, 1935), 188, 262, 213; PF's annotated edition, TDA. Helen Darbishire's edition of *The Manuscripts of Milton's Paradise Lost, Book I,* was published in 1931.
32. *HA,* 273; Kathleen Tillotson to PF, 2 April 1984, HR II, 9–1. The story about the scripts being bound in vellum was repeated in interviews by Jean Fisher, Barbara Craig and Elisabeth Barnett.
33. For PF's student journalism, see Edmund Gordon, "PF's Juvenilia," *TLS,* 2 July 2010, 14–15, and Dean Flower and Linda Henchey, "PF's Unknown Fiction," *Hudson Review,* vol. 61, no. 1 (Spring 2008).
34. PK articles: "Place aux Dames: For First Years Only," *Isis,* 29 April 1936, 5; "On Going Abroad," *Cherwell,* 23 May 1936, 78; "Books in General: The Literature of Detection," *Cherwell,* 19 June 1937, 188; "A Spot of Bother," *Cherwell,* 19 June 1937, 190; "A Desirable Resident," *Cherwell,* 6 February 1937, 58; "A Curious Incident," *Cherwell,* 6 March 1937, 149; "Beefsteak Damned Good," *Cherwell,* 15 May 1937, 55; "I Was Afraid," *Cherwell,* 27 February 1937, 134; "Look, Stranger," *Cherwell,* 14 May 1938, 48; "Wicked Words," *Cherwell,* 10 June 1939, 128.
35. *Isis,* 2, 9, 16 February 1938; Conrad Cherry, "ABC at the BBC: An Account of a Spelling Bee," *Isis,* 2 February 1938; "Hard Spells on the Air," *The Times,* Monday, 24 January 1938.
36. *HA,* 172.
37. "Place aux Dames: In the News, Miss Penelope Knox (Somerville)," *Isis,* 19 May 1938, 10.
38. Helen Knox, interview MS, 7 January 2004.
39. Barbara Craig, interview MS, 20 February 2004.
40. PK to Hugh Lee, 8 July [1940], *L,* 11; Oliver Breakwell to Hugh Lee, [?] December 1939, Hugh Lee archive.
41. PK to Hugh Lee, *L,* 11; Barbara Craig, interview MS, 20 February 2004.
42. Peter Conradi, *Iris Murdoch: A Life* (HarperCollins, 2001), 88.
43. *KB,* 219–20.

CHAPTER FOUR

Love and War

1. All quotations not otherwise identified in chapter 4 are from *Human Voices.*
2. PK to Hugh Lee, 5, 13 October 1939, *L,* 4–6.
3. Hugh Lee to HL, 19 December 2004.
4. PK, "At the Pictures," *Punch,* 18 September, 9 and 23 October, 6 and 13 November 1940.
5. PK, "War on Wit," *TLS,* 18 February 1939.
6. BH to HL, 6 March 2010.
7. PK to Hugh Lee, 11 June 1940, *L,* 9.
8. PK to Hugh Lee, September 1940, *L,* 15.
9. Ministry of Food: See Susan Foreman, *Loaves & Fishes: An Illustrated History of the Ministry of Agriculture, Fisheries and Food, 1889–1989* (HMSO, 1989); Ministry of Food/Imperial War Museum websites.
10. Harold Roots to PF, n.d., HR II, 9.1.

11. PK to Hugh Lee, 26 November 1940, *L,* 20.

12. Asa Briggs, *The History of Broadcasting in the United Kingdom,* vol. 3: *The War of Words* (OUP, 1995), 24, 71.

13. *HA,* 473–75.

14. PK to Hugh Lee, 24 September, 6 and 15 October 1940, *L,* 16, 17, 18.

15. Paul Fussell, *Wartime: Understanding and Behaviour in the Second World War* (OUP, 1989), 181–82.

16. George Orwell, March 1942, quoted in Briggs, *History of Broadcasting,* 20.

17. HR II, 6, 8–13.

18. See Briggs, *History of Broadcasting,* 268–89, citing Freddie Grisewood, *My Story of the BBC* (1959), 121; *HA,* 474.

19. PK to Hugh Lee, 19 March 1941, *L,* 22; information on the BBC in 1940s from Ros Goulder to HL, 3 November 2012.

20. For Murrow, Liddell, Sackville-West, see Briggs, *History of Broadcasting,* 266 ff.; PF, interview HL, "The View from Here," BBC Radio 4, 20 January 1995.

21. A. S. Byatt to HL, 14 September 2010.

22. *HA,* 475.

23. PK to Hugh Lee, September 1940, *L,* 14.

24. Briggs, *History of Broadcasting,* 41, 10–11.

25. Ibid., 220; A. J. P. Taylor, *English History, 1914–1945* (Pelican, 1970), 594.

26. *KB,* 244, 246.

27. *KB,* 243.

28. Mavis Batey, "Dilly Knox: A Reminiscence," *Cryptologia,* no. 32 (2008); 104–30; Taylor and Francis, 117; *KB,* 226.

29. *KB,* 229; Batey, "Dilly Knox," 112; Charlotte Knox to HL, 18 July 2010.

30. *KB,* 232, 248; Batey, "Dilly Knox," 111.

31. *KB,* 244.

32. PK to Hugh Lee, 15 October 1940, 2 December 1940, *L,* 18, 21.

33. Obituary, *The Times,* 9 June 1994; Helen Knox, interview MS, 7 January 2004; *KB,* 246.

34. PK to Hugh Lee, 15 October 1940, *L,* 18; Hugh Lee to HL, 15 January 2010.

35. Oliver Breakwell to Hugh Lee, 17 July 1940.

36. PK to Hugh Lee, 28 October 1940, *L,* 18.

37. PF to Mandy Kirkby, 17 June 1997, *L,* 482; *County Louth Archaeological Society Journal,* vol. 12, no. 1 (1949): 2; information re Fitzgeralds and Lyons from Tina.

38. Because DF was born in Malaya and had Irish parents, he had difficulties in getting a British passport when, in the 1970s, immigration restrictions were being tightened up.

39. Family information, Tina, TD, VF.

40. WC, interview MS, 20 February 2004; Jean Talbot [Fisher], interview MS, 8 January 2004.

41. Abbot of Downside, reference for DF to Irish Guards, 7 November 1939, VF archive.

42. Hugh Lee thought Eamon ugly and unpleasant, and noted his heavy drinking as a young man. Hugh Lee to HL, 15 January 2010.

43. Helen Knox, interview MS, 7 January 2004.

44. Robert Conquest to HL, 27 March 2010.

45. Jasmine Blakeway to HL, 27 September 2010.

46. Report on D. L. J. Fitzgerald, VF archive.

47. *The Times,* 27 May 1942, "Forthcoming Marriages," col. C.

48. Jasmine Blakeway to HL, 27 September 2010.

49. Elizabeth Bowen, *The Heat of the Day* (1949).

50. *HA,* 475.

51. *Punch,* 22 July 1942, 60; 12 August 1942, 126.

52. *KB,* 249–51; DF, military record, VF archive; DF, *History of the Irish Guards* (Gale & Polden, 1949).

53. DF, *History,* 118, 121; DF, military records, VF archive; Robert Conquest to HL, 27 March 2010.

54. Jasmine Blakeway to HL, 27 September 2010; DF, *History,* 385, 538.

55. DF, *History,* 237–38, 255–56.

56. Ibid., 359.

57. Jean Talbot [Fisher] interview MS, 8 January 2004; VF to HL, 11 February 2010.

58. VF to HL, 11 February 2010.

59. PF to Maria, 6 May 1974, *L,* 146.

60. Janet Probert [Russell] to PF, 14 June 1956; Janet to Hugh Lee, 7 July 2008.

61. PF to Beryl Radley, 31 October 1945, BBC.

62. *Punch,* 13 December 1944, 513; 29 January 1947, 26; 13 January 1943, 40; 21 April 1943, 341; 29 March 1944, 276; 19 January 1944, 60; 3 December 1947, 542.

63. PF to Miss Leggett, 23 October 1945; PF to Beryl Radley, 29 September 1945; PF to Helen ——, 31 July 1946, BBC.

64. Annual allowance from EVK, Helen Knox interview MS, 7 January 2004; PF to Beryl Radley, 19 June 1947; Ursula Keeble, memo, 9 January 1948, BBC.

65. WC interview MS, 20 February 2004; Helen Knox interview MS, 7 January 2004.

66. Janet Probert to PF, 14 June 1956.

67. *HA,* 214.

68. *I,* 191–92; *BS,* 33.

69. BH to HL, 6 March 2010; BH and Helen Knox, interview MS, 7 January 2004.

70. *KB,* 261.

71. PF, preface to Rose Macaulay, *The World My Wilderness* (1983); *HA,* 303.

72. Janet Probert to PF, 14 June 1956.

73. PF to Tina, 12 January 1987, *L,* 76.

74. PF to Ursula Keeble, 8 August 1947, PF to Mollie [Reynolds?], 24 July 1947, BBC.

CHAPTER FIVE

The World

1. *WR,* June 1951.

2. PF to Maria, 18 May 1975, TDA.

3. "Coming Shortly," *Woman's Hour,* 17 January 1951, 1 November 1945, BBC.

4. PF, postcard, 14 April 1946; postcard, 9 June 1947; PF to Mollie [Reynolds], 8 August 1948, BBC.

5. PF to Ivan Gilman, 2 January 1951; Schools Service, 22 May 1951, 18 September 1953, 20 November 1953, 16 January 1956, 26 February 1953, BBC.

6. "General Science," 27 October 1959, 12 October 1949, rebroadcast 30 January 1959, BBC.

7. PF to Robert [Gittings], 20 September [1951], BBC; *HA,* 236–37; PF to Ursula [Keeble], 10 August 1949, BBC.

8. *Woman's Hour,* 10 August 1948, BBC.

9. PF to Miss Foulger, 24 May 1950, BBC.

10. *Woman's Hour,* 17 January 1951, 2 April 1952, 21 March 1951, 7 February 1951, BBC.

11. "Books to Read," Overseas Service, 22 March 1949, BBC.

12. *Woman's Hour,* 12 March 1952; *Bookshelf,* 3 February 1949, BBC.

13. This method is recommended by Elizabeth David in *Italian Food* (Macdonald, 1954), 84. The mother in the typescript of *GC* does the same thing.

14. Harvey Frost to PF, 10 October 1999, TDA; memories of Chestnut Lodge: Jasmine Blakeway, Helen Knox, William Knox, BH, Deborah Chorlton, VF, Tina, Maria.

15. PF to CC, 23 April [1992], *L,* 497.

16. *KB,* 265.

17. Malcolm Muggeridge, *Like It Was: The Diaries of Malcolm Muggeridge,* ed. John Bright-Holmes (Collins, 1981), 264, 454–56.

18. Helen Knox and BH, interview MS, 7 January 2004; *KB,* 261.

19. Hulton Press: Tom Hopkinson, *Of This Our Time* (Hutchinson, 1982); David Reed, *The Popular Magazine in Britain and the United States, 1880–1960* (British Library, 1997), 185; Sally Morris and Jan Hallwood, *Living with Eagles: Marcus Morris, Priest and Publisher* (Lutterworth Press, 1998); Tom Burns, *The Use of Memory: Publishing and Further Pursuits* (Sheed & Ward, 1993).

20. Richard Cockett, *David Astor and The Observer* (Deutsch, 1991), 159. Clifford Makins was *Private Eye*'s "Lunchtime O'Booze."

21. Helen Knox, interview MS, 7 January 2004.

22. *The Times,* 4 August 1950, 6, col. C.

23. PF to Ivan Gilman, 8 January 1951, BBC.

24. John Lehmann, 1950, quoted in Peter Brooker and Andrew Thacker, *The Oxford Critical and Cultural History of Modernist Magazines,* vol. 1 (OUP, 2009), 680.

25. Raleigh Trevelyan to HL, 25 July 2010.

26. *WR,* January, February, August, September–November, December 1951; January, April 1952.

27. *WR,* "Medardo Rossi," "PMF," June 1951.

28. PF to EVK and MK, 10 October [1950/1951?], TDA.

29. "PMF and DF," "Spanish Painted Sculpture," *WR,* July, August 1952.

30. "PMF," *WR,* "The Unsophisticated Arts," February 1952.

31. *WR,* January 1953.

32. *WR,* June 1951; "DF" "Resolutions," *WR,* January 1952; "DF" "The Chart of Half-Baked Ideas," *WR,* February 1952.

33. "A Letter from Tisshara," and "The Feast of the Writers in Tisshara," *WR,* March and July 1951; see Dean Flower and Linda Henchey, "Penelope Fitzgerald's Unknown Fiction," *Hudson Review,* no. 1 (Spring 2008): 2–18.

34. PF, postcard, 24 January 1952, BBC.

35. *Queen Mary* passenger list, October 1952, TDA; information re 36 Amherst Road, Port Washington, Michael J. Roberts to HL, 15 August 2011; Mexico trip memories: VF to HL and VF interview MS; *HA,* 494–98.

36. PF to Tina, 12 January [1987], *L,* 77.

37. *WR,* April–May 1953.
38. "DF and PMF" "Editorial," *WR,* April–May 1953.
39. *WR,* November 1952.
40. David Painting to PF, 14 August 1990, HR, II, 7, 5; PF to David Painting, 20 August 1990.
41. Francesca Zawadzki to HL, August 2010; PF to Maria, February 1974, TDA.
42. "Jassy of Juniper Farm," *Swift,* 1957–58, TDA.
43. PF to EVK and MK, 13 April [1953], *L,* 213.
44. PF to CC, 2 March [1997], *L,* 501. The first giant panda arrived in England in 1958.
45. Helen Knox, WC, interviews MS; Jasmine Blakeway to HL, 17 March 2010.
46. *KB,* 268; PF to CC, 15 March 2000, *L,* 517.
47. Maria to HL, 1 October 2009.
48. PF to Frank Kermode, 2 November [1979], *L,* 452. See Flower and Henchey, "Penelope Fitzgerald's Unknown Fiction," on "The Mooi."
49. DF, "The Soldier in My Throat," *Lilliput,* vol. 41, no. 5 (November 1957), reprinted in *Hudson Review,* vol. 61, no. 1 (Spring 2008).
50. PF to Maria, 5 August 1972, *L,* 115.
51. *HA,* 495.

CHAPTER SIX
The Bookshop

1. All quotations in chapter 6 not otherwise identified are from *The Bookshop.*
2. *HA,* 476.
3. Nikolaus Pevsner, with Enid Radcliffe, *Suffolk: The Buildings of England* (1961, 1974), 432; Norman Scarfe, *A Shell Guide to Suffolk* (Faber, 1960), 155; PF to Mandy Kirkby, 19 May 1995, *L,* 480.
4. *HA,* 477.
5. According to Deborah Chorlton, her aunt, a lucid ninety-six-year-old, said: "Somebody lent them a house" in Southwold; Deborah Chorlton to HL, 2010.
6. *HA,* 476.
7. PF to RO, 2 November 1979, *L,* 373; VF, interview MS, 5 March 2004.
8. *HA,* 476; Maria, interview MS, 13 February 2004.
9. Phyllis Neame to PF, 19 November, 10 December 1978, HR 1, 4.10.
10. Iris Birtwistle, interview MS, 9 January 2004.
11. Christina Fitzgerald, *Mrs. Killick's Luck,* illustrated by Mary Shepard, foreword by Stevie Smith (Frederick Books, Methuen, 1960).
12. PF, interview with Annie Reynolds, *Island,* Spring 1992, 39.
13. PF to CC, 2 September 1997, *L,* 505.
14. *HA,* 477.
15. PF to Tina, 12 January [1987], *L,* 77.
16. Stevie Smith, "Parents," in *Not Waving But Drowning,* 1957.
17. Helen Knox thought that a friend of Desmond's paid for VF to go to Downside. Helen Knox, interview MS. VF thought the school waived the fees.
18. *KB,* 264.
19. HR I, 5.15.
20. HR I, 5.15 and TDA.

CHAPTER SEVEN
Clinging On for Dear Life

1. All quotations in chapter 7 not otherwise identified are from *Offshore*.
2. *HA,* 478. The minesweeper was in fact a motor torpedo boat, with a proud ex-naval owner.
3. PF to CC, 25 February 1998, *L,* 506.
4. Memories of life on *Grace* from interviews (HL and MS) with Tina, Maria, VF, Janet Probert, WC, Jean Fisher, Iris Birtwistle and Jasmine Blakeway.
5. VF, interview MS, 5 March 2004.
6. Janet Probert to Hugh Lee, 9 July 2008.
7. *HA,* 508.
8. *HA,* 478.
9. *HA,* 498.
10. *O,* 59, says it is six months before the spring of 1962, and on *O,* 100, Richard (aged 39), says he was born in 1922: so it is autumn 1961. But *O,* 71, says that Mrs. Stirling will be 100 in 1965 and is now 97: so it is 1962. And on *O,* 39, Martha's (aged 12) birth date is 1951: so it is 1963. In the manuscript, the date of O is 1961. HR, I, 8.7.
11. HR I, 8.7.
12. Ibid.; PF interview, Joan Acocella, "Assassination on a Small Scale," *New Yorker,* 7 February 2000, 85.
13. Josephine Pullein-Thompson to HL, 21 August 2010; FK to HL, 12 February 2010.
14. Robert Conquest to HL, 27 March 2010.
15. VF to HL, June 2009, 11 February 2010; interview MS, 5 March 2004. Details of DF court case: London Metropolitan Archive, Mansion House Justice Room Records, CLA/004; *The Times,* 4 July, 12 December 1962.
16. Jasmine Blakeway to HL, 17 March 2010; Antonia Southern to HL, 23 March 2010.
17. FK, Josephine Pullein-Thompson, to HL. A solicitor at the firm of Theodore Goddard, a friend of PF's nephew William Knox, also told William and Belinda Knox that DF went to prison and "disappeared from the scene." BH to HL, 6 March 2010.
18. VF to PF, January [1963], TDA.
19. PF to Rachel Hichens, 18 December 1962; PF to RO, 25 February 1981, *L,* 384.
20. Diana Ladas was descended from a banking family, had been in the Ministry of Economic Warfare in Cairo, married Alexis Ladas, a Greek war refugee, whom she left, knew Lawrence Durrell, taught at Westminster Tutors, was deputy head at Queen's Gate and owned a converted oast house near Burwash in Sussex. She let the Fitzgeralds use the oast house and also lent them a car. Andrea Ladas to HL, 19 January 2012.
21. *HA,* 478.
22. Suzanne Spratt to PF, 1 July 1963, TDA; DF, diary, Maria archive. Sinking of *Grace:* information from Tina, Maria, VF, Iris Birtwistle, Lis Barnett and Jasmine Blakeway. Romilly Saumarez-Smith to HL, 22 May 2010.
23. "In the Forefront of Children's Care Since World War II," wisearchive.co.uk; S. Fitzpatrick, P. Kemp and S. Klinker, *Single Homelessness* (Joseph Rowntree Foundation, 2000); P. Dunleavy, *The Politics of Mass Housing in Britain* (OUP, 1981); VF, Maria, Tina, to HL and interviews with MS; DF, diary, 1964, Maria archive.

24. PF to Tina, [Easter, 1964], *L,* 33.

25. PF to Ivan Gilman, 23 June 1964; Ivan Gilman to PF, 26 June 1964; Ivan Gilman memo, 26 June 1964, BBC.

26. PF to Tina, [Easter, 1964], *L,* 33. Tina notes on her grandmother's funeral on 29 September 1964, TDA; DF, diary, 29 September 1964, Maria archive.

CHAPTER EIGHT
Family Matters

1. PF to Maria, 20 January [1973], *L,* 123.

2. VF interview MS, 3 March 2004; Helen Knox interview MS, 7 January 2004.

3. PF ms. on VF, TDA.

4. Tina and Maria, diaries, 1964, 1965, 1966, TDA.

5. PF ms. on VF, TDA.

6. VF to Tina, n.d. [March 1965], TDA.

7. John Henderson, Director, International Teacher Training Institute, to PF, 29 April 1965; Notebook "Teacher Training: English as a Foreign Language," n.d., TDA.

8. VF to PF, 30 March 1965, TDA.

9. Tina, diary, 5 May 1965, TDA.

10. VF to PF, undated letters [March–June 1965], TDA.

11. VF to Tina, 12 October and 24 November 1965, 21 January 1966, TDA.

12. DF, diary, 3, 12 January 1966, Maria archive.

13. PF, diary, 1966, TDA.

14. VF, interview MS, 5 March 2004.

15. PF to Tina, 9 April 1966, *L,* 39.

16. PF to Tina, 23 August 1966, *L,* 40; Angelines Fitzgerald to HL, 16 March 2010.

17. DF, diary, 9 December 1967, "Valpy & Angie arrive."

18. Angelines Fitzgerald to HL, 16 March 2010.

19. Tina, diary, 5 January 1968, TDA.

20. PF to Tina, 8 July [1968], TDA.

21. PF to Tina, 29 July [1968], TDA.

22. Angelines Fitzgerald to HL, 16 March 2010.

23. PF to Tina, 24 March [1968], *L,* 55.

24. DF to Tina, 19 November 1968, TDA.

25. PF to Tina, 12 October [1968], *L,* 59.

26. PF to Maria, 14 May [1973], *L,* 135.

27. PF to Maria, 26 October [1972], *L,* 118.

28. PF to Maria, 5 August 1972, *L,* 115; 10 June [1973], *L,* 137.

29. DL to Maria, 19 February 1974, Maria archive.

30. PF to Tina, 20 January [1993], TDA.

31. Untitled, undated notes on Valpy, TDA.

32. PF to Tina, 8 July [1968], TDA; PF to Tina, 7 April 1965, *L,* 35; PF to Maria, 20 January [1973], *L,* 122.

33. PF to Maria, 14 May [1973], *L,* 135; PF to Tina, 1 August [1967], *L,* 43; 24 March [1968], *L,* 54; 13 April [1968], *L,* 58.

34. PF to Maria, 23 January [1972], *L*, 199.
35. Maria, Tina, TD, interviews with HL and MS; Maria to HL, 10 January 2012; Maura Dooley to HL, May 2012.
36. PF to Maria, 23 November [1974], *L*, 155.
37. TD, ms., "Memories of Penelope," 1974?, TDA.
38. PF to Maria, 12 February [1972], *L*, 111.
39. HL interviews with Charlotte, William and Timothy Knox, 18, 28 July, August 2010.
40. Lis Barnett to HL, 1 October 2010; BH to HL, 6 March 2010; William Knox to HL, 4 April 2010.
41. MK to PF, 15 February 1972, TDA.
42. PF to Maria, 23 November [1974], *L*, 155.
43. Helen Knox, interview MS, 7 January 2004; Colin Peck to HL, 12 August 2010; BH to HL, 6 March 2010.
44. William Knox to HL, 4 April 2010; BH to HL, 6 March 2010; Helen Knox, interview MS, 7 January 2004.
45. PF to Tina, 9 August [1967], *L*, 46; [August 1967], *L*, 50.
46. PF to Maria, 5 August [1969], *L*, 100.
47. PF to Maria, 23 July [1972], *L*, 113.
48. DF diary entries, 30 January 1965, 5 January, 6 April 1967, 19 April 1969, 11 January 1966, Maria archive.
49. DF to Tina, 19 November 1968, TDA.
50. DF to PF, n.d.; 15 May 1972; 17 July 1973, TDA.
51. *Alpenblumenfibel*, 1963, TDA.
52. Maria to HL, 11 May 2012.
53. PF to Tina, [summer 1969], *L*, 69.
54. PF to Maria, 27 February [1973], *L*, 128; DF, diary, 10 May 1969, Maria archive; PF to Tina, 13 April [1968], 58.
55. DF, diary, 18 January 1965; *L*, 121, 130, 134, 165.
56. PF to Maria, 12 February 1972, *L*, 111.
57. PF to Tina, [August 1967], *L*, 50.
58. PF to Maria, [1970], *L*, 103; 26 July [1972], *L*, 114; The Revd Ian Reid to PF, 12 August 1970, TDA; "Beehernz," *ME*, 60.

CHAPTER NINE
The Teacher

1. *HA*, 479. All quotations in chapter 9 not otherwise identified are from *At Freddie's*.
2. PF, Teaching notebook, 1969, TDA.
3. PF to Maria, "Sunday" [6 May 1974], *L*, 145.
4. *HA*, 479–80.
5. Rena Fogel to HL, 11 July 2011.
6. Elizabeth de Leeuw, *Queen's Gate: An Unschooly School* (Antony Rowe, 2007), 226, 233.
7. PF to Maria, 20 January [1973], *L*, 123.
8. PF to Maria, Sunday 20 [February 1973], *L*, 126.
9. PF to Maria, 6 January [1972], *L*, 106.

10. A. S. Byatt, preface to *L*, 2008, ix–xiii; *The Times*, 18 July 2008; A. S. Byatt to HL, 31 August 2010.

11. Antonia Southern to HL, 23 March 2010.

12. A. S. Byatt, preface to *L*; A. S. Byatt to HL, 31 August 2010; A. S. Byatt in "Listen with Writers," *Guardian*, 22 December 2012; Penelope Lively to HL, 19 October 2010.

13. Jane Darwin to HL, 16 May 2010.

14. PF to Tina, 20 January [1993], TDA.

15. PF to Maria, [late 1973], *L*, 142; 12 February [1972], *L*, 111; 12 June [1974], *L*, 147; 3 June [1975], *L*, 172.

16. PF, Teaching notebook, 1966, TDA.

17. PF to Maria, 26 October [1972], *L*, 117.

18. Jane Martineau, diary, 1965, Jane Martineau.

19. Jane Martineau to HL, 6 May 2010.

20. Nicola-Rose Virgin to HL, 9 July 2010.

21. Edward St. Aubyn to HL, 24 April 2012. Other reminiscences of PF as teacher, to HL from Henrietta Heald, Romilly Saumarez Smith, Patrick Marber, Nicola-Rose Virgin, Joe Coughlan, Wanda Carter, Tiffany Daneff, William Sieghart.

22. Antonia Byatt Jr. to HL, 31 August 2010; Jane Martineau to HL, 6 May 2010; Jane Martineau to PF, 27 March 1998; PF to Jane Martineau, 2 April 1998.

23. Lucy Wadham to HL, 10 January 2010.

24. Linda Thomas to PF, n.d. [22 August], TDA.

25. Nicola-Rose Virgin [then Sworder], "Theme of Losing and Finding in Winter's Tale: Essay for Mrs. Fitzgerald," 1984–85, Nicola-Rose Virgin.

26. Jane Martineau essays, 1965–66, Jane Martineau.

27. Lucy Wadham to HL, 10 January 2010; Oxford General Entrance Paper, November 1974, with *Innocence* papers, HR I, 7.22.

28. PF, Teaching notebook, late 1960s, HR I, 10.10.

29. PF, Teaching notebook, probably 1970, TDA.

30. Reading notes for teaching, 1968–69, HR I, 10.10.

31. PF Teaching notebook, late 1960s, HR I, 10.10.

32. PF, Notebook, drafts for *AF*, HR I, 5.10.

33. Ibid.

34. For Lilian Baylis, see Richard Findlater, *Lilian Baylis: The Lady of the Old Vic* (Allen Lane, 1975), and Elizabeth Schaefer, *Lilian Baylis: A Biography* (University of Hertfordshire, 2006).

35. PF to RO, 13 April [1982], *L*, 391. AF may have been partly inspired by Val May's *Tribute to a Lady* (1975), his affectionate and funny portrait of Baylis, performed at a gala when the National Theatre left the Old Vic.

36. Maev Kennedy, "Ellen Terry's Beetlewing Gown Back in Limelight," *Guardian*, 12 March 2011. The gown has been restored and is on show at her last home, Smallhythe Place in Kent.

37. HR I, 5.10.

38. Ibid.

39. PF to RO, 28 August [1981], *L*, 389.

40. *Hamlet*, Act II, scene ii; HR I, 5.10.

41. PF to RO, 28 August [1981], *L,* 389.

42. PF typescript for blurb, July 1981, annotated for RO: "This is the best I can do. I'll settle for anything, though." HCA.

43. *HA,* 306.

44. HR I, 5.10.

45. PF interview, *Island,* Spring 1992, 41: "I meant to indicate that he'd kill himself "; PF interview, Joan Acocella, *New Yorker,* 7 February 2000, 86: "Jonathan dies, she said. He kills himself, accidentally, leaping off the wall. But nobody had grasped this, she added, and that was her fault."

46. *HA,* 5, 10.

47. HR I, 6.15, 6.16.

48. PF, notes on a visit to Stevie Smith, 30 January 1969, TDA.

49. "Thirteen Poems by PF," *LRB,* 3 October 2002, 26–27.

50. HR II, 8.2; PF to Tina, [early 1969], *L,* 63; Hughes was working on, and reading from, *The Life and Songs of the Crow* (1966) through the 1960s and early 1970s. *Crow* was published in 1972.

51. *L,* 522.

52. PF to Tina, 4, 8 January [1971], TDA; HR I, 10.8; *HA,* 470.

53. *HA,* 386.

CHAPTER TEN
The Useful Arts

1. "Foreword," EBJ. All quotations in chapter 10 not otherwise identified are from *Edward Burne-Jones.*

2. Ms., "Introduction" [to *EBJ,* pb, 1989], HR I, 8.6; interview, *Island,* Spring 1992, 38.

3. *KB,* 45.

4. Lu, 378; Ms., "Introduction," HR I, 8.6.

5. William Morris, *News from Nowhere* (Nonesuch Press, 1934), 91. (This edition was given to PF by Tina in 1968, "during her first term at Oxford," Maria archive.) See "Art Nouveau," *WR,* January 1953.

6. Mavis Batey to HL, 19 March 2010; Jasmine Blakeway to HL, 17 March 2010.

7. SP to HL, 16 May 2010.

8. PF to Maria, 20 February [1973], *L,* 127.

9. 17–24 July 1971, 14–23 July 1973, 20–22? August, September 1974, PF entries in visitors' book, St. Deiniol's [now Gladstone Library]; PF to Tina, 10, 14 July [1969], *L,* 65, 67.

10. PF to Tina, 14 July [1969], *L,* 68.

11. PF to Maria, 6 May [1974], *L,* 145; DF, diary, Maria archive. HR I, 10.6, "Autobiography"; VF to PF, 7 February 1971, TDA; PF to Maria, 23 June [1973], *L,* 138.

12. PF to Maria, 12 February [1972], *L,* 111; PF to Oliver Knox, 3 March 1997, Charlotte Knox archive; Mary Chamot, Obituaries, *Independent,* 17 May 1993, *The Times,* 21 May 1993; *Oxford Dictionary of National Biography* entry, Dennis Farr.

13. HR I, 5.9, 5.12, 6.11, 8.13.

14. HR I, 8.13.

15. HR I, 6.9.

16. RO, memo, 29 January 1979, HCA.

17. HR I, 7.2. Undated but mid-1980s.

18. *GC,* 45.

19. PF to Frank Kermode, 3 October [1995], *L,* 453.

20. *HA,* 121, 133.

21. PF to Maria, 11 October [1973], *L,* 140.

22. William Morris Society to PF, 26 May 1994, Maria archive.

23. PF letters to Mary Lago, *L,* 294–329.

24. *HA,* 105–11; William Morris, *The Novel on Blue Paper* (Journeyman Press, London, 1982), 78.

25. Mary Lago, ed., *Burne-Jones Talking: His Conversations, 1895–98, Preserved by His Studio Assistant Thomas Rooke* (John Murray, 1982), Maria archive; Stephen Wildman and John Christian, *Edward Burne-Jones: Victorian Artist-Dreamer* (Metropolitan Museum of Art, 1998), 178, 250, 260, 321; Fiona MacCarthy, *The Last Pre-Raphaelite: Edward Burne-Jones and the Victorian Imagination* (Faber, 2011), 597. EBJ had two reissues, by Hamish Hamilton in 1989 and by Sutton Publishing in 2003 (a bad edition full of misprints).

26. *TLS,* 12 December 1975; *The Economist,* 27 September 1975.

27. PF to Maria, 26 October [1972], [6 March 1974], *L,* 117, 144; VF to HL, 11 February 2010.

28. "Most treasured things," Knox family papers, TDA; *HA,* 210–11.

29. PF to Maria, 12 February [1972], *L,* 111; 1 March 1974, *L,* 143.

30. *Independent,* 24 September 1994.

31. DF, diary, 1973, Maria archive.

32. PF to Maria, 24 October [1973] *L,* 141.

33. Ibid.

34. Tina, 1974 diary, TDA.

35. Richard Usborne to PF, 2 April 1978, HR I, 1.13; Dean of Bristol to PF, 20 December 1974, HR I, 1.18; Revd Murray Macdonald, 14 October 1974, HR I, 1.18; David Kahn to PF, 13 March 1977, HR I, 1.19; J. Winterbotham to PF, 12 December 1974, HR I, 1.19; PF to Maria, 6 October [1974], *L,* 150; PF to Muggeridge, 30 October 1977, *L,* 254.

36. PF to Oliver Knox, 25 January 1975, Charlotte Knox archive.

37. PF to Maria, 5 April [1975], *L,* 164.

38. PF to Maria, [April 1973], *L,* 166.

39. Harold Macmillan to PF, 19 November 1977, *L,* 249; Macmillan's memo, 3 September 1975, HR I, 1.5.

40. PF to Maria, 10 May [1975], *L,* 168; *ME,* 25–36.

41. PF to Tina, [1974], *L,* 70; PF to Maria, 20 October 1974, *L,* 151; Tina to HL, 14 August 2009; TDA.

42. PF to Maria, [30 May 1975], *L,* 170.

43. DF to Tina, 11 June 1975, TDA.

44. *Island,* Spring 1992, 38; Acocella, *New Yorker,* 7 February 2000, 85; *Independent,* 24 September 1994, and many other examples.

45. PF to Richard Garnett, 10 September [1977], *L,* 240.

46. PF to WC, 16 October [1976], *L,* 174. Maria to HL, May 2012.

47. DF, diary, July 1975, Maria archive.

48. Tina to HL, 19 February 2010.

49. Maria to HL, May 2012.
50. DF, diary, September 1975; Tina to HL, 19 February 2010; Maria to HL, May 2012.
51. DF, diary, 1975–76; PF to MK [February–March 1976], *L*, 224.
52. Mary would leave half her estate in 2000 to Rawle's widow, Helen, enough for her to afford sheltered housing (BH to HL, 6 March 2010). The other half was left to PF, but as PF predeceased MK, her half was inherited equally by PF's children.
53. DF, *Irish Guards*, 1949: see chapter 4, note 52.
54. DF, diary, June 1976; PF to Richard Garnett, 18 June 1976, *L*, 233.
55. DF, diary, July–August 1976; VF to PF and DF, 9 July 1976, TDA; PF to Richard Garnett, 7 August [1976], *L*, 234; PF to Oliver Knox, 16 August [1976], Charlotte Knox archive.
56. PF to WC, 16 October [1976], *L*, 174.

CHAPTER ELEVEN
Enigmas

1. All quotations in chapter 11 not otherwise identified are from *The Golden Child*.
2. PF to Mandy Kirkby, 17 June 1997, *L*, 481.
3. *Independent Books*, 24 September 1994.
4. Stoddard Martin, ed., *Colin Haycraft, 1929–1994, Maverick Publisher* (Duckworth, 1995), 121.
5. Frank Kermode, "The Duckworth School of Writers," *LRB*, vol. 2, no. 22 (20 November 1980), 18–19.
6. See Martin, *Colin Haycraft*.
7. Anna Haycraft to PF, 3 December 1976, Colin Haycraft to PF, 30 March 1977, HR I, 4.12.
8. PF to Richard Garnett, 16 September 1977, *L*, 241.
9. VF to PF, 17 January 1977, TDA.
10. PF to Richard Garnett, 16 September 1977, *L*, 241.
11. PF to FK, 20 January [1978], *L*, 264.
12. Jasmine Blakeway to HL, 17 March 2010.
13. Ms. of "The Iron Bridge," TDA.
14. PF to FK, 25 February [1978], *L*, 268; PF to RO, 14 June [1979], 371; PF to FK, 12 April [1978], *L*, 269, [1984], *L*, 286, 29 January [1978], *L*, 264, 25 February [1978], *L*, 268, 19 January [1979], *L*, 279; *HA*, 321.
15. L. P. Hartley, *The Go-Between* (Penguin, 1972), PF copy, and notes on LPH, TDA; PF to FK, 12 April [1978], *L*, 269–70.
16. PF to FK, 25 February [1978], *L*, 268, 29 October [1979], *L*, 281, 29 January [1978], *L*, 264; RO, Memo re PF, 29 January 1979, HCA.
17. PF to Colin Haycraft, 11 April [1978], *L*, 255; PF to FK, 25 February [1978], *L*, 266. PF interviews with Francis Wyndham (28 July 1979), Princess Clary (winter 1978); *HA*, 327–28; PF to Colin Haycraft, 16 February [1979], *L*, 260.
18. PF to RO, 14 June [1979], *L*, 370; Lord David Cecil to PF, 16 April 1977, HR II, 4.8.
19. FK to PF, 1 March 1978, HR II, 4.8; FK to HL, 12 February 2010. PF to FK, 29 January [1978], *L*, 264, 22 June [1978], *L*, 272.
20. PF notes on Francis Wyndham, 28 July 1979, on Hamilton, 5 September 1979, on Clary, winter 1978, on Powells, 28 February 1979, on Cecil [July 1979], HR II, 4.3–4; PF to FK, 2 March [1979], *L*, 276.

21. Notes on LPH, TDA.

22. PF to FK, 12 February [1978], *L,* 265; to Colin Haycraft, 11 April [1978], *L,* 256.

23. Examples: PF to Michael Holroyd, 18 September 1984, *L,* 472; PF to Howard Woolmer, 25 May [1988], *L,* 349.

24. Alan Hollinghurst to PF, 15 June 1981, Miranda Seymour to PF, 27 July 1992, HR II, 4.9.

25. *HA,* 329.

26. Notes on interview with Patric Dickinson, HR I, 7.16 [?] August 1979; notes on PB, HR I, 6.14–6.16; TDA; correspondence with Howard Woolmer, *L,* 330–69.

27. PF to Howard Woolmer, 29 November 1978, *L,* 331; 12 October [1988], *L,* 352; *HA,* 168.

28. J. C. Trewin, "Uncommon Quartet," *Times,* 27 October 1977; Malcolm Muggeridge, "A Family and Its Humour," *TLS,* 28 October 1977; H. R. F. Keating, "Crime," *Times,* 6 October 1977; T. J. Binyon, "Goldrush," *TLS,* 7 October 1977.

29. PF to Richard Garnett, 31 December [1977], *L,* 242.

30. PF, "My China Diary," December 1977, TDA.

31. Interview with PF, Clare Boylan, *Guardian,* 21 November 1991.

CHAPTER TWELVE
The Prize

1. PF to FK, 29 October [1979], *L,* 280–81.

2. PF to FK, 3 November 1978, *L,* 197.

3. Dust jacket, B, 1978; PF to CC, 7 December 1987, *L,* 490.

4. "High Spirits," interview with PF, Amazon.com, 1997, TDA.

5. PF to RO, 14 April 1983, *L,* 400.

6. For example, PF to Mary Lago, 1 January 1987, *L,* 313.

7. Clare Boylan, interview with PF, *Guardian,* 21 November 1991, 26.

8. PF to Richard Garnett, 11 March 1978, *L,* 243.

9. Epigraph to *BF.*

10. PF to FK, 22 June [1978], *L,* 272; PF to A. L. Barker, 8 March [1994], *L,* 440.

11. Colin Haycraft to PF, 6 April 1978, HR I, 4.8; Phyllis Neame to PF, 19 November 1978, HR I, 4.9.

12. Derek Parker, *The Times,* 2 November 1973; William French, "Signs of Malaise in the State of BritLit," *Toronto Globe and Mail,* 3 May 1979, 17; Norman Shrapnel, "Women's Novels," *Guardian,* 26 October 1978; Valentine Cunningham, "Suffocating Suffolk," *TLS,* 17 November 1978, 9; PF to FK, 3 November 1978, *L,* 273–74; Auberon Waugh, *Evening Standard,* 19 December 1978; Richard Mayne, *Critics' Forum,* cited in Richard Ollard, memo, Collins, January 1979, HCA.

13. PF in *Contemporary Authors Autobiography Series,* vol. 10 (1989), 101–9; *HA,* 467–80.

14. PF to RO, 11 October [1980], *L,* 381.

15. *L,* xxvi; PF to FK, 24 November [1978], *L,* 274–75.

16. PF to FK, 24 November [1978], *L,* 274–75; PF to Colin Haycraft, 1 November [1978], *L,* 258.

17. PF to FK, 3 November [1987], *L,* 273.

18. June Braybrooke to FK, 13 December 1978, HR [R 15095] I.4.

19. PF to WC, 5 January [1979], *L,* 178–79; PF to FK, 19 January [1979], *L,* 276.

20. PF to Colin Haycraft, 19 January [1979], *L,* 259.

21. Colin Haycraft to PF, 23 January 1979, HR II, 9.4.

22. PF to Colin Haycraft, 24 January [1979], *L*, 259–60.

23. PF to FK, 13 April [1979], *L*, 278. *"E pur si muove"* ("and yet it moves") was famously supposed to have been muttered by Galileo at his trial, after his recantation of the theory that the earth moves round the sun.

24. Annie Hallam, Beyack & Conway, to PF, 7 June 1979, annotated by PF in HR I, 4.8.

25. PF to Colin Haycraft, 16 February [1979], *L*, 260.

26. PF to FK, 13 April [1979], *L*, 278.

27. PF to RO, 26 August [1991], *L*, 413.

28. PF to RO, 28 October [1989], HCA.

29. On RO: SP, obituary, *Guardian*, 7 February 2007; SP to HL, 16 May 2010; Mary Ollard to HL, 2010; Philip Gwyn Jones to HL, 16 March 2010; Tim Knox to HL, August 2010.

30. RO to PF, 15 January 1979, HR I, 1.21.

31. PF to Colin Haycraft and to RO, 24 January 1979, *L*, 260, 370.

32. RO, memo, 29 January 1979, HCA.

33. PF to RO, 14 March [1980], *L*, 379; PF to RO 2 November [1979], *L*, 374.

34. *Bookseller*, 9 April 1979, HR I, 1.21.

35. Shepard left MK part of the interest income from his accumulated royalties, but not the rights in the *Winnie-the-Pooh* illustrations themselves, which went to his son's widow and her daughter. Then Disney drove a hard bargain for the rights. The same kind of thing happened when Disney bought the rights to *Mary Poppins*, which MK (as Mary Shepard) had illustrated. She derived very little benefit from the Disney adaptation.

36. PF to BH, 19 October [1979], BH archive.

37. *O*, 1979, dust jacket.

38. Briggs, Levin, jacket copy, HV, 1st ed.; Hinde, cited RO, memo re HV, April 1980, HCA. See also HL, *Observer*, 2 September 1979; Myrna Blumberg, *The Times*, 24 November 1979; Victoria Glendinning, "Between Land and Water," *TLS*, 23 November 1979; PF to RO, 9 September [1979], *L*, 372.

39. Frank Kermode, "Booker Books," *LRB*, 22 November 1979, 12–13.

40. PR to RO, 2 November [1979], *L*, 374.

41. Susannah Clapp to HL, 13 February 2010; PF to RO, 10 October [1979], *L*, 373; Briggs, jacket copy of *HV*, 1st ed.; *HA*, 479; Hilary Spurling, "Dry-Eyed Marathon," *Observer*, 4 November 1979.

42. PF to FK, 29 October [1979], *L*, 280–81.

43. *The Book Programme: Literary Prizes*, BBC TV, 24 October 1979, director Antony Roose, producer Sue Mallinson.

44. William Webb, *Guardian*, 24 October 1979, HR I. 1.24; Hilary Spurling, "Dry-Eyed Marathon," *Observer*, 4 November 1979.

45. RO to Bernard Levin, 3 December 1979; F. I. Chapman to RO, 27 November 1979, HCA; PF to RO, 29 February 1980, *L*, 377, 11 October 1980, *L*, 381; PF to RO, 2 November [1979], *L*, 373, 23 August [1981], *L*, 388.

46. Glenys Roberts, *Evening News*, 25 October 1979, HR I, 1.24.

47. PF to BH, 26 October 1979, BH archive.

48. Paperback contract, 25 October 1979, HR I, 1.21; Magnum Books letter to RO, 14 December 1979, HCA.

49. PF to RO, 14 March [1980], *L*, 380.

50. PF to RO, 11 October [1980], *L*, 381.

51. PF to Howard Woolmer, April 1980, *L*, 334; PF to RO, 11 October [1980], *L*, 381.

52. PF to FK, 29 October [1979], *L*, 282; PF to RO, 20 November [1980], *L*, 382.

53. RO, memo; *HV* contract, April 1980, HCA.

54. EBJ notes; HR I, 6.2; *EBJ*, ch 9. "Dimmie": notebook, HR I, 5.13.

55. PF to RO, 4 September 1980, 11 October 1980, *L*, 380, 381. Bernard Levin, "Love at the BBC," *Sunday Times*, 28 September 1980; FK, "A War On," *Spectator*, 27 September 1980; Frank Kermode, "The Duckworth School of Writers," *LRB*, 20 November 1980.

56. *HA*, 499.

57. PF to RO, 28 August 1981, *L*, 389.

58. RO, memo, 14 July 1981, to Christopher Maclehose, Ian Chapman, Mark Bonham Carter, Michael Hyde et al., HCA.

59. PF to RO, 23 August 1981, *L*, 388, 13 April [1982], *L*, 391; John Sutherland, "Nationalities," *LRB*, 6 May 1982; Nick Shrimpton, "The Ice Age Cometh," *Sunday Times*, 28 March 1982; Anthony Thwaite, "Stagers Old and New," *Observer*, 28 March 1982.

CHAPTER THIRTEEN
The Ventriloquist

1. All quotations in chapter 13 not otherwise identified are from *Charlotte Mew and Her Friends*.

2. PF to RO, 16 April [1981], *L*, 385.

3. PF to RO, 23, 28 August [1981], *L*, 388–89; Tina to HL, 17, 20 June 2012.

4. PF to Mary Lago, 20 January 1980, *L*, 300; PF to RO, 16 July [1982], *L*, 394; PF to Howard Woolmer, 7 October 1981, *L*, 335.

5. PF to RO, 8 October [1983], *L*, 396, 27 July [1981], *L*, 388; PF to Liz Barnett, [1985–86], *L*, 211; PF to RO, 23 April [1982], *L*, 393; PF to RO, 14 November 1983, *L*, 400.

6. PF to RO, 23 January [1982], *L*, 391.

7. PF to Mary Lago, 26 April [1982], *L*, 301; Tina to HL, 19 February 2010, 20 June 2012.

8. PF to BH, 22 December [1982], BH archive.

9. PF to RO, [autumn 1981], *L*, 390; PF to Mary Lago, 9 August [1982], *L*, 302, 28 September [1982], *L*, 303.

10. On Clifton Hill: Tina to HL, 11 September 2010, Maria to HL, 1 October 2009; Desmond Maxwell to HL, 11 September, 28 October 2010; Perdita Dawson to HL, 28 July 2010; Antonia Southern to HL, 23 March 2010.

11. PF on Milton Abbot, *HA*, 443–49.

12. "The Prescription," *LRB*, December 1982, *ME*, 71–82; "Worlds Apart," *Woman*, 1983, *Hudson Review*, vol. 61, no. 1 (spring 2008).

13. Susannah Clapp to HL, 13 February 2010.

14. *HA*, 97–100, 238, 252, 246–52.

15. *HA*, 171–84.

16. PF to Howard Woolmer, 23 October [1983], *L*, 338.; RO to PF, 6 October 1980, HCA; PF to RO, 13, 16 July [1982], *L*, 393, 395, 8 October 1983, *L*, 398. Joy Grant, *Harold Morro and Poetry Bookshop* (Routledge and Kegan Paul, 1967), is not listed in PF's bibliography to *CM*, though she names Grant in her acknowledgements.

17. PF to Michael Holroyd, 18 September 1984, *L*, 472; PF to FK [c. 1984], *L*, 286; PF to Howard Woolmer, 25 May [1988], *L*, 349, on giving up on the biography of LPH.

18. PF to FK, [c. 1984], *L*, 286; PF to Mary Lago, 28 February 1983, *L*, 304.

19. "The Changeling," *CM* (Flamingo, 2002), 234. The U.S. and U.K. Flamingo paperbacks of *CM* contained PF's selection of Charlotte Mew poems; the Collins 1984 first edition did not.

20. The "split self" theory also runs through "Charlotte Mew," *Oxford Dictionary of National Biography* (OUP, 1997).

21. Cf. Val Warner, "Introduction," *Charlotte Mew: Collected Poems and Prose* (Virago, 1981), and Elaine Showalter, *Daughters of Decadence* (Virago, 1983).

22. PF reports what follows in Dawson Scott's diary as "Are all geniuses perverts?" But according to Dawson Scott's diaries, edited by her daughter, she wrote: "Is then genius one form of sex?" Marjorie Watts, *Mrs. Sappho: The Life of C. A. Dawson Scott* (Duckworth, 1987), 58.

23. PF to RO, 8 October [1983], *L*, 398.

24. *HA*, 160.

25. On the PB: Bowen, Plomer, Lehmann, Grigson, Macaulay, in *Coming to London,* ed. John Lehmann (Phoenix House, 1957); Alida Monro, ed., *Collected Poems of Harold Monro* (Duckworth, 1970); Joy Grant, *Harold Monro and the Poetry Bookshop* (Routledge & Kegan Paul, 1967); Helen Carr, *The Verse Revolutionaries* (Cape, 2009); Dominic Hibberd, *Harold Monro: Poet of the New Age* (Palgrave, 2001); Matthew Hollis, *Now All Roads Lead to France: The Last Years of Edward Thomas* (Faber, 2011).

26. Harold Monro, ed., *The Monthly Chapbook,* PB, vol. 1, no. 1 (July 1929).

27. Val Warner, "Introduction," *Charlotte Mew: Collected Poems and Prose,* xii; *The Rambling Sailor,* PB, 1929; Harold Monro, ed., *Twentieth-Century Poetry* (Chatto, 1929); Siegfried Sassoon to Sydney Cockerell, 31 May 1932, in *The Best of Friends: Further Letters to Sydney Cockerell,* ed. Viola Meynell and Rupert Hart-Davis (1956).

28. "Some day . . .": "The Quiet House," *Charlotte Mew, Complete Poems* (Penguin, 2000), 38.

29. Cf. Angela Leighton, in *Victorian Women Poets* (Harvester, 1992), 271, on "a sense of uncertainty, of a mind following casual trains of thought, inconsistent, wavering, and doubting," and Ian Hamilton in his *Charlotte Mew: Selected Poems* (Bloomsbury, 1999), 11, on "the intensity and pitch of Mew's address, her wobbly metres, her zigzag lineation."

30. "Dimmie" notebook, HR I, 5. 13.

31. Ibid.

32. On "Mewing" with Cooper, Josephine Pullein-Thompson to HL, 21 August 2010; Jonathan Barker to HL, 26 January 2010; SP to HL, 16 May 2010; PF to RO, 4 September [1980], *L*, 380, 8 October [1983], *L*, 397–99, 9 December [1983], *L*, 400; PF to Howard Woolmer, 8 September 1987, *L*, 347.

33. John Gross, *Observer,* 29 July 1984.

34. PF to WC, 1 July [1998], *L*, 201; PF to RO, 28 March [1985], *L*, 402; CC to HL, 16 April 2010; PF to CC, 12 September and 17 October 1987, *L*, 487, 489.

35. PF to CC, 4 August 1988, 15 June [1992], *L*, 493, 498.

CHAPTER FOURTEEN
Innocence

1. All quotations in chapter 14 not otherwise identified are from *Innocence*.

2. *HA*, 480, 1989.

3. *Island,* Spring 1992, 39. Cf.: "The moment comes when you have to step outside your own experience because you have used everything you want to write about and maybe many things which are too painful for you to mention." *British Writers at Alcalá,* The British Council, 1995, vol. 1, 88.

4. Eleanor Wachtel, interview with PF, *Writers & Company,* 21 April 1996; *HA,* 480.

5. *Island,* Spring 1992, 41.

6. Jeremy Lewis, *Sunday Telegraph,* 15 August 1990.

7. Lu, 380, 384.

8. PF to SP, 20 February [1986], HCA. Blurb to first edition of *I,* 1986.

9. HR I, 7.22.

10. *WR,* Petroni, September 1951; Petroni, September–November 1951; Moravia, September 1951, January 1952, April 1952. Raleigh Trevelyan to HL, 25 July 2010.

11. PF copy of *The Companion Guide to Florence,* TDA.

12. Jane Martineau to HL, 6 May 2010.

13. FK to HL, 12 February 2010; Josephine Pullein-Thompson to HL, 21 August 2010; PF to FK, 23 May 1983, *L,* 284.

14. PF to SP, 20 February [1986], HCA.

15. Eve Borsook, *The Companion Guide to Florence* (Fontana, 1966, 1973); HR I, 2.3.

16. Examples of small errors in *I:* the Villa Valmorana is just outside Vicenza, not Verona; Piero da Cortona should be Pietro; the quotation from Dante's *Vita nuova* misses out a word; there are no angels in the Pontormo *Visitation;* the Cassa del Mezzogiorno should be "per il Mezzogiorno"; it should be "Marchesa," not "Marquesa," "salsa," not "salza," etc.

17. PF to FK, 30 August [1986], *L,* 287; HR I, 6.12; *HA,* 189.

18. HR I, 7.21.

19. HR I, 6.12.

20. PF to SP, 8 July 1986, HCA; SP to PF, 13 August 1986, HR II, 9.6.

21. Philip Howard, "A Romance with a View," *The Times,* 2 October 1986; Valentine Cunningham, "Skulls Beneath the Skin," *Observer,* 7 September 1986; Christopher Hawtree, "A Troubled Morality," *Telegraph,* 12 September 1986; John Gross, "Books of the Times," *New York Times,* 28 April 1987; Anne Duchêne, "Do No Evil, Mean No Evil," *TLS,* 12 September 1986; C. K. Stead, "Chiara Ridolfi," *LRB,* 9 October 1986.

CHAPTER FIFTEEN
The Beginning of Spring

1. All quotations in chapter 15 not otherwise identified are from *The Beginning of Spring.*

2. PF to SP, 21 March 1986, HCA.

3. PF to Howard Woolmer, October [1987], *L,* 348.

4. Typescript of talk for Somerville College [1990], beginning "When I suggested the title The Beginning and End of It I was, I admit, thinking about myself, so you'll have to forgive a few reminiscences. Worse still I've been asked to come and speak as a writer and I can only speak to you as an old writer who's never been a young one, because I started so late in life, and therefore missed the most dramatic part of a writer's life." TDA.

5. "Have Public Libraries Outlived Their Usefulness?" Royal Society of Literature, 21 October 1993, Chair, Melvyn Bragg, with PF, HL and Douglas Mason.

6. PL to HL, 19 October 2010, 9 September 2011.

7. PF to PL, 8 March 1981; 21 January, 199?; 9 August 1999; 25 January [1998].

8. SP to Richard Burgess, 29 April 1987, HCA. For PF's relations with her publishers: SP to HL, 16 May 2010; Karen Duffy to HL, 16 March 2010; letters between PF and SP and in-house memos, HCA; SP archive.

9. SP to HL, 16 May 2010; SP, memorial address, 10 October 2000.

10. PF to SP, 15 October [1989], HCA.

11. PF to SP, 9 November [1986], HCA.

12. SP to PF, November 1986, HCA.

13. PF to SP, 21 November [1986], HCA.

14. SP to PF, 27 November 1986, HCA.

15. SP, memorial address, 10 October 2000.

16. Maura Dooley to HL, May 2012.

17. Edward Blishen to PF, [August 1984], HR II, 9.1.

18. PF on J. L. Carr, typescript of tribute at Northamptonshire Libraries, October 1994, TDA; *HA*, 380–87.

19. Margaret Crane to HL, 19 November 2010; Brenda Benghen to HL, 26 November 2010.

20. Maura Dooley to HL, May 2012.

21. PF to FK, April 1984, *L*, 285.

22. Programme for PEN Writers' Day, 28 March 1987, HR I 4.2: guest speaker, Doris Lessing; Amos Oz, interviewed by HL;. PF to Howard Woolmer, 3 April 1987, *L*, 343.

23. PF to FK, 1 April 1984, *L*, 285.

24. PF to Hugh Lee, 21 February [1986], *L*, 27.

25. FK to HL, 12 February 2010; Josephine Pullein-Thompson to HL, 21 August 2010.

26. Ray Watkinson to Josephine Pullein-Thompson, 11 May 1983, HR, PEN archive.

27. FK to HL, 12 February 2010; Josephine Pullein-Thompson to HL, 21 August 2010, 15 October 2010; Elizabeth Paterson, PEN report on 1983 Italian congress, May 1983.

28. HR II, 9.5, 3 February 1987.

29. PF, diary, 28 July 1986, TDA.

30. HR I, 7.3 [late 1980s].

31. PF to MK, "Sat morning" [November 1986], *L*, 226. Most of PF's letters to Mary were lost at the time of Mary's death in 2000.

32. PF, diary, 1986: to Jean and Mike Talbot, 13 April 1986, to WC and Mike Conder, October 1986, TDA.

33. PF to Hugh Lee, *L*, 23–36, 1978–86; Hugh Lee to HL, 15 January 2010.

34. Jasmine Blakeway to HL, 17 March 2010.

35. PF, diary, 20 October 1988, TDA.

36. *HA*, 154–71, 319–26.

37. *HA*, 317.

38. *HA*, 393–98; PR to WC, 27 May [1980], *L*, 180.

39. *HA*, 307, 240.

40. *HA*, 235.

41. PF to RO, 30 May [1986], *L*, 404.

42. *HA*, 63.

43. PF to Carmen Callil, 21 October 1995.

44. PF to PL, 9 August 1999, PL archive.

45. Ms., n.d. [1990?], "Where Novels Come From," and notes towards talks on "How Novelists Work," TDA. Part of these notes became "Daisy's Interview," in *How Novelists Work,* ed. Maura Dooley (Seren, 2000), 37–44, *HA,* 510–24, but without the section on *BS.*
46. Ibid.
47. Ibid.
48. PF to PL, 9 August 1999, PL archive.
49. HR I, 6.13; Harvey Pitcher, *The Smiths of Moscow* (Swallow House Books, 1984), 28; Aylmer Maude, *The Life of Tolstoy: The Later Years* (Constable, 1911), 649, 653.
50. *Baedeker's Russia, 1914,* 147.
51. Ronald Hingley, *Russian Writers and Society, 1825–1904* (Weidenfeld & Nicolson, 1967), 161; *Russian Writers and Soviet Society, 1917–1978* (Weidenfeld & Nicolson, 1979), 99.
52. Hingley, *Russian Writers and Society,* 176–78.
53. Pitcher, *The Smiths of Moscow,* 53.
54. PF to Harvey Pitcher, 6 March 1988, *L,* 442.
55. Pitcher, *The Smiths of Moscow,* 41, 87.
56. Eugenie Fraser, *The House by the Dvina: A Russian Childhood* (Mainstream, Edinburgh, 1984), 84, 140, 150.
57. Ibid., 130.
58. *The Times Russian Supplement,* 15 December 1911, 37.
59. HR I, 6.13.
60. HR I, 4.2.
61. HR I, 4.2. *HA,* 393–98.
62. HR I, 4.2.
63. SP to PF, 8 February 1988, HR II, 9.5. The Flamingo paperback of *HV* (1988) was still referring to "her seventh novel, *Nellie and Lisa.*"
64. Andrew Sinclair, "Mortar Board and Boiler Suit," *The Times,* 15 September 1988; Margaret Walters, "Women's Fiction," *LRB,* 13 October 1988; Anita Brookner, "Moscow Before the Revolution," *Spectator,* 1 October 1988; other reviews in *BS,* Flamingo, 1989.
65. PF to Hugh Lee, 29 October 1988, *L,* 28.
66. PF to RO, 16 February [1989], *L,* 407.
67. *LRB,* June 1989, October 1990, May 1994.
68. PF to Oliver Ready, 8 December 1999, printed in the *Moscow Times,* 18 December 1999, in "Millennium's Greatest Reads?" "A Clean Sheet" is a terrifying surreal fable.
69. PF to Oliver Ready, 8 December 1999, enlarged on in a review of Chandler's translation of Platonov's *The Return* in *Prospect,* August–September 1999.

CHAPTER SIXTEEN
The Gate of Angels

1. All quotations in chapter 16 not otherwise identified are from *The Gate of Angels.*
2. PF to Mary Lago, 16 September 1986, *L,* 312, 18 August 1988, *L,* 316; PF to Howard Woolmer, 15 June 1988, *L,* 350.
3. PF to Mary Lago, 18 August 1988, *L,* 316; PF to Howard Woolmer, 15 June 1988, *L,* 350; Howard Woolmer to HL, 27 August 2012; PF notebook, "My Takings," entry for 9 October 1996, "Howard Woolmer (for Texas Humanities Library), £1,859.63," TDA.
4. PF to SP, 27 November 1987, HCA; PF to Mary Lago, 10 February 1988, *L,* 315.

5. PF, appointment diary, February 1990, TDA.

6. VF to HL, 11 February 2010, 23 January 2013, 1 February 2013.

7. Valpy Gregory Fitzgerald to HL, June 2010.

8. PF to Tina, [October 1989], *L*, 84; PF to RO, 1 February [1989], *L*, 406, 5 October [1989], *L*, 409.

9. PF to Luke Dooley, n.d., TDA; Luke Dooley to HL, 2010.

10. Notes for talk at Somerville College, 1990s, HR II, 1.2.

11. Ms. of talks, "How Novels Work" and "Where Novels Come From," given at Somerville College, Edinburgh Festival and elsewhere in early 1990s, TDA. A short version of the talk was published as "Daisy's Interview" in *How Novelists Work,* ed. Maura Dooley (Seren Books, 2000), 37–44, reprinted with slight alterations as "How I Write: Daisy's Interview," *HA,* 510–17.

12. "Daisy's Interview," Dooley, ed., *How Novelists Work,* 38. (Revised in *HA,* 512.)

13. "She is drawn to men who don't say a lot, but carry on and like best to be left in peace—what used to be called 'decent sorts.'" PF interviewed by Jeremy Lewis, *Sunday Telegraph,* 1 August 1990.

14. HR II, 3.12.

15. "Daisy's Interview."

16. "PF vista por PF," in *British Writers at Alcalá de Henoses,* vol. 1, ed. Ricardo Sola Buil and Luis Alberto Lázaro (British Council, 1995), 83–96.

17. The novel's dates vary between March and February and between 1912 and 1911. Also, a character called Skippey is referred to as Shippey throughout chapter 6.

18. *Eliza* notebook, TDA, n.d. HR II, 3.11; "Daisy's Interview."

19. Undated "Memo Book" with notes for *GA, BS* and early notes for *BF,* TDA.

20. PF to Bridget Nichols, 26 February 2000, *L*, 455.

21. *KB,* 56, 60, 84.

22. PF to Richard Holmes, 20 July 1997, *L*, 479.

23. *KB,* 79; *HA,* 192–200.

24. PF to Bridget Nichols, 26 February 2000, *L*, 455.

25. Lu, 384.

26. "Daisy's Interview."

27. Samir Okasha, *Philosophy of Science: A Very Short Introduction* (OUP, 2002), 59.

28. See Lloyd Motz and J. H. Weaver, *The Story of Physics* (Plenum, 1989), 184, 217–21, 237–39; Okasha, *Philosophy of Science,* 8, 58–70; Iwan Rhys Morris, *When Physics Became King* (University of Chicago, 2005), 237, 242, 273; E. N. da C. Andrade, *Rutherford and the Nature of the Atom* (Doubleday, 1964), 25, 48; Roger Newton, *How Physics Confronts Reality* (World Scientific Publishing, 2009), v, 33, 132; David Wilson, *Rutherford: Simple Genius* (Hodder & Stoughton, 1983), 5, 308; Ernst Mach, *The Analysis of Sensations,* ed. Thomas Szasz (Dover, 1959); Eric Scerri, *The Periodic Table: A Very Short Introduction* (OUP, 2011), 72–76.

29. Lu, 384.

30. "PF vista por PF," in Burl and Lazaro, eds., *British Writers at Alcalá,* 83–96.

31. Sebastian Faulks, "Blind Alleys to Equality," *Independent on Sunday,* 19 August 1990; Anita Brookner, "Daisy Pulls It Off," *Spectator,* 11 September 1990; John Bayley, "Innocents at Home," *NYRB,* 9 April 1992.

32. PF to SP, 15 September [1990], *L*, 423.

33. *Sunday Times,* 16 September, 15 October 1990.
34. PF to SP, 24 October [1990], *L,* 423; SP to PF, October 1990, HR II, 9.5.
35. Kate Kellaway, "Atoms, Angels and the Mach Factor," *Observer,* 12 August 1990; "Who's Reading Whom," *Sunday Times,* 14 October 1990.
36. PF to SP [1991], *L,* 429; PF to CC, 25 March 1992, *L,* 496; PF on *Punch, HA,* 201–10.
37. "Curriculum Vitae," 1989, *HA,* 467–80.
38. Notes for "How Novels Begin" and "How Novelists Work," TDA.
39. Lu, 387.
40. Jonathan Keates to HL, 7 February 2010.
41. Valentine Cunningham to HL, 20 October 2010; PF to CC, 3 December 1998, *L,* 509.
42. PF to SP, 24 October [1990], *L,* 424; PF to Tina, October 1989 [but dated 1990–91?], *L,* 85; judging notebook, HR II, 10.
43. PF to Hugh Lee, 26 January [1992], *L,* 28; PF to SP, 24 October, 6 November [1990], *L,* 423, 425.
44. Kazuo Ishiguro to HL, 1 February 2010; PF to Mary Lago, 15 June 1991, *L,* 317.
45. Judging notebook, HR II, 10.
46. J. L. Carr to PF, 22 December 1993, TDA.
47. *HA,* 289, 405, 412.
48. PF to Julian Barnes, 23 March 1993, *L,* 469; "Julian Barnes," one-page ms., HR II, 1.1.
49. PF to RO, 24 August [1990], *L,* 41; 26 August [1991], *L,* 413; Joanna and Sydney Price, re Highgate Institute, to HL, summer 2010; PF to Tina, August [1989], *L,* 80; "10 July (I think) [1999]," *L,* 93; PF to Oliver and Patty Knox, 13 June 1991; PF to SP, 4 March [1991], *L,* 427, Charlotte Knox archive.
50. PF to RO, 1 February [1989], *L,* 405; PF to SP, 2 February [1991], *L,* 426.
51. Karen Duffy to HL, 7 June 2010. PF to Karen Duffy, n.d., KD archive.
52. PF to WC, Friday [1991], *L,* 183.
53. *HA,* 457.
54. *HA,* 461.
55. PF to RO, 25 January [1993] *L,* 415; PF to Lis Barnett, 17 May [1996], *L,* 217; PF to Rachel Hichens [1995], *L,* 216; PF to WC, 15 June [1997], 15 December 1994, *L,* 320, 19 November [1996], *L,* 324; PF to WC, 29 December 1994, *L,* 186.
56. Rachel Hichens to PF, 13 June 1994, TDA; *The Times,* 9 June 1994; PF to Helen Knox, 23 February 1998, *L,* 230; PF to WC, 29 December 1994, *L,* 186.

CHAPTER SEVENTEEN
The Blue Flower

1. All quotations in chapter 17 not otherwise identified are from *The Blue Flower.*
2. Two of PF's best critics, Julian Barnes and Frank Kermode, praise this first page. "Julian Barnes remembers Penelope Fitzgerald," *Guardian,* 26 July 2008, revised in *Through the Window* (Vintage, 2012); Frank Kermode, "Dark Fates," *LRB,* 5 October 1995.
3. Joan Acocella, "Assassination on a Small Scale," *New Yorker,* 7 February 2000; Jackie Wullschlager, "Heywood Finds a Subtle Winner," *Financial Times,* 15 June 1996. There are German nineteenth-century musical settings of Novalis's *Hymns* by Louise Reichardt, Alphons Diepenbrock, Alma Mahler and Schubert, among others.
4. D. H. Lawrence, "The Fox," 1923, in *Three Novellas* (Penguin, 1960), PF copy, TDA.

5. Ms. of talks, "How Novels Work" and "Where Novels Come From," TDA, HR I, 1.7. II, 1.8.
6. Eleanor Wachtel, interview with PF, *Writers & Company,* Canadian Broadcasting Corporation, 21 April 1996.
7. PF to Frank Kermode, 3 October 1995, *L,* 453.
8. HR I, 2.3.
9. "Dimmie" notebook, HR I, 5.13: see chapter 12.
10. PF to Alberto Manguel, 14 September 1998, *L,* 475.
11. Jeremy Adler, "News of the Golden Age," *TLS,* 15 June 2012, 3–4.
12. For Novalis, see: Frederich Beiser, *The Romantic Imperative: The Concept of Early German Romanticism* (Harvard, 2003); J. M. Bernstein, *Classic and Romantic German Aesthetics* (Cambridge, 2003); Dennis F. Mahoney, ed., *The Literature of German Romanticism* (Camden House, 2004); Dennis F. Mahoney, *The Critical Fortunes of a Romantic Novel* (Camden House, 1994); Géza von Molnár, *Romantic Vision, Ethical Context: Novalis and Artistic Autonomy* (University of Minnesota, 1987); H. S. Reiss, *The Political Thought of the German Romantics* (Blackwell, 1955); William Rose, *Men, Myths and Movements in German Literature* (Allen & Unwin, 1931); James Sheehan, *German History, 1770–1866* (Clarendon Press, 1989). Richard Holmes's review of *BF,* "Paradise in a Dream," *NYRB,* 17 July 1997, cites Coleridge's notebook reference to the "Flower" seen in a dream.
13. *Henry of Ofterdingen: A Novel by Novalis,* trans. Palmer Hilty (Waveland Press, 1964, 1990); Mahoney, *Critical Fortunes,* 7–8, 87; Molnár, *Romantic Vision,* 102, Rose *German History,* 195–98; Sheehan, *Men, Myths and Movements,* 333.
14. HR II, 2.4.
15. PF to Mary Lago, 24 June 1995, *L,* 322.
16. Ms. notes for talk on *BF,* n.d., HR II, 1.7.
17. *HA,* 475.
18. *"Wie sie so sanft ruhn alle die Seligen":* Friedrich Beneken and August Stockmann, trans. H. W. Longfellow.
19. HR II, 1.7.
20. Wachtel, interview with PF, *Writers & Company.*
21. Ms. of "How Novels Work" and "Where Novels Come From," TDA, HR I, 1.7. II, 1.8.

CHAPTER EIGHTEEN
Last Words

1. Ms. notes for a talk on biography, "Writing About Human Beings" [1990], TDA.
2. PF to SP, 8 April 1993, SP to PF, 27 October 1994, SP archive.
3. PF to Mary Lago, 24 June [1995], *L,* 322; PF to RO, 29 November [1994], *L,* 417.
4. Frank Kermode, "Dark Fates," *LRB,* 5 October 1995.
5. Philip Hensher, "The Sweet Smell of Success," *Spectator,* 11 April 1998, 33–34; Philip Hensher to HL, 12 November 2012, citing unseen letter from PF to Philip Hensher.
6. Carol Shields to PF, 22 January 1998, HR II, 9.3; Candia McWilliam to PF, 18 November 1995, HR II, 9.2.
7. Alberto Manguel to PF, 6 July 1998, TDA; 3 September 1998, HR II, 9.3; PF to Manguel, 12 July 1998, 14 September 1998, *L,* 475–76.

8. PF to CC, [1 January 1997], *L,* 500. ("The stars are with the voyager wherever he may sail;/The moon is constant to her time,/The sun will never fail;/But follow, follow round the world,/The green earth and the sea;/So love is with the lover's heart,/Wherever he may be.")

9. SP to PF, 10 July 1997, SP archive.

10. PF to CC, 3 December 1998, *L,* 509; CC to HL, 5 February, 16 April 2010.

11. Michael Hofmann, "Nonsense Is Only Another Language," *New York Times,* 13 April 1997; Gerhard Schulz to PF, April 1997, HR II, 9.2; Editor's Choice, *New York Times,* 7 December 1997.

12. Richard Holmes, "Paradise in a Dream," *NYRB,* 17 July 1997.

13. Richard Eder, "Nouvelle Novalis," *Los Angeles Times,* 13 April 1997.

14. PF to CC, 14 May [1998], *L,* 508; *Los Angeles Times,* 25 March 1998; Janet Silver to PF, 18 August 1998, HR II, 9.4; James Marcus to HL, 16 October 2012, http:#housemirth .blogspot.com/2005/04; Janice Harayda, *The Plain Dealer,* 29 March 1998; PF to WC, 15 June [1997], 27 December [1998], *L,* 201, 203.

15. SP to PF, 4 December 1996, SP archive.

16. PF to Karen Duffy, 17 June [1996], Karen Duffy archive; PF to Oliver Knox, 26 June [1996], Charlotte Knox archive. On the Heywood Hill prize: Jackie Wullschlager, "Heywood Finds a Subtle Winner," *Financial Times,* 15 June 1996; Anita Brookner, "Thoughts on a Dry Brain in a Dry Season," *Spectator,* 22 June 1996.

17. PF to WC, 28 March [199], *L,* 204.

18. PF to WC, 17 May [1999], 13 January [2000], *L,* 205–8; BH to HL, 6 March 2010.

19. Philip Hensher to HL, 12 November 2012.

20. Julian Barnes, "The Deceptiveness of Penelope Fitzgerald," *Through the Window: Seventeen Essays (and One Short Story)* (Vintage, 2012), 2–3, by permission of the author.

21. Maggie Fergusson to HL, 25 August 2012.

22. *Daily Telegraph,* 27, 28 February, 7 March 1998; *Guardian,* 7 March 1998; PF to WC, 1 April [1998], *L,* 199.

23. SP to HL, 16 May 2010.

24. PF to Mandy Kirkby, 13 January 2000, HR II, 9.5. "Our Lives Were Only Lent to Us" and "The Likeness" were added to the 2001 paperback edition of *ME.*

25. PF to SP, n.d. [10 January], SP archive.

26. Goethe, "Gefunden." There are many musical settings of this poem; she may be referring to Richard Strauss's Op. 56.

27. PF to Tina, [1999], *L,* 90.

28. "Last Words," *End Games: Late Work Considered,* ed. Robert Stewart (Oxford: Sonth Bank Centre, 1988); *HA,* 525–31.

29. *HA,* 424, 21, 434, 387, 28–35.

30. S. J. Dubney to PF, 15 October 1998, HR II, 9.4.

31. *KB,* xxiii–xxiv.

32. *Salon,* 28 April 1999, HR II, 6.7; Ronald Schwarz, ed., *A Writers' Guide to Great Books* (1998), HR II, 8.10; W. H. Smith, 150th anniversary author poll, HR II, 8.10; *Mail on Sunday,* 30 July 1998, HR II, 8.10; HL interview with PF, 26 March 1997; Folio Society, 3 September 1998, HR II, 8.12.

33. PF to Lu, 3 June [1995], 7 March [1999]; Lu, 377–92. Interviews with PF: HL, 26 March

1997, for *New Writing,* 1998; HL, "The View from Here," producer Erin Riley, BBC Radio 4, 20 January 1995 (when I asked her what she was working on after *BF*); "The Man in the Back Row Has a Question," *Paris Review,* 1998; Eleanor Wachtel, interview with PF, *Writers & Company,* Canadian Broadcasting Corporation, 21 April 1996; Arthur Lubow, "An Author of a Certain Age," *New York Times,* 15 August 1999; Sylvia Brownrigg, *Newsday,* August 1997; Joan Acocella, "Assassination on a Small Scale," *New Yorker,* 7 February 2000; Humphrey Carpenter, BBC Radio 4, "Visiting Lives," 21 November 1998.

34. HR II, 8.6; published as "In Praise of the Family," *Good Housekeeping,* December 1990, 56–57.
35. PF to Tina [n.d.], TDA.
36. Card to Sophie Lake, Maria archive.
37. PF to SP, 6 March [1999], SP archive; PF to Karen Duffy, 28 September [1998], Karen Duffy archive.; SP to PF, 24 January 1995, SP archive; PF to Michael Holroyd, 21 February [2000], *L,* 473.
38. PF to Tina, 10 July, "I think" [1999], *L,* 94; PF to WC, 28 March [1999], *L,* 204, 12 July [1998], *L,* 201.
39. Tina to HL, 2 July 2012; David Hubbard to HL, 13 October 2010; PF to CC, 29 March [2000], *L,* 520.
40. "Offshore: A Celebration of the Life and Work of Penelope Fitzgerald," 19 April 2001, *News from the RSL,* 23 June 2002.
41. PF to RO, 5 October 1989, *L,* 409.
42. HL interviews with PF: Edinburgh Festival, 16 August 1989; "The View from Here," BBC Radio 4, 20 January 1995; on *BF,* at York, 10 October 1995; 26 March 1997, interview for *New Writing,* vol. 7 (British Council/Vintage, 1998); Chair, "Writers at Work," University of York, 8 May 1997.
43. HR II, 8.6. A magician called Oswald Williams worked with "Maskelyne's Mysteries" in shows in London in the 1920s; PF may have seen him. "Maskelyne's Mysteries" was also, from 1926 to 1950, the name of a magic set with accessories and instructions for conjuring tricks and making magic.

Index

Hermione Lee is a biographer, critic, teacher of literature and president of Wolfson College, Oxford. She has written literary biographies of *Willa Cather* (1989, revised 2008), *Virginia Woolf* (1996) and *Edith Wharton* (2007), and critical books on Elizabeth Bowen, Philip Roth and Virginia Woolf. Her collection of essays on life-writing, *Body Parts,* was published in 2005 and her *Very Short Introduction to Biography* in 2009. She is a Fellow of the British Academy and the Royal Society of Literature, and a Foreign Honorary Member of the American Academy of Arts and Sciences. She was made a CBE for services to literature in 2003. She lives in Oxford and Yorkshire.

A NOTE ON THE TYPE

This book was set in Adobe Garamond. Designed for the Adobe Corporation by Robert Slimbach, the fonts are based on types first cut by Claude Garamond (c. 1480–1561). Garamond was a pupil of Geoffroy Tory and is believed to have followed the Venetian models, although he introduced a number of important differences, and it is to him that we owe the letter we now know as "old style." He gave to his letters a certain elegance and feeling of movement that won their creator an immediate reputation and the patronage of Francis I of France.

Composed by North Market Street Graphics,
Lancaster, Pennsylvania

Printed and bound by Berryville Graphics,
Berryville, Virginia

Rockenthien no longer jolly

Harmo.
Dietmahler?

Schöben do Rockenthiens go?

~~tauter~~ Freiherr put off going to Jena although
a brave man. At length takes whole family, par
to get rid of uncle who is ~~still~~ staying at weissenfels
Fritz already in Jena staying with Dietmahler schiegel?
First go to Schöben. Randy ~~as~~ ~~she~~ now 2 hours from Jena
St Anton, Karl? Sidonie remember sledges &c. Bernhard
had not wanted to come, but neither had he wanted to
left with his uncle

Gemüthet   although
~~hastily~~ as ever, ~~but~~ ~~like~~ like all H. properties, spar
~~froaty~~ form?

FREIHERRS OFFER   that he ~~wrong~~
                                    was in on the way
this time FRITZ had a persistent dream that he was back a
Jena, back on ~~the walk up to the dwelling~~ field (on Fichte's lect
it came to him that he should not be doing. became he had ne
that his friend Hardenberg lived only 2 hours ~~ride~~ away. at sch
~~he~~ ~~named · walked back into the town~~ but his house w
~~he~~ did not arrive until it was dark. He knocked at the doo
the Freiherr comes back ~~at schöben~~ could, they've had 3rd & most
painful operation had ~~doesn't~~ a right to be in room, &
Starke had told him afterwards that one more operation
~~but give her schöben~~ might
was
Hardenberg

next chap
B. points out that the sacrifice is pointless

HOUSE (large)

Great house thickly surrounded
with trees—already at bottom
of valley, damp & dark, 3, 4
great chimney stacks a lot of
it not in use. steward lived in par house?

BARN

SCHLÖBEN [schossgut schlöben. bei Jena]
~~over~~ smaller than ~~or~~ Oberwiederstadt
in a valley, you drop down to it from the hills
don't know if there's a village but (from R. to l.
chapel, ~~road between~~ stream with bridges ROAD
between lines of planted poplars. the great HOUSE
surrounded by ~~large~~ windows
trees, in front, wall bedroom? of servant
(black & white)
& a ~~lot~~ farm buildings. large, some with
prob: barns, & with chimneys prob: bedroom
for bailiff &c. plain [tiled] ROOFS.
Another church seen in distance, but no
indication of extent of land

Trees everywhere look like willows & birches not
fruit trees

Can one grazing let out. Anton.